Coding

ALL-IN-ONE

3rd Edition

by Chris Minnick, Luca Massaron, Paul McFedries, John Paul Mueller, John Shovic, and Alan Simpson

for dummies®
A Wiley Brand

Coding All-in-One For Dummies®, 3rd Edition

Published by: **John Wiley & Sons, Inc.,** 111 River Street, Hoboken, NJ 07030-5774, www.wiley.com

For general information on our other products and services, please contact our Customer Care Department within the U.S. at 877-762-2974, outside the U.S. at 317-572-3993, or fax 317-572-4002. For technical support, please visit https://hub.wiley.com/community/support/dummies.

Wiley publishes in a variety of print and electronic formats and by print-on-demand. Some material included with standard print versions of this book may not be included in e-books or in print-on-demand. If this book refers to media that is not included in the version you purchased, you may download this material at http://booksupport.wiley.com. For more information about Wiley products, visit www.wiley.com.

Library of Congress Control Number: 2026947680

ISBN 978-1-394-44918-7 (pbk); ISBN 978-1-394-44920-0 (ebk); ISBN 978-1-394-44919-4 (ebk)

SKY10164655_080526

Contents at a Glance

Table of Contents

Introduction

Welcome to the third edition of *Coding All-in-One For Dummies!* Not much has changed in coding since the second edition came out in 2022, so I'm not sure why you're reading this introduction.

JUST KIDDING.

In 2022, few people had any idea that generative AI was about to change the world, seemingly overnight. The first mainstream AI coding assistant, GitHub Copilot, was available only to a limited audience, and the second edition of this book had no content about using AI tools in coding.

All that has changed in this edition. Learning to code as well as coding itself is now all about making use of AI tools to code faster and better. This book is your guide to the coding fundamentals that will help you get the most out of using AI coding tools.

So, yes, things have changed. A lot. The good news is you don't need to become a robot (or learn to speak fluent binary) to keep up. In the pages ahead, you'll learn the fundamentals and then let AI do the heavy lifting, while you stay in charge of the steering wheel, the brakes, and the "no, we are *not* deploying that" button.

About This Book

This book gives an overview of programming to readers with little to no coding experience. In plain English, you learn how code in several of the most popular programming languages can accomplish useful tasks. You also discover how to get coding help from artificial intelligence. The topics covered include:

- A description of what coding is and answers to common questions related to code
- The basics of Python
- Working with data and machine learning using Python

- Coding with AI tools
- Building basic websites using the three most common languages: HTML, CSS, and JavaScript
- Getting started with advanced JavaScript and the React front-end library

As you read this book, keep the following in mind:

- The book can be read from beginning to end, but feel free to skip around if you like. If a topic interests you, start there. You can always return to previous chapters, if necessary.
- At some point, you'll get stuck, and the code you write will not work as intended. Do not fear! There are many resources to help you, including support forums, others on the internet, and me! I love to receive email from readers, and I always respond. You can reach me at `chris@minnick.com`.
- Code in the book appears in a monospaced font like this: `<h1>Hi there!</h1>`.

Foolish Assumptions

I do not make many assumptions about you, the reader, but I do make a few.

I assume you don't have previous programming experience. To follow along, then, you only need to be able to read, type, and follow directions. I try to explain as many concepts as possible using examples and analogies you already know.

I assume you have a computer running the latest version of Google Chrome. The examples in the book that require a browser have been tested and optimized for the Chrome browser, which is available for free from Google. Even so, the examples work also in the latest version of Firefox, Safari, and Microsoft Edge.

I assume you have access to an internet connection. Some of the examples in the book can be done without an internet connection, but most require one.

For the minibooks on Python and data analysis, I assume you can download and install the Python programming language and its associated programming libraries, both of which are available for free.

Icons Used in This Book

Here are the icons used in the book to flag text that should be given extra attention or can be skipped.

TIP

This icon flags useful information or explains a shortcut to help you understand a concept.

TECHNICAL STUFF

This icon explains technical details about the concept being explained. The details might be informative or interesting, but they aren't essential to your understanding of the concept at this stage.

REMEMBER

Try not to forget the material marked with this icon. It signals an important concept or process that you should keep in mind.

WARNING

Watch out! This icon flags common mistakes and problems that can be avoided if you heed the warning.

Beyond the Book

A lot of extra content that you won't find in this book is available at `www.dummies.com`. Go online to find the following:

- **The source code for the examples:** The source code is organized by book and chapter. The best way to work with a chapter is to download all the source code for it at one time. You can find the code at `www.dummies.com/go/codingaiofd3e`.
- **The book's cheat sheet:** Simply navigate to `www.dummies.com` and search for *Coding All-in-One For Dummies Cheat Sheet.* From there, you'll be able to access several helpful articles about coding.
- **Updates:** Code and specifications are constantly changing, so the commands and syntax that work today may not work tomorrow. You can find updates and corrections by visiting `www.dummies.com/go/codingaiofd3e`.

Where to Go from Here

All right, now that all the administrative stuff is out of the way, it's time to get started. You can totally do this. Congratulations on taking your first step into the world of coding!

1

Getting Started with Coding

Contents at a Glance

IN THIS CHAPTER

» **Understanding how programming works**

» **Perusing a few programming languages**

» **Taking a peek under the coding hood**

» **Figuring out why you'd want to learn to code**

» **Learning how code is used in the real world**

Chapter 1
What Is Coding?

Everybody should learn to program a computer because it teaches you how to think.

—STEVE JOBS

Okay, I'll admit it: I'm not one of those look-before-you-leap types. I'm a dedicated leaper. With almost every new thing I learn, my philosophy is that I learn best when I *do* the thing. I usually just jump in, get my hands dirty, make mistakes, fix them, and before long, I develop a feel for this new hobby or skill.

Note, though, that I said I do that with *almost* every new thing I learn. I don't do it when I'm learning something related to coding. Why not? "Just jumping in" is a lousy strategy for learning to code because the mistakes you make are dumb ones that teach you nothing (as opposed to smart mistakes that you can learn from). When it comes to learning anything related to code, it's always best to start with the basics and work your way slowly and steadily to competency, then proficiency, then mastery.

This chapter is your look-before-you-leap introduction to coding. Here you explore what coding is and how it works. You discover the myriad reasons why it's good to learn to code, and you investigate quite a few real-world uses for coding.

Programming: Making a Computer Do Your Bidding

A computer is a machine that follows instructions. Or, to put a finer point on it, a computer is a machine that does nothing until someone or something tells it what to do. That might sound surprising. After all, computers cost many hundreds, sometimes even thousands, of dollars, and are positively bristling on the inside with electronic gadgetry. Surely something so expensive and so complex must be capable of doing some useful tasks on its own.

Nope.

Sure, when you turn on a new computer for the first time, some hieroglyphics appear on the screen, and you eventually end up in Windows or macOS or some other desktop. Doesn't that so-called boot process mean that the computer is doing something on its own?

Again, nope.

When you turn on a computer, it automatically loads a set of instructions that tell the computer what it must do to get the hardware (keyboard, mouse, screen, and so on) up and running and to get the operating system (Windows or macOS or whatever) loaded. That set of instructions is known as the computer's *firmware,* which is a special type of program embedded in the computer hardware. When the firmware has completed its job, it calls the *bootloader,* which loads the operating system.

Okay, that's all fine, but where did the firmware and bootloader come from? I'm glad you asked because at long last I can get to the point of all this: Someone coded them.

Some very smart person versed in the esoterica of computer hardware and system software programmed the firmware, and some other just as smart person coded the bootloader. So, let me repeat myself: Computers can't do anything unless someone or something tells them what to do. And the way you tell a computer what to do is via code.

Coding firmware or a bootloader is hideously complex and requires years of study. Happily, you won't be going anywhere near that level of complexity in this book.

Whew! But everything you do learn here will be a variation on the overall theme of this section: telling a computer what you want it to do using code.

These days, "telling the computer what to do" often occurs in partnership with AI tools. You might describe the goal in plain English, have an AI assistant suggest a first draft, and then refine it yourself into code that you can run, test, and maintain. Even with great AI help, the programmer's job doesn't disappear — it shifts to being clear about what you want, checking the results, and making sure the finished program is correct and safe. Think of it this way: Code is the set of instructions that ultimately gets executed by the computer. Prompts are instructions you give to an AI system to help you *produce* or *transform* that code. Prompts are powerful, but they're not a substitute for understanding what the program does because you're still responsible for the output.

Am I talking about making a computer do anything you want? Alas, no, although that would be very useful! When you code, you're given a set of tools for the job; the tools you work with vary depending on the language you're using. As I discuss later in this book, the tools you get with Python (refer to Book 2) are much different than the tools you get with JavaScript (check out Book 6). As an analogy, the types of home projects you'd take on would be very different depending on whether you had a carpenter's toolbox or a sewing kit.

REMEMBER

But no matter how you code — no matter what programming tools you have at your disposal — you're almost always doing one (or sometimes both) of the following:

- **Solving a problem:** One of the most common reasons that a piece of code gets written is because the coder had a pain point or an inefficiency in their life and saw a way to use code to make their life easier or more streamlined.
- **Creating something new:** Another common reason to start coding is when you get a great idea and want more than anything to bring that idea to life.

No matter what you work on in your coding career, you're almost always doing one (or both) of these things — solving problems, creating new stuff, or combining the two to make something that's both new *and* improved.

What Is a Programming Language?

Python and JavaScript are programming languages. Okay, fine, but what does it mean to call something a *programming language?* To understand this term, you need look no further than the language you use to speak and write. At its most fundamental level, human language is composed of two things — words and rules:

- The words are collections of letters that have a common meaning among all the people who speak the same language. For example, the word *book* denotes a type of object; the word *heavy* denotes a quality; and the word *read* denotes an action.
- The rules are the ways in which words can be combined to create coherent and understandable concepts. If you want to be understood by other speakers of the language, you have only a limited number of ways to throw two or more words together. "I read a heavy book" is an instantly comprehensible sentence, but "Book a I read heavy" is gibberish.

The key goal of human language is being understood by someone else who is listening to you or reading something you wrote. If you use the proper words to refer to things and actions, and if you combine those words according to the rules, the other person will understand you.

A programming language works in more or less the same way. That is, it, too, has words and rules:

- The words are a set of terms that refer to the specific things that your program works with or the specific ways in which those things can be manipulated. These words are known as *reserved words* or *keywords.*
- The rules are the ways in which the words can be combined to produce the desired effect. In the programming world, these rules are known as the language's *syntax.*

The crucial concept here is that just as the fundamental purpose of human language is to be understood by another person, the fundamental purpose of a programming language is to be understood by whatever machine is processing the language. The key, however, is that being understood by the machine really means being able to *control* the machine. That is, your code sentences are commands that you want the machine to carry out.

The Role of Programming Languages

Let's say you travel to Igboland in Nigeria and want to ask a local for directions to the nearest bathroom. If that person speaks only Igbo (the native language of Igboland), one solution would be to find someone who speaks both English and Igbo and ask that person to translate your request as well as the response. Problem solved!

The person who can translate your English into Igbo is called an *interpreter*, and that task is essentially how we're able to program a computer. The problem is that a computer understands only its native language, which is called *machine language* and consists of 1s and 0s. (I won't get into this topic here, but if you're curious to know more, check out the sidebar "How computers work: A crash course for would-be coders.") A very simple machine language instruction to a computer might look something like this:

```
10111000 00000001 00000000 00000000 00000000
10111111 00000001 00000000 00000000 00000000
01001000 10111110 00000000 01100000 01100000
00000000 00000000 00000000 00000000 00000000
10111010 00001101 00000000 00000000 00000000
00001111 00000101 10111000 00111100 00000000
00000000 00000000 00110001 11111111 00001111
00000101
```

Yikes! No sane human wants to deal with something as weird as machine language, so one of the first things that engineers did after computers were invented was to come up with two remarkable inventions:

- A way of representing machine-language instructions as human-understandable English words
- A way of converting those English words back into the machine language that the computer understands

The first invention is called a *programming language* and consists of, in part, English (or, sometimes, English-like) words such as `if`, `while`, and `return`. You use these generally comprehensible terms to construct *statements*, which are commands that you want the computer to carry out on your behalf.

For example, the preceding machine language code began life, in part, as the following statement:

```
printf("Hello, World!");
```

This statement, which is written in the C programming language, outputs the text *Hello, World!* C is an example of a *high-level language*, which describes any programming language that abstracts away the mind-numbing complexity of the computer's native machine language.

HOW COMPUTERS WORK: A CRASH COURSE FOR WOULD-BE CODERS

You might have heard someone say, with great authority, that "computers operate by processing 1s and 0s." If, upon hearing that, you were flummoxed, let me tell you that your reaction is utterly normal. It really *is* incomprehensible to us mere mortals that computers, which can do all these incredible things, perform those wonders by slinging around just two values: 1 and 0. What's behind this mystery?

At the lowest level, a computer is basically a collection of billions of unimaginably teensy components called *transistors,* which operate essentially as on/off switches for electrical current. When a transistor allows electrical current to pass through, by convention, that state is represented by a 1. When a transistor blocks electrical current from passing through, by convention, that state is represented by a 0. Each 1 or 0 is called a *binary digit,* or *bit.* One bit offers only two options: 1 or 0. Combining two bits offers four options: 00, 01, 10, or 11. Skipping ahead, I can tell you that combining eight bits offers 256 options, from 00000000 to 11111111 and every combo in between. A string of eight bits is called a *byte,* and the 256 possible byte values are enough to code every letter, every number, every punctuation mark, plus a few other standard symbols that make up the American Standard Code for Information Interchange (ASCII) table. The uppercase letter *H,* for example, is 01001000 in binary. So, combine eight transistors, set them so that they form the byte 01001000, and you've got the letter *H* stored on your circuit board (which might be a memory module).

Do you need to memorize the byte values for every letter, number, and symbol to code a computer? No, not even close! In fact, the history of coding can be seen as moving farther and farther away from how information is physically stored using transistors to being able to make the computer do your bidding using relatively simple English words.

C is a notoriously difficult language to learn, so aside from a brief mention in Chapter 3, I steer clear of it in this minibook. Instead, you learn two languages that reside at an even higher (read: easier) level than C: Python (covered in Book 2) and JavaScript (tackled in Book 6). You also learn how to write code with the assistance of AI (starting in Chapter 4 of this minibook).

The second of the inventions I mentioned is called either an *interpreter* or a *compiler*, depending on the programming language. (I explain the difference between interpreters and compilers in Chapter 3 of this minibook.) Either way, the purpose of this invention is to take the English-like code of a programming language and convert it to something (such as machine language) that the computer can read and run. All of this happens behind the scenes, so, as a coder, you never have to lay your eyes on a single 1 or 0 (unless it's part of your Python or JavaScript code, of course).

Understanding How Code Is Written and Executed

At this very early stage of your programming career, the process of coding might seem more than a little mysterious, possibly even downright puzzling. After all, from the outside, a computer is a mystifying machine, so the idea that you can somehow *control* this inscrutable hunk of electronica might seem the stuff of fantasy. Or even if you've already convinced yourself that you can make a computer do your bidding, *how* you do that might still have you scratching your head.

Perhaps the secret to being able to code a computer is having the right equipment, something like needing a loom for weaving or a lathe for woodworking.

Nope, you're way off. Maybe the most surprising thing about code is that it's nothing but text. (To keep things simple, for now I'm ignoring non-text files such as images and videos that you might incorporate in, say, a web page.) Ever used Notepad in Windows or TextEdit on a Mac? Those bare-bones text files are essentially what you use to write your code.

REMEMBER

To describe the programming process in its most generic terms, I like to use what I call the "three-and-a-half Rs" of coding — write, run, revise, and repeat:

- **Write:** In a text file, you write your code as a series of statements, each of which is essentially an instruction to the interpreter or compiler for whatever programming language you're using.
- **Run:** You invoke the programming language's interpreter or compiler and tell it to process the code in the text file you wrote. The interpreter or compiler then executes the code, and the results appear, which could be the program's output or one or more error messages.
- **Revise:** Based on the results of the run, you edit your code to fix any errors that crop up or to improve your code.
- **Repeat:** You write more code (to, say, add new functionality), run it, revise it as needed, and then repeat the cycle until your program or app or web page or whatever is complete.

That's the bird's-eye view. The next two sections bring things slightly closer to the ground by looking at the coding processes specifically for Python and JavaScript.

How Python code works

I go into a pleasing amount of detail about Python in the chapters that make up Book 2, so here I just provide you with a quick overview of the Python coding process:

1. **Using a text editor or code editor, write your Python language statements in a plain text file.**

   When you save your text file for the first time, be sure to name the file with the `.py` file extension, which identifies it as a Python file.

2. **At the command line, type** python**, a space, and the name of the Python file, and then press Enter or Return.**

   For example, the following runs a file named `hello.py`:

   ```
   python hello.py
   ```

   The `python` part of the command invokes the Python interpreter, which processes the content in the Python file one statement at a time. Note that the Python interpreter is available on your computer only if you have installed Python, as I describe in Book 2, Chapter 1.

   The interpreter then displays the results of the code, which might be some output you defined or one or more error messages.

   TECHNICAL STUFF

   As I discuss in Book 2, Chapter 1, you can execute Python code in other ways, including an interactive Python shell that enables you to run one Python statement at a time and code editors that enable you to run Python code from the editor's development environment.

3. **Return to your code editor and modify the code as needed based on the results of the most recent run, especially to troubleshoot any errors that cropped up.**

4. **Repeat Steps 1 through 3 as required until your Python program is complete.**

How JavaScript code works

JavaScript is the subject of Books 6 and 7, so I'll just whet your appetite here with a short-and-sweet review of the JavaScript coding process:

1. **Using a text editor or code editor, write your JavaScript language statements in a plain text file.**

I assume for simplicity that you want to run your JavaScript statements in a web page (that is, an HTML file, which usually uses the `.html` file extension), so there are two ways to go:

- *Create an external JavaScript file:* Save your text file using the `.js` file extension, which identifies it as a JavaScript file, and then modify your web page code to tell the browser about the file. For example, the following tags reference a file named `hello.js`:

  ```
  <script src="hello.js"></script>
  ```

- *Embed the JavaScript code inside the HTML file:* Your JavaScript statements reside within a `<script></script>` block:

  ```
  <script>
     // JavaScript statements go here
  </script>
  ```

REMEMBER

If this rapid-fire overview is confusing, don't sweat it for now. I discuss all this in more careful detail in Book 6.

2. **Open the HTML file in a web browser or, if the HTML file is already open in the browser, refresh the page.**

   The web browser contains a built-in JavaScript interpreter, so as soon as the browser loads the HTML file, it begins processing the JavaScript code one statement at a time. The browser then displays the results of the code, which might be some output you defined, a web page modification, or one or more error messages.

3. **Switch back to your code editor and edit the code as required, given what happened when you opened or refreshed the HTML file.**

   In particular, be sure to tackle any errors that cropped up.

4. **Repeat Steps 1 through 3 as required until your JavaScript code is running the way you want it.**

Why Learn to Code? Let Me Count the Ways

Since you're reading this book, I think it's safe to assume that you want to learn how to code. If that's true, feel free to skip merrily over the rest of this section. However, if you're still on the fence, trying to decide whether you want to spend the time and effort to learn to code, have I got a section for you!

If you're short on time, my immediate answer to the question "Should I learn to code?" is a real timesaver: Yes, absolutely! If you still need to be convinced, let the next few sections serve as my long answer.

Coding isn't just for nerds

You might have an image of a stereotypical coder in your head, one that no doubt envisages some not-recently-washed nerd sitting in a dank, dimly lit basement surrounded by empty pizza boxes and crushed energy drink cans. Ah, so you *have* seen photos of my office!

I'm sure many coders fit that stereotype, but most don't, and you certainly don't have to stop bathing and ruin your diet to code.

Lots of nerds code, but not all coders self-identify as nerds, so if the geeky reputation of coding is holding you back, forget about it. You can code just as you are.

Coding teaches you how to think

While it's true that the essence of coding is writing instructions for a computer to follow, it's not like writing a list of items for your spouse to pick up when they go to the grocery store. That is, you can't just pick up the coding equivalent of a pen and start writing things down as they pop into your head. Coding requires multiple kinds of thought, so in a sense, coding teaches you how to think.

For example, when you're considering how to tackle a coding project, it always helps if you can break down the project into smaller, more manageable chunks. Similarly, computers are relentlessly logical beasts, so successful coding requires that you use your logical reasoning skills to think like the computer. Every program ever written contains errors, so a big part of coding is troubleshooting problems, which requires understanding how your code works. Converting an idea in your head into code that brings the idea to life is a task that requires large doses of imagination.

REMEMBER

All these skills — breaking down problems, logical reasoning, troubleshooting problems, critical thinking, and imagination — not only make you a good coder but are also tremendously useful outside programming. Whether it's business, finance, science, or trying to assemble some piece of IKEA furniture with its inscrutable instructions, the thinking skills you hone via coding will help with whatever you're doing.

Coding is fun and creative

In the preceding section, I mentioned that getting code to run requires a logical, channel-the-computer approach. I stand by that, but I'll also admit that "think like the computer" isn't a clarion call for fun. That's okay, though, because thinking logically is only part of what it takes to get a program running. Most of us associate creativity with artistic endeavors, but I'm here to tell you that coding is one of the most creative skills you can learn.

For starters, every non-trivial coding project you work on will present you with hurdles that at first seem insurmountable but will soon yield to some creative problem-solving.

But coding creativity really begins with designing and implementing whatever idea has fired your imagination. Want to make a game? Design a website? Create an app? Craft some digital artwork? Whatever it is, coding enables you to take almost any idea, no matter how pie-in-the-sky it might seem to you now, and turn it into an actual, working project that you and others can play, run, or view. Believe me when I tell you that building things from scratch and watching them come to life not only gives your creativity circuits a workout but is also the very definition of fun.

You can build (almost) anything you can imagine

Being able to code is like having a superpower: If you can imagine something, you can build it. Want to create a website for your side hustle? Code it. Have an idea for an awesome game? Make it. Need an app to remind you to drink water? Build it. (Then send it to me. I could really use that app!)

When you learn to code, you give yourself the near-magical ability to create something out of nothing. This ability is incredibly rewarding because now you're not just *using* apps — you're *making* them.

REMEMBER

Scoot over to the "Real-World Uses of Coding" section, later in the chapter, for a few practical and useful project ideas.

Coding is a universal language

When people with different native languages want to communicate, they can sometimes use another language that they have in common. That common language is called a *lingua franca.*

In today's technical world, code often acts as a kind of lingua franca because programming is one of the few skills that work the same across every industry and country. A JavaScript developer in Japan writes the same kind of code as one in Canada. A Python script written in the U.S. can be used by someone in Germany.

This means coding opens up opportunities around the world. If you ever dream of working internationally (or remotely for a global company), coding can help you get there.

Coding opens the door to high-paying jobs

Coding is one of the best ways to land a great job that pays well. Even in the age of AI, software is still being built everywhere, but the work is shifting. AI can speed up routine coding, so entry-level roles are more competitive. However, coding gives you leverage in almost any industry — finance, healthcare, entertainment, agriculture, education — because those fields still need people who can define problems clearly, build reliable solutions, and double-check results.

AI doesn't make learning to code pointless. It makes the fundamentals *more* important. If you can read, test, and debug code, you can use AI as a turbocharger instead of a crutch. That mix — automation plus human judgment — is what employers want.

Here are just a few example careers:

- Software developer
- Web developer
- Data scientist
- Cybersecurity analyst
- AI or machine-learning engineer

But you need a computer science degree, right? Not necessarily. Plenty of people who become professional programmers are self-taught using books just like this one!

You don't have to be a pro to benefit from learning to code

Yep, I get it: Being a professional programmer isn't for everyone. It might be the hours, the constant sitting, all that screentime, or whatever. Turning pro is one coding path, but it's not the only one. Whatever field you work in (or want to work in), having even basic coding know-how can give you an edge over your peers.

For example, if you work in marketing, knowing how to code can enable you to automate reports and analyze customer data. If you work in finance, coding can help you write scripts to track stock prices and investments. If healthcare is your field, knowing how to code can help you manage patient data efficiently. If you're an educator, you can use code to create fun and interactive learning tools for students.

Whatever your career, knowing how to code is a bonus skill that makes you more valuable, more productive, and more creative.

Coding is easier to learn than ever before

Back in the dim mists of time, otherwise known as the twentieth century, learning to code was hard. A few dedicated hobbyists taught themselves to program, mostly using a relatively simple language called BASIC, but the vast majority of programmers learned to code by obtaining expensive college degrees that required reading enormous textbooks filled with abstruse technical jargon and recondite computer science theory.

Today? Ah, today we have beginner-friendly languages like Python and JavaScript that enable *anyone* to learn to code, no fancy-schmancy college degree required. We even have AI-powered coding assistants that can help with the more technical parts so you can focus on the big picture. Forget the jargon and the theory. If you can think reasonably logically and you can break down a problem into smaller challenges, you can learn to code.

Coding is the future

Back in 2011, the venture capitalist Marc Andreessen wrote an op-ed piece titled "Why software is eating the world." He meant that software was and is transforming entire industries and disrupting traditional ways of doing business. He predicted that software would become a crucial and more deeply baked-in component of company operations, products, and services.

However, before software can eat anything, it has to be coded. Before software can be embedded into every facet of business, someone has to program it. Software is all around us now and will soon be ubiquitous. Learning to code now future-proofs your skills, ensuring that you stay relevant in this rapidly evolving, being-eaten-by-software world.

Real-World Uses of Coding

The overall theme of this chapter has been that coding, at its most basic, is just cajoling a computer into performing some task. As the early chapters in Book 2 (Python) and Book 6 (JavaScript) show, it's not that hard to write code that makes a computer do something trivial, such as display text on the screen. Simple and straightforward examples are a great learning tool and an easy way to build your coding confidence, but they lack, well, substance.

After writing and running a few such examples, you might start to wonder whether that's all there is to coding. Is programming all bun and no hamburger? All sizzle and no steak? Are any vegetarians still reading this?

Fortunately, even beginner-welcoming languages such as Python and JavaScript can be used to build useful and fun projects. You build some in this book a bit later, but for now I want to give you a taste of what's possible. Here, broken down into five development categories, are a few things that folks in the real world are building using Python:

- **Automation:** Python can automate boring, repetitive tasks like renaming files, sending emails, and scraping data from websites. For example, a marketer can write a Python script to automatically send out weekly email reports instead of doing it manually.
- **Data science:** Big-time firms such as Google, Netflix, and Facebook use Python to analyze the massive amounts of data they generate. Many business users take advantage of Python libraries such as Pandas and NumPy to help them make sense of customer behavior, market trends, and sales predictions.
- **Machine learning:** This branch of AI enables computers to learn from data and make decisions or predictions without being programmed. Python-based machine-learning tools such as TensorFlow and scikit-learn enable companies to develop AI-powered systems, such as recommendation engines (I'm looking at *you*, Netflix suggestions).
- **Scientific computing and engineering:** NASA and other scientific institutions take advantage of Python to create complex simulations and calculations. Python also helps engineers analyze large datasets in fields such as genetics, physics, and climate modeling.
- **Web development:** Python is used to build web applications using tools such as Django and Flask, and companies such as Instagram and Spotify rely on Python-based web services. However, in web development, Python is most often called upon for building server systems for handling chores such as data storage, user authentication, and security.

Here are some projects that coders in the real world are building using JavaScript, arranged into five development categories:

- **Web page development:** A sprinkling of JavaScript turns a boring web page into something interactive and dynamic. Browser-based JavaScript can request data from a server, display that data on the page, and handle user input. For example, when you type some text in a web page search box, and a list of matching items appears lickety-split, that tells you that JavaScript is working feverishly in the background to fetch and display those search results.
- **Web server development:** A JavaScript tool called Node.js runs on many web servers and is used for *back-end* tasks, such as dealing with data, authenticating users, and providing cloud services. Behemoth companies such as LinkedIn and PayPal use Node.js to power their web apps.
- **Mobile apps:** JavaScript tools are available that enable developers to build mobile apps. Using the framework React Native, Facebook and Instagram (and many others) use JavaScript to offer apps that work on both iOS and Android devices.
- **Games:** JavaScript tools such as Phaser.js enable developers to use JavaScript to build games that run either in the browser or on mobile devices.
- **Smart devices:** JavaScript is used to program smart home devices, such as lights, security cameras, and thermostats. And with Node.js, developers can connect JavaScript applications to Internet of Things (IoT) systems.

IN THIS CHAPTER

- » Getting to know variables, data types, and objects
- » Building your own expressions and functions
- » Controlling code with conditionals and loops
- » Adding comments for readability
- » Debugging the inevitable errors

Chapter 2 Essential Coding Concepts

Well begun is half done.

—ARISTOTLE

A certain class of programmer self-identifies as a kind of high priest of software, versed, unlike us laypeople, in the esoteric and arcane rites of programming. While it's certainly true that top-level software engineers are impressively knowledgeable about the systems they code; these high priest types want you to believe that only a select group is capable of doing *any* kind of programming.

You're about to find out just how untrue that is. Coding, far from being a rarefied intellectual pursuit available only to an elite few, is a democratic craft that anyone can learn. As proof, I offer up this chapter, which demonstrates that true coding requires understanding just a handful of programming concepts: variables, data types, expressions, conditionals, loops, functions, and objects. Oh, sure, the high priests know a few dozen more programming ideas. But with this chapter's accessibly small list of coding concepts, you can build a lifetime's worth of apps, websites, games, or whatever you like. Your path to becoming a true coder — ignore those blustering high priests over there — begins now.

Storing Stuff in Variables

By default, your programs live a life without the benefit of short-term memory. In the case of Python and JavaScript, the interpreter executes your code one statement at a time, until no more statements are left to process. It all happens in the perpetual present. Ah, but note that I refer to this lack of short-term memory as the *default* state of your scripts. You have the power to give your scripts the gift of short-term memory.

But why would a script need short-term memory? Because one of the most common concepts that crops up when coding is the need to store a temporary value for use later. In most cases, you want to use that value a bit later in the same script. However, you may also need to use it in some other script, to populate an HTML form (if you're coding a web page) or as part of a larger or more complex calculation. For example, if you're constructing a shopping cart script, you may need to calculate taxes on the order. To do that, you must first calculate the total value of the order, store that value, and then later take a percentage of it to work out the tax.

In programming, the way you save a value for later use is by storing it in a variable. A *variable* is a small chunk of computer memory set aside for holding program data. The good news is that the specifics of how the data is stored and retrieved from memory happen well behind the scenes, so it isn't something you ever have to worry about.

Declaring variables

The process of creating a variable is called *declaring* in programming terms. All declaring really means is that you're supplying the variable with a name and telling the browser to set aside a bit of room in memory to hold whatever value you end up storing in the variable.

How you declare a variable depends on the programming language you're coding in. Python is nice and simple because you just set the name of the variable equal to the value you want it to store initially:

```
cookies_eaten = 3
```

This statement declares a variable named cookies_eaten and sets the variable's value to 3.

Most other languages require a bit more info. Here's a variable declared in Java (not the same as JavaScript; check out Chapter 3 in this minibook if you don't believe me):

```
float interestRate = 0.05
```

The added float keyword declares the variable with the floating-point data type. Skip ahead to the "Dealing with Data Types" section to find out what on Earth the phrase *floating-point* refers to.

REMEMBER

Variable names can't include spaces, so when a name requires two or more words, most coders smush the words together and capitalize the first letter of every word after the first. This combination of lowercase and uppercase letters is called *camel case* (because it creates humps in the text; no, seriously).

Many languages enable you to declare a variable without also assigning it a value. Here's an example using the Go language:

```
var interestRate float32
```

Note the var keyword, which is short for *variable* and is a common keyword for declaring variables. You then assign a value to the variable later in your code:

```
interestRate = 0.05
```

Including variables in other statements

With a variable declared and assigned a value, you can then use that variable in other statements. When the interpreter comes across the variable, it goes to the computer's memory, retrieves the current value of the variable, and then substitutes that value into the statement. The following code presents an example:

```
interestRate = 0.05
interestRate = interestRate / 12
```

This code declares a variable named interestRate with the value 0.05; it then divides that value by 12 and stores the result in the variable.

TECHNICAL STUFF

If the second statement is something you've never come across before, it probably looks a bit illogical. How can something equal itself divided by 12? The secret to understanding such a statement is to remember that the interpreter always evaluates the right side of the statement — that is, the expression to the right of the equals sign (=) — first. In other words, it takes the current value of `interestRate`, which is `0.05`, and divides it by `12`. The resulting value is what's stored in `interestRate` when all is said and done. For a more in-depth discussion of operators and expressions, fast-forward to the "Constructing Expressions" section.

Getting your head around arrays and lists

Variables are a fundamental aspect of coding, but it's easy to use them inefficiently. For example, consider the following declarations:

```
day1 = "Monday"
day2 = "Tuesday"
day3 = "Wednesday"
day4 = "Thursday"
day5 = "Friday"
day6 = "Saturday"
day7 = "Sunday"
```

These are string variables (check out "Dealing with Data Types" to learn what a string is), and together they store a collection of related things (days of the week, in this case). Whenever you find you have multiple variables storing related or similar items, you can group all those items into a single variable called an *array*, or in Python, a *list*.

You can enter as many values as you want into the array or list, and the programming language tracks each value using an *index number*. For example, the first value you add is given the index 0. (For obscure reasons, programmers since time immemorial have numbered lists of things starting with 0 instead of 1.) The second value you put into the array or list is index 1; the third value gets 2; and so on. You can then access any value in the array or list by specifying the index number you want.

You have to declare the array or list, and how you do that depends on the language. Here's an example list from Python:

```
days = ["Monday", "Tuesday", "Wednesday", "Thursday",
        "Friday", "Saturday", "Sunday"]
```

The square brackets ([and]) tell the interpreter that every item between the brackets is part of the list assigned to the variable days.

In most programming languages, you reference an array or a list item using the array or list name followed by the item's index number in square brackets. For example, days[0] refers to "Monday" and days[6] refers to "Sunday". (A few languages — most notably Visual Basic and Visual Basic for Applications — use regular parentheses instead of square brackets.)

Dealing with Data Types

In programming, a variable's *data type* specifies what kind of data is stored in the variable. The data type is a crucial idea because it determines not only how two or more variables are combined (for example, mathematically) but also whether they can be combined at all. *Literals* are a special class of data type, and they cover values that are fixed (even if only temporarily). For example, consider the following variable assignment statement:

```
todaysQuestion = "Who let the dogs out?"
```

Here, the text Who let the dogs out? is a literal string value. All programming languages support three kinds of literal data types: numeric, string, and Boolean. The next three sections discuss each type.

Working with numeric literals

The two basic numeric literals are integers and floating-point numbers:

- **Integers:** These numbers don't have a fractional or decimal part. So you represent an integer using a sequence of one or more digits, as in these examples:

```
0
42
2001
-20
```

- **Floating-point numbers:** These numbers do have a fractional or decimal part. Therefore, you represent a floating-point number by first writing the integer part, followed by a decimal point, followed by the fractional or decimal part, as in these examples:

```
0.07
3.14159
-16.6666667
7.6543e+21
1.234567E-89
```

TECHNICAL STUFF

The last two floating-point examples require a bit more explanation. They use *exponential notation*, which is an efficient way to represent really large or really small floating-point numbers. Exponential notation uses an `e` (or `E`) followed by the *exponent*, which is a number preceded by a plus sign (+) or a minus sign (–).

You multiply the first part of the number (that is, the part before the `e` or `E`) by 10 to the power of the exponent. Here's an example:

```
9.87654e+5
```

The exponent is 5, and 10 to the power of 5 is 100,000. Multiplying 9.87654 by 100,000 results in the value 987,654.

Here's another example:

```
3.4567e-4
```

The exponent is –4, and 10 to the power of –4 is 0.0001. Multiplying 3.4567 by 0.0001 results in the value 0.00034567.

Working with string literals

A *string literal* is a sequence of one or more letters, numbers, or punctuation marks, enclosed in either double quotation marks (`"`) or single quotation marks (`'`). Here are some examples:

```
"Coding For Dummies"
'Literally a string literal'
""
"What's the deal with airline peanuts?"
```

REMEMBER

The string `""` (or `''` — two consecutive single quotation marks) is called a *null string* or an *empty string*. It represents a string that doesn't contain any characters.

The final example shows that it's okay to insert — or *nest* — one or more instances of one of the quotation marks (such as ') inside a string enclosed by the other quotation mark (such as "). Being able to nest quotation marks comes in handy when you need to embed one string inside another, which is a common coding situation. Here's a JavaScript example:

```
onsubmit="processForm('testing')";
```

However, it's illegal to insert in a string one or more instances of the same quotation mark that encloses the string, as in this example:

```
"This is "illegal" in every programming language."
```


Working with Boolean literals

Booleans are the simplest of all the literal data types because they can assume only one of two values: `true` or `false`. That simplicity may make it seem as though Booleans aren't particularly useful, but the capability to test whether a particular variable or condition is true or false is invaluable in programming.

You can assign Boolean literals directly to a variable, like this:

```
taskCompleted = true
```

Alternatively, you can work with Boolean values implicitly by using expressions (refer to the section "Constructing Expressions" to learn more). For example, in most languages, you can test whether two items are *equal* by using the == operator:

```
currentMonth == "August"
```

The comparison expression `currentMonth == "August"` asks the following: Is the value of the `currentMonth` variable equal to the string `"August"`? If it is, the expression evaluates to the Boolean value `true` (or `True` in some languages); if it's not, the expression evaluates to `false` (or `False` in some languages).

REMEMBER

When you want to assign a value to a variable, you use a single equals sign (=), which is known in the programming trade as the *assignment operator.* When you want to compare two things to determine whether they're equal, you use two equals signs (==), which coders refer to as the *equal to operator.*

Constructing Expressions

An *expression* is a collection of symbols, words, and numbers that performs a calculation and produces a result. That's a nebulous definition, I know, so I'll make it more concrete.

When your check arrives after a restaurant meal, one of the first things you probably do is take out your smartphone and use the calculator to figure out the tip amount. The service and food were good, so you're thinking 20 percent is appropriate. With phone in hand, you tap in the bill total, tap the multiplication button, tap 20%, and then tap Equals. Voilà! The tip amount appears on the screen, and you're good to go.

A programming expression is something like this kind of procedure because it takes one or more inputs, such as a bill total and a tip percentage, and combines them in some way — for example, by using multiplication. In expression lingo, the inputs are called *operands,* and they're combined by using special symbols called *operators:*

- **operand:** An input value for an expression. An operand is the raw data that the expression manipulates to produce its result. The operand could be a number, a string, a variable, a function result (refer to "Organizing Code into Functions," later in this chapter), or an object property (check out "Introducing Objects," later in this chapter).
- **operator:** A symbol that represents a particular action performed on one or more operands. For example, the * operator represents multiplication, and the + operator represents addition.

Assuming that your code has already declared a variable named `billTotal` that holds the bill total, as well as a variable named `tipPercentage` that holds the percentage you want to tip, here's an expression that calculates a tip amount and assigns the result to a variable named `tipAmount`:

```
tipAmount = billTotal * tipPercentage
```

The expression is everything to the right of the equals sign (=). Here, `billTotal` and `tipPercentage` are the operands, and the multiplication sign (*) is the operator.

REMEMBER

Another analogy I like to use for operands and operators is a grammatical one — that is, if you consider an expression to be a sentence, the operands are the nouns (the things) of the sentence and the operators are the verbs (the actions) of the sentence.

Building numeric expressions

Calculating a tip amount on a restaurant bill is a mathematical calculation, so you may be thinking that code expressions are going to be mostly mathematical. If I were standing in front of you and happened to have a box of gold stars on me, I'd certainly give you one because, yes, math-based expressions are probably the most common type you'll come across.

A mathematical calculation is often called a *numeric expression,* and it combines numeric operands and arithmetic operators to produce a numeric result. Every programming language's basic arithmetic operators are more or less the same as those found in your smartphone's calculator app or on the numeric keypad of your computer's keyboard, plus a couple of extra operators for more advanced work. Table 2-1 lists the basic arithmetic operators you can use in your code expressions.

TABLE 2-1 Basic Arithmetic Operators

Operator	Name	Example, where `n = 10`	Result
+	Addition	`n + 4`	`14`
++	Increment	`n++`	`11`
–	Subtraction	`n - 4`	`6`
–	Negation	`- n`	`-10`
--	Decrement	`n--`	`9`
*	Multiplication	`n * 4`	`40`
/	Division	`n / 4`	`2.5`
%	Modulus	`n % 4`	`2`

REMEMBER

Although most programming languages (including JavaScript) support the increment (++) and decrement (--) operators, some languages (including Python) don't.

Almost all programming languages support a few extra operators that combine some of the arithmetic operators and the assignment operator, which is the humble equals sign (=) that assigns a value to a variable. Table 2-2 lists these *arithmetic assignment* operators.

TABLE 2-2 Arithmetic Assignment Operators

Operator	Example	Equivalent
+=	`x += y`	`x = x + y`
-=	`x -= y`	`x = x - y`
*=	`x *= y`	`x = x * y`
/=	`x /= y`	`x = x / y`
%=	`x %= y`	`x = x % y`

Building string expressions

A *string expression* is one where at least one of the operands is a string, and the result of the expression is another string. String expressions are straightforward in the sense that there is only one operator to deal with: the *concatenation* operator, which in most languages (including Python and JavaScript) is `+`. You use this operator to combine (or *concatenate*) strings in an expression. For example, the expression `"Java" + "Script"` returns the string `"JavaScript"`.

Yep, it's unfortunate that the concatenation operator is identical to the addition operator because this similarity can lead to some confusion. For example, the expression `2 + 2` returns the numeric value `4` because the operands are numeric. However, the expression `"2" + "2"` returns the string value `22` because the two operands are strings.

Building comparison expressions

You use *comparison expressions* to compare the value of two or more numbers, strings, variables, function results, object properties, or object method results. If the expression is true, the expression result is set to the Boolean value `true`; if the expression is false, the expression result is set to the Boolean value `false`. You'll use comparisons with alarming frequency in your code, so it's important to understand what they are.

Table 2-3 summarizes the comparison operators used in most programming languages.

In Table 2-3, note that JavaScript uses `===` instead of `==` (and `!==` instead of `!=`). JavaScript supports `==` (and `!=`), but for too-geeky-to-get-into reasons (until you get to Book 6), your JavaScript code should only ever use `===` (and `!==`).

TABLE 2-3 Comparison Operators

Operator	Name	Example	Result
==	Equal to	10 == 4	false
!=	Not equal to	10 != 4	true
>	Greater than	10 > 4	true
<	Less than	10 < 4	false
>=	Greater than or equal to	10 >= 4	true
<=	Less than or equal to	10 <= 4	false
===	Strictly equal to (JavaScript)	"10" === 10	false
!==	Strictly not equal to (JavaScript)	"10" !== 10	true

Building logical expressions

You use *logical expressions* to combine or manipulate Boolean values, particularly comparison expressions. For example, if your code needs to test whether two different comparison expressions are both true before proceeding, you can do that with a logical expression.

Table 2-4 lists the most common logical operators.

TABLE 2-4 Logical Operators

<table>
<tr><th>Operator</th><th>Name</th><th>General Syntax</th><th>Returned Value</th></tr>
<tr><td>&& or and</td><td>AND</td><td>expr1 && expr2
or
expr1 and expr2</td><td>true if both expr1 and expr2 are true; false otherwise</td></tr>
<tr><td>|| or or</td><td>OR</td><td>expr1 || expr2
or
expr1 or expr2</td><td>true if one or both of expr1 and expr2 are true; false otherwise</td></tr>
<tr><td>! or not</td><td>NOT</td><td>!expr
or
not expr</td><td>true if expr is false; false if expr is true</td></tr>
</table>

In the Operator column of Table 2-4, note that most programming languages (JavaScript is one of them) use the symbols `&&`, `||`, and `!`. Just a few languages (Python is one of them) use the words `and`, `or`, and `not`.

Making Decisions with Conditionals

One of the most common coding conundrums is controlling when part of your code runs. For example, you might want a particular set of statements to run only if today is Monday. Similarly, you might want some division code *not* to run if the divisor is equal to `0`. Because constraints such as the day of the week and whether a value is a particular number are used as conditions that dictate when or if some code will execute, this programming logic is called *conditional execution*, and the language features you use are called *conditionals*.

Making simple true/false decisions

The most basic test is the simple true/false decision (which could also be thought of as a yes/no or an on/off decision). In this case, your program looks at a certain condition, determines whether it's currently true or false, and acts accordingly. Comparison and logical expressions (covered in the preceding section) play a big part here because they always return a `true` or `false` result.

In all programming languages, simple true/false decisions are handled by the `if` statement, which has a similar syntax in most languages. You can use the *single-line* syntax:

```
if (expression) statement
```

or the *block* syntax:

```
if (expression) {
    statement1
    statement2
    ...
}
```

REMEMBER

Syntax refers to the symbols, keywords, and structures that define how code must be written and formatted in a particular programming language to be correctly interpreted and executed by a compiler or interpreter.

In both cases, *`expression`* is a comparison or logical expression that returns `true` or `false`, and *`statement`*, *`statement1`*, *`statement2`*, and so on represent the code to run if *expression* returns `true`. If *expression* returns `false`, the code doesn't run the statements.

For example, suppose your code includes variables named `totalCookies` and `totalApples` that hold, respectively, the number of cookies and the number of apples the user ate this week. In your analysis, it's vital that you calculate the user's cookies-to-apples ratio (hey, it's your analysis):

```
cookiesToApples = totalCookies / totalApples
```

That's fine, but your code will generate an error if `totalApples` equals `0` since dividing by `0` is illegal. To prevent that error, you can use an `if` statement:

```
if (totalApples != 0) {
    cookiesToApples = totalCookies / totalApples
}
```

If `totalApples` isn't `0`, the expression `totalApples != 0` returns `true`, so the division statement runs. If, instead, `totalApples` is `0`, the expression `totalApples != 0` returns `false`, so the division statement doesn't run and no error occurs.

TIP

Note that in the block syntax, I've been indenting the statements by four spaces. This increases the readability of the code by making it clear which statements belong to the block (that is, the part between the braces: { and }). Some programmers use two spaces, but four makes the indentation clearer. (If someone tells you to use tabs instead of spaces, ignore them.)

Branching with if . . . else statements

Using the `if` statement to make decisions adds a powerful new weapon to your coding arsenal. However, the simple version of `if` suffers from an important limitation: A `false` result only bypasses one or more statements; it doesn't execute any of its own. This is fine in many cases, but there will be times when you need to run one group of statements if the condition returns `true` and a different group if the condition returns `false`. To handle these scenarios, you need to use an `if...else` statement, which, again, has a similar syntax in most languages:

```
if ( expression ) {
     statements-if-true
} else {
     statements-if-false
}
```

The *expression* is a comparison or logical expression that returns `true` or `false`. *statements-if-true* represents the block of statements you want your code to run if *expression* returns `true`, and *statements-if-false* represents the block of statements you want executed if *expression* returns `false`.

As an example, consider the following code:

```
if (currentDay == "Monday") {
    discountRate = 0.25
} else {
    discountRate = 0.1
}
discountedPrice = regularPrice * (1 - discountRate)
```

This code calculates the discounted price of an item, where the discount depends on whether the current day is Monday. Assume that earlier in the code, the script set the value of the current day (`currentDay`) and the item's regular price (`regularPrice`). An `if...else` statement checks whether `currentDay` equals `Monday`. If it does, `discountRate` is set to `0.25`; otherwise, `discountRate` is set to `0.1`. Finally, the code uses the `discountRate` value to calculate `discountedPrice`.

Automating Repetitive Tasks with Loops

It's one thing to write code that gets the job done, but your goal as a coder should always be to write code that gets the job done as efficiently as possible. Efficient programs run faster, take less time to code, and are usually (not always, but usually) easier to read and troubleshoot.

One of the best ways to introduce efficiency into your coding is to look for areas where you're essentially repeating the same code over and over. For example, consider the following code:

```
total = 0
total = total + 1
total = total + 2
total = total + 3
total = total + 4
total = total + 5
total = total + 6
total = total + 7
```

```
total = total + 8
total = total + 9
total = total + 10
```

This code first declares a variable named `total` and sets it equal to `0`. The next line adds `1` to the total, the next line adds `2`, and so on down to the final line, which adds `10` to the total. Besides being a tad useless, this code reeks of inefficiency because most of the code consists of repeatedly adding a value to the `total` variable.

To make code such as this more efficient, you can use a *loop*, which is a programming structure that repeats one or more statements for as long as you need it to. Quite a few different loop types are available, which tells you how important loops are to the coding process. I won't go through the different loop types here. Refer to Book 2, Chapter 5, to learn about looping in Python, and Book 6, Chapter 5, to get the goods on JavaScript loops.

For now, I'll hint at the loop wonders to come by introducing you to one of the most common loop types: the `while` loop, which uses the following syntax:

```
while ( expression ) {
    statements
}
```

Here, *`expression`* is a comparison or logical expression (that is, an expression that returns `true` or `false`) that, as long as it returns `true`, tells your code to keep executing the *`statements`* in the block.

Essentially, the programming language interpreter handles a `while` loop as follows: "Okay, as long as *`expression`* remains `true`, I'll keep running through the loop statements, but as soon as *`expression`* becomes `false`, I'm out of there."

Here's a closer look at how a `while` loop works:

1. Evaluate the *`expression`* in the `while` statement.
2. If *`expression`* is `true`, continue with Step 3; if *`expression`* is `false`, skip to Step 5.
3. Execute each of the statements in the block.
4. Return to Step 1.
5. Exit the loop (that is, execute the next statement that occurs after the `while` block).

The following code demonstrates how to use `while` to rewrite the inefficient code I presented earlier in this section:

```
total = 0
num = 1

while (num <= 10) {
    total = total + num
    num = num + 1
}
```

The code begins by initializing the `total` variable to `0`, as before. To control the loop, the code declares a variable named `num` and initializes it to `1`, which means the expression `num <= 10` is `true`, so the code enters the `while` block, adds `num` to `total`, and then increments `num`. This is repeated until the 11th time through the loop, when `num` is incremented to `11`, at which point the expression `num <= 10` becomes `false` and the loop is done.

Organizing Code into Functions

Imagine, if you will, cooking a dish that you make up as you go along. You assemble the ingredients you need, perform all the prep work and cooking, and then enjoy the resulting meal. A month or so later, you remember that the meal you thought up was delicious, so you repeat the process: You assemble the ingredients (perhaps with some slight variations this time), perform all the prep work and cooking (hoping you remember the steps correctly), and then once again chow down on the resulting dish.

That second time also produced a good meal, but there's an extra cognitive load involved because you're trying to remember what you did the first time. If it's a meal you think you'll cook a lot, just making it up from scratch every time is hard. A much better and easier way to go would be to write a recipe that has the following characteristics:

- It has a name.
- It has a list of ingredients.
- It has a set of instructions.
- It produces a dish.

In coding, the equivalent of a recipe is called a function, and every programming function has recipe-like features:

- It has a name.
- It has a list of inputs called *arguments.*
- It has a set of statements that it runs.
- It produces a result.

A *function*, then, is a group of statements that are separate from the rest of the program and that perform a designated task. (Technically, a function can perform any number of chores, but as a rule it's best for each function to focus on a specific task.) When your program needs to perform that task, you tell it to run — or *execute*, in programming vernacular — the function.

The way you define a function varies depending on the programming language, but in the simplest case (used in languages such as JavaScript, PHP, and Visual Basic), the basic structure of a function looks like this:

```
function functionName ([ arguments ]) {
    statements
}
```

where

- **`function`** identifies the block of code that follows it as a function. (Some languages use `func`, others use `fun`, Python uses `def`, and some languages don't bother with a keyword.)
- ***`functionName`*** is a unique name for the function. In most languages, function names must begin with a letter or an underscore (_); the rest of the function name can include any letter, any number, or the underscore; and you can't use any other characters, including spaces, symbols, and punctuation marks.
- ***`arguments`*** are zero or more values that are passed to the function and act as variables within the function. Arguments (or *parameters,* as they're sometimes called) are typically one or more values that the function uses as the raw materials for its tasks or calculations. You always enter arguments between parentheses after the function name, and you separate multiple arguments with commas. If you don't use arguments, you must still include the parentheses after the function name.
- ***`statements`*** are the code that performs the function's tasks or calculations.

TIP

When I present the syntax of a function that includes one or more optional arguments, I surround those arguments with square brackets — `[` and `]` — to let you know.

TIP

Note how the *`statements`* line in the example is indented slightly from the left margin. This standard and highly recommended programming practice makes your code easier to read. This example is indented four spaces, which is enough to do the job but isn't excessive. Some programmers use two spaces.

Note, too, the use of braces (`{` and `}`). These are used in many languages (including JavaScript) to enclose the function's statements within a block, which tells you (and the interpreter or compiler) where the function's code begins and ends.

Here's an example function:

```
function getDiscountedPrice (currentDay, regularPrice) {
    if (currentDay == "Monday") {
        discountRate = 0.25
    } else {
        discountRate = 0.1
    }
    discountedPrice = regularPrice * (1 - discountRate)
    return discountedPrice
}
```

This function is named `getDiscountedPrice` and accepts two arguments: `currentDay` and `regularPrice`. Inside the function, the code sets the `discountRate` based on the day of the week, performs the calculation, and then uses the `return` statement to send the result back. Back to where? Back to whichever statement executed — or *called* — the function.

Here's a slightly more complete example that demonstrates this function being called:

```
function getDiscountedPrice (currentDay, regularPrice) {
    if (currentDay == "Monday") {
        discountRate = 0.25
    } else {
        discountRate = 0.1
    }
    discountedPrice = regularPrice * (1 - discountRate)
    return discountedPrice
}
```

```
dayOfWeek = "Friday"
listPrice = 19.95
reducedPrice = getDiscountedPrice(dayOfWeek, listPrice)
```

The final three statements declare and initialize the `dayOfWeek` and `listPrice` variables, and then call the `getDiscountedPrice` function, passing the values of the `dayOfWeek` and `listPrice` variables as arguments. The value returned by the function is stored in the `reducedPrice` variable.

Introducing Objects

Only the simplest programs do nothing but assign values to variables and calculate expressions. To go beyond these basic programming beginnings — that is, to write truly useful programs — your code needs to manipulate things. Okay, I know *things* is annoyingly unspecific, but what your code manipulates depends on what the program was designed to do.

Take JavaScript as an example. JavaScript was designed from the start to manipulate the web page that it's displaying. That's what browser-based JavaScript is all about, and that manipulation can come in many forms:

- Add text and HTML attributes to an **element**.
- Modify a CSS **property** of a class or other selector.
- Store some data in the browser's internal **storage.**
- Validate a **form's** data before submitting it.

The bold items in this list are examples of the things you can work with, and they're special for no other reason than that they're programmable. In coding parlance, these programmable things are called *objects*.

You can work with objects in your code in any of the following three ways:

- You can read and make changes to the object's *properties.*
- You can make the object perform a task by activating a *method* associated with the object.
- You can define a procedure that runs whenever a particular *event* happens to the object.

To help you understand objects and their properties, methods, and events, I'll put them in real-world terms. Specifically, consider your computer as though it were an object:

- If you wanted to describe your computer as a whole, you'd mention things like the name of the manufacturer, the price, the size of the hard drive, and the amount of RAM. Each of these items is a *property* of the computer.
- You can also use your computer to perform tasks such as writing letters, crunching numbers, and coding programs. These are the *methods* associated with your computer.
- A number of things happen to the computer that cause it to respond in predefined ways. For example, when the On button is pressed, the computer runs through its Power On Self-Test, initializes its components, and so on. The actions to which the computer responds automatically are its *events*.

These properties, methods, and events give you an overall description of your computer.

But your computer is also a collection of objects, each with its own properties, methods, and events. The hard drive, for example, has various properties, including its speed and data-transfer rate. The hard drive's methods are actions such as storing and retrieving data. A hard drive event may be a scheduled maintenance task, such as checking the drive for errors.

In the end, you have a complete description of the computer: its appearance (its properties), how you interact with it (its methods), and to what actions it responds (its events).

In most programming languages, you reference an object's properties and methods using *dot notation*, as shown using the syntax in the following generic expressions:

```
object.property
object.method()
```

where

- ***object*** is the object that has the property or method.
- ***property*** is the name of the property you want to work with.

» ***method*** is the name of the method you want to run. Note that some methods are function-like in that they accept one or more arguments.

For example, consider the following JavaScript expression:

```
document.location
```

This expression refers to the `document` object's `location` property, which holds the address of the document (usually a web page) currently displayed in the browser window.

Because a property always contains a value, you're free to use property expressions in just about any type of statement and as an operand in an expression. You can assign a property value to a variable and, in many cases, you can assign a new value to the object property.

Methods that return values are similar: You can use them in expressions and assign their results to variables.

Documenting Code with Comments

A program that consists of just a few lines is usually easy to read and understand. However, your programs won't stay that simple for long, and these more complex creations will be correspondingly more difficult to read. (This difficulty will be particularly acute if you're looking at the code a few weeks or months after you first wrote it.) To help you decipher your code, it's good programming practice to make liberal use of comments throughout the script. A *comment* is text that describes or explains a statement or group of statements. Comments are ignored by the interpreter or compiler, so you can add as many as you deem necessary.

For short, single-line comments, use either the double-slash (`//`) or a hash symbol (`#`). Most programming languages (including JavaScript) support `//`, but some (such as Python) require `#`.

Put the `//` (or the `#`) at the beginning of the line and then type your comment after it (with a space in between for readability). Here's an example:

```
// Calculate the discounted price
discountedPrice = regularPrice * (1 - discountRate)
```

It's fine to use // (or #) for two or three comment lines in a row. However, most programming languages support multiple-line comments that begin with the /* symbol and end with the */ symbol. Here's an example:

```
/*
This code is released under the Creative Commons Zero
v1.0 Universal (CC0 1.0) license. To the fullest extent
permitted by law, I (the author) have dedicated this work
to the public domain.

This means:
- You are free to copy, modify, distribute, and use this
   code, for any purpose, even commercially.
- No permission or attribution is required, but giving
   credit is appreciated.
- This code is provided "as-is," without any warranties
   or guarantees.

For more details, refer to:
https://creativecommons.org/publicdomain/zero/1.0/
*/
```

WARNING

Although it's fine to add quite a few comments when you're just starting out, you don't have to add a comment to everything. If a statement is trivial or its purpose is glaringly obvious, forget the comment and move on. If you're not sure whether to comment some code, go ahead and add the comment, particularly while you're just getting started building a program. Adding copious comments to your new code is a great way to organize your thoughts and keep your code readable. You can always go back later and delete comments that you no longer need.

Debugging Code and Handling Errors

It usually doesn't take too long to get short scripts and functions up and running. However, as your code grows larger and more complex, errors inevitably creep in. In fact, it has been proven mathematically that any code beyond a minimum level of complexity will contain at least one error and probably quite a lot more.

Many of the bugs that crawl into your code will consist of simple typos that you can fix quickly, but others will be more subtle and harder to find. For the latter — whether the errors are incorrect values returned by functions or problems with the overall logic of a script — you need to be able to get inside your code to scope out what's wrong.

The good news is that most programming languages have a ton of top-notch tools that can remove some of the burden of program problem solving, which is known as *debugging* in the coding trade.

Understanding error types

When a problem occurs, you first need to determine what kind of error you're dealing with. The three basic error types are syntax errors, runtime errors, and logic errors:

- **Syntax errors:** These errors arise from misspelled or missing keywords, incorrect punctuation, or mangled indentation in Python.
- **Runtime errors:** Runtime errors occur during the execution of a program. They generally mean that the interpreter or compiler has stumbled upon a statement that it can't figure out. A runtime error might be caused by trying to use an uninitialized variable in an expression.
- **Logic errors:** If your code zigs instead of zags, the cause is usually a logic error, which is a flaw in the logic of your script. It might be a loop that never ends or a function that doesn't return a value. Logic errors are usually the toughest to pin down because you don't get an error message to give you a clue about what went wrong and where.

Taking a look at some debugging techniques

Debugging effectively is closer to an art than a science and something you'll acquire an intuitive feel for as you become more experienced as a coder (which is the same thing as saying "as you become more experienced dealing with the inevitable errors in your code"). I talk about language-specific debugging techniques in Book 2 (Python) and Book 6 (JavaScript), and I talk about techniques and tools for using AI to help with debugging in Book 4, Chapter 4. In the meantime, here's a general look at the three main debugging techniques:

- **Pausing code execution:** In this technique, you temporarily stop your code, which puts the code into *break mode* to let you examine certain elements, such as the current values of variables or object properties. Break mode also lets you execute program code one statement at a time (refer to the next item in this list) so that you can monitor the flow of the script. If you know approximately where an error or a logic flaw is occurring, you can enter break mode at a specific statement in the program by setting a *breakpoint* on that statement.

- **Stepping through your code:** One of the most common (and most useful) debugging techniques is to step through the code one statement at a time. Doing so lets you get a feel for the program flow to make sure that things such as loops and function calls are executing properly. You can use three main techniques:
  - *Step one statement at a time:* Executes the current statement and then pauses on the next statement. If the current statement to run is a function call, stepping takes you into the function and pauses at the function's first statement. You can then continue to step through the function until you execute the last statement, at which point the browser returns you to the statement after the function call.
  - *Step over some code:* For a statement that calls a function, executes the function normally without stepping into it, and then resumes break mode at the next statement *after* the function call.
  - *Step out of some code:* Takes you immediately out of a function that you've stepped into. This is handy when you've accidentally stepped into a function that you'd meant to step over.
- **Monitoring script values:** Many runtime and logic errors are the result of (or, in some cases, can result in) variables assuming unexpected values. If your program uses or changes these elements in several places, you'll need to enter break mode and monitor the values of these elements to figure out where things go awry.

More debugging strategies

Debugging your programs can be a frustrating job, even for relatively small apps. Here are a few tips to keep in mind when tracking down programming problems:

- **Indent your code for readability.** All code is immeasurably more readable when you indent the code in each statement block. Readable code is that much easier to trace and decipher, so your debugging efforts have one less hurdle to negotiate. How far you indent is a matter of personal style, but two or four spaces is typical:

```
function myFunction() {
    Each statement in this function
    block is indented four spaces.
}
```

If you nest one block inside another, indent the nested block by another four spaces:

```
function myFunction() {
    Each statement in this function
    block is indented four spaces.
    while ( something <= somethingElse ) {
        Each statement in this nested while
        block is indented another four spaces.
    }
}
```

Note that when you code in Python, nesting block statements with consistent indentation is required.

- **Break down complex tasks.** Don't try to solve all your problems at once. If you have a large program or function that isn't working right, test it in small chunks to try to narrow down the problem.
- **Break up long statements.** One of the most complicated aspects of script debugging is making sense out of long statements (especially expressions). It's usually best to keep your statements as short as possible. After you get things working properly, you can often recombine statements for more efficient code.
- **Comment out problem statements.** If a particular statement is giving you problems, temporarily deactivate it by turning the statement into a comment (check out "Documenting Code with Comments" for more info). If you have a number of consecutive statements you want to skip, you can turn them all into a multiline comment.
- **Use comments to document your scripts.** Speaking of comments, it's a programming truism that good code — meaning (at least in part) code that uses clear variable and function names and a logical structure — should be self-explanatory. However, almost every piece of non-trivial code contains sections that, when you examine them later, aren't immediately obvious. For those sections, it's another programming truism that you can never add enough explanatory comments. The more comments you add to complex and potentially obscure chunks of your code, the easier your programs will be to debug.

IN THIS CHAPTER

- » Getting your first looks at Python and JavaScript
- » Peeking at a few other languages
- » Learning how each language is used
- » Figuring out interpreters versus compilers

Chapter 3
Getting to Know Some Programming Languages

There are only two kinds of languages: the ones people complain about and the ones nobody uses.

—BJARNE STROUSTRUP (INVENTOR OF C++)

Long-time coders tend to be a tad, well, opinionated about certain aspects of programming. Some of these aspects are reasonably described as trivial, such as whether two or four spaces should be used to indent code and whether strings should be delineated with double quotes (") or single quotes ('). More substantively, most experienced coders will defend their choice of programming editor to the death (which is only a slight exaggeration). Coders spend an inordinate amount of time waging these and other so-called holy wars over non-holy subjects such as braces, semicolons, and commas.

But these battles have nothing on those that surround programming languages, which spark some of the most intense holy wars in tech. Coders can be fiercely loyal to their favorite languages, sometimes to the point of raving lunacy. The web is littered with the rubble of scorched-earth battles over the merits of C versus C++, Python versus Ruby, and JavaScript versus TypeScript.

Happily, this chapter doesn't rehash any of these ancient (and fundamentally irresolvable) language wars. What you *do* get in this chapter is an introduction to the most popular and the most useful languages around today. Although the rest of this book delves into Python and JavaScript in more depth, you really can't go wrong if you decide to learn any of the languages that I mention in this chapter (with a few noted exceptions).

Ranking Programming Languages

When it comes to choosing a programming language to learn, it's best to first decide what you want to make, then find a language that can make it happen, preferably with a learning curve that's not too long and not too steep.

If, after all that, you're still not sure, another useful angle for comparing languages is to look up where each language ranks in terms of popularity or usage. The web has tons of such rankings, but two are considered to be the most useful:

- **TIOBE Index (`www.tiobe.com/tiobe-index/`):** Measures the popularity of programming languages by counting the number of search engine queries for each language (using data from Google, Bing, Yahoo!, Wikipedia, Amazon, YouTube, and Baidu), as well as the number of skilled engineers, courses, and third-party vendors mentioning a language. The TIOBE Index is updated monthly. (For what it's worth, TIOBE stands for *The Importance of Being Earnest*, which is the title of an Oscar Wilde play.)
- **IEEE Spectrum (`https://spectrum.ieee.org/top-programming-languages-2025`):** Ranks programming languages based on usage and demand by aggregating data from GitHub (a site for code repositories), Stack Overflow (a site for code discussions), Google Search trends, social media mentions, Reddit, IEEE Xplore (academic papers), and Indeed (job postings). The IEEE Spectrum ranking is updated annually.

Neither is perfect, but together they give you a reasonable sense of the popularity of a programming language. I provide both rankings for each language I mention in this chapter. (The TIOBE Index rankings are from March 2026 and the IEEE Spectrum rankings are from 2025.)

Assembly: Close to the Machine

Back in Chapter 1 of this minibook, I talked about how computers use 1s and 0s internally and that, at the most fundamental level, computers respond to instructions written in machine code. But writing raw machine language is like trying to have a dinner conversation using only Morse code — sure, it's *technically* possible, but nobody in their right mind would think it's a good idea.

To get away from the inefficiency and tedium of trying to communicate with a computer in its native tongue, a British computer scientist named Kathleen Booth invented something called assembly language way back in the 1940s. Assembly language acts as a kind of bridge between human-understandable code and the raw binary instructions that a computer executes.

For example, a typical machine code instruction looks like this:

```
01001000 11000111 11000000 00000101 00000000 00000000 00000000
```

Yuck! Now here's the assembly code equivalent:

```
mov rax, 5
```

Hmm, well, okay, I guess that's every bit as incomprehensible to you as the machine code, but at least you're dealing with letters and with numbers beyond those unfathomable 1s and 0s.

The key point is that assembly language is easier to write than pure machine code because instead of memorizing binary patterns (as if!), you use short commands called *mnemonics*, such as `mov` for moving data and `add` for addition.

In the preceding example, the instruction is telling the computer to move (`mov`) the value `5` into the register (a small storage area in the CPU) named RAX (`rax`).

Here's a longer example:

```
mov rax, 5
mov rbx, 3
add rax, rbx
```

This code puts `5` into register RAX and `3` into register RBX, and then adds the contents of RBX to RAX, which in this case means that RAX now holds the value `8`.

REMEMBER

Assembly allows for fine control over the computer's central processing unit (CPU). High-level languages such as Python hide the details of how the CPU executes code, but assembly lets you optimize performance and interact directly with hardware. Therefore, assembly is foundational for understanding how computers work. If you ever want to dive deep into cybersecurity, embedded systems (task-specific computers squirreled inside larger devices such as medical devices and industrial machines), or operating systems, you'll need to get your hands dirty with assembly code.

REMEMBER

Unlike Python or JavaScript, which work on any computer, assembly language is specific to the type of CPU you're using. An Intel x86 processor understands different assembly instructions than an ARM (Advanced RISC Machine) processor (like the one in most smartphones). This means that learning assembly is often tied to a particular CPU architecture.

If you want to give assembly a whirl (how brave of you!), here are some next steps:

- **Decide which architecture you want to write for.** The architecture will be either x86 for Windows programs or ARM for M-series Macs, Raspberry Pi boards, and most smartphones and smart home devices.
- **Look at simple examples, preferably *lots* of them.** Many online resources provide basic assembly programs.
- **Get yourself an assembler.** An *assembler* is a compiler for translating assembly code into machine code. Examples include NASM (Netwide Assembler) and MASM (Microsoft Macro Assembler) for x86, and ARMASM (ARM Assembler) for ARM.
- **Experiment in a sandbox.** Websites like Try It Online (`https://tio.run/`) and Compiler Explorer (`https://godbolt.org/`) enable you to choose an assembler, write assembly code for it, and compile the code. (It's called a *sandbox* because it's a place where you can play with the code without fear of wrecking anything.)

Since time immemorial, programming teachers have introduced students to a language by offering a "Hello, World!" program, which is generally used as an example of the simplest working program in the language. Who am I to break with tradition? Therefore, for each language I introduce in this chapter, I provide a "Hello, World!" example. Here's one for x86 (64-bit) assembly language written for the Linux operating system:

```
section .data
    msg db "Hello, World!", 0 ; Define the string to print

section .text
    global _start ; Set the program entry point

_start:
    mov rax, 1    ; Set syscall to 1 (sys_write)
    mov rdi, 1    ; Set the file descriptor to 1 (stdout)
    mov rsi, msg  ; Store a pointer to the message
    mov rdx, 13   ; Store the message length
```

```
    syscall         ; Execute the system call

    mov rax, 60     ; Set syscall to 60 (sys_exit)
    mov rdi, 0      ; Set the exit code to 0
    syscall         ; Execute the system call
```

Note that, in assembly code, a semicolon marks the start of a comment. So in the preceding code, any text to the right of a semicolon is a comment describing the code to the left of the semicolon.

REMEMBER

All the code in this chapter is available with this book's example files. Head back to the Introduction to learn how to get your mitts on those files.

What about rankings? Not surprisingly, assembly doesn't rank near the top in any ranking, but neither is it mired anywhere near the bottom:

TIOBE Index: 19th

IEEE Spectrum: 23rd

Python: No Experience Required

By far the most common complaint I hear about learning programming is how finicky coding can be. Forget a brace (`{` or `}`) or a semicolon (`;`) or some other rarely used punctuation mark, and your program fails miserably. That's a valid criticism for most programming languages because they tend to be *syntax-heavy*, which means they have a seemingly endless list of complex and strict rules about what goes where.

Fortunately, there are exceptions to these exacting languages. One such exception is Python, one of the most popular and beginner-friendly programming languages in the world. Designed from the ground up to be easy to read and write, Python is the antithesis of all those persnickety languages.

Python's emphasis is on simplicity and readability, which makes it a great choice for anyone just getting started with coding. Unlike all those other programming languages that are defined by their labyrinthine syntax and overly meticulous rules, Python is forgiving and intuitive. That easygoing nature enables beginners to focus on learning core programming concepts and to get programs up and running quickly without getting bogged down by syntactical complexities.

To give you just the teensiest taste, here's a complete, working "Hello, World!" program in Python:

```
message = "Hello, World!"
print(message)
```

Here, `print()` is a built-in Python function that outputs text to the screen. After running this program, the text `Hello, World!` appears on your screen.

Because Python is so popular, a vast community of developers is out there ready to answer questions, write tutorials, offer coding challenges, and generally provide whatever support you need on your quest to learn the Python language. Python's popularity also means a rich ecosystem of prefabricated Python code — called *libraries* — exists to enable you to create programs that perform sophisticated tasks such as data analysis without having to code everything from scratch. Nice.

If Python was just easy to read and write, it would be a worthy candidate for your first programming language. But Python is also extremely flexible and versatile, which means you can use it for an eye-popping variety of tasks:

- **Automate everyday tasks.** Python saves time by automating repetitive tasks. With just a few lines of code, you can rename multiple files at once, automatically send emails or reminders, or scrape information from websites.
- **Work with and analyze data.** If you like numbers or want to explore data, Python makes it easy to create simple charts and graphs and analyze basic statistics (like averages, trends, or word frequency).
- **Build simple games.** Python lets you dip your toes into game development. As a beginner, you can create a text-based adventure game or a guess-the-number game. With libraries such as Pygame, you can even start adding graphics to your games as you progress.
- **Create simple apps.** Python makes it easy to build small applications that help you stay organized. For example, you could make a to-do list app to track your tasks or build a basic calculator.
- **Interact with online data sources.** Even as a beginner, you can use Python to pull in real-time data from the internet, including live weather updates for your city, fun facts, random jokes, or recent news headlines.
- **Experiment with AI and machine learning.** Python is a major player in AI, and beginners can start with simple chatbots that respond to user input, a program that predicts numbers based on past data, or a script that recognizes common words in text. Make no mistake: AI is an advanced topic, but Python makes it easy to experiment as you learn.

- **Build your own websites.** Python is used in web development with frameworks like Flask and Django. (A *framework* is a library that makes it easy to build websites by providing prefabricated code to handle common tasks such as database interactions and user authentication.)
- **Control hardware and IoT projects.** You can use Python to control a Raspberry Pi to make small gadgets, automate home devices (like turning lights on and off), and even read sensor data from small machines.

If Python sounds like the right choice for your first foray into coding, head on over to Book 2, where I take you through everything you need to know to get started with this beginner-friendly language.

Rankings:

TIOBE Index: 1st

IEEE Spectrum: 1st

JavaScript: The Glue that Binds the Web

When you surf the web, each page you visit consists of text, images, and maybe a video or two. How all that data is structured on the page is the job of a technology called Hypertext Markup Language, or HTML. How all that data looks on the page is the job of a technology called Cascading Style Sheets, or CSS. Together, HTML and CSS make up the *front end* of the web. Check out Book 5 to learn the details of how to write HTML and CSS.

But have you ever wondered where all that data comes from? Sometimes the data is added directly to the page, but in this modern age, more often than not, the data comes from a database that resides on a special computer called a *web server.* The database and the code that works with the data make up the *back end* of the web.

JavaScript is the secret sauce that brings the front end and the back end together to create the vast majority of web pages you visit today. JavaScript is the default programming language used for coding websites today. JavaScript is, first and foremost, a front-end web development language. That is, JavaScript runs inside the web browser and has access to everything on the page: text, images, HTML tags, CSS properties, and more. Having access to all the web page stuff means that you can use code to manipulate, modify, and even add and delete web page elements.

But although JavaScript runs in the browser, it's also a popular choice for running backend code. With JavaScript, you can send data to the server to store that data in a database, and you can request data from the server and then use code to display that data on the web page. (You learn about running backend code and accessing server-side data with JavaScript in Book 8.)

JavaScript, then, is the backbone of the modern web, powering everything from interactive websites to web applications and even mobile and desktop apps. It's a versatile and beginner-friendly programming language that enables developers to add dynamic behavior to web pages, making it one of the most essential languages for anyone interested in coding.

What makes JavaScript a great starter language is that it enables beginners to write, run, and troubleshoot code directly in a web browser without needing any special setup or tools. As long as you have access to a web browser (it doesn't even have to be online), you can experiment with code and display the results instantly. But you need a special browser, right? Nope. JavaScript is the only programming language supported by all modern web browsers, so you can use any browser you like.

Happily, the syntax of JavaScript is straightforward, especially for fundamental coding constructs such as variables, loops, and conditionals. That straightforwardness makes JavaScript an excellent language for learning core programming concepts.

Want a sample? Okay: Here's a complete, working "Hello, World!" program in JavaScript:

```
let message = "Hello, World!";
console.log(message);
```

Here, `console.log()` is a JavaScript function built into web browsers that prints messages to the console (an output area in a web browser's development tools). In this case, after running this program, the text `Hello, World!` appears in your browser's console.

JavaScript is one of the best programming languages for beginners because you can start creating fun and useful projects almost immediately. Whether you're interested in building websites, making interactive elements, or even experimenting with simple games, JavaScript has something exciting for you. Here's what you can expect to do as a beginner:

- **Make web pages interactive.** If you've ever clicked a button on a web page and something changed — such as a menu appeared, a pop-up showed up, or a form responded to your input — that's JavaScript at work. You can also show and hide sections of a page or create a simple image slideshow.

- **Build fun mini-projects.** JavaScript enables you to quickly build small projects that you — and anyone else who has access to your site — can use. Need a countdown timer for an event? JavaScript can do it. Want a random joke generator that shows a new joke when you click a button? That's JavaScript at work.
- **Create simple games.** Even as a beginner, you can start making basic games with JavaScript. With a bit of coding, you can create a number-guessing game where the user has to guess the correct number, a rock-paper-scissors game that plays against the computer, or a simple quiz where users can answer questions and get a score.
- **Add cool features to your pages.** Once you get comfortable, you can start adding features that make your pages more dynamic and engaging. For example, you could add a dark mode toggle that switches between light and dark themes, or you could add a search bar that filters page content.
- **Connect to online data.** JavaScript can pull information from the internet in real time. Even as a beginner, you can learn how to connect to online sources to display random facts or quotes, show the latest news headlines or weather updates, or build a simple app around online data (such as a list of movies or books).

If you're interested in exploring the possibilities of JavaScript, check out Book 6, where you can learn everything you need to know to get started in the world of JavaScript coding.

Rankings:

TIOBE Index: 6th

IEEE Spectrum: 6th

Sneaking a Peek at a Few Other Popular Languages

By a conservative estimate, something like 700 programming languages are in existence, with at least 100 languages in active use. 100! That's way too many to get your head around, so in this section I offer potted descriptions of the ten languages that I think are the most useful to know about.

C

C is a powerful, low-level programming language that has been around since the 1970s. It's known for its speed, efficiency, and direct access to hardware (that's what *low-level* means), making it a foundational language in computer science. Lots of modern languages, including C++ (covered next), Java, and Python, are influenced by C.

C is a fast and efficient language, making it great for performance-critical applications. C doesn't have a bunch of fancy features, so its programs tend to be super-compact. All these features are why C is the code underlying many of today's most complex projects:

- **Operating systems:** Windows, macOS, and Linux are all primarily written in C.
- **Embedded systems:** Smart devices, IoT devices, and device firmware are routinely coded in C.
- **Game development:** Game engines such as Unreal Engine are written in C.
- **Compilers and interpreters:** Many programming language compilers and interpreters are written in C. For example, the most widely used Python interpreter, called CPython, is written in C.
- **High-performance applications:** Many databases, networking tools, and scientific computing tools use C for maximum performance.

But coding in C is not for the faint of heart. There are no built-in safety features, so C, unlike newer languages, doesn't protect against common programming mistakes like buffer overflows (where a program writes more data to a memory area — called a *buffer* — than the area can hold, causing adjacent memory to be overwritten, often disastrously). Also with C, the developer has to allocate and free memory manually, which can lead to memory leaks (gradual increases in memory usage caused by failing to release no longer needed memory).

Here's a "Hello, World!" example in C:

```
#include <stdio.h>

int main() {
    char message[] = "Hello, World!";
    printf("%s\n", message);
    return 0;
}
```

Rankings:

TIOBE Index: 2nd

IEEE Spectrum: 8th

C++

As its name implies, C++ (pronounced "SEE-plus-plus") is an extension of C, adding object-oriented programming (OOP) features while maintaining the speed and efficiency of C. *OOP* is a programming philosophy based on the concept of objects (refer to Chapter 2 of this minibook) which, when used correctly, can make code more organized, easier to reuse, and easier to scale. Many modern languages use OOP principles, including Python, JavaScript (partially), C#, Kotlin, PHP, and Swift.

Like C, C++ runs close to the hardware, making it great for performance-critical applications. But with the addition of OOP features, C++ code is more reusable and more organized, and supports both high-level and low-level programming. C++ is widely used for high-performance applications and system programming:

- **Game development:** Lots of game-related code is written in C++ because game engines and interfaces have to be fast and require access to hardware.
- **High-performance software:** Many financial trading systems and scientific computing applications are coded in C++ for high performance.
- **Operating systems and embedded systems:** C++ is used to code many Windows components and the firmware for many IoT devices.
- **Web browsers:** The core components of browsers such as Chrome and Firefox are written in C++.
- **Graphics and virtual reality (VR) applications:** Many 3D rendering applications and VR simulations use C++.

On the downside, C++ has a huge learning curve and is far more complex than Python or even Java. As with C, developers must manually manage the allocation and release of memory, problems with which can lead to bugs and memory leaks. For these reasons, writing and debugging C++ code can take longer than in higher-level languages.

Here's a "Hello, World!" example in C++:

```
#include <iostream>

int main() {
    std::string message = "Hello, World!";
    std::cout << message << std::endl;
    return 0;
}
```

Rankings:

- TIOBE Index: 3rd
- IEEE Spectrum: 3rd

C#

C# (pronounced "SEE-sharp") is a modern, high-level programming language developed by Microsoft. It's heavily used for Windows applications, game development, and web services, and runs on the .NET framework. (.NET — it's pronounced DOT-net — is a software development platform created by Microsoft. It provides the tools, libraries, and a runtime environment needed to build and run Windows applications, web apps, and services. .NET also supports cross-platform development across Windows, macOS, and Linux using the unified .NET platform.)

You might be thinking that since C++ was an extension of C, C# must be an extension of C++. Yes and no. C# does extend C++ by automating the allocation and release of memory, so it removes the burden of manual memory management. But C# also removes the features found in both C and C++ that give developers low-level access to the hardware.

C# is an OOP language that's relatively easy to learn (at least compared to C++) and has strong error checking. It's a must if you ever want to get into Windows application development because it works seamlessly with .NET. C# is popular today not only for Windows applications but also for game development, Azure cloud computing services, enterprise software, and web development.

Here's a "Hello, World!" example in C#:

```
using System;

class Program {
    static void Main() {
```

```
        string message = "Hello, World!";
        Console.WriteLine(message);
    }
}
```

Rankings:

TIOBE Index: 5th

IEEE Spectrum: 5th

Go

Go (also called Golang) is a modern, open-source programming language developed by Google in 2009. It was designed to be a relatively easy language to learn by offering developers simple, clean, and easy-to-read code with a minimum of fussy rules (such as the semicolons that C and Java require at the end of each statement).

Go is a compiled language, so the resulting files are super-fast. Go is also cross-platform because you can compile your code to run on Windows, macOS, or Linux. That performance is why Go is very popular and is used for multiple areas of development:

- **Cloud computing and DevOps:** Go is used by big-time cloud concerns such as Docker, Kubernetes, and Terraform. (DevOps is a set of practices and tools that integrate software development — the Dev part — and IT operations — the Ops part — to improve collaboration, automate workflows, and accelerate software delivery.)
- **Web development:** Go is a popular language for coding back-end application programming interfaces (APIs) and microservices. (An *API* is software that enables different apps to communicate with each other. A *microservice* is a program that performs a specific task — such as user authentication — and is part of a larger application consisting of multiple such services.)
- **Networking and distributed systems:** Go code is fast and scalable (able to expand without running into problems), so it can handle large numbers of users.
- **High-performance applications:** Go is the language-of-choice when companies such as Google, Uber, and Dropbox feel the need for speed.
- **Command-line tools:** Go is great for building automation scripts that run from the command prompt.

Here's a "Hello, World!" example in Go:

```
package main

import "fmt"

func main() {
    var message string
    message = "Hello, World!"
    fmt.Println(message)
}
```

Rankings:

TIOBE Index: 16th

IEEE Spectrum: 10th

Java

Java is a powerful and widely used programming language best known for enabling developers to create "write once, run anywhere" code. That is, Java programs can run as-is on different devices (Windows PCs, Macs, mobile devices, you name it). How is that possible? It's all thanks to a chunk of software called the Java Virtual Machine (JVM), which acts as a kind of translator between your Java code and each device's operating system.

REMEMBER

So, Java and JavaScript are close language cousins, right? Nope. Other than both being coding languages, the two have little in common. As I like to say, Java is to JavaScript what ham is to hamburger.

Java has a bit of a learning curve, is one of those syntax-heavy languages I mentioned earlier, and requires the installation of a special development kit to get started, so it's not an ideal language for beginners.

To give you a taste, here's a "Hello, World!" example in Java:

```
public class HelloWorld {
    public static void main(String[] args) {
        String message = "Hello, World!";
        System.out.println(message);
    }
}
```

That code is quite a bit denser than the equivalent code in JavaScript and especially Python.

However, experienced Java developers love its clear syntax and strong error checking, which is why Java is a very popular language used all over the place:

- **Android app development:** Many Android apps are built with Java.
- **Web applications:** Java is used to build apps in banking, e-commerce, and enterprise systems.
- **Game development:** Java is a very popular choice for mobile and desktop games.
- **Big data and cloud computing:** Java is used in back-end services for handling large-scale applications.

Rankings:

TIOBE Index: 4th

IEEE Spectrum: 2nd

Kotlin

Kotlin is a modern, concise, and safe programming language developed by JetBrains. Google has anointed Kotlin as the preferred language for Android app development. Kotlin is designed to be easier to read and write than Java while maintaining high performance. Kotlin is also fully interoperable with Java, which means it works seamlessly with existing Java projects.

Even though Kotlin code can be a bit slower than the equivalent Java code and even though Kotlin does have a relatively steep learning curve, it's one of the fastest-growing languages today, and developers are using it for lots of things:

- **Android app development:** Kotlin is the primary language for coding modern Android apps.
- **Web development:** You can use Kotlin libraries such as Ktor and Spring Boot to build back-end web applications, APIs, and microservices.
- **Cross-platform apps:** With Kotlin Multiplatform, you can share code between Android, iOS, and web apps.

» **Data science and machine learning:** You can use Kotlin libraries such as Kotlin for Data Science to crunch data and KotlinDL (where DL is short for deep learning) to build AI applications.

Here's a "Hello, World!" example in Kotlin:

```
fun main() {
    val message: String = "Hello, World!"
    println(message)
}
```

Rankings:

TIOBE Index: 20th

IEEE Spectrum: 13th

PHP

PHP (the name is a recursive acronym for PHP: Hypertext Preprocessor) is a server-side scripting language designed for web development. (*Server-side* refers to operations that run on a server. The opposite is *client-side*, which refers to code that runs on a *client*, a system used to access a server. In web development, a web server represents the server side, and the web browser represents the client side.) PHP is widely used for building dynamic websites and web applications and is designed to work seamlessly with databases such as MySQL (pronounced "MY-ess-kew-ell" or sometimes "MY-sequel").

PHP is a beginner-friendly language with relatively simple syntax. Its syntax shares similarities with JavaScript, such as the use of braces and semicolons, so if you learn one, you'll be able to pick up the other quickly. (Someone who can code both the client-side and the server-side is well on their way to becoming what's known in the trade as a *full-stack developer*.)

Although PHP has been around forever (the first version was released way back in 1995!), it remains a powerful and popular language for many different uses:

» **Server-side web development:** PHP is designed to handle web forms, user authentication, database chores, and pretty much anything else required for web development on the server. About 75 percent of websites use PHP, including WordPress, Facebook, and Wikipedia.

» **Content management systems:** A CMS is software that enables users to create, edit, manage, and publish digital content, such as a blog. Many bigtime

CMS platforms — including WordPress, Drupal, and Joomla — are built using PHP.

- **Ecommerce websites:** PHP is the engine behind lots of sites that enable ecommerce, including WooCommerce and Magento.
- **APIs and back-end services:** Many developers use PHP to create APIs, and a PHP framework called Laravel helps developers create web apps.
- **Automating web tasks:** PHP is widely used for automating routine web chores such as form handling, file uploads, and sending email.

While newer languages like server-side JavaScript (Node.js) are growing in popularity, PHP still powers a massive chunk of the web and remains a great choice for anyone who wants to learn server-side web development.

Here's a "Hello, World!" example in PHP:

```
<?php
$message = "Hello, World!";
echo $message;
?>
```

Rankings:

TIOBE Index: 13th

IEEE Spectrum: 12th

Rust

Rust is a systems programming language known for its speedy performance and memory safety. It was built originally by a team at Mozilla (developer of the Firefox web browser) but is now an open-source project led by the Rust Foundation. Rust is widely used for developing high-performance, safe, and reliable software. Unlike C and C++, Rust offers developers built-in tools for preventing memory leaks and memory-related program crashes.

The blazing speed of Rust programs (they're comparable to C and C++ programs) and the safety of the code mean that Rust is rapidly finding lots of adherents in the high-end coding world:

- **Systems programming:** Rust is widely viewed as a modern alternative to C and C++ for operating system development.

- **WebAssembly:** Rust is often used to create WebAssembly code, which is high-performance, compiled code that runs in the web browser.
- **Embedded systems:** Rust provides safe and efficient code for IoT devices.
- **Game development:** Rust is used in many high-performance game engines.
- **Networking and cloud services:** Rust enables developers such as Amazon Web Services and Cloudflare to create fast, safe back-end services.
- **Cybersecurity and blockchain:** Rust is popular with developers who need to build secure applications and cryptographic tools.

Rust is powerful and complex, but it's becoming very popular, so it would be a great language to learn if you want a career in coding. If you're interested, you can check out my book *Rust All-in-One For Dummies*.

Here's a "Hello, World!" example in Rust:

```
fn main() {
    let message = "Hello, World!";
    println!("{message}");
}
```

Rankings:

TIOBE Index: 14th

IEEE Spectrum: 14th

Swift

Released in 2014 by Apple, Swift is a modern, fast, and safe programming language created for coding apps across Apple's major operating systems: iOS, iPadOS, macOS, tvOS, and watchOS. Swift is designed to be easy for beginners while powerful enough for professionals. Swift combines a clean and readable syntax reminiscent of Python, the speed of C thanks to being a compiled language, and some of the modern features of JavaScript. If you want to code apps only in the Apple ecosystem, you might want to take a close look at Swift.

Here's a "Hello, World!" example in Swift:

```
let message = "Hello, World!"
print(message)
```

Rankings:

TIOBE Index: 21st

IEEE Spectrum: 16th

TypeScript

TypeScript is just JavaScript with extra features that enable you to specify a data type when you declare a variable and to warn you when you try to mix data types. To understand why this is useful, first check out a basic variable declaration in JavaScript:

```
let message = "Hello, World!";
```

All is good: You're just storing a string literal in a variable named `message`. But later in the same program, your code could do this:

```
message = 42;
```

Now, instead of a string literal, you're using the same `message` variable to store a numeric literal. JavaScript is totally fine with that.

JavaScript might not protest at this mixing of data types, but such mixing can lead to problems in complex programs or when you use a method that requires a particular data type (such as a string). To avoid such woes, Microsoft invented TypeScript, which enables developers to specify a data type when they declare a variable. Here's an example:

```
let message: string = "Hello, World!";
console.log(message);
```

Here, `message` is the variable name, and the extra `: string` characters specify that `message` can only contain string data. If, later in the same program, your code tried to assign a number to the `message` variable, TypeScript would display an error message.

Rankings:

TIOBE Index: 32nd

IEEE Spectrum: 7th

Grokking the Difference between Interpreted and Compiled Languages

No matter which programming language you use, all programs must be translated into something that a computer understand and execute. The coding world uses two different tools to do this translating: compilers and interpreters.

A *compiler* is a software program that translates the entire source code of a program into machine code (sometimes called *binary*) before execution. The resulting machine code file can then be run repeatedly without further translation. The main advantages of compiled code are that it runs very fast and the compiler will let you know if your code contains syntax errors. The main disadvantage of compiled code is that the larger and more complex the code, the longer the compilation time. Compiled languages include C, C++, Go, Rust, and Swift.

An *interpreter* is a software program that translates and executes the source code one statement at a time, rather than converting the entire program into machine code beforehand. The interpreter reads and executes source code directly, so interpreted code runs slower because the translation happens at runtime. The interpreter stops executing the code at the first error it trips over. Interpreted languages include Python, JavaScript, and PHP.

Some languages use both a compiler and an interpreter. That is, the original code is compiled, and then the compiled code is executed using an interpreter. Languages that use both a compiler and an interpreter include C#, Java, and Kotlin.

IN THIS CHAPTER

» Automating repetitive tasks

» Getting help with syntax

» Testing your programs

» Enhancing your learning with AI

» Pair programming with AI

Chapter 4
How Coding Benefits from AI

The real problem is not whether machines think but whether men do.

—B.F. SKINNER

If you're a programmer or learning to program, *generative artificial intelligence* (also known as *GenAI*) can help you be more productive, make fewer mistakes, and learn new skills and languages faster, as you discover in this chapter. In the process, you work with some tools to get a taste of what's available. All the topics in this chapter are described in detail in later chapters.

Although you might be able to use AI to generate working computer programs without knowing how to code, I strongly discourage you from doing this — especially if you plan to deploy anything you generate. Generative AI systems are improving quickly and can produce useful code, but they don't truly understand programming concepts or context the way a human developer does. As a result, code generated without sufficient knowledge can contain security vulnerabilities, functional errors, or subtle flaws that are difficult to detect and fix.

TIP

If you're just starting out on your journey to learn to code, parts of this chapter might not make sense to you just yet. Feel free to skip this chapter for now and come back to it after you've had some practice with coding in Books 2 and 3. But I recommend that you read through this chapter now to gain some valuable context (and tools) as you set out to learn to code.

Banishing Boring Tasks

One of the most basic and useful things you can do with generative AI models is to use them to generate the types of code programmers lovingly refer to as boilerplate code.

TECHNICAL STUFF

The term *boilerplate* dates to the 19th century, when steel plates were used as templates for making steam boilers. The term was also used to describe prepared text such as advertisements and syndicated columns that were distributed to newspapers on metal printing plates.

Boilerplate code is the stuff that's the same or nearly the same in every file or every project. No one likes to write boilerplate code, but we have to do it because the code we want to write (the fun stuff) won't work without the boilerplate.

Spotting boring tasks

To identify tasks that can be automated with AI, think about the tasks that you do repeatedly in multiple projects. JavaScript developers might select an element in the browser window, such as a button, and attach an event listener to it to perform some action when a user interacts with that element. Or they might do something more complex, such as writing the code for a database-driven application that handles creating, reading, updating, and deleting (CRUD) tasks.

For web developers and designers, a simple example of boilerplate code that can be automated is the basic structure of an HTML page. Every valid HTML page starts with a document type declaration followed by an HTML element, and then a head element (including several internal elements, such as the title and meta tags), and then a body element.

Letting AI write the template

You can minimize the work required to generate a simple HTML template in many ways, such as by using a code snippet or searching the web for an example.

However, if you want to create a custom boilerplate that includes some structure and gives you a good start on the design of a future website, you could simply ask your AI. For example, I gave ChatGPT the following request:

```
Please generate an HTML template with a style element that
uses flexbox to create a three-column layout with a sample
top navigation bar and a footer.
```

Listing 4-1 shows the code that ChatGPT generated.

LISTING 4-1: ChatGPT's First Attempt

```
<!DOCTYPE html>
<html lang="en">
<head>
    <meta charset="UTF-8">
    <meta name="viewport" content="width=device-width,
  initial-scale=1.0">
    <title>Three Column Layout</title>
    <style>
        body {
            margin: 0;
            padding: 0;
            font-family: Arial, sans-serif;
        }
        .container {
            display: flex;
            flex-direction: column;
            min-height: 100vh;
        }
        header {
            background-color: #333;
            color: #fff;
            padding: 10px 0;
            text-align: center;
        }
        nav {
            background-color: #444;
            color: #fff;
            padding: 10px 0;
            text-align: center;
        }
        .main-content {
            flex: 1;
```

(continued)

LISTING 4-1: *(continued)*

```
            display: flex;
            justify-content: space-between;
            padding: 20px;
        }
        .sidebar {
            flex-basis: 20%;
            background-color: #f0f0f0;
            padding: 20px;
        }
        .content {
            flex-basis: 60%;
            background-color: #fff;
            padding: 20px;
        }
        .aside {
            flex-basis: 20%;
            background-color: #f0f0f0;
            padding: 20px;
        }
        footer {
            background-color: #333;
            color: #fff;
            padding: 10px 0;
            text-align: center;
        }
    </style>
</head>
<body>
    <div class="container">
        <header>
            <h1>Top Navigation Bar</h1>
        </header>
        <nav>
            <ul>
                <li> <a href="#">Home</a> </li>
                <li> <a href="#">About</a> </li>
                <li> <a href="#">Services</a> </li>
                <li> <a href="#">Contact</a> </li>
            </ul>
        </nav>
        <div class="main-content">
            <div class="sidebar">
                <h2>Sidebar</h2>
```

```
            <p>This is the sidebar content.</p>
        </div>
        <div class="content">
            <h2>Main Content</h2>
            <p>This is the main content area.</p>
        </div>
        <div class="aside">
            <h2>Aside</h2>
            <p>This is the aside content.</p>
        </div>
    </div>
    <footer>
        <p>Footer</p>
    </footer>
  </div>
</body>
</html>
```

The resulting HTML generated by my request (also known as a *prompt*) matched fairly well with what I would have done if I'd written it by hand. Figure 4-1 shows the resulting web page when I saved the generated HTML markup in a file and opened it in a browser without modifying it.

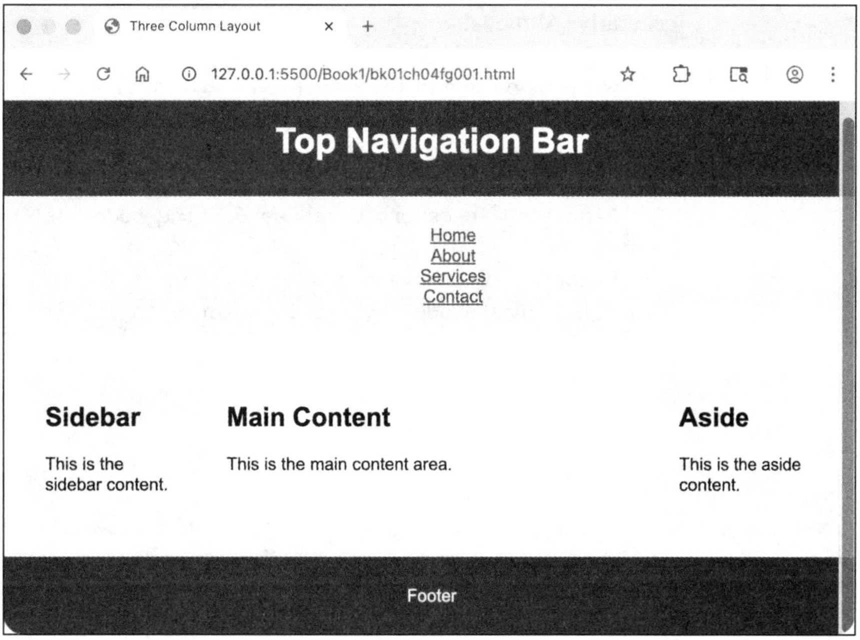

FIGURE 4-1: A ChatGPT-generated HTML template.

How Coding Benefits from AI

Crafting CRUD with AI

One of the most common tasks in any computer program is accessing a data source and writing functions for performing operations with the data source. The basic operations you can do with any data source are creating a record, reading a record, updating a record, and deleting a record. The collective name for the code that makes these operations possible is the wonderfully evocative acronym CRUD. Most people don't enjoy writing CRUD.

In this section, you use generative AI to reduce the amount of work it takes to generate some CRUD. To get started with this exercise, you need to have access to an interface for chatting with a generative AI model such as Anthropic Claude, ChatGPT, Google Gemini, or Microsoft Copilot. If you don't have an account with any of these services yet, follow the instructions in Book 4, Chapter 2 to sign up for ChatGPT.

Then, once you have a chat window in front of you, start with a short request to the generative model to see what it will do. Although pretty much any generative AI chatbot today (whether or not it's optimized for coding) can do a competent job with simple coding requests, starting simple ensures that you don't waste time crafting a detailed prompt if the service you're using won't or can't fulfill your request.

Once you have an initial response from the AI model, determine whether the response shows any promise. If you didn't get a response, try using a different generative AI model.

Here is the beginning of the response I got from ChatGPT to my initial prompt, which was "Write JavaScript functions for performing CRUD operations for a database table named todo-list:"

```
// Simulated in-memory database for the todo-list
const todoListDB = [];
// Function to Create a new todo item
function createTodoItem(title, description) {
  const newItem = {
    id: todoListDB.length + 1,
    title,
    description,
    completed: false,
  };
  todoListDB.push(newItem);
  return newItem;
}
```

Because I failed to provide enough information about my desired application, ChatGPT used an array as if it were a database, which is unlikely to be what is needed here. If you manage to get a promising response to your initial prompt, give the model additional details.

REMEMBER

The process of refining your instructions to a GenAI model and providing context and examples is called *prompt engineering.* Book 4, Chapter 2 covers the process of prompt engineering in detail.

For example, my next step would be to tell ChatGPT that this is a Node.js application that will be working with a MongoDB database and that it should use Mongoose. (You learn about Node.js, MongoDB, and Mongoose in Book 8.) When I prompted ChatGPT with that information, it gave me a much better response.

This time, ChatGPT responded with a complete Node.js application that connects to a local database and can perform CRUD operations. Listing 4-2 shows the regenerated code.

LISTING 4-2: ChatGPT's Second Attempt

```
const mongoose = require('mongoose');
// Connect to MongoDB
mongoose.connect('mongodb://localhost/todo-list', {
  useNewUrlParser: true,
  useUnifiedTopology: true,
});
// Define a TodoItem schema
const todoItemSchema = new mongoose.Schema({
  title: String,
  description: String,
  completed: Boolean,
});
// Create a TodoItem model
const TodoItem = mongoose.model('TodoItem', todoItemSchema);
// Function to Create a new todo item
async function createTodoItem(title, description) {
  const newItem = new TodoItem({
    title,
    description,
    completed: false,
  });
  try {
    await newItem.save();
    return newItem;
```

(continued)

LISTING 4-2: (continued)

```
  } catch (error) {
    throw error;
  }
}
// Function to Read all todo items
async function getAllTodoItems() {
  try {
    const todoItems = await TodoItem.find();
    return todoItems;
  } catch (error) {
    throw error;
  }
}
// Function to Read a specific todo item by ID
async function getTodoItemById(id) {
  try {
    const todoItem = await TodoItem.findById(id);
    return todoItem || null;
  } catch (error) {
    throw error;
  }
}
// Function to Update a todo item by ID
async function updateTodoItem(id, updatedData) {
  try {
    const updatedItem = await TodoItem.findByIdAndUpdate(id,
   updatedData, { new: true });
    return updatedItem;
  } catch (error) {
    throw error;
  }
}
// Function to Delete a todo item by ID
async function deleteTodoItem(id) {
  try {
    const deletedItem = await TodoItem.findByIdAndRemove(id);
    return deletedItem || null;
  } catch (error) {
    throw error;
  }
}
```

This isn't bad at all. I like that ChatGPT (mostly) used the latest JavaScript syntax, properly handled errors that may happen, and wrote good comments. I've seen human-written code that's much worse. However, parts of this generated code won't work with the latest version of MongoDB because the code uses functions that have been removed. I resolved this problem by installing a slightly older version (7.1.0) of Mongoose.

The real test, however, is whether the code runs. After it generated the CRUD functions, ChatGPT provided some examples of how they can be used. These examples are shown in Listing 4-3.

LISTING 4-3: Example Usage Code from ChatGPT

```
// Example usage:
(async () => {
  try {
    const newItem = await createTodoItem("Buy groceries", "Milk,
  eggs, and bread");
    console.log("Created item:", newItem);
    const allItems = await getAllTodoItems();
    console.log("All items:", allItems);
    const itemToUpdate = await getTodoItemById(newItem._id);
    if (itemToUpdate) {
      const updatedItem = await updateTodoItem(itemToUpdate._id,
  { completed: true });
      console.log("Updated item:", updatedItem);
    }
    const deletedItem = await deleteTodoItem(newItem._id);
    console.log("Deleted item:", deletedItem);
  } catch (error) {
    console.error("Error:", error);
  } finally {
    mongoose.disconnect();
  }
})();
```

If Node.js and MongoDB are installed on your development machine, you can try out this code by copying Listings 4-2 and 4-3 into a file and saving it with the .js extension.

Before you run the application, you need to initialize the directory containing the .js file as a Node package by entering the following in a terminal window:

```
npm init -y
```

Then install Mongoose by entering the following:

```
npm install mongoose @7.1.0
```

Next, run the program by entering **node** followed by the file name, like this:

```
node listing0402.js
```

Figure 4-2 shows what happened when I ran this program.

FIGURE 4-2: Running my Node.js application.

To verify that ChatGPT's code worked, I commented out the code that deletes the created record, ran the Node.js application again, and then started the Mongo shell and looked at the contents of the `todo-list` collection, as shown in Figure 4-3.

```
chrisminnick — mongosh mongodb://127.0.0.1:27017/?directCo...

test> use todo-list
switched to db todo-list
todo-list> show collections
todoitems
todo-list> db.todoitems.find()
[
  {
    _id: ObjectId("69aaf0854cb1eb553eabe53f"),
    title: 'Buy groceries',
    description: 'Milk, eggs, and bread',
    completed: true,
    __v: 0
  }
]
todo-list> 
```

FIGURE 4-3: Viewing the collection's contents in MongoDB.

Helping with Syntax

A large part of the work involved in computer programming is simply remembering or looking up the rules that define the structure of a programming language, also known as its *syntax*. Each language or code library has its own way of doing things. Once you know the basics of how a programming language works (such as how to create a function, use basic operators, and write loops), you need to know what built-in functions are available in your environment (whether it's a browser or a mobile operating system) and what parameters and types of data they expect to receive. That's a lot to remember, and no programmer I've ever met can remember everything there is to remember about one programming language, much less several programming languages. With the help of GenAI tools, you can have instant access to the collected knowledge of millions of coders.

You may be asking yourself at this point, "But is it ethical for AI to harvest everyone's code like that?" This topic is hotly debated and the subject of at least one lawsuit. I explore legal and ethical issues having to do with GenAI throughout this book.

Stop remembering trivial details

When I teach programming, my students often ask me questions about syntax and application programming interfaces (APIs) rather than how something works. When I get a question about syntax, I answer the question if I can without looking it up; otherwise, I encourage students to "Google it." These days, I'm just as likely to answer "Ask AI." Not knowing how to do something with code is fine. What's not fine is not using all the tools you have available! With time and experience, remembering syntax just starts to happen.

TIP

When writing software, one of the best skills is knowing how and where to look for answers. And most of the time, the best place is through a search engine. Because search engines employ machine learning to determine the best results to show in response to queries, we've been using AI for coding for some time now.

Hinting at code mastery

One of the oldest forms of computer-assisted coding is code completion. Microsoft introduced its implementation of code completion, IntelliSense, in Visual Studio in 1996. These types of tools work by suggesting functions and methods that partially match something you've started typing, as shown in Figure 4-4. Traditional code completion functionality doesn't employ GenAI, and its suggestions can often be frustratingly incorrect. However, if you need help with the syntax or spelling (or don't want to type the full names of functions), code completion is useful.

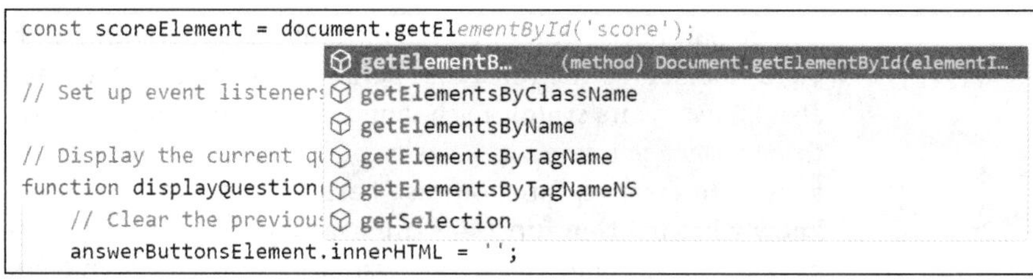

FIGURE 4-4: Code completion is often helpful.

Generative AI takes code completion to the next level by offering suggestions based on its training. When integrated into your IDE, tools such as GitHub Copilot (`https://github.com/copilot`) or Cursor (`https://cursor.com`) can suggest entire statements or functions, rather than just single function calls.

GenAI models trained on large datasets of code can offer multiple suggestions based on what other programmers have written; libraries, classes, and functions you've imported into the current file; and even other files that are open in your IDE or in your code repository.

Figure 4-5 shows a suggestion from Copilot based on the fact that I named my file validatePhoneNumber.js.

WARNING

Unfortunately, in this instance, the suggested function isn't great. It only validates the (XXX) XXX-XXXX format and will fail, for example, if a user enters a phone number as XXX-XXX-XXXX or with any non-U.S. phone number.

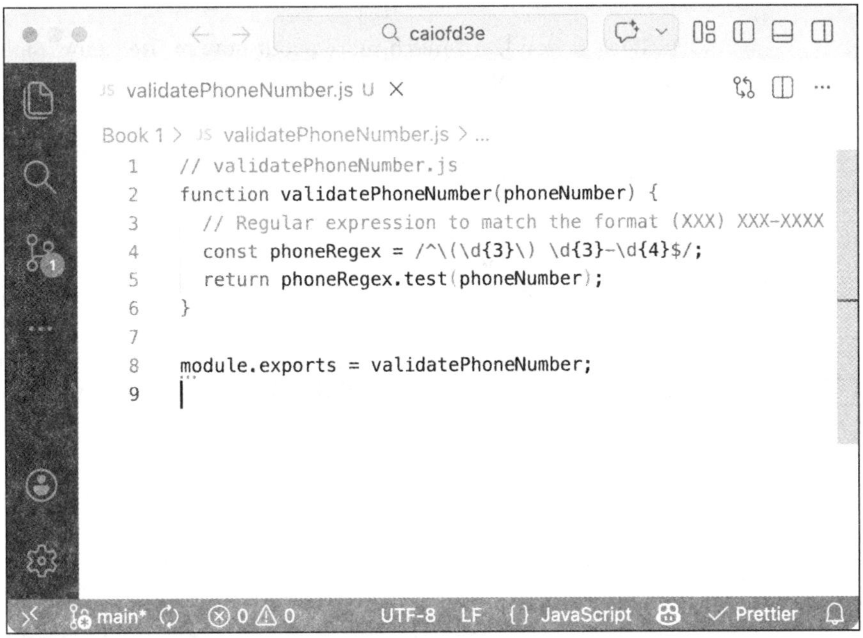

FIGURE 4-5: Copilot's suggested phone number validation function.

However, more context can coax the model into returning a better response. When I provided a comment describing what I was trying to do, the model returned a much better suggestion, as shown in Figure 4-6. While not perfect and far too wordy, at least this suggestion gets me closer to what I'm looking for.

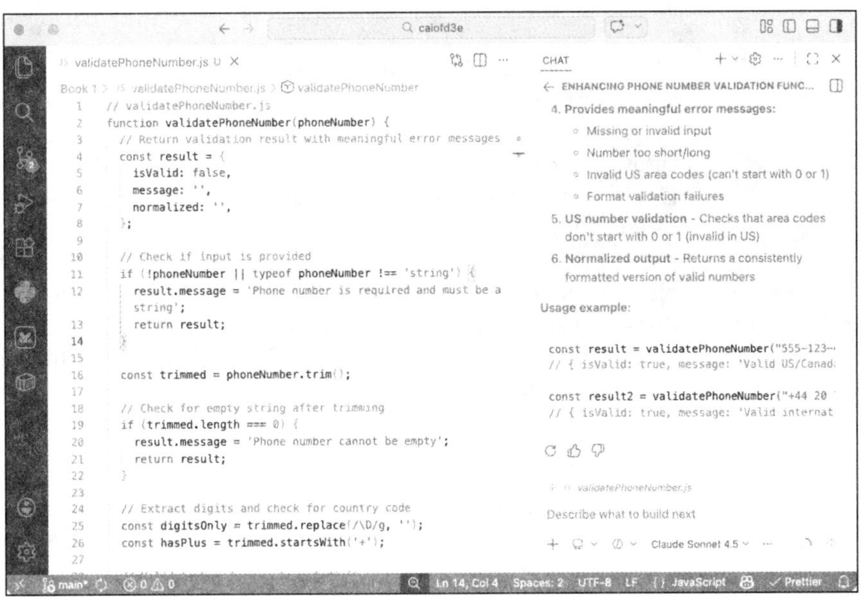

FIGURE 4-6: GenAI models do better when given context.

In Book 4, you learn much more about how to use GenAI tools to write, format, translate, and optimize your code.

Adapting to new syntax

Like code hint features in IDEs, GenAI can help you learn or remember the syntax for functions or methods. For example, Copilot will give you hints as you type; you can ignore these by continuing to type or accept them by pressing Tab.

For example, I have trouble remembering the order of the arguments to pass to JavaScript's `Array.reduce` method. Figure 4-7 shows a Copilot hint for starting the method.

```
export function calculateTotal(itemsInCart) {
  return itemsInCart.reduce((total, item) => total + item.price * item.quantity, 0);
}
```

FIGURE 4-7: Getting syntax support from Copilot.

You can also use GenAI chat interfaces to learn about new syntax. But keep in mind that the model you're using may have been trained on data that predates the existence of the function or method you're seeking help with. For example, GPT-3.5's training data cutoff date is September 2021, so the model has no knowledge of events or technologies developed after that date. Figure 4-8 shows what happened when I asked GPT-3.5 about a feature of JavaScript introduced in 2022.

GPT-3.5 is ancient (from the perspective of a technology timeline), however, and you're unlikely to have to use it. (Although you could if you wanted to see how rough we had it way back in 2023.) Newer models have a more recent training data cutoff and can take advantage of later information derived from web searches. Figure 4-9 shows ChatGPT's response to the same question but with the model set to GPT-4.

WARNING

Also remember that, in response to a query, a GenAI model may just invent something that sounds plausible but is incorrect. ChatGPT's tendency to make up facts and people is legendary. However, in cases where something is as rule-based as a computer language, it usually gets the facts right. You should have a certain amount of distrust of any AI-generated code and always verify it.

FIGURE 4-8: GPT-3.5 doesn't know about recent additions to JavaScript.

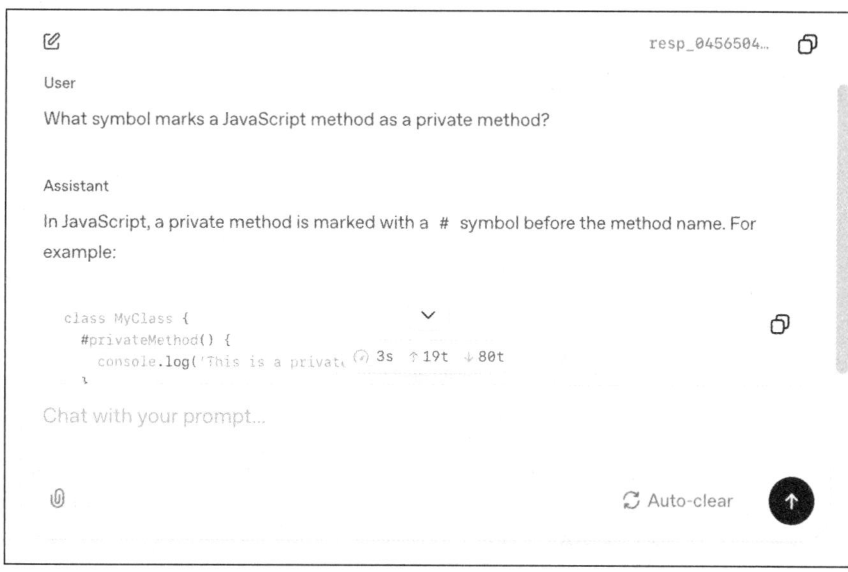

FIGURE 4-9: GPT-4 generates a correct answer when asked about new syntax.

Figure 4-10 shows ChatGPT's response to my question about a non-existent JavaScript method.

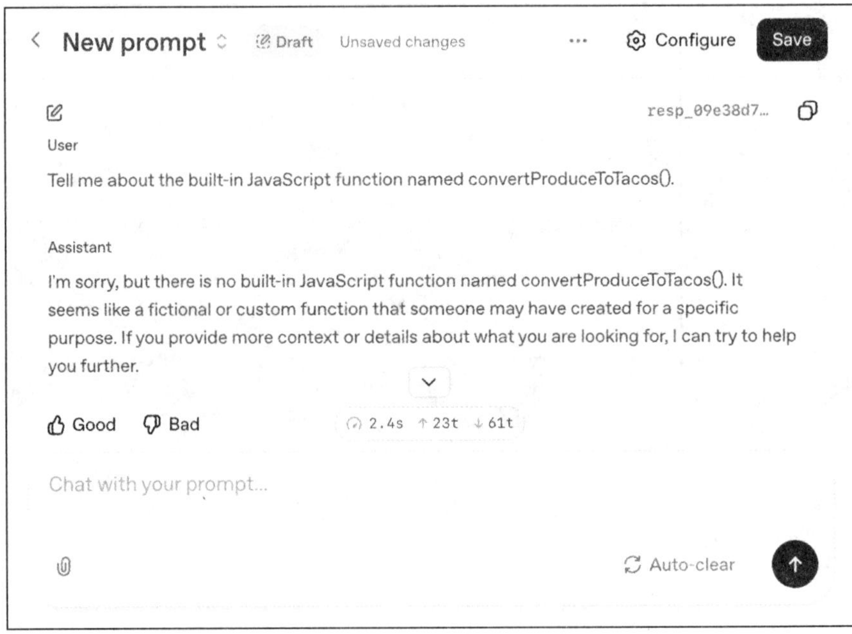

FIGURE 4-10: ChatGPT is usually correct about programming language syntax basics.

Linting with AI

Linters are tools that flag programming errors, bugs, and style issues. The technical name for the job that linters do is static code analysis. The *static* part of *static code analysis* refers to the fact that these tools check the code without compiling or running it. Using a linter can help you improve the quality of your code.

Detecting bad code with static code analysis

To use an AI chatbot as a linter, you can prompt the model with your code and ask it what's wrong with it. Since GenAI models have been trained on a large quantity of working code, they're generally good at finding typos, inconsistencies, and code that doesn't look right.

Simply write something like "What's wrong with this code?" and then paste in the code that's not working. Figure 4-11 shows Google Gemini's response to my question about a function with several typos and examples of bad coding style.

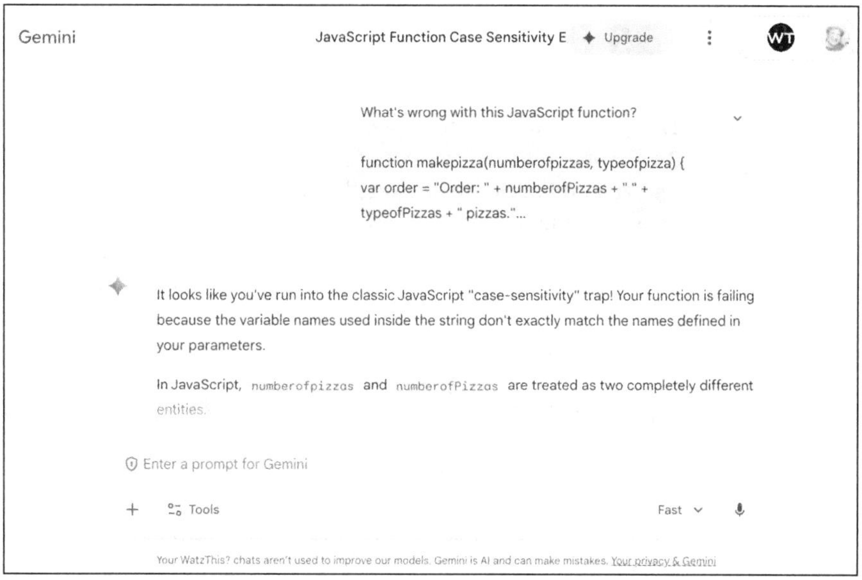

FIGURE 4-11: Using Gemini as a linter.

Integrating AI with static code analysis

Because programming languages have strict rules, linters don't necessarily need to use AI to detect bad code. However, linting tools that make use of AI can provide functionality that's not possible with standard code linters, such as

- Detailed natural-language explanations of what's wrong with your code
- Defining new rules using natural language
- Fixing problematic code or refactoring problematic code or both

Many linters that aren't AI-enhanced can automatically fix certain kinds of problems with your code, and defining new rules generally isn't difficult. The potential for providing detailed descriptions as well as improving your code is promising.

Several tools add AI to existing linters. For example, eslint-ai (available at `https://github.com/iamando/eslint-ai`) is an open-source project that uses AI to enhance the errors returned by the most popular JavaScript linter, ESLint.

Using eslint-ai requires you to have an account and an API key from OpenAI, and using the tool may result in OpenAI charges. However, GitHub Copilot and other tools include features for cleaning, fixing, and improving your code as part of their standard subscriptions. Book 4, Chapter 4 covers linting and debugging with AI in detail.

Using AI as a Tutor

The question of whether generative AI should be used in education is hotly debated. On the one hand, AI chatbots and AI-enhanced search engines often provide customized and accurate answers to questions that traditional search engines can't. These broader concerns become especially relevant when the subject is learning to code because AI can both support understanding and shortcut the practice that coding requires. In this section, I touch on some of the pros and cons of using AI to learn to code.

Studying AI's potential in education

AI can be a useful tool for someone who is learning to code. Just as search engines, online tutorials, and coding books are used today by both new and experienced programmers, AI chatbots and coding assistants are increasingly seen as normal and essential tools.

Whether you're learning from older technologies (such as books or a human instructor) or the latest GenAI model, there's no substitute for gaining experience through writing code or through interacting with more experienced programmers.

Avoiding potential pitfalls

GenAI models and the chatbots that make use of them don't know how to code. All they do is crunch the numbers based on their training and tell you the next most likely word. Even with this seemingly simple functionality, AI chatbots are often surprisingly accurate and human-sounding.

WARNING

Although efforts are underway to make GenAI models properly express themselves when they have doubts about their answers, today's models are supremely confident in their answers, even when they are completely wrong or are just making things up. The popular term for answers GenAI makes up with no basis in truth is *hallucination*, although I prefer the term *fabrication*. Never fully trust a GenAI model. You should always test and verify any code output you get, especially before using it in a production environment.

Pairing Up with AI

Pair programming is a software development technique in which two programmers team up at one computer. In pair programming, one person acts as the *driver* and handles all the typing, while the other acts as the *navigator* and makes sure the driver is headed in the right direction. Ideally, both programmers are equally skilled and switch roles between navigator and driver as needed to take advantage of each person's strengths. However, pair programming also works well when one of the programmers is more experienced (known as expert-novice) or where both programmers are inexperienced (novice-novice).

Pair programming helps team members share knowledge and learn to work together, and it leads to fewer mistakes and better code.

Overview of pair programming styles

Depending on the skill levels of the programmers, several variations of pair programming might be used:

- **Driver-navigator:** This style of pair programming is the most common. In driver-navigator, the driver handles the typing while the navigator looks at the big picture and keeps an eye out for mistakes being made by the driver.
- **Backseat navigator:** In this style, the driver still does the typing, and the navigator takes a more active role and dictates instructions, such as when to create a file or method, or what to name a variable. This style works best when the navigator is a more experienced programmer.
- **Tour guide:** In the tour guide style, the driver is the expert programmer. They handle the typing and explain to the navigator at every step what they're doing and why.
- **Ping-pong:** The ping-pong style is designed for test-driven development as a pair. The first person writes a piece of code designed to verify that a feature works as expected (a *test*). The second programmer writes the code to make the test pass. Then the second programmer writes a new test, and the first programmer writes the code to make it work. This style usually requires two expert developers.

Understanding the pros and cons of pair programming with AI

In AI pair programming, you're the navigator who sets the direction and does the strategic thinking. You communicate the project's goal to the AI through comments and code that you write. As you type, the AI navigator suggests snippets and code blocks. With each suggestion, you have to decide whether to accept the suggestion, write your own solution, or ask your AI assistant to try again.

Following are some of the benefits of pair programming with an AI partner:

- You (the coder) can spend less time looking up syntax and typing repetitive or boilerplate code.
- The AI assistant is available whenever you are.
- The AI assistant is fast.
- The GenAI model behind the assistant is trained on many different programming languages and programming styles, potentially giving you access to solutions you might not have otherwise considered.

The cons of pair programming with AI may include the following:

- Team members each working individually with an AI partner don't get the knowledge-sharing benefits of traditional pair programming.
- AI-suggested code may not be accurate or up-to-date with the latest syntax or coding styles.
- AI-suggested code may contain security flaws or other types of issues that a human coding partner would easily spot.

WARNING

Pair programming with AI works best for coders who know their language and have experience writing code without the use of AI. As you're coding, remember that your partner (the GenAI model) speaks confidently but may not always be right.

2 Python from Scratch

Contents at a Glance

IN THIS CHAPTER

» Installing Python, VS Code, Copilot, and Jupyter Notebooks

» Using interactive mode

» Writing, debugging, and running Python code

» Creating a Jupyter notebook

Chapter 1
Introducing Python

Code is read much more often than it is written.

—GUIDO VAN ROSSUM (CREATOR OF PYTHON)

Python is a great language to know if you're looking for a good job in programming, or if you want to expand your existing programming skills into exciting, cutting-edge technologies such as artificial intelligence (AI), machine learning (ML), data science, or robotics, or even if you're just building apps in general. Plus, Python is relatively easy to learn, and everything you need to learn (and do) in Python is free.

In this chapter, you learn how to install Python and Visual Studio Code (VS Code) and how to install extensions in VS Code for Python development. In the process, you set up GitHub Copilot so you can get AI assistance as you're learning to code. Next, you discover several places where you can write Python code, including in interactive mode, in Python code files, and in Jupyter Notebook.

You're probably anxious to get started on more advanced topics such as data science, artificial intelligence, robotics, or whatever, but learning those topics will be easier if you have a good understanding of the many tools available to you — and the skills to use them.

Getting the Tools for Success

To learn Python, you need a Python interpreter and an editor. The *editor* lets you type the code, and the *interpreter* lets you run that code. If you've already started learning Python and are happy with the editor and interpreter you've been using, you're welcome to continue using them and ignore my suggestions.

In this section, you install the Visual Studio Code editor and the latest version of Python. You also configure an AI assistant and the Jupyter Notebook interactive Python development environment.

TIP

As of this writing, the latest version of Python is 3.14. By the time you're reading this, there will likely be a more recent version. However, most of what's in Python is the same across all recent versions, and the code you learn in this book will work with Python 3.10 or any newer version.

Installing Python and VS Code

If you're just getting started, I suggest that you use Microsoft's *Visual Studio Code editor* — also known as *VS Code.* Here are the main reasons why it's my favorite editor:

- It's an excellent editor for learning coding.
- It's an excellent editor for writing code professionally and is used by millions of professional programmers and developers.
- It's relatively easy to learn and use.
- It works pretty much the same on Windows, Mac, and Linux.
- It's free.
- It integrates well with GitHub Copilot and other AI coding assistants, so you can use generative AI to speed both learning and coding.

To use VS Code as your editor for Python, you need to download and install Python, VS Code, and a VS Code extension. Here are the steps to download and install Python and VS Code:

1. **Use any web browser to browse to `www.python.org/downloads`.**
2. **Click the Download Python button.**

   The file is saved to your Downloads folder.
3. **To install Python, open the Downloads folder, double-click the downloaded file, and follow the onscreen instructions, and accept any suggested defaults during the installation process.**
4. **Browse to `https://code.visualstudio.com/` and download the current version of VS Code for your operating system.**
5. **To install VS Code, open the Downloads folder, double-click the icon for the downloaded file, and follow the onscreen instructions.**

After VS Code is installed, you should be able to start it like any other app in your system. In Windows, click Start and look on the Start menu for the Visual Studio Code icon. On a Mac, you will find VS Code in the Applications folder or in Spotlight.

Next, you need to install the VS Code Python extension:

1. **Open VS Code.**
2. **Click the Extensions icon, shown in Figure 1-1.**

   The Extensions sidebar appears.
3. **Enter** Python **in the Search box at the top of the Extensions panel.**

   The results in the Extensions sidebar will change as you type.
4. **In the left sidebar, click the Install button next to the Python extension from Microsoft (see Figure 1-1).**

When you've finished installing the Python extension, you might notice that both Python and Pylance were added as extensions to VS Code. Don't worry; that's normal. Pylance just gives you some additional capabilities that make it easier to learn and write Python code in the VS Code editor.

Using GitHub Copilot

GitHub Copilot is an AI tool that can write code for you. It uses AI models from other providers such as OpenAI, Anthropic, and Google, is geared toward working with code. It's automatically installed when you install VS Code.

Extensions icon Install the Python extension from Microsoft

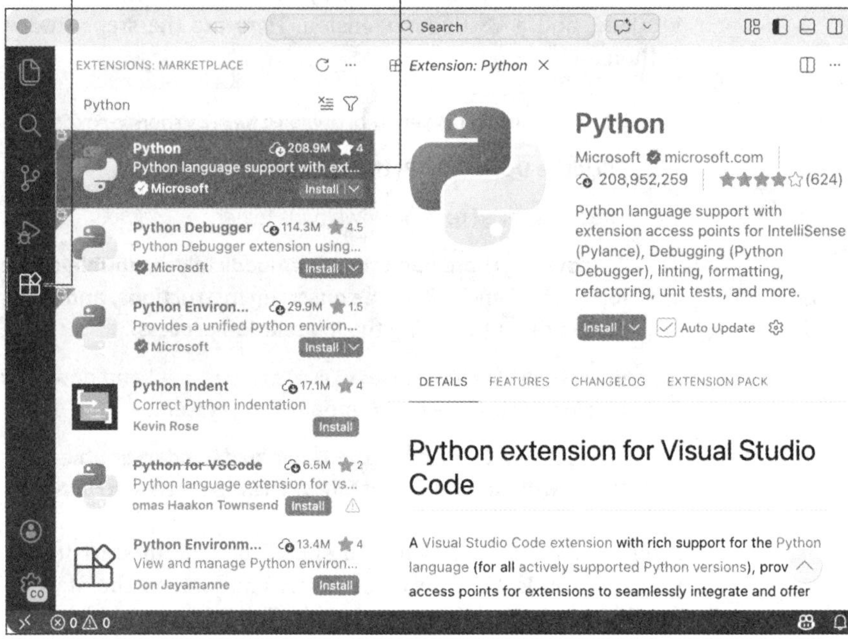

FIGURE 1-1: Getting the Python extension in VS Code.

GitHub offers a limited version of Copilot for free. Its paid plans start at $10 a month. Don't sign up for a paid account yet because you may find that the free features are all you need right now.

Here's how to enable GitHub Copilot in VS Code:

1. **Open VS Code.**
2. **Click the Copilot icon in the lower-right corner, as shown in Figure 1-2.**
3. **In the pop-up window, click the Use AI Features button.**

   A chat pane appears on the right, as shown in Figure 1-3.

   TIP

   You can open the chat pane at any time by clicking the speech bubble icon to the right of the search box at the top of VS Code.

   Note that the Copilot icon now reads Signed Out. You can use a trial version of GitHub Copilot without logging in. If you have a GitHub account, you can log in to enable additional AI features, but my advice is to start with the free trial until you're sure you need more.

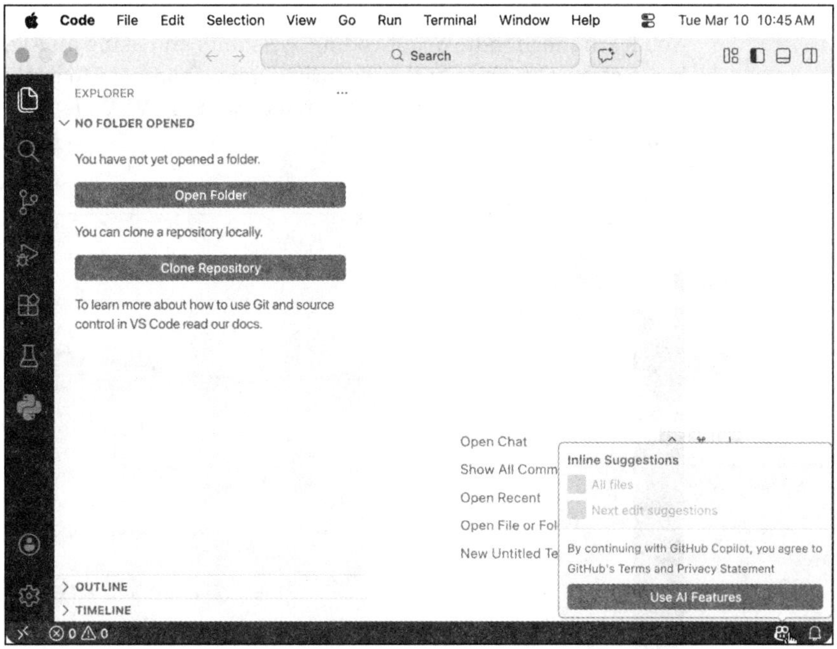

FIGURE 1-2: Revealing the Use AI Features button.

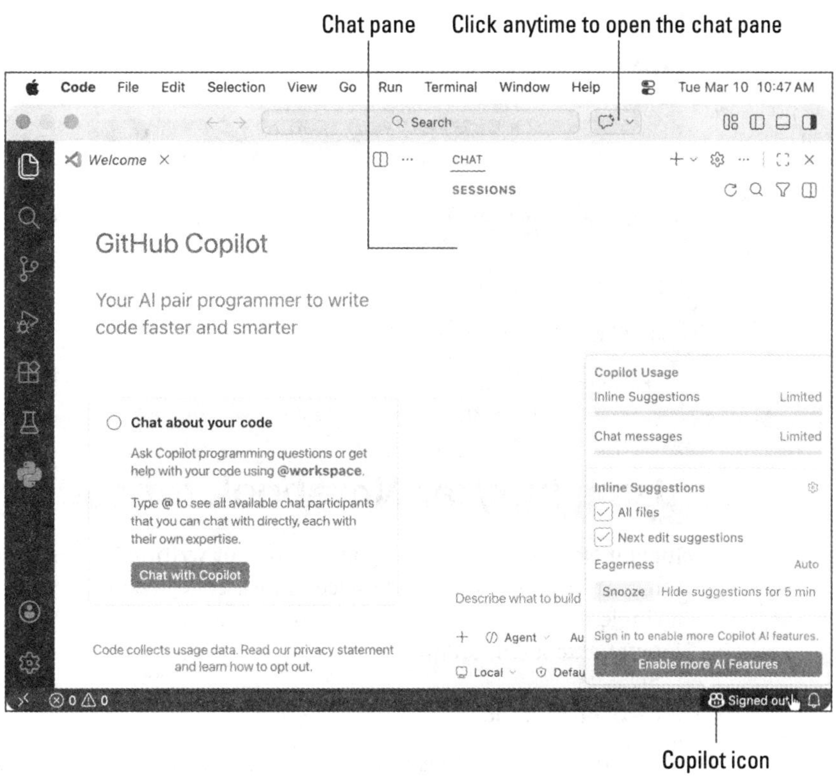

FIGURE 1-3: You can enable more features by logging in.

You learn much more about coding assistants and using an AI chatbot to help you write code in Book 4. In the meantime, take a moment to explore GitHub Copilot. One great way to find out what Copilot can do in VS Code is to ask it yourself, as shown in Figure 1-4.

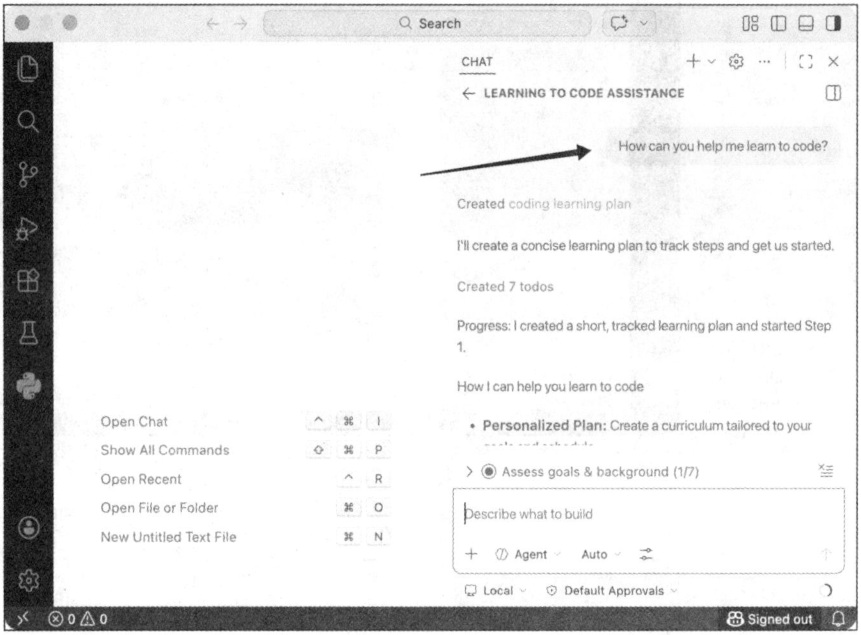

FIGURE 1-4: Asking Copilot how it can help you.

You can also use the following AI services to write Python code:

- ChatGPT, `chatgpt.com`
- Claude, `https://claude.ai/login`
- Gemini, `gemini.google.com/app`

Using Jupyter Notebook for coding

Jupyter Notebook is another popular tool for writing Python code and is also great for learning Python because it combines code, results, and explanatory text in a single document. You can use Jupyter Notebook inside VS Code. To install the Jupyter extension, follow these steps:

1. **Open VS Code.**
2. **Click the Extensions icon in the left sidebar.**

3. **In the Search box, enter** Jupyter.

4. **Click the Install button to install the Jupyter extension from Microsoft, as shown in Figure 1-5.**

   You see instructions for using Jupyter on the Welcome page to the right. But you needn't do anything right this minute.

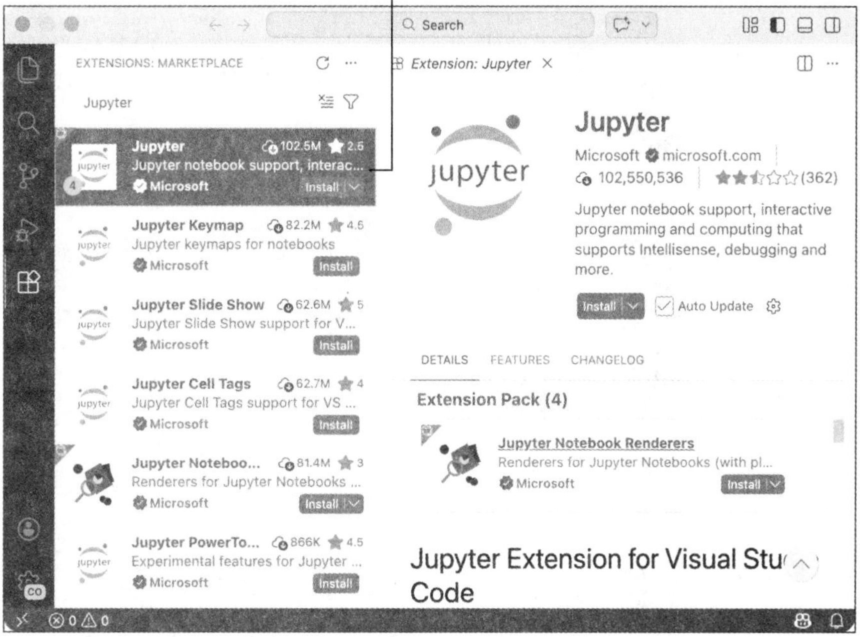

FIGURE 1-5: Install the Jupyter extension in VS Code.

Verifying your setup

If you've made it through all the steps for installing extensions in this chapter, VS Code is ready to go:

1. **Open VS Code.**

2. **Click the Extensions icon in VS Code (refer to Figure 1-1).**

3. **In the left sidebar, find the Python, Copilot, and Jupyter extensions.**

   You will also see various additional extensions that were automatically installed when you installed Python and Jupyter.

4. **If any windows are open to the right of the Extensions pane, you can close those now by clicking the X in their tab.**
5. **Click the Explorer icon at the top of the left sidebar in VS Code.**

   You see the window shown in Figure 1-6. This is where you will be managing your folders and files in the next section.

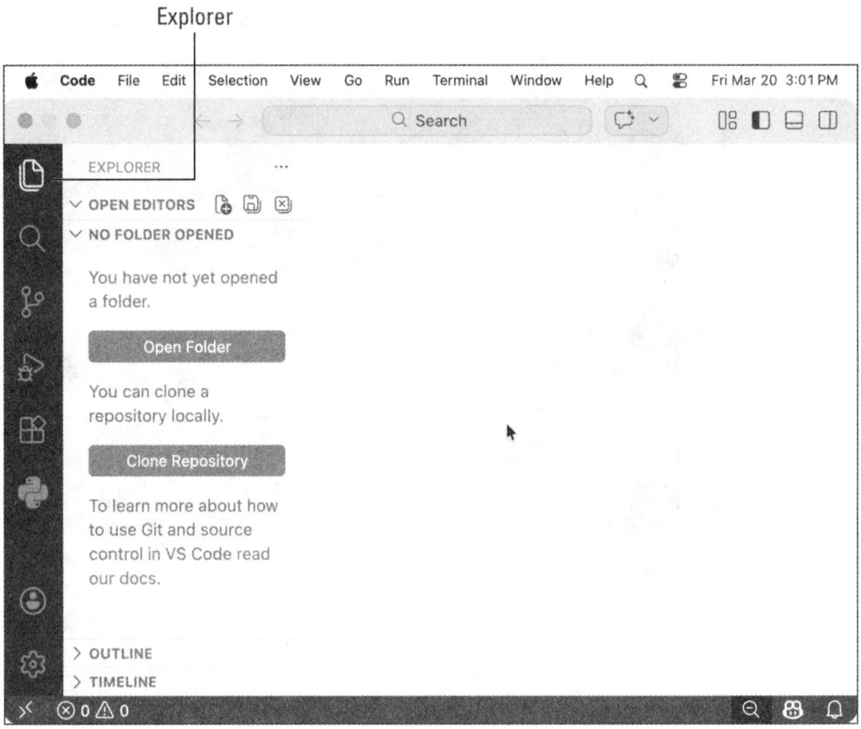

FIGURE 1-6: VS Code is ready!

Next, you delve a bit deeper into Python and using the tools you now have available on your computer.

Using Python's Interactive Mode

One way to get some experience with using Python is to just start typing some commands interactively. The Terminal pane in VS Code is a great place to type Python code. So that's where you'll start.

Opening Terminal

To use Python interactively with VS Code, follow these steps:

1. **Open VS Code, if necessary.**
2. **On the menu bar, choose Terminal ➪ New Terminal.**

   A new window opens at the bottom of VS Code, with the Terminal tab selected, as shown in Figure 1-7.

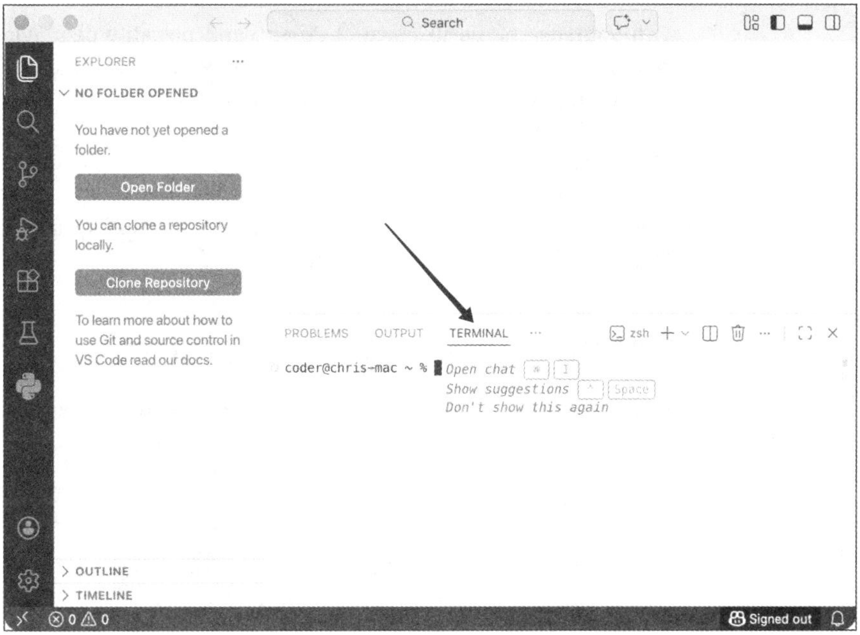

FIGURE 1-7: The Terminal pane in VS Code.

COLORS AND ICONS IN VS CODE

In this book, the VS Code Terminal pane is displayed as black text against a white background, but you can use any color scheme you like. If you want to switch to black on white, as shown in this book, choose File (Windows) or Code (Mac) ➪ Preferences ➪ Theme ➪ Color Theme ➪ Light (Visual Studio).

The first prompt you see is typically for your computer's operating system, and it likely shows the username of the account you're using. For example, on a Mac, it may look like the following,

```
Coder@My-Computer ~ %
```

with the name of your computer replacing `My-Computer`. In Windows, the prompt is likely

```
C:\Users\Coder>
```

with your username in place of `Coder`, and possibly displaying a different path than `C:\Users`. Depending on your Windows version and current configuration, you might instead see the following prompt:

```
PS C:\Users\xxx>
```

where *xxx* is your user name. This prompt just means that you're using PowerShell. You don't need to change anything.

Getting your Python version

At the operating system command prompt, type the following and press Enter to see what version of Python you're using. Note the space before the first hyphen:

```
python --version
```

You should see something like Python 3.*x*.*x* (where each *x* is a number representing the version of Python you're using).

If you see an error message on a Mac, such as `Command Not Found`, enter this command instead:

```
python3 --version
```

If you're using Windows and you see an error message, enter this command instead:

```
py --version
```

Using the Python interpreter

The *Python interpreter* is a command-line interface where you can enter Python code directly. To access the Python interpreter, type **python** (or **python3** or just **py**) in Terminal and press Enter. You'll know you're in the right place when the prompt changes to three greater-than signs (>>>).

Entering commands in the Python interpreter is the same as typing them anywhere else. You must type the command correctly and then press Enter. For example, suppose you type the command

```
howdy
```

After you press Enter, you'll see some techie gibberish that is trying to tell you that the interpreter doesn't know what "howdy" means, so it can't do anything. Nothing has broken. You're just back to another >>> prompt, where you can try again, as shown in Figure 1-8.

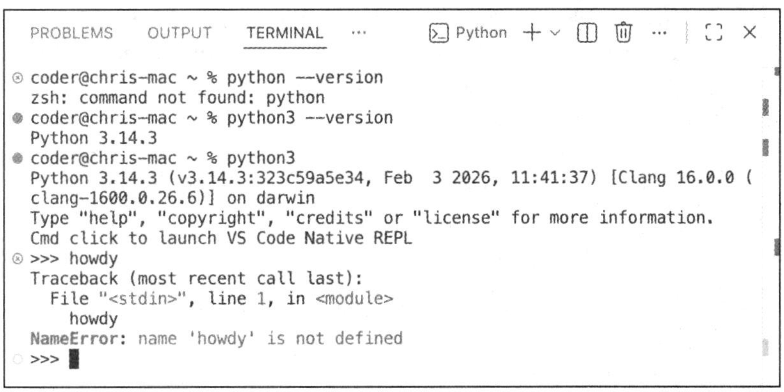

FIGURE 1-8: Python doesn't know what *howdy* means.

Getting built-in help

To use the built-in help system in Python, simply type **help** as a command in the Python interpreter and press Enter. You see the following:

```
Type help() for interactive help, or help(object) for help about object.
```

The interpreter is telling you to type **help** followed by an empty pair of parentheses, or type **help** with a specific word in parentheses (`object` is the example given). Go ahead and type the following:

```
help()
```

After you press Enter, the screen provides some information about using Python's interactive help, as shown in Figure 1-9.

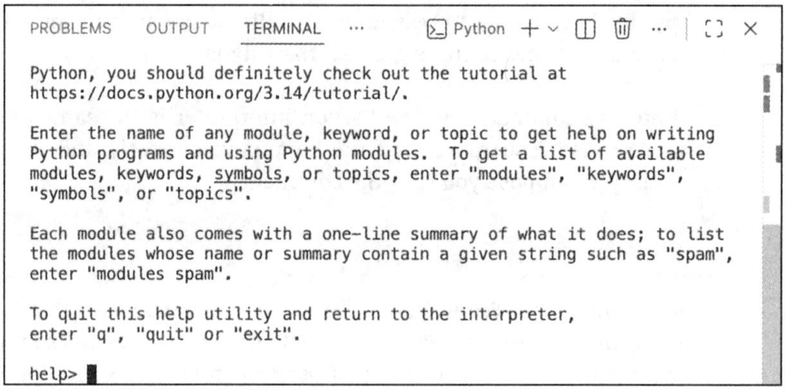

FIGURE 1-9: Python's interactive help utility.

The `help>` prompt at the bottom of the window tells you that you're no longer in the Python interpreter (which always shows `>>>`) but are now in a new area that provides help. As described on the screen, you can enter the name of any module, keyword, or topic to get help with that term.

For example, Python uses certain keywords that have special meaning in the language. To get a list of those keywords, just type the following at the `help>` prompt:

```
keywords
```

After you press Enter, you see a list of keywords, as shown in Figure 1-10.

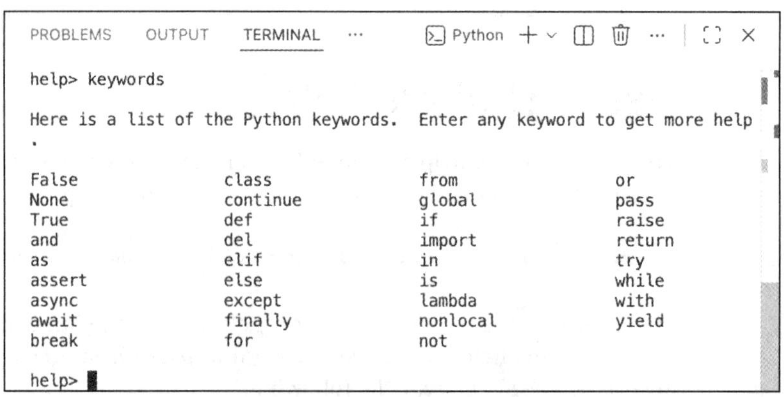

FIGURE 1-10: Getting help with keywords.

Above the list of keywords is a message telling you that you can type any keyword at the `help>` prompt for more information about that keyword. For example, entering the `class` keyword provides information about Python classes, as shown in Figure 1-11.

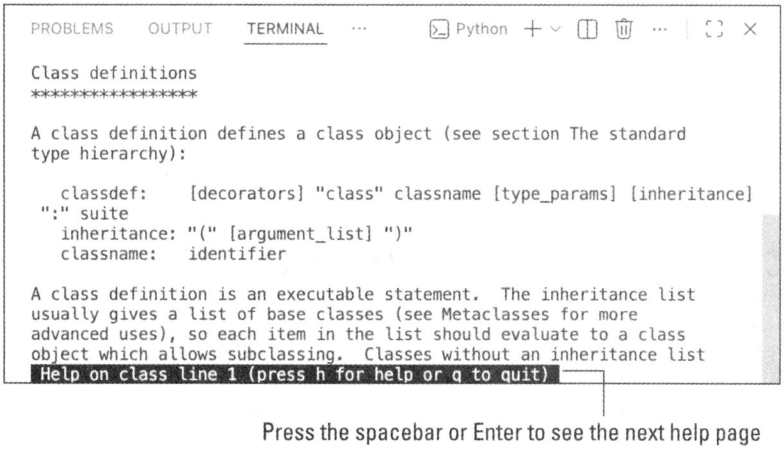

FIGURE 1-11: Getting help with the `class` keyword.

All the technical jargon in the help text might leave you flummoxed. But as you learn about new concepts in Python, realize that you can use the interactive help for guidance.

TIP

See the bar at the bottom of Figure 1-11? Every time you see that bar (or `-- More --`), you can press the spacebar or Enter to get to the next page of help. Eventually you'll get to the end of the help text.

Exiting interactive help and Python

To exit the help system when you're at the `help>` prompt, type **quit** (or **q**) and press Enter. You return to the normal Python interpreter prompt (`>>>`). If you're at the Python interpreter prompt and want to get back to the operating system prompt, type **exit()** and press Enter.

Note that if you make a mistake, such as forgetting the parentheses, you'll get some help on the screen. For example, if you type **exit** and press Enter, you'll see

```
Use exit() or Ctrl-Z plus Return to exit.
```

You'll know you've exited the Python interpreter when you see the operating system prompt rather than `>>>` at the end of the Terminal pane, as shown in Figure 1-12.

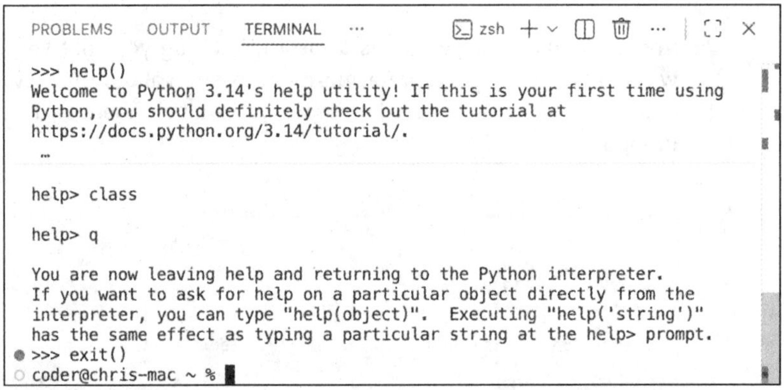

FIGURE 1-12: Getting back to the operating system prompt.

Writing and Debugging Python Code

TIP

Before working with Python, it's a good idea to create a folder to store all the Python code that you write in this book so that it's all together in one place and easy to find when you need it. You can put this folder anywhere you like and name it whatever you like.

In Windows or macOS, navigate to the folder that will contain the new folder. (You can use Desktop, Documents, or any other folder.) Right-click an empty place in the folder and choose New Folder (Mac) or New ⇨ Folder (Windows). Type the folder name and press Enter. To follow along with the examples in this chapter, name your folder `CODINGAIO`.

Opening a folder in VS Code

Now that you have a folder for the code you'll be writing, you need to open that folder in VS Code. Follow these steps:

1. **Open VS Code using the Start menu in Windows or Spotlight on a Mac.**
2. **Click File ⇨ Open Folder or click the Open Folder button in the Explorer panel.**

   A file browser window opens.
3. **Navigate to the location where you created your code folder, and click the name of the folder.**
4. **Click the Open (macOS) or Select Folder (Windows) button in the file browser.**

   The name of the currently open folder appears near the top of the Explorer pane at the left side of the VS Code window (see Figure 1-13).

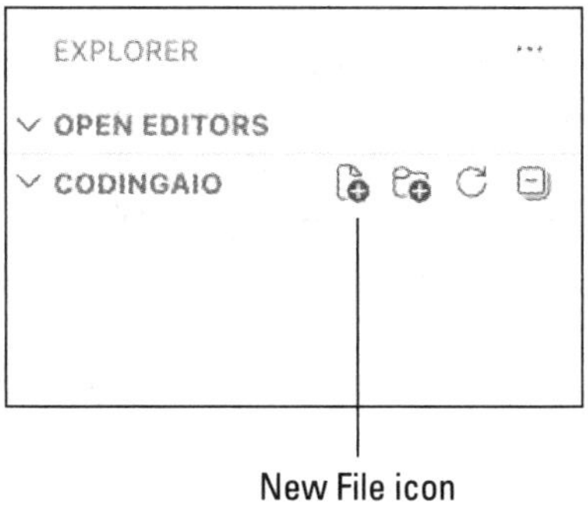

FIGURE 1-13: The currently open folder is CODINGAIO.

Although you can run Python code interactively in the Python interpreter — as you did earlier in this chapter — most programming is done by writing code in a Python script file that ends with the `.py` extension. This approach allows you to save, edit, and organize your code, making it easier to develop larger projects or revisit your work later.

To create a `.py` file at any time, follow these steps:

1. **If you haven't already done so, open VS Code and your `CODINGAIO` folder.**
2. **If the Explorer pane isn't open, click the Explorer icon, which is at the top of the sidebar.**
3. **To create a file in your `CODINGAIO` folder, click the New File icon to the right of the folder name (refer to Figure 1-13).**
4. **Type the filename, including the `.py` extension, and press Enter.**

   To follow along with the example, type **hello.py**.

   The new file opens, and you can see its name in the tab on the right. The larger area below the tab is the editor, where you type the Python code. The filename also appears under the `CODINGAIO` folder name in the Explorer pane because that's where it's stored.

Writing Python code

Now that you have a `.py` file open, you can use it to write some Python code. As is typical when learning a new programming language, you'll start by typing a simple Hello World program. Here are the steps:

1. **Click just to the right of line 1 in the editing area.**
2. **Type the following:**

```
print("Hello World")
```

As you're typing, you might see *IntelliSense text,* which shows you information about what you're typing. (Exactly how much information you see depends on whether you're using Copilot.) You don't have to do anything with the IntelliSense text, so just keep typing or press the Esc key to dismiss it.

3. **Press Enter after you've typed the line.**

The new line of code is displayed on the screen. You might also notice a few other changes, as shown in Figure 1-14:

- The Explorer icon sports a circled 1 or a dot, indicating that you have one unsaved change.
- The `hello.py` name in the tab displays a black dot, which indicates that the file has unsaved changes.

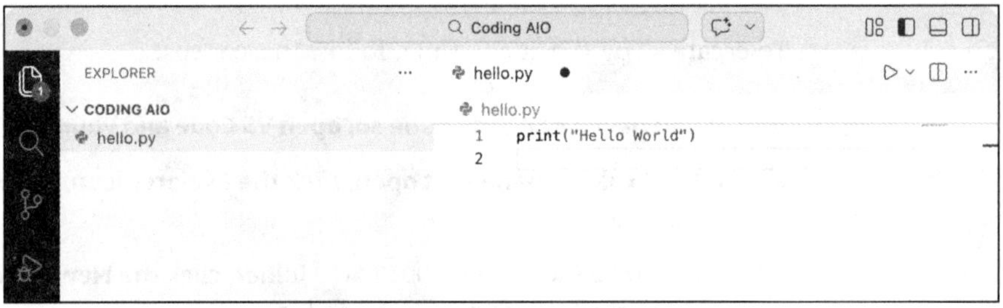

FIGURE 1-14: The `hello.py` file contains some Python code and has unsaved changes.

Saving your code

Code you type in VS Code is not saved automatically. There are two ways to deal with this. The first method is to try to remember to save anytime you make a change that's worth saving. Then simply choose File ➪ Save or press Ctrl+S in Windows or ⌘+S on a Mac.

I prefer the second method, which is to use Auto Save to automatically save changes. To enable Auto Save, choose File ➪ Auto Save. The next time you open the File menu, you'll see a check mark next to Auto Save, which tells you that Auto Save is turned on. To turn off Auto Save, just choose File ➪ Auto Save again.

Running Python in VS Code

To test your Python code in VS Code, you need to run it. The easiest method is to right-click the file's name (`hello.py` in this example) and choose Run Python File in Terminal, as shown in Figure 1-15.

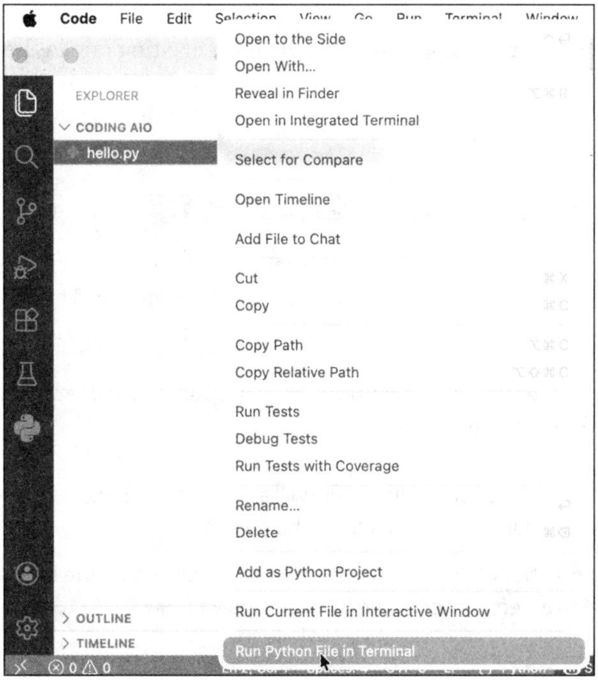

FIGURE 1-15: Run `hello.py`.

The first time you run Python code in a new VS Code project, VS Code will prompt you to choose your Python interpreter. This step is necessary because many Python programmers have multiple versions of Python installed. Even if you have only one version of Python on your computer, you'll still be asked to select it. Choose the version of Python you downloaded and installed at the beginning of this chapter. Typically, it will be marked as Recommended.

The Terminal pane opens along the bottom of the VS Code window. You see a command prompt followed by a command to run the code in the Python interpreter (`python.exe` for Windows or `python3` for macOS). Below that, you see the output of the program (the words *Hello World* in this example) and then another prompt, as shown in Figure 1-16.

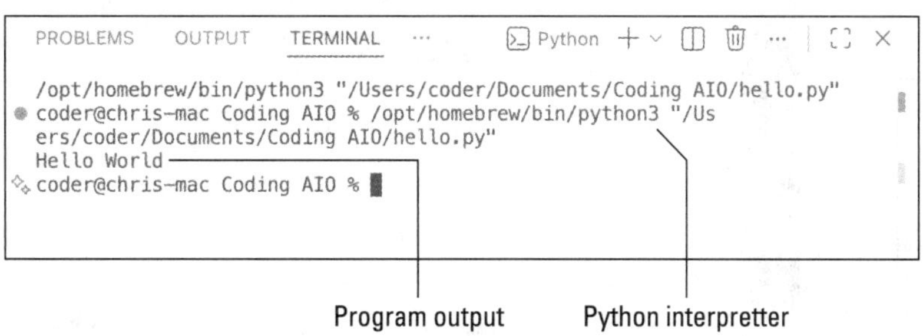

FIGURE 1-16: Output from `hello.py`.

This "Hello World" program is not the most exciting one in the world, but at least now you know how to write, save, and execute a Python program in VS Code, a skill you'll be using often as you continue through this book.

Learning simple debugging

REMEMBER

When you're first learning to write code, you're bound to make a lot of mistakes. Mistakes are no big deal — you won't break anything. The code just won't work as expected.

Before you attempt to run some code, you might see several screen indications of an error in your code:

- The number of errors in the file will appear in red next to the filename in the Explorer pane at the left side of the screen.
- The number of errors or warnings will also appear in the blue status bar near the lower-left corner of the VS Code app window.
- The bad code will have a wavy underline.

In Figure 1-17, I typed `PRINT` in all uppercase. But Python is case sensitive, and the correct command is `print`.

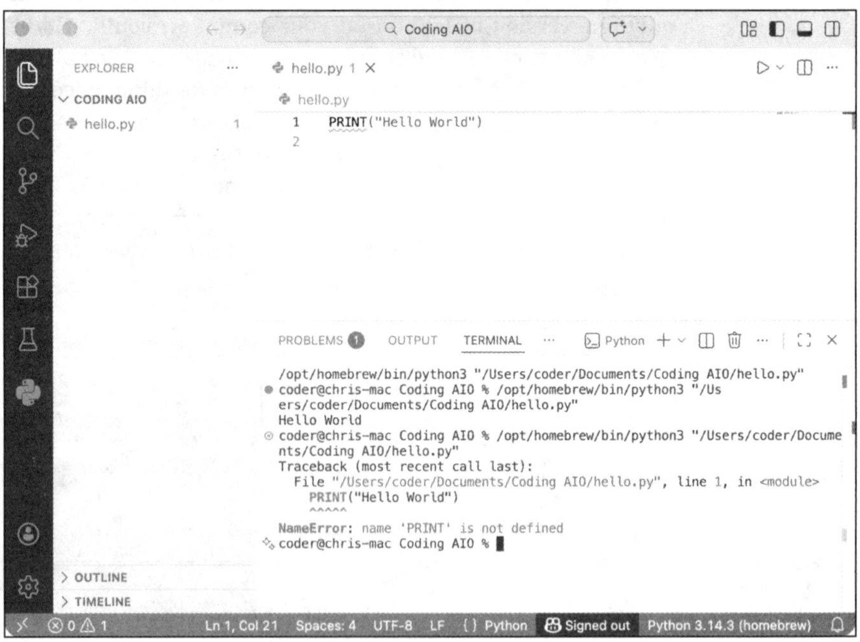

FIGURE 1-17: `PRINT` is typed incorrectly in `hello.py`.

To run the code, you must fix the error. In this example, I would just replace `PRINT` with `print`, and then save the change (unless I've turned on Auto Save). Then I can right-click and choose Run Python File in Terminal to run the corrected code.

Closing a file

When you're finished working with a program or file in VS Code, you can close it by clicking the X next to the filename in its tab or by choosing File ➪ Close Editor.

When the Explorer pane is open, the name of the file will still be visible in the Explorer pane on the left side of the VS Code window. Just click the filename whenever you want to reopen the file in the editor.

Writing Code in a Jupyter Notebook

In this section, you learn how to create, save, and open a Jupyter notebook.

Creating a folder for Jupyter Notebook

A Jupyter Notebook folder is no different than any other folder, so you can create it using whatever method you normally use in your operating system. I put mine in the `Coding AIO` folder that I created to keep all the files for this book in one place:

1. **Open your `CODINGAIO` folder (or whatever folder you created for working with files in this book) in Finder (Mac) or Explorer (Windows).**
2. **Right-click an empty spot in that folder and choose New ➪ Folder (Windows) or New Folder (Mac).**
3. **Type** Jupyter Notebooks **as the folder name and press Enter.**

Now you can create a notebook, as discussed next.

Creating a Jupyter notebook

You can create Jupyter notebooks, as well as run their code, in VS Code. If you created the `Jupyter Notebooks` folder in your `CODINGAIO` folder in the preceding section, you should see that folder name in VS Code's Explorer pane when the `CodingAIO` folder is open in VS Code. If you did create that folder but don't see it in VS Code, click the Refresh Explorer icon (a round arrow) just to the right of the `CodingAIO` folder name at the top of the Explorer pane.

To create a Jupyter notebook, follow these steps:

1. **Open VS Code.**
2. **In the Explorer pane, click the folder you created in the preceding section.**
3. **Right-click the folder and select New File to create a file in the `Jupyter Notebooks` folder.**
4. **Type** 01 Notebook.ipynb **as the filename.**

   REMEMBER

   It's important to get the filename extension — `.ipynb` — right so that the file will be recognized as a Jupyter Notebook.

   After you type the filename and press Enter, the file opens as a Jupyter Notebook in the editor to the right, as shown in Figure 1-18.

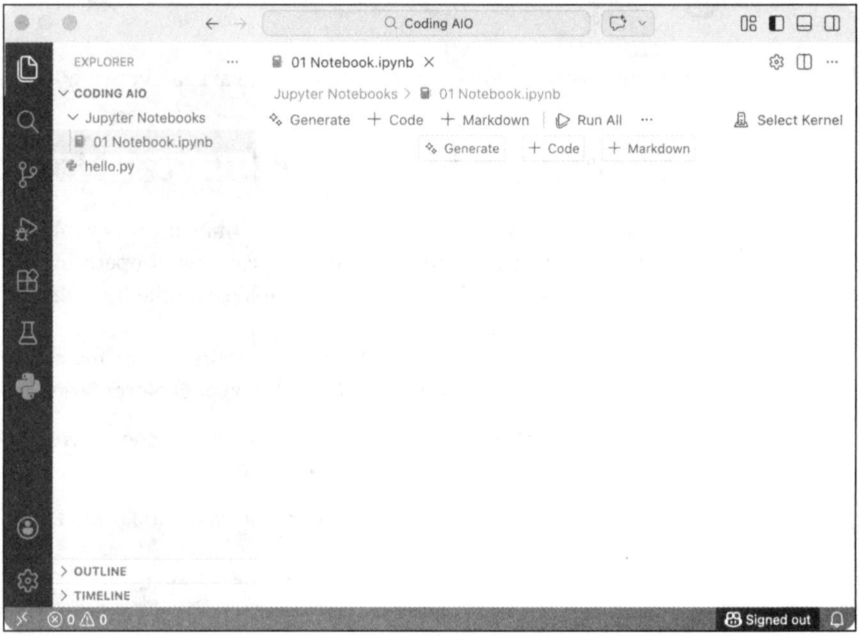

FIGURE 1-18: A Jupyter notebook.

REMEMBER

If you didn't turn on Auto Save, as mentioned earlier, you'll need to save your changes manually as you go along when you work with the notebook in the next sections.

Typing and running code in a notebook

At the top of the notebook are three buttons: Generate, Code, and Markdown. The first button, Generate, opens a prompt area where you can tell Copilot what you want so it can write the code for you. I recommend that you leave that one alone until you know more about Python. The other two buttons create different types of typing areas, called *cells*, in a Jupyter notebook.

Click the Code button to create a *code cell*, which is a cell that can execute Python code. It always has a right-pointing triangle near its top-left corner (see Figure 1-19), which you can use to run any Python code you type in the cell.

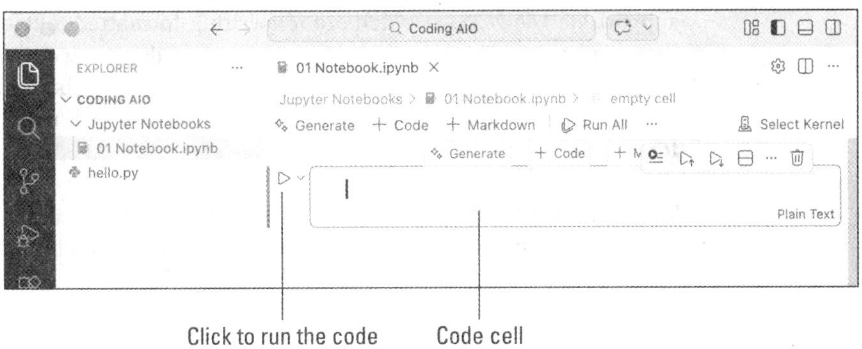

FIGURE 1-19: Your first code cell.

Right now, you should see one code cell, and you can use it to type and run some Python code:

1. **Click in the code cell to the right of the triangle and type the following code:**

```
print("Hello World")
```

2. **To run the code, simply click the Run icon (the right-pointing triangle to the left of the code) or the Run All button above the code.**

   If you're prompted to choose a Python interpreter, just choose the one you last downloaded (typically shown as the Recommended option), and install any needed extensions it suggests.

Assuming that your code has no errors, the output from the Python program (the words *Hello World*) appears just below the code in the Jupyter notebook, as shown in Figure 1-20.

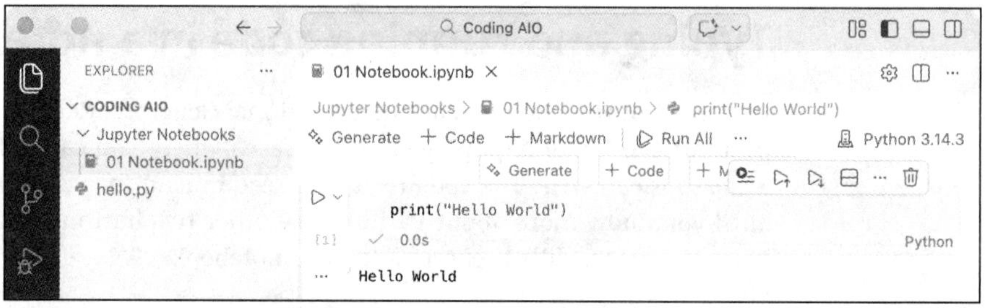

FIGURE 1-20: Successfully running your first code cell.

Using markdown cells

So far, you've used a code cell, which runs Python. But Jupyter notebooks also support *markdown cells,* which are for writing formatted text — notes, headings, lists, and even simple tables. Markdown cells don't execute Python; they help you explain what your code is doing and make your notebook easier to read later. Markdown cells are similar to code comments, but with many more options for formatting.

To add a markdown cell, click the Markdown button near the top of the notebook. A new cell appears, as shown in Figure 1-21, and you can type your text.

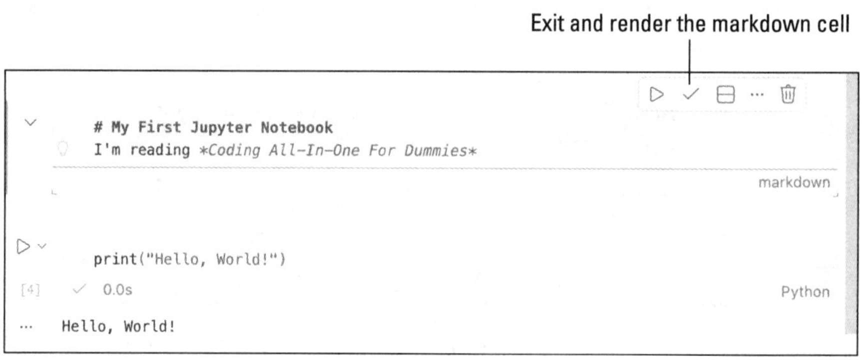

FIGURE 1-21: Markdown cells explain and organize the code.

When you have finished typing in the markdown cell, click outside the cell, press the Esc key, or click the check mark icon (see Figure 1-22). VS Code replaces the markdown characters with formatted text.

Here are a few markdown basics you can try in a markdown cell:

- **Headings:** Type `#` for a main heading, `##` for a subheading, and so on.
- **Emphasis:** Use `**bold**` for bold and `*italic*` for italic.

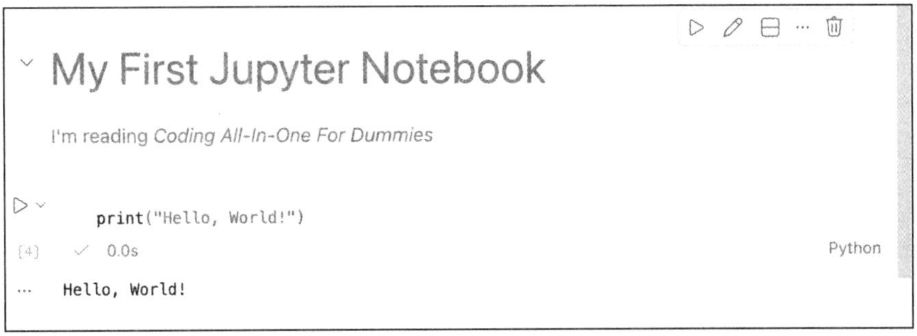

FIGURE 1-22: A notebook with a formatted markdown cell.

- **Lists:** Start a line with * or – for a bulleted list or with `1.` for a numbered list.
- **Code formatting:** Use backticks for inline code, like `` `print("Hello")` ``. For a multiline code block, put three backticks on a line by themselves before and after the code.

Why bother including markdown cells? Because notebooks are often shared (or revisited weeks later). A few well-placed markdown cells can turn a pile of code into a readable story: what you're trying to do, what data you're using, what results you got, and what the next step should be. A common pattern is to use a markdown heading for each task (for example, load data, clean data, analyze, plot results), followed by one or more code cells that do that work.

Closing a Jupyter notebook

Each notebook you create has its own file. You can close a notebook as you would a `.py` file. Click the X in the tab next to the notebook's filename, or choose File ➪ Close Editor. To reopen a notebook, click its filename in the Explorer pane.

IN THIS CHAPTER

» Understanding the design principles of Python

» Coding more easily with Python modules

» Working with data types

» Manipulating data types with operators

» Creating variables

Chapter 2

Understanding Python's Building Blocks

You might not think that programmers are artists, but programming is an extremely creative profession. It's logic-based creativity.

—JOHN ROMERO, VIDEO GAME DEVELOPER AND PROGRAMMER

Whether you want to code a website, analyze data, or create a script to automate something, this chapter gives you the basics you need to get started on your journey. As when learning any language, you need to understand the individual words so that you can start building sentences and, finally, the blocks of code that will enable your app to work. You also need to know something about what's considered good style in your chosen language. To help you understand Python's style, you learn about its guiding principles as well as the basic programming language design principle that Python employs. You also discover the words of the Python language: its various data types, operators, and variables.

The Zen of Python

The *Zen of Python*, shown in Figure 2-1, is a list of the guiding principles for the design of the Python language. These principles are hidden in an *Easter egg*, which is a term for something in a programming language or an app that is not easy to find and is an inside joke to people who have learned enough of the language or app to be able to find the Easter egg.

```
PROBLEMS    OUTPUT    DEBUG CONSOLE    TERMINAL

PS C:\Users\Alan\OneDrive\AIO Python> python
Python 3.11.4 (tags/v3.11.4:d2340ef, Jun  7 2023, 05:45:37) [MSC v.1934 64 bit (AMD64)] on win32
Type "help", "copyright", "credits" or "license" for more information.
>>> import this
The Zen of Python, by Tim Peters

Beautiful is better than ugly.
Explicit is better than implicit.
Simple is better than complex.
Complex is better than complicated.
Flat is better than nested.
Sparse is better than dense.
Readability counts.
Special cases aren't special enough to break the rules.
Although practicality beats purity.
Errors should never pass silently.
Unless explicitly silenced.
In the face of ambiguity, refuse the temptation to guess.
There should be one-- and preferably only one --obvious way to do it.
Although that way may not be obvious at first unless you're Dutch.
Now is better than never.
Although never is often better than *right* now.
If the implementation is hard to explain, it's a bad idea.
If the implementation is easy to explain, it may be a good idea.
Namespaces are one honking great idea -- let's do more of those!
>>> 
```

FIGURE 2-1: The Zen of Python.

To get to the Easter egg, follow these steps:

1. **Open VS Code and then open your `Coding AIO` folder.**
2. **If the Terminal pane isn't open, choose View ➪ Terminal.**

   If View ➪ Terminal is dimmed, you can create a new Terminal by choosing Terminal ➪ New.
3. **Type** python **and press Enter to get to the Python prompt (>>>).**

   If you get an error, type **python3** (on a Mac) or **py** (in Windows).
4. **At the** >>> **prompt, type** import this **and press Enter.**

   The list of aphorisms appears. You may have to scroll up and down to see them all. The general idea they express is to always try to make the code more human-readable than machine-readable.

The Zen of Python is sometimes referred to as *PEP 20*, where *PEP* stands for *Python Enhancement Proposals*. Many other PEPs exist; you can find them all at `https://peps.python.org`.

Introducing Object-Oriented Programming

There are different approaches to designing languages. One of the most successful and widely used models is *object-oriented programming*, or *OOP*, which is a design philosophy that tries to mimic the real world in the sense that it consists of objects with properties as well as methods (actions) that those objects perform.

For example, any one car is an object. Different cars have different properties, such as make, model, year, color, and size. And yet they all serve the same purpose: to get us from point A to point B. All cars have certain methods (things they can do) in common. You can drive them, steer them, speed them up, slow them down, adjust the inside temperature, and more by using controls in the car that you manipulate with your hands.

An *object* in an object-oriented programming language isn't a physical thing, like a car, because it exists inside a computer. An object is strictly software. In Python, you can have a *class* (which you can think of as an object creator, such as a car factory) that can produce many different kinds of objects (cars). All these objects can be manipulated through the controls they have in common (steering wheel, brakes, accelerator, and gearshift).

Python is an object-oriented language. The core language consists of controls (in the form of words) that you use to work with all kinds of objects — in your own and other people's programs. However, you need to learn the core language. Similarly, after you know how to drive one car, you pretty much know how to drive them all.

Why Indentations Count

One feature that makes Python different from many other languages is that it uses indentations rather than parentheses and curly braces to indicate blocks, or chunks, of code. If you're familiar with a language such as JavaScript, you know that you have to do a bit of wrangling with parentheses and braces to control what's inside what.

For example, here's some JavaScript code. If you're familiar with the Magic 8 Ball toy, you may have a sense of what this program is doing. But that's not what's important. Just note all those parentheses, curly braces, and semicolons:

```
document.addEventListener('DOMContentLoaded', function () {
  let question = prompt('Ask magic 8 ball a question');
  let answer = Math.floor(Math.random() * 8) + 1;
  if (answer == 1) {
    alert('It is certain');
  } else if (answer == 2) {
    alert('Outlook good');
  } else if (answer == 3) {
    alert('You may rely on it');
  } else if (answer == 4) {
    alert('Ask again later');
  } else if (answer == 5) {
    alert('Concentrate and ask again');
  } else if (answer == 6) {
    alert('Reply hazy, try again');
  } else if (answer == 7) {
    alert('My reply is no');
  } else if (answer == 8) {
    alert('My sources say no');
  }
});
```

In JavaScript, the parentheses and curly braces are required because they identify where chunks of code begin and end. The indentations for readability are optional.

Here's that JavaScript code written in Python:

```
import random
question = input("Ask magic 8 ball a question")
answer = random.randint(1, 8)
if answer == 1:
    print("It is certain")
elif answer == 2:
    print("Outlook good")
elif answer == 3:
    print("You may rely on it")
elif answer == 4:
    print("Ask again later")
elif answer == 5:
    print("Concentrate and ask again")
elif answer == 6:
    print("Reply hazy, try again")
elif answer == 7:
    print("My reply is no")
```

```
elif answer == 8:
    print("My sources say no")
print("The end")
```

In Python, indentation determines the structure of your program. The indentation level of each line tells Python which block of code that line belongs to. Using the wrong indentation can cause errors or, worse, silently change what your program does without any error message. That said, when you read well-written Python code as a human, this structure tends to work in your favor: It's relatively easy to see what's going on because you're not distracted by a lot of extra punctuation marks such as curly braces.

Writing Python Comments

Before you type any code, you should start with a *comment,* which is text in the program that Python ignores when the program runs. Comments are there for people: They help teammates understand what your code is intended to do, and they help *you* remember why you wrote the code a certain way when you come back to it days, weeks, or months later.

Because a comment isn't code, you can use any wording you want. However, to identify the text as a comment, you must start the line with a pound sign (`#`). If the comment is short (one line), the pound sign is all you need. Often you'll see it followed by a space, as in the next example, but the space is optional:

```
# This is a Python comment
```

In VS Code, comments are usually displayed in a different color from your code, making them easy to spot. The color depends on which theme you're using.

You might also come across triple-quoted strings (""" or ''') in Python code, but these aren't true comments. However, when a triple-quoted string appears as the first statement in a function, class, or module, Python treats it as a docstring: a built-in way to document what that code does.

Putting Python Modules to Work

One of the secrets to Python's success is that it's composed of a simple, clean, core language. That's the part you need to learn first. In addition to that core language, many modules (also written in the core language) are available that you can grab for free and access from your own code.

Most modules are for a specific application, such as science, artificial intelligence, or working with dates and time. The beauty of using modules is that other people have spent a lot of time creating, testing, and fine-tuning those modules, so that you don't have to. You simply import the module into your Python file and use the module's capabilities as instructed in the module's documentation.

For example, the sample Magic 8 Ball program in the preceding section starts with this line:

```
import random
```

The core Python language has nothing built into it to generate a random number. But someone figured out how to do it and made the code freely available. Starting your program with `import random` tells the program that you want to use the capabilities of the random number module to generate a random number.

Then, later in the program, you generate a random number between 1 and 8 with this line:

```
answer = random.randint(1, 8)
```

The syntax for importing a module is

```
import modulename [as alias ]
```

where *`modulename`* is the name of the module you want to import, and *`alias`* is a nickname you can assign to the module. Anything in square brackets is optional.

TIP

For the alias, most people use a short name that's easy to type and remember so that they don't have to type a long name every time they want to access the module's capabilities. For example, instead of typing `import random` to import that module, you could import it and give it a nickname such as `rnd`, which is shorter:

```
import random as rnd
```

Then, in subsequent code, you wouldn't use the full name, `random`, to refer to the module. Instead, you'd use the short name, `rnd`:

```
answer = rnd.randint(1, 8)
```

REMEMBER

You can type the `import` line any place you type Python code: at the Python command prompt (>>>), in a `.py` file, or in a Jupyter notebook. In a `.py` file, always put `import` statements first (after a module docstring) so that their capabilities are available to the rest of the code.

Understanding Python Data Types

You deal with written information all the time and probably don't think about the difference between numbers and text. For example, everyone knows that 1 + 1 = 2. The same doesn't apply to letters and words. The expression A+A doesn't necessarily equal B or AA or anything else because letters and words aren't quantities.

In programming, a type of data (such as text or a number) is called, appropriately enough, a *data type.* In this section, you learn about Python's basic data types: numbers, strings, and Boolean.

Numbers

Numbers in Python must start with a number digit, (0–9), a dot (period), which is a decimal point, or a hyphen (-), used as a negative sign for negative numbers. A number can contain only one decimal point. It should not contain letters, spaces, dollar signs, or anything else that isn't part of a normal number. Table 2-1 shows examples of good and bad Python numbers.

TABLE 2-1 Examples of Good and Bad Python Numbers

Number	Good or Bad?	Reason
1	Good	A whole number (integer)
1.1	Good	A number with a decimal point
1234567.89	Good	A large number with a decimal point and no commas
–2	Good	A negative number, as indicated by the starting hyphen
.99	Good	A number that starts with a decimal point because it's less than 1
$1.99	Bad	Contains a dollar sign
12,345.67	Bad	Contains a comma
1101 3232	Bad	Contains a space
91740-3384	Bad	Contains a hyphen
123-45-6789	Bad	Contains two hyphens
123 Oak Tree Lane	Bad	Contains spaces and words
(267)555-1234	Bad	Contains parentheses and a hyphen
127.0.0.1	Bad	Only one decimal point is allowed

If you're worried that the number rules won't let you work with dollar amounts, zip codes, addresses, or anything else, stop worrying. You can store and work with *all* kinds of information, as you'll see shortly.

TIP

The vast majority of the numbers you use will probably match one of the first four examples of good numbers. However, if you happen to be looking at code used for more advanced scientific or mathematical applications, you might occasionally see numbers that contain the letter *e* or the letter *j*. That's because Python supports three different types of numbers, as discussed in the sections that follow.

Integers

An *integer* is any whole number, positive or negative. There's no limit to its size. Numbers such as 0, −1, and 999999999999999 are all valid integers. From your perspective, an integer is any valid number that doesn't contain a decimal point.

Floats

A *floating-point number,* often called a *float,* is any valid number that contains a decimal point. Again, there is no size limit: 1.1, −1.1, and 123456.789012345 are all valid floats.

If you work with very large scientific numbers, you can put an *e* in a number to indicate the power of 10. For example, 234e3 means 234×10^3, or 234,000, and 2.34e3 means 2.34×10^3, or 2,340. Python treats any number written this way as a float, even if there's no decimal point. If you're not using it in your day-to-day work now, chances are you'll never need it in Python either.

Complex numbers

Just about any kind of number can be expressed as an integer or a float, so being familiar with these two types is sufficient for just about everyone. Note, though, that Python also supports *complex numbers,* which always end with the letter *j,* which is the *imaginary* part of the number. If you have no idea what I'm talking about, you're normal — only people deep in math land care about complex numbers. But if you see something like z = 2 + 3j, realize that *j* after the 3 indicates that 3 is to be treated as imaginary.

Words (strings)

Strings are sort of the opposite of numbers. With numbers, you can add, subtract, multiply, and divide because the numbers represent quantities. Strings are for just about everything else. A name, an address, or even the name of a number (such as *eleven*) is a string in Python (and in computers in general). It's called a *string* because it's a string of characters (letters, spaces, punctuation marks, and maybe some numbers). To us, a string usually has some meaning, such as a person's name or address. But to a computer, if a piece of information is not something on which it can do arithmetic, it's just a string of characters.

Unlike numbers, a string must always be enclosed in quotation marks. You can use either double (") or single (') quotation marks. The following are valid strings:

```
"Hi there, I am a string"
'Hello world'
"123 Oak Tree Lane"
"(267)555-1234"
"18901-3384"
```

Note that it's fine to use numeric characters (0–9) as well as hyphens and dots (periods) in strings, as long as they are enclosed in quotation marks.

WARNING

A word of caution: If a string contains an apostrophe (single quote), the entire string should be enclosed in double quotation marks like this:

```
"Mary's dog said Woof."
```

The double quotation marks are necessary to avoid confusion about where the string starts and ends.

Similarly, if the string contains double quotation marks, enclose the entire thing in single quotation marks to avoid confusion:

```
'The dog of Mary said "Woof".'
```

The first single quotation mark starts the string, the second one ends it, and the double quotation marks cause no confusion because they're inside the string.

So what if you have a string that contains both single and double quotation marks, like this:

```
Mary's dog said "Woof".
```

This deserves a resounding "hmm." The solution involves something called *escape characters* because, in a sense, they allow you to escape (avoid) the special meaning of a character such as a single or double quotation mark. To escape a character, precede it with a backslash (\). Make sure you use a backslash (the one that leans back toward the previous character), not a forward slash (/).

Continuing with the last example, you could enclose the entire string in single quotation marks, and then escape the apostrophe (which is the same character) by preceding it with a backslash:

```
'Mary\'s dog said "Woof".'
```

Or you could enclose the entire string in double quotation marks, and escape the quotation marks in the string:

```
"Mary's dog said \"Woof\"."
```

Another common use of the backslash is to use `\n` to add a newline character (a line break) on the screen. For example, this string

```
"The old pond\nA frog jumped in,\nKerplunk!"
```

would look like this when displayed:

```
The old pond
A frog jumped in,
Kerplunk!
```

Booleans

A third data type in Python is called a *Boolean* (named after mathematician George Boole) and can be one of two values: `True` or `False`.

In Python code, people store `True` and `False` values in *variables* (placeholders in code described later in the chapter) using a format similar to this:

```
x = True
```

or this:

```
x = False
```

Booleans are most useful when making decisions in your code. For example, you might store whether a user is logged in, and then use that value to control what your program does next:

```
is_logged_in = True
if is_logged_in:
    print("Welcome back!")
```

```
else:
    print("Please log in.")
```

Here, Python checks whether `is_logged_in` is `True` and prints the appropriate message.

TIP

You know `True` and `False` are Boolean because they are not enclosed in quotation marks (as a string would be) and are not numbers. Also, the initial cap is required.

Working with Python Operators

As mentioned, in Python and computers in general, information is one of the following data types: number, string, or Boolean. You also use computers to *operate* on that information, meaning to do any necessary math, comparisons, searches, or whatever to help you find information and organize it in a way that makes sense to you.

Python offers many different *operators* for working with and comparing types of information. This section offers a brief summary of them.

Arithmetic operators

Arithmetic operators, as the name implies, are for doing arithmetic: addition, subtraction, multiplication, division, and more. Table 2-2 lists Python's arithmetic operators.

TABLE 2-2 Python's Arithmetic Operators

Operator	Description	Example
+	Addition	1 + 1 = 2
–	Subtraction	10 – 1 = 9
*	Multiplication	3 * 5 = 15
/	Division	10 / 5 = 2.0
%	Modulus (remainder after division)	11 % 5 = 1
**	Exponent	3**2 = 9
//	Floor division	11 // 5 = 2

The first four items in the table are the same as you learned in elementary school. The last three are a little more advanced:

- The *modulus* operation returns the remainder after division. For example, 11 % 5 is 1 because if you divide 11 by 5, you get 2 remainder 1.
- The *exponent* means "raised to the power of." For example, 3**2 is 3^2 (or 3 squared), which is 3*3, or 9. For another example, 3**4 is 3*3*3*3, or 81.
- *Floor division,* indicated by //, is integer division in that anything after the decimal point is truncated (cut off), without rounding. For example, in regular division, 9/5 is 1.8. But 9//5 is 1 because .8 is chopped off — it isn't rounded to 2.

Comparison operators

Computers can make decisions, but these decisions aren't judgment calls or anything human-like that. Computer decisions are based on absolute facts that are based on comparisons. The *comparison operators* that Python offers for writing code that makes a decision are listed in Table 2-3.

TABLE 2-3 **Python Comparison Operators**

Operator	What It Means
<	Less than
<=	Less than or equal to
>	Greater than
>=	Greater than or equal to
==	Equal to
!=	Not equal to
is	Object identity
is not	Negated object identity

The first few are self-explanatory. The last two are tricky because they concern Python objects, which we haven't talked about yet. We get to those in Chapters 5 and 6 of this minibook. For now, it's best to stick with the basics.

Boolean operators

Boolean operators work with Boolean values (`True` or `False`) and are used to determine whether something is `True` or `False`. Table 2-4 summarizes the Boolean operators.

TABLE 2-4 Python Boolean Operators

Operator	Code Example	What It Determines
or	x or y	Either x or y is true
and	x and y	Both x and y are true
not	not x	x is not true

Python Style Guide (PEP 8) recommends that you put a space before and after each operator.

Creating and Using Variables

A *variable* is simply a placeholder for information that may vary (change). In your code, a variable is represented by a variable *name* rather than a specific piece of information. For example:

```
extended_price = quantity * unit_price
```

The variables are `extended_price`, `quantity` and `unit_price`. No matter what numbers you plug in for them, you get the correct `extended_price`. For example, if you buy three turtle doves for $1.00 apiece, your `extended_price` is $3.00 (3 * $1.00). If you buy two dozen roses for $1.50 apiece, `extended_price` is $36 because 1.5 * 24 is 36.

Using valid variable names

In Python, you can make up your own variable names, but they must conform to the following rules to be recognized as variable names:

- The variable name must start with a letter or an underscore (_).
- After the first character, you can use only letters, numbers, or underscores.

- Variable names are case sensitive, so any reference to that variable must use the same uppercase and lowercase letters.
- Variable names can't be enclosed in, or contain, single or double quotation marks.
- The variable name can't be the same as a Python keyword.
- Python style conventions recommend that you use only lowercase letters in variable names and use an underscore to separate multiple words.

REMEMBER

You often see variable names that don't conform to that last style. For example, in *camel case* formatting — in which the first letter is lowercase and new words are capitalized — you might see something like `extendedPrice` or `unitPrice`.

Creating variables in code

To create a variable, you use the following syntax (order of things):

```
variablename = value
```

where *`variablename`* is the name you make up. You can use *x* or *y*, as people often do in math, but in larger programs, it's a good idea to give your variables meaningful names, such as `sales_tax` or `user_name`, so that you can remember what you're storing in the variable.

The *`value`* is whatever you want to store in the variable. It can be a number, a string, a Boolean `True` or `False` value, or the result of a calculation.

The = sign is the *assignment operator* and is so named because it assigns the value (on the right) to the variable (on the left). For example, in the following, you're storing the number `10` in a variable named `x`. In other words, you're assigning the value `10` to the `x` variable:

```
x = 10
```

And here, you're putting the string `Alan` in a variable named `user_name`:

```
user_name = "Alan"
```

Manipulating variables

Much of computer programming revolves around storing values in variables and manipulating that information with operators. Following are some simple examples.

```
quantity = 10
unit_price = 1.99
extended_price = quantity * unit_price
print(extended_price)
```

This code creates some variables, stores some values in them, and calculates a new value, `extended_price`, based on the contents of the `quantity` and `unit_price` variables. The last line displays the contents of the `extended_price` variable on the screen.

Now that you know something about Python and its data types and operators, it's time to learn how to work with these different tools. In the next chapter, you will learn about working with numbers.

IN THIS CHAPTER

» Exploring Python's built-in number tools

» Importing the `math` module

» Making numbers presentable

Chapter 3 Working with Numbers

Form and function are one.

—FRANK LLOYD WRIGHT

In the computer world, *numbers* are numbers you can add, subtract, multiply, and divide. Python also differentiates between whole numbers (integers) and numbers that contain a decimal point (floats). Words (textual information such as names and addresses) are stored as strings, which is short for "strings of characters." In addition to numbers and strings, there are Boolean values, which can be either `True` or `False`. We also have to deal with dates and times, which are yet another type of information.

In this chapter, you build on what you learned about the number data type in the preceding chapter by digging into Python's built-in functions for calculations, exploring additional tools in the `math` module, and learning practical ways to format numeric output for people to read. In Chapter 4, you shift from numbers to strings (text), and Chapter 5 shows you how to work with dates.

Calculating with Built-In Functions

A *function* in Python is similar to a function in a calculator, in that you pass something to the function and the function passes something back. For example, with the square root function, you provide a number, and the function tells you the square root of that number.

Python functions generally have the following syntax:

```
variablename = function_name ([ param, param ])
```

Because most functions return some value, you typically start by defining a variable to store what the function returns. Next is = and the function name, followed by a pair of parentheses. Inside the parentheses, you may pass zero or more values (called *arguments*) to the function.

For example, the `abs()` function accepts one number and returns the absolute value of that number. If you're not a math nerd, this just means that the `abs()` function converts negative numbers to positive numbers.

For example, in Figure 3-1, I created a variable named `x` and assigned it the value –4. Then I created a variable named `y` and assigned it the absolute value of `x` using the `abs()` function. Printing `x` shows its value, –4, which hasn't changed. Printing `y` shows 4, the absolute value of `x` as returned by the `abs()` function. You can try this out for yourself in a Jupyter notebook, at the Python prompt, or in a `.py` file in VS Code.

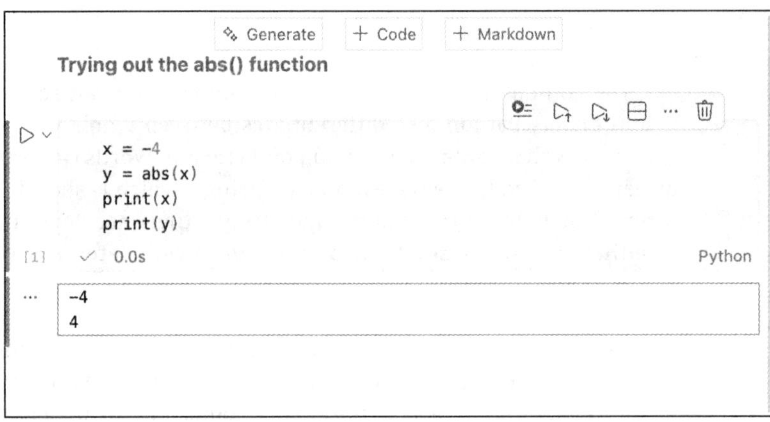

FIGURE 3-1: Trying out the `abs()` function.

Even though a function always returns one value, some functions accept two or more values. For example, the `round()` function takes one number as its first argument. The second argument is the number of decimal places to which you want to round that number. In the example in Figure 3-2, I created a variable named `x` with a whole lot of digits after the decimal point. Next, I created a variable named `y` to return the same number rounded to two decimal places. Then I printed both results.

FIGURE 3-2: Trying out the `round()` function.

Python has many built-in functions for working with numbers, as shown in Table 3-1. Some may not mean much to you if you're not into math in a big way, but don't let that intimidate you. If you don't understand what a function does, chances are it's not doing something relevant to the kind of work you do. But if you're curious, you can always search the web for *python* followed by the function name for more information. For a more extensive list, search for *python 3 built-in functions.*

TABLE 3-1 **Some Built-In Python Functions for Numbers**

Built-In Function	What It Does
`abs(x)`	Returns the absolute value of number *x* (converts negative numbers to positive).
`bin(x)`	Returns a string representing the value of *x* converted to binary.
`float(x)`	Converts a string or number *x* to the float data type.
`format(x, y)`	Returns *x* formatted according to the pattern specified in *y*. This older syntax is still in Python, but f-strings are generally preferred in current Python versions.
`hex(x)`	Returns a string containing *x* converted to hexadecimal, prefixed with `0x`.
`int(x)`	Converts *x* to the integer data type by truncating (not rounding) the decimal portion and any digits after it.
`max(x, y, z, ...)`	Takes any number of numeric arguments and returns whichever is the largest.
`min(x, y, z, ...)`	Takes any number of numeric arguments and returns whichever is the smallest.
`oct(x)`	Converts *x* to an octal number, prefixed with 0o to indicate octal.
`round(x, y)`	Rounds the number *x* to *y* number of decimal places.
`str(x)`	Converts the number *x* to the string data type.
`type(x)`	Returns a string indicating the data type of *x*.

Figure 3-3 shows examples of the Python syntax to use for the built-in math functions.

```
>>> pi=3.14159265358979323846264338327950
... x=128
... y=345.67890987
... z=-999.9999
... print(abs(z))
... print(int(z))
... print(int(abs(z)))
... print(round(pi,4))
... print(bin(x))
... print(hex(x))
... print(oct(x))
... print(max(pi,x,y,z))
... print(min(pi,x,y,z))
... print(type(pi))
... print(type(x))
... print(type(str(y)))
...
999.9999
-999
999
3.1416
0b10000000
0x80
0o200
345.67890987
-999.9999
<class 'float'>
<class 'int'>
<class 'str'>
>>>
```

FIGURE 3-3: Playing around with built-in math functions at the Python prompt.

You can also *nest* functions — meaning that you can put functions inside functions. For example, when `z = -999.9999`, the expression `print(int(abs(z)))` prints the integer portion of the absolute value of `z`, which is `999`. The original number is converted to positive, and then the decimal point and everything to its right are chopped off.

Still More Math Functions

In addition to the built-in functions, Python has others that you can import from the `math` module. If you need them in an app, put `import math` near the top of the `.py` file or Jupyter cell to make those functions available to the rest of the code. To use them at the command prompt, first enter the `import math` command.

One of the functions in the `math` module is the `sqrt()` function, which gets the square root of a number. Because it's part of the `math` module, you can't use it without importing that module first. For example, if you enter the following, you'll get an error because `sqrt()` isn't a built-in function:

```
print(sqrt(81))
```

Even if you do two commands like the following, you'll still get an error because you're treating `sqrt()` as a built-in function:

```
import math
print(sqrt(81))
```

To use a function from a module, you have to import the module and precede the function name with the module name and a dot. The following example shows what works and what doesn't:

```
# This causes an error - sqrt() is not a built-in function
print(sqrt(81))

# This also causes an error - sqrt() still needs the module name

import math
print(sqrt(81))

# This works - import the module and use the module name as a prefix
import math
print(math.sqrt(81))
```

Running the last example gives you

```
9.0
```

Note that `math.sqrt()` always returns a float, so the result is 9.0 rather than 9.

The `math` module offers a lot of trigonometric and hyperbolic functions, powers and logarithms, angular conversions, and constants such as `pi` and `e`. I don't delve into all of them because advanced math isn't relevant to most people. You can check them by searching the web for *python 3 math module functions*. Table 3-2 offers examples that might prove useful in your own work.

The constants `pi`, `e`, and `tau` aren't typical functions into which you pass a value. Each is a constant that always returns the same value. You can assign the value returned by any constant to a variable of your choosing. Figure 3-4 shows some examples of using constants from the `math` module.

TABLE 3-2 **Some Functions from the Python Math Module**

Function	What It Does
`math.acos(x)`	Returns the arccosine of *x* in radians.
`math.atan(x)`	Returns the arctangent of *x*, in radians.
`math.atan2(y, x)`	Returns the arc tangent of *y* divided by *x* in radians.
`math.ceil(x)`	Returns the ceiling of *x*, the smallest integer greater than or equal to *x*.
`math.cos(x)`	Returns the cosine of *x* radians.
`math.degrees(x)`	Converts angle *x* from radians to degrees.
`math.e`	Returns the mathematical constant *e* (2.718281. . .).
`math.exp(x)`	Returns *e* raised to the power *x*, where *e* is the base of natural logarithms.
`math.factorial(x)`	Returns the factorial of *x*.
`math.floor(x)`	Returns the floor of *x*, the largest integer less than or equal to *x*.
`math.isnan(x)`	Returns `True` if *x* is not a number; otherwise returns `False`. More specifically, this function returns `True` if *x* contains NaN, a special value in Python used as a placeholder for numeric variables that don't contain a number.
`math.log(x, y)`	Returns the logarithm of *x* to base *y*.
`math.log2(x)`	Returns the base-2 logarithm of *x*.
`math.pi`	Returns the mathematical constant `pi` (3.141593 . . .).
`math.pow(x, y)`	Returns *x* raised to the power y.
`math.radians(x)`	Converts angle *x* from degrees to radians.
`math.sin(x)`	Returns the sine of *x*, (when *x* is expressed in radians).
`math.sqrt(x)`	Returns the square root of *x*.
`math.tan(x)`	Returns the tangent of *x* radians.
`math.tau`	Returns the mathematical constant tau (6.283185 . . .).

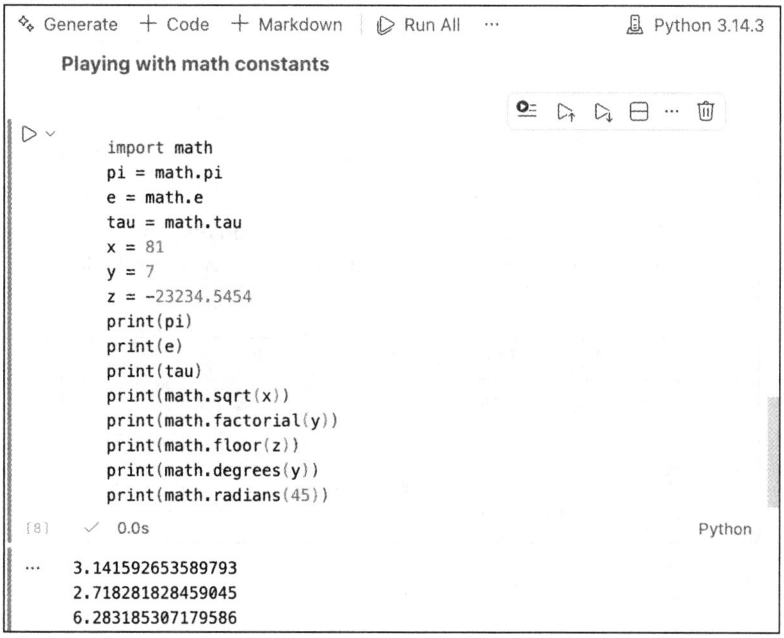

FIGURE 3-4: More playing around with built-in math constants.

Formatting Numbers

Over the years, Python has offered different methods for displaying numbers in formats familiar to us humans. For example, most people would rather see dollar amounts expressed in the format $1,234.56 rather than 1234.56006595069540569540 5959. The easiest way to format numbers in Python, starting with version 3.6, is to use f-strings.

Formatting with f-strings

Format strings, or f-strings, are the easiest way to format data in Python. All you need is `f` followed by text or an expression enclosed in quotation marks. Here's an example:

```
f"Hello {username}"
```

The `f` before the first quotation mark tells Python that what follows is a format string. Inside the quotation marks, the text, called the *literal part,* is displayed literally (exactly as typed in the f-string). Anything in curly braces is the *expression part* of the f-string, a placeholder for what will appear when the code executes.

Inside the curly braces, you can have an *expression* (a formula to perform some calculation, a variable name, or a combination of the two). For example:

```
username = "Quincy"
print(f"Hello, {username}!")
```

When you run this code, the `print` function displays the word `Hello`, followed by a space, followed by the contents of the `username` variable, as shown in Figure 3-5.

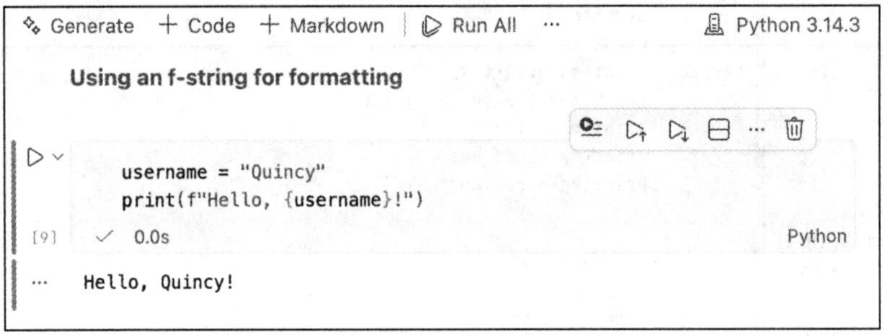

FIGURE 3-5: A super simple f-string for formatting.

Here is another example of an expression — the formula `quantity` times `unit_price` — inside the curly braces:

```
unit_price = 49.99
quantity = 30
print(f"Subtotal: ${quantity * unit_price}")
```

When executed, the output is

```
Subtotal: $1499.7
```

That $`1499.7` isn't an ideal way to show dollar amounts. Typically, we like to use commas in the thousands place, and two digits for the pennies, as in the following:

```
Subtotal: $1,499.70
```

Fortunately, f-strings provide you with the means to do this formatting, as you learn next.

Showing dollar amounts

To get a comma to appear in the dollar amount and display pennies as two digits, you can use a format string inside the curly braces of an expression in an f-string.

The format string starts with a colon and needs to be placed inside the closing curly brace, right up against the variable name or the value.

To show commas in thousands place, use a comma in your format string right after the colon, like this:

```
:,
```

Using the current example, you would do the following:

```
print(f"Subtotal: ${quantity * unit_price:,}")
```

Executing this statement produces this output:

```
Subtotal: $1,499.7
```

To display the pennies as two digits, follow the comma with

```
.2f
```

The `.2f` means "two decimal places, fixed" (never more or less than two decimal places). The following code will display the number with commas and two decimal places:

```
print(f"Subtotal: ${quantity * unit_price:,.2f}")
```

Here's what the code displays when executed:

```
Subtotal: $1,499.70
```

Perfect! That's exactly the format I want. So anytime you want to show a number with commas in the thousands place and exactly two digits after the decimal point, use an f-string with the format string `.2f`.

INTERNATIONALIZING PYTHON

For help with internationalization, Python supports the POSIX (Portable Operating System Interface) standard, which enables developers to write software that can be used on multiple operating systems. One part of POSIX allows you to display currency amounts in local formats.

(continued)

(continued)

Type **import locale** at the top of your code to import the module. Then use `locale.setlocale()` to define the country, and `locale.currency()` to display the number. You can also set `grouping` to `True` to include thousands separators in languages that support that. For example, the following code stores a number in a variable named `sample_amount`. Then it sets the locale for France (`fr_FR`) and uses `locale.currency()` to show that number in French currency format:

```
import locale
# Just some random number to work with
sample_amount = 1234.56
# Set the locale to French (France)
locale.setlocale(locale.LC_ALL, "fr_FR")
# Use locale.currency() to show sample amount in locale format
print(locale.currency(sample_amount, grouping=True))
```

As you might imagine, the locale module is huge because it covers all the different countries. But simply searching the web for *Python internationalization* should get you to the information you need to handle cultural formatting in your app.

Formatting percent numbers

Now, suppose your app applies sales tax. The app needs to know the sales tax rate, which should be expressed as a decimal number. So if the sales tax rate is 6.5 percent, it has to be written as 0.065 (or .065, if you prefer) in your code, like this:

```
sales_tax_rate = 0.065
```

It's the same amount with or without the leading zero, so just use whichever format works for you.

Simply using a `print()` function displays the number as Python stores it:

```
sales_tax_rate = 0.065
print(f"Sales Tax Rate {sales_tax_rate}")
Sales Tax Rate 0.065
```

When displaying the sales tax rate for people to read, however, you'll probably want to use the more familiar 6.5% format rather than .065. You can use the same idea as with fixed numbers (`.2f`), replacing the `f` for fixed numbers with `%`, like this:

```
print(f"Sales Tax Rate {sales_tax_rate:.2%}")
```

Running this code multiplies the sales tax rate by 100 and follows it with a percent sign (`%`), as you can see in Figure 3-6.

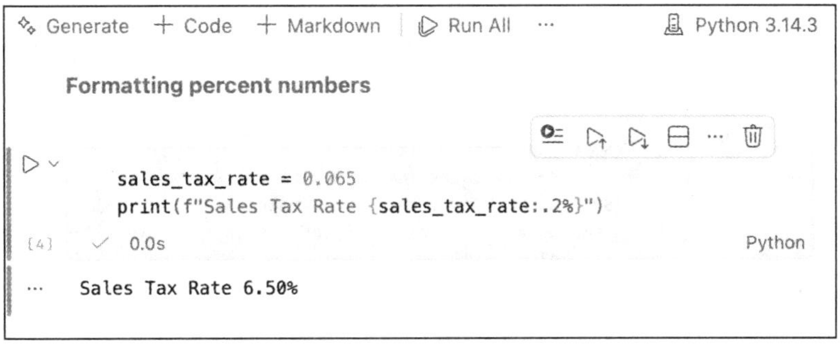

FIGURE 3-6: Formatting a percentage number.

In both of the previous examples, I used `2` for the number of digits, but you can display any number of digits you want, from none to whatever level of precision you need. For example, using `.1%`, as in the following:

```
print(f"Sales Tax Rate {sales_tax_rate:.1%}")
```

displays this output when the line is executed:

```
Sales Tax Rate 6.5%
```

Replacing `1` with a `9`, like this:

```
print(f"Sales Tax Rate {sales_tax_rate:.9%}")
```

displays the percentage with nine digits after the decimal point:

```
Sales Tax Rate 6.500000000%
```

You don't need to use an f-string only inside a call to the `print` function. You can execute an f-string and save the result in a variable that you can display later.

The format string itself is like any other string in that it must be enclosed in single, double, or triple quotation marks. When using triple quotation marks, you can use either three single quotation marks or three double quotation marks. It doesn't matter which you use as the outermost quotation marks on the format string; the output is the same, as you can see in Figure 3-7. Make sure you end the string with the same characters you used to start the string.

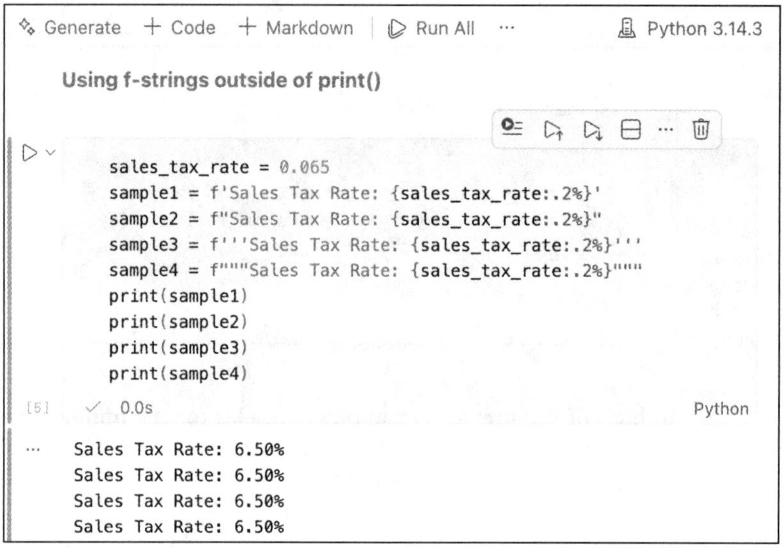

FIGURE 3-7: An f-string can be encased in single, double, or triple quotation marks.

Making multiline format strings

If you want to have multiline output, you can add line breaks to your format strings in a few ways:

» **Use \n.** You can use a single-line format string with \n any place you want a line break. Just make sure you put the \n in the literal portion of the format string, not inside curly braces. For example:

```
user1 = "Alberto"
user2 = "Babs"
user3 = "Carlos"
output = f"{user1}\n{user2}\n{user3}"
print(output)
```

When executed, this code displays:

```
Alberto
Babs
Carlos
```

» **Use triple quotation marks (single or double).** If you use triple quotation marks around your format string, you don't need to use \n. You can just break the line in the format string wherever you want it to break in the output. For example, look at Figure 3-8; the format string is in triple quotation marks and contains multiple line breaks. The output from running the code has line breaks in the same places.

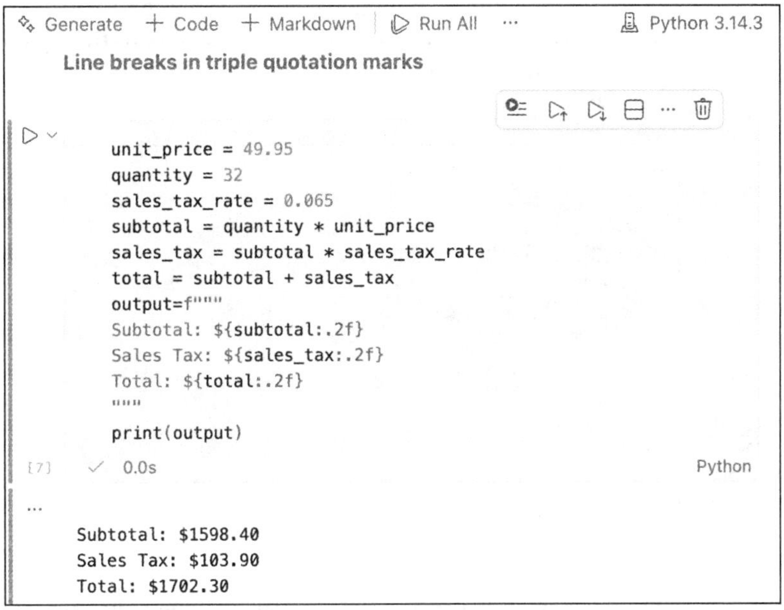

FIGURE 3-8: A multiline f-string enclosed in triple quotation marks.

As you can see, the output honors the line breaks and even the blank spaces in the format string. Unfortunately, it's not perfect — in real life, I would right-align the numbers so that the decimal points line up. All is not lost, though, because with format strings you can also control the width and alignments of your output.

Formatting width and alignment

You can control the width of your output (and the alignment of content within that width) by following the colon in your f-string with < (for left-aligned), ^

(for centered), or > (for right-aligned). Put any of these characters right after the colon in your format string. For example, the following will make the output 20 characters wide, with the content right-aligned:

```
:>20
```

In Figure 3-8, all the dollar amounts are left-aligned, because that's the default. To right-align numbers, which is how you usually see dollar amounts, you use `>` in an f-string. To make the numbers the same width, specify a number after the `>` character.

For example, in Figure 3-9, each f-string includes `>9`, which makes each displayed number right-aligned and 9 characters wide. The output, which you can see at the bottom of the figure, makes all the numbers align to the right, with their dollar signs neatly aligned to the left. The spaces to the right of each dollar sign ensure that each number is exactly nine characters wide.

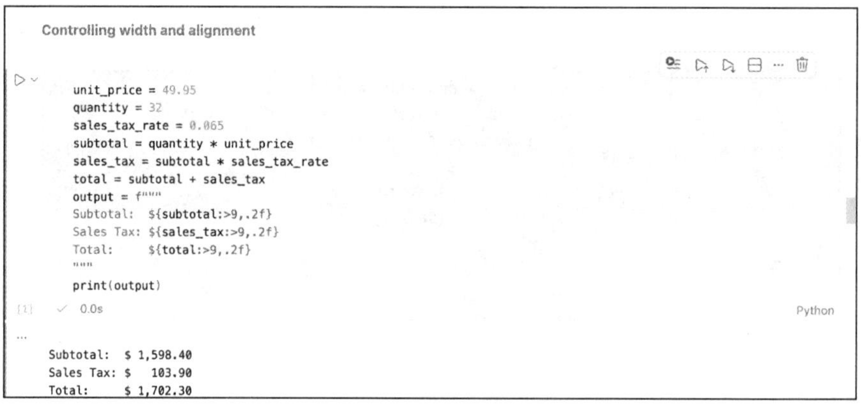

FIGURE 3-9: All dollar amounts are right-aligned within a width of nine characters (>9).

You may look at Figure 3-9 and wonder why the dollar signs aren't aligned right next to their numbers. The dollar signs are part of the literal string, outside the curly braces, so they aren't affected by `>9` inside the curly braces.

Realigning the dollar signs is a little more complicated because the `,.2f` formatting can be used only on a number. You can't attach $ to the front of a number unless you change the number to a string — but then it wouldn't be a number anymore, so `.2f` wouldn't work.

But complicated doesn't mean impossible; it just means inconvenient. You can convert each dollar amount to a string in the current format, stick the dollar sign on that string, and then format the width and alignment on this string. For example, the following code creates a variable named `s_subtotal` containing a dollar sign immediately followed by the dollar amount, with the dollar sign just to the left of the first digit and no spaces after the dollar sign:

```
s_subtotal = "$" + f"{subtotal:,.2f}"
```

In this code, I assume that the `subtotal` variable contains some number. If the number were `1598.402`, `f"{subtotal:,.2f}"` would format the number in a fixed two-decimal-places format with a comma in the thousands place, like this:

```
1,598.40
```

The output is a string rather than a number because an f-string always produces a string.

The following part of the code adds a dollar sign to the front (in Python, putting two strings together is called *concatenation*, and it uses the same operator as the addition operation):

```
"$"+
```

So now the output is `$1,598.40`. That final formatted string is stored in a new variable named `s_subtotal`. (The leading `s_` is a reminder that this is the string equivalent of the subtotal number, not the original number.)

To display that dollar amount right-aligned with a width of nine digits, use `>9` in a new format string to display the `s_subtotal` variable, like this:

```
f"{s_subtotal:>9}"
```

Figure 3-10 shows a complete example, including the output from running the code. All the numbers are right-aligned with the dollar signs in the usual place.

TIP

Anytime you need a reminder about the complicated `print f` stuff, just ask ChatGPT or other generative AI for a reminder. For example, you can ask it to *write python print f for right-aligned currency numbers with two decimal places* or *write a python print f for two-digit percentage values.* Then copy and paste whatever AI produces into your own code, and adjust it to your current needs.

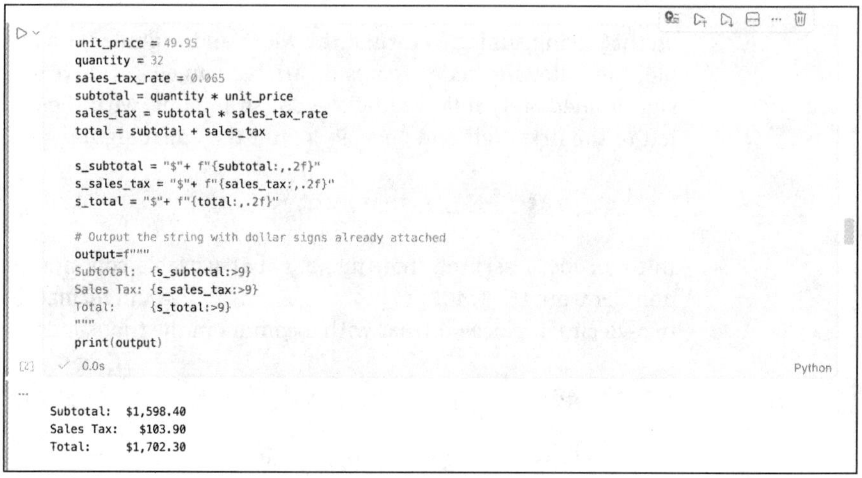

FIGURE 3-10: All the dollar amounts neatly aligned.

IN THIS CHAPTER

» Joining strings

» Finding a string's length

» Using string operators

» Discovering string methods

Chapter 4
Manipulating Strings

The problem with words is that you never know whose mouths they've been in.

—DENNIS POTTER

In Python and other programming languages, words and chunks of text are called *strings,* short for "a string of characters." A string has no numeric meaning or value. (I discuss the basics of strings in Chapter 2 in this minibook.) In this chapter, you learn Python coding skills for working with strings.

Concatenating Strings

You can join strings by using a plus sign (+). The process of doing so is called *string concatenation* in nerd-o-rama world. One thing that catches beginners off guard is the fact that a computer doesn't know a word from a bologna sandwich. So when you join strings, the computer doesn't automatically put spaces where you'd expect them. For example, in the following code, `full_name` is a concatenation of the first three strings:

```
first_name = "Bart"
middle_init = "J"
last_name = "Simpson"
full_name = first_name + middle_init + last_name
print(full_name)
```

When you run this code to print the contents of the `full_name` variable, you can see that Python did join them in one long string:

```
BartJSimpson
```

Because Python won't automatically put in spaces where you think they should go, you have to put them in yourself. The easiest way to represent a single space is by using a pair of quotation marks with one space between them, like this:

```
" "
```

If you forget to put the space between the quotation marks, like the following, you won't get a space in your string because there's no space between the quotation marks:

```
""
```

You can put multiple spaces between the quotation marks if you want multiple spaces in your output, but typically one space is enough. In the following example, I put a space between `first_name` and `last_name`. I also stuck a period and space after `middle_init`:

```
first_name = "Bart"
middle_init = "J"
last_name = "Simpson"
full_name = first_name + " " + middle_init + ". " + last_name
print(full_name)
```

The output of this code, which is the contents of that `full_name` variable, looks more like the kind of name you're used to seeing:

```
Bart J. Simpson
```

Of course, as an alternative to concatenating all the components and spaces together in a new string, you can simply display the name in the desired format using an f-string, as in the following code. The only difference is that you don't have a variable named `full_name` to work with in your code:

```
print(f"{first_name} {middle_init}. {last_name}")
```

Getting the Length of a String

To determine how many characters are in a string, you use the built-in `len()` function (short for *length*). The length includes spaces because spaces are characters, each one having a length of 1. An empty string — that is, a string with nothing in it, not even a space — has a length of 0.

Here are some examples. In the first line, you define a variable named `s1` and put an empty string in it (a pair of quotation marks with nothing in between). The `s2` variable gets a space (a pair of quotation marks with a space between). The `s3` variable gets a string with some letters and spaces. Then, three `print()` functions display the length of each string:

```
s1 = ""
s2 = " "
s3 = "A B C"
print(len(s1))
print(len(s2))
print(len(s3))
```

Following is the output from that code, when executed. The output makes perfect sense when you understand that `len()` measures the length of strings as the number of characters (including spaces) in the string:

```
0
1
5
```

Working with Common String Operators

Python offers several operators for working with sequences of data. One weird thing about strings in Python (and in most other programming languages) is that when you're counting characters, the first character counts as 0, not 1. This makes no sense to us humans, but computers count characters that way because it's the most efficient method. So even though the string in Figure 4-1 is five characters long, the last character in that string is the letter *E*, because the first character is number 0. Go figure.

```
ABCDE
01234
```

FIGURE 4-1: Character positions in a string start at 0, not 1.

Table 4-1 summarizes the Python operators for working with strings.

TABLE 4-1 **Python Sequence Operators That Work with Strings**

Operator	What It Does
`x in s`	Returns `True` if the string *x* exists somewhere in string *s*.
`x not in s`	Returns `True` if *x* is not contained in string *s*.
`s * n` or `n * s`	Repeats string *s* *n* times.
`s[i]`	The character at position *i* within string *s*.
`s[i:j]`	A slice from string *s* beginning with the character at position *i* up to (but excluding) the character at position *j*.
`s[i:j:k]`	A slice of *s* from *i* to *j* with step *k*, where *k* is the distance between any characters. For example, setting *k* to 2 displays every other character. Setting *k* to 3 returns every third character, and so forth.
`min(s)`	The smallest (lowest) character of string *s*.
`max(s)`	The largest (highest) character of string *s*.

In Python, selecting a single element from a sequence (such as a letter in a string) is called *indexing*. Selecting a range of elements is called *slicing*.

Figure 4-2 shows examples of using the string operators in Jupyter Notebook. When the output of a `print()` function doesn't look right, keep in mind two important facts about strings in Python:

- The first character is always number `0`.
- Every space counts as one character, so don't skip spaces when counting.

Playing around with string operators

```
s = "Abracadabra Hocus Pocus you're a turtle dove"
# Is there a lowercase letter t in string s?
print("t" in s)
# Is there an uppercase letter t in string s?
print("T" in s)
# Is there no uppercase T in string s?
print("T" not in s)
# Print 15 hyphens in a row
print("-" * 15)
# Print first character in string s
print(s[0])
# Print characters 33 - 39 from string s
print(s[33:40])
# Print every third character from string s starting at zero
print(s[0:44:3])
# Print the lowest character in string s (a space is lower than any letter)
print(min(s))
# Print the highest character in string s
print(max(s))
# Where is the first uppercase P in string s?
print(s.find("P"))
# Where is the first lowercase O in the latter half of string s?
print(s.index("o", 22,44))
# How many lowercase letter "a"s are in string s?
print(s.count("a"))
```

[35] Python

FIGURE 4-2: Playing around with string operators in Jupyter Notebook.

You may have noticed that `min(s)` returns a blank space, meaning that the blank space character is the lowest character in that string. But what exactly makes the space "lower" than the letter *A* or the letter *a*? The simple answer is the letter's *Unicode code point*. Every character you can type at your keyboard, and many additional characters, has a number assigned by the Unicode Consortium so computers all over the globe can display, store, and process text consistently.

Figure 4-3 shows a chart of Unicode code points for many common characters. Spaces and punctuation characters are lower than the uppercase letter *A* because they have smaller code points. Uppercase letters are lower than lowercase letters because they have smaller code points. Are you wondering what happened to the characters assigned to numbers 0–31? These numbers have characters too, but they are control characters and are nonprinting and invisible, such as when you hold down the Ctrl key and press another key.

Python offers two functions for working with Unicode code points. The `ord()` function takes a character as input and returns its Unicode code point. For example, `print(ord("A"))` returns `65`, because uppercase *A* has a code point of 65. The `chr()` function does the opposite: you give it a number, and it returns the character at that code point. For example, `print(chr(65))` displays `A`.

Unicode contains a vast range of characters beyond those found on a standard keyboard. For example, code point 00A3 is the British pound sterling symbol (£). To print a Unicode character in Python, precede the code point with `\u` and enclose it in quotation marks. For example, `print('\u00A3')` prints the £ symbol.

Number	Character	Number	Character	Number	Character
32	[space]	65	A	97	a
33	!	66	B	98	b
34	"	67	C	99	c
35	#	68	D	100	d
36	$	69	E	101	e
37	%	70	F	102	f
38	&	71	G	103	g
39	'	72	H	104	h
40	(	73	I	105	i
41	)	74	J	106	j
42	*	75	K	107	k
43	+	76	L	108	l
44	,	77	M	109	m
45	-	78	N	110	n
46	.	79	O	111	o
47	/	80	P	112	p
48	0	81	Q	113	q
49	1	82	R	114	r
50	2	83	S	115	s
51	3	84	T	116	t
52	4	85	U	117	u
53	5	86	V	118	v
54	6	87	W	119	w
55	7	88	X	120	x
56	8	89	Y	121	y
57	9	90	Z	122	z
58	:	91	[	123	{
59	;	92	\	124	|
60	<	93	]	125	}
61	=	94	^	126	~
62	>	95	_	127	□
63	?	96	`	128	€
64	@				

FIGURE 4-3: Unicode code points for common characters.

Using Methods to Manipulate Strings

In Python, every piece of text you use is stored in a *str object* (pronounced "string object"). All str objects can do certain things or have certain actions performed on them, such as changing their case or counting specific letters. These built-in actions are called *str methods.*

The general syntax of str object methods is as follows:

```
string.methodname(params)
```

where *string* is the string you're analyzing, *methodname* is the name of a method from Table 4-2, and *params* refers to any parameters that you need to pass to the method (if required). The leading `s` in the first column of Table 4-2 means "any string," be it a literal string enclosed in quotation marks or the name of a variable that contains a string.

You can play around with these methods in a Jupyter notebook, at the Python prompt, or in a `.py` file. Figure 4-4 shows some examples in a Jupyter notebook using four variables named `s1`, `s2`, `s3`, and `s4` as strings to experiment with. The result of running the code appears below the code.

TABLE 4-2 Key Built-In Methods for Python Strings

Method	What It Does
`s.capitalize()`	Returns a string with the first letter capitalized and the rest lowercase.
`s.count(x[, y[, z]])`	Returns the number of times string *x* appears in string `s`. Optionally, you can add *y* as a starting point and *z* as an ending point to search a portion of the string.
`s.endswith(x[,y[,z]])`	Returns True if string *s* ends with string *x*, or `False` otherwise. If *y* and *z* are provided, checks within the slice from position *y* to position *z*.
`s.find(x[, y[, z]])`	Returns a number indicating the first position at which string *x* can be found in string *s*. Optional *y* and *z* parameters allow you to limit the search to a portion of the string. Returns `-1` if none are found.
`s.index(x[, y[, z]])`	Similar to `s.find` but raises a "substring not found" error if string *x* can't be found in string *s*.
`s.isalpha()`	Returns `True` if *s* is at least one character long and contains only letters (A–Z or a–z) and printable Unicode characters.
`s.isdecimal()`	Returns `True` if *s* is at least one character long and contains only numeric characters (0–9).
`s.islower()`	Returns `True` if *s* contains letters and all those letters are lowercase.
`s.isnumeric()`	Returns `True` if *s* is at least one character long and contains only numeric characters (0–9).
`s.isprintable()`	Returns `True` if string *s* contains only printable characters. Spaces are considered printable, but newlines and tabs are not.
`s.istitle()`	Returns `True` if string *s* contains letters and the first letter of each word is uppercase followed by lowercase letters.
`s.isupper()`	Returns `True` if all letters in the string are uppercase.
`s.lower()`	Returns *s* with all letters converted to lowercase.
`s.lstrip()`	Returns *s* with any leading whitespace (spaces, tabs, newlines) removed.
`s.replace(x, y)`	Returns a copy of string *s* with string *x* replaced by string *y*.
`s.rfind(x[, y[, z]])`	Returns the position of the last occurrence of string *x* in string *s*, or `-1` if not found. If *y* and *z* are provided, searches within the slice from position *y* to position *z*.
`s.rindex(x[,y[,z]])`	Same as `s.rfind` but raises an error if the substring isn't found.
`s.rstrip()`	Returns string *s* with any trailing whitespace removed.

(continued)

TABLE 4-2 ***(continued)***

Method	What It Does
`s.startswith(x[,y[,z]])`	Returns `True` if string `s` begins with string `x`, or `False` otherwise. If *y* and *z* are provided, checks within the slice from position *y* to position *z*.
`s.strip()`	Returns string *s* with leading and trailing whitespace removed.
`s.swapcase()`	Returns string *s* with uppercase letters converted to lowercase and lowercase letters converted to uppercase.
`s.title()`	Returns string *s* with the first letter of every word capitalized and all other letters lowercase.
`s.upper()`	Returns string *s* with all letters converted to uppercase.

```
s1 = "There is no such word as schmeedledorp"
s2 = "    a b c    "
s3 = "ABC"
s4 = "The cat in the hat sat on the mat."
# Capitalize first letter, the rest lowercase
print(s3.capitalize())
# Count the number of spaces in s1
print(s1.count(" "))
# Find the dot in S4
print(s4.find("."))
# Is s2 all lowercase letters?
print(s2.islower())
# Convert s3 to all lowercase letters
print(s3.lower())
# Strip leading characters from s2
print(s2.lstrip())
# Strip leading and trailing characters from s2
print(s2.strip())
# Swap the case of letters in s1
print(s1.swapcase())
# Show s1 in title case (initial letter of each word capitalized)
print(s1.title())
# Show s1 in uppercase letters
print(s1.upper())
```

[39] Python

```
Abc
6
33
True
abc
a b c
a b c
tHERE IS NO SUCH WORD AS SCHMEEDLEDORP
There Is No Such Word As Schmeedledorp
THERE IS NO SUCH WORD AS SCHMEEDLEDORP
```

FIGURE 4-4: Playing around with Python string functions.

REMEMBER

Don't bother trying to memorize or even make sense of every string method. Remember, you can always ask generative AI to list all the string operators and functions for you. Or search the web for *python string methods* to find out what's available.

IN THIS CHAPTER

» Handling dates

» Handling times

» Combining dates and times

» Finding time differences

» Handling time zones

Chapter 5
Managing Dates and Times

Time is an illusion.

— ALBERT EINSTEIN

In the world of computers, we often use dates and times for scheduling or for calculating when something is due or how many days it's past due. We sometimes use timestamps to record exactly when a user did something or when an event occurred. Surprisingly, Python does not have built-in data types for dates and times as it does for strings and numbers. Instead of built-in data types, Python provides the `datetime` module, which includes classes for working with dates and times.

In this chapter, you get a practical tour of Python's `datetime` module: how to create and use `date`, `time`, and `datetime` values, how to format them for display, and how to do date math with `timedelta` so you can calculate things like deadlines and time differences. You also learn the basics of time zones and what it means for a datetime to be *naïve* versus *aware.*

Checking Out the datetime Module

The `datetime` module provides an easy way to work with dates and times in Python. It provides three ways of storing information about dates, times, and time zones:

- **`datetime.date`:** A date consisting of month, day, and year (but no time information).
- **`datetime.time`:** A time consisting of hour, minute, second, microsecond, and optionally time zone information if needed (but no date).
- **`datetime.datetime`:** A single item of data consisting of date, time, and, optionally, time zone information.

As with any module, you must import the `datetime` module before you can use it. You do that using `import datetime`. And as with any import, you can add an alias (nickname) that's easier to type, such as `import datetime as dt`.

I talk about each of these data types separately in the sections that follow.

Working with Dates

The `datetime.date` data type is ideal for working with dates when time isn't an issue. You can create a date object in two ways. You can get today's date from the computer's internal clock by using the `today()` method. Or you can specify a year, month, and day (in that order) inside parentheses.

REMEMBER

When specifying the month or day, don't use a leading zero. Python doesn't allow leading zeros in integer literals, so 2030,04,01 causes an error before `datetime.date()` receives the values. Write April 1, 2030 as `2030, 4, 1`.

After importing the `datetime` module, you can use `date.today()` to get the current date from the computer's internal clock. Or use `date(`*`year, month, day`*`)` syntax to create a date object for some other date. The following code shows both methods:

```
# Import the datetime module, nickname dt
import datetime as dt
# Store today's date in a variable named today.
today = dt.date.today()
# Store some other date in a variable called last_of_twenties
last_of_twenties = dt.date(2029, 12, 31)
print(last_of_twenties)
```

YOUR COMPUTER DATE AND TIME

Your computer gets its internal date and time from NTP (Network Time Protocol), a set of rules for communicating between computers over the internet and for synchronizing their clocks to the Coordinated Universal Time (UTC). The `datetime` information is tailored to your time zone and takes into account the daylight saving time of your location (if applicable).

Try it by typing the code in a Jupyter notebook, at the Python prompt, or in a `.py` file. Use the `print()` function to see what's in each variable, as shown in Figure 5-1. Your `today` variable won't be the same as in the figure; it will be the date you try this.

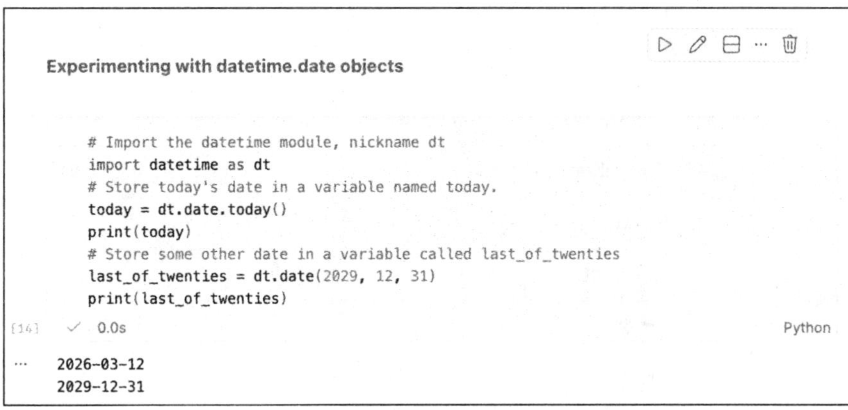

FIGURE 5-1: Experiments with `datetime.date` objects in a Jupyter notebook.

You can isolate any part of a date object by using `.month`, `.day`, or `.year`. For example, in the same Jupyter cell or Python prompt, execute this code:

```
print(last_of_twenties.month)
print(last_of_twenties.day)
print(last_of_twenties.year)
```

Each of the three components of that date appears on a separate line:

```
12
31
2029
```

As you saw in Figure 5-1, the default date display is *yyyy-mm-dd*, but you can format dates and times however you want. Use f-strings, which I discuss in Chapter 3 of this minibook, along with the directives shown in Table 5-1, which includes the format for dates as well as for times, as I discuss later in this chapter. For directives that show local dates and times, the format depends on your location. For example, using %x to display December 18, 2030 would show 12/18/30 in the U.S., but 18/12/2030 in countries where it's more common to show the day first, rather than the month.

TABLE 5-1 **Formatting Strings for Dates and Times**

Directive	Description	Example
%a	Weekday, abbreviated	Sun
%A	Weekday, full	Sunday
%w	Weekday number 0-6, where 0 is Sunday	0
%d	Number day of the month 01–31	31
%b	Month name abbreviated	Jan
%B	Month name full	January
%m	Month number 01–12	01
%y	Year without century	29
%Y	Year with century	2029
%H	Hour 00–23	23
%I	Hour 00–12	11
%p	AM/PM	PM
%M	Minute 00–59	01
%S	Second 00–59	01
%f	Microsecond 000000-999999	495846
%z	UTC offset	-0500
%Z	Time zone	EST
%j	Day number of year 001–366	300
%U	Week number of year, Sunday as the first day of week, 00–53	50
%W	Week number of year, Monday as the first day of week, 00–53	50

Directive	Description	Example
%c	Local version of date and time	Mon Dec 31 23:59:59 2029
%x	Local version of date	12/31/29
%X	Local version of time	23:59:59
%%	A % character	%

TECHNICAL STUFF

Some tutorials tell you to format dates and times by using `strftime` rather than f-strings, and that's a valid method. I stick with the newer f-strings here because I find them more readable than calling `strftime` directly.

When using format strings, make sure you put spaces, slashes, and anything else you want between directives. For example, this line:

```
print(f"{last_of_twenties:%A, %B %d, %Y}")
```

displays the following when executed:

```
Monday, December 31, 2029
```

To show the date in the *mm/dd/yyyy* format, use `%m/%d/%Y`, like this:

```
todays_date = f"{today:%m/%d/%Y}"
```

The output will be the current date for you when you try it, with a format like the following:

```
03/12/2029
```

Here are a few more examples you can try with different dates:

- %a, %b %d %Y outputs Fri, Jun 01 2029
- %x outputs 06/01/29
- %m-%d-%y outputs 06-01-29
- This %A %B %d outputs This Friday June 01
- %A %B %d is day number %j of %Y outputs Friday June 01 is day number 152 of 2029

Working with Times

If you want to work strictly with time data, use the `datetime.time` class. The basic syntax for defining a time object using the `time` class is

```
variable = datetime.time([ hour [, minute [, second [, microsecond ]]]])
```

Note how all the arguments are optional. For example, you can use no arguments:

```
midnight = dt.time()
print(midnight)
```

This code stores the time as `00:00:00`, which is midnight. To verify that it's really a time, entering `print(type(midnight))` displays the following:

```
<class 'datetime.time'>
```

This tells you that midnight, or 00:00:00, is a `time` object from the `datetime` class.

The fourth optional value you can pass to `time()` is `microseconds` (millionths of a second). For example, the following code puts a time that's a millionth of a second before midnight in the `almost_midnight` variable and then displays that time onscreen with a `print()` function:

```
almost_midnight = dt.time(23, 59, 59, 999999)
print(almost_midnight)
23:59:59.999999
```

You can use format strings with the time directives in Table 5-1 to format the time. Here are some examples using `23:59:59:999999` as the sample time:

- %I:%M %p outputs 11:59 PM
- %H:%M:%S and %f microseconds outputs 23:59:59 and 999999 microseconds
- %X outputs `23:59:59`

Working with Dates and Times

Sometimes you want to work only with dates, and sometimes you want to work only with times. But often you want to pinpoint a moment in time using both the date and the time. For that, use the `datetime` class of the `datetime` module.

This class supports a `now()` method that can grab the current date and time from the computer clock, as follows:

```
import datetime as dt
right_now = dt.datetime.now()
print(right_now)
```

What you see on the screen from the `print()` function depends on when you execute the code. On March 12, 2026 at 10:39 AM, the `datetime` value is

```
2026-03-12 10:39:32.437367
```

with 32.437367 seconds tacked on.

You can define a `datetime` also by using any of the following parameters. Note that `year`, `month`, and `day` are required. The rest are optional and set to 0 if you omit them:

```
datetime(year, month, day, [hour [, minute [, second [, microsecond ]]]])
```

Here is an example using 11:59 PM on December 31 2029:

```
import datetime as dt
new_years_eve = dt.datetime(2029, 12, 31, 23, 59)
print(new_years_eve)
```

Here is the output of that `print()` statement with no formatting:

```
2029-12-31 23:59:00
```

Following are examples of formatting the datetime using directives shown previously in Table 5-1:

- %A, %B %d at %I:%M%p outputs Monday, December 31 at 11:59PM
- %m/%d/%y at %H:%M outputs 12/31/29 at 23:59
- %I:%M %p on %b %d outputs 11:59 PM on Dec 31
- %x outputs 12/31/29
- %c outputs Mon Dec 31 23:59:00 2029
- %m/%d/%y at %I:%M %p outputs 12/31/29 at 11:59 PM
- %I:%M %p on %m/%d/%y outputs 11:59 PM on 12/31/29

Calculating Timespans

Sometimes just knowing the date or time isn't enough. You need to know the duration, or *timespan*, as it's typically called in the computer world. In other words, not the date, not the o'clock, but the "how long" in terms of years, months, weeks, days, hours, minutes, or whatever. For timespans, the Python `datetime` module includes the `datetime.timedelta` class.

A `timedelta` object is created automatically when you subtract a date, time, or datetime from another one to determine the duration between them. For example, suppose you create a couple of variables to store dates, one for New Year's Day and another for Memorial Day. Then you create a third variable named `days_between` and put in it the difference you get by subtracting the earlier date from the later date, as follows:

```
import datetime as dt
new_years_day = dt.date(2030, 1, 1)
memorial_day = dt.date(2030, 5, 27)
days_between = memorial_day - new_years_day
print(days_between)
print(type(days_between))
```

So what exactly is `days_between` in terms of a data type? If you print its value, you get `146 days, 0:00:00`. In other words, there are 146 days between those dates. The `0:00:00` is time, but because I didn't specify a time of day for either date, the time digits are all set to `0`. If you use the Python `type()` function to determine the data type of `days_between`, you see that it's a `timedelta` object from the `datetime` class, as follows:

```
146 days, 0:00:00
<class 'datetime.timedelta'>
```

The `timedelta` calculation happens automatically when you subtract one date from another to get the time between. You can also define any `timedelta` (duration) using this syntax:

```
datetime.timedelta(days,seconds,microseconds,milliseconds,minutes,hours,weeks)
```

If you provide an argument name, you must include a number after the equal sign (=). If you omit an argument, its value is set to `0`.

To get an understanding of how the time difference is calculated, try the following code. After importing the `datetime` module, create a date using `.date()`. Then create a `timedelta` object using `.timedelta`. If you add a `date` and a `timedelta`, you get a new date — in this case, a date that's 146 days after 1/1/2030:

```
import datetime as dt
new_years_day = dt.date(2030, 1, 1)
duration = dt.timedelta(days=146)
print(new_years_day + duration)
2030-05-27
```

Of course, you can subtract, too. For example, if you start with a date of 5/27/2030 and subtract 146 days, you get 1/1/2030, as shown here:

```
import datetime as dt
memorial_day = dt.date(2030, 5, 27)
duration = dt.timedelta(days=146)
print(memorial_day - duration)
2030-01-01
```

Calculating the timespan (time difference) works with datetimes, too. If you're looking for a duration that's less than a day, just give both datetimes the same date. For example, consider the following code and the results of the subtraction:

```
import datetime as dt
start_time = dt.datetime(2030, 3, 31, 8, 0, 0)
finish_time = dt.datetime(2030, 3, 31, 14, 34, 45)
time_between = finish_time - start_time
print(time_between)
print(type(time_between))
6:34:45
<class 'datetime.timedelta'>
```

I know that 6:34:45 is a time duration of 6 hours, 34 minutes, and 45 seconds for two reasons. One, it's the result of subtracting one moment of time from another. Two, printing the `type()` of that data type tells me it's a `timedelta` object (a duration), not an o'clock time.

Here is another example using datetimes with different dates: One is the current datetime, and the other is a date of birth with the time down to the minute (March 31, 1995 at 8:26 AM). To calculate age, subtract the birthdate from the current time, `now`:

```
import datetime as dt
now = dt.datetime.now()
birthdatetime = dt.datetime(1995, 3, 31, 8, 26)
```

```
age = now - birthdatetime
print(age)
print(type(age))
```

The result will vary, depending on when you run the code. But the format will be as follows:

```
11403 days, 21:47:04.355252
<class 'datetime.timedelta'>
```

The tiny seconds value stems from the fact that `datetime.now` grabs the date and time from the computer's clock down to the microsecond.

You don't always need microseconds or even seconds in your `timedelta` object. For example, say you're trying to determine someone's age. You could start by creating two dates, one named `today` for today's date and another named `birthdate` that contains the birthdate. The following example uses a birthdate of December 31, 2000:

```
import datetime as dt
today = dt.date.today()
birthdate = dt.date(2000, 12, 31)
delta_age = (today - birthdate)
print(delta_age)
```

In this example, I use `today=dt.date.today()` to set the `today` variable to the current date. The `dt.date.today()` method is similar to `datetime.now`, which I used previously, but it contains only today's date, not the time. The last two lines of code create a variable named `delta_age` and print what's in the variable. If you run this code, you'll see something like the following output (but it won't be exactly the same because your `today` date will be whatever today's date is when you run the app):

```
9301 days, 0:00:00
```

Say what you really want is the age in years. You can convert `timedelta` to a number of days by tacking `.days` onto `timedelta` and putting that in another variable called `days_old`. Printing `days_old` and its type shows you that `days_old` is an `int`, a regular old integer that you can use in math calculations.

For example, in the following code, the `days_old` variable receives the value `delta_age.days`, which is `delta_age` from the preceding line converted to a number of days:

```
delta_age = (today - birthdate)
days_old = delta_age.days
print(days_old, type(days_old))
9301 <class 'int'>
```

To get the number of years, divide the number of days by 365. If you want just the number of years as an integer, use the floor division operator (//) rather than regular division (/). (*Floor division* removes the decimal portion from the quotient, so you get a whole number.) You can put the result of that calculation in another variable if you like. For example, in the following code, the `years_old` variable contains a value calculated by dividing `days_old` by 365:

```
years_old = days_old // 365
print(years_old)
```

If you want the number of months, too, you can ballpark that by taking the remainder of dividing the days by 365 to get the number of days left. Then floor divide that value by 30 (because on average, each month has about 30 days) to get a good approximation of the number of months. Use % rather than / for division to get just the remainder after the division. Figure 5-2 shows the sequence of events in a Jupyter notebook, with comments to explain what's going on.

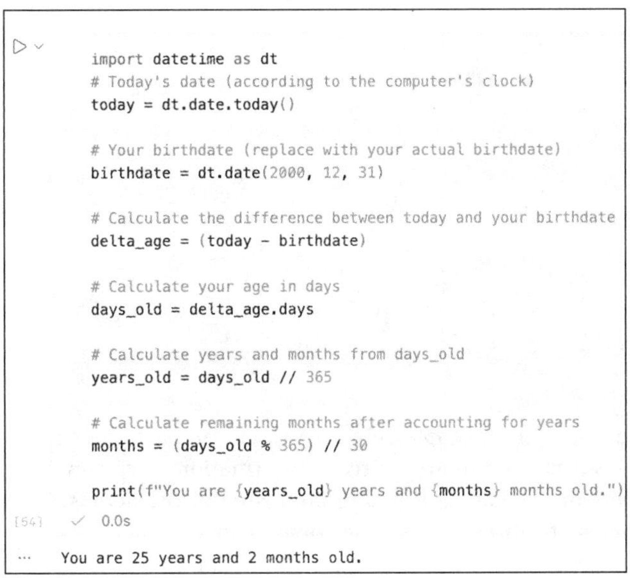

FIGURE 5-2: Calculating age in years and months from a `timedelta` object.

> **TIP** Generative AI can write complicated date-and-time code for you, too. For example, you can ask Copilot in VS Code, ChatGPT, or another service to *write python code to calculate the time between two dates* or *write python code to display the current date and time in USA format.*

Working with Time Zones

As you know, when it's noon in your neighborhood, it's not noon everywhere. Figure 5-3 shows a map of all the time zones. If you want a closer look, simply search the web for *time zone map.* The time and even the day change depending on your location. To keep time consistent across locations, computers often use Coordinated Universal Time (UTC), a global time standard. You may also hear UTC called Zulu time, especially in military and aviation contexts. Greenwich Mean Time (GMT) is a time zone based on the prime meridian at 0 degrees longitude, near the center of the time zone map in Figure 5-3.

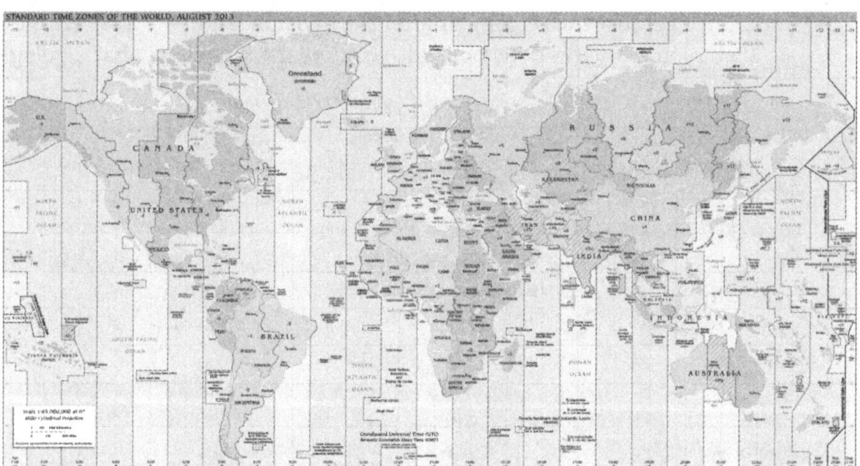

FIGURE 5-3: Time zones.

These days, most people rely on the tz database (sometimes called the Olson Database) as the primary source of information about time zones. Search for *Olson database* or *tz database* if you're interested in the details. Table 5-2 shows some examples of United States time zones. The left column is the official name from the database. The second column shows the more familiar name. The last two columns show the offset from UTC for standard time and daylight saving time.

TABLE 5-2 Sample Time Zones from the Olson Database

Time Zone	Common Name	UTC Offset	UTC DST Offset
Etc/UTC	UTC	+00:00	+00:00
Etc/UTC	Universal	+00:00	+00:00
America/Anchorage	US/Alaska	–09:00	–08:00
America/Adak	US/Aleutian	–10:00	–09:00
America/Phoenix	US/Arizona	–07:00	–07:00
America/Chicago	US/Central	–06:00	–05:00
America/New_York	US/Eastern	–05:00	–04:00
America/Indiana/Indianapolis	US/East-Indiana	–05:00	–04:00
Pacific/Honolulu	US/Hawaii	–10:00	–10:00
America/Indiana/Knox	US/Indiana-Starke	–06:00	–05:00
America/Detroit	US/Michigan	–05:00	–04:00
America/Denver	US/Mountain	–07:00	–06:00
America/Los_Angeles	US/Pacific	–08:00	–07:00
Pacific/Pago_Pago	US/Samoa	–11:00	–11:00

So why am I telling you all this? Because Python lets you work with two different types of datetimes:

- **Naïve datetime:** Any datetime that does not include information that relates it to a specific time zone
- **Aware datetime:** A datetime that includes time zone information

The `timedelta` objects and dates that you define with `.date()` are always naïve. Any time or datetime you create as `time()` or `datetime()` objects will also be naïve, by default. But with those two you have the option of including time zone information, which is useful if, for example, you're showing event dates to an audience in multiple time zones.

When you get the time from your computer's system clock, it's for your time zone, but you don't have an indication of what that time zone *is*. However, you can tell the difference between your local time and UTC time by comparing the local time to the UTC time and then subtracting the difference. The function for getting UTC time versions of Python prior to 3.12 is `utcnow()`. In current Python versions, `datetime.datetime.utcnow()` is deprecated because it returns a *naïve* datetime (no time zone). Figure 5-4 shows both ways of calculating the difference between your time zone and UTC.

```
here_now = dt.datetime.now()

# --- Legacy approach (naïve datetimes; utcnow() is deprecated
import datetime as dt
utc_now = dt.datetime.utcnow() # deprecated in Python 3.12+
time_difference = utc_now - here_now
print(f"My time : {here_now:%I:%M:%S %p}")
print(f"UTC time : {utc_now:%I:%M:%S %p}")
print(f"Time difference: {time_difference}")

# --- Python 3.12+ approach (timezone-aware datetimes) ---
local_now = dt.datetime.now().astimezone()
utc_now = dt.datetime.now(dt.UTC)
time_difference = utc_now - local_now
print(f"My time : {local_now:%I:%M:%S %p %Z} ({local_now:%z})")
print(f"UTC time : {utc_now:%I:%M:%S %p %Z} ({utc_now:%z})")
print(f"Time difference: {time_difference}")
```

```
✓ 0.0s
My time : 12:04:06 PM
UTC time : 07:04:06 PM
Time difference: 7:00:00.000189
My time : 12:04:06 PM PDT (-0700)
UTC time : 07:04:06 PM UTC (+0000)
Time difference: 0:00:00.000030
```

FIGURE 5-4: Determining the difference between your time and UTC time.

When I ran that code, the current time was 12:04PM and the UTC time was 7:04PM. The difference was 7:00:00, which means seven hours (no minutes or seconds). My time is earlier, so my time zone is UTC – 7.

TECHNICAL STUFF

I'm in Pacific Standard Time (PST), which is always UTC-8. However, during daylight saving time in the United States (the second Sunday in March to the first Sunday in November), the clocks in my state are set to Pacific Daylight Time (PDT), which is UTC-7. Things would be much easier if we'd just do away with daylight saving time!

Note that the deprecated `utcnow()` function still works in current versions of Python (as of this writing), but it is displayed with a line through it in VS Code, and a warning message appears when you run code containing it.

REMEMBER

Functions that have been deprecated aren't recommended for use in new code, because the function will be removed in a future version of Python. Deprecation is a way of saying: "We have a better way to do this now, but we're giving you some time to learn that new way and to update your old code."

If you want to work directly with time zone names, you'll need to import `gettz` (short for *get time zone*) from the `tz` class of the `dateutil` package. So in your code, right after the line where you `import datetime`, use `from dateutil.tz import gettz` like this:

```
# import datetime and dateutil tz
import datetime as dt
from dateutil.tz import gettz
```

Afterward, you can use `gettz('` *name* `')` to get time zone information for any time zone. Replace *name* with the name of the time zone from the Olson database, for example, `America/New_York` for US Eastern time, or `Etc/UTC` for UTC time.

In Figure 5-5, I am getting the current date and time by using `datetime.now()` with five different time zones — UTC and four U.S. time zones.

```
# import datetime as dt
import datetime as dt
# import timezone helpers from dateutil
from dateutil.tz import gettz

#UTC time right now
utc=dt.datetime.now(gettz('Etc/UTC'))
print(f"{utc:%A %D %I:%M %p %Z}")

#USA Eastern time
eastern=dt.datetime.now(gettz('US/Eastern'))
print(f"{eastern:%A %D %I:%M %p %Z}")

#USA Central time
central=dt.datetime.now(gettz('US/Central'))
print(f"{central:%A %D %I:%M %p %Z}")

#USA Mountain time
mountain=dt.datetime.now(gettz('US/Mountain'))
print(f"{mountain:%A %D %I:%M %p %Z}")

#USA Pacific time
pacific=dt.datetime.now(gettz('US/Pacific'))
print(f"{pacific:%A %D %I:%M %p %Z}")
[59]  ✓ 0.0s
```

FIGURE 5-5: The current date and time for five time zones.

TECHNICAL STUFF

If you research Python time zones online, you'll probably find that many people recommend using the `arrow` module rather than the `dateutil` module. I don't get into all that here because `arrow` isn't part of your initial Python installation and this book is hefty enough. (If I tried to cover everything, you'd need a wheelbarrow to carry the book around.)

IN THIS CHAPTER

» Storing data in your Python code

» Controlling Python with conditionals and loops

» Finding out first-hand why beginners love Python

Chapter 6

Storing Data and Controlling Your Code

There should be one — and preferably only one — obvious way to do it.

—TIM PETERS

Coders — from grizzled veterans to the greenest rookies — love Python. They take to it because Python code is clean, clear, and easy to write and read (at least compared to other programming languages). But coders stay with Python because the language has an inherent elegance, an undeniable grace that sets it apart from other languages. Python code sparks joy.

In this chapter, you get your first glimpse at just how delightfully different Python is from other languages by looking at three common coding structures that Python implements uniquely: lists, conditionals, and loops.

Storing Stuff in Lists

A variable usually stores a single item of data, such as a grade, a day of the week, or the name of a Kardashian. But it's extremely common for your code to work with two or more (usually many more) items of related data, such as the grades for an entire class, every day of the week, or the names of everyone in a particular family.

Sure, you *could* create a separate variable for each item, but Python offers a faster, simpler, *and* more powerful way: the list. A *list* is a collection of items that resides in a single container. That description might sound underwhelming at the moment, but as I hope to show in the sections that follow, lists are a big deal in the Python world.

Making a list

You construct a list by starting with a pair of square brackets `[` and `]`, and then filling those brackets with the values you want to store, separated by commas. A list can hold just about anything: numbers, strings, Booleans — even other lists, as shown in the following example:

```
shopping_list = ["milk", "eggs", "bread", "Snickerdoodles"]
lucky_numbers = [7, 11, 548834]
mixed_bag = ["hello", 3.14, True, 42]
```

You can store as many items as you want and, as demonstrated in the third example, the items don't need to be the same data type (though using a single data type per list usually makes your coding life easier).

If you ever need to know how many items are in a list (that actually comes up a lot), use the `len()` function:

```
len( list )
```

Where *`list`* is the name of the list. To try out `len()`, add the following line to the preceding example:

```
print(len(shopping_list))
```

When you run this command after creating the shopping_list list, you'll see `4` printed to the terminal, which is the number of items in `shopping_list`.

Making a list from a range of numbers

When you need a list that's a collection of numbers, the `range()` function is a great tool:

```
range( stop )
range( start , stop [, step ])
```

start is the first number you want in the range. If you specify only the *stop* argument, Python uses `0` as the *start* value. *stop* is the last number you want in the range, minus one. For example, if you set *stop* to `10`, the last number in the range will be `9`. *step* is the difference between each number in the range. The default value is `1`.

`range()` gets you a range data type, so to turn that object into a proper list, use the `range()` function as an argument for the `list()` conversion function. Here are some examples you can try out in Python's interactive mode:

```
>>> list(range(10))
[0, 1, 2, 3, 4, 5, 6, 7, 8, 9]
>>> list(range(1, 6))
[1, 2, 3, 4, 5]
>>> list(range(2, 20, 2))
[2, 4, 6, 8, 10, 12, 14, 16, 18]
```

As you learn in Book 2, Chapter 1, you can get to Python's interactive mode by opening a terminal and entering **python** (or **python3** or **py** in some cases). The `>>>` characters at the beginning of each of the previous code lines aren't things you type; they indicate that you should run these commands in the Python interactive mode, at the `>>>` prompt.

You don't need to run these examples at the Python prompt, however. If you like, you could save them in a `.py` file or in a Jupyter notebook and run them that way.

To reverse the range, use the `reversed()` function:

```
>>> list(reversed(range(10)))
[9, 8, 7, 6, 5, 4, 3, 2, 1, 0]
```

Getting an item from a list

List items are numbered according to their position in the list, and that number is called the *index*. The first item in the list has index `0`, the second item has index `1`, and so on.

So, you can grab something from a list by specifying the item's index number in square brackets after the list name. Here are some examples:

```
>>> print(shopping_list[0])
milk
>>> print(shopping_list[2])
bread
```

To get multiple items, you can *slice* the list with `list[start:end]`, where `list` is the name of the list, `start` is the index of the first item you want, and *end* is the index of the item that comes after the last item you want. Python returns the items as a list:

```
>>> print(shopping_list[1:3])
['eggs', 'bread']
```

If you ask for an index that doesn't exist, Python throws a little tantrum:

```
>>> print(shopping_list[5])
IndexError: list index out of range
```

Changing an item in a list

Once you create a list, its items aren't set in stone. Python geeks like to say that lists are *mutable*, which is an eye-roll-inducing way of saying they're changeable. To change an item in a list, you set that item to the new value, like so:

```
>>> shopping_list[1] = "chocolate"
>>> print(shopping_list)
['milk', 'chocolate', 'bread', 'Snickerdoodles']
```

Adding and removing list items

Another way that lists are changeable is that you're free to add new items to the list and remove existing items from the list. Python offers a couple of ways to mess with the contents of a list in these ways, as I describe in the next two sections.

Adding list items

In Python, you can use the `append()` method to add an item to the end of the list or the `insert()` method to shoehorn an item into a list at a specific index:

```
list .append( item )
list .insert( index , item )
```

list is the list object in which you want to add the item. *item* is the item you want to add. *index* is the position within *list* where you want *item* to appear when using the `insert()` method.

Here are some examples:

```
>>> shopping_list = ["milk", "eggs", "bread", "Snickerdoodles"]

>>> shopping_list.append("butter")
>>> print(shopping_list)
['milk', 'eggs', 'bread', 'Snickerdoodles', 'butter']

>>> shopping_list.insert(1, "coffee")
>>> print(shopping_list)
['milk', 'coffee', 'eggs', 'bread', 'Snickerdoodles', 'butter']
```


Removing list items

If you need to prune a list, you can use the `pop()` method to either remove the item that's at the end of the list or remove an item at a specified index, or you can use the `remove()` method to remove the first item that matches a value that you specify:

```
list .pop([ index ])
list .remove( item )
```

list is the list object from which you want to remove the item. *index* is the position within *list* of the item you want to expunge. If you leave out *index*, `pop()` removes the last item in the list. *item* is the item you want to remove.

REMEMBER

Note that `pop()` not only removes an item from the list but also returns that item, which you could then store in a variable for later use.

Here are some examples:

```
>>> shopping_list = ["milk", "eggs", "bread", "Snickerdoodles"]

>>> last_item = shopping_list.pop()
>>> print(last_item)
Snickerdoodles
```

```
>>> print(shopping_list)
['milk', 'eggs', 'bread']

>>> first_item = shopping_list.pop(0)
>>> print(first_item)
milk

>>> print(shopping_list)
['eggs', 'bread']

>>> shopping_list.remove("eggs")
>>> print(shopping_list)
['bread']
```

Searching in a list

Want to know if something's in a list? Use the `in` keyword:

```
item in list
```

`item` is the item you're looking for, and *`list`* is the list object in which you're looking.

If the item does appear somewhere in the list, the `in` expression returns `True`; otherwise, you get `False`. Here's an example:

```
>>> shopping_list = ["milk", "eggs", "bread", "Snickerdoodles"]

>>> print("bread" in shopping_list)
True

>>> print("rutabaga" in shopping_list)
False
```

More Ways to Store Stuff: Tuples and Dictionaries

When you're just getting started, there are two other Python data structures that you probably won't use all that often but are worth knowing in case you come across them in someone else's code. As you get more experienced with Python, you'll come to rely on these useful data structures (they're also Python data types): the tuple and the dictionary.

Storing unchanging data in a tuple

A *tuple* is a data structure that enables you to store multiple items in a single variable. Yes, I know, that sounds just like a list. However, there's one big difference: Tuples can't be changed (yep, the nerds insist on describing them as *immutable*). Once you forge a tuple, it's locked in. No changing items, no adding items, and no removing them. That sounds restrictive, but a tuple is a useful thing to have around when you're working with data that must never change.

For example, if you're making a game in which you have to track player positions on a 2D plane using (x, y) coordinates (where x is the horizontal position and y is the vertical position), the following conditions are true:

- A given position only has two values: x and y.
- You don't want either x or y to be changed accidentally.
- You don't want a third value added to the position.
- You do want the capability to change both values at once (for example, when a player's position changes).

You can meet all these conditions by storing a player's current position in a tuple:

```
player_position = (125, 280)
```

Tuple values can be any valid Python data type, including strings, numbers, Booleans, lists, dictionaries (discussed in the next section), functions (refer to Chapter 7 of this minibook), and even other tuples. And, yes, you're free to mix and match data types within a single tuple.

As with lists, tuple values are indexed, with the first value at index `0`, the second at index `1`, and so on. You use the index in square brackets to extract that value from a tuple. Here's an example:

```
player_position = (125, 280)
x = player_position[0]
y = player_position[1]
print(f"The player is at position ({x}, {y}).")
```

TIP

Python supports tuple *unpacking*, where you assign variables to each item in the tuple. That is, rather than this:

```
x = player_position[0]
y = player_position[1]
```

You can do this:

```
x, y = player_position
```

You can't change a single element in a tuple, nor can you add elements to or delete elements from a tuple. What you *can* do is replace the entire tuple. So, for example, if the player's position changes, you can update the entire tuple:

```
player_position = (160, 210)
```

What else can you do with a tuple? You can find out how many items it contains using `len()`:

```
>>> print(len(player_position))
2
```

Also, you can *iterate* (a fancy-schmancy programming term that means *loop*) through a tuple using a `for` loop, as in this example:

```
quiz_answers = (
    "Rumpelstiltskin",
    "bullet bra",
    "antidisestablishmentarianism",
    "Senegalese",
    42)
for answer in quiz_answers:
    print(answer)
```

Looking up data in a dictionary

A *dictionary* is a data structure that enables you to store multiple items in a single variable. Yes, I know, that sounds just like a list or a tuple. However, in a dictionary, each item is actually a pair: the value you want to store and a label that describes the value. That label is called a *key*, so these pairs are known as *key-value pairs*.

That label is important because it can make your code more readable. For example, it's not at all clear what the following refers to:

```
person[0]
```

But even without looking at the rest of the code, it's pretty obvious what the following means:

```
person["age"]
```

Here are the general steps to follow to build a dictionary:

1. **Type an opening curly brace ({).**
2. **Type a key, which can be a string surrounded by quotation marks, a number, or a tuple.**

   You'll almost always use a string for the key. Also note that within a dictionary, the keys must be unique.
3. **Type a colon (:), a space, and then type the value.**

   The value can be any valid Python data type, including a string, a number, a Boolean, a list, a tuple, or even a dictionary.
4. **Type a comma, then press Enter or Return.**
5. **Repeat Steps 2 through 4 for each item you want to store in the dictionary.**
6. **Type a closing curly brace (}).**

Here's an example to make things more concrete:

```
person = {
    "name": "Alice",
    "age": 30,
    "is_student": False
}
```

The keys are `"name"`, `"age"`, and `"is_student"`, and the values are `"Alice"`, `30`, and `False`.

To get a value from a dictionary, use the key in square brackets:

```
>>> print(person["age"])
30
```

Dictionary values are changeable, and you update a value by setting its key to the new value:

```
>>> person["age"] = 31
```

You can also add a new key/value pair on-the-fly:

```
>>> person["email"] = "alice@somewhere.com"
```

You can use `del` to remove a key:

```
>>> del person["is_student"]
```

To iterate through a dictionary, you have a couple of choices. First, you can loop through just the keys:

```
for key in person:
    print(key)
```

Or you can loop through both the keys and the values:

```
for key, value in person.items():
    print(key, "=", value)
```

YET ANOTHER DATA STRUCTURE: SETS

One of the reasons pros such as data analysts and data scientists love Python is that it offers a seemingly endless menu of ways to store and mess around with data. So far in this chapter I've covered lists, tuples, and dictionaries. But you may hear Pythonistas talking about the "big four" data structures that every coder should know. What's missing? An occasionally handy data structure called the *set*, which stores only unique values and doesn't impose any order on its items.

You create a set by surrounding a comma-separated list of items (which can be numbers, strings, Booleans, or tuples) with braces ({ and }):

```
fave_fruits = {"peach", "apple", "orange", "cherry"}
```

You can then check if a value is in the set:

```
if "apple" in fave_fruits:
    print("Apple is a favorite fruit!")
```

But perhaps the handiest use of sets is to extract just the unique values from a collection by running `set(collection)`, where *collection* is a list, string, range, or tuple. Here's an example:

```
str = "it was the best of times it was the worst of times"

# Extract the individual words into a list
words = str.split()

# Use set() to get just the unique words
unique_words = set(words)

print(unique_words)
```

Here's the output:

```
{'best', 'was', 'the', 'worst', 'it', 'of', 'times'}
```


Conditionals in Python

The way you make your code do something smart is to create a conditional statement, where your code executes one or more statements only if a certain condition is met. In Python, you use three keywords to set up your conditionals: `if`, `else`, and `elif`.

The basic if statement

The simplest Python conditional involves using `if` all by itself:

```
if expression :
    statement1 ;
    statement2 ;
    ...
```

Here, *expression* is a comparison or logical expression that returns `True` or `False`, or a Boolean value. Note, too, that Python requires a colon (`:`) immediately after *expression*. Next, *statement1*, *statement2*, and so on represent the Python statement or statements the interpreter will run if *expression* returns `True`. If *expression* returns `False`, Python skips over the statements.

Here's an example:

```
score = int(input("What was your score? "))
if score >= 80:
    print(f"Wow, your score was {score}.")
    print("Nice job!")
```

If the condition (`score >= 80`) returns `True`, Python runs the two indented `print()` statements; otherwise, Python skips them.

REMEMBER

How does Python know which statements to run if the condition returns `True`? Those statements form the *`if` block*, and that block is defined as every statement after the colon (`:`) that is indented by the same number of spaces from the beginning of the `if` statement. In other words, in Python, indentation isn't an optional stylistic choice to make your code more readable — it's how Python knows what belongs to the `if` block.

REMEMBER

Python doesn't care how many spaces you use to indent, just as long as you use the same number of spaces within the block. For ideal readability of your code, the recommended number of indentation spaces is four.

Consider the following example:

```
is_raining = input("Is it raining (if not, just press Enter)? ")

if is_raining:
    print("Bring an umbrella!")
print("Have a great day!")
```

Pressing Enter (or Return) at the `input()` prompt returns an empty input that's equivalent to `False`; any other input (such as `y`, `yes`, or `cats and dogs!`) is equivalent to `True`. When the variable `is_raining` is `True`, the `if` statement prints `Bring an umbrella!` to the screen. However, since the next `print()` statement (the one that prints `Have a great day!`) isn't indented, it's not part of the `if` block, so it will run no matter whether the `is_raining` variable is `True` or `False`.

Adding an else statement

An `if` statement all by its lonesome runs one or more statements when its condition returns the value `True` and lightly leaps over those statements if the condition returns `False`. But what if, when the condition returns `False`, you want Python to run a *different* set of statements? Ah, to handle that scenario, you need to augment the `if` statement with an `else` statement:

```
if expression :
     statement-if-true1 ;
     statement-if-true2 ;
    ...
else:
     statement-if-false1 ;
     statement-if-false2 ;
    ...
```


The *expression* is either a comparison or logical expression that returns `True` or `False`, or a Boolean. *statement-if-true*1, *statement-if-true*2, and so on define the block of statements that Python executes if *expression* returns `True`; *statement-if-false*1, *statement-if-false*2, and so on define the block of statements that Python executes if *expression* returns `False`.

Here's an example:

```
score = int(input("What was your score?"))

if score >= 80:
    print(f"Wow, your score was {score}")
    print("Nice job!")
else:
    print(f"Too bad, your score was {score}")
    print("Keep practicing!")
```

Even more choices with the elif statement

Making a this-or-that decision using `if`/`else` statements is extremely common in programming, so you'll turn to that structure again and again in your projects. But sometimes the world presents you with multiple conditions that your code has to somehow take into account. With a test score, for example, it's not enough to just check whether the score was greater than or equal to 80. Your code probably also has to check for scores greater than or equal to 90, 70, and so on.

When you need to check multiple conditions, that's where Python's `elif` (short for "else if") statement shines:

```
if expression1 :
     statement-if-expression1-true1 ;
```

```
    statement-if-expression1-true2 ;
   ...
elif expression2 :
    statement-if-expression2-true1 ;
    statement-if-expression2-true2 ;
   ...
else:
    statement-if-false1 ;
    statement-if-false2 ;
   ...
```

Python first tests *expression1*. If *expression1* returns `True`, Python runs the *statement-if-expression1-true* block and skips over everything else. If *expression1* returns `False`, Python then tests *expression2*. If *expression2* returns `True`, Python runs the *statement-if-expression2-true* block and skips over everything else. Otherwise, if all the `if` and `elif` tests return `False`, Python runs the *statement-if-false* block.

Feel free to add as many `elif` statements as you need. Here's an example:

```
score = int(input("What was your score? "))

if score > 90:
    print(f"Woot, your score was {score}.")
    print("You get an A+")
elif score >= 80:
    print(f"Wow, your score was {score}.")
    print("You get an A.")
elif score >= 70:
    print(f"Not bad, your score was {score}.")
    print("You get a B.")
elif score >= 60:
    print(f"Okay, your score was {score}.")
    print("You get a C.")
elif score >= 50:
    print(f"Hmm, your score was {score}.")
    print("You get a D.")
else:
    print(f"Oh, snap, your score was {score}.")
    print("You get an F.")
```

Python Loops

As you code larger and more complex programs, one conundrum that will come up again and again is repetitive code. Here's an example:

```
shopping_list = ["milk", "eggs", "bread", "Snickerdoodles"]

print(f"Don't forget to buy {shopping_list[0]}")
print(f"Don't forget to buy {shopping_list[1]}")
print(f"Don't forget to buy {shopping_list[2]}")
print(f"Don't forget to buy {shopping_list[3]}")
```

This code displays the following:

```
Don't forget to buy milk
Don't forget to buy eggs
Don't forget to buy bread
Don't forget to buy Snickerdoodles
```

So, yep, the code works just fine, but all those `print()` statements are a drag to type. Imagine if the shopping list had a dozen items on it or *two* dozen. Forget about it!

Whenever you come across repetitive code like this, it's time to get Python to do some of the heavy lifting by using a *loop*, which is code that handles all the repetition for you.

Looping through a collection of things

One of the main types of Python loop is the `for` loop, which goes through every item in a collection, which could be just about any set of things you can define in Python, including a list, a string, a tuple, a dictionary, a set, or a range of numbers. Here's the general syntax:

```
for item in collection :
    statement1 ;
    statement2 ;
    ...
```

Here, *`item`* is a variable that stores an item from *`collection`* (which is a list, a string, a range, or another Python collection), and *`statement1`*, *`statement2`*, and so on represent the Python statements the interpreter will run for each item. These statements must be indented four spaces from the `for` statement.

REMEMBER

Any item that you can loop through using `for` is known in the Python trade as an *iterable.*

Here's an example:

```
shopping_list = ["milk", "eggs", "bread", "Snickerdoodles"]

for product in shopping_list:
    print(f"Don't forget to buy {product}")
```

This code displays the following:

```
Don't forget to buy milk
Don't forget to buy eggs
Don't forget to buy bread
Don't forget to buy Snickerdoodles
```

Look at that: You get the same output as before, but you had to type the `print()` statement only once. Sweet! What's happening here is that Python is going through the items in `shopping_list` one by one. For each item, it stores the item's value in the `product` variable, which is then available to your code within the `for` block. The first time through the loop, `product` is given the value `milk`, the second time through, `product` is set to `eggs`, and so on.

You can loop through strings too:

```
for letter in "Hello":
    print(letter)
```

Here's the output:

```
H
e
l
l
o
```

When you need to loop a set number of times, the `range()` function will get the job done:

```
for i in range(5):
    print(f"Loop number {i}")
```

Here's the output:

```
Loop number 0
Loop number 1
Loop number 2
Loop number 3
Loop number 4
```

Looping while a condition is True

The other main type of Python loop is the `while` loop, which repeats one or more statements as long as a specified condition returns `True`:

```
while expression :
    statement1 ;
    statement2 ;
    ...
```

Here, *`expression`* is a comparison or logical expression that returns `True` or `False`, or a Boolean value. *`statement1`*, *`statement2`*, and so on represent the Python statements the interpreter will run as long as *`expression`* returns `True`. (These statements must be indented four spaces from the `while` statement.) The general idea is that something in the `while` block will update a value used in *`expression`*, such as a counter variable. Eventually, one pass through the `while` block will update that value in such a way that *`expression`* now returns `False` instead of `True`, and the `while` loop ends.

Here's an example:

```
counter = 0

while counter < 3:
    print(f"The loop counter is now: {counter}")
    counter += 1
```

This code initializes a variable named `counter` to `0`. In the `while` statement, the expression `counter < 3` returns `True`, so Python runs the statements inside the `while` block: The current value of `counter` is printed, and then the value of `counter` is increased by `1`. The code then loops back to the `while` statement, rechecks the `counter < 3` expression, and repeats for as long as that expression returns `True`. After the third time through the loop, the value of `counter` is now `3`, which means `counter < 3` returns `False`, and the loop shuts down.

Here's the output

```
The loop counter is now: 0
The loop counter is now: 1
The loop counter is now: 2
```

Interrupting loop execution

TIP

If you ever need to exit a loop before it's finished, use the `break` statement:

```
while True:
    value = input("Type a number (or q to quit): ")
    if value == "q":
        break
    else:
        print(f"The cube of your number is {int(value) ** 3}")
```

This code uses `while True` to set up an endless loop. After getting a value from the user, the code uses `if` to check whether that value was `"q"` (for quit). If it was, the code uses `break` to quit the loop; otherwise, it continues with the rest of the loop.

A slightly different case is when you need a loop to skip the rest of the code in the current loop because of some condition. To skip the rest of a loop and returns to the beginning, use the `continue` statement:

```
tax_factors = [1.05, 1.08, 1.04, 0.00, 1.03]
price = 100.00
for factor in tax_factors:
    if factor == 0:
        continue
    else:
        original_price = price / factor
        tax_rate = int((factor - 1) * 100)
        print(f"The price less {tax_rate}% tax is ${original_price:.2f}")
```

This code loops through the items in the `tax_factors` list. If it comes across an item that equals `0`, it uses `continue` to skip the rest of the loop (and thereby avoid an illegal division by zero) and return to the beginning for the next item. Here's the output:

```
The price less 5% tax is $95.24
The price less 8% tax is $92.59
The price less 4% tax is $96.15
The price less 3% tax is $97.09
```

Example: Build Your Own Survey Bot

To complete this chapter, I offer the following example, shown in Listing 6-1, which demonstrates most of the concepts I present in this and previous chapters in this minibook, including variables, data types, expressions, strings, lists, conditionals, and loops. I added lots of comments to help you understand what the code is doing.

LISTING 6-1: A Simple Survey Bot

```
# Simple Survey Analyzer

print("Welcome to the Super Quick Survey!")
print("----------------------------------")

# Store the survey questions in a list
questions = [
    "What's your name? ",
    "How old are you? ",
    "What's your favorite programming language so far? "
]

# Create an empty list to store the answers
answers = []
# Loop through the questions
for question in questions:

    # Get the answer to the next question
    answer = input(question)

    # Add the answer to the answers list
    answers.append(answer)

# Unpack the answers into variables
name = answers[0]
age = int(answers[1])
language = answers[2]

# Respond based on their input
# The \n in the string prints a blank line
print(f"\nThanks, {name}! Here's your survey summary:\n")

print(f"You are {age} years old.")

# Add some conditional feedback
# about their age
```

(continued)

LISTING 6-1: (continued)

```
if age < 18:
    print("You're off to an early start – awesome!")
elif age > 60:
    print("Proving it's never too late to learn!")
else:
    print("Perfect time in life to be learning something new!")

print(f"\nYou enjoy coding in {language}.")

# Add some conditional feedback about
# their programming language choice
if language.lower() == "python":
    print("Great choice – Python is beginner-friendly and powerful!")
elif language.lower() == "javascript":
    print("Nice! JavaScript makes the web come alive.")
else:
    print(f"{language}? Very cool. Every language has its own superpower.")

print("\nThanks for taking the survey!")
```

Type the program into a .py file, or open it from the files you can download at `www.dummies.com/go/codingaiofd3e`. Then run it to see what it does! Once you understand the program, try making some changes or improvements yourself using the Python you've learned so far.

IN THIS CHAPTER

» Defining and calling functions

» Wrapping your head around variable scope

» Installing and importing Python modules

» Working with external code libraries

» Reusing data stored in files

Chapter 7
Reusing Code

Good programmers know what to write. Great ones know what to reuse.

—ERIC S. RAYMOND

One of the secrets to programming productivity is also one of the oldest pieces of advice in the world: *Don't reinvent the wheel!* If you or someone else has already solved a particular programming puzzle, use that solution instead of re-solving the puzzle every time you come across it.

Avoiding reinventing wheels in coding generally involves reusing existing code as much as possible. If you've already written some code, you can structure it so that you can easily reuse it elsewhere. If you find code in one of Python's public code repositories, you can bring that code into your Python file.

This chapter marks a turning point in your Python path where you go from writing one-off bits of code in Chapters 1 through 6 of this minibook to creating efficient, reusable, and powerful programs. This chapter is all about teaching you how to use functions to break your code into reusable chunks; how to use modules to expand your Python toolkit without having to write new code; how to use libraries to borrow useful tools that others have made; and how to reuse data by writing it to and reading it from files.

Making Your Code More Efficient with Functions

One of the superpowers of a good coder is to always be on the lookout for inefficient places in your code. If you've declared a bunch of variables for similar data, perhaps you could bring all those variables into a single list (covered in Chapter 6). If you have to repeat some code for each item in a string or list or for a specified number of times, write the code once and wrap it in a `for` or `while` loop (also covered in Chapter 6).

Another way to write ridiculously efficient code is to look for a collection of statements that you need to run frequently. For example, suppose your program, given a price, needs to calculate a final cost that includes tax and shipping. Listing 7-1 shows a program that works well for a very particular problem, namely calculating the tax and shipping for a single price.

LISTING 7-1: Calculating Shipping and Tax for a Single Price

```
# Get the price
price = float(input("Enter the price: "))

# Calculate 7% tax
tax = price * 0.07

# Is the price at least $50?
if price >= 50:

    # If so, charge a flat rate for shipping
    shipping = 5.00
else:

    # Otherwise, charge 10% of the price for shipping
    shipping = price * 0.1

# Calculate the total
total = price + tax + shipping

print(f"Total with tax and shipping: ${total:.2f}")
```

That code works fine for a single price, but what if you have to calculate the total for ten prices, or a hundred? Not fun! The efficient solution is to wrap the code inside a function, which has the following general syntax in Python:

```
def function_name ([ parameters ]):
     statement1
     statement2
     ...
    return value
```

`def` identifies the block of code that follows it as a function. `def` is short for *define*. *`function_name`* is a unique name for the function. The naming rules and guidelines that I outline for variables in Chapter 5 also apply to function names.

`parameters`, which are optional, are one or more comma-separated variable names listed in the function definition. When you call the function, you pass in *arguments* (the actual values) that get assigned to these parameters. If you don't use parameters, you must still include the parentheses after the function name.

`statement1`, *`statement2`*, and so on represent the code that performs the function's tasks or calculations.

`return` *`value`* sends *`value`* back as the result of the function, where *`value`* is something calculated or in some other way determined by your function statements. Note that if the function doesn't use a return value, you can forgo the `return` statement.

TIP

It's common to mix up the terms *parameters* and *arguments* when talking about functions. Here's an easy way to keep them straight: Think of a function like a restaurant recipe card. The *parameters* are the blanks on the card, for example "___ cups of flour," "___ teaspoons of salt." The blank shows what the cook expects to be filled in. The *arguments* are what you pour in when you make the dish, for example, 2 (cups of flour) and 1 (teaspoon of salt). Use the same recipe with different amounts (arguments), and you might end up with a cookie, a cake, or a culinary disaster.

As with conditionals and loops (refer to Chapter 6), you tell Python which statements are included in the function by indenting them (four spaces is the standard indentation).

To run a function, your code uses the function name, followed by the arguments (the values you pass in) in parentheses, if any. These arguments are assigned to the function's parameters. (If the function doesn't require arguments, you still need to include the parentheses.) Here's an example:

```
def get_user_name():
    name = input("What's your name? ")
    return name

your_name = get_user_name()
print(f"Nice to meet you, {your_name}!")
```

This code defines a `get_user_name()` function, which prompts the user for their name and then returns that name. When the function is called using `get_user_name()`, the return value is stored in the `your_name` variable, which is then printed to the screen.

For the earlier example of calculating a total including tax and shipping, all the calculation code can go inside a function. In Listing 7-2, I shoehorned the calculations inside a function named `calculate_total()`:

LISTING 7-2: Defining a Function for Calculating a Total

```
def calculate_total(price):

    # Calculate 7% tax
    tax = price * 0.07

    # Is the price at least $50?
    if price >= 50:

        # If so, charge a flat rate for shipping
        shipping = 5.00
    else:

        # Otherwise, charge 10% of the price for shipping
        shipping = price * 0.1

    # Calculate the total
    total = price + tax + shipping

    # Return the total
    return total

counter = 0
```

```
while (counter < 3):
    # Get the price
    price = float(input("Enter the price: "))

    # Get the total with tax and shipping
    total = calculate_total(price)

    print(f"Total with tax and shipping: ${total:.2f}")

    counter += 1
```

Following the function, a `while` loop asks for a price and then calls `calculate_total()` with `price` as the argument. The function result is stored in the `total` variable, which is then printed to the screen as before. The loop repeats this two more times before quitting. I added the loop to demonstrate that with the calculation code handily stored in the `calculate_total()` function, you can reuse that function as many times as you need.

WARNING

Because Python is an interpreted language, it reads your code from top to bottom, like reading a recipe as you cook. So, if you try to call a function before it's defined, Python will look confused and throw an error. That's why, in the examples I've shown so far, the statements that call the function come after the function.

Getting the Hang of Variable Scope

You may be tempted to think that once you declare a variable, you can then use that variable anywhere later in the same program. It makes sense. For example, suppose you declare a variable as the first statement of a function inside your program. Python is an interpreted language that processes one statement at a time from top to bottom, so once Python has processed your function variable declaration, you should be able to use that variable as needed anywhere later in the program, all the way to the end of the file. Right?

Nope. Welcome to the world of variable scope, where you learn who can access what, when, and where.

What is variable scope, anyway?

Variable scope — often shortened to just *scope* — defines where in the program a variable can be used and where it can't be used. To put it another way, a variable's scope determines which statements and functions can access and work with the variable. Scope is just a fancy way of saying, "Where does this variable exist?" or "Where can this variable be used?"

You definitely want to care about scope in your Python scripts for several reasons:

- **You may need to use the same variable in multiple functions.** For example, a function may use a variable to store the result of a calculation, and other functions may also need to use that result. In this case, you'd set up the scope of the variable so that it's accessible to multiple functions.
- **You may want to use the same variable name in multiple functions.** If these variables are otherwise unrelated, you'll want to make sure that there is no confusion about which variable you're working with. In other words, you'll restrict the scope of each variable to the function in which it is declared.
- **It helps with debugging.** When a Python program zigs instead of zags, understanding the scope of the variables involved can be crucial to figuring out the problem.

Python lets you establish two types of scope for your variables:

- Global scope
- Function scope

The next two sections describe each type in detail.

Global: The "everyone's invited" scope

When a variable has *global scope*, the variable has the following properties:

- The variable is declared outside any function.
- The variable is available to be used in any statement after the declaration.
- In particular, the variable is available to be used inside any function defined after the variable declaration.

Here's an example:

```
message = "Hello, scope world!"  # global variable

def greet():
```

```
    print(message)  # works just fine

greet()
```

Here, even though the `print(message)` statement resides in the `greet()` function, that function can still access the `message` variable because it was defined outside any function and therefore has global scope.

Local: The "for function eyes only" scope

When a variable has *local scope*, the variable has the following properties:

- The variable is declared inside a function.
- The variable is available to be used in any statement that comes after the declaration in the same function.
- The variable is unavailable to any statements outside that function.

Here's an example:

```
def greet():
    user_name = input("What's your name? ") # local variable
    print(f"Hi, {user_name}!")  # works just fine

greet()

print(user_name)  # Not gonna happen
```

Here's a sample output:

```
What's your name? Dweezil
Hi, Dweezil!
Traceback (most recent call last):
  File "chapter07/example05.py", line 7, in <module>
    print(user_name)  # Not gonna happen
          ^^^^^^^^^
NameError: name 'user_name' is not defined
```

Whoops! Here, the `user_name` variable is declared in the `greet()` function. This declaration makes `user_name` a local variable, so the `print()` statement in the `greet()` function works as expected. However, when the code tries to use the `user_name` variable outside the function in the final `print()` statement, the Python interpreter implodes with `NameError: name 'user_name' is not defined` because outside the function, Python has no idea what `user_name` is — that variable lives and dies inside `greet()`.

WARNING

So why not just make everything a global variable? That may seem like a reasonable way to go, and it's true that global variables can be handy. However, if you use them too much, your code gets messy and hard to manage. It's like leaving all your clothes on the floor instead of putting them in drawers. If a variable is only ever used inside a function, make it a local variable and save global variables for those relatively rare times you need a value throughout your program.

Listing 7-3 demonstrates when you should use a global variable:

LISTING 7-3: Demonstrating Local and Global Variables

```
app_title = "Awesome App"  # Global variable

def show_welcome():
    print(f"Welcome to {app_title}!")
def show_goodbye():
    print(f"Thanks for using {app_title}! Goodbye!")

show_welcome()
show_goodbye()
```

Here's the output:

```
Welcome to Awesome App!
Thanks for using Awesome App! Goodbye!
```

In this example, the `app_title` variable has global scope, so both functions can use the variable without any problem.

Avoiding Wheel Reinvention with Modules

When you get some experience with Python, you'll start noticing all kinds of puzzles in the form of what appear to be gaps in the language. If you've gone through Chapter 5 of this minibook, you already know how to solve some of these puzzles.

How do you calculate how many days are between two dates? How do you calculate the square root of a number? How do you find the mean or the standard deviation of a list of numbers? How do you generate a random number between 1 and 6 to simulate a dice roll for a game?

Sure, with a lot of effort and a lot of Googling, you might be able to solve these puzzles yourself, but you'd just be reinventing some very difficult wheels. That's because Python comes with an impressively large toolbox full of prewritten code, all of which is available for you to use in your Python programs. This toolbox is called the *standard library*, and you access this library using special Python files called modules.

A *module* is a file containing prefab Python code — such as functions or constants — that you can bring into any project instead of writing the code from scratch. There are modules available to plug all the "gaps" I just mentioned:

- The `datetime` module, which you learn about in Chapter 5, enables you to work with dates and times, including calculating the number of days between two dates.
- The `math` module offers a huge number of math-related functions, including one that calculates the square root of a number.
- The `statistics` module provides a ton of stats functions, including ones that calculate the arithmetic mean and the standard deviation of a sample.
- The `random` module offers functions for generating random values, including one function that can generate a random integer between any two values.

REMEMBER

Who codes all these modules? Most of what you'll find in the standard library is created and maintained by the Python Software Foundation (PSF) and a team of core Python developers from around the world. It's a community-driven effort, and many of the modules have been around (and evolving) for years. So, as you dive into these modules, if you ever find yourself thinking, "Dang, this is handy," remember that you're standing on the shoulders of giants — dedicated and skilled Python coders who built a bunch of useful tools so you don't have to.

TIP

To browse a complete list of the modules available in the standard library, surf to `https://docs.python.org/3/library/`. Here you find modules organized by category, including data types, numeric and mathematical modules, generic operating system services, and internet data handling.

Want a sneak peek? Here's a tiny sample:

Module	Used For
math	Math functions and constants
random	Random numbers and choices
datetime	Manipulating dates and times
os	Interacting with the operating system
sys	Getting info about the Python system
time	Sleep, timestamps, and more
statistics	Calculating mean, median, and other stats
json	Working with JSON data

Importing a module

Python's standard library modules are separate parts of the language, and to use any module, you must import it into your Python program. To *import* a module means to make the module's code available to your Python program.

To import an entire module, you have two choices:

```
import module
import module as alias
```

module is the name of the module in the standard library. *alias* is a nickname that you use to refer to the module instead of the name *module*. In most cases, your alias will be something shorter or easier to type (or both) than the module's name.

For example, to import the statistics module, you'd include the following in your Python program (usually at the top of the file):

```
import statistics
```

Alternatively, you can import statistics using an alias, such as stats:

```
import statistics as stats
```

TECHNICAL STUFF

WHAT HAPPENS WHEN YOU IMPORT A MODULE?

Suppose you include something like the following in your code:

```
import math
```

What's really happening here? Behind the scenes, Python performs the following steps:

1. It finds the `math.py` file in the standard library.
2. It loads and runs the `math.py` code.
3. It creates a module object, which acts like a container full of whatever functions, classes, and constants are defined in the module.
4. It assigns the name `math` to that container. If you specify an alias with the `import` statement, Python assigns that alias to the container instead.

Now your module is ready for action.

TIP

After you import a module, you can display a list of all the stuff inside that module by running the `print(dir(`*`module`*`))` statement, where *`module`* is the name of the imported module:

```
import math
print(dir(math))
```

Using a module

Once you've imported a module, it's available to your program as an object. That means you can use Python's standard dot notation to access all the goodies the module provides, such as functions, constants, data structures (such as lists), and classes:

```
module . function ()
module . constant
module . list
module . class
```

Here, *`module`* is the name of the imported module or its alias, and *`function`*`()`, *`constant`*, *`list`*, or *`class`* is the name of the module element you want to use.

For example, the statistics module offers a mean() function that returns the arithmetic mean of some collection of numbers. Listing 7-4 shows how to put that function through its paces:

LISTING 7-4: Using the mean() Function

```
# Import the statistics module to use the mean() function
import statistics

# Store the test scores in a list
test_scores = [77, 65, 82, 71, 90, 53, 68, 79, 47, 77]

# Calculate the mean value of the test scores
test_mean = statistics.mean(test_scores)

print(test_mean) # Output: 70.9
```

The key here is the second-last statement, which uses statistics.mean(test_scores) to run the statistics module's mean() function on the test_scores list.

Similarly, a common bit of logic needed in certain games is calculating the distance between two points on the 2D plane. If both points are represented as (x, y) tuples (refer to Chapter 6), you take the difference between the *x* values, square that difference, take the difference between the *y* values, square that difference, sum those two squares, and then take the square root of that sum. This is the good old Pythagorean theorem in action. Listing 7-5 implements this algorithm:

LISTING 7-5: Calculating the Distance between Points on a 2D Plane

```
# Import the math module to use the sqrt() function
import math

# Define two points as (x, y) tuples
point1 = (3, 4)
point2 = (7, 1)

# Calculate the difference between the x values
dx = point2[0] - point1[0]

# Calculate the difference between the y values
dy = point2[1] - point1[1]
```

```
# Apply the Pythagorean theorem:
# distance = √(dx² + dy² )
distance = math.sqrt(dx**2 + dy**2)

print(f"The distance between the points is: {distance:.2f}")
```

Importing part of a module

You don't always have to import an entire module. Your code will be a little cleaner and easier to understand if you import just the part of the module — such as a particular function, constant, or class — you need:

```
from module import element
```

Here, *module* is the name of the module, and *element* is the name of the module element you want to import. When you import only part of a module, you no longer need to use the dot notation; just refer to the *element* name directly.

For example, Listing 7-5 requires only the `sqrt()` function, so the `import` statement could have been this:

```
from math import sqrt
```

In that case, the distance calculation changes to this:

```
distance = sqrt(dx**2 + dy**2)
```

TIP

You can specify more than one element. If you do, be sure to separate them with commas, as in this example:

```
from math import sqrt, pi, pow
```

Rolling your own modules

Although you'll usually import modules from Python's standard library, nothing is stopping you from building your own library of reusable Python code and using `import` to bring any part of that library into your projects.

Creating and using your own modules requires just three steps:

1. **Create a text file and populate it with the functions, constants, lists, and other data that you want to make available to other Python files.**

2. **Save your text file as a Python (`.py`) file.**

   For simplicity's sake, save this module in the same folder as whatever file or files you'll be using to import the module.

3. **In another Python file, import your module by adding the statement `import module`, where *module* is the name of the file you saved in Step 2 minus the `.py` extension.**

For example, I could create a module that includes the `calculate_total()` function (from the "Making Your Code More Efficient with Functions" section) by saving the `calculate_total()` function from Listing 7-2 and saving it in a file named `my_calculators.py`:

```
def calculate_total(price):

    # Calculate 7% tax
    tax = price * 0.07

    # Is the price at least $50?
    if price >= 50:

        # If so, charge a flat rate for shipping
        shipping = 5.00
    else:

        # Otherwise, charge 10% of the price for shipping
        shipping = price * 0.1

    # Calculate the total
    total = price + tax + shipping

    # Return the total
    return total
```

Listing 7-6 shows how to import the new module into a separate file.

LISTING 7-6: **Using the my_calculators Module**

```
import my_calculators

counter = 0

while (counter < 3):
    # Get the price
```

```
    price = float(input("Enter the price: "))

    # Get the total with tax and shipping
    total = my_calculators.calculate_total(price)

    print(f"Total with tax and shipping: ${total:.2f}")

counter += 1
```

This code imports the `my_calculators` module, and then uses `my_calculators.calculate_total()` to call the module's `calculate_total()` function.

Reuse Heaven: Installing External Libraries

Python comes with a ton of useful built-in features, and importing modules from Python's standard library (which I cover in the preceding section) gives you access to a wide range of powerful tools. Depending on the types of projects you're looking to build, having these two code sources at your disposal may give you everything you need.

But probably not.

If you have a project that grabs data from a website or a server; displays attractive charts; works with Excel files; involves building a chatbot; or is related to creating any kind of reasonably sophisticated game, you're going to need some help.

Fortunately, that help is almost always just a few clicks away in the form of an external library. An *external library* is custom Python code that someone wrote and shared with the world. These libraries aren't included with Python by default, nor are they part of Python's standard library, but you can download and install them in seconds. Think of them as plug-ins or expansion packs for your Python powers.

REMEMBER

Most Python libraries live on the Python Package Index (PyPI), which is like the App Store for Python code. You can browse and search the entire index of libraries by steering your favorite browser to `https://pypi.org`. Be warned, though: The site is home to hundreds of thousands (yes, you read that right: *hundreds of thousands*) of libraries — everything from game engines to machine learning toolkits.

Installing a library

Python includes a tool called `pip` (short for Pip Installs Packages; yep, it's a recursive acronym). `pip` is your personal library installer.

To install a library, you open your terminal or command prompt, exit the Python REPL if you have a session running, and type the following:

```
pip install library
```

In macOS Terminal, you may need to run this command, instead:

```
pip3 install library
```

Here, replace *`library`* with the name of the Python library you want to install. For example, one of the most popular libraries is `requests`, which enables a Python program to make requests to websites and application programming interfaces (APIs). You install `requests` by running the following command at the terminal:

```
pip install requests
```

Or, in macOS Terminal:

```
pip3 install requests
```

Importing and using a library

Once you've convinced `pip` to install a library, you use the library in your Python code just as though it was a module. That is, you first import the library using the `import` statement:

```
import library
import library as alias
```

`library` is the name of the installed library. *`alias`* is a nickname that you use to refer to the library instead of the name *`library`*. In most cases, your alias will be something shorter or easier to type (or both) than the library's name.

For example:

```
import requests
```

You then use dot notation to access the library's functions, constants, lists, and classes:

```
library . function ()
library . constant
library . list
library . class
```

Listing 7-7 uses `requests.get` to connect to the Random Joke API:

LISTING 7-7: Getting a Random Joke

```
import requests

# Get a random joke
response = requests.get("https://official-joke-api.appspot.com/random_joke")

if response.status_code == 200:
    print("I was able to connect to the API no problem.")
    joke = response.json()
    print(f"{joke['setup']} {joke['punchline']}")

else:
    print("Something went wrong. This is not a joke.")
```

REMEMBER

Before the program in Listing 7-7 will work, you need to install the `requests` library by entering `pip install requests` (or `pip3 install requests`) in Terminal.

Reusing Data by Writing and Reading Files

In Chapter 6, I talk about storing data in a list, a tuple, and a dictionary. These data structures are extremely useful, but their utility ends when the program's done. That is, if you've plopped some data in a list or whatever, that data evaporates as soon as the Python interpreter executes the final statement of the program.

This chapter has been all about reusing code both to make your programs more efficient and more powerful, and to make coding those programs much faster and easier. But all the benefits of reusing code apply equally to reusing data — and the more data you have, the greater the benefit.

But how do you reuse data? The key is to store that data in its own file outside any Python program. You can use Python to write the data to its own file, or you might already have data in some format, such as a text file. Python also offers ways to read the data in that file, which enables you to reuse the data by bringing it into any Python program.

Reading and writing files turns your little Python script into something that can

- Save data between runs
- Keep a log of user activity
- Save and load settings or configurations
- Store progress in a game or project
- Generate reports
- Build real-world tools like notepads or file converters

In this section, you learn how to work with files on your computer using Python, so your programs can save and retrieve — in short, *reuse* — data, just like the pros.

Opening a file

In Python, you work with files using the `open()` function:

```
open( file , mode )
```

file is the name of the file you want to work with, surrounded by quotation marks. If the file is in the same folder as your program, just provide the filename. Otherwise, you need to specify the path to the file.

mode is an optional letter, surrounded by quotation marks, that indicates how you want Python to open the file. Most of the time, you'll use either `w` (for write mode; refer to "Writing data to a file") or `r` (for read mode, which is the default; refer to "Reading data from a file").

You always use `open()` in the following context:

```
with open( file , mode ) as alias :
    statement1
    statement2
    ...
```

alias is a temporary name you use in your code to refer to the file you opened. *statement1*, *statement2*, and so on represent the code you use to manipulate the open file in some way. Note that each of these statements must be indented from the `with` statement by the same number of spaces.

When the `with` block is complete, Python automatically closes the file.

Writing data to a file

To write some data to a file, the `open()` function uses `"w"` (short for *write*) as the *mode* argument, and the `with` block uses the open file object's `write()` method to write a string to the open file, as shown in Listing 7-8.

LISTING 7-8: Writing a Limerick to a File

```
with open("limerick.txt", "w") as file:
    file.write("Limerick #1\n")
    file.write("There once was a coder named Ray\n")
    file.write("Who wrote Python all night and day\n")
    file.write("Through one missing colon\n")
    file.write("His sanity was stolen\n")
    file.write("Now code just makes him run away\n")
    file.write("\n")
```

The code in Listing 7-8 opens a file named `limerick.txt` in write mode (`"w"`) using the alias `file`. If `limerick.txt` doesn't exist, Python creates it; if `limerick.txt` does exist, Python overwrites it (so you want to be careful here that you don't overwrite a file you don't want to trash). Then a series of `file.write()` methods writes a few strings to the open file. The `\n` text at the end of each string is called the *newline* character and ensures that the next string added to the file begins on its own line.

TIP

If you have an existing file, you may prefer to add new content to it rather than overwrite it. No problem! Just open the file in append mode, where your `open()` function uses `"a"` (short for *append*) as the *mode* argument, as shown in Listing 7-9.

LISTING 7-9: Opening a File in Append Mode

```
with open("limerick.txt", "a") as file:
    file.write("Limerick #2\n")
    file.write("There once was a coder named Pete\n")
    file.write("His code was quite incomplete\n")
```

Reading data from a file

If you have an existing file that has data you want to use in a program, you can read the contents of that file by using the `open()` function with `"r"` (short for *read*) as the *mode* argument. The `with` block uses the open file object's `read()` method to grab the entire contents of the open file. Listing 7-10 shows an example:

LISTING 7-10: Reading a File

```
with open("limerick.txt", "r") as file:
    content = file.read()
    print(content)
```

This example opens the `limerick.txt` file from the preceding section in read mode (`"r"`) using the alias `file`. The `file.read()` method grabs everything from the file and stores it in the `content` variable, which is then printed.

REMEMBER

Read mode is the default, so if you leave out the *mode* argument, Python assumes you want to open the file in read mode.

TIP

Sometimes it's better to read a file one line at a time. You can do that with ease using a `for` loop that runs through each line in the open file, as shown in Listing 7-11.

LISTING 7-11: Reading a File One Line at a Time

```
with open("limerick.txt", "r") as file:
    for line in file:
        no_newline = line.strip()
        print(no_newline)
```

The `strip()` method removes whitespace characters at the beginning and end of a string. In this case, `strip()` removes each newline character that Python automatically adds to the end of each line, so you don't get empty spaces between lines.

TIP

It's often useful to read all the file data at once and append each line of the file as an item in a list. You can do that with the file object's `readlines()` method. Listing 7-12 shows an example.

LISTING 7-12: Reading a File to Create a List

```
with open("limerick.txt", "r") as file:
    lines = file.readlines()
    for line in lines:
        print(line.strip())
```

Example: Building a Quotations Archive

To complete this chapter, Listing 7-13 presents some code for an example program that creates and maintains an archive of quotations. The archive is stored in a text file, uses several modules from the standard library, and corrals most of the code into functions to keep things organized and readable.

LISTING 7-13: A Program to Create and Maintain an Archive of Quotations

```
# Import the necessary modules
import random
from datetime import date

# Create a constant for the name of the text file
QUOTATIONS_FILE = "quotations.txt"

# This function displays the app menu
def show_menu():
    print("\nWelcome to the Quotations Archive!\n")
    print("What would you like to do?")
    print("1. View all quotations")
    print("2. Add a new quotation")
    print("3. Get a random quotation")
    print("4. Quit")

# This function reads the quotations from the file
# and returns them as a list
def read_quotations():
    # Start with an empty list
    quotations = []

    # Check if the file exists before trying to read it
    if not file_exists(QUOTATIONS_FILE):
        # If the file doesn't exist, return an empty list
        return quotations
```

(continued)

LISTING 7-13: (continued)

```
    # Open the file in read mode
    with open(QUOTATIONS_FILE, "r") as file:
        # Read each line from the file
        for line in file:
            # Strip whitespace and add the line to the list
            quotations.append(line.strip())

    # Return the list of quotations
    return quotations

# This function checks if the file exists
# and returns True or False
def file_exists(filename):

    # Import the os module to check for file existence
    import os

    # Use os.path.exists to check if the file exists
    # and return the result
    return os.path.exists(filename)

# This function saves a new quotation to the file
def save_quotation(quotation):
    # Open the file in append mode
    with open(QUOTATIONS_FILE, "a") as file:

        # Get the current date and format it as YYYY-MM-DD
        today = date.today().isoformat()

        # Write the quotation and the date to the file
        file.write(f"{quotation} (added on {today})\n")

# This function asks for a new quotation
def add_new_quotation():

    # Prompt the user for a new quotation
    quotation = input("Enter your quotation: ")

    # Save the quotation to the file
    save_quotation(quotation)

    # Inform the user that it has been saved
    print("Quotation saved!")

# This function displays all saved quotations
```

```
def view_all_quotations():

    # Read the quotations from the file
    quotations = read_quotations()

    # Check if there are any quotations
    if not quotations:
        # If not, inform the user
        print("No quotations saved yet.")
    else:
        # If there are, display them
        print("\nYour saved quotations:")
        for quotation in quotations:
            print(f"- {quotation}")

# This function displays a random quotation
def show_random_quotation():
    # Read the quotations from the file
    quotations = read_quotations()

    # Check if there are any quotations
    if not quotations:
        # If not, inform the user
        print("No quotations to show. Try adding some first!")
    else:
        # If there are, choose one at random
        # and display it
        print("\nHere's a random quotation:")
        print(random.choice(quotations))

# This function is the main loop of the program
def main():
    # Loop until the user chooses to quit
    while True:

        # Show the menu and get the user's choice
        show_menu()
        choice = input("Choose an option (1-4): ")

        # Check the user's choice,
        # then call the appropriate function
        if choice == "1":
            # Display all the quotations
            view_all_quotations()
        elif choice == "2":
            # Prompt for a new quotation
            add_new_quotation()
```

(continued)

Reusing Code

LISTING 7-13: ***(continued)***

```
        elif choice == "3":
            # Display a random quotation
            show_random_quotation()
        elif choice == "4":
            # Exit the program
            print("Goodbye! Keep those quotations coming.")
            # Exit the loop to quit the program
            break
        else:
            # Handle a choice that's not 1-4
            print("Invalid option. Please try again.")

# Run the main function to start the program
main()
```

Figure 7-1 shows the quotation archive program running in a terminal window.

```
chapter7 — Python listing0717.py — 70×30
Welcome to the Quotations Archive!

What would you like to do?
1. View all quotations
2. Add a new quotation
3. Get a random quotation
4. Quit
Choose an option (1-4): 1

Your saved quotations:
- "Talk is cheap. Show me the code." - Linus Torvalds (added on 2026-0
3-13)
- "Make it work, make it right, make it fast." - Kent Beck (added on 2
026-03-13)
- "The 3 virtues of a programmer: Laziness, impatience, and hubris." -
 Larry Wall (added on 2026-03-13)
- "People think that computer science is the art of geniuses but the a
ctual reality is the opposite, just many people doing things that buil
d on each other, like a wall of mini stones." (added on 2026-03-13)
- "A clever person solves a problem. A wise person avoids it." (added
on 2026-03-13)

Welcome to the Quotations Archive!

What would you like to do?
1. View all quotations
2. Add a new quotation
3. Get a random quotation
4. Quit
Choose an option (1-4):
```

FIGURE 7-1: Running the Quotations Archive program.

The code is liberally sprinkled with comments, so it should be straightforward to follow what it's doing. Here are a few not-so-straightforward things to watch out for:

- The archive file (`quotations.txt`) must be in the same folder as the Python file.
- The name of the archive file (`quotations.txt`) is used several times in the code. To avoid having to edit all those instances if you decide to change the filename, the program defines the constant `QUOTATIONS_FILE` and sets it equal to the filename as a string. Using all-uppercase letters for the names of constants is standard programming practice.
- The `file_exists()` function imports the `os` module and uses the `path` object's `exists()` method to determine whether the quotations archive file exists.
- In the `show_random_quotation()` function, the `random` module's `choice()` function is used to grab a random item from the list of quotations.
- The `main()` function defines the overall logic of the program, which is a common Python organizing structure. In this program, `main()` uses a `while True` loop to display the menu, prompt the user to choose a menu option, and handle the input by calling the appropriate function. Using `while True` means the loop runs until the user cancels the program by choosing the Quit menu option. At that point, the `while` loop is exited by running the `break` statement.

3 Python for Data and AI

Contents at a Glance

IN THIS CHAPTER

» Understanding what data science is and why it matters

» Seeing how data science, big data, and AI connect

» Following the data science pipeline from raw data to insight

» Meeting the Python libraries that power data science

» Installing and verifying your data science dependencies

Chapter 1

What Is Data Science?

Errors using inadequate data are much less than those using no data at all.

—CHARLES BABBAGE

If you've read Book 2, you already know Python. You can write functions, work with lists and dictionaries, loop through data, and pull in external libraries. That's a solid base, and it's just what you need to enter one of today's most sought-after tech careers: data science.

This minibook puts those Python skills to work on real problems. You load datasets, clean messy data, visualize patterns, and build your first predictive model. By the time you're done, you'll have a working understanding of the full data science workflow and the tools professionals use every day.

But before diving into code, it's worth taking a chapter to understand what data science is, how it works as a process, and which Python libraries you'll be reaching for throughout this minibook. That context will make everything that follows click faster.

Defining Data Science

You might think that understanding data science involves complex equations and requires an advanced degree. In practice, though, data science is something far more accessible: It's the process of extracting useful insights from data. This process might mean figuring out why sales dropped last quarter, predicting which customers are likely to cancel their subscriptions, identifying fraudulent transactions in real time, or helping a streaming service recommend what to watch next.

How data science got its name

The term *data science* is surprisingly recent. William S. Cleveland coined it in 2001 in a paper titled "Data Science: An Action Plan for Expanding the Technical Areas of the Field of Statistics." The International Council for Science formally recognized the field a year later, and Columbia University began publishing the *Journal of Data Science* in 2003.

The name is new, but the core concepts are very old. For thousands of years, people have been using statistics, which is the mathematical foundation of data science, to identify patterns in data. For example, the historian Thucydides describes Athenian soldiers in the fifth century BC carefully counting bricks in an unplastered section of a city wall and then averaging those counts across multiple soldiers to estimate the wall's full height. This is an early example of data collection, reducing errors, and making inferences, which are the essential parts of data science that we still practice 2,500 years later.

What's new isn't the math. It's the scale of the data, the power of the computers, and the libraries available that make the process practical for anyone who can write a few lines of Python.

What data scientists do

Data scientists rarely work alone, and for good reason: the job requires a wide range of skills. In practice, teams often divide the work across three broad competency areas:

- **Data capture:** Obtaining data by connecting to databases, pulling information from APIs, and loading files. This process also requires a strong understanding of the domain to identify which questions are valuable to explore.
- **Analysis:** Applying statistical methods and algorithms to find patterns, test hypotheses, and draw conclusions that wouldn't be visible from simply reading the raw numbers.

- **Presentation:** Translating findings into visualizations and plain language so that people who weren't part of the analysis can understand and act on the results.

Over the course of this minibook, you touch on all three areas.

Data science, big data, and AI

Data science is not an isolated discipline; it combines statistics, software development, and domain expertise, and it directly supports the fields of machine learning and artificial intelligence.

You may have heard the term *ETL* (extract, transform, and load), which describes the process of pulling data from multiple sources, converting it into a consistent format, and loading it somewhere useful for analysis. You follow this process in Chapter 3 of this minibook when you load your first datasets.

The outputs of data science analysis often feed directly into AI applications. When a music service learns your listening preferences and starts suggesting artists you've never heard of but end up loving, that's data science at work upstream of an AI recommendation system. When a hospital system flags a patient's test results as potentially indicating a condition before symptoms appear, that's data science informing a clinical AI tool. The pipeline from raw data to insight to automated action is one of the most consequential technology systems of our time.

The Data Science Pipeline

Data science is partly art and partly engineering. The art is in knowing which questions to ask, which patterns to look for, and how to present findings compellingly. The engineering is in the repeatable set of steps that transforms raw, messy data into a reliable, interpretable result.

This process is called the *data science pipeline*, and understanding it gives you a map for everything else in this minibook.

Step 1: Preparing the data

Real-world data is rarely clean. It arrives from multiple sources in different formats, and with missing values, duplicate records, inconsistent naming conventions, and all manner of other problems. Before you can analyze data, you have to prepare it, which involves loading it, examining it, cleaning it, and transforming it into a form your tools can work with.

Many experienced data scientists spend 70 to 80 percent of their time on data preparation. Chapters 2 and 3 of this minibook focus on data preparation.

Step 2: Exploring the data

Once your data is in reasonable shape, you explore it. *EDA*, or *exploratory data analysis*, involves calculating descriptive statistics, looking at distributions, spotting outliers, and visualizing relationships between variables before committing to any particular modeling approach.

EDA is where you ask: What does this data look like? Are there patterns? Anything surprising? Anything that seems wrong? It's an iterative process in which you form a hypothesis, look at the data, revise your hypothesis, and look again. Chapter 4 of this minibook covers the EDA tools you'll use most: descriptive statistics and visualization.

Step 3: Learning from the data

With a solid understanding of the data, you can apply algorithms to find deeper patterns and make predictions. This is the machine learning part of data science, in which you train a model on your data so that it can generalize to new examples. Chapter 5 walks you through this process.

Step 4: Visualizing

Numbers tell a story, but most people need a picture to see it. Visualization is woven throughout the pipeline, from EDA to model evaluation. A well-constructed chart can reveal in seconds what a table of numbers might obscure completely.

Step 5: Obtaining insights and data products

The pipeline doesn't end until you've extracted something useful such as a decision, a recommendation, a prediction, or a report. The goal is never to produce a model; it's to answer a question or solve a problem. A data product is what gets deployed. Examples of data products include a pricing algorithm, a spam filter, or a dashboard that updates in real time.

The Python Data Science Ecosystem

You may have started learning Python for general programming, or maybe data science was the goal from the start. Either way, you've chosen the right language. Python is the dominant tool in data science for a straightforward reason: Its ecosystem of scientific libraries is unmatched.

Other languages can perform data science tasks. R has deep statistical roots. Julia is fast. MATLAB is widely used in engineering and research. But Python is unique in that it's simultaneously a powerful general-purpose language *and* the best-supported environment for data science. You can write the data pipeline, build the model, create the API that serves predictions, and build the web interface that displays them — all in the same language.

Python's power in data science comes from a collection of specialized libraries you import into your programs. You've already used libraries in Book 2 (the statistics module, datetime, and others). The data science libraries work the same way, just at a much larger scale. This section introduces the main libraries you'll encounter in this minibook.

NumPy

NumPy (`numpy.org`) is the foundation of scientific computing in Python. Its central feature is the *n-dimensional array* (or *ndarray*), which is an efficient and fast data structure for storing and operating on large collections of numbers. Whereas a Python list is flexible but relatively slow when you're doing math on thousands of values, a NumPy array is designed for that kind of work.

NumPy also provides functions for linear algebra, random-number generation, and mathematical operations that can be applied to entire arrays at once. Almost every other data science library is built on top of NumPy.

pandas

pandas (`pandas.pydata.org`) builds on NumPy to provide data structures and analysis tools designed for real-world data. Its central object is the *DataFrame,* which is like a spreadsheet that you can manipulate with Python code. You can load a CSV file into a DataFrame with one line of code. DataFrames make it simple to filter rows, calculate column statistics, handle missing values, merge datasets, and export the result.

If NumPy is the engine, pandas is the dashboard. It's the library you'll use most for day-to-day data work.

Matplotlib

Matplotlib (`matplotlib.org`) is Python's foundational plotting library. It gives you precise control over every element of a chart, including axes, labels, colors, line styles, and legends. With Matplotlib, you can produce publication-quality figures. You'll use Matplotlib in Chapter 4 to visualize your data during exploratory analysis and to communicate findings in Chapter 5.

Scikit-learn

Scikit-learn (`scikit-learn.org`) is the go-to library for machine learning in Python. It provides a consistent, well-designed interface for dozens of algorithms along with tools for evaluating model performance and preparing data. Chapter 5 introduces Scikit-learn and walks you through training your first predictive model.

SciPy

SciPy (`scipy.org`) provides additional scientific computing tools built on NumPy: optimization, integration, signal processing, statistics, and more. You won't use SciPy directly much in this minibook, but it works in the background as part of the ecosystem, and you'll encounter references to it as you go deeper into data science.

REMEMBER

You don't need to master all these libraries at once. This minibook focuses on the ones you'll use every day and introduces them in context, as you need them. By the end of Chapter 5, each of them will feel familiar.

TIP

All the code in this minibook is written for Jupyter Notebook, which you're already familiar with from Book 2. Open a new notebook, and you're ready to go.

Installing the Libraries

Before you move on to Chapter 2, let's make sure you're all set to run Python code. If you followed the steps to install Python, VS Code, and get started with Jupyter Notebook in Book 2, Chapter 1, you're all set. If you haven't set up Python yet, or if it's been a while, visit Chapter 1 of Book 2 now and come back here when you're done.

Do the following to install the libraries:

1. **Open VS Code and download the code for this book at `www.dummies.com/go/codingaiofd3e`.**
2. **Open the Book3 folder, and then open the Chapter 1 file (`chapter_01_what_is_data_science.ipynb`).**
3. **In the Chapter 1 file, find and run the two code cells by clicking the arrow to their left (the execute cell icon).**

   The first code cell installs the libraries you'll learn about in the rest of this minibook. The second one confirms that the libraries are installed and that you're ready to move on to Chapter 2.

   When everything is ready and installed, you'll see the screen shown in Figure 1-1.

```
import sys
import platform

print(f"Python version: {sys.version}")
print(f"Platform:       {platform.platform()}")
print()

packages = ['numpy', 'pandas', 'sklearn', 'matplotlib']

for name in packages:
    try:
        module = __import__(name)
        version = getattr(module, '__version__', 'unknown')
        display_name = 'scikit-learn' if name == 'sklearn' else name
        print(f"{display_name:15}: {version}")
    except ImportError as e:
        print(f"{name:15}: NOT INSTALLED ({e})")
```

```
[2]  ✓ 25.4s                                                    Python

...  Python version: 3.14.4 (main, Apr  7 2026, 13:13:20) [Clang 21.0.0 (clang-2100.0.123.102)]
     Platform:       macOS-26.3.1-arm64-arm-64bit-Mach-O

     numpy          : 2.4.4
     pandas         : 3.0.2
     scikit-learn   : 1.8.0
     matplotlib     : 3.10.8
```

FIGURE 1-1: The libraries are installed!

If you encounter any issues while installing the libraries or running the demo, remember that you can ask your favorite AI assistant for help. Or if you don't mind waiting a bit longer, feel free to email me, and I'll do my best to help. (You'll find my email address in the Introduction.)

IN THIS CHAPTER

» Working with NumPy arrays for fast numerical computing

» Loading and inspecting data with pandas DataFrames

» Looking for messy data

» Cleaning up duplicates and missing values

» Filtering, selecting, and aggregating your data

Chapter 2
Processing Your Data

It is a capital mistake to theorize before one has data. Insensibly one begins to twist facts to suit theories, instead of theories to suit facts.

—ARTHUR CONAN DOYLE

In Book 2, Chapter 6, you learn about storing data in Python using lists, dictionaries, and tuples. These structures work fine for general programming but show their limits when you work with thousands or millions of rows of numbers. They're slow. They require explicit loops. And they weren't designed with mathematical operations in mind.

This chapter introduces two libraries that solve that problem: NumPy and pandas. These are the tools you'll reach for every time you touch data in a professional setting. NumPy gives you fast, compact numerical arrays. pandas builds on top of NumPy to give you the DataFrame — a table-based data structure that makes loading, cleaning, filtering, and summarizing real-world data feel almost effortless.

By the end of this chapter, you'll be able to load a dataset, understand its shape, find and fix problems in it, and pull out the slice of data you need for analysis.

TIP

You don't have to type the source code for this chapter; using the downloadable source is a lot easier. The source code for this chapter is in the `chapter_02_working_with_data.ipynb` file in the Book3 folder at `www.dummies.com/go/codingaiofd3e`.

NumPy: The Foundation of Data Science in Python

NumPy (`numpy.org`), which is short for Numerical Python, is the bedrock library for scientific computing in Python. Almost every other data science library is built on top of it. Understanding what NumPy does and why it matters is the first step in learning about data science with Python.

Arrays versus lists

The core feature of NumPy is the *ndarray*, or *n-dimensional array.* At first glance, ndarray looks like a Python list, but there's a critical difference under the hood.

Python lists can hold anything, including a mix of strings, numbers, and other lists. But that flexibility comes with a cost because Python must check the type of every item each time it processes the list. NumPy arrays, on the other hand, contain elements of a single type. That constraint lets NumPy store the data in a tight block of memory and operate on all of it at once.

ndarrays are fast and concise. The following example shows a comparison between doubling numbers in a list and doubling numbers in a NumPy array:

```
import numpy as np

# Python list approach – requires a loop
values = [1, 2, 3, 4, 5]
doubled = [x * 2 for x in values]
# Output: [2  4  6  8 10]
```

```
# NumPy approach - operates on the whole array at once
arr = np.array([1, 2, 3, 4, 5])
doubled = arr * 2
print(doubled)
# Output: [2  4  6  8 10]
```

The NumPy approach doesn't require a loop. It's just a single operation applied to every element simultaneously. This process, called *vectorization*, is one of the reasons why Python is so popular for writing data science code.

Creating NumPy arrays

You create a NumPy array by passing a Python list (or list of lists) to `np.array()`:

```
import numpy as np

# 1-D array
temps = np.array([72.1, 68.4, 74.5, 70.2, 69.8])

# 2-D array (3 rows, 4 columns)
grid = np.array([[1, 2, 3, 4],
                 [5, 6, 7, 8],
                 [9, 10, 11, 12]])

print(grid.shape)    # (3, 4) - 3 rows, 4 columns
print(grid.dtype)    # int64 - all elements are integers
print(grid.size)     # 12 - total number of elements
```

NumPy also provides shortcuts for creating common arrays:

```
np.zeros((3, 3))        # 3x3 array of zeros
np.ones((2, 5))         # 2x5 array of ones
np.arange(0, 10, 2)     # [0, 2, 4, 6, 8]
np.linspace(0, 1, 5)  # [0.0, 0.25, 0.5, 0.75, 1.0]
```

Basic array math

NumPy makes it easy to apply math functions across an entire dataset at once:

```
arr = np.array([10, 20, 30, 40, 50])

print(arr.mean())   # 30.0
print(arr.sum())    # 150
```

```
print(arr.min())    # 10
print(arr.max())    # 50
print(arr.std())    # Standard deviation: 14.14...
```

These one-liners replace what would otherwise be several lines of loop-based Python. For datasets with millions of rows, an operation takes seconds rather than minutes.

TIP

You'll rarely build NumPy arrays by hand in real data science work. More often, NumPy arrays appear automatically as the underlying structure when you work with pandas DataFrames, Matplotlib plots, or Scikit-learn models. Knowing what a NumPy array is helps you understand what's happening in those higher-level tools.

Creating a DataFrame Using pandas

If NumPy is the engine, pandas (`pandas.pydata.org`) is the dashboard. It takes NumPy's speed and adds the structures and tools you need to work with real-world data: loading files, handling missing values, filtering rows, and summarizing columns.

The two central objects in pandas are:

- **Series:** A one-dimensional labeled array (think of a single column of data)
- **DataFrame:** A two-dimensional labeled table (think of a spreadsheet or a database table)

Most of the time, you'll work with a DataFrame.

One of the simplest ways to create a DataFrame in pandas is by passing a dictionary of lists, where each key represents a column name and its associated values form the data for that column:

```
import pandas as pd

data = {
    'name': ['Alice', 'Bob', 'Carol', 'Dave'],
    'age': [25, 32, 28, 45],
    'score': [88.5, 92.0, 79.5, 85.0]
}
```

```
df = pd.DataFrame(data)
print(df)
Output:
    name  age  score
0  Alice   25   88.5
1    Bob   32   92.0
2  Carol   28   79.5
3   Dave   45   85.0
```

Each column in a DataFrame is a Series. The leftmost column, which contains 0, 1, 2, 3 in the preceding example, is the *index*, which labels each row. You can set the index to any column that makes sense as a row identifier.

In practice, you rarely build DataFrames from dictionaries. Instead, you load them from files. I cover this technique in Chapter 3. For now, you just need to know what a DataFrame looks like so you can work with the examples in this chapter.

Validating Your Data

When you receive a dataset, you can never assume it's clean. Real data comes from databases, spreadsheets, and systems designed by different people at different times, and it shows. Duplicate records, missing values, and inconsistent types are the norm, not the exception. You must always validate your data before analyzing it.

Getting the lay of the land

The first thing to do with any new DataFrame is to ask: What's in here? pandas gives you several tools to find out quickly, as shown in the following example:

```
import pandas as pd

# Load the built-in Titanic dataset for these examples
url = "https://raw.githubusercontent.com/datasciencedojo/
  datasets/master/titanic.csv"
df = pd.read_csv(url)

print(df.shape)   # (891, 12) — 891 rows, 12 columns
print(df.dtypes)  # data type of each column
print(df.head())  # first 5 rows
```

```
print(df.tail())  # last 5 rows
print(df.describe())  # summary statistics for numeric columns
print(df.info())  # column names, types, and non-null counts
```

When you run this code, you see several kinds of output, and each answers a different sanity-check question about your DataFrame. First, `df.shape` shows the DataFrame's *shape* (its dimensions) as a two-item tuple: *(rows, columns)*. In the preceding example, `df.shape` is `(891, 12)`, meaning the dataset has 891 rows (records) and 12 columns (features).

Next, `df.dtypes` prints one line per column, showing the data type assigned by pandas (for example, integers for IDs, floats for prices, and object for text).

After that, `df.head()` and `df.tail()` print previews of the first and last five rows, which help you confirm that the data loaded correctly, the column names look right, and there aren't obvious formatting issues (such as shifted columns, extra header rows, or junk footer lines).

Finally, `df.describe()` prints a table of summary statistics for numeric columns, and `df.info()` prints a compact report showing the DataFrame's columns, data types, and how many values are present (non-null) in each column. The outputs from `df.info()` and from `df.describe()` are especially useful when you want to assess data quality quickly.

The `df.info()` report includes a non-null count for each column. Compare those counts to the total number of rows (from `df.shape`). If the DataFrame has 891 rows but a column only has 200 non-null values, that column is mostly missing, and you'll need to decide whether to fill in those missing values, drop the column, or restrict your analysis to rows where that field exists. Even smaller gaps matter, too: A column with 891 rows but only 880 non-null values can still break calculations or models if you don't handle the missing entries.

The `df.describe()` table helps you spot numeric problems at a glance. Look at `count` first (it should match the total rows for fully populated numeric columns), and then scan `min` and `max` for impossible values (negative ages, fares that are orders of magnitude larger than the rest, and so on). If the mean and the 50% (median) are far apart, the distribution is likely skewed, which may affect how you summarize or model that variable.

Together, `info()` and `describe()` give you a fast way to find the columns that deserve attention before you do any serious analysis: columns with lots of missing values, columns stored as the wrong type (for example, numbers stored as `object`), and columns that contain outliers or suspicious ranges.

Finding and removing duplicates

Duplicate rows are a subtle problem. They silently overweight certain observations, making your analysis treat some data points as more important than they are. pandas makes finding and removing duplicate rows straightforward:

```
import pandas as pd

df = pd.DataFrame(
    {"name": ["Alice", "Bob", "Carol", "Bob"], "score":
  [88.5, 92.0, 79.5, 92.0]}
)

# Find duplicate rows - returns True for duplicates
print(df.duplicated())
# 0    False
# 1    False
# 2    False
# 3     True

# Show only the duplicated rows
print(df[df.duplicated()])

# Remove duplicates, keeping the first occurrence
df_clean = df.drop_duplicates()
print(df_clean)
```

The `drop_duplicates()` method returns a new DataFrame with the duplicate rows removed. The original DataFrame is unchanged unless you assign the result back to `df`.

Creating a data map

Before you dive into analysis, it's worth creating a quick data map. A *data map* is a statistical overview of your dataset that helps you spot potential problems: columns that are mostly missing, variables with suspiciously wide ranges, or features that barely vary.

The `describe()` method gives you a table of summary statistics for each numeric column (count, mean, standard deviation, min, max, and percentiles) at a glance. But you can also use `groupby()` to get statistics broken down by category:

```
import pandas as pd
import numpy as np
```

```
# Load the Titanic dataset
url = "https://raw.githubusercontent.com/datasciencedojo/
   datasets/master/titanic.csv"
df = pd.read_csv(url)

# Group by a categorical column and get stats on a numeric
   column
group_stats = df.groupby("Pclass")["Fare"].describe()
print(group_stats)
```

In this example, `groupby()` groups the *Titanic* passengers by `Pclass` (passenger class: first, second, and third class) and then calculates descriptive statistics for the `Fare` column in each group. In other words, instead of getting one summary of fares for the entire ship, you get three separate summaries (one for each class) so you can compare how ticket prices differ across the categories.

The output you should expect looks like a small table for each class value (1, 2, and 3), with the same fields you saw in `describe()`: count, mean, std, min, 25%, 50% (median), 75%, and max. Think of `group_stats` (the table returned by `groupby(...).describe()`) as a compact profile of the fare distribution for each class — how many fares are present, what a typical fare looks like, and how spread out the values are.

To look for missing data, start with `count`. For each class, `count` tells you how many non-missing fare values were available for that group. If you know a class has, say, 200 passengers but the fare `count` is much lower, that's a strong signal that the `Fare` column is missing values for many passengers in that class. In data science, we use the word *missingness* to refer to the absence of data values in a dataset. You can also compare the counts across classes: if one class has a noticeably smaller count than the others, missingness may be concentrated in that segment of the dataset (which can bias any comparisons you make later).

To look for outliers (or data entry issues), scan `min` and `max` and compare them to the quartiles. If `max` is far above 75%, that group likely contains a small number of unusually high fares. These values could be legitimate (for example, a few very expensive first-class tickets) or a sign of an error (such as a misplaced decimal or mixed currency). `std` (standard deviation) also provides a quick spread check: Very large values relative to the mean usually mean the group has widely varying fares, which is often driven by outliers.

REMEMBER

A data map doesn't tell you that the data is correct. It tells you whether analysis is likely to succeed and where you need to look more closely. Think of a data map as a preflight checklist before your analysis takes off.

Dealing with Missing Data

Missing data is nearly universal in real datasets. A survey respondent left a field blank. A sensor failed for an hour. A database migration left some records incomplete. Whatever the cause, you have to decide what to do about it before you analyze anything.

Finding missing values

pandas represents missing values as `NaN` (not a number). You can think of `NaN` as a special placeholder that means there isn't a value here. If you include a `NaN` in a calculation, the result often becomes `NaN` too, which is why it's important to find and handle missing values before you do math with your data. The `isnull()` method identifies missing values:

```
import pandas as pd
import numpy as np

s = pd.Series([10, 20, np.nan, 40, None])

print(s.isnull())
# 0    False
# 1    False
# 2     True
# 3    False
# 4     True

# Count missing values per column in a DataFrame
print(df.isnull().sum())
```

The last line is one of the most useful single lines in data science, telling you how many values are missing for each column in your DataFrame. That information instantly tells you which columns need attention.

Your three options: Fill, drop, or impute

Once you've found missing values, you have three choices:

- **Drop the rows (or columns) with missing values.** This approach is the simplest and is reasonable when the missing data is a small fraction of the total.

```
df_clean = df.dropna() # drop any row with at least one NaN
df_clean = df.dropna(axis=1) # drop any column with at
  least one NaN
```

- **Fill missing values with a fixed value.** Common choices for a fixed value are the column mean, median, or zero — or a domain-appropriate placeholder such as Unknown for a text column.

```
# Fill a numeric column's NaN values with the column mean
df['Age'] = df['Age'].fillna(df['Age'].mean())

# Fill a text column's NaN values with a placeholder
df['Cabin'] = df['Cabin'].fillna('Unknown')
```

- **Impute using a model.** Scikit-learn's SimpleImputer can replace missing values with the column mean, median, or most frequent value, and it can also add a binary indicator column so your model knows which values were filled in:

```
import numpy as np
import pandas as pd

from sklearn.impute import SimpleImputer

data = pd.DataFrame({"age": [25, np.nan, 32, 41, np.nan,
  28]})

imp = SimpleImputer(strategy="mean")
imp.fit(data)
data_filled = imp.transform(data)
print(data_filled)
```

There's no universally right answer. Dropping rows works when you have plenty of data and few missing values. Filling with the mean is quick but introduces assumptions. Imputation with a model is the most sophisticated approach and tends to produce the best results for machine-learning pipelines.

TIP

Never ignore missing data and hope for the best. Most analysis functions in pandas will simply exclude NaN values by default, which can silently skew your results in ways that are hard to detect later.

Slicing and Dicing: Filtering and Selecting Data

You may not need to work with all the data in a dataset. Perhaps you want to look at a particular column, such as age, or focus only on a set of rows that have all the columns you care about filled in (such as age and fare). You perform two steps to obtain only the data you need to perform a particular task:

1. Filter rows to create a subset of the data that meets the criterion you select (such as all the people between the ages of 5 and 10).
2. Select data columns that contain the data you need to analyze. For example, you probably don't need the individuals' names unless you want to perform some analysis based on name.

The act of slicing and dicing data gives you a subset of the data suitable for analysis. This section describes various ways to obtain specific pieces of data to meet particular needs.

Slicing rows

You can slice data in several ways. In this section, you slice data from a row of 2-D or 3-D data. Suppose that a 2-D array contains temperatures (x-axis) over a specific time frame (y-axis). Slicing a row means seeing the temperatures at a specific time. In a dataset, you can think of each row as one record, such as one customer, one patient, or one day's worth of measurements.

If a 3-D array has an axis for place (x axis), product (y axis), and time (z axis), you could see sales for items over time. If you want to track whether sales of an item are increasing and where they are increasing, you could slice a row, which would show you all the sales for one specific product for all locations at any time:

```
x = np.array(
    [
        [
            [1, 2, 3],
```

```
            [4, 5, 6],
            [7, 8, 9],
        ],
        [
            [11, 12, 13],
            [14, 15, 16],
            [17, 18, 19],
        ],
        [[21, 22, 23], [24, 25, 26], [27, 28, 29]],
    ]
)
x[1]
```

In this case, the example builds a 3-D array. It then slices row 1 of that array to produce the following output:

```
array([[11, 12, 13],
       [14, 15, 16],
       [17, 18, 19]])
```

Slicing columns

Using the examples from the preceding section, slicing columns would obtain data at a 90-degree angle from rows. In other words, when working with the 2-D array, you would want to see the times at which specific temperatures occurred. Likewise, you may want to see the sales of all products for a specific location at any time when working with the 3-D array.

In some cases, you may associate columns with features in a dataset. The following example demonstrates how to perform this task using the same array as in the preceding section:

```
x = np.array(
    [
        [
            [1, 2, 3],
            [4, 5, 6],
            [7, 8, 9],
        ],
        [
            [11, 12, 13],
            [14, 15, 16],
            [17, 18, 19],
```

```
        ],
        [[21, 22, 23], [24, 25, 26], [27, 28, 29]],
    ]
)
x[:, 1]
```

Note that the indexing now occurs at two levels. The first index refers to the row. Using a colon (:) for the row means to use all the rows. The second index refers to a column. In this case, the output will contain column 1:

```
array([[ 4,  5,  6],
       [14, 15, 16],
       [24, 25, 26]])
```

REMEMBER

This is a 3-D array, so each column contains all the z-axis elements. What you see is every row — 0 through 2 for column 1 with every z-axis element 0 through 2 for that column.

Dicing

Dicing a dataset means to perform both row and column slicing such that you end up with a data wedge. For example, when working with the 3-D array, you may want to see the sales of a specific product in a specific location at any time. The following example performs this task using the same array as in the previous two sections:

```
x = np.array([[[1, 2, 3], [4, 5, 6], [7, 8, 9],],
              [[11,12,13], [14,15,16], [17,18,19],],
              [[21,22,23], [24,25,26], [27,28,29]]])
print(x[1,1])
print(x[:,1,1])
print(x[1,:,1])
print(f"\n{x[1:2, 1:2]}")
```

This example dices the array in four ways. First, you get row 1, column 1. Of course, what you may want is column 1, z axis 1. If that's not quite right, you could always request row 1, z axis 1 instead. Then again, you may want rows 1 and 2 of columns 1 and 2. Here's the output of all four requests:

```
[14 15 16]
[ 5 15 25]
[12 15 18]
[[[14 15 16]]]
```

Aggregating Data

Aggregation means combining multiple rows into summary statistics. You can aggregate across a dataset or within groups. It's one of the most frequent operations in exploratory data analysis.

Simple column statistics

The following code example shows how to compute quick, descriptive statistics for each column in a dataset. Using a small helper routine, you summarize numeric fields with common measures (such as count, mean, standard deviation, minimum/maximum, and percentiles) so you can validate data quality and get an at-a-glance sense of scale and distribution before deeper analysis:

```
print(df['Fare'].mean())     # average fare
print(df['Age'].median())    # median age
print(df['Survived'].sum()) # total survivors (1s)
print(df['Pclass'].value_counts()) # count of each class
```

Grouping and aggregating

The real power of pandas aggregation comes from `groupby()`. It splits the DataFrame into groups based on a column's values, and then applies a function to each group:

```
# Average fare by passenger class
print(df.groupby('Pclass')['Fare'].mean())
# Survival rate by sex
print(df.groupby('Sex')['Survived'].mean())
# Multiple stats at once
print(df.groupby('Pclass')['Age'].agg(['mean', 'median',
   'count']))
```

Output from the survival rate by sex:

```
Sex
female    0.742038
male      0.188908
Name: Survived, dtype: float64
```

In just two lines of code, you can see a striking pattern: Women survived at nearly four times the rate of men on the *Titanic*. That's the value of aggregation — it reveals meaningful differences between groups without the need to manually scan or sort rows.

Putting It Together

Here's a short end-to-end example that uses everything from this chapter on a real dataset:

```
import pandas as pd
import numpy as np

# Load the data
url ="https://raw.githubusercontent.com/datasciencedojo/
  datasets/master/titanic.csv"
df = pd.read_csv(url)

# 1. Get the lay of the land
print(f"Shape: {df.shape}")
print(f"\nMissing values:\n{df.isnull().sum()}")

# 2. Drop duplicates
df = df.drop_duplicates()

# 3. Handle missing values
df['Age'] = df['Age'].fillna(df['Age'].median())
df['Embarked'] = df['Embarked'].fillna('S')  # most common port
df = df.drop(columns=['Cabin'])  # too many missing to be useful

# 4. Select the columns we care about
df = df[['Survived', 'Pclass', 'Sex', 'Age', 'Fare']]

# 5. Aggregate: survival rate by class
print("\nSurvival rate by passenger class:")
print(df.groupby('Pclass')['Survived'].mean().round(2))
```

And here's the output:

```
Shape: (891, 12)

Missing values:
```

```
Age          177
Cabin        687
Embarked       2
...

Survival rate by passenger class:
Pclass
1    0.63
2    0.47
3    0.24
Name: Survived, dtype: float64
```

In under 20 lines of code, you load data, check what is in the data, handle missing values, and then narrow the DataFrame to the relevant columns for your analysis. You'll do this type of data-cleaning and exploration workflow at the start of every data science project.

TIP

pandas has a one-page cheat sheet covering the most common operations and maintained by the official documentation team at `pandas.pydata.org/Pandas_Cheat_Sheet.pdf`. It's one of the most-referenced documents in all of data science, so it's worthwhile to print it or keep it open in a browser tab.

IN THIS CHAPTER

» Using Scikit-learn's built-in datasets for instant practice data

» Loading the many formats of data

» Working with large datasets

Chapter 3
Getting Your Data

Truth is stranger than fiction, but it is because Fiction is obliged to stick to possibilities; Truth isn't.

—MARK TWAIN

Before you can clean, explore, or model data, you have to get it into Python. That sounds obvious, but in practice it's one of the first places new data scientists get stuck. Where does the data come from? How do you get it into a DataFrame? What if the file is on a server, not on your computer?

This chapter answers those questions. You learn to load data from the most common sources — Scikit-learn's built-in practice datasets, CSV files, Excel spreadsheets, tab-delimited text files, and URLs on the web. Along the way, you'll also see how to take a manageable sample from a dataset that's too large to work with all at once.

REMEMBER

Data scientists use the word *features* for what a spreadsheet user would call *columns*, and *cases* (or observations) for what they'd call *rows*. Both terms refer to the same thing: Features are the variables that describe each item in your dataset, and cases are the individual items themselves.

Using Scikit-learn's Built-In Datasets

The fastest way to get data into Python is to load a dataset that's already there. Scikit-learn is a machine-learning library that ships with a collection of small, clean, ready-to-use datasets called *toy datasets.* They're complex enough for meaningful practice but small enough to run quickly on any computer.

These datasets are ideal for learning because they require no file management, no internet connection, and no cleanup. One line of code and your data is ready.

Iris dataset

The Iris dataset is one of the most famous in all of machine learning. It contains measurements of 150 iris flowers across three species, with four features per flower: sepal length, sepal width, petal length, and petal width. This is a classification problem. Can you predict the species from the measurements?

```
from sklearn.datasets import load_iris

iris = load_iris()

print(type(iris))          # Bunch - a dictionary-like object
print(iris.feature_names)  # ['sepal length (cm)', 'sepal width
                             (cm)', ...]
print(iris.target_names)   # ['setosa', 'versicolor',
                             'virginica']
print(iris.data.shape)     # (150, 4) - 150 rows, 4 features
```

Scikit-learn datasets come back as Bunch objects — essentially dictionaries with named attributes. The data lives in `iris.data` (a NumPy array of features) and `iris.target` (a NumPy array of labels). To work with Bunch objects using pandas, convert them to a DataFrame:

```
import pandas as pd
from sklearn.datasets import load_iris

iris = load_iris()

df = pd.DataFrame(iris.data, columns=iris.feature_names)
df['species'] = iris.target
print(df.head())
```

The preceding code displays the first five cases (also known as rows) from the iris dataset, as shown in Figure 3-1.

```
   sepal length (cm)  sepal width (cm)  petal length (cm)  petal width (cm)  \
0                5.1               3.5                1.4               0.2
1                4.9               3.0                1.4               0.2
2                4.7               3.2                1.3               0.2
3                4.6               3.1                1.5               0.2
4                5.0               3.6                1.4               0.2

   species
0        0
1        0
2        0
3        0
4        0
```

FIGURE 3-1: The first five cases from Scikit-learn's iris dataset.

Other useful built-in datasets

Scikit-learn includes several other datasets worth knowing:

```
from sklearn.datasets import (load_diabetes, fetch_california_
  housing, load_breast_cancer, load_wine)

# Regression: predict disease progression from health metrics
diabetes = load_diabetes()

# Regression: predict California house prices
housing = fetch_california_housing()

# Classification: predict whether a tumor is malignant or benign
cancer = load_breast_cancer()

# Classification: predict wine variety from chemical composition
wine = load_wine()
```

Each loads with the same pattern: `.data` for features, `.target` for labels, `.feature_names` for column names, and `.DESCR` for a full description of the dataset.

To see the full documentation for a dataset, print its DESCR attribute:

```
print(housing.DESCR)  # prints a detailed description of the
   dataset
```

TIP

When you're experimenting with a new technique or algorithm, always start with a clean built-in dataset. It removes all the uncertainty about whether problems in your results come from the code or from messy data. Once the technique is working on clean data, move to your real dataset.

Loading Other Types of Files and URLs

Built-in datasets are great for practice, but real-world projects usually start with a file (or a link) someone hands you. In this section, you learn the core pandas tools for getting data into a DataFrame from common sources: CSV files, Excel workbooks, tab-delimited text files, and data hosted on the web (including JSON from simple APIs). By the end, you'll be able to take nearly any "Here's the data" input and turn it into something you can clean, explore, and model.

Loading CSV files

Outside of built-in datasets, the comma-separated values (CSV) file is the most common data format you'll encounter. It's a plain text file in which each row is a record and fields are separated by commas. Almost every database, spreadsheet application, and data repository can export to CSV.

pandas reads CSV files with a single function: read_csv(). The following code shows how to read a CSV file:

```
import pandas as pd

df = pd.read_csv('titanic.csv')
print(df.shape)   # (891, 12)
print(df.head())
```

pandas automatically treats the first row as a header, assigns an integer index, and infers each column's data type. That's the default behavior, and it works correctly for most well-formed CSV files.

However, CSV files are rarely perfectly formatted. For example, you may get a CSV file that has semicolons instead of commas, or that doesn't specify names for the columns. To adjust the way `read_csv()` imports your CSV file, you can pass options to it. Here are the options you'll use most often:

```
# File uses semicolons instead of commas
df = pd.read_csv('data.csv', sep=';')

# First column should be the row index
df = pd.read_csv('data.csv', index_col=0)

# File has no header row - provide column names manually
df = pd.read_csv('data.csv', header=None,
                 names=['age', 'income', 'label'])

# Read only certain columns
df = pd.read_csv('data.csv', usecols=['age', 'income'])

# Specify what strings represent missing values
df = pd.read_csv('data.csv', na_values=['N/A', 'missing', '-'])

# Read only the first 1,000 rows (useful for previewing large
  files)
df = pd.read_csv('data.csv', nrows=1000)
```

After loading, always call `df.info()` and `df.describe()` to confirm that the data loaded as expected. Check that the column types are correct, that missing values were detected, and that the number of rows and columns matches what you anticipated.

TIP

If `read_csv()` raises an encoding error, which can occur with files created on older Windows systems, add `encoding='latin-1'` or `encoding='utf-8-sig'` as a parameter. Encoding problems are common with exported data from legacy systems.

Loading Excel files

Excel files are ubiquitous in business settings. Unlike CSV, they can contain multiple worksheets, formatted cells, formulas, and charts. However, pandas reads only the data and ignores all formatting.

The simplest way to read an Excel file is to use `pd.read_excel()`:

```
import pandas as pd

# Read the first sheet by default
df = pd.read_excel('sales_data.xlsx')

# Read a specific sheet by name
df = pd.read_excel('sales_data.xlsx', sheet_name='Q3')

# Read a specific sheet by position (0-indexed)
df = pd.read_excel('sales_data.xlsx', sheet_name=1)

# Read all sheets - returns a dictionary of DataFrames
all_sheets = pd.read_excel('sales_data.xlsx', sheet_name=None)
print(all_sheets.keys())  # dict_keys(['Q1', 'Q2', 'Q3', 'Q4'])
df_q1 = all_sheets['Q1']
```

For large Excel files you'll access multiple times, opening the file once and parsing sheets as needed is more efficient:

```
xls = pd.ExcelFile('sales_data.xlsx')
df = xls.parse('Q3', index_col=None, na_values=['NA'])
```

TIP

To read .xlsx files, you may need the openpyxl library installed (`pip install openpyxl`). For older .xls files, install xlrd instead (`pip install xlrd`). If you're not sure which format you have, check the file extension. The modern Excel file format uses the .xlsx extension.

Loading tab-delimited text files

Some data files, such as those from databases and older statistical software, use tabs (rather than commas) to separate fields. pandas can read these tab-delimited text files with `read_table()` (where tabs are the default separator) or with `read_csv()` by setting `sep='\t'` to tell pandas that the columns are separated by tab characters. The following code shows the syntax for each method:

```
import pandas as pd

# Using read_table() - tab is the default separator
df = pd.read_table('data.txt')
```

```
# Equivalent using read_csv() with explicit separator
df = pd.read_csv('data.txt', sep='\t')

print(df)
```

Both approaches produce the same result: a DataFrame with the first row treated as a header and each tab-delimited field as a column.

Loading data from the web

You don't always need to download a file before loading it. `pd.read_csv()` accepts a URL directly. As long as the URL points to a raw CSV file, pandas fetches and loads it in one step:

```
import pandas as pd

url = "https://raw.githubusercontent.com/datasciencedojo/
  datasets/master/titanic.csv"
df = pd.read_csv(url)
print(df.shape)  # (891, 12)
```

This approach is useful with data repositories like GitHub, government open data portals, and dataset hosting sites. Many public datasets are available as direct CSV links.

If your data comes from a web API and the response is formatted as JSON instead of CSV, pandas can handle that as well:

```
import pandas as pd

# Read a JSON API response directly into a DataFrame
url ="https://data.cityofchicago.org/resource/ijzp-q8t2.json"
df = pd.read_json(url)
```

For more complex API interactions, such as authentication, pagination, or adding request headers, you typically use the requests library to fetch the data first and then parse it into a DataFrame.

REMEMBER

When loading data from the web, be mindful of file size. Calling `pd.read_csv(url)` downloads the entire file before doing anything with it. For large remote files, it's better to download them locally first and then load from disk. This approach is faster and prevents re-downloading the file each time you run the code.

Sampling Large Datasets

Sometimes a dataset is simply too large to work with all at once, either because it's slow to process or because your computer doesn't have enough memory to hold it. In that situation, taking a representative sample lets you develop and test your analysis on a manageable subset before scaling up.

The easiest way to sample a DataFrame is with the built-in `sample()` method:

```
import pandas as pd

df = pd.read_csv('large_dataset.csv')

# Take a random sample of 1,000 rows
sample = df.sample(n=1000, random_state=42)

# Take a random 10% of rows
sample = df.sample(frac=0.1, random_state=42)

print(sample.shape)
```

The `random_state` parameter seeds the random-number generator so that you get the same sample every time you run the code. This is important for reproducibility — if your results changed each time you ran the code due to a different sample, it would become difficult to debug your analysis or share it with others.

For very large files that don't fit in memory, you can use `read_csv()` to load the files in chunks:

```
# Load 10,000 rows at a time, process each chunk separately
chunk_list = []
for chunk in pd.read_csv('huge_file.csv', chunksize=10000):
# Do some processing on each chunk
    filtered = chunk[chunk['value'] > 0]
    chunk_list.append(filtered)

# Combine all processed chunks
df = pd.concat(chunk_list)
```

Processing a large file in chunks and then concatenating the results is a standard technique for handling data that exceeds available memory.

CHOOSING THE RIGHT LOADING METHOD

Data Source	Function	Notes
Scikit-learn built-in	`load_iris()`, `fetch_california_housing()`, and so on	Best for learning and experimentation
CSV file (local or URL)	`pd.read_csv()`	Most common; handles many separators
Excel file	`pd.read_excel()`	Specify sheet name if using multiple sheets
Tab-delimited text	`pd.read_table()` or `pd.read_csv(sep='\t')`	Common database export format
JSON (API or file)	`pd.read_json()`	Common for web APIs
SQL database	`pd.read_sql()`	Requires a database connection

Once your data is in a DataFrame, the workflow is the same regardless of where it came from. You should validate the data, clean it, explore it, and model it. The source matters only during the loading step.

IN THIS CHAPTER

- » Understanding the Exploratory Data Analysis (EDA) philosophy
- » Summarizing numeric data with key descriptive measures
- » Plotting with Matplotlib basics
- » Matching questions to appropriate chart types
- » Quantifying correlations between variables

Chapter 4
Exploring Data Analysis

The combination of some data and an aching desire for an answer does not ensure that a reasonable answer can be extracted from a given body of data.

—JOHN TUKEY

In Chapter 3, you learn how to get data into Python. In Chapter 5, you train a machine-learning model. But there's a step between those two that data scientists take every time, without exception, before touching any algorithm: exploratory data analysis, or EDA.

EDA is the process of understanding your data before you attempt to model it. You examine distributions, identify anomalies, explore relationships between variables, and develop hypotheses, using a combination of summary statistics and visualization.

The process sounds straightforward, but you'll often encounter surprises: variables that turn out to be much more correlated than expected, outliers that can sabotage a model, or patterns that point to a different analytical approach than you originally planned.

This chapter introduces the tools and mindset of EDA, centered on two Python libraries: pandas for computing statistics and Matplotlib for visualizing them.

REMEMBER

You don't have to type the source code for this chapter; using the downloadable source is a lot easier. The source code for this chapter appears in the `chapter_04_exploring_and_visualizing.ipynb` file, which you can download at `www.dummies.com/go/codingaiofd3e`.

The EDA Philosophy

EDA was developed at Bell Labs by the statistician John Tukey, who wanted to promote exploration of data based on the data itself, rather than testing assumptions that were formed before the data was collected. His argument was that looking at the data openly, without preconceptions, leads to better questions and ultimately better science.

That spirit translates directly to modern data science. Before running any algorithm, you want to:

- Describe your variables (central tendency, spread, distribution shape)
- Understand relationships between variables
- Spot unusual values or unexpected patterns
- Identify which variables are likely to be useful for prediction and which are redundant

The purpose of EDA is not to deliver a final outcome; instead, it guides every decision that comes afterward. Training a model without EDA is simply guessing, while training a model after careful EDA means making an informed decision.

REMEMBER

GIGO, or garbage in, garbage out, is the oldest saying in data science. Even the most advanced algorithm will produce useless results if the data being used contains uncorrected issues. EDA helps you find and address these problems before they affect your analysis.

Defining Descriptive Statistics for Numeric Data

The first action to take with the data is to produce synthetic measures to determine what is going on with it. You can start by calculating a few simple summary numbers, such as the maximum and minimum values, and then use those to choose sensible ranges (also known as *intervals*) to explore.

During your exploration, you use a simple but useful dataset, the Palmer Penguins dataset. Dr. Kristen Gorman and the Palmer Station Long-Term Ecological Research (LTER) program collected this dataset in the Palmer Archipelago, Antarctica. The dataset contains detailed information about three species of penguins: Adélie, Gentoo, and Chinstrap. It includes various measurements, such as the penguins' bill length, bill depth, body mass, and flipper length. You can load it by using the following code, which will select a few variables:

```
import numpy as np
import pandas as pd

def load_palmer_penguins(no_missing=True):
    url = "https://raw.githubusercontent.com/"
    url += "allisonhorst/palmerpenguins/main/"
    url += "inst/extdata/penguins.csv"
    numeric_features = [
        "bill_length_mm", "bill_depth_mm",
        "flipper_length_mm", "body_mass_g"]
    target = ["species"]
    data = pd.read_csv(url)
    if no_missing:
        data = data.dropna()
    return data[numeric_features + target]

penguins = load_palmer_penguins(no_missing=True)
```

Having loaded the Palmer Penguins dataset into a pandas DataFrame, as a last preparatory activity before starting data exploration, you can check your pandas and NumPy versions:

```
print(f"Your pandas version is: {pd.__version__}")
print(f"Your NumPy version is {np.__version__}")
```

REMEMBER

NumPy, Scikit-learn, and especially pandas are under constant development, so it's a good idea to check the product version numbers before you start working with EDA. Using an older or a newer version could cause your output to differ from that shown in the book or cause some commands to fail. I'm using pandas version 3.0.2 and NumPy version 2.4.4.

TIP

This chapter presents a series of pandas and NumPy commands that help you explore the structure of data. Even though applying single explorative commands grants you more freedom in your analysis, it's nice to know that you can obtain most of these statistics using the `describe()` method applied to your `pandas` DataFrame; for example, you might use `print(penguins.describe())` when you're in a hurry in your data science project.

Measuring central tendency

When starting EDA, the first measures to calculate for numeric variables are the mean and median. They can provide an estimate when the variables are centered and somewhat symmetric.

Using pandas, you can quickly compute both the means and median. Here is the command for getting the mean from the penguins `DataFrame`:

```
print(penguins.mean(numeric_only=True))
```

Here is the resulting output for the mean statistic:

```
bill_length_mm          43.992793
bill_depth_mm           17.164865
flipper_length_mm      200.966967
body_mass_g           4207.057057
dtype: float64
```

Similarly, here is the command that will output the median:

```
print(penguins.median(numeric_only=True))
```

You then obtain the median estimates for all the variables:

```
bill_length_mm          44.5
bill_depth_mm           17.3
flipper_length_mm      197.0
body_mass_g           4050.0
dtype: float64
```

The *median* provides the central position in the series of values. When creating a variable, the median is less influenced by anomalous cases or by an asymmetric distribution of values around the mean. What you should note here is that the mean is not centered (no variable is zero mean) and the median of body mass is different from the mean, which requires further inspection.

When checking for central tendency measures, you should

- » Verify whether the means are zero
- » Check whether the means are different from each other
- » Note whether the median is different from the mean

Measuring variance and range

As a next step, you should check the variance by using its square root, the standard deviation. The standard deviation is as informative as the variance, but comparing to the mean is easier because it's expressed in the same unit of measure. The *standard deviation* is a good indicator of whether a mean is a suitable indicator of the variable distribution because it tells you how the values of a variable distribute around the mean. The higher the standard deviation, the farther you can expect some values to appear from the mean.

To see how spread out each measurement is, use `std()` to compute the standard deviation for the numeric columns:

```
print(penguins.std(numeric_only=True))
```

Following is the printed output for each variable:

```
bill_length_mm          5.468668
bill_depth_mm           1.969235
flipper_length_mm      14.015765
body_mass_g           805.215802
dtype: float64
```

You should also check the *range*, which is the difference between the maximum and minimum values for each quantitative variable. The range tells you the difference in scale among variables:

```
print(penguins.max(numeric_only=True)
      - penguins.min(numeric_only=True))
```

Here is the output of the preceding command:

```
bill_length_mm         27.5
bill_depth_mm           8.4
flipper_length_mm      59.0
body_mass_g          3600.0
dtype: float64
```

For `body_mass_g`, the range is 3,600g — from the lightest penguin at 2,700g to the heaviest at 6,300g. That range is more than double. Combined with the mean-median difference, the wide body-mass range and the mean-median gap strongly suggest that the dataset contains meaningfully different groups. Time to look at the data visually.

Getting Started with Matplotlib

Matplotlib is Python's foundational plotting library. It's widely used for creating a variety of static, animated, and interactive visualizations. It serves as the backbone for many other plotting libraries and is a standard tool for data visualization tasks in the Python ecosystem. With Matplotlib, you can generate everything from simple line charts and bar graphs to complex heatmaps and 3D plots, making it highly versatile for both beginners and advanced users.

To use Matplotlib, you first need to ensure that it is installed in your Python environment. If you're working in a Jupyter Notebook or a Python script, you can install Matplotlib using `pip`, the Python package installer. Open your terminal or command prompt, and run the following command:

```
pip install matplotlib
```

After installation, you will be able to import the library and start creating plots. Matplotlib's flexibility means that you can customize nearly every aspect of your plots, including colors, labels, and figure sizes, which are essential for producing publication-quality graphics.

Once Matplotlib is installed, you can import it. The standard import pattern looks like this:

```
import matplotlib.pyplot as plt
%matplotlib inline
```

The %matplotlib inline line is a Jupyter Notebook command that renders plots directly in the notebook rather than in a separate window. Almost every Matplotlib script you'll ever write will start with these two lines.

Your first plot

Time to create your first plot. The following code creates a simple line plot showing values from a list of numbers:

```
values = [1, 5, 8, 9, 2, 0, 3, 10, 4, 7]

plt.plot(range(1, 11), values)
plt.xlabel('Entry')
plt.ylabel('Value')
plt.title('My First Plot')
plt.show()
```

The process of creating a plot usually follows a clear sequence: You define your data, use a plot function, add labels, and then call `plt.show()`. Although `xlabel()`, `ylabel()`, and `title()` aren't required for the code to run, you should almost always include them. Labels turn a picture into a readable chart by telling your audience what each axis represents and what they're looking at; without them, even a correct plot is easy to misinterpret.

Figure 4-1 shows the chart that results from this code.

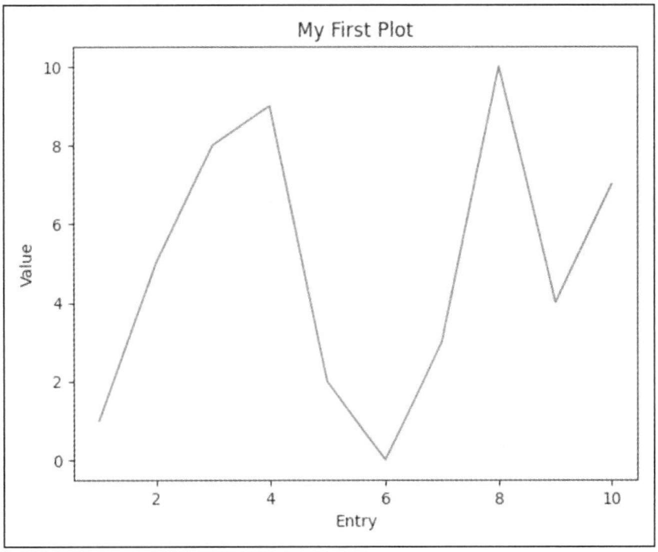

FIGURE 4-1: Your first plot.

Multiple lines and legends

When visualizing data, it's common to compare multiple series in the same chart to explore relationships or trends. Matplotlib makes this easy. You can plot several lines by calling `plt.plot()` multiple times, each with its own data and label.

To distinguish the different lines, you can add a legend that automatically identifies each series. The following plots two data sets in one figure and displays a legend for clarity:

```
values1 = [1, 5, 8, 9, 2, 0, 3, 10, 4, 7]
values2 = [3, 8, 9, 2, 1, 2, 4, 7, 6, 6]

plt.plot(range(1, 11), values1, label='Series A')
plt.plot(range(1, 11), values2, label='Series B')
plt.legend()
plt.show()
```

Each call to `plt.plot()` adds another line. Adding `label=` to each call and then calling `plt.legend()` generates a legend. This is the pattern for any multiline chart. The chart produced by this code is shown in Figure 4-2.

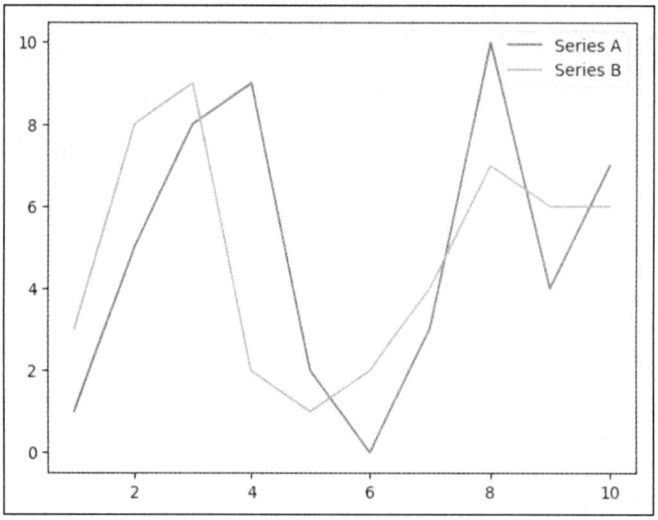

FIGURE 4-2: Plotting multiple series.

Saving your work

When you need to save a copy of your work for later reference or to use it as part of a larger report, you use the `plt.savefig()` function, as shown in the following code:

```
import matplotlib.pyplot as plt
%matplotlib auto

values = [1, 5, 8, 9, 2, 0, 3, 10, 4, 7]
plt.plot(range(1,11), values)
plt.ioff()
plt.savefig('MySamplePlot.png', format='png')
```

In this case, you must provide a minimum of two inputs. The first input is the filename. You may optionally include a path for saving the file. The second input is the file format. In this case, the example saves the file in Portable Network Graphic (PNG) format, but you have other options: Portable Document Format (PDF), Postscript (PS), Encapsulated Postscript (EPS), and Scalable Vector Graphics (SVG).

REMEMBER

Note the presence of the `%matplotlib auto` command. This call removes the inline display of the graph. You have options for other Matplotlib backends, depending on which version of Python and Matplotlib you use. For example, some developers prefer the `notebook` backend to the `inline` backend because it provides additional functionality. However, to use the `notebook` backend, you must also restart the kernel, and you may not always see what you expect. To see the backend list, use the `%matplotlib -l` command. In addition, calling `plt.ioff()` turns plot interaction off.

Choosing the Right Chart

Different data and different questions call for different chart types. Here are the four you'll use most in EDA:

- Bar charts
- Histograms
- Boxplots
- Scatterplots

This section explains how to use Matplotlib to create each type of chart.

Bar charts: Comparing categories

Bar charts are the right choice when you want to compare a numeric value across categories. The following example creates a bar chart comparing the average body mass of penguins by species:

```
# Average body mass by species
species_mass = penguins.groupby('species')['body_mass_g'].mean()

plt.bar(species_mass.index, species_mass.values,
  color=['steelblue', 'coral', 'mediumseagreen'])
plt.xlabel('Species')
plt.ylabel('Average Body Mass (g)')
plt.title('Average Body Mass by Penguin Species')
plt.show()
```

The output from this code is shown in Figure 4-3.

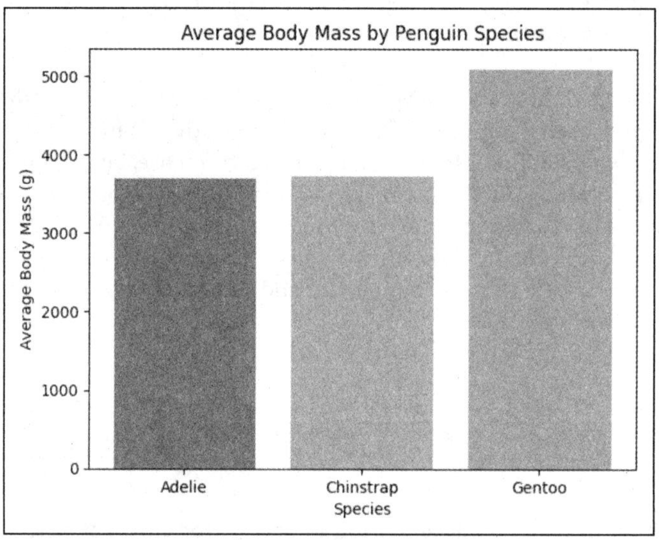

FIGURE 4-3: A bar chart.

You can immediately see that Gentoo penguins are substantially heavier than Adélie or Chinstrap — confirming the hunch that different species were pulling the overall mean upward.

Histograms: Showing distributions

Histograms show how values are distributed across a range. They divide data into *bins* (value ranges) and count how many observations fall in each bin. Use them when you want to understand the shape of a single variable. For example:

```
plt.hist(penguins['body_mass_g'], bins=30, color='steelblue',
   edgecolor='white')
plt.xlabel('Body Mass (g)')
plt.ylabel('Count')
plt.title('Distribution of Penguin Body Mass')
plt.show()
```

Figure 4-4 shows the resulting histogram.

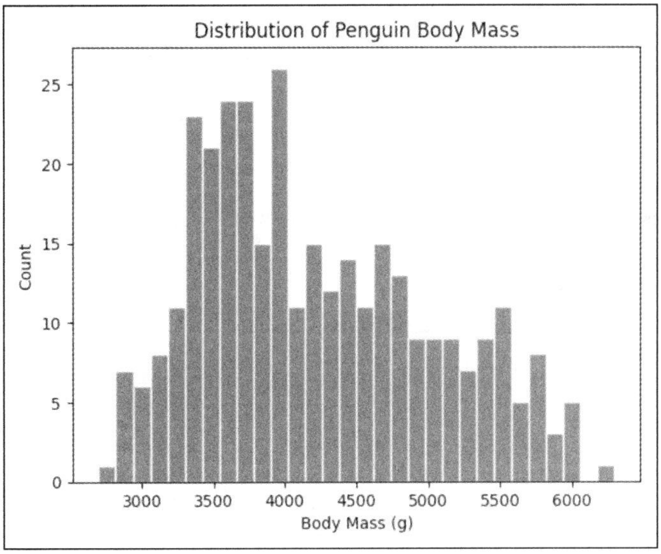

FIGURE 4-4: Histograms show distributions.

The resulting histogram reveals something interesting: The distribution has two visible peaks, rather than a single bell curve. These peaks are a strong signal that the data has distinct subgroups — exactly what you'd expect if different species have very different body masses.

TIP

The number of bins matters. Too few and the histogram looks like a few tall bars that hide the distribution's shape; too many and you get a noisy, spiky chart. Experiment with different values: 20 to 40 bins is a reasonable starting range for most datasets.

Boxplots: Comparing group distributions

A *boxplot* shows the distribution of a variable at a glance. The box spans the 25th to 75th percentile (the *interquartile range*, or IQR), the line through the middle is the median, the *whiskers* (the lines that extend from the box to show the typical low and high values) extend to 1.5× the IQR, and individual dots beyond the whiskers are potential outliers.

Boxplots really shine when you want to compare a distribution across groups:

```
# Separate body mass values by species
adelie = penguins[penguins['species'] =='Adelie']['body_mass_g']
chinstrap = penguins[penguins['species'] =='Chinstrap']
    ['body_mass_g']
gentoo = penguins[penguins['species'] =='Gentoo']['body_mass_g']

plt.boxplot([adelie, chinstrap, gentoo],
            tick_labels=['Adélie', 'Chinstrap', 'Gentoo'])
plt.ylabel('Body Mass (g)')
plt.title('Body Mass Distribution by Species')
plt.show()
```

The boxplot created by this code is shown in Figure 4-5.

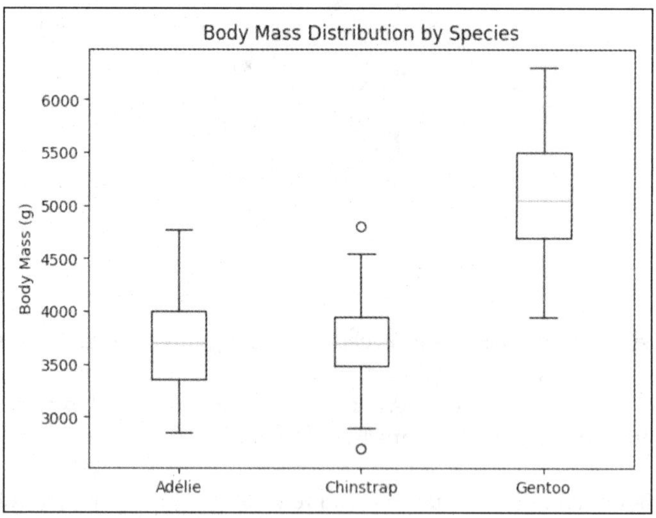

FIGURE 4-5: Boxplots compare distributions across groups.

The three boxplots side by side tell a clear story: Adélie and Chinstrap penguins have similar overlapping body mass distributions, while Gentoo penguins are substantially heavier, with barely any overlap. Any points outside the whiskers are flagged as potential outliers, meaning they represent individual penguins that are unusually large or small compared to others in their species.

REMEMBER

Outliers shown in a boxplot are not necessarily errors. They are unusual values that deserve closer inspection. Some may be data entry mistakes, while others are genuine extreme observations that are scientifically meaningful. You should never delete outliers.

Scatterplots: Exploring relationships between variables

A *scatterplot* places each observation as a point on a two-dimensional plane, with one variable on each axis. The pattern of points reveals whether and how the two variables relate to each other. For example:

```
# Color each point by species
palette = {'Adelie': 'steelblue', 'Gentoo': 'coral',
           'Chinstrap': 'mediumseagreen'}
colors = [palette[s] for s in penguins['species']]

plt.scatter(penguins['bill_length_mm'],
            penguins['flipper_length_mm'],
            c=colors, alpha=0.6)
plt.xlabel('Bill Length (mm)')
plt.ylabel('Flipper Length (mm)')
plt.title('Bill Length vs. Flipper Length by Species')
plt.show()
```

Figure 4-6 shows the result of running this code.

The color-coded scatterplot reveals something striking: The three species form visually distinct clusters. Gentoo penguins (orange) cluster in the upper right, showing longer bills and longer flippers. Adélie penguins (blue) cluster in the lower left. Chinstrap penguins (green) sit in between, with longer bills but shorter flippers than Gentoo.

The fact that the scatterplot separates the three species into distinct clusters is a critical EDA finding: It shows that bill length and flipper length are both useful features for distinguishing species. This kind of insight guides which features to select before training a model. Never select features automatically without first understanding what they represent.

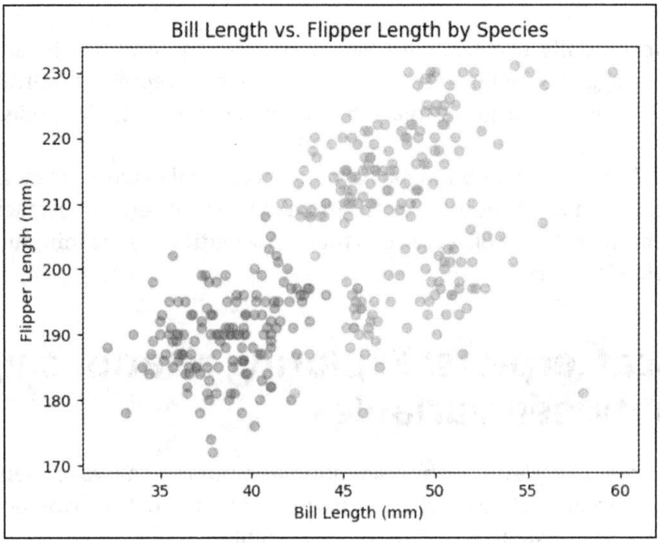

FIGURE 4-6: Scatterplots reveal relationships.

Measuring Correlations

Visualization reveals patterns, but you also want to quantify relationships between variables. *Correlation* measures how strongly two variables move together, on a scale from –1 (perfectly inverse) to +1 (perfectly proportional). A correlation near 0 means the variables move independently.

pandas calculates every pair of numeric columns (also known as the *full correlation matrix*) in one line:

```
print(penguins.select_dtypes('number').corr().round(2))
```

The output from the preceding code is shown in Figure 4-7.

The correlation between `flipper_length_mm` and `body_mass_g` is 0.87, which is very strong. Larger penguins tend to have larger flippers. The strong negative correlations between `bill_depth_mm` and the other measurements should also be examined, since this is likely due to species differences. Each species appears to have distinct bill proportions.

TIP

Squaring a correlation coefficient gives you the percentage of variation in one variable that is explained by the other. A correlation of 0.87 means that roughly 76% (0.87^2) of the variation in body mass is shared with flipper length — a remarkably strong relationship.

Calculating the full correlation matrix

```
print(penguins.select_dtypes('number').corr().round(2))
```

[17] Python

```
                   bill_length_mm  bill_depth_mm  flipper_length_mm  \
bill_length_mm               1.00          -0.23               0.65
bill_depth_mm               -0.23           1.00              -0.58
flipper_length_mm            0.65          -0.58               1.00
body_mass_g                  0.59          -0.47               0.87

                   body_mass_g
bill_length_mm            0.59
bill_depth_mm            -0.47
flipper_length_mm         0.87
body_mass_g               1.00
```

FIGURE 4-7: The correlation matrix for the Penguin dataset.

Numbers are useful, but a heatmap makes patterns in the correlation matrix immediately visible.

A *heatmap* is a visual representation of data where values are depicted by color. In the context of a correlation matrix, a heatmap uses varying shades to show the strength and direction of relationships between pairs of variables. Darker or more intense colors often indicate stronger correlations, while lighter colors reveal weaker relationships. This shading makes it much easier to spot patterns and trends compared to scanning through rows of numbers. For example:

```
import matplotlib.pyplot as plt
import numpy as np

corr = penguins.select_dtypes('number').corr()
fig, ax = plt.subplots(figsize=(6, 5))
im = ax.imshow(corr, cmap='coolwarm', vmin=-1, vmax=1)
plt.colorbar(im)

labels = corr.columns
ax.set_xticks(range(len(labels)))
ax.set_yticks(range(len(labels)))
ax.set_xticklabels(labels, rotation=45, ha='right', fontsize=9)
ax.set_yticklabels(labels, fontsize=9)

# Annotate each cell with its correlation value
for i in range(len(labels)):
    for j in range(len(labels)):
        ax.text(j, i, f'{corr.iloc[i, j]:.2f}',
                ha='center', va='center', fontsize=8)
```

```
plt.title('Correlation Matrix – Palmer Penguins')
plt.tight_layout()
plt.show()
```

Figure 4-8 shows the heatmap that results from this code.

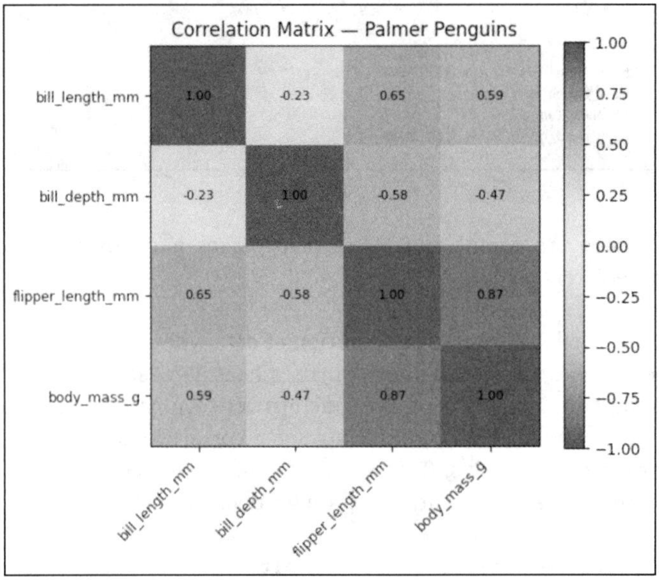

FIGURE 4-8: Visualizing a correlation matrix with a heatmap.

A Complete EDA Workflow

Here's a complete EDA workflow, written as one runnable script:

```
import numpy as np
import pandas as pd
import matplotlib.pyplot as plt

# 1. Load data
url = ("https://raw.githubusercontent.com/allisonhorst/"
"palmerpenguins/main/inst/extdata/penguins.csv")
penguins = pd.read_csv(url).dropna()
penguins = penguins[['bill_length_mm', 'bill_depth_mm',
'flipper_length_mm', 'body_mass_g', 'species']]
```

```
# 2. Describe the data
print(penguins.describe())
print("\nMissing values:", penguins.isnull().sum().sum())

# 3. Distribution of a key variable
penguins['body_mass_g'].hist(bins=30)
plt.title('Body Mass Distribution')
plt.xlabel('Body Mass (g)')
plt.show()

# 4. Compare groups with boxplot
groups = [penguins[penguins['species'] == s]['body_mass_g']
for s in penguins['species'].unique()]
plt.boxplot(groups, tick_labels=penguins['species'].unique())
plt.title('Body Mass by Species')
plt.ylabel('Body Mass (g)')
plt.show()

# 5. Explore a relationship
palette = {'Adelie': 'steelblue', 'Gentoo': 'coral',
           'Chinstrap': 'mediumseagreen'}
colors = [palette[s] for s in penguins['species']]
plt.scatter(penguins['bill_length_mm'], penguins['body_mass_g'],
            c=colors, alpha=0.6)
plt.xlabel('Bill Length (mm)')
plt.ylabel('Body Mass (g)')
plt.title('Bill Length vs. Body Mass by Species')
plt.show()

# 6. Correlation matrix
print("\nCorrelation matrix:")
print(penguins.select_dtypes('number').corr().round(2))
```

Each step of the EDA workflow generates questions that the next step answers. By the time you've completed the workflow, you'll know your data well enough to make informed decisions about which model to try, which features to use, and what preprocessing the data might need.

In Chapter 5, you use the insights gained from this EDA, especially the clear separability of species based on bill and flipper measurements, to train your first machine-learning model.

IN THIS CHAPTER

» Understanding what machine learning does

» Meeting Scikit-learn's consistent fit/predict/score workflow

» Training a linear regression model on real housing data

» Seeing a complete machine-learning workflow

» Continuing your data science journey

Chapter 5

Your First Machine-Learning Model

Artificial intelligence is the study of how to make real computers act like the ones in the movies.

—ANONYMOUS

You've loaded data. You've cleaned it. You've explored it with statistics and charts. You understand your dataset's shape, patterns, and potential. Now it's time for the part that makes data science genuinely powerful: training a model that learns from that data and makes predictions on new examples it's never seen before.

This chapter guides you through the entire machine-learning workflow, starting with raw data, moving through model training, and finishing with evaluation, all using Scikit-learn and the California Housing dataset. By the end of this chapter, you will have trained your first predictive model, learned how to evaluate it properly, and gained a clear understanding of how to apply this workflow to new problems.

What Machine Learning Actually Does

Machine learning is often described in mystical terms, with algorithms that learn and models that understand data. In reality, machine learning is much more concrete and, once you see how it works, surprisingly intuitive.

A *machine-learning model* is a mathematical function that maps inputs to outputs. You train it by showing it many examples of those inputs paired with their correct outputs. The algorithm adjusts the function's internal parameters until its predictions match the known outputs as closely as possible. When training is done, you hand the model new inputs it's never seen, and it uses what it learned to predict the corresponding outputs.

There are two fundamental types of prediction problems:

- **Regression:** Predicting a continuous number. How much will this house sell for? What will tomorrow's temperature be? How many units will we sell next quarter?
- **Classification:** Predicting a category. Is this email spam or not? Which species is this penguin? Will this customer churn?

The algorithm you select depends on what you want to predict. This chapter highlights linear regression as the simplest and most interpretable regression model, using housing price prediction as the example problem.

Working with Scikit-learn

Scikit-learn (`scikit-learn.org`) provides dozens of machine-learning algorithms, but they all share the same interface. Once you know how to use one, you effectively know how to use all of them.

Every Scikit-learn algorithm follows the same three-step pattern:

- **Instantiate:** Create the model object, optionally passing configuration parameters.

» **Fit:** Train the model on your data using `.fit(X, y)`.

» **Predict or score:** Use the trained model with `.predict(X_new)` or `.score(X, y)`.

That's it. The same three steps apply regardless of which algorithm you use. One of Scikit-learn's greatest strengths is its consistent API, allowing you to switch algorithms with only minimal changes to your code.

The following snippet shows the basic Scikit-learn workflow: instantiate an estimator, fit it on training data, and then use it to predict (or score) on new data:

```
# The universal Scikit-learn pattern
from sklearn.some_module import SomeAlgorithm

model = SomeAlgorithm()                    # 1. Instantiate
model.fit(X_train, y_train)                # 2. Fit (train)
predictions = model.predict(X_test)        # 3. Predict
score = model.score(X_test, y_test)        # or Score
```

Setting up the features and the target

Machine learning requires you to separate your data into two pieces:

» **`X` is the feature matrix.** The input variables your model will learn from. `X` is always a 2-D array or DataFrame, where rows are observations and columns are features.

» **y is the target vector.** The output you want the model to predict. y is always a 1-D array, one value per row in `X`.

For this chapter, you use the California Housing dataset, a classic resource containing census data from California districts where the goal is to predict the median house value in each district.

The next example loads Scikit-learn's built-in California Housing dataset and converts it to the standard format you'll use throughout this chapter: a Pandas DataFrame of features (`X`) and a series target (`y`), followed by a quick shape check and preview:

```
import pandas as pd
from sklearn.datasets import fetch_california_housing


def load_california_housing():
```

```
    dataset = fetch_california_housing()
    X = pd.DataFrame(data=dataset.data,
                     columns=dataset.feature_names)
    y = pd.Series(data=dataset.target, name='MedianHouseValue')
    return X, y

X, y = load_california_housing()

print(f"Features: {X.shape}")   # (20640, 8)
print(f"Target:   {y.shape}")   # (20640,)
print(X.head())
```

Output:

```
Features: (20640, 8)
Target:   (20640,)
MedInc      HouseAge  AveRooms  AveBedrms  Population  AveOccup  Latitude  Longitude
0  8.3252   41.0      6.984127  1.023810   322.0       2.555556  37.88     -122.23
1  8.3014   21.0      6.238137  0.971880   2401.0      2.109842  37.86     -122.22
...
```

The eight features are median income (MedInc), house age, average rooms, average bedrooms, population, average occupancy, latitude, and longitude. The target (y) is the median house value in units of $100,000. For example, a value of 1.5 means $150,000.

REMEMBER

The number of rows in X must equal the number of elements in y. Each row in X is paired with the corresponding element of y. That pairing is how the algorithm learns which inputs produce which outputs. Never shuffle one without also shuffling the other.

Scaling your features

Many machine-learning algorithms, such as linear regression, perform better and are easier to interpret when features are on comparable scales. MedInc ranges from about 0.5 to 15, while Population ranges from 3 to 35,000. That 1000x difference in scale can cause some algorithms to over-weight certain features simply because of their larger numbers.

Standardization fixes this by transforming each feature so it has a mean of 0 and a standard deviation of 1. Scikit-learn's StandardScaler does this automatically:

```
from sklearn.preprocessing import StandardScaler

scaler = StandardScaler()
scaler.fit(X) # Learn the mean and std from the data
X_scaled = scaler.transform(X) # Apply the transformation
```

Note the two-step pattern: Use `fit()` first to learn the statistics, and then use `transform()` to apply them. This separation is important. When you later evaluate test data, you use `transform()` only, and you should never call `fit()` again on test data because that would allow information from the test set to influence your scaling parameters.

Scikit-learn's pipeline bundles preprocessing and modeling into a single object, ensuring that you fit preprocessing steps (like scaling) on the training data and then reuse those same learned parameters to transform test or new data before making predictions:

```
from sklearn.linear_model import LinearRegression
from sklearn.preprocessing import StandardScaler
from sklearn.pipeline import Pipeline

model = Pipeline(steps=[
    ('scaler', StandardScaler()),
    ('regression', LinearRegression())
])
```

A pipeline is a sequence of steps applied in order. When you call `fit()`, it first scales the data and then trains the regression model. When you use `predict()`, it scales new data by using the same learned parameters and then produces predictions. Using a pipeline is considered a best practice because it helps prevent one of the most common sources of errors in machine learning: accidentally applying preprocessing inconsistently between training and prediction.

Training the Model

With the pipeline set up, training requires a single line:

```
model.fit(X, y)
print(f"Training R² score: {model.score(X, y):.3f}")
```

Here is the output:

```
Training R² score: 0.606
```

The model has been trained. The `score()` method returns R^2 (R-squared), which is a measure of how well the model's predictions match the actual values. R^2 ranges from 0 to 1: an R^2 of 0 means the model is no better than simply predicting the mean for every house; an R^2 of 1 means perfect predictions. A score of 0.606 means the model explains about 61% of the variation in house prices using the eight available features.

At first glance, 61% accuracy sounds decent, but there's a problem with evaluating a model on the same data you trained it on.

Splitting data into training and test sets

When you score a model on its training data, you're asking: "How well did it memorize what it already saw?" That's not what you care about. You care about: "How well will it perform on houses it has never seen?"

These two questions can have very different answers. Some models, especially complex ones, are remarkably good at memorizing training data while performing poorly on new data. Memorization of training data is called *overfitting*, and it's one of the central challenges of machine learning.

The standard solution is to split your data into two separate sets *before* training:

- **Training set (~80%)**: What the model learns from
- **Test set (~20%)**: Not used for training the model; used only to evaluate the finished model

Scikit-learn's `train_test_split()` splits the dataset into training and testing sets in one line:

```
from sklearn.model_selection import train_test_split

X_train, X_test, y_train, y_test = train_test_split(
    X, y, test_size=0.20, random_state=42)

print(f"Training set: {X_train.shape}")  # (16512, 8)
print(f"Test set:     {X_test.shape}")   # (4128, 8)
```

The random_state parameter seeds the random split so you get the same split every time. This step is important for reproducibility. The split is random rather than sequential, which prevents problems that arise when data is ordered in some way (such as chronologically or geographically).

Now train on the training set and evaluate on the test set:

```
from sklearn.metrics import mean_absolute_error

# Train on training data only
model.fit(X_train, y_train)

# Evaluate on both sets
train_score = model.score(X_train, y_train)
test_score  = model.score(X_test, y_test)

# Also compute mean absolute error on the test set
y_pred = model.predict(X_test)
mae = mean_absolute_error(y_test, y_pred)

print(f"Train R²:  {train_score:.3f}")
print(f"Test R²:   {test_score:.3f}")
print(f"Test MAE:  {mae:.3f} ($100k units)")
```

Here is the output:

```
Train R²:  0.613
Test R²:   0.576
Test MAE:  0.533 ($100k units)
```

The training and test scores are close to each other. That's a good sign! When they're very close, it means the model is generalizing well; it didn't just memorize the training data. The mean absolute error (MAE) of 0.533 means the model's predictions are off by about $53,300 on average. For a house-price prediction model using only eight features, that first result is reasonable.

REMEMBER

The gap between training score and test score is a key diagnostic. A small gap (as here) suggests that the model is generalizing well. A large gap — high training score, much lower test score — is a signature of overfitting; the model memorized the training data instead of learning general patterns.

Getting a reliable estimate by using cross-validation

A single train/test split has a limitation: The result depends on *which* 20% ended up in the test set. A lucky or unlucky random split can make the model look better or worse than it actually is.

Cross-validation solves this by repeating the split multiple times and averaging the results. The most common approach is *k-fold cross-validation*. Here's how it works:

1. Divide the data into *k* equal-sized groups (folds) — typically 10.
2. Reserve one fold as the test set; train on the remaining *k–1* folds.
3. Record the test score.
4. Repeat *k* times, using each fold as the test set exactly once.
5. Average the *k* scores. That average is a stable, reliable estimate of model performance.

The next code snippet creates a 10-fold split (with shuffling for randomness) and uses `cross_val_score()` to train and score the model on each fold. It then prints the individual R^2 scores along with their mean and standard deviation:

```
from sklearn.model_selection import cross_val_score, KFold
import numpy as np

cv = KFold(n_splits=10, shuffle=True, random_state=42)

scores = cross_val_score(model, X, y, cv=cv, scoring='r2',
  n_jobs=-1)

print(f"CV R² scores: {scores.round(3)}")
print(f"Mean R²:  {np.mean(scores):.3f}")
print(f"Std R²:   {np.std(scores):.3f}")
```

Here is the output:

```
CV R² scores: [0.581 0.57  0.634 0.595 0.616 0.603 0.591 0.64
  0.578 0.594]
Mean R²:  0.600
Std R²:   0.022
```

The mean R^2 of 0.600 across 10 folds, with a standard deviation of just 0.008, indicates that the model consistently explains about 60% of the variance in house prices regardless of which 10% is held out. The mean R^2 across the 10 folds provides a trustworthy estimate and is much more reliable than relying on a single train/test split.

TIP

Cross-validation uses all your data for both training and evaluation (just not at the same time), which means you get a better performance estimate compared to using a single split. The tradeoff is computation time; performing a 10-fold CV takes ten times as long to run as a single train/test evaluation. For small-to-medium datasets, this increased time is rarely an issue.

Interpreting what the model learned

R^2 tells you how well the model predicts. The model's *coefficients* tell you what it learned — which features matter most and in which direction.

Because the features were standardized before training, the coefficients can be compared directly. A larger absolute value indicates that the feature has a greater effect on the prediction.

The next snippet refits the full pipeline on all available data, extracts the linear regression coefficients, and prints one coefficient per feature so you can interpret both the direction (positive versus negative) and the relative strength of each predictor (because the inputs were standardized).

```
# Re-fit on all data to get stable coefficient estimates
model.fit(X, y)

# Extract coefficients from the regression step in the pipeline
coefficients = model.named_steps['regression'].coef_

for feature, coef in zip(X.columns, coefficients):
    print(f"{feature:12}: {coef:+.3f}")
```

The output follows:

```
MedInc      : +0.830
HouseAge    : +0.119
AveRooms    : -0.266
AveBedrms   : +0.306
Population  : -0.005
```

```
AveOccup    : -0.039
Latitude    : -0.900
Longitude   : -0.871
```

Here's how to interpret the most important coefficients:

- **MedInc (+0.830):** This is the strongest positive predictor. When the median income in a district is higher, it strongly predicts higher house values, which is not surprising.
- **Latitude (−0.900) and Longitude (−0.871):** These are the largest coefficients by absolute value. Location is the most influential factor; houses in certain parts of California are worth much more than in other areas, regardless of their other characteristics.
- **AveRooms (−0.266):** The negative coefficient for average rooms is unexpected because more rooms would typically suggest higher prices. This unusual result is probably due to multicollinearity. In dense urban areas, the average room count per dwelling is lower, yet prices are higher, which creates an artificial negative relationship. This subtlety in interpretation is something exploratory data analysis, such as examining a correlation matrix like the one you built in Chapter 4, can help you anticipate.

TIP

Linear regression coefficients are not the same as feature importances. A large coefficient means that a unit change in that standardized feature produces a large change in the prediction — but it doesn't tell you whether that relationship is causal. Correlation is not causation, and regression coefficients are measures of correlation.

The Complete End-to-End Workflow

Here is the full pipeline from raw data to evaluated model, all in one place:

```
import numpy as np
import pandas as pd
import matplotlib.pyplot as plt
from sklearn.datasets import fetch_california_housing
from sklearn.linear_model import LinearRegression
from sklearn.preprocessing import StandardScaler
from sklearn.pipeline import Pipeline
```

```
from sklearn.model_selection import train_test_split,
  cross_val_score, KFold
from sklearn.metrics import mean_absolute_error

# 1. Load data
dataset = fetch_california_housing()
X = pd.DataFrame(dataset.data, columns=dataset.feature_names)
y = pd.Series(dataset.target, name='MedianHouseValue')

# 2. Split into train and test
X_train, X_test, y_train, y_test = train_test_split(
    X, y, test_size=0.20, random_state=42)

# 3. Define the model pipeline
model = Pipeline(steps=[
    ('scaler', StandardScaler()),
    ('regression', LinearRegression())
])

# 4. Train
model.fit(X_train, y_train)

# 5. Evaluate on test set
y_pred = model.predict(X_test)
print(f"Test R²:  {model.score(X_test, y_test):.3f}")
print(f"Test MAE: {mean_absolute_error(y_test, y_pred):.3f}
  ($100k)")

# 6. Cross-validate for a stable estimate
cv = KFold(n_splits=10, shuffle=True, random_state=42)
scores = cross_val_score(model, X, y, cv=cv, scoring='r2')
print(f"CV R²: {np.mean(scores):.3f} ± {np.std(scores):.3f}")

# 7. Visualize predictions vs. actual values
plt.figure(figsize=(6, 5))
plt.scatter(y_test, y_pred, alpha=0.3, s=10)
plt.plot([0, 5], [0, 5], 'r--', linewidth=1)  # perfect
  prediction line
plt.xlabel('Actual Value ($100k)')
plt.ylabel('Predicted Value ($100k)')
plt.title('Linear Regression: Predicted vs. Actual')
plt.tight_layout()
plt.show()
```

The final scatterplot, shown in Figure 5-1, shows predicted values versus actual values. A scatterplot is one of the most informative diagnostics for a regression model. Points that fall along the red dashed line represent perfect predictions. The spread around that line reveals where and how much the model makes errors. A good model creates a tight cluster of points along the diagonal, while a poor model results in a scattered cloud or systematic curves that indicate patterns the model failed to capture.

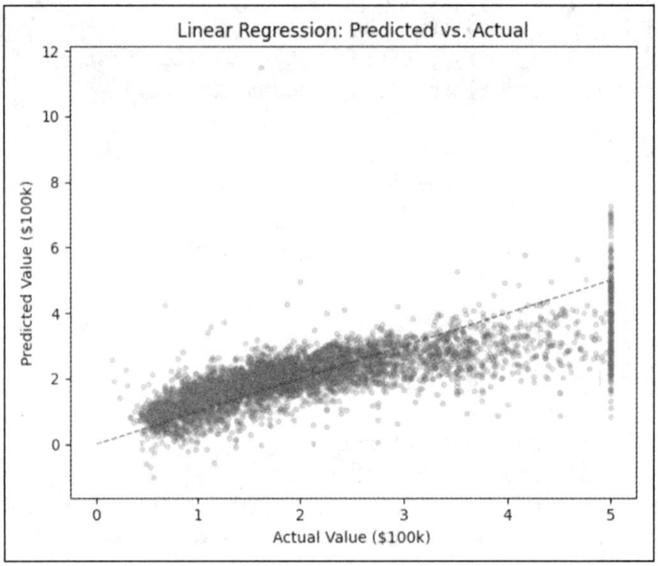

FIGURE 5-1: Predicted values versus actual values.

Where to Go from Here

Linear regression is just the beginning. The same Scikit-learn workflow, which includes the methods `fit()`, `predict()`, and `score()`, is compatible with every algorithm in the library. Once you understand this pattern, you can start to explore:

- **Classification:** Logistic regression, decision trees, and random forests to predict categories rather than numbers
- **Regularization:** Ridge and Lasso regression for variants of linear regression that prevent overfitting on high-dimensional data

- **Ensemble methods:** Random forests and gradient boosting, models that combine many simple models for stronger predictions
- **Clustering:** K-means and hierarchical clustering to find structure in unlabeled data
- **Deep learning:** Neural networks via Keras/TensorFlow for image recognition, natural language, and complex sequential data

Each of these topics builds directly on the foundation you've built in this minibook. The pipeline stays the same; only the algorithms inside it change.

TIP

The documentation at `scikit-learn.org` is well-written and features a User Guide that offers conceptual explanations alongside the API reference. The example gallery is an excellent resource for learning how various algorithms are used in real-world situations. Bookmark this site; you'll return to it often.

4

Coding with AI

Contents at a Glance

IN THIS CHAPTER

» Defining AI terms

» Processing natural language

» Interpreting transformers and tokens

» Knowing the limitations of AI

» Practicing responsible AI

Chapter 1

Parsing Machine Learning and Deep Learning

A little learning is a dangerous thing; drink deep, or taste not the Pierian spring.

—ALEXANDER POPE

In this chapter, I cover just enough AI vocabulary and "what's going on under the hood" to help you use today's AI coding tools effectively. You don't need to be a mathematician to benefit from AI-assisted development, but understanding a few core ideas (models, training, tokens, and context windows) will help you get better results and spot mistakes faster.

Decoding Machine and Deep Learning

When you first encounter a generative AI tool such as ChatGPT or Anthropic's Claude, it can seem like magic. Some people even speculate that generative AI tools are conscious and capable of thinking and having emotions. Knowing how these tools were created and how they work will quickly dispel that notion — or make you think differently about consciousness, but that's a subject for a philosophy book, not a coding book.

Defining key concepts

Before you can dip your toes into understanding how the latest AI systems are capable of writing code and generating complex responses to natural-language input, I need to present some vocabulary. People often use the terms *AI, machine learning, deep learning,* and *generative AI* interchangeably, but these fundamental terms are different (see Figure 1-1):

- **Artificial intelligence (AI)** is the use of computer science and data to solve problems. AI encompasses everything from expert systems and decision trees, which simulate the judgment and behavior of humans using a complex series of if-then statements, to machine learning, computer vision, and natural-language processing.
- **Machine learning** is a type of AI that focuses on developing and using computer systems that can learn and adapt without following explicit instructions. Machine learning can solve problems that would be prohibitively expensive to solve by programmers writing the algorithms by hand.
- **Deep learning** is a type of machine learning based on artificial neural networks. The word *deep* in *deep learning* doesn't indicate that it produces inherently more profound or mysterious AI. Rather, it refers to the use of multiple layers of algorithms (artificial neurons) in the neural network. I explain artificial neural networks and layers in the next section.
- **Generative AI (GenAI)** are AI systems that can generate new content based on the data used to train them. Some form of GenAI has been around since the 1960s. In recent years, the content created by GenAI is of a high enough quality to be more than a novelty, thanks to the use of deep learning.

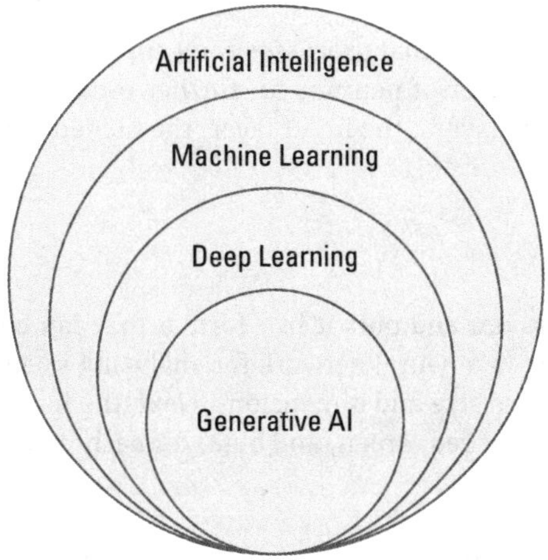

FIGURE 1-1: The relationship between fields in AI.

Thinking about neural networks

The idea behind deep learning is to teach computers to process data based on how we think our brains work. In a human brain, cells called *neurons* form a complex and massive interconnected network. Using chemical reactions and electrical currents, neurons send signals to each other to enable us to learn and process information.

Neural networks in deep learning, also known as *simulated neural networks* or *artificial neural networks,* consist of artificial neurons called nodes that form layers, as shown in Figure 1-2.

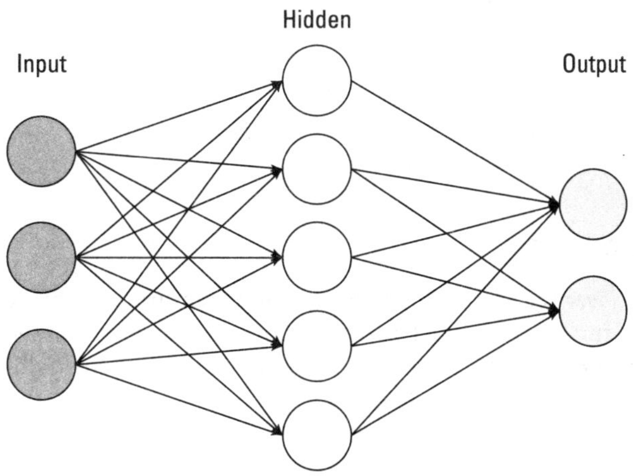

FIGURE 1-2: Nodes are arranged in layers.

Each *node* is a software module that processes some input and determines whether to pass it on to the next layer of neurons for further processing. A simple neural network consists of three layers: the input layer, the hidden layer, and the output layer.

Input layer

The *input layer* receives data and puts it in a format that can be used by the hidden layers. For example, in a neural network for analyzing images, the images are first converted to the same size and dimensions. Next, the input layer takes in the pixel values (the amount of red, green, and blue) for each image and passes them along to the hidden layer.

TECHNICAL STUFF

In the preceding example, the number of neurons in the input layer is determined by the number of pixels in the image. If the neural network will be processing color images, the number of pixels is multiplied by 3 for each of the pixel values (red, green, and blue) to get the number of neurons. For example, the image shown in Figure 1-3 has a width of 56 pixels and a height of 56 pixels. I've magnified the image so you can see the individual pixels. An input layer for working with this image would have 56 × 56 × 3, or 9,408, neurons.

FIGURE 1-3: A color image containing 3,136 pixels requires a 9,408-neuron input layer.

Czar/Wikimedia Commons/Public domain

Hidden layer

A *hidden layer* receives data from the input layer or other hidden layers and processes it further to extract features from the image, such as color, shape, and texture. More complex tasks require more neurons in the hidden layers. A neural network can have many hidden layers.

Output layer

Neural networks must have at least one *output layer*, which provides the final result of the calculations from the hidden layers.

Figure 1-4 shows a simple artificial neural network that determines whether or not a photo contains a hot dog. This type of problem is known as a binary classification because the output from this neural network is either 1 (hot dog) or 0 (not hot dog).

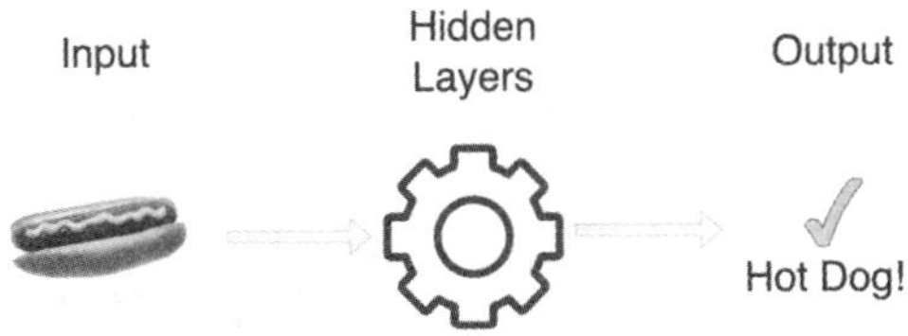

Czar/Wikimedia Commons/Public domain

FIGURE 1-4: Is it a hot dog?

But how does the neural network determine whether the photo contains a hot dog? That's where its training comes in.

Training and testing models

Before a neural network can perform a task, it must be trained. In the case of the hot dog classifier, the neural network can be trained by analyzing thousands of pictures of hot dogs as well as an equal number of things that aren't hot dogs. Each photo must be labeled ("hot dog" or "not hot dog"). From these pictures, the neural network can make certain conclusions about what a picture of a hot dog contains. For example, a picture of a hot dog generally will contain a lighter-colored area (the bun) surrounding a darker-colored cylindrical shape (the hot dog), as shown in Figure 1-5.

As the layers of the neural network analyze pictures, values called weights and biases are assigned to each neuron in the network. The *weight* determines the strength of the connection between two nodes in the network. The *bias* determines the threshold at which a node is activated. Weights and biases adjust how much a neuron will contribute to the final result.

The weights and biases that the model learns from the training data are called *parameters*. The complexity of a model can be described by how many parameters it has. More complex models have more parameters because they're able to learn more complex patterns in data. You can think of parameters as similar to the synapses that connect neurons in a human brain.

How accurately a model can make predictions (whether or not a new picture contains a hot dog, for example) is based on the quality and quantity of data that was used to train it.

FIGURE 1-5: Many pictures of hot dogs have similar characteristics.

Small models that make relatively simple predictions, such as whether or not a photograph contains a hot dog, can be created quickly, and the risks of messing up such a model are unlikely to be catastrophic.

Complex models, such as climate models and models of systems of the human body, can take months or years to train, and getting them wrong can have expensive or life-threatening consequences. Some of the challenges of training neural networks include the following:

- Complex neural networks can involve terabytes of training data and billions of parameters. Training a large neural network is computationally expensive.
- Neural networks can learn their training data too well, which is called *overfitting.* When overfitting occurs, the model will be able to ace tests about the data it was trained on but will have a hard time generalizing to new data (which is the point of a model).
- Because of the number of parameters in a model, it can be difficult for people to figure out how a neural network is making predictions. Being able to understand how a model makes predictions is called *interpretability.*

Demystifying Natural-Language Processing

Natural-language processing (NLP) is the branch of AI concerned with giving computers the capability to understand human language in written and spoken form. NLP can be further divided into two subsets:

- **Natural-language understanding (NLU)** is the analyzing of text and speech to figure out the meaning of sentences.
- **Natural-language generation (NLG)** is concerned with giving computers the capability to write.

NLP is used for a wide variety of purposes, including the following:

- **Machine translation:** Translating text from one language to another
- **Speech recognition:** Understanding spoken language and translating it into text
- **Text summarization:** Generating summaries of longer texts, such as books, articles, or briefs
- **Question answering:** Answering questions asked in natural language
- **Sentiment analysis:** Identifying the sentiment of text, for example, whether it's positive, negative, or neutral
- **Computer programming:** Writing or assisting with the writing of computer programs

REMEMBER

Human language includes not only the languages we use for communicating with each other (such as English, French, and Greek) but also the languages we use for communicating with computers (such as C++, Python, JavaScript, and Haskell).

History of NLP

Natural-language processing has been around since the first experiments in automatic translation in the 1950s. The creators of the first automatic translation machine predicted that the problem of machine translation would be solved within a few years. However, it ended up taking much longer, and we still haven't perfected it.

Early natural-language processing systems relied on a list of handwritten rules that the computer applied to the data it received. The ELIZA chatbot, created in the 1960s, could have a somewhat convincing conversation with a human by following rules and responding as a non-directive psychotherapist. Although ELIZA was created as a joke, it successfully demonstrated that natural-language conversations between people and computers were possible. Figure 1-6 shows a typical conversation with ELIZA.

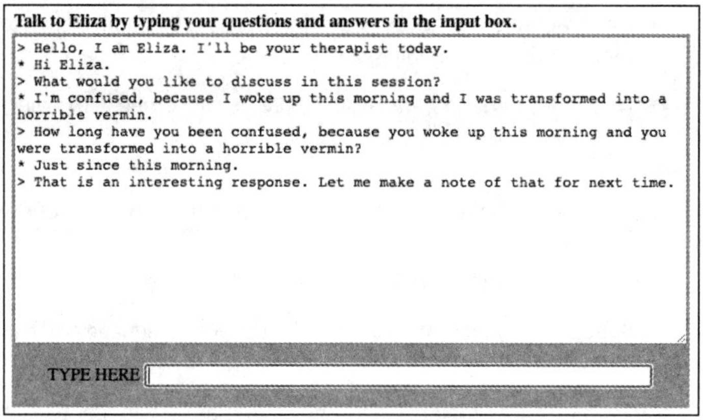

FIGURE 1-6: Early NLP was based on rules.

Machine-learning algorithms and increased computing power led to advances and new techniques for natural-language processing starting in the late 1980s.

In the 1990s, Richard Wallace created the ALICE chatbot. ALICE is similar to ELIZA in that it uses pattern-matching rules. The operator of an ALICE chatbot could add rules, which made it useful for customer service applications such as answering questions about a company's products. Figure 1-7 shows an example conversation with ALICE.

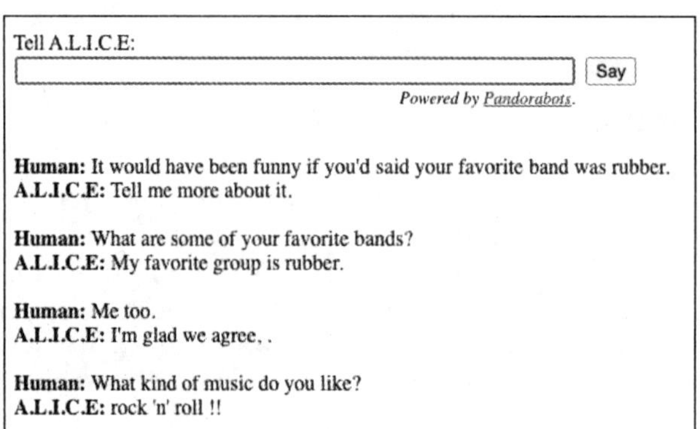

FIGURE 1-7: An example of an Alice chatbot.

The growth of the internet made large collections of text readily available for training models. As a result of all this data, new techniques were created in the 1990s and 2000s that depended on statistical analysis of large datasets.

Machine learning models made it possible for natural-language processing systems to be trained without having to hand-code rules. Further advances in machine learning, including neural networks, made virtual assistants such as Apple's Siri and Amazon's Alexa possible in the 2010s and eventually enabled the remarkable advances in natural-language processing that made tools such as ChatGPT possible.

Overcoming the challenges of NLP

In the past, creators of NLP systems focused on breaking down human languages into rules. The idea was that if you could give a computer access to a language's dictionary and a grammar book, it would know that language.

Human language is tricky because meaning depends on context, culture, and intent — not just dictionary definitions and grammar rules. Modern NLP works well because it learns patterns from huge amounts of real language instead of relying on a brittle set of handcrafted rules.

The fact that a box of chips and wires can understand any of what we say is incredible. Until recently, it seemed that computers were doomed to understand only a formal and limited subset of human languages, and that chatting with an AI assistant would always be a frustrating and disappointing experience.

So what changed? The biggest breakthrough in NLP was when researchers decided to throw out the rules and start teaching computers to talk the way we teach babies to talk: namely, by exposing them to language and letting them figure things out.

Understanding supervised and unsupervised learning

Supervised learning relies on *labeled data,* which is data annotated with tags that describe what the data is. For example, if you want to train a model to recognize spam email messages, you could create a dataset containing millions of email messages, each labeled either "spam" or "not spam." However, the process of labeling data can be costly and time-consuming.

Unsupervised learning is the process of finding patterns in unlabeled data. With unsupervised learning, algorithms sort through unlabeled data looking for patterns. Unsupervised language-learning models can be trained on very large datasets to create large language models (LLMs). Unlike supervised learning, unsupervised learning can be done inexpensively and quickly.

You'll see many NLP techniques mentioned in articles and documentation. Older approaches (logistic regression, naïve Bayes, decision trees) can still be useful, but today's general-purpose chatbots and coding assistants — especially transformer architectures — are typically based on deep learning.

Transformer models learn context by tracking relationships in sequential data (such as the words in a sentence). Transformer models are the breakthrough that has revolutionized NLP in recent years. I tell you more about how transformers work in the next section.

Understanding Transformers

Transformer models use a self-attention mechanism to find dependencies between inputs and outputs. To understand what that means, you first need to know what attention and self-attention are in machine learning. Read on!

Learning to pay attention

The mathematical technique that transformer models use is called attention. The goal of *attention* is to allow the model to focus on important parts of the input while generating its output. As people, we do this naturally. When you read a sentence or look at an image, you can easily see which parts of the sentence or image are the most important in terms of understanding it.

When the idea of attention first became popular, it was combined with recurrent neural networks (RNNs). But RNN models have to consider words in sequence one at a time, which is a slow process. Even worse, RNNs tend to assign more importance to recent words and the ends of sentences.

Another side effect of considering words one at a time is that you lose important context. Consider this sentence:

> The player swung his bat, and he ran to first base.

Anyone with a passing familiarity with baseball will know that *bat* refers to a baseball bat and that *he* refers to the player. Considered one word at a time, however, a language model can't make the same connections.

This is where the idea of self-attention comes in. *Self-attention* allows a model to learn information about an input sequence from the input sequence itself. With self-attention, a transformer model finds relationships between the words *player* and *bat* as well as between *player* and *he.*

Figure 1-8 shows a visualization of the connections a transformer model makes between the word *he* in the example sentence and the other words in the sentence. Darker lines indicate a stronger connection.

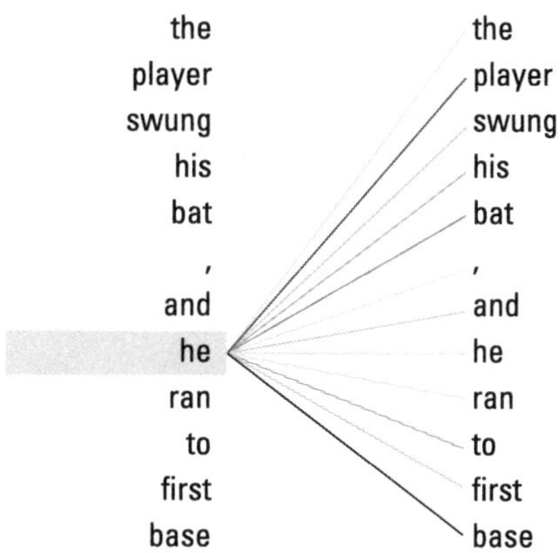

Created in BertViz by Chris Minnick

FIGURE 1-8: Visualizing self-attention.

TECHNICAL STUFF

The visualization in Figure 1-8 was created using a tool called BertViz. You can learn more about how BertViz works and try it out yourself at `https://github.com/jessevig/bertviz`.

Self-attention was first proposed as a solution for improving large language models in the paper "Attention Is All You Need." This paper, published in 2017, led to the giant leaps forward in transformer models that we've seen in recent years.

Getting tokens

You may be surprised to learn that language models can understand only numbers; they don't read or understand words as we do. When you ask an NLP system a question, your input must first be converted into a sequence of numbers called *tokens*. You can think of tokens as the language equivalent of pixels in an image.

These tokens are read by a model's input layer and then processed through the hidden layers to predict and output responses to your prompts.

Hidden layers are the layers between the input and output layers that process data and learn features of it.

Text can be converted to tokens in a variety of ways. One common method is *word tokenization*, which simply creates a token for each word in the text. Transformer models use *sub-word tokenization*, which converts text into common sequences of characters, such as *token* and *ize*. Using smaller units improves the model's performance.

To see how OpenAI converts text to tokens, go to OpenAI's Tokenizer at `https://platform.openai.com/tokenizer`. Figure 1-9 shows the list of tokens that were generated when I entered the sentence *Transformer models use sub-word tokenization.*

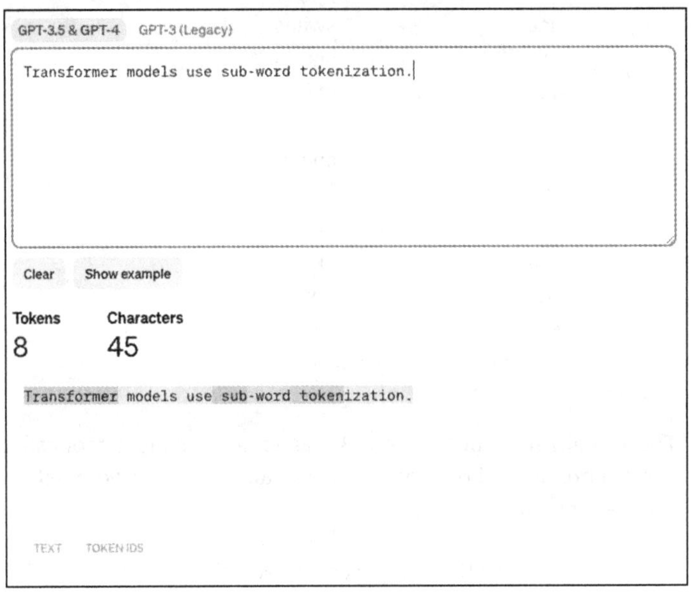

FIGURE 1-9: Tokenizing a prompt.

ChatGPT

After the text is tokenized, it's encoded into token IDs. The token IDs created from the text in Figure 1-9 are shown in Figure 1-10.

TECHNICAL STUFF

Token IDs are input into a neural network as a sequence of numbers called a *numerical vector*.

Being aware of tokens and the tokenization of your input is important. If you're using a model through an API, the combined number of tokens in your input and the model's response determines how much you pay for the service.

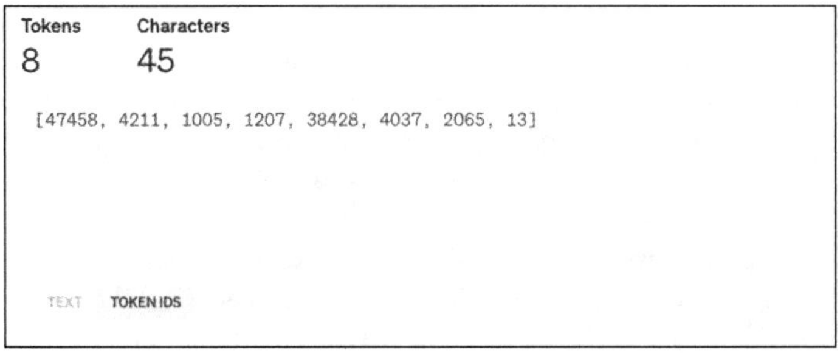

FIGURE 1-10: Tokens are represented as token IDs.

ChatGPT

In addition, the NLP system you're using may have a *token limit,* which is the maximum number of tokens the model will consider while generating its response. Your input and the model's responses contribute to the number of tokens used by a conversation. In a long conversation with an LLM, or if you input an excessively long prompt, the token limit may be exceeded. In this case, the model will "forget" earlier prompts in the conversation, and you'll need to repeat any instructions you included at the beginning.

Token limits are imposed on a model to prevent it from running out of memory, to shorten the model's response time, and to reduce the amount of computation required to train and deploy the model.

Ethical Considerations and Responsible AI

AI has enormous potential to improve people's lives — and to cause harm. Laws regarding the development and use of AI are still being argued over and drafted. Guidelines have been and are being developed by companies and organizations concerned about the negative potential of AI.

Both developers and users of AI models and systems that use those models have a responsibility to use these new technologies in a way that follows best practices. One guide to best practices for developers of AI models is Google's Responsible AI Practices document, which is available at `https://ai.google/responsibility/responsible-ai-practices`. Google recommends four best practices for AI: fairness, interpretability, privacy, and safety and security.

Fairness: Because computer programs have access to much more information than a person, AI systems used for making decisions or for generating content can be more fair and inclusive than decision-making tools based on human judgment. However, because they're trained on data created by humans, AI models have a tendency to learn and sometimes amplify the biases of their training data.

Furthermore, there's no standard definition of fairness. Making a model fair in every language, culture, and situation is a difficult, and perhaps impossible, task. The *fairness best practice* encourages those working with AI to aim for continuous improvement towards "fairer" systems.

Interpretability: *Interpretability* refers to the level to which we can question, understand, and trust an AI system. When people make decisions, they use their experience, intuition, and logic. Often, it's impossible for a person to say exactly what inputs went into their final decision. AI, on the other hand, theoretically has the capability to list the information that went into a prediction. Because a generative AI model may be based on billions of parameters, debugging and understanding the decisions it makes isn't always possible. However, the *interpretability best practice* demands and provides specific recommendations for how to incorporate interpretability into AI systems.

Privacy: The training data and prompts we give AI models can sometimes be sensitive. For example, training data may contain personally identifying data, medical data, private financial information, or photos of people taken without permission. AI models, and generative AI models in particular, can reveal aspects of data they've been exposed to. AI developers, as well as people who use these models, have a responsibility to protect people's privacy and to provide users with the ability to control their data, even absent laws that require it. *Privacy best practices* include collecting and handling training data responsibly, processing data locally (rather than on a server) when appropriate, and considering how a model's construction and access can affect privacy.

Safety and security: *Safety and security best practices* make sure that AI systems behave as they're supposed to regardless of what prompts or inputs a person with bad intentions gives them. For example, ChatGPT has proactive restrictions regarding hate speech and generating content that may be harmful to people. Attackers are constantly looking for new ways to get GenAI systems to produce restricted output. Developers must balance necessary restrictions for safety and security with the flexibility to handle unusual inputs and generate useful responses.

Illuminating Generative AI Models

A *generative AI model* is a model that is trained on content (such as images or text) and can use that content to make predictions to generate new content. OpenAI's GPT-3.5, the model behind the first public version of ChatGPT, is a generative model for natural-language processing. By leveraging what it's learned about how people talk and write, it can accurately predict what the next word or sentence should be in response to input.

For example, if you provide the words *peanut butter and* to an LLM, it will most likely predict that the next words should be *jelly sandwich.* The LLM doesn't have any experience with eating or making peanut butter and jelly sandwiches, but it has analyzed a lot of text, and the most common way to finish the phrase *peanut butter and* is with *jelly sandwich.*

Recognizing AI's Limitations

As impressive as they are, transformer models don't know how to code — they know only how to look for patterns in sequential data (such as sentences, statements, or functions). When you train a generative model on enough data, it becomes very good at finding patterns and making predictions, but it does have limitations, and you should never trust the output of a chatbot (or any AI system) entirely.

Here are the limitations you're most likely to run into when using AI for coding:

- **AI can be confidently wrong.** Models may hallucinate details (such as a library API that doesn't exist).
- **AI can struggle with math and long chains of reasoning.** Always verify calculations and edge cases with tests or a calculator.
- **AI has a limited working memory.** If a conversation or file is too long, earlier constraints can fall out of the context window.
- **AI can reflect bias from training data.** Be cautious with outputs that affect people (hiring, lending, healthcare, safety decisions).
- **AI can introduce security issues.** Treat generated code as untrusted until you review it and run tests and linters.

Unintended consequences can result from biased or poorly constrained systems. A classic example is Microsoft's Tay chatbot (2016), which was manipulated into posting offensive content and was taken offline about 16 hours after launch.

IN THIS CHAPTER

» Engineering prompts

» Talking code with chatbots

Chapter 2
Coding with Chatbots

A problem well-stated is a problem half-solved.

—CHARLES KETTERING

Large language models (LLMs) enable computers to understand and generate human languages with astonishing accuracy. *Chatbots* are easy-to-use interfaces to LLMs that enable conversations with a generative AI model. Using a chatbot, anyone can converse with an LLM in a way that's similar to how you would message a friend or coworker. (To learn about how machine learning and LLMs work, check out Chapter 1.)

Because the generative AI models that underlie AI chatbots have been trained on an enormous amount of text, it can sometimes seem like the chatbots are omniscient. However, after some time working with chatbots and sometimes getting responses that are incoherent or plainly wrong, you'll realize that they're not.

In this chapter, you learn how to use several popular AI chatbots to generate programming code. You also learn how to get better results by improving the inputs, or prompts, that you give an LLM.

Improving Your Prompts

Prompt engineering is the art and science of developing and optimizing prompts to use LLMs more effectively. By learning about prompt engineering, you'll not only become better at getting what you want out of LLMs but also gain a greater appreciation for what LLMs can and can't do.

Deciphering the elements of a prompt

Prompts can be simple, such as the completion request *bread and*, or complex and multi-part. Prompts may include all or just some of the following elements:

- **Instruction:** A task you want the model to do. For example, *Translate the following text into Spanish.*
- **Context:** Additional information or files that the model should consider while generating the response. The files you have open in neighboring tabs while using GitHub Copilot are examples of context.
- **Input data:** The input or question you want the AI to answer or respond to. If your instruction is to translate some text to Spanish, the input data would be the text you want translated.
- **Output format:** The type or format in which the model should provide the output. Examples of output formats are JSON data, tab-delimited data, and markdown format.

Open-ended versus closed-ended prompts

Prompts may be either open-ended or closed-ended. *Closed-ended prompts* ask for a specific and targeted response, such as:

- Write a function to validate an email address input.
- Check this function for bugs.
- What is the tallest building in Indianapolis?

Open-ended prompts are designed to generate expansive responses, such as:

- Write an email to my landlord telling him that I'm moving out if he doesn't fix the leak.

- Draft an outline for an article about nutrition and school lunches.
- Write a story about a magician squirrel in the style of Dr. Seuss.

Using different types of prompts

An LLM will do its best to return an accurate completion for any prompt that you give it. However, there are types of prompts that can be used for different purposes, as you explore in this section.

Zero-shot prompting

In a *zero-shot prompt*, you don't give the model context or examples of what you're looking for, but instead rely entirely on its training. An example of a zero-shot prompt is:

```
What is the capital of Maine?
```

For simple questions or tasks, many LLMs can do zero-shot prompting. As your requests become more complex, however, you'll need to move on to other forms of prompts.

TIP

As models have become larger, an increasing number of tasks can be accomplished using simple zero-shot prompts. However, if you want an LLM to do a task involving math or complex reasoning, you may have better success with one of the prompt types described in the following sections.

Few-shot prompting

Few-shot prompting, in which you include one or more examples of the type of output you're looking for, is especially useful for code style and data shape. For example, if you want the model to generate test cases in `pytest` style, give it one or more example tests that match your conventions and then ask it to produce more in the same style:

```
Example (few-shot):
Here is one pytest test that matches my style:
def test_slugify_basic():
    assert slugify("Hello, world!") == "hello-world"
Now write 5 more tests for edge cases (unicode, repeated spaces,
  empty string, punctuation-only, leading/trailing dashes).
```

If you're tempted to ask the model to "show your work," it's usually more effective to ask for a brief plan, assumptions, and tests. That keeps the output actionable without turning the conversation into pages of fragile reasoning text.

Prompting like a pro

Although prompting a language model often involves trial and error, you can improve your prompts by remembering the following tips:

- **Be specific about constraints.** Name the language and version (Python 3.12+), libraries (`pandas`, `pytest`), and any non-negotiables (no new dependencies, must be type-checked).
- **Provide a concrete example.** Show a small input-output pair, a failing test, or a snippet that demonstrates the style you want.
- **Ask for tests.** For code generation, ask the model to create (or update) unit tests first, and then implement the code to satisfy them.
- **Prefer small diffs.** Ask for the smallest possible change that fixes the bug or adds the feature, and apply it in steps you can review.
- **Provide cues.** Indicate where and how the model should provide its completion when possible. For example, when asking a model to summarize an article, you might write the following to get the model to respond with a bulleted list:
- **Verify, and then iterate.** Run tests and linters, read the diff, and ask for revisions ("make it smaller," "add tests," "handle errors") until it meets your requirements.

Using Chatbots for Coding Tasks

Chatbots are great for interactive help, generating pieces of code, and brainstorming ideas. They're generally tuned to be more creative than dedicated coding assistants. A side effect of this increased creativity is that chatbots are more likely to make mistakes and may be more limited in how well they work in large coding projects.

General-purpose chatbots such as OpenAI's ChatGPT, Anthropic's Claude, Google's Gemini, and Microsoft's Copilot change frequently and are getting better at coding with each new model version. Don't worry about which chatbot to use for coding. All of today's chatbots are far better at coding than they were even a year ago, so focus less on model names and more on whether the tool is giving you consistent, testable output.

Many chatbots let you set *persistent preferences* (sometimes called *custom instructions*). The exact UI changes over time, but the idea is simple: Tell the assistant how you want it to behave so you don't have to repeat yourself in every chat:

Following is an example custom instruction:

> You are a helpful senior Python developer and tutor.
>
> Use Python 3.12+ syntax and standard libraries unless I ask otherwise.
>
> I prefer small, testable changes. Include pytest tests when relevant.
>
> If you're not sure, say so and suggest how to verify (docs, tests, or a quick experiment).

Setting custom instructions such as these saves time and friction: You get consistent defaults (language, libraries, tone, and level of detail) without restating them for every prompt. They also help the model tailor its answers to your goals, whether you want quick code-only snippets, step-by-step tutoring, or a "small diffs and tests" workflow, so the output is easier to trust, review, and reuse. Still, it's important to recognize the limits of chat-style help. Coding tasks that demand more control and capabilities, such as navigating a large codebase, running tools, editing multiple files, and verifying results, require different tools, and that's what agents are about, as you learn in the next chapter.

IN THIS CHAPTER

» Progressing from chatbots to agents

» Understanding your project's requirements

» Coding a prototype with prompts

» Blending your code with AI-generated code

» Tips for generating better code

Chapter 3
Progressing from Plan to Prototype

A goal without a plan is just a wish.

—ANTOINE DE SAINT-EXUPÉRY

Although it's possible to work with an AI coding assistant to generate working code and even entire programs, acceptable results are far from guaranteed. The quality of the results you'll get depends on several factors, including the LLM you use, the input you give the model, your own coding skills, and how clearly you've defined the project's requirements.

This chapter focuses on one of the most important skills in AI-assisted development: turning a vague idea into a clear plan that an AI (and your future self) can follow. You learn lightweight ways to capture requirements, generate a first prototype, and iterate safely with tests and small changes.

Developing with AI Agents

AI agents offer a more dynamic and capable approach compared to traditional chatbots. They can handle complex tasks by automating processes that would otherwise require manual intervention, making them invaluable for development workflows. Developers can focus on higher-level problem solving while the agent takes care of repetitive or multistep operations.

Agents can plan a change, edit multiple files, run commands or tests, and present a set of proposed modifications for your review. Tools like Claude Code are designed around this workflow. AI agents can dramatically increase the speed of coding work. However, allowing an AI agent to make large changes that you don't fully understand is risky.

The key to using agents effectively is to make use of their capabilities while not giving up control of the direction of the code and important decisions involved in writing code. A reliable agent workflow looks like this:

- **Constrain the task.** Point the agent at a specific folder/file and a single goal (for example, `"add tests for slugify()"`).
- **Clearly state what you want it to do.** Describe your requirements or project goals, and ask the agent to repeat the acceptance criteria before starting to code.
- **Prefer tests first.** Ask the agent to write or update tests, and then implement the code to satisfy them.
- **Review diffs and rerun checks.** Read the changes like a code review and rerun your tests and linters before you accept the result.

Here's an example of a good agent-task prompt:

> Act as an agent working in my repository.
>
> Goal: implement `slugify(text)` according to the spec below.
>
> Constraints: Python 3.12+, standard library only, small diffs.
>
> First: Write `pytest` tests from the acceptance criteria.
>
> Then: Implement the function and run the tests.
>
> Finally: Summarize changes and list any assumptions or follow-ups.

Understanding Project Requirements

If you've ever been thrown into working on a new project that you don't fully understand, you can identify with what a coding assistant would feel like all the time — if a coding assistant could feel anything. Although coding assistants have seen a lot of code, the only way they can be helpful to you is if they have context about the particular requirements of the code you're writing.

Software requirements

When starting to work with a coding assistant, think about what you need to know before working on a project. Specifically, you need to know the following:

- What will the software do?
- Who are you building the software for?
- Who will use the software?
- Where and how will the software do what it does?
- How will the user interact with the software?
- What languages and technologies will you use to build the software?
- What are the goals of the software?
- Are there any legal or regulatory standards that the software must comply with?

In the world of software development, we call the answers to these questions the *software requirements.* You can specify your project's software requirements by using a *software requirements specification (SRS),* which is a document that describes, in detail, what the planned software will do and how it will be expected to perform. For small projects, a full SRS is usually not necessary. However, some sort of documentation of requirements is essential to any project, and figuring out the requirements for yourself is essential to being able to communicate them to another developer or to an AI coding assistant.

Software requirements can be divided into three broad categories: domain requirements, functional requirements, and non-functional requirements.

Domain requirements

Domain requirements are particular to the category, purpose, or industry in which the software will be used. It's possible for a piece of software to be functional and user-friendly without being acceptable for use because it doesn't meet domain requirements. For example, if you develop an online banking app that doesn't meet the legal and regulatory requirements that apply to online banking apps, it doesn't fulfill its requirements.

Functional requirements

Functional requirements define how the software system behaves and are generally defined using specific responses to inputs or conditions. These statements of functional requirements are called use cases or user stories.

A *use case* is a detailed description of a functional requirement. It defines, using natural language, the ways in which a user can interact with a system (such as a piece of software or a website) and how the system will respond.

The details specified in a use case include the following:

- The goal
- Whether the user (called the *actor* in use cases) is human or another system
- Preconditions that must be present for the use case (for example, the user must be logged in)
- The series of steps the system will take
- Alternative steps (for example, what happens when the user isn't logged in)
- What happens after the steps are complete (also known as *postconditions*)

Use cases are no longer common in modern software development due to the popularity of agile software development, in which functional requirements are specified with user stories.

User stories are generally informal one-sentence statements, written from the user's point of view. They contain the who, what, and why of an outcome that the users want to accomplish with the system. User stories are often written using the following format:

> As a [persona], I [want to], [so that].

For example:

> As a user, I want to be able to reset my password if I forget it, so I can regain access to my account.

This format, however, is not required when writing user stories. It's also common, especially during the initial process of documenting functional requirements, to see less structured statements that may eventually be turned into user stories.

Whether you decide to write use cases or user stories, the following are examples of functional requirements:

- The system must allow users to create an account.
- The system must allow users to log in with a username and password.
- The system must allow users to click a forgot password link to reset their password.
- After a user signs up for an account, they'll see a login page where they can enter their username and password to log in.
- When a user successfully signs in, they'll see the newsfeed page.
- The newsfeed page presents the user with a list of the latest posts made by other users.
- At the bottom of the newsfeed page, users can enter text into an input field and click a submit button to create a new post.

You don't need to capture every detail of the functional requirements for the SRS. However, stating who will be using the system, what needs to be built, and why it needs to be built will give you more clarity as you're writing code and will give your AI assistant more context.

Non-functional requirements

Non-functional requirements relate to the quality of the software system, including security, maintainability, reliability, scalability, and reusability. Prioritizing non-functional requirements often involves considering the different assumptions and constraints that apply to the project.

Assumptions are factors that are believed to be true but aren't confirmed. Following are the categories of assumptions:

- **Technical assumptions** relate to technology, such as hardware, operating systems, and infrastructure. For example, a technical assumption may be that the user's computer will have a certain amount of RAM.

- **Operational assumptions** have to do with user or organizational behavior and factors. For example, an operational assumption for this book is that the reader is a computer programmer (or wants to be one).
- **Business assumptions** focus on the business context in which the project will be used, such as business policies and market conditions that may affect the design or functionality of the software.
- **Environmental assumptions** are external factors that may affect the software, such as cultural, social, or geographical factors or availability of a stable internet connection.

Constraints restrict the options available to developers of a system. Types of constraints include the following:

- **Interface constraints** define the limitations that the software's user interface puts on the project. If you're developing a mobile app, the size of the mobile device screens places limits on the functionality and design of the app.
- **Performance constraints** define specific performance criteria that the software must meet. For example, you might define a percentage of uptime or a maximum time for the website to finish loading.
- **Operating constraints** relate to existing organizational processes, policies, or practices. Examples include whether the company where the software will be deployed allows the use of certain software libraries or the organization's policies regarding the use of AI coding assistants.
- **Life cycle constraints** have to do with maintainability, portability, and the ongoing life of the software after it's built.
- **Economic constraints** involve the budget for building and operating the software. Finances are a major limitation of any project.

TIP

Specifying software requirements is an important part of any project and, with the emergence of AI coding assistants, a skill that every software developer should have. Many books have been written about software requirements, but the most essential one is *Software Requirements*, 3rd Edition (Microsoft Press) by Karl Wiegers and Joy Beatty.

Writing a spec

To demonstrate the process, I'll use a small but realistic example: a `slugify(text)` function. The goal is not to build an entire app but to use an AI assistant to turn requirements into working code in small, testable steps.

Here's a prompt you can use to generate a first draft spec for `slugify(text)`:

> Act as an experienced software project manager.
>
> Ask me questions, and then produce a concise spec using these sections: Goal, Inputs, Outputs, Behavior, Examples, Constraints, and Tests/Acceptance Criteria.

After a short back-and-forth, you should have a clear first draft of your requirements. Before you generate any code, look over the spec and add the missing bits that AIs usually gloss over: edge cases, error handling, and what "done" means (tests/acceptance criteria).

Here's the spec that I came up with for `slugify(text)`:

```
# Spec: slugify(text)
## Goal
Turn a string into a URL-friendly slug.
## Behavior
- lowercase
- replace whitespace runs with a single '-'
- remove punctuation
## Examples
- "Hello, world!" → "hello-world"
## Tests / acceptance criteria: include unicode, empty string,
   punctuation-only
```

Once you have a spec, you're ready to start the prototype loop.

A minimal prototype loop (Python-first)

The details of your stack will change, but the prototype loop stays the same: Write a spec, generate a small slice of code, and validate it with automated checks. In practice, developers often start with a small Python module and a few tests before building the UI.

A reliable loop looks like this:

- **Write spec:** Define inputs, outputs, and edge cases (use the SDD template earlier in this chapter).
- **Test:** Write a few failing tests that capture the acceptance criteria.
- **Implement:** Ask your assistant (or agent) for the smallest change that makes the tests pass.
- **Verify:** Run tests, lint/format, and review diffs before you move on.

For example, if your spec includes the example behavior `"Hello, world!"` → `"hello-world"`, start by capturing that as a test:

```
from myproj.text import slugify
def test_slugify_basic():
    assert slugify("Hello, world!") == "hello-world"
```

Then implement the smallest amount of code to satisfy the test. For example:

```
import re
import unicodedata
def slugify(text: str) -> str:
    text = unicodedata.normalize("NFKD", text).encode("ascii",
   "ignore").decode("ascii")
    text = text.lower()
    text = re.sub(r"[^a-z0-9\s-]", "", text)
    text = re.sub(r"[\s-]+", "-", text).strip("-")
    return text
```

Note what's missing: You don't need to build a server or a user interface yet. These parts can be added later, after you've tested and trusted your main logic.

Generating code from the spec

Once you have a spec (and ideally a couple of tests), you can ask an assistant to generate code that fits *your* constraints. The trick is to keep the request small and verifiable.

Here's an example prompt that will work in a chat or as a prompt to an agent:

> Implement `slugify(text)` in Python.
>
> Constraints: Python 3.12+, standard library only.
>
> Acceptance criteria:
>
> > "Hello, world!" becomes "hello-world"
> >
> > Collapse multiple spaces into one hyphen.
> >
> > Remove punctuation.
> >
> > Handle unicode input reasonably (document your approach).
>
> Also provide 3 to 5 `pytest` tests, including empty string and punctuation-only.

After you get the code back, run the tests immediately. If anything fails, paste the failure output back to the assistant and ask for a minimal fix. This generate-test-fix cycle is faster (and safer) than repeatedly asking the model to rewrite the entire solution.

Tips and Tricks for Code Generation

The results you get from a generative AI model will vary widely, based on your prompts, the context and input you provide to the model, the specific LLM you use, the settings provided to the model, and more.

As you become more comfortable working with an AI coding assistant, you'll start to become more familiar with what it can and can't do. If you follow certain practices, however, you can get the LLM to generate good code more reliably. In this section, I tell you some of the tips and tricks that I've found to be most helpful, as well as a few practices that will end up costing you more time than it's worth to use the AI.

Use acceptance criteria and tests

If you want consistent results from AI, make "done" measurable. Put acceptance criteria in your prompt, turn them into tests, and treat the assistant's output like a pull request:

- **Start with examples.** A couple of input-output examples (like the `slugify()` cases) prevent the model from guessing your intent.
- **Ask for tests first.** Even a handful of tests will catch many subtle mistakes and regressions.
- **Prefer small modifications.** Tell agents to keep changes scoped. Small patches are easier to review and less likely to introduce unrelated bugs.
- **Make the computer do the arguing.** When the assistant claims something works, let tests, linters, and type checkers confirm it.

Don't stop coding

While AI can generate complete functions, or even working programs, it works best when you take the lead. Keep your skills up-to-date and use AI as a tool to help you write more code, rather than as a tool that will write your code for you.

Not only will the AI learn from you and write better code, but you'll also be able to fully understand the code you're writing, which is essential to creating high-quality software.

Be specific

When prompting a coding assistant to generate code, or when asking a question about how to do something, be as specific as possible. When you're exploring an idea that you don't yet know how to code, it can be helpful to start with a vague prompt to generate ideas. But once you understand the problem and the domain, ask for details.

Think in steps

Complex requests are much more likely to result in unacceptable responses. Instead, break down every problem into its smallest units. Instead of saying, "How do I write an Instagram clone?" start with a plan (which you should consider writing as an SRS) and then with a small piece, such as the new user signup page.

Ask follow-up questions

If you're unsure about how a piece of generated code works or if a response is unexpected, ask the AI assistant to clarify, explain, or try again. For example, if a function generated by the AI doesn't look quite right to you, but you don't know exactly what's wrong with it, ask the AI to provide several other ways that the function might be written. Just as you might watch several YouTube videos before finding the best solution to a problem, having your AI assistant generate options can be a great way to figure out what will work best. If you don't like the responses one AI assistant gives you, try another AI assistant. Or try feeding the code generated by one AI assistant to another one, asking it to improve the code.

Check the official documentation

Remember that coding assistants are trained on publicly available code, and the LLM behind the assistant may have a training data cutoff date. As a result, code generated by an LLM may use deprecated syntax, an older version of a library, or libraries that are no longer recommended. If a code assistant uses syntax or a library that you're not familiar with, check the official documentation to make sure you're using it correctly.

Use examples and context

Although the latest LLMs have amazing capabilities, they aren't mind readers. If you want the output from a request to be in a specific format, give the AI an example of that format. If the code you ask the AI to generate will integrate with some other function or service, provide the relevant information to the AI as context.

Prioritize security

Chatbots and coding assistants may use your input to train the underlying model. To be certain that no sensitive or personally identifying information will show up in suggestions given to other users of the LLM, always anonymize sensitive data. For example, if you ask the AI to summarize a long email, remove or change the email addresses and names from the email before submitting it as input to an LLM.

Keep learning

Working with a chatbot or a coding assistant is a great way to get answers to coding questions, but it's no substitute for staying up-to-date the same way programmers always have — by talking with other programmers, engaging in online forums on StackOverflow, Reddit, and Hacker News, watching videos, taking classes, and reading high-quality books like the one you have in front of you!

Keep your tools updated

AI coding tools are evolving quickly. Make sure that you have the latest version of whatever tools you're using. If you learn about a new tool that seems promising (through any of the sources mentioned in the preceding tip), try it out. If a new tool or IDE works better for you than the one you've been using, consider switching to it.

Be mindful of AI's limitations

As you see repeatedly in this book, LLMs aren't perfect or omniscient. They were trained on a lot of data and can make predictions based on patterns they find. If you're writing code that's unlike anything the AI has seen before, it will be of little help to you.

IN THIS CHAPTER

» Finding and eliminating bugs

» Refactoring and improving code quality

» Testing your code with AI assistance

» Translating between programming languages

» Optimizing performance

» Documenting and maintaining your code

Chapter 4

Fixing and Optimizing Code with AI

If debugging is the process of removing software bugs, then programming must be the process of putting them in.

— EDSGER W. DIJKSTRA

Writing software is only partly about producing new code. Most of a developer's time goes into everything that surrounds it: finding bugs, cleaning up messy code, writing tests, translating code from one language or platform to another, making it run faster, documenting how it works, and maintaining it over the long haul. In this chapter, you learn how AI tools can take some of the tedium out of those tasks and, in many cases, produce a credible first pass for you.

The principles in this chapter outlast any particular tool. Models and IDE plug-ins come and go, but the underlying ideas have been remarkably stable for decades:

what a bug is, what a code smell looks like, what a good test does, and what kinds of maintenance software needs. Modern AI changes how much of that work you can delegate and how carefully you need to verify what comes back.

Finding and Eliminating Bugs

The term debugging dates back to Admiral Grace Hopper, who in the 1940s removed an actual moth from a computer and noted that she was debugging it. Today you're far more likely to encounter logical bugs than literal insects, but the goal is the same: locate the defect, understand it, and fix it without introducing new problems.

Before you can remove bugs, you need to know what kind you're dealing with. Most defects fall into a handful of familiar categories.

Knowing your bugs

Software bugs come in many varieties, but most of them fall into one of the following types:

- Syntax errors are incorrect or missing characters that prevent the program from compiling or running.
- Runtime errors don't stop the program from starting, but they cause it to crash while running.
- Functional bugs occur when a feature doesn't do what it was designed to do. A search box that returns no results when it should is a common one.
- Logical bugs come from flawed business logic. Assigning a value to the wrong variable or computing the wrong total falls into this category.
- Workflow bugs involve the user's navigation through the app. A link that goes to the wrong page or a step that's skipped in a wizard is a workflow bug.
- Unit-level bugs are small, easy-to-fix defects contained in a single function. Missing input validation on an email field is one common type.
- Integration bugs appear when individual units that each work correctly behave badly together, often because they exchange data in slightly different formats.

» Out-of-bound bugs occur when a user interacts with the software in an unexpected way. Entering 9999 in a field that expects a value from 1 to 10 is a classic case.

» Security bugs make the software vulnerable to attacks or data leaks. They might not block normal usage, but they're the highest-priority bugs to fix.

WARNING

All non-trivial software has bugs. Aiming for bug-free code is unrealistic, and the attempt tends to produce missed deadlines, ballooning budgets, and demoralized teams. Aim instead for software that fails gracefully, reveals problems quickly, and can be fixed without drama.

Preventing bugs with static analysis

Debugging is frustrating, so it pays to prevent bugs before you write them. Static code analysis tools, more commonly called linters, read your code without running it and flag patterns that often turn into defects. A code formatter cares about tabs, spaces, and indentation. A linter cares about the shape of your code and your adherence to good conventions.

ESLint for JavaScript and TypeScript, Pylint and Ruff for Python, RuboCop for Ruby, and similar tools for other languages all work the same way. They apply a list of rules to your source files and report violations. Most modern IDEs and editors run them continuously in the background, underlining problems with a red squiggly line as you type.

REMEMBER

Debugging fixes problems that occur while your code is running. Linting fixes problems in your code that exist before it runs. Time spent on the second kind tends to reduce time spent on the first.

AI coding assistants pair well with linters. When the linter flags a problem you don't understand, you can ask a chat assistant to explain what the rule is, why it matters, and how to fix it. Many editors now offer one-click "Fix with AI" actions that propose a corrected version of the offending code. Review the proposed fix before accepting it. AI tools sometimes change more than you asked them to, and not always for the better. (For more on working with chat assistants, see Book 4, Chapter 2.)

TIP

If your linter and your code formatter ever disagree about whitespace or layout, adjust the linter rules. Don't waste time refereeing between two automated tools when one of them is happy to be overruled.

Debugging with AI

Even with good formatting and a strict linter, problems slip through. When they do, two techniques have always been the workhorses of debugging: logging and breakpoints.

Logging is the process of writing messages from your running program so you can see what it did. In JavaScript, you use `console.log()`. In Python, the `print()` statement or the logging module does the same job. Logs are particularly useful for tracking down problems that only show up in production or in long-running processes.

Breakpoints let you pause a running program at a chosen line and inspect the state of its variables. Every major IDE and every modern browser has a built-in debugger that supports breakpoints, step-over, step-into, and a call-stack view. Learning to use one well is one of the most valuable investments a developer can make.

AI changes the picture in how quickly you can move from "something is wrong" to a likely cause. Paste the misbehaving function into a chat assistant, along with enough context to explain what the code is supposed to do, and you'll often get a plausible diagnosis and a candidate fix in seconds. Coding agents that can read your whole project and run your code (Claude Code, Cursor's agent mode, Aider, and similar tools) take this a step further. They can reproduce the bug, edit several files, run the tests, and present a diff for you to review.

TIP

When you ask an AI assistant to fix a bug, include the error message, the smallest code snippet that demonstrates the problem, and a short description of what you expected to happen. The more context you provide, the more likely the response is to be useful.

Don't trust the first answer blindly. AI assistants will sometimes "fix" code by silently changing behavior you actually wanted, or by editing more than you asked. Treat every suggested change like it was made by a junior developer: read it, understand it, and run your tests before merging.

Automating dependency hygiene

A surprising number of bugs, and most security vulnerabilities, aren't in code you wrote. They're in libraries you depend on. Modern projects can have hundreds or thousands of dependencies, and every one of them is a potential source of trouble.

Services like Snyk, GitHub's Dependabot, and Renovate continuously scan your dependency tree, flag known vulnerabilities, and open pull requests that upgrade affected packages. Most of these tools also perform code analysis to identify common security antipatterns: SQL injection risks, unsafe deserialization, secrets committed to the repo, and others.

REMEMBER

Node packages and many other ecosystems use semantic versioning (semver) in the form X.Y.Z. The first number signals a breaking change, the second adds new functionality without breaking the old, and the third is a bug-fix patch. Always read the changelog before merging a major-version upgrade. The auto-generated PR may compile but break behavior elsewhere.

Upgrading an out-of-date dependency to its latest patch version is a near-perfect candidate for full automation: low risk, high frequency, and tedious to do by hand. Bigger upgrades and code-level fixes still deserve a human in the loop.

Refactoring and Improving Code Quality

Refactoring is the process of changing the structure of code without changing what it does. You refactor to make code easier to read, easier to extend, or easier to test. Refactoring is also a major source of bugs, which is why you should do it in small steps, with tests and version control as a safety net.

Recognizing code smells

A code smell, as defined by Kent Beck and Martin Fowler, is a surface indication that usually corresponds to a deeper problem in the system. Code smells aren't always bugs, but they're worth paying attention to because they often grow into bugs over time. Fowler's classic book *Refactoring* groups them into a few broad families.

- **Dispensables** are bits of code that don't need to exist: duplicate code, dead code that no one calls anymore, lazy classes that barely do anything, comments that explain what the code already says, and "oddball" alternate solutions to a problem that's already solved elsewhere.
- **Bloaters** are pieces of code that have grown larger than they should be: giant classes that do too many things, functions with twelve parameters, and primitive obsession (using a string or number where a small object would be clearer).
- **Abusers** misuse a language feature: tangled if/else chains where polymorphism would be cleaner, switch statements stretching for hundreds of lines, temporary fields used only under particular circumstances.

» **Couplers** connect parts of the code too tightly: feature envy (a method that pokes at another object's internals more than its own), message chains that traverse many objects to get a single value, and middleman classes that exist only to delegate to another class.

» **Change preventers** are smells that make change painful: divergent change (one class has to be edited for many unrelated reasons) and shotgun surgery (one small change forces edits in many classes).

Other smells worth knowing include magic numbers (hard-coded values with no explanation), inconsistent or uncommunicative names, and excessive global state. None of these will stop your program from running today, but each one will slow down whoever has to read the code tomorrow.

Detecting smells and refactoring with AI

Code smells are normally caught during a code review. AI assistants do well at this kind of work. They can read a file or a whole repository, flag common smells, and propose specific refactors. A prompt as simple as "Review this file and list any code smells you see, with line numbers and a short explanation" will often return a useful list.

Be aware that AI reviews are non-deterministic. Ask the same question twice, and you may get two different lists. Run the review a few times if you want broader coverage, and treat the results as suggestions to investigate rather than commands to follow.

TIP

Leading questions like "What's wrong with this code?" will almost always produce a list of things that are "wrong," even when the code is fine. Trust your own judgment, especially on style questions. The output is often more confident than its training data warrants.

Refactoring safely

Refactoring has a habit of breaking things that were working. Three safety nets protect you:

» **Version control.** Commit early, commit often, and do refactoring work on a branch. If a refactor goes sideways, you can throw the branch away.

» **Tests.** A good test suite tells you within seconds whether a refactor changed behavior. If you don't have tests for the code you're about to refactor, write them first.

» **Small steps.** Make one change, run the tests, and commit. Avoid combining refactors with feature work in the same commit. When something breaks, you want to be able to identify which change caused it.

Coding agents are well suited to mechanical refactors: extracting a function, renaming a variable across files, splitting a long function into smaller ones, or moving code into a new module. Ask the agent to make one named refactor, run the tests, and report back. If the tests pass and the diff looks right, accept it. If not, revert and try a different approach.

Working with code formatters

Formatting your code consistently is the cheapest way to make it more readable. Prettier (for JavaScript and TypeScript), Black (for Python), gofmt (for Go), and rustfmt (for Rust) are all opinionated: you give up some control over style in exchange for never needing to think about formatting your code again.

Formatters are rule-based, not AI-based, and that's a feature. When you want a deterministic, predictable transformation that makes a file conform to a team's style guide, a rule-based tool will produce the same result every time. AI assistants are better suited to tasks that require some judgment.

TIP

Knowing when to use an AI tool versus a rule-based tool is just as important as knowing how to use either kind. Reach for AI when the task requires interpretation. Reach for a deterministic tool when you want certainty.

Testing Your Code

Of all the programming tasks that AI can help with, testing may be the safest. Running a test doesn't change your code; it only checks whether the code does what you say it does. Writing tests with AI assistance is trickier, because the quality of the tests depends heavily on how clearly you've described what the code is supposed to do.

Writing a test plan

A test plan describes what you're going to test, how you'll test it, and how you'll know when you're done. On a small or personal project, it might be a paragraph in a README. On a regulated project in aviation, medical devices, or financial systems, it's a formal document with a schedule, exit criteria, and a sign-off process.

Whichever end of that spectrum you're on, the same questions apply:

- **What are you testing?** Identify the features and behaviors that matter most.
- **How will you test it?** Decide which mix of unit tests, integration tests, end-to-end tests, performance tests, and security tests is appropriate.
- **Where will the tests run?** Some tests run on a developer's laptop. Others need a staging environment that mirrors production.
- **When are you done?** Define the exit criteria. "All tests pass" is a start, but you'll also want coverage targets, performance budgets, and a no-known-critical-bugs threshold.
- **Who owns it?** On large projects, the QA team owns the test plan. On small projects, you do. The plan should always have an owner.

AI can jump-start the planning process. Ask a chat assistant to analyze your code and propose a test plan, or to brainstorm edge cases for a particular function. You'll get a useful starting list, which you can revise and add to based on what you know about the system.

Generating tests with AI

Once you have a plan, AI can write a lot of the boilerplate. Modern coding assistants do well at producing tests in popular frameworks: Jest, Vitest, and Playwright for JavaScript and TypeScript; pytest for Python; JUnit for Java; RSpec for Ruby. Open a function, ask the assistant to write tests for it, and you'll usually get something close to working in seconds.

The trap is that an AI-generated test will verify the function as it is, including any bugs. Consider a Python function called sum_numbers(a, b) that returns the string "a + b" instead of an integer. Ask an AI to test it, and you may get tests that confirm it correctly returns the string "1 + 2" when given 1 and 2. The test may pass, but the function is still wrong.

WARNING

AI writes tests that verify the function you have, not the function you intended. To test for intent, you need to spell out what the function is supposed to do in the prompt or in a clear docstring at the top of the function.

Once your tests run, a coverage report shows which lines of code your tests actually exercise. Coverage tools come built into most test frameworks. Use coverage as a guide to where you're undertested, not as a goal in itself. A coverage figure of 100 percent doesn't mean the code is correct, only that every line ran at least once.

Test-driven development with AI

Test-driven development (TDD) inverts the usual order: you write a test that describes the behavior you want, run it to confirm it fails, then write the minimum code needed to make the test pass. Then you refactor and repeat. The cycle is often summarized as red, green, refactor.

TDD is a surprisingly good fit for AI-assisted coding. The tests give the AI a precise, machine-checkable specification of what the code should do. Write the test yourself, then ask the assistant to make it pass. Because the test is concrete, the AI is less likely to drift into doing the wrong thing. When it does, the test fails, and you know immediately.

REMEMBER

In AI-assisted TDD, you write the tests and the AI writes the code. If the AI writes both, it's likely to produce code and tests that agree with each other and miss what you actually wanted.

Translating Code Between Languages

Translating code from one programming language to another is one of the things people most want AI to do for them, and one of the riskiest things to ask. When it works, it can save weeks of tedious work. When it doesn't, you end up with a slightly different program that's hard to debug, because no one fully understands either version.

When (and when not) to translate

Translating code between languages is worth the trouble when there's a compelling reason: a platform that doesn't support the original language, a runtime that's being retired, a security model that requires a different stack. "The new language is cooler" is not a good reason. A working program in an old language is almost always more valuable than a half-working program in a fashionable one.

Translation between dialects (JavaScript to TypeScript, Python 2 to Python 3, Java to Kotlin) tends to be much more reliable than translation between fundamentally different languages, because the underlying execution model is shared. Translation between paradigms (functional Haskell to imperative Go, say) is the riskiest case and the one where AI is most likely to produce code that compiles but misbehaves.

Preparing code for translation

Whatever the source and target languages, some housekeeping first will make the translation smoother:

- **Back up your original code.** This is the most important step. You need a known-good version to revert to.
- **Comment and document thoroughly.** Good comments give the AI context about the intent of each function, not just its mechanics.
- **Clean and refactor first.** Translate clean code, not messy code. Remove dead code, simplify complex bits, and resolve obvious smells before the translation.
- **Enforce a consistent style.** Run a linter and a formatter. Consistent code is easier for human readers and AI tools to parse.
- **Use descriptive names.** Variables named user_email translate better than variables named x1 or x2.
- **Modularize.** Translating a single 4,000-line file all at once is far harder than translating thirty 130-line modules one at a time.
- **Flag language-specific features.** Decorators, macros, async/await semantics, exception models, and similar features often don't map cleanly. Identify them up front so you can think about each case deliberately.

Verifying translated code

Treat translated code as freshly written code, not as something that's already been tested. Before you trust it, work through the same checks you'd apply to any new code:

- **Read it.** Take the time to understand what the AI produced. If you can't read it, you can't maintain it.
- **Run the tests.** Port your existing test suite alongside the code. If you didn't have tests before, write them now. This is exactly the situation they protect against.
- **Cross-reference output.** Feed the original and the translation the same inputs and compare the outputs. Differences are bugs.
- **Lint and review.** Run a linter for the new language and have someone (or another AI) review the result.

» **Re-do the security review.** Different languages and runtimes have different vulnerabilities. A web app converted to a mobile app has a completely different threat model.

WARNING

Don't ask an AI to translate code into a language you don't know. You won't be able to tell whether the result is idiomatic, secure, or even correct. Translation is one of the cases where AI's confidence outruns its reliability.

Optimizing Performance

Optimization is the process of making code do the same job faster, with less memory, or with less network or disk activity. Almost all code can be improved on at least one of these axes. Improving them costs time, risks new bugs, and often doesn't matter.

Profile before you optimize

Donald Knuth's famous warning that "premature optimization is the root of all evil" is one of the most quoted lines in computing. What Knuth meant is that programmers waste enormous amounts of effort optimizing things that don't matter (shaving microseconds off code that runs once a day) while ignoring the parts of the program that genuinely are slow.

The fix is to profile first. A profiler measures how long each function takes and how often it runs, so you can see exactly where your program spends its time. Profilers exist for every major language: cProfile and Scalene for Python, the V8 inspector for Node.js, JFR for Java, and perf for native code. Run one, look at the top of the report, and you'll usually find that 80 percent of the runtime happens in 20 percent of the code.

REMEMBER

Optimize the slow parts. Leave the rest alone. Code clarity is usually more valuable than a marginal speed improvement, especially given how much hardware speeds up every year.

AI-assisted optimization

Once a profiler has told you where the bottleneck is, an AI assistant can help with the harder question of what to do about it. Show it the slow function and the profile output and ask for ways to make it faster. Common suggestions include caching results, replacing a quadratic algorithm with a linear one, batching I/O, moving work off the request path, and replacing pure-Python loops with vectorized NumPy or Pandas operations.

Scalene combines the two steps. It profiles the code and then asks a language model to propose optimizations for the slowest lines. Treat the suggestions as starting points. Implement one at a time, re-run the profiler, and confirm that the change actually helped. Optimizations that look obvious sometimes make things worse, because modern CPUs and JIT compilers are smarter than you'd think.

TIP

Before you optimize, ask whether you should. If users haven't complained about performance and the program is fast enough for the job, your time is probably better spent elsewhere. If users are complaining, optimization rises to the top of the list.

Documenting Your Code

Documentation is the part of programming that everyone agrees is important and nobody enjoys. AI doesn't completely solve that problem, but it reduces the time and willpower required to write reasonable docs, which often means the difference between docs that exist and docs that don't.

Internal versus external documentation

Software documentation comes in two broad flavors. Internal documentation is for the people who build and maintain the software: comments, architecture diagrams, requirements documents, design notes, status reports, and runbooks. External documentation is for the people who use the software: README files, tutorials, FAQs, troubleshooting guides, API references, and release notes.

Each kind matters, and each benefits from AI assistance in different ways. Internal documentation is mostly about capturing decisions and context that aren't obvious from the code itself. External documentation is mostly about explaining the software clearly to someone who hasn't seen it before.

Generating comments and API docs

Modern AI coding assistants do a respectable job of generating comments and documentation strings from existing code. Highlight a function and ask for a

JSDoc, docstring, or Javadoc comment, and you'll get one in seconds. The output is often longer than it needs to be, so trim it down to the parts a reader actually needs.

Two pieces of advice keep AI-generated comments useful. Comments should explain why the code is the way it is, not just what it does. The code already shows what it does. Use comments to capture the constraints, trade-offs, and historical context that aren't visible. And remember to regenerate the comment when the code changes. Stale comments are worse than no comments.

For API documentation, the OpenAPI Specification (OAS) is the de facto standard for describing REST APIs. Swagger, Postman, ReadMe, and Redocly can turn an OAS file into an interactive API reference. AI assistants do well at generating an initial OAS file from your route handlers and at keeping it in sync as the API evolves. Validate the generated spec by importing it into one of these tools and exercising the endpoints. A spec that compiles but doesn't match your real API is worse than no spec at all.

Visual documentation and diagrams

Diagrams (sequence diagrams, architecture diagrams, entity-relationship diagrams, state machines) are some of the most useful documentation you can produce. They're also the kind that most people skip because they're tedious to draw. Two techniques make them easier.

The first is text-based diagramming. Mermaid, PlantUML, and similar tools let you describe a diagram in a few lines of text and render it as an image. AI assistants do well at generating these descriptions. A prompt like "Write a Mermaid sequence diagram for the login flow in this file" will usually produce a workable first draft.

The second is to use a diagramming tool with built-in AI assistance, like draw.io's smart templates or the diagram features in modern documentation platforms. Describe what you want in natural language, and the tool generates a starting point that you can edit.

WARNING

Don't use generative AI for diagrams that need to be accurate to the pixel, like annotated screenshots that call out specific UI elements. Image-generation models still struggle with text and exact placement. For those, use a screenshot tool with manual annotations.

Maintaining Code Over Time

Software is never finished. After planning, coding, testing, documenting, and deploying, the maintenance phase begins, and it never ends. By most accounts, professional developers spend nearly half their time on maintenance work. It isn't the most glamorous part of the job, but it's the part that keeps the lights on.

The four types of maintenance

Software maintenance is traditionally divided into four categories. Done well and in combination, they keep software healthy over its lifetime.

- **Corrective maintenance,** also known as software repair, is the work of fixing bugs and errors discovered after deployment. It's always reactive, triggered by a bug report from a tester or an end user.
- **Adaptive maintenance** keeps software working as the world around it changes. Operating systems get upgraded, dependencies release new versions, third-party APIs change, browsers deprecate features, and your app has to keep up.
- **Perfective maintenance** enhances the software based on user feedback and new requirements. New features fall here, as does removing features that no one uses anymore.
- **Preventative maintenance** is proactive: refactoring messy code, updating documentation, increasing test coverage, and tightening security before any of those things turn into a bug. Of the four types, this is the one most often skipped and most often regretted.

Managing technical debt

Technical debt is the cost of future work created when you choose a quick, limited solution today instead of a better one that would take longer. Some technical debt is unavoidable, especially in the early phases of a project when you're trying to ship a proof of concept. It accumulates interest. The longer you ignore it, the more it costs to fix.

Common causes of technical debt include:

- Starting development before requirements are clear.
- Business pressure to ship something, anything, this quarter.

- Years of incremental changes that each made sense in isolation but no longer add up to a coherent design.
- Skipping tests, which encourages quick fixes that hide problems.
- Skipping documentation, which guarantees that the next developer misunderstands the code.
- Postponing required refactoring, usually because product owners would rather have new features than maintenance.

AI-assisted code quality tools like Code Climate, SonarQube, and CodeScene measure technical debt by analyzing your repository against a battery of rules and reporting on complexity, duplication, test coverage, and maintainability. They give you a grade, a list of issues, and an estimate of how long it would take to resolve them. Combined with an AI coding assistant that can do the refactoring, they make it realistic to pay down debt incrementally instead of in one large rewrite.

Using AI across the maintenance lifecycle

Every kind of maintenance work in this chapter benefits from AI assistance:

- **Corrective maintenance:** AI can read stack traces, propose fixes, and run regression tests. Dependency scanners can automate routine security updates.
- **Adaptive maintenance:** When a dependency or API changes, AI can read the changelog or migration guide and propose the edits your code needs.
- **Perfective maintenance:** AI helps brainstorm enhancements, draft new tests, and refactor old code so that new features can land cleanly.
- **Preventative maintenance:** AI is genuinely good at the tedious side of preventative work: generating tests for previously untested code, writing missing docstrings, identifying code smells, and proposing safe refactors.

AI is fast, willing, and often wrong. It works best with tests, version control, and your own judgment in the loop. Used carefully, it makes the unglamorous parts of software development genuinely faster. Used carelessly, it generates new technical debt as fast as it pays off the old. The choice is yours.

5 Basic Web Coding

Contents at a Glance

IN THIS CHAPTER

- » Learning the purpose of HTML
- » Understanding basic HTML structure
- » Adding headlines, paragraphs, hyperlinks, and images
- » Formatting web page text
- » Creating a basic HTML website

Chapter 1 Exploring Basic HTML

A chain is no stronger than its weakest link, and life is after all a chain.

—WILLIAM JAMES

HTML, or *HyperText Markup Language,* is used in every single web page you browse on the internet. Because the language is so foundational, a good first step for you is to start learning HTML.

In this chapter, you discover HTML, including HTML structure and how to make text appear in the browser. Next, you find out how to format text and display images in a web browser. Finally, you create your own, and possibly first, HTML website. You may find that HTML without additional styling appears plain and doesn't look like the websites you normally visit on the internet. After you code a basic website using HTML, you use additional languages in later chapters to add even more style and functionality to your websites.

What Does HTML Do?

HTML is the language used to give structure to a website. HTML was designed for creating structured documents, such as a letter, a book, or a scientific paper that you might create using a word processor. Whether you use Microsoft Word, Apple

Pages, or another application, your word processor has a main window in which you type text content and a menu or toolbar with multiple options to structure and style that text (see Figure 1-1). Using your word processor, you can create headings and subheadings, write paragraphs, insert pictures, create footers, and so forth. Similarly, you can use HTML to structure text that appears on websites.

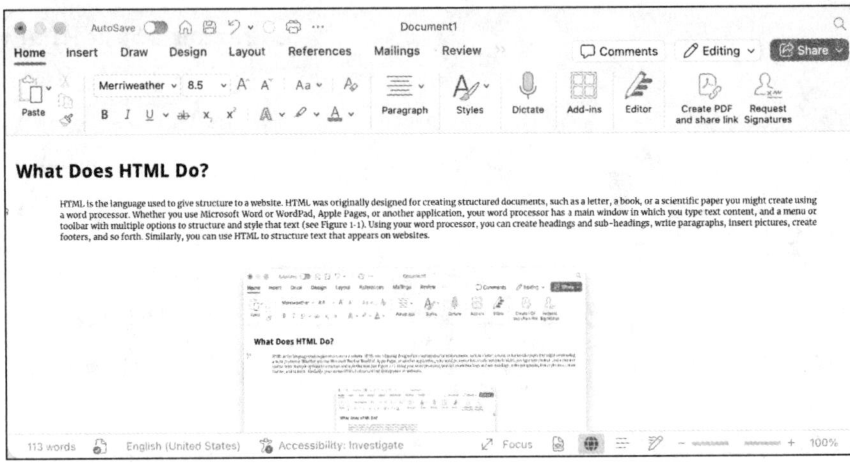

FIGURE 1-1: The layout of a word processor.

Markup language documents, like HTML documents, are just plain text files. Unlike documents created with a word processor, you can view an HTML file using any web browser on any type of computer.

REMEMBER HTML files are plain text files that appear styled only when viewed with a browser. By contrast, the rich text file format used by word processors adds unseen formatting commands to the file. As a result, HTML written in a rich text file won't render correctly in the browser.

Understanding HTML Structure

HTML follows a few rules to ensure that a website is always displayed in the same way, no matter which browser or computer is used. Once you understand these rules, you'll be better able to predict how the browser will display your HTML pages and to diagnose your mistakes when the browser displays your web page differently than you expected.

TIP

You can use any browser to display your HTML files. The current leading browsers, including Microsoft Edge, Mozilla Firefox, Google Chrome, and Apple Safari, are all updated often, are generally fast, and support and consistently render the widest variety of HTML tags. In addition to these four, there are a number of more niche browsers to explore, including Opera, DuckDuckGo, Brave, and Vivaldi. Each of these browsers has its own focus (such as privacy or customizability). It can be fun and rewarding to explore the possibilities!

Identifying elements

The basic building blocks of HTML are called *elements*. Elements give meaning and structure to web pages. The browser recognizes an element if the following three conditions exist:

- **The element has a name that's a letter, word, or phrase with special meaning.** For example, `h1` is an element recognized by the browser to mark text as a header. By default, a header is displayed in a browser with bold text and an enlarged font size.
- **The element's name is enclosed with a left-angle bracket (`<`) and right-angle bracket (`>`).** An element enclosed in this way is called a *tag* (such as `<h1>`).
- **An opening tag (`<element>`) is followed by a closing tag (`</element>`).** Note that the closing tag differs from the opening tag by the addition of a forward slash after the first left bracket and before the element (such as `</h1>`).

REMEMBER

Some HTML elements are *void elements* (such as `br` and `img`), which means they don't have closing tags. In HTML, you can write them as `<br>` and `<img ...>`; you may also see a trailing slash (such as `/>`) in some examples, but it isn't required in HTML.

When all three conditions are met, web browsers will display the text between the opening and closing tags using some predefined style, or the browser will take some other action based on the content of the element. If one of these conditions is not met, the browser will try to figure out what you meant to do, but the result may not be what you expect.

For a better understanding of these three conditions, look at the following example code:

```
<h1>This is a big heading with all three conditions</h1>
h1 This is text without the < and > sign surrounding the tag /h1
<rockstar>This is text with a tag that has no meaning to the browser</rockstar>
This is regular text
```

You can see how a browser displays this code in Figure 1-2.

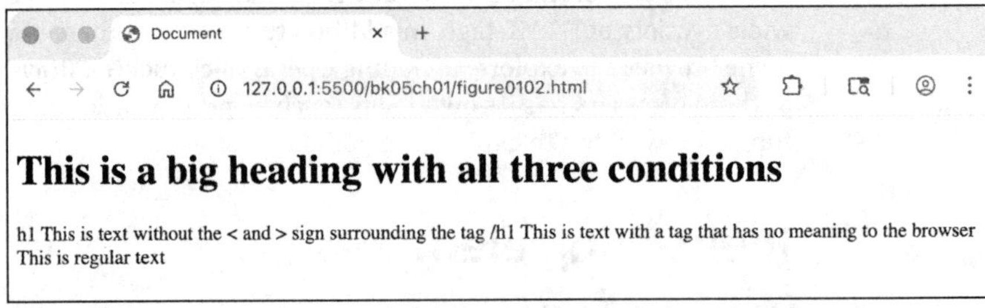

FIGURE 1-2: The example code displayed in a browser.

The browser applies a header effect to "This is a big heading with all three conditions" because `h1` is a header element and all three conditions for a valid HTML element exist:

- The browser recognizes the `h1` element.
- The `h1` element name is surrounded by a left-angle bracket (`<`) and a right-angle bracket (`>`).
- The opening tag (`<h1>`) is followed by text and then a closing tag (`</h1>`).

TIP

Note how the `h1` tags are not displayed in the heading. The browser will never display the text of a tag in a properly formatted HTML element.

The remaining lines of code are displayed as plain text because each is missing one of the conditions. On the second line of code, the `<h1>` tag is missing the left and right brackets, which violates the second condition. The third line of code violates the first condition because `rockstar` is not a recognized HTML element. (Once you finish this chapter, however, you might feel like a rockstar!) Finally, the fourth line of code is displayed as plain text because it has no opening tag preceding the text and no closing tag following the text, which violates the third condition.

REMEMBER

Every left-angle bracket must be followed by the element name and then a right-angle bracket. In addition, every opening HTML tag must be followed with a closing HTML tag.

Over 100 HTML elements exist, and you'll learn about the most important elements in the following sections. For now, don't worry about memorizing individual element names.

WARNING

HTML is a forgiving language, and browsers may properly render it even if you're missing pieces of code, like a closing tag. However, if your code has too many errors, your page won't display correctly.

Featuring your best attribute

Attributes provide additional ways to modify the behavior of an element or specify additional information. Usually, but not always, you set an attribute equal to a value enclosed in quotes. Here's an example using the `title` attribute and the `hidden` attribute:

```
<h1>Web Development</h1>
<p title="HyperText Markup Language">
  Hover over <abbr>HTML</abbr> to see more info
</p>
<p>This page has a secret message.</p>
<p hidden>You found it! But browsers won&apos;t display this.</p>
```

The `title` attribute provides advisory information about the element that many browsers display when the mouse cursor hovers over the affected text (in other words, a *tooltip*). In this example, the `<abbr>` element wraps the word HTML inside a `<p>` tag that has a title attribute set to `'HyperText Markup Language'`. In a browser, when you place your mouse cursor over the word `HTML`, the text `HyperText Markup Language` might appear as a tooltip. (See Figure 1-3.) Because tooltips are not always available on touch devices and might not be read consistently by assistive technology, don't rely on `title` to communicate critical information.

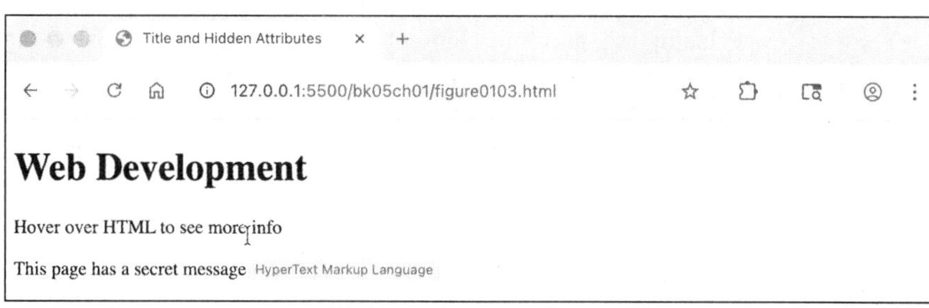

FIGURE 1-3: A heading with `title` attribute has a tooltip.

The `hidden` attribute indicates that the element is not currently relevant, so the browser won't render it. In this example, the hidden message never appears in the browser window because the `hidden` attribute is in the opening `<p>` tag. Developers often use `hidden` to temporarily hide content that might be shown later (for example, after a user clicks a button). Note that hiding content is not a security feature because users can still view the page source. If you need to submit a value in a form without letting the user edit it, use a hidden form control such as <input type="hidden" name="eventTime" value="7:00pm">.

You don't have to use one attribute at a time. You can include multiple attributes in the opening HTML tag, like this:

```
<p title="HyperText Markup Language" lang="en">HTML</p>
```

This example uses the title attribute and the lang attribute. The lang attribute is set to "en" to specify that the content of the element is in the English language.

REMEMBER

When including multiple attributes, separate each attribute with one space.

Keep the following rules in mind when using attributes:

- Always include the attribute in the opening HTML tag.
- Multiple attributes can modify a single element.
- If the attribute has a value, use the equals sign (=) and enclose the value in quotes.

Standing head, title, and body above the rest

HTML files are structured in a specific way so browsers can correctly interpret the files' information. A standard, well-formed HTML page typically includes the following core pieces: the DOCTYPE declaration, which appears once and doesn't have a closing tag, and four elements whose opening and closing tags appear once:

- **!DOCTYPE html** must appear first in your HTML file, and it appears only once. This tag lets browsers know which version of HTML you're using. In this case, it's the latest version, HTML5. No closing tag is necessary for this element.
- **html** represents the *root,* or beginning, of an HTML document. The <html> tag is followed by first an opening and closing <head> tag, and then an opening and closing <body> tag.
- **head** contains other elements that specify general information about the page, including the title.
- **title** defines the title in the browser's title bar or page tab. Search engines like Google often use the page title as the clickable headline in search results, which can influence how your page is understood.

- **body** contains the main content of an HTML document. Text, images, and other content listed between the opening and closing body tag are displayed by the browser.

Here is an example of a properly structured HTML file with these five pieces (see Figure 1-4):

```
<!doctype html>
<html>
  <head>
    <title>My First Web Page</title>
  </head>
  <body>
    <h1>Welcome to HTML</h1>
    <p>HTML stands for HyperText Markup Language.</p>
    <h2>What is HTML?</h2>
    <p>HTML is the standard language for creating web pages.</p>
    <h2>Why Learn HTML?</h2>
    <p>HTML is the foundation of all websites on the internet.</p>
  </body>
</html>
```

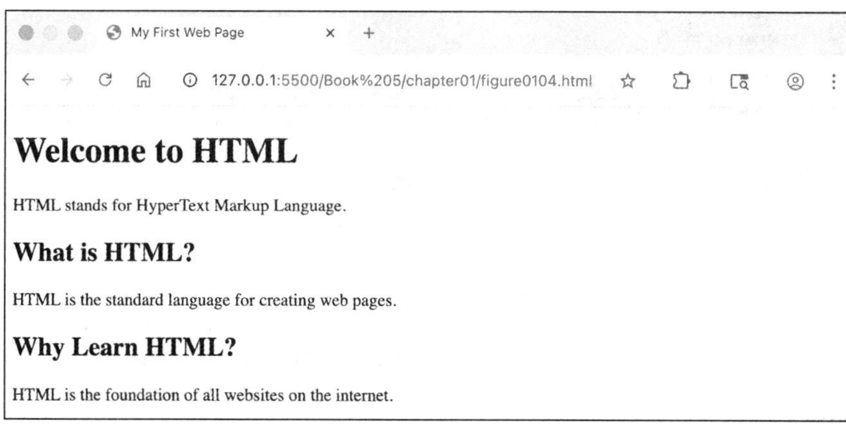

FIGURE 1-4: A web page created with basic HTML elements.

TIP

I highly recommend that you use spaces to indent and separate your tags. Doing so helps you and others read and understand your code. These spaces are only for you and any other human who reads the code, however. As far as your browser is concerned, you could run all your HTML together on one line. (Don't do this, though. The next person who reads your code will be most unhappy.)

HISTORY OF HTML

A computer engineer, Tim Berners-Lee, wanted academics to be able to easily access academic papers and collaborate with each other. To accomplish this goal, in 1989 Mr. Berners-Lee created the first version of HTML, which had the same hyperlink elements you find in this chapter, and hosted the first website in 1991. Unlike with most other computer software, Mr. Berners-Lee made HTML available royalty-free, allowing widespread adoption and use around the world.

Shortly after creating the first iteration of HTML, Mr. Berners-Lee formed the W3C (World Wide Web Consortium), which is a group of people from academic institutions and corporations who define and maintain the HTML language. The W3C continues to develop the HTML language and has defined more than 100 HTML elements, far more than the 18 that Mr. Berners-Lee originally created. The latest version of HTML is HTML5, and it has considerable functionality. In addition to supporting elements from previous HTML versions, HTML5 allows developers to write code for browsers to play audio and video files, easily locate a user's physical location, and build charts and graphs.

REMEMBER

The example had multiple `h2` and `p` elements but only one opening and closing `html`, `head`, `title`, and `body` tag.

Getting Familiar with Common HTML Tasks and Elements

Your browser can interpret over a hundred HTML elements, but most websites use just a few elements to do most of the work in the browser. For example, think of your favorite news website. Have one in mind? Now connect to the internet, open your browser, and type the address of that website. Bring this book with you, and take your time — I can wait!

In the event you can't access the internet right now, check out the article from *The New York Times* in Figure 1-5.

Look closely at the news website on your screen (or the one in Figure 1-5). Four HTML elements are used to create the majority of the page:

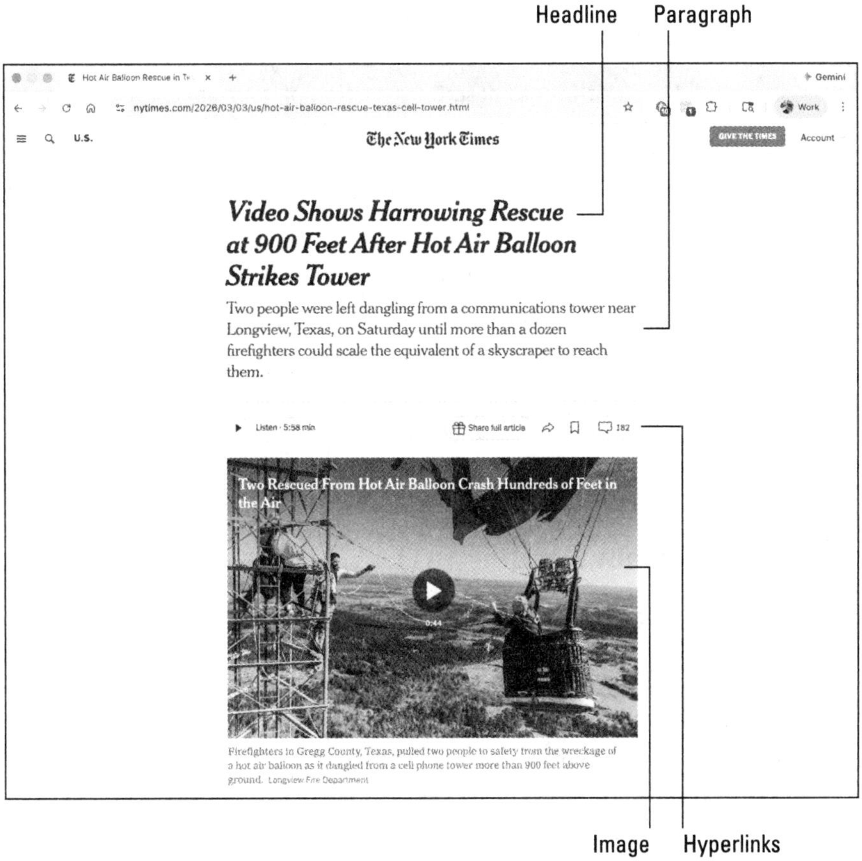

FIGURE 1-5: An article from *The New York Times* with headline, paragraphs, hyperlinks, and images.

- **Headlines:** Headlines are displayed in bold and have a larger font size than the surrounding text.
- **Paragraphs:** Each story is organized into paragraphs with whitespace dividing each paragraph.
- **Hyperlinks:** The site's homepage and article pages have links to other stories and links to share the story, bookmark it, or comment on it.
- **Images, video, and audio:** Writers and editors place images, video, and audio throughout the story, but also look for site images like icons and logos.

The following sections explain how to write code to create some of these common HTML features.

Writing headlines

Use headlines to describe a section of your page. HTML has six levels of headings (see Figure 1-6):

- **h1** is used for the most important heading. There should only be one h1 on a page.
- **h2** is used for subheadings.
- **h3 to h6** are used for less important headings.

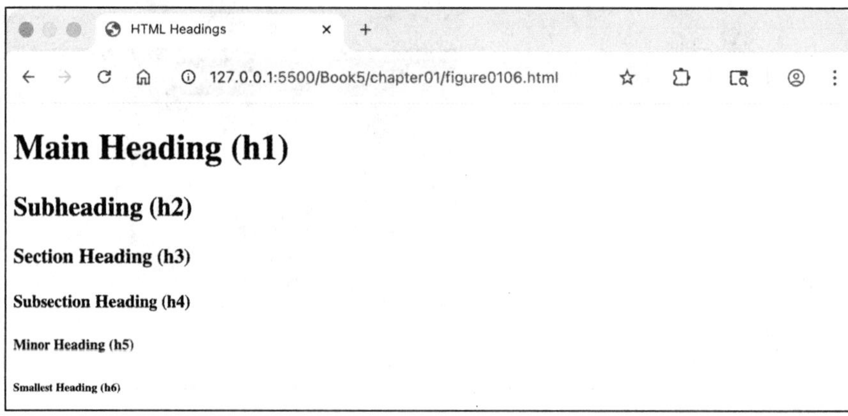

FIGURE 1-6: Headings created using elements `h1` through `h6`.

The browser renders `h1` headings with a font size larger than `h2`'s, which in turn are larger than `h3`'s. Headings start with an opening heading tag, the heading text, and then the closing heading tag, as follows:

```
<h1>Heading text here</h1>
```

Here are some additional code examples showing various headings:

```
<h1>Main Heading (h1)</h1>
<h2>Subheading (h2)</h2>
<h3>Section Heading (h3)</h3>
<h4>Subsection Heading (h4)</h4>
<h5>Minor Heading (h5)</h5>
<h6>Smallest Heading (h6)</h6>
```

REMEMBER

Always close what you open. With headings, remember to include a closing heading tag, such as `</h1>`.

Organizing text in paragraphs

To display text in paragraphs, you can use the p element: Place an opening <p> tag before the paragraph and a closing tag after it. The p element takes text and inserts a line break after the closing tag.

TIP

To insert a single line break after any element, use the <br> tag. The br tag is a void element, so it doesn't use a closing tag.

Paragraphs start with an opening paragraph tag, followed by the paragraph text and then the closing paragraph tag:

```
<p>Paragraph text here</p>
```

Here are some additional examples of coding a paragraph (see Figure 1-7):

```
<p>Armstrong: Okay. I'm going to step off the LM now.</p>
<p>Armstrong: That's one small step for man; one giant leap for mankind.</p>
<p>Armstrong: Yes, the surface is fine and powdery. I can kick it up loosely
   with my toe. It does adhere in fine layers, like powdered charcoal, to the
   sole and sides of my boots.</p>
```

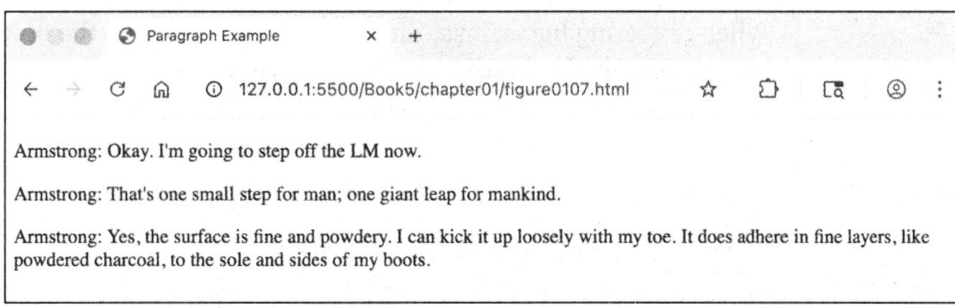

FIGURE 1-7: Text displayed in paragraphs using the p element.

Linking to your heart's content

Hyperlinks are one of HTML's most valuable features. Web pages that include hyperlinked references to other sources allow the reader to access those sources with just a click, a big advantage over printed pages.

Hyperlinks have two parts:

- **Link destination:** The web page the browser visits once the link is clicked.
- **Link description:** The words used to describe the link.

To create a hyperlink, start with an opening anchor tag (<a>), which has the `href` attribute. Then add the value of the `href` attribute, which is the website the browser will go to once the link is clicked. Then add the closing anchor tag.

The resulting HTML should look like this:

```
<a href="website url">Link description</a>
```

Here are three more examples of coding a hyperlink (see Figure 1-8):

```
<a href="https://www.wikipedia.org">Free online encyclopedia</a>
<a href="https://www.weather.gov">National Weather Service</a>
<a href="https://www.nasa.gov">Space exploration and science</a>
```

FIGURE 1-8: Three hyperlinks created using the a element.

When rendering hyperlinks, the browser will underline the link and color the link blue by default. To change these default properties, see Chapter 3 in this minibook.

REMEMBER

The <a> tag does not include a line break after the link.

Adding images

Images spruce up otherwise plain HTML text pages. To include an image on your web page — your own or someone else's — you need a URL that points to an image file. Websites like Google Images (`images.google.com`) and Flickr (`www.flickr.com`) allow you to search for online images based on keywords. When you find an image you like, look for the image's address or URL (many sites offer a share or copy link option), or download the image and host it in a way that matches the site's terms.

WARNING

Make sure you have permission to use an online image. Many sites (including Flickr) let you filter by license (for example, Creative Commons), but you still need to follow the license requirements. Also, be careful about *hotlinking*, which is linking directly to an image hosted on someone else's server. The link can break if the URL changes, and some sites block hotlinking or disallow it in their terms. When in doubt, host the image yourself (with permission) or use an approved image host or CDN (content delivery network).

TIP

If you want to use an image that has not already been uploaded to the internet, you can use a site like `www.imgur.com` to upload and host the image. After uploading, you can copy the direct image URL and use it in your HTML.

To include an image, use the `<img>` tag and define the source of the image using the `src` attribute. You should also include an `alt` attribute that briefly describes the image for readers who can't see it (including people using screen readers). In HTML, `img` is a void element, so it doesn't have a closing tag; you may see a trailing slash (such as `/>`) in some examples, but it isn't required in HTML. See Figure 1-9:

```
<img src="https://upload.wikimedia.org/wikipedia/commons/8/87/Ada_Lovelace.jpg"
   alt="Ada Lovelace" />

<img src="https://upload.wikimedia.org/wikipedia/commons/5/55/Grace_Hopper.jpg"
   alt="Grace Hopper"/>
```

FIGURE 1-9: Images of Ada Lovelace, who is considered the first computer programmer, and Grace Hopper, who invented the compiler, rendered using `<img>`.

TIP

The `img` tag is a void element, which means a separate `</img>` closing tag is not used. For better performance and a steadier page layout, many sites also specify an image's `width` and `height` (or use CSS) so the browser can reserve space before the image finishes loading.

Making HTML Pretty

Now that you know how to display basic text and images in a browser, you should understand how to further customize and style them. HTML has basic capabilities to style content, and later chapters show you how to use CSS to style and position your content down to the last pixel. Here, however, I explain how to do some basic text formatting in HTML, and then you'll build your first web page.

Highlighting with bold, italics, underline, and strikethrough

HTML allows for basic text styling using the following elements:

- `strong` marks important text, which the browser displays as bold.
- `em` marks emphasized text, which the browser displays as italicized.
- `u` marks text as underlined.
- `del` marks deleted text, which the browser displays as strikethrough.

REMEMBER

The underline element is not typically used for text because it can lead to confusion. Hyperlinks, after all, are underlined by default.

To use these elements, start with the element's opening tag, followed by the affected text and then a closing tag, as follows:

```
< element name >Affected text </element name >
```

Here are some examples (see Figure 1-10):

```
<p>
      Grace Hopper, <strong>a US Navy rear admiral</strong>, popularized the
      term "debugging."
    </p>
    <p>
      Alan Turing wrote a paper called
      <em>Computing Machinery and Intelligence</em>.
    </p>
    <p>
      Donald Knuth wrote a book called
      <u>The Art of Computer Programming</u>.
    </p>
```

```
<p>
  Tim Berners-Lee created a system called <del>Mesh</del> World Wide Web.
</p>
<p>
  Margaret Hamilton developed software for the
  <del><em>Lunar</em></del> <em>Apollo</em> program.
</p>
```

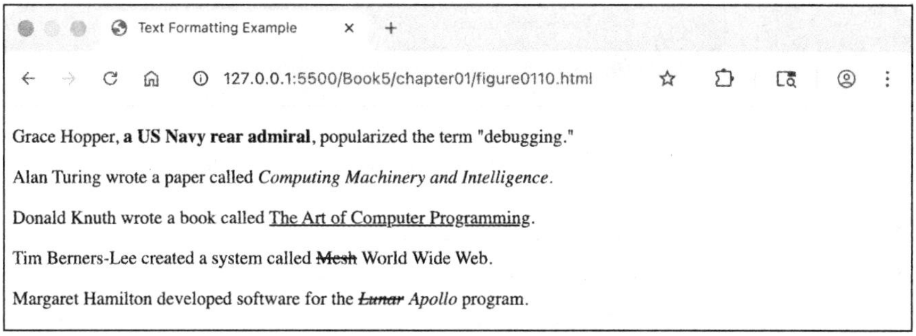

FIGURE 1-10: Sentences formatted using bold, italics, underline, and strikethrough.

TIP

You can apply multiple effects to text by using multiple HTML tags. Always close the most recently opened tag first and then the next most recently used tag. For an example, look at the last line of code in Figure 1-10 and the tags applied to the word *Lunar*.

Raising and lowering text with superscript and subscript

Reference works like *Wikipedia* and technical papers often use superscript for footnotes and subscript for chemical names. To apply these styles, use the following elements:

- **sup** for text marked as superscript
- **sub** for text marked as subscript

Start with the element's opening tag, followed by the affected text and then a closing tag as follows:

```
< element name >Affected text </element name>
```

Here are two examples (see Figure 1-11):

```
<p>The University of Pennsylvania announced to the public the first
electronic general-purpose computer, named ENIAC, on February 14,
1946.<sup>1</sup> </p>
<p>The Centers for Disease Control and Prevention recommends drinking
several glasses of H<sub>2</sub>O per day.</p>
```

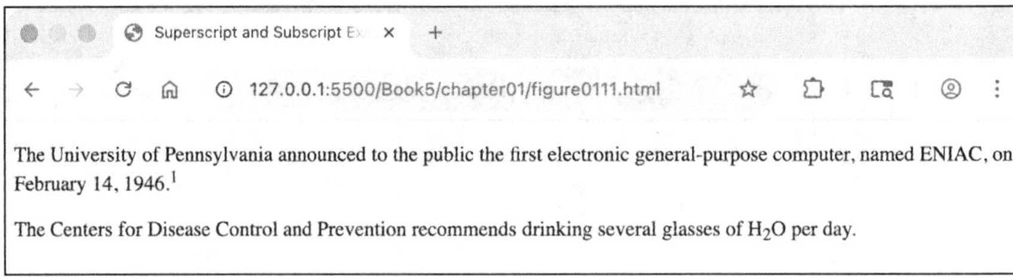

FIGURE 1-11: Text formatted to show superscript and subscript effects.

TIP

When using the superscript element to mark footnotes, use an `<a>` anchor tag to link directly to the footnote so the reader can view the footnote easily.

Building Your First Website Using HTML

Now that you understand the basics of HTML, you can put that knowledge to use by creating a website. You can practice directly on your computer by following these steps:

1. **Open any text editor, such as Notepad (on a PC) or TextEdit (on a Mac).**

   On a PC running Microsoft Windows, you can open Notepad from the Start menu, or press the Windows key and type **Notepad** in the search box.

   On a Macintosh, select the Spotlight Search (hourglass icon on the top-right corner of the toolbar), and type **TextEdit**.

2. **Enter into the text editor any of the code samples in this chapter, or create your own combination of the code.**
3. **Save the file and make sure to include `.html` at the end of the filename.**
4. **Double-click the file to open it in your default browser.**

TIP

Visual Studio Code (VS Code) is a specialized text editor created specifically for writing code. You can download it (for macOS, Windows, or Linux) at `code.visualstudio.com`. See Book 2, Chapter 1 for complete instructions on installing VS Code.

IN THIS CHAPTER

» Organizing content in a web page

» Writing HTML lists

» Creating HTML tables

» Filling out HTML forms

Chapter 2
Getting More Out of HTML

I'm controlling, and I want everything orderly, and I need lists.

—SANDRA BULLOCK

Even your best content needs structure to increase readability for your users. This book is no exception. Consider the "In This Chapter" bulleted list of items at the top of this chapter, or the table of contents at the beginning of the book. Lists and tables make things easier for you to understand at a glance. By mirroring the structure you find in a book or magazine, web elements let you precisely define how content, such as text and images, appears on the web.

In this chapter, you find out how to use HTML elements such as lists, tables, and forms, and how to know when these elements are appropriate for your content.

Organizing Content on the Page

Readability is the most important principle for organizing and displaying content on your web page. Your web page should allow visitors to easily read, understand, and act on your content. The desired action you have in mind for your visitors may be to click on and read additional content, share the content with others, or perhaps make a purchase. Poorly organized content will lead users to leave your website before engaging with your content.

Figures 2-1 and 2-2 show two examples of website readability. Figure 2-1 is a search on `Craigslist.org` for an apartment in Portland, Oregon. The search results are structured like a list, and you can limit the content displayed using the filters and search forms. Each listing has multiple attributes, such as a description, the number of bedrooms, the neighborhood, and, most importantly, the price. Comparing similar attributes from different listings takes some effort — notice the jagged line your eye must follow.

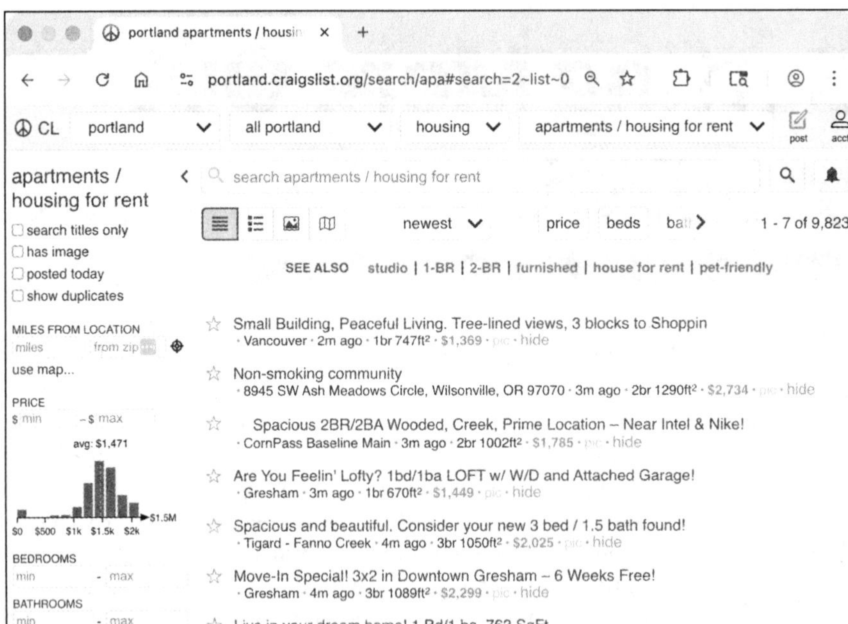

FIGURE 2-1: A `Craigslist.org` listing of apartments in Portland.

Figure 2-2 shows the results of a search at `Kayak.com` for flights from Portland to London. As with the Craigslist search results, you can limit the content displayed by using filters and search forms. Additionally, each flight listing has multiple attributes, including price, carrier, departure time, landing time, and duration, which are similar to the attributes of the apartment listings. Comparing similar attributes from different flights is much easier with the Kayak layout, however. Note how the content, in contrast to Craigslist's, has a layout that allows your eye to follow a straight line down the page, so you can easily rank and compare options.

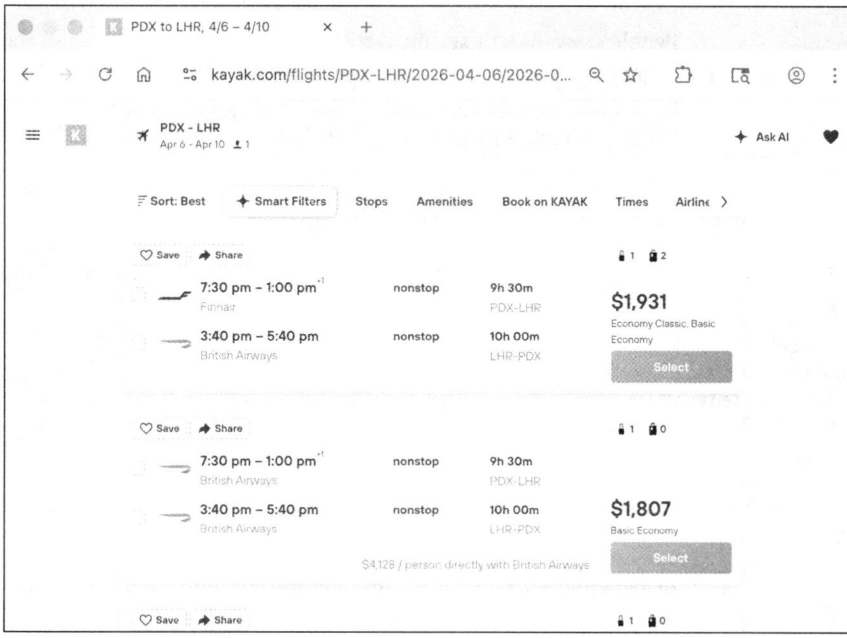

FIGURE 2-2: A Kayak.com listing of flights from Portland to London.

TIP

Don't underestimate the power of simplicity when displaying content. Although Craigslist's content layout may look almost too simple, the site remains one of the most visited websites in the United States, with tens of millions of monthly users. `Reddit.com` is another example of a popular website with a simple layout.

Before displaying your content, ask yourself a few questions:

- **Does your content have one attribute with related data that follows sequential steps?** If so, consider using lists.
- **Does your content have multiple attributes suitable for comparison?** If so, consider using tables.
- **Do you need to collect input from the visitor?** If so, consider using forms.

Don't let these choices overwhelm you. Choose one, see how your visitors react, and if necessary, change how you display the content. The process of evaluating one version against another version of the same web page is called *A/B testing.*

Listing Data

People have used lists on websites for decades to convey related or hierarchical information. In Figure 2-3, left, you can see an older version of `Yahoo.com` that uses bulleted lists to display various categories. Figure 2-3, right shows a recent `Food.com` recipe page, which uses lists to display various ingredients.

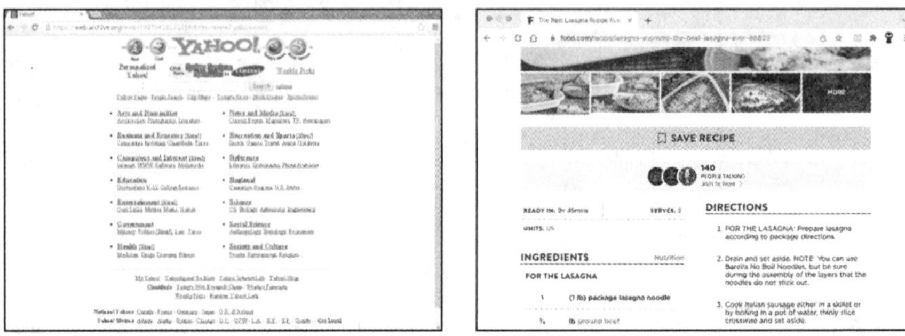

FIGURE 2-3: Yahoo!'s 1997 homepage using an unordered list (left) and a `Food.com` recipe using an ordered list (right).

Lists begin with a symbol, an indentation, and then the list item. The symbol can be a number, a letter, a bullet, or no symbol at all.

Creating ordered and unordered lists

Here are the two most popular types of lists:

- **Ordered:** Ordered lists are numerical or alphabetical lists in which the sequence of list items is important.
- **Unordered:** These lists are usually bulleted lists in which the sequence of list items has no importance.

You create lists by specifying the type of list as ordered or unordered and then adding each list item using the `li` tag, as shown in the following steps:

1. **Specify the type of list.**

   Add opening and closing list tags that specify either an ordered (`ol`) or unordered (`ul`) list, as follows:

   - `ol` to specify the beginning and end of an ordered list
   - `ul` to specify the beginning and end of an unordered list

2. **For each item in the list, add an opening `<li>` tag and a closing `</li>` tag.**

For example, here's an ordered list:

```
<ol>
      <li> List item #1 </li>
      <li> List item #2 </li>
      <li> List item #3 </li>
</ol>
```


Nesting lists

Additionally, you can nest lists within lists. A list of any type can be nested inside another list. To nest a list, replace the list item tag `<li>` with a list type tag, either `<ol>` or `<ul>`.

The example code in Listing 2-1 shows an HTML page with several lists, including nested lists.

LISTING 2-1: Using and Nesting Lists

```
<!doctype html>
<html lang="en">
  <head>
    <meta charset="UTF-8"/>
    <meta name="viewport" content="width=device-width, initial-scale=1.0"/>
    <title>Ordered and Nested Lists</title>
  </head>
  <body>
    <!-- ordered and nested lists example -->
    <h1>Step-by-Step Recipe: Classic Chocolate Chip Cookies</h1>
    <div>
      <ol>
        <li>
          Gather and measure all dry ingredients:
```

(continued)

LISTING 2-1: ***(continued)***

```
          <ol>
            <li>2 1/4 cups all-purpose flour</li>
            <li>1 teaspoon baking soda</li>
            <li>1 teaspoon salt</li>
          </ol>
        </li>
        <li>
          Prepare wet ingredients in a large mixing bowl:
          <ol>
            <li>1 cup (2 sticks) softened butter</li>
            <li>3/4 cup granulated sugar</li>
            <li>3/4 cup packed brown sugar</li>
            <li>2 large eggs</li>
            <li>2 teaspoons vanilla extract</li>
          </ol>
        </li>
        <li>
          Combine dry and wet ingredients:
          <ol>
            <li>Gradually beat flour mixture into butter mixture</li>
            <li>Stir in 2 cups chocolate chips</li>
            <li>Mix until well combined</li>
          </ol>
        </li>
        <li>
          Bake the cookies:
          <ol>
            <li>Preheat oven to 375°F (190°C)</li>
            <li>
              Drop rounded tablespoons of dough onto ungreased cookie sheets
            </li>
            <li>Bake for 9 to 11 minutes or until golden brown</li>
            <li>
              Cool on baking sheet for 2 minutes, then transfer to wire rack
            </li>
          </ol>
        </li>
      </ol>
    </div>
  </body>
</html>
```

Figure 2-4 shows the code from Listing 2-1 when it's opened in a web browser.

FIGURE 2-4: The page produced by the code in Listing 2-1.

Putting Data in Tables

Tables help further organize text and tabular data on the page. The table format is especially appropriate when displaying pricing information, comparing features across products, or anytime columns or rows share a common attribute. Tables act as containers and can hold and display any type of content, including text, such as headings and lists, as well as images. For example, the table in Figure 2-5 includes additional content and styling, such as icons at the top of each column, gray background shading, and rounded buttons. This content and styling can make tables online different from tables in books.

Basic table structuring

A table comprises several parts, as shown in Figure 2-6.

You create a table by following these steps:

1. **Define a table with the `table` element.**

   To do this, add the opening and closing `<table>` tags.

2. **Divide the table into rows with the `tr` element.**

   Between the opening and closing `table` tags, create opening `<tr>` tags and closing `</tr>` tags for each row of your table.

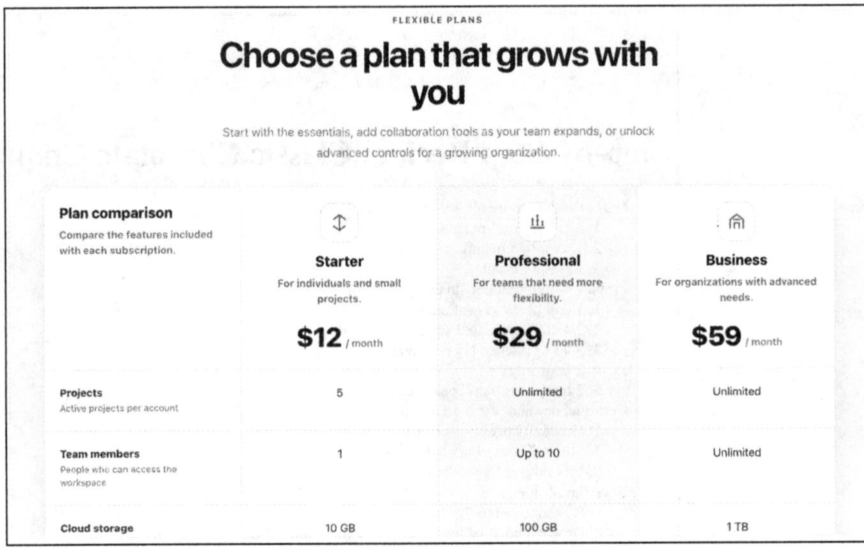

FIGURE 2-5: HTML tables being used to display pricing information.

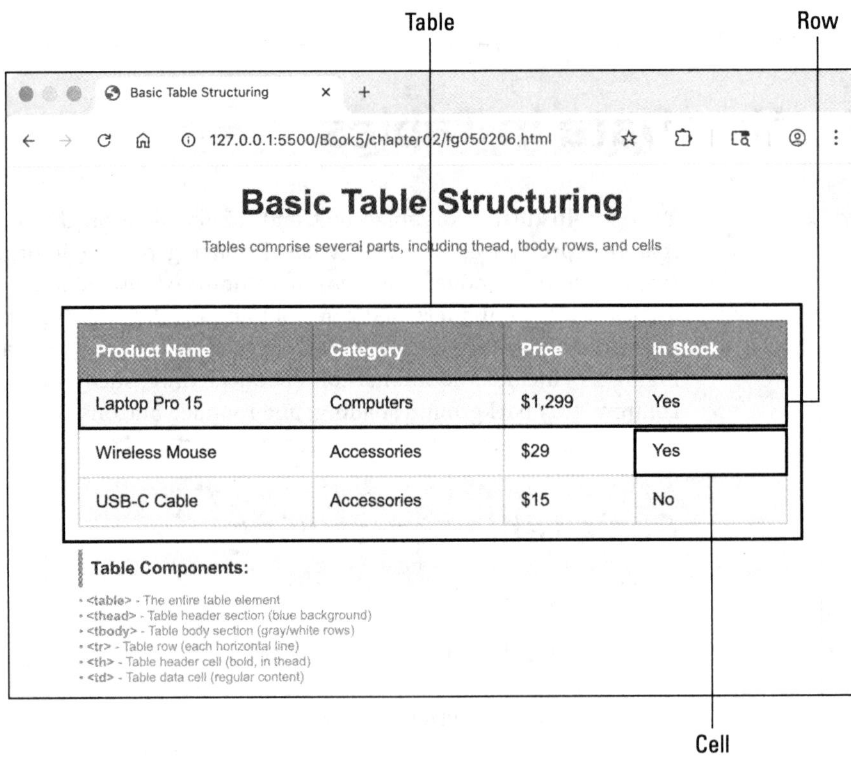

FIGURE 2-6: The different parts of a table.

3. **Divide rows into cells by using the `td` element.**

   Between the opening and closing `tr` tags, create opening and closing `td` tags for each cell in the row.

4. **Highlight cells that are headers by using the `th` element.**

   Specify cells that are headers by replacing the `td` element with a `th` element.

REMEMBER

Your table should have only one opening and closing `<table>` tag, but you can have one or more table rows (`tr`) and cells (`td`).

The following example code shows the syntax for creating the table shown in Figure 2-6:

```
<table>
  <thead>
    <tr>
      <th>Product Name</th>
      <th>Category</th>
      <th>Price</th>
      <th>In Stock</th>
    </tr>
  </thead>
  <tbody>
    <tr>
      <td>Laptop Pro 15</td>
      <td>Computers</td>
      <td>$1,299</td>
      <td>Yes</td>
    </tr>
    <tr>
      <td>Wireless Mouse</td>
      <td>Accessories</td>
      <td>$29</td>
      <td>Yes</td>
    </tr>
    <tr>
      <td>USB-C Cable</td>
      <td>Accessories</td>
      <td>$15</td>
      <td>No</td>
    </tr>
  </tbody>
</table>
```

TIP

After you decide how many rows and columns your table will have, make sure to use an opening and closing <tr> tag for each row and an opening and closing <td> tag for each cell in the row.

Stretching table columns and rows

Tables are commonly used for data-heavy components such as reports, schedules, and invoices — places where users need to scan rows and compare columns. For example, imagine an invoice table, such as the one shown in Figure 2-7. You might include a section header such as Labor or Parts that stretches across multiple columns, and you might also want a single Order # cell to cover several line items that all belong to the same order.

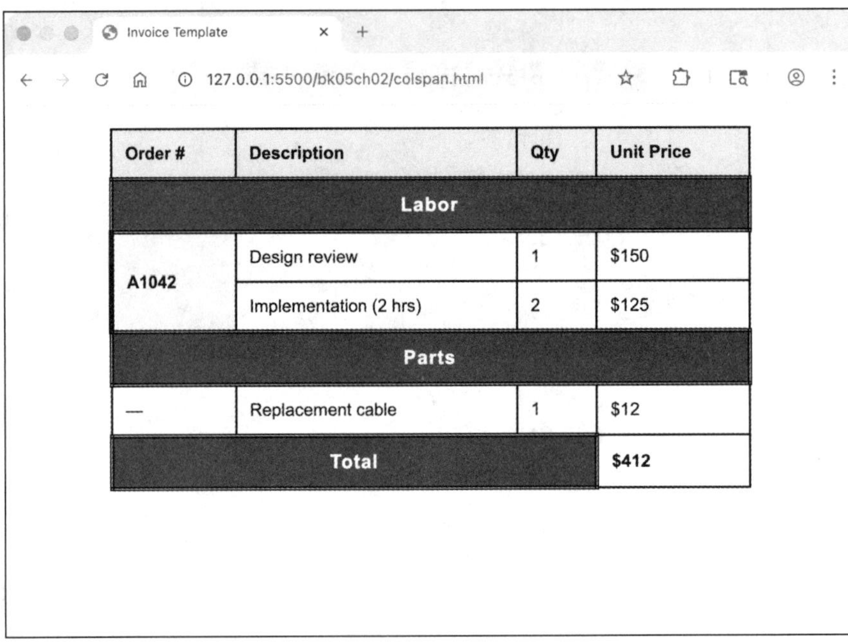

FIGURE 2-7: An invoice in a table with columns of different sizes.

TECHNICAL STUFF

Stretching a cell across columns or rows is called *spanning.* Spanning lets you represent grouped or hierarchical data without repeating the same labels over and over.

Use the `colspan` attribute when one cell should cover multiple columns (left to right). Use the `rowspan` attribute when one cell should cover multiple rows (top to bottom). In both cases, the value is the number of columns or rows you want that cell to span.

The following code is a simplified invoice table. In the Labor row, I use `colspan` to create a section header across the full width of the table. In the Order #A1042 cell, I use `rowspan` to label multiple line items that belong to the same order:

```
<table>
      <tr>
        <th>Order #</th>
        <th>Description</th>
        <th>Qty</th>
        <th>Unit Price</th>
      </tr>
      <tr>
        <th colspan="4">Labor</th>
      </tr>
      <tr>
        <td rowspan="2">A1042</td>
        <td>Design review</td>
        <td>1</td>
        <td>$150</td>
      </tr>
      <tr>
        <td>Implementation (2 hrs)</td>
        <td>2</td>
        <td>$125</td>
      </tr>
      <tr>
        <th colspan="4">Parts</th>
      </tr>
      <tr>
        <td>—</td>
        <td>Replacement cable</td>
        <td>1</td>
        <td>$12</td>
      </tr>
      <tr>
        <td colspan="3"><strong>Total</strong></td>
        <td><strong>$412</strong></td>
      </tr>
    </table>
```

REMEMBER

If you set a column or row to span more columns or rows than are present in the table, the browser will insert additional columns or rows, changing your table layout.

TIP

For Figure 2-7, I applied some styles to the basic HTML table to make it look presentable for the book. CSS helps size, style, and align individual columns and rows, as well as entire tables. You learn about CSS in Book 5, Chapters 3 and 4.

Filling Out Forms

Forms allow you to capture input from your website visitors. Until now, we have displayed content as-is, but capturing input from visitors allows you to do the following:

- **Modify existing content on the page.** For example, price and date filters on airline websites allow for finding a desired flight more quickly.
- **Store the input for later use.** For example, a website might use a registration form to collect your email, username, and password information to allow you to access the site at a later date.

Understanding how forms work

Forms use the following process to pass information entered by a user to a server:

1. The browser displays a form on the client machine.
2. The user completes the form and presses the submit button.
3. The browser submits the data collected from the form to a server.
4. The server processes and stores the data and sends a response to the client machine.
5. The browser displays the response, usually indicating whether the submission was successful.

TIP

See Book 1, Chapter 2 for an additional discussion about the relationship between the client and server.

REMEMBER

A full description of how the server receives and stores data (Steps 3 to 5) is beyond the scope of this book. I discuss what happens on the server in Book 8. For now, all you need to know is that server-side programming languages such as Python, PHP, and Ruby are used to write scripts that receive and store form submissions.

TABLE 2-1 **Selected Form Attributes**

Attribute Name	Possible Values	Description
type	checkbox email submit text password radio (a complete list of values has been omitted here for brevity)	Defines the type of input field to display in the form. For example, text is used for free text fields, and submit is used to create a submit button.
value	text	The initial value of the input control.

Forms are flexible and can record a variety of user inputs. Input fields used in forms can include free text fields, radio buttons, checkboxes, drop-down menus, range sliders, dates, phone numbers, and more (See Table 2-1.). Additionally, input fields can be set to initial default values.

TIP

View the entire list of form input types and example code at developer.mozilla.org/en-US/docs/Learn_web_development/Extensions/Forms/HTML5_input_types.

Creating basic forms

You create a basic form by following these steps:

1. **Define a form with the form element.**

   Start by adding an opening <form> tag and closing </form> tag.

2. **Using the action attribute, specify in the form element where to send form data.**

   Add an action attribute to your opening <form> tag and set it equal to the URL of a script that will process and store the user input.

3. **Using the method attribute, specify in the form element how to send form data.**

   Add a method attribute to your opening <form> tag and set it equal to POST.

TECHNICAL STUFF

The `method` attribute is set equal to `GET` or `POST`. The technicalities of each are beyond the scope of this book, but, in general, `POST` is used for storing sensitive information (such as a credit card number), whereas `GET` is used to allow users to bookmark or share with others the results of a submitted form (for example, an airline flight listing).

4. **Provide a way for users to input and submit responses with the `input` element.**

   Between the opening `<form>` and closing `</form>` tags, create one `<input>` tag.

REMEMBER

Your form should have only one opening and closing `<form>` tag, but at least two `<input>` tags to collect and submit user data.

5. **Specify input types using the `type` attribute in the `input` element.**

   For this example, set the `type` attribute equal to `"text"`.

TIP

The `<input>` element is a void element, so it doesn't have a closing tag. You learn about two other void elements, `<br>` and `<img>`, in Book 5, Chapter 1.

6. **Create another `<input>` tag and set the `type` attribute equal to `submit`.**

Listing 2-2 shows the HTML for a contact form that uses several different types of inputs. Figure 2-8 shows what it looks like in a browser (with some CSS styling applied to make it look nice).

REMEMBER

You can find the complete form, including the CSS I used to style it, in the code for this book, which you can download from the URL in the book's introduction.

LISTING 2-2: A Contact Form

```
<form
  action="mailto:chris@minnick.com"
  method="POST"
  enctype="text/plain"
>
  <div class="form-group">
    <label for="name">Full Name:</label>
    <input
      type="text"
      id="name"
      name="name"
      placeholder="Enter your full name"
      required
```

```
  />
</div>

<div class="form-group">
  <label for="email">Email Address:</label>
  <input
    type="email"
    id="email"
    name="email"
    placeholder="your.email@example.com"
    required
  />
</div>

<div class="form-group">
  <label for="phone">Phone Number:</label>
  <input
    type="tel"
    id="phone"
    name="phone"
    placeholder="(555) 123-4567"
  />
</div>

<div class="form-group">
  <label for="subject">Subject:</label>
  <select id="subject" name="subject">
    <option value="">Select a topic...</option>
    <option value="general">General Inquiry</option>
    <option value="support">Technical Support</option>
    <option value="billing">Billing Question</option>
    <option value="feedback">Feedback</option>
  </select>
</div>

<div class="form-group">
  <label>Preferred Contact Method:</label>
  <div class="radio-group">
    <label
      ><input
        type="radio"
        name="contact-method"
        value="email"
        checked
```

(continued)

LISTING 2-2: (continued)

```
        />
        Email</label
      >
      <label
        ><input type="radio" name="contact-method" value="phone"/>
        Phone</label
      >
      <label
        ><input type="radio" name="contact-method"
  value="either"/>
        Either</label
      >
    </div>
  </div>

  <div class="form-group">
    <label for="message">Message:</label>
    <textarea
      id="message"
      name="message"
      placeholder="Type your message here..."
      required
    ></textarea>
  </div>

  <div class="form-group">
    <div class="checkbox-group">
      <label>
        <input type="checkbox" name="newsletter" value="yes"/>
        Subscribe to our newsletter
      </label>
    </div>
  </div>

  <input type="submit" value="Send Message"/>
</form>
```

TECHNICAL STUFF

The `action` attribute in this form is set equal to `mailto`, which signals to the browser to send an email using your default mail client (such as Outlook or Gmail). If your browser isn't configured to handle email links, this form won't work. Ordinarily, forms are submitted to a server to process and store the form's contents, but in this example form, the contents are submitted to the user's email application.

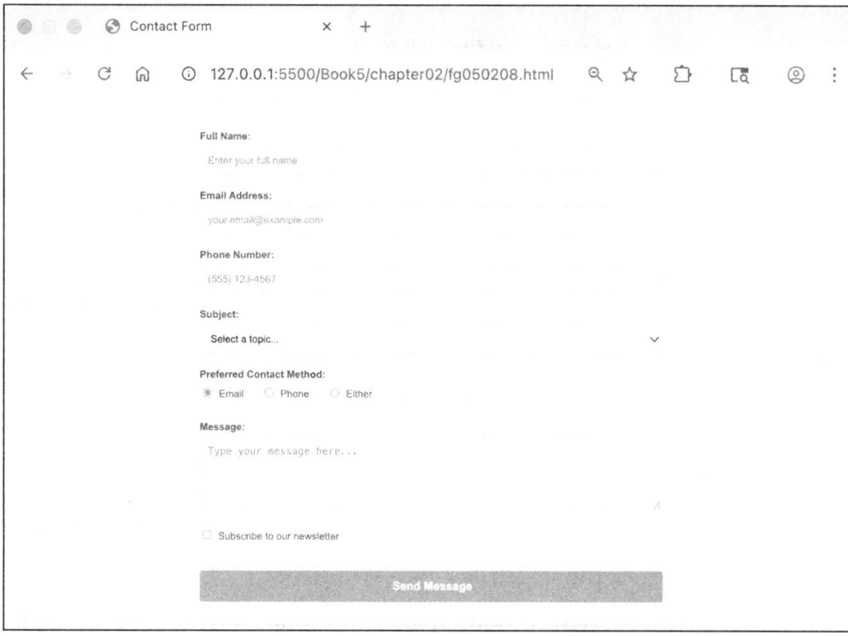

FIGURE 2-8: A form with one user input and a submit button (Send Message).

WARNING

Using `mailto:` to send the results of a form is not recommended for use on publicly available websites. Because `mailto:` makes your email address available to anyone who visits a website, it's very easy for bulk emailers (aka spammers) to automate the process of gathering email addresses that are used as the values of `mailto:` form actions. This automated process of gathering information from public websites is called *scraping.*

Practicing with HTML

Now that you understand how to use HTML lists, tables, and forms, it's time to practice them on your own computer! Follow these steps:

1. **Open Visual Studio Code.**

   Visual Studio Code (VS Code) is a specialized text editor specifically for writing code. You can download it (for macOS, Windows, or Linux) at `code.visualstudio.com`. See Book 2, Chapter 1 for complete instructions on installing and using VS Code.

2. **Create a new file and type or paste any of the code samples in this chapter or create your own combination of the code.**

   You can find all the code from this chapter in the code download for this book, which is available at `www.dummies.com/go/codingaiofd`.

3. **Once you have finished, save the file, making sure to include `.html` at the end of the filename.**

Next, you install an extension in VS Code that will make previewing HTML and CSS much easier:

1. **Open Visual Studio Code.**
2. **Go to the Extensions view.**

   To do so, click the Extensions icon on the activity bar (usually on the left side) or press Ctrl+Shift+X (Windows and Linux) or Cmd+Shift+X (macOS).

3. **In the search box, type Live Server.**
4. **Find the extension named Live Server by Ritwick Dey and click its Install button to add Live Server to VS Code.**
5. **Open the HTML file you want to preview.**
6. **Right-click anywhere in the HTML file and select Open with Live Server.**

   Your default web browser will open and display a live preview of your HTML file. Any changes you save in VS Code will automatically update in the browser.

IN THIS CHAPTER

» Understanding CSS and its structure

» Formatting text size, color, and style

» Styling images

» Using CSS in three different contexts

Chapter 3
Understanding the Elements of Style

To achieve style, begin by affecting none.

—E.B. WHITE

The examples in the preceding chapters in this minibook are simple, like websites you may have seen in a previous era. Websites you browse today are different, and they have a more polished look and feel. Numerous factors enabled this change. Twenty-five years ago, most people connected to the internet using a very slow connection, and niceties like large graphics and interesting typefaces were sacrificed in the name of improved loading speeds. Today, you likely use a very fast internet connection and a powerful computer. Programmers have used this extra bandwidth and speed to write code to further customize and style websites.

In this chapter, you discover modern techniques to style websites using Cascading Style Sheets (CSS). First, you learn basic CSS structure and then the CSS rules to style your content. Finally, you'll see how to apply these rules to your websites.

What Does CSS Do?

CSS styles HTML elements with greater control than HTML does. Take a look at Figure 3-1. On the left, Facebook appears as it currently exists. On the right, the same Facebook page is shown without the CSS styling; all the images and text are left-justified, borders and shading have disappeared, and text has minimal formatting.

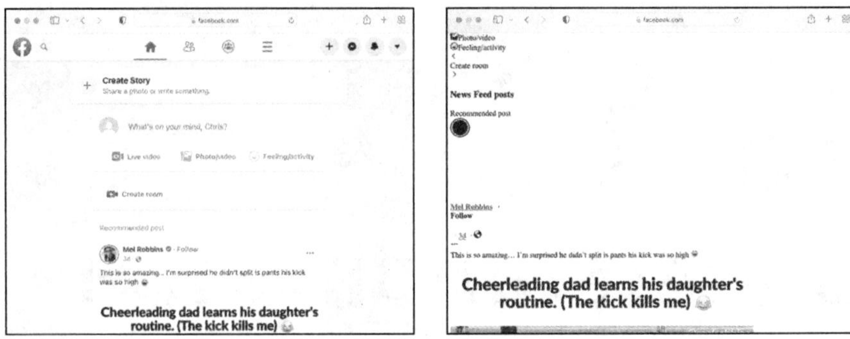

FIGURE 3-1: Facebook with CSS (left) and without (right).

CSS can style almost any HTML tag that creates a visible element on the page, including all the HTML tags used to create headings, paragraphs, links, images, lists, and tables, which you learned about in previous chapters. Specifically, CSS allows you to style:

- Text size, color, style, typeface, and alignment
- Link color and style
- Image size and alignment
- List bullet styles and indentation
- Table size, shading, borders, and alignment

REMEMBER

CSS styles and positions the HTML elements that appear on a web page. However, some HTML elements (for example, `<head>`) aren't visible on the page and aren't styled using CSS.

You may wonder why creating a separate language like CSS to handle styling was considered a better approach than expanding the capabilities of HTML. There are three reasons:

- **History:** CSS was created four years after HTML as an experiment to see whether developers and consumers wanted extra styling effects. At the time, it was unclear whether CSS would be useful, and only some major browsers supported it. As a result, CSS was created separately from HTML to allow developers to build sites using just HTML.

- **Code management:** Initially, some CSS functionality overlapped with existing HTML functionality. However, specifying styling effects in HTML results in cluttered and messy code. For example, to specify a particular font typeface in HTML, you had to wrap text in a `<font face="...">` tag. Styling a single paragraph this way is easy, but applying the font to a series of paragraphs (or an entire page or website) quickly becomes tedious. By contrast, CSS requires the typeface to be specified only once, and it automatically applies to all paragraphs. This feature makes it easier for developers to write and maintain code. In addition, separating the styling of the content from the content itself allows search engines and other automated website agents to more easily process the content on web pages.
- **Accessibility:** Web browsers aren't the only place where web pages are used. Web pages are also used by screen readers for the blind, text-to-speech applications, smart speakers, and much more. Different kinds of devices require different types of styling. By separating style (CSS) from structure (HTML), web pages become much more flexible, and the content of the web page can be used more easily by more people.

CSS Structure

CSS follows a set of rules so that websites are displayed consistently across browsers and devices. Sometimes, because of varying support of the CSS standard, browsers can and do display web pages differently. Nevertheless, generally speaking, CSS helps users have a consistent experience across modern browsers.

TIP

Every web browser interprets CSS rules to style your HTML. For the best results, keep your browser up to date and test your pages in multiple modern browsers (for example, Chrome, Safari, Firefox, and Edge).

Choosing the element to style

CSS continues to evolve and support increased functionality, but the basic syntax for defining CSS rules remains the same. CSS modifies HTML elements with rules that apply to each element. These rules are written as follows:

```
selector {
    property : value ;
}
```

A CSS rule is composed of three parts:

- **Selector:** The HTML element you want to style.
- **Property:** The feature of the HTML element you want to style. For example, font typeface, image height, or color.
- **Value:** The options for the property that the CSS rule sets. For example, if `color` were the property, the value would be `red`.

The selector identifies which HTML element you want to style. In HTML, an element is surrounded by angle brackets, but in CSS, the selector stands alone. The selector is followed by a space, an opening left curly bracket ({), a property with a value, and then a closing right curly bracket (}). The line break after the opening curly bracket and before the closing curly bracket is not required by CSS — in fact, you could put all your code on one line with no line breaks or spaces. Developers follow the line break convention to make CSS easier to modify and read.

TIP

On most keyboards, you can find curly brackets to the right of the P key.

The following code shows you an example of CSS modifying a specific HTML element. The CSS code appears first, followed by the HTML code that it modifies:

The CSS:

```
h1 {
   font-family: cursive;
}
```

And now the HTML:

```
<h1>Largest IPOs in US History</h1>
<ul>
  <li>2014: Alibaba Group - $25.0B</li>
  <li>2010: General Motors - $23.1B</li>
  <li>2008: Visa Inc. - $19.7B</li>
  <li>2021: Rivian Automotive - $13.7B</li>
  <li>2012: Meta (Facebook) - $16.0B</li>
  <li>2019: Uber Technologies - $8.1B</li>
  <li>2020: Snowflake Inc. - $3.4B</li>
  <li>2020: Airbnb - $3.5B</li>
</ul>
```

The CSS selector targets and styles the HTML element with the same name (in this case, `<h1>` tags). For example, in Figure 3-2, the "Largest IPOs in US History" heading is created using the opening and closing `<h1>` tag and styled using the `h1` selector and the `font-family` property with the `cursive` value.

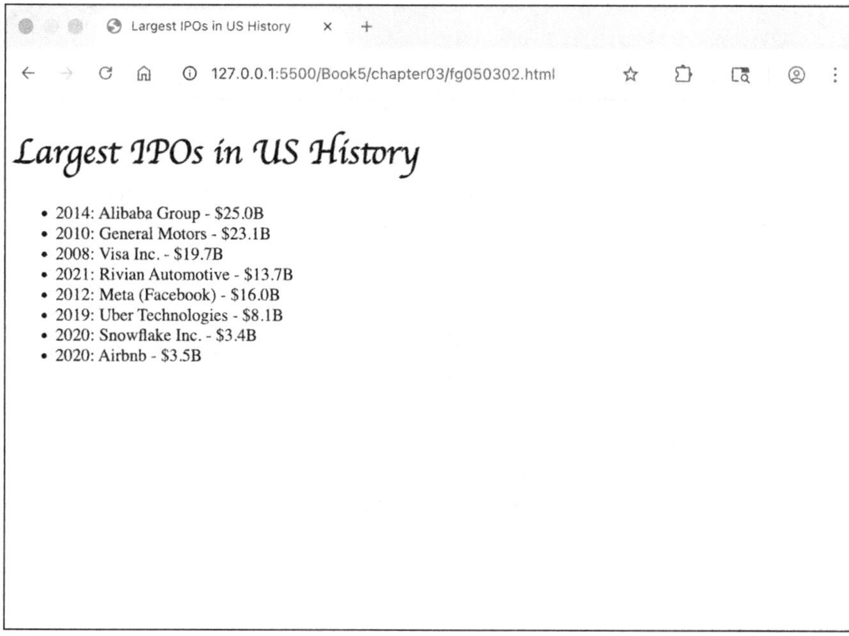

FIGURE 3-2: CSS targeting the heading `h1` element.

REMEMBER

CSS uses a colon (`:`) instead of the equals sign (=) to set values of CSS properties.

TIP

The font in Figure 3-2 likely doesn't appear to be `cursive`, as defined in the preceding code, because `cursive` is the name of a generic font family, not a specific font. Generic font families are described later in this chapter.

My property has value

CSS syntax requires that a CSS property and its value appear within opening and closing curly brackets. After each property is a colon, and after each value is a semicolon. This combination of property and value together is called a *declaration*, and a group of properties and values is called a *declaration block*.

Let's look at a specific example with multiple properties and values:

```
h1 {
    font-size: 15px;
    color: blue;
}
```

In this example, CSS styles the `h1` element, changing the `font-size` property to `15px` and the `color` property to `blue`.

TIP

You can improve the readability of your code by putting each declaration (each property/value combination) on its own line. Additionally, adding spaces or tabs to indent the declarations also improves readability. Note that adding line breaks and indentions doesn't affect browser performance.

Hacking CSS on your favorite website

In Book 5, Chapter 2, you modified a news website's HTML code. In this chapter, you modify its CSS. Let's take a look at some CSS rules in the wild. In this example, you change the CSS on `www.huffpost.com` (or your news website of choice) using the Chrome browser. Just follow these steps:

1. **Using a Chrome browser, navigate to your favorite news website, ideally one with many headlines, as shown in Figure 3-3.**

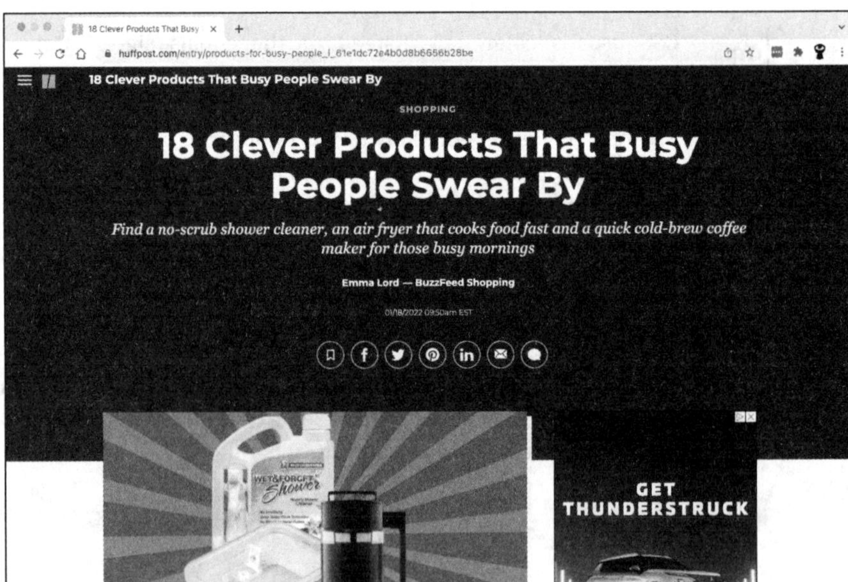

FIGURE 3-3: The Huffington Post website before modification.

2. **Place your mouse pointer over a headline and right-click. From the menu that appears, select Inspect, as shown in Figure 3-4.**

   A window opens at the bottom of your browser.

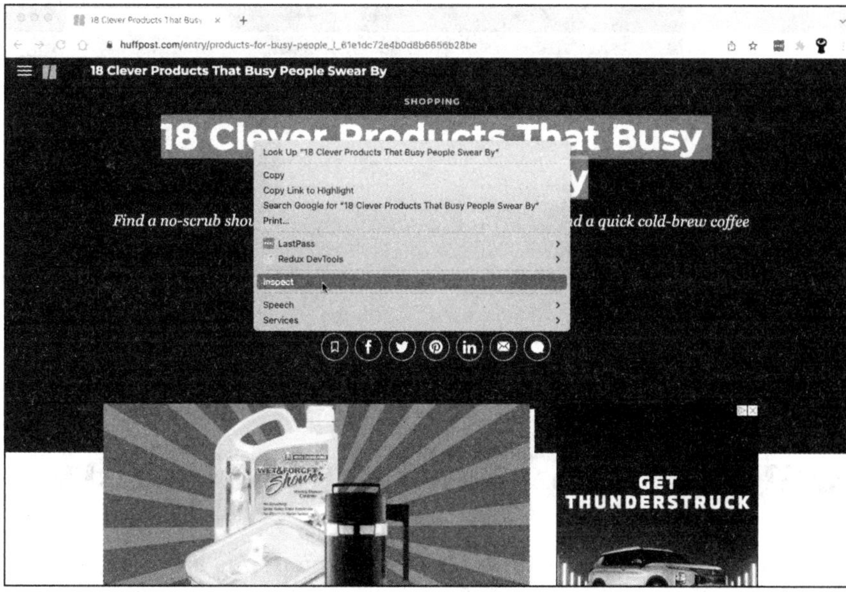

FIGURE 3-4: Inspecting the website's headline.

3. **On the right side of the window, click the Styles tab to see the CSS rules being applied to HTML elements.**

4. **Change the color of the headline by using CSS.**

   To do this, first find the `color` property in the `element.style` section. In that property, note the square color box displaying a sample of the current color. Click this box and change the value by selecting a new color from the pop-up menu, and then press Enter.

   Your headline now appears in the color you picked, as shown in Figure 3-5.

   TIP

   If the `element.style` section is blank, and no `color` property appears, you can still add a color manually. To do so, click once in the `element.style` section, and when the blinking cursor appears, type **color: purple**. The headline changes to purple.

TIP

As with HTML, you can modify any website's CSS using Chrome's Inspect feature. Most modern browsers, including Firefox, Edge, Safari, and Opera, have a similar feature.

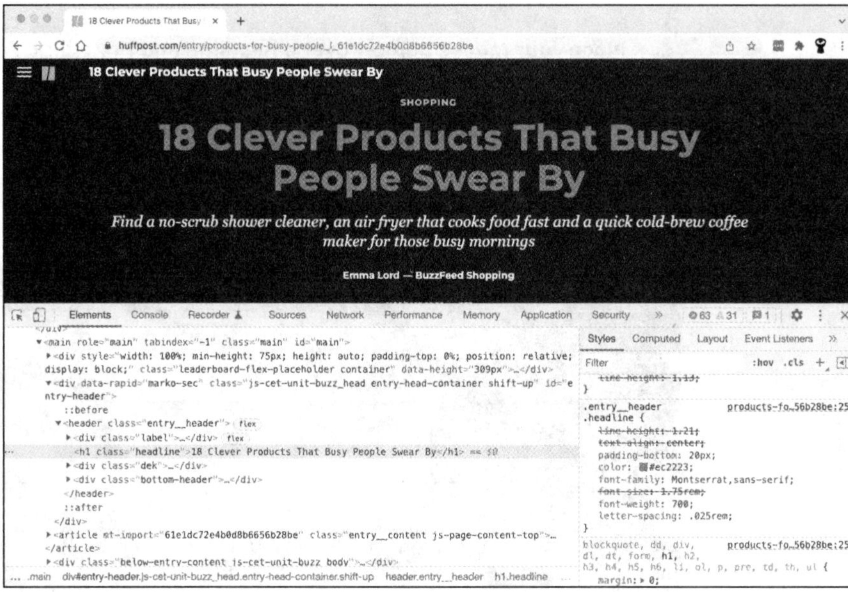

FIGURE 3-5: Changing the CSS changes the color of the headline.

Common CSS Tasks and Selectors

Although CSS includes over 150 properties and many values for each property, only a handful of CSS properties and values do the majority of the work on modern websites. In the preceding section, when you hacked the CSS on a live website, you changed the heading color — a common task in CSS. Other common tasks performed with CSS include:

- Changing font size, style, font family, and decoration
- Customizing links, including color, background color, and link state
- Adding background images and formatting foreground images

Font gymnastics: Size, color, style, family, and decoration

CSS lets you control text in many HTML elements. The most common text-related CSS properties and values are shown in Table 3-1. I describe these properties and values more fully in the sections that follow.

TABLE 3-1 Common CSS Properties and Values for Styling Text

Property Name	Possible Values	Description

`font-size`	`pixels (#px)`
	`%`
	`em (#em)`
		Specifies the size of text measured either in pixels, as a percentage of the containing element's font size or with an em value, which is calculated by the desired pixel value divided by the containing element font size in pixels. For example: `font-size: 16px;`

`color`	name hex code rgb value	Changes the color of the text specified by using a name (`color: blue;`), a hexadecimal code (`color: #0000FF;`), or an RGB (red, green, and blue) value (`color: rgb(0,0,255);`).
`font-style`	`normal` `italic`	Sets the font to appear in italics (or not).
`font-weight`	`normal` `bold`	Sets the font to appear as bold (or not).
`font-family`	`font name`	Sets the font typeface. For example: `font-family: serif;`

`text-decoration`	`none`
	`underline`
	`line-through`
		Sets the font to have an underline or strikethrough (or not).

Setting font-size

You can set the size of a font with CSS's `font-size` property. You have a few options for setting the font size, and the most common one is to use pixels, as in the following:

```
p {
  font-size: 16px;
}
```

In this example, I use the `p` selector to size the paragraph text to 16 pixels. One disadvantage of using pixels to size your font occurs when users who prefer a large font size for readability have changed their browser settings to a default font size value that's larger than the one you specify on your site. In these situations, the font size specified in the browser takes precedence, and the fonts on your site will not scale to adjust to these preferences.

Percentage-sizing and em values, the other options to size your fonts, are considered more accessibility-friendly. The default browser font size of normal text is

16 pixels. With percentage-sizing and em values, fonts can be sized relative to the user-specified default. For example, the CSS for percentage-sizing looks like this:

```
p {
   font-size: 150%;
}
```

In this example, I use the `p` selector to size the paragraph text to 150 percent of the default size. If the browser's default font size was set at 16 pixels, this paragraph's font would appear sized at 24 pixels (150 percent of 16).

TECHNICAL STUFF

A `font-size` equal to `1px` is one *CSS pixel*, which is an abstract unit and not necessarily the same as a single physical pixel on a screen. As a result, the physical size of text can vary by device, zoom level, and display density.

Setting the color

The `color` property sets the color in one of three ways:

- **Name:** You can reference 147 colors by name. You can reference common colors, such as black, blue, and red, along with uncommon colors, such as burlywood, lemon chiffon, thistle, and rebeccapurple.

  TECHNICAL STUFF

  Rebecca Meyer, the daughter of prominent CSS standards author Eric Meyer, passed away in 2014 from brain cancer at the age of six. In response, the CSS standardization committee approved adding a shade of purple called rebeccapurple to the CSS specification in Rebecca's honor. All major internet browsers have implemented support for the color.

- **Hex code:** Colors can be defined by component parts of red, green, and blue, and when hexadecimal code is used, over 16 million colors can be referenced. In the following code example, I set the `h1` color equal to `#FF0000`. After the hashtag, the first two digits (`FF`) refer to the red in the color, the next two digits (`00`) refer to the green in the color, and the final two digits (`00`) refer to the blue in the color.
- **RGB value:** Just like hex codes, RGB values specify the red, green, and blue component parts for over 16 million colors. RGB values are the decimal equivalent to hexadecimal values.

  TIP

  Don't worry about trying to remember hex codes or RGB values. You can easily identify colors using an online color picker such as the one at `www.w3schools.com/colors/colors_picker.asp`.

The following example shows all three types of color changes:

```
p {
   color: red;
}
h1 {
   color: #FF0000;
}
li {
   color: rgb(255,0,0);
}
```

REMEMBER

`li` is the element name for a list item in ordered and unordered lists.

TIP

All three colors in the preceding code example reference the same shade of red. For the full list of colors that can be referenced by name, go to `www.w3.org/TR/css-color-3/#svg-color`.

Setting font-style and font-weight

The `font-style` property can set text to italics, and the `font-weight` property can set text to bold. For each of these properties, the default is `normal`, which doesn't need to be specified. In the following example, the paragraph is styled so that the font appears italicized and bold:

```
p {
   font-style: italic;
   font-weight: bold;
}
```

Setting font-family

The `font-family` property sets the typeface used for text. The property is set equal to one font or to a list of fonts separated by commas. Your website visitors will have a variety of different fonts installed on their computers. The `font-family` property displays your specified font only if that font is already installed on their system.

The `font-family` property can be set equal to two types of values:

- **Font name:** A font name is the name of a specific font that you (and, presumably, the viewer of the web page) have on your computer. Common font names include Times New Roman, Arial, and Courier.

» **Generic font family:** Modern browsers usually define one installed font for each generic font family. These five generic font families are
  - *Serif* (Times New Roman, Palatino)
  - *Sans-serif* (Helvetica, Verdana)
  - *Monospace* (Courier, Andale Mono)
  - *Cursive* (Comic Sans, Florence)
  - *Fantasy* (Impact, Oldtown)

When using `font-family`, it's best to define two or three specific fonts followed by a generic font family as a fallback in case the fonts you specify aren't installed, as in the following example:

```
p {
   font-family: "Times New Roman", Times, serif;
}
```

In this example, the paragraph's font family is defined as Times New Roman. If Times New Roman isn't installed on the user's computer, the browser uses Times. If Times isn't installed, the browser will use any available font in the generic serif font family.

TIP

When using a font name with multiple words (such as Times New Roman), enclose the font name in quotes.

Setting text-decoration

The `text-decoration` property sets font underlining or strikethrough. By default, the property is equal to none, which doesn't have to be specified. In the following example, any text with an `h1` heading is underlined, whereas any text inside a paragraph tag is made strikethrough:

```
h1 {
    text-decoration: underline;
}
p {
    text-decoration: line-through;
}
```

Customizing links

In general, browsers display links as blue underlined text. Originally, this default behavior minimized the confusion between content on the page and an interactive link. Today, almost every website styles links in its own way. Some websites don't underline links; others retain the underlining but style links in colors other than blue; and so on.

REMEMBER

You use the HTML anchor element (`a`) to create a link. The text between the opening and closing anchor tag, is the link description, and the URL set in the `href` attribute is the address the browser visits when the link is clicked.

The anchor tag has four states:

- **`link`:** A link that a user hasn't clicked or visited
- **`visited`:** A link that a user has clicked or visited
- **`hover`:** A link that the user hovers the mouse cursor over without clicking
- **`active`:** A link the user has begun to click but hasn't yet released the mouse button

CSS can style each of these four states, most often by using the properties and values shown in Table 3-2.

TABLE 3-2 Common CSS Properties and Values for Styling Links

Property Name	Possible Values	Description
`color`	name hex code `rgb value`	Specifies the link color by using a name (`color: blue;`), a hexadecimal code (`color: #0000FF;`), or an RGB value (`color: rgb(0,0,255);`).
`text-decoration`	none `underline`	Sets a link to have an underline (or not).

The following example styles links in a way that's similar to the way they're styled in articles on Wikipedia, where links appear blue by default, underlined on a mouse cursor hover, and orange when active. As shown in Figure 3-6, the first link to Chief Technology Officer of the United States appears underlined, as it would if my mouse cursor was hovering over it. Also, the link to Google appears orange, as it would if it were active and my mouse were clicking it.

```
a:link {
    color: rgb(6,69,173);
    text-decoration: none;
}
a:visited {
    color: rgb(11,0,128)
}
a:hover {
    text-decoration: underline
}
a:active {
    color: rgb(250,167,0)
}
```

FIGURE 3-6: `Wikipedia.org` page showing `link`, `visited`, `hover`, and `active` states.

REMEMBER

Remember to include the colon between the `a` selector and the link state.

The various link states are known as *pseudo-class selectors*. Pseudo-class selectors add a keyword to CSS selectors and allow you to style a special state of the selected element.

Adding background images and styling foreground images

You can use CSS to add background images behind HTML elements. Most commonly, the `background-image` property is used to add background images to individual HTML elements such as `div`, `table`, and `p`, or (when applied to the `body` element) to entire web pages.

TIP

Background images with smaller file sizes load more quickly than larger images. This is especially important if your visitors commonly browse your website using a mobile phone, which typically has a slower data connection.

The properties and values in Table 3-3 show the options for adding background images.

TABLE 3-3 CSS Properties and Values for Background Images

Property Name	Possible Values	Description
`background-image`	`url("URL")`	Adds a background image from the image link specified at *URL*.

`background-size`	`auto`
	`contain`
	`cover`
	`width height (#px, %)`
		Sets the background size according to the value:
		`auto` (default value) displays the image as originally sized.
		`contain` scales the image's width and height so that it fits inside element.
		`cover` scales the image so element background isn't visible.
		Background size can be set by also specifying the width and height in pixels or as a percentage.

`background-position`	`keywords` `position (#px, %)`	Positions the background in the element by using keywords or an exact position. Horizontal keywords (`left, right, center`) and vertical keywords (`top, center`, and `bottom`) are available. The placement of the background can also be exactly defined by using pixels or a percentage to describe the horizontal and vertical position relative to the element.

(continued)

TABLE 3-3 ***(continued)***

Property Name	Possible Values	Description
background-repeat	repeat repeat-x repeat-y no-repeat	Sets the background image to *tile*, or repeat, as follows: horizontally (repeat-x) vertically (repeat-y) horizontally and vertically (repeat) don't repeat (no-repeat).
background-attachment	scroll fixed	Sets the background to scroll with other content (scroll) or to remain fixed (fixed).

Setting background-image

As shown in the following example, the background-image property can set the background image for the entire web page or a specific element:

```
body {
     background-image:
     url("https://upload.wikimedia.org/wikipedia/commons/e/e5/
     Chrysler_Building_Midtown_Manhattan_New_York_City_1932.jpg
     ");
}
```

TIP

You can find background images at sites such as images.google.com, www.flickr.com, or publicdomainarchive.com.

WARNING

Check image copyright information to see if you have permission to use the image, and comply with the image's licensing terms, which can include attributing or identifying the author. Additionally, is preferable to download the image and host and link to the image on your own server. (Directly linking to images on other servers is called *hotlinking.*)

TIP

If you prefer a single-color background instead of an image, use the background-color property. This property is defined in much the same way as the background-image property. Just set it equal to a color name, an RGB value, or a hex code, as I describe earlier in this chapter in the section "Setting the color."

Setting background-size

By specifying exact dimensions using pixels or percentages, the background-size property can scale background images to be smaller or larger, as needed.

In addition, this property has three dimensions commonly used on web pages, as follows (see Figure 3-7):

- **`auto`:** This value maintains the original dimensions of an image.
- **`cover`:** This value scales an image so all dimensions are greater than or equal to the size of the container or HTML element.
- **`contain`:** This value scales an image so all dimensions are less than or equal to the size of the container or HTML element.

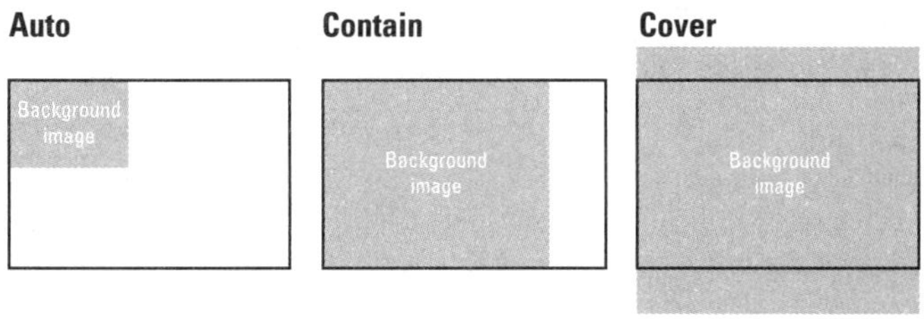

FIGURE 3-7: Setting the background size to three different values.

Setting background-position

The `background-position` property sets the initial position of the background image. The default initial position is in the top-left corner of the web page or specific element. You change the default position by specifying a pair of keywords or position values, as follows:

- **Keywords:** The first keyword (`left`, `center`, or `right`) represents the horizontal position, and the second keyword (`top`, `center`, or `bottom`) represents the vertical position.
- **Position:** The first position value represents the horizontal position, and the second value represents the vertical. Each value is defined using pixels or percentages, representing the distance from the top left of the browser or the specified element. For example, `background-position: center center` is equal to `background-position: 50% 50%`. (See Figure 3-8.)

Setting the background-repeat

The `background-repeat` property sets the direction the background will tile as follows:

- **`repeat`:** This value (the default) repeats the background image both horizontally and vertically.

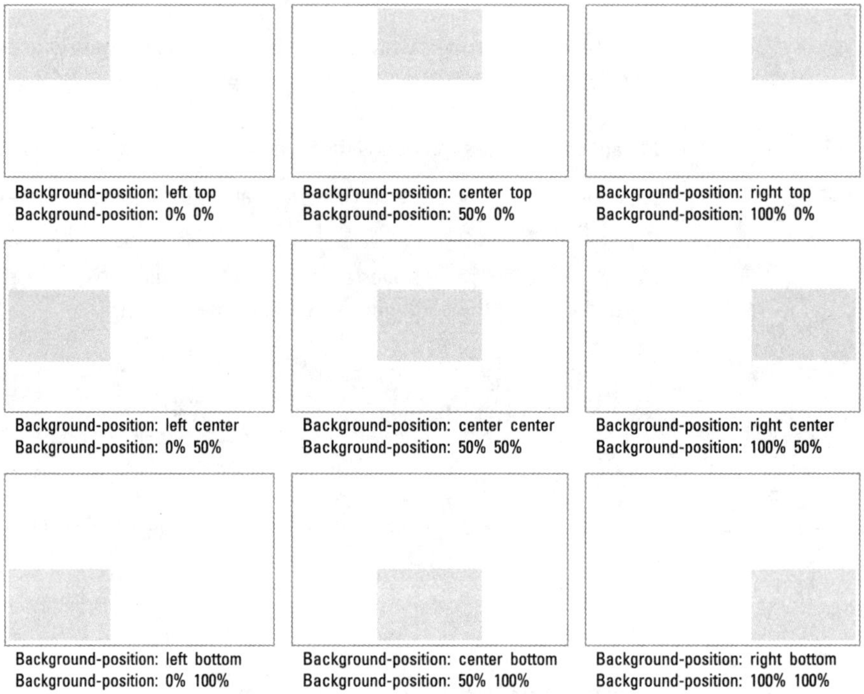

FIGURE 3-8: The initial background image positions specified using keywords or position.

- **`repeat-x`:** This value repeats the background image only horizontally.
- **`repeat-y`:** This repeats the background image only vertically.
- **`no-repeat`:** This value prevents the background from repeating.

Setting the background-attachment

The `background-attachment` property sets the background image to move (or not) when the user scrolls through content on the page. The property can be set to

- **`scroll`:** The background image moves when the user scrolls.
- **`fixed`:** The background image doesn't move when the user scrolls.

The following code segment uses several of the properties discussed earlier to add a background image that stretches across the entire web page, is aligned in the center, does not repeat, and does not move when the user scrolls.

```
<style>
  body {
    background-image: url('https://images.pdimagearchive.org/
   collections/maria-catharina-prestel/maria-catharina-prestel-
   00010.jpg?width=1580&height=800');
    background-size: cover;
    background-position: center center;
    background-repeat: no-repeat;
    background-attachment: fixed;
  }
</style>
```

Figure 3-9 shows a web page that uses previous CSS to display a painting as the page background.

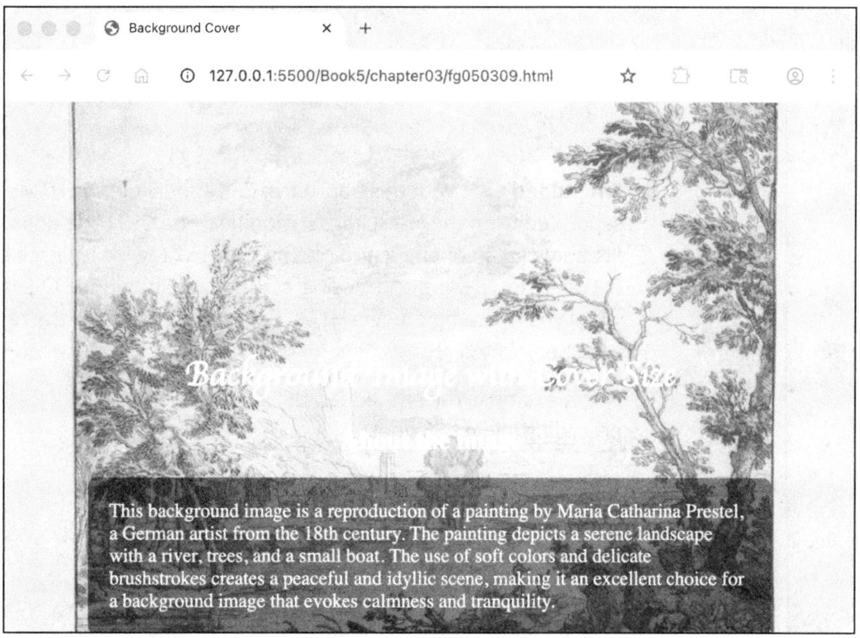

FIGURE 3-9: An image set as the background for the entire page.

Getting Stylish

The CSS rules discussed in this chapter give you a taste of a few common styling properties and values. Although you aren't likely to remember every property and value, with practice, the property and value names will come to you naturally.

After you understand the basic syntax, the next step is to incorporate CSS into your web page and try your hand at styling HTML elements.

There are three ways to apply CSS to a website to style HTML elements:

- **Inline CSS:** CSS can be specified in an HTML file on the same line as the HTML element it styles. This method requires placing the `style` attribute inside the opening HTML tag. Generally, inline CSS is the least preferred way of styling a website because the styling rules are frequently repeated. Here's an example of inline CSS:

```
<!DOCTYPE html>
<html>
<head>
   <title>Record IPOs</title>
</head>
<body>
   <h1 style="color: red;">Alibaba IPO expected to be biggest IPO of all
   time</h1>
</body>
</html>
```

- **Embedded CSS:** With this approach, CSS appears in the HTML file but is separated from the HTML tags it modifies. The CSS code appears in the HTML file between an opening and closing `<style>` tag, which itself is located between an opening and closing `<head>` tag. Embedded CSS is usually used when you're styling a single HTML page differently from the rest of your website.

  In this example, the embedded CSS styles the header red, just like the preceding inline CSS does:

```
<!DOCTYPE html>
<html>
<head>
 <title>Record IPOs</title>
 <style>
 h1 {
       color: red;
 }
 </style>
</head>
<body>
   <h1>Alibaba IPO expected to be biggest IPO of all time</h1>
</body>
</html>
```

» **Separate style sheets:** CSS can be specified in a separate *style sheet* — that is, in a separate file. Using a separate style sheet is the preferred approach to storing your CSS because it makes maintaining the HTML file easier and allows you to quickly make changes. In the HTML file, the `<link>` tag is used to refer to the separate style sheet and has the following attributes:

- `href`: Specifies the CSS filename
- `rel`: Should be set equal to `"stylesheet"`

TECHNICAL STUFF

All three ways of styling HTML elements with CSS can be used with contradictory styles. For example, say your inline CSS styles `h1` elements as red, whereas embedded CSS styles them as blue, and a separate style sheet styles them as green. To resolve these conflicts, inline CSS has the highest priority and overrides all other CSS rules. If no inline CSS is specified, embedded CSS has the next highest priority. And finally, in the absence of inline or embedded CSS, the styles in a separate style sheet are used. In the example, with the presence of all three styles, the `h1` element text would appear red because inline CSS has the highest priority and overrides the embedded CSS blue styling and the separate CSS green styling.

The following example uses a separate CSS style sheet to style the header red, as in the previous two examples:

CSS: style.css

```
h1 {
     color: red;
}
```

HTML: index.html

```
<!DOCTYPE html>
<html>
<head>
 <title>Record IPOs</title>
 <link href="style.css" rel="stylesheet">
</head>
<body>
   <h1>Alibaba IPO expected to be biggest IPO of all time</h1>
</body>
</html>
```

Practicing with CSS

Now that you understand the basics of using CSS, it's time to practice on your own computer! Follow these steps:

1. **Open Visual Studio Code.**

   Visual Studio Code (VS Code) is a specialized text editor created for writing code. You can download it (for macOS, Windows, or Linux) at `code.visualstudio.com`. See Book 2, Chapter 1 for instructions on installing and using VS Code.

2. **Create a new file and type or paste any of the code samples you have seen in this chapter, or create a new HTML file using the structure you learned in Chapter 1:**

```
<!DOCTYPE html>
<html lang="en">
<head>
  <meta charset="UTF-8">
  <meta name="viewport" content="width=device-width,
   initial-scale=1.0">
  <title>Document</title>
</head>
<body>

</body>
</html>
```

REMEMBER

   You can find all the code in this chapter at `www.dummies.com/go/codingaiofd`.

3. **Save your file as index.html (or any other name ending in .html).**

4. **Add an opening `<style>` tag and a closing `</style>` tag in the `head` element of your HTML file.**

5. **Add some content to the `<body>` element of your HTML file.**

   For example, you could create a list of your favorite foods, like the following:

```
<h1>My Favorite Foods</h1>
<ul>
  <li>Sushi</li>
  <li>Pizza</li>
  <li>Pickle Soup</li>
</ul>
```

6. **Define styles for some of the elements in your HTML document.**

   For example, to make all the text in your web page red, you can use the following CSS rule:

   ```
   body {
      color: red;
   }
   ```

7. **Make as many CSS rules as you like, using what you've learned in this chapter, and save your file to see them in the preview window.**

8. **Create a file in your project and give it a name ending with `.css` (such as `styles.css`).**

9. **Replace your embedded CSS in `index.html` with a link to your new `.css` file.**

   For example, if your CSS file is named `styles.css` and is in the same folder as your HTML file, your link tag would look like this:

   ```
   <link href="styles.css" rel="stylesheet">
   ```

10. **Use the Live Server VS Code extension, which you installed in Chapter 2 of this minibook, to preview your styled web page.**

IN THIS CHAPTER

» Formatting lists and tables

» Styling web pages using parent and child selectors

» Naming pieces of code using `id` and `class`

» Using the box model to position HTML elements on the page

Chapter 4
Next Steps with CSS

Style is the difference between a circle and the way you draw it.

—PABLO PICASSO

In this chapter, you continue building on the CSS you worked with in Book 2, Chapter 3. So far, the CSS rules you've seen in the preceding chapter applied to the entire web page, but now they get more specific. You find out how to style several more HTML elements, and how to use advanced selectors to select and style specific parts of a web page. Finally, you read about how professional web developers use CSS and the box model to control the positioning of elements on the page.

Before diving in, remember the big picture: HTML puts content on the web page, and CSS styles and positions that content. Instead of trying to memorize every rule, use this chapter to understand CSS basics.

TIP

There is no better way to learn than by doing, so feel free to try out new style properties as you go through this chapter. If you've built a web page already, you can use this chapter as a reference when you have questions about specific elements you're trying to style.

Styling (More) Elements on Your Page

In this section, you discover common ways to style lists and tables. In the preceding chapter, CSS properties and rules, like `color` and `font-family`, can apply to any HTML element containing text. By contrast, some of the CSS shown here is used only to style lists, tables, and forms.

Styling lists

In Book 5, Chapter 2, you created ordered lists, which start with markers like letters or numbers, and unordered lists, which start with markers like bullet points. By default, list items in an ordered list use numbers (for example, 1, 2, 3), whereas list items in unordered lists use a solid black circle (●).

These defaults may not be appropriate for all circumstances. In fact, the two common tasks when styling a list are

- **Changing the marker used to create a list:** For unordered lists, like this one, you can use a solid disc, an empty circle, or a square bullet point. For ordered lists, you can use numbers, Roman numerals (uppercase or lowercase), or case letters (upper or lower).
- **Removing the marker from list items:** For example, it's common to remove the bullets from bulleted lists when you're creating a list of links, such as in a navigation menu.

You can accomplish either of these tasks by using the properties in Table 4-1 with an `ol` or `ul` selector to modify the list type.

TABLE 4-1 Common CSS Properties and Values for Styling Lists

Property Name	Possible Values	Description

`list-style-type`
(unordered list)
	`disc`
	`circle`
	`square`
	none
		Sets the markers used to create list items in an unordered list to disc (●), circle (o), square (■), or none (which removes the marker).

Property Name	Possible Values	Description
`list-style-type` (ordered list)	`decimal` `upper-roman` `lower-roman` `upper-alpha` `lower-alpha`	Sets the markers used to create list items in an ordered list to decimal (1, 2, 3), uppercase Roman numerals (I, II, III), lowercase Roman numerals (i, ii, iii), uppercase letters (A, B, C), or lowercase letters (a, b, c).
`list-style-image`	`url("URL")`	When URL is replaced with the image link, the property sets an image as the marker used to create a list item.

Listing 4-1 shows an HTML page with CSS rules that modify lists and list items.

LISTING 4-1: Modifying List Styles

```
<html>
  <head>
    <title>Figure 4-1: Lists</title>
    <style>
      ul {
        list-style-type: square;
      }

      ol {
        list-style-type: upper-roman;
      }

      li {
        font-size: 27px;
      }
    </style>
  </head>
  <body>
    <h1>World&apos;s Highest Mountains</h1>
    <ul>
      <li>Mount Everest: 29,032 feet (8,849 meters)</li>
      <li>K2: 28,251 feet (8,611 meters)</li>
      <li>Kangchenjunga: 28,169 feet (8,586 meters)</li>
    </ul>

    <h1>Planets in Order from the Sun</h1>
    <ol>
```

(continued)

LISTING 4-1: *(continued)*

```
      <li>Mercury: the smallest and closest planet</li>
      <li>Venus: the hottest planet in our solar system</li>
      <li>Earth: our home planet with abundant water</li>
    </ol>
  </body>
</html>
```

Study the HTML in Listing 4-1 along with the rendered web page shown in Figure 4-1. You'll see that the following style changes were made to the default list styles:

- Changed the marker in an unordered list to a square by using `list-style-type`.
- Changed the marker in an ordered list to uppercase Roman numerals again by using `list-style-type`.
- Changed the font size of the list items by using `font-size`.

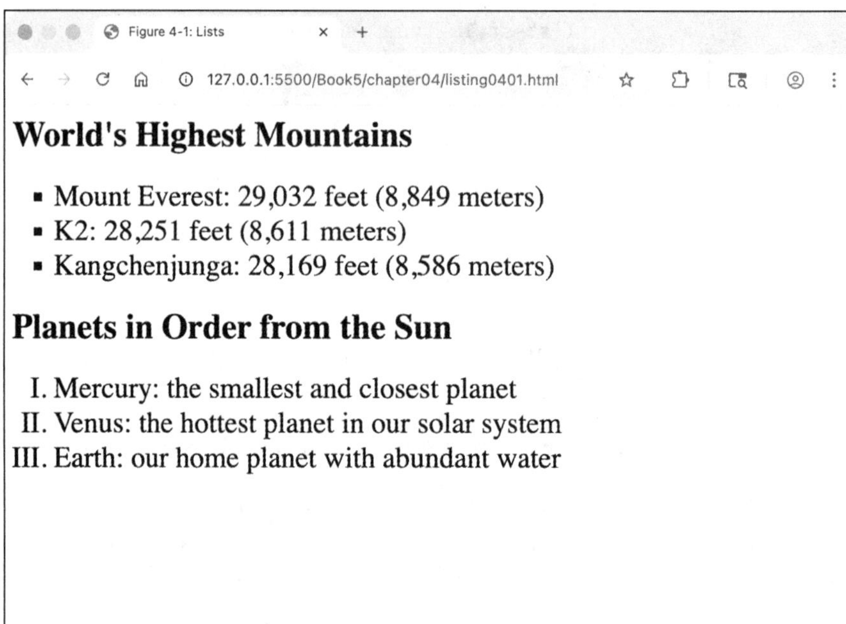

FIGURE 4-1: Ordered and unordered lists modified to change the marker type.

REMEMBER

You can apply CSS in three ways: with inline CSS using the `style` attribute, with embedded CSS using an opening and closing `<style>` tag, and in a separate CSS style sheet. In many modern projects, styles are also bundled or scoped per component by build tools or frameworks, but they still end up as CSS rules applied to elements through selectors.

Designing tables

In Book 5, Chapter 2, you find out how to create basic tables. By default, the width of these tables expands to fit content inside the table, content in individual cells is left-aligned, and no borders are displayed.

These defaults may not be appropriate for all circumstances. Some older HTML attributes used to modify these defaults are now considered *deprecated,* which means that an attribute or a feature is no longer recommended for use and may be removed in future browser versions. Although deprecated attributes might work in some browsers for now, relying on them is risky because support can be dropped at any time, which would result in incorrectly displayed tables. As a safer alternative, CSS can style tables with greater control.

Three common tasks CSS can perform for tables are

- Setting the width of a table, table row, or individual table cell with the `width` property
- Aligning text in the table with the `text-align` property
- Displaying borders in the table with the `border` property

These properties are outlined in Table 4-2.

TABLE 4-2 Common CSS Properties and Values for Styling Tables

Property Name	Possible Values	Description
`width`	*`pixels`* (#px) %	Width of the table measured either in pixels on-screen or as a percentage of the browser window or container tag.

`text-align`	`left`
	`right`
	`center`
	`justify`
		Position of text relative to the table according to the value of the attribute. For example, `text-align="center"` positions the text in the center of the table cell.

(continued)

TABLE 4-2 ***(continued)***

Property Name	Possible Values	Description

`border`	`width`
	`style`
	`color`
		Defines three properties in one: `border-width`, `border-style`, and `border-color`. The values must be specified in this order: width (pixel), style (none, dotted, dashed, solid), and then color (name, hexadecimal code, RGB value). For example, `border: 1px solid red`.

In Listing 4-2, the table is wider than the text in any cell, the text in each cell is centered, and borders are applied to the table, header cells, and data cells:

LISTING 4-2: An HTML Table

```
<html>
  <head>
    <title>Figure 4-2: Tables</title>
    <style>
      table {
        width: 100%;
        max-width: 700px;
        margin: 0 auto;
        border-collapse: collapse;
      }
      table,
      th,
      td {
        text-align: center;
        border: 1px solid black;
      }
    </style>
  </head>
  <body>
    <table>
      <caption>
        Desktop browser market share (February 2026)
      </caption>
```

```
      <tr>
        <th>Source</th>
        <th>Chrome</th>
        <th>Safari</th>
        <th>IE and Edge</th>
        <th>Firefox</th>
        <th>Opera</th>
      </tr>
      <tr>
        <td>StatCounter</td>
        <td>73.26%</td>
        <td>6.18%</td>
        <td>11%</td>
        <td>4.2%</td>
        <td>2.23%</td>
      </tr>
      <tr>
        <td>W3Counter</td>
        <td>77.4%</td>
        <td>8.0%</td>
        <td>3.2%</td>
        <td>1.7%</td>
        <td>0.3%</td>
      </tr>
    </table>
  </body>
</html>
```

TIP

The HTML `<caption>` tag and the CSS `border-collapse` property further style the table. The `<caption>` tag adds a title to the table. Although you can create a similar effect using the `<h1>` tag, `<caption>` associates the title with the table. The CSS `border-collapse` property can have a value of `separate` or `collapse`. The `separate` value renders each border separately (refer to Book 2, Chapter 2, Figure 2-9), whereas `collapse` draws a single border when possible, as shown in Figure 4-2.

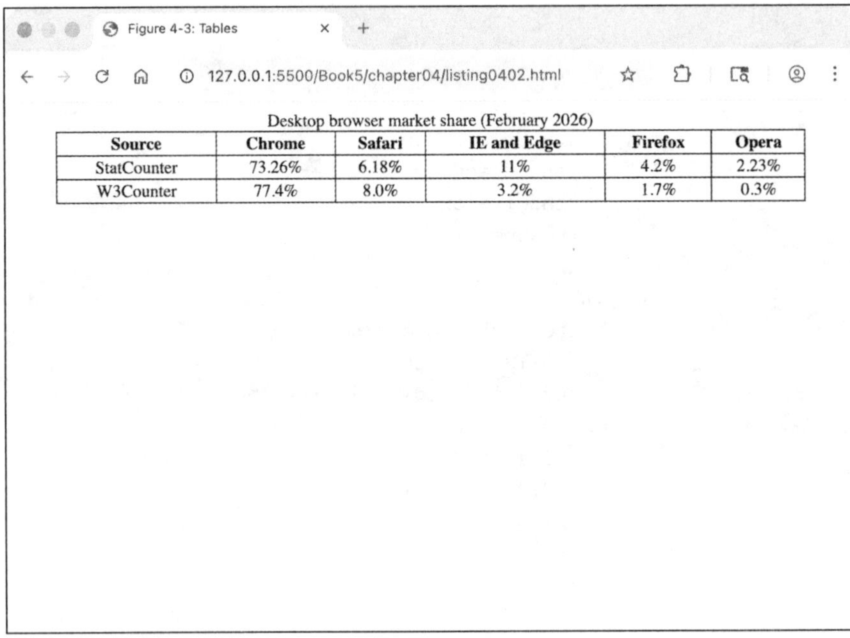

Source	Chrome	Safari	IE and Edge	Firefox	Opera
StatCounter	73.26%	6.18%	11%	4.2%	2.23%
W3Counter	77.4%	8.0%	3.2%	1.7%	0.3%

FIGURE 4-2: A table with width, text alignment, and border modified with CSS.

Selecting Elements to Style

Currently, the CSS you have seen styles every HTML element that matches the CSS selector. For example, in Figure 4-3, the `table` and `td` selectors have a `text-align` property that centers text in every table cell. Depending on the content, you may want to center the text in the header row but left-align text in subsequent rows. Here are two ways to do so:

- » Style specific HTML elements based on their position to other elements
- » Name HTML elements and then style elements only by name

Styling specific elements

When styling specific elements, it's helpful to visualize the HTML code as a family tree with parents, children, and siblings. In Listing 4-3, the tree starts with the `html` element, which has two children `head` and `body`. The `head` has a child element called `title`. The `body` has `h1`, `ul`, and `p` elements as children. Finally, the `ul` element has `li` elements as children, and the `p` element has `a` elements as children.

LISTING 4-3: A Typical HTML Document

```
<html>
  <head>
    <title>Figure 4-3: DOM</title>
  </head>
  <body>
    <h1>Useful Learning Resources</h1>
    <ul>
      <li>
        <a href="https://example.com/tutorials">Tutorials</a>
      </li>
      <li>
        <a href="https://example.com/reference">Reference</a>
      </li>
      <li>
        <a href="https://example.com/community">Community Q&amp;A</a>
      </li>
    </ul>

    <h1>Featured Links</h1>
    <p>
      <a href="https://example.com/news" id="featured">Weekly Web
  Dev News</a>
    </p>
    <p><a href="https://example.com/events">Local Events
  Calendar</a></p>
  </body>
</html>
```

Figure 4-3 shows how the code appears in the browser.

Figure 4-4 shows a depiction of the code using the tree metaphor.

TECHNICAL STUFF

The HTML tree is called the *DOM* or *document object model.*

Child selector

The links in the "Featured Links" section of the code in the preceding section are immediate children of the paragraph tags. If you want to style just those links, you can use the *child selector*, which selects the immediate children of a specified element. A child selector is created by listing the parent selector, a greater-than sign (>), and then the child selector.

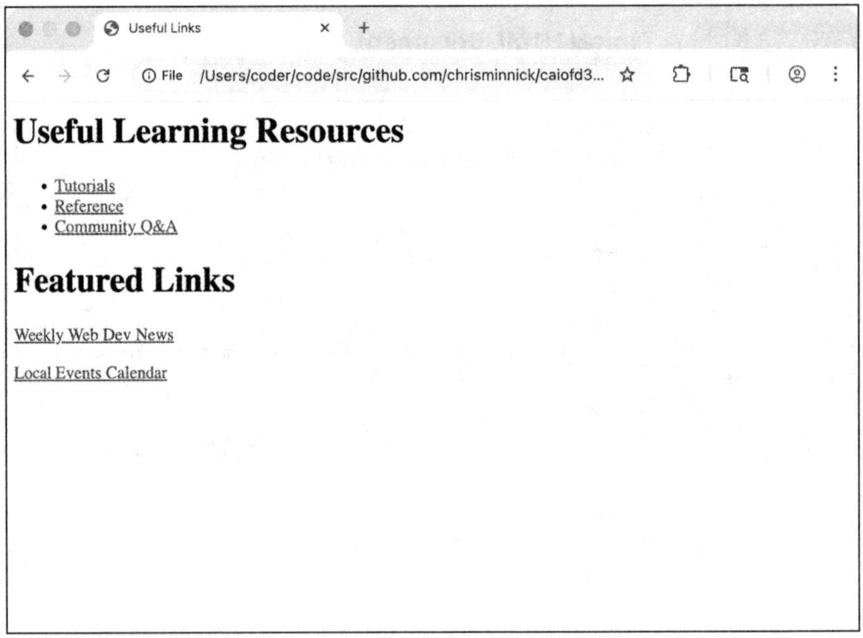

FIGURE 4-3: Two groups of links (browser view).

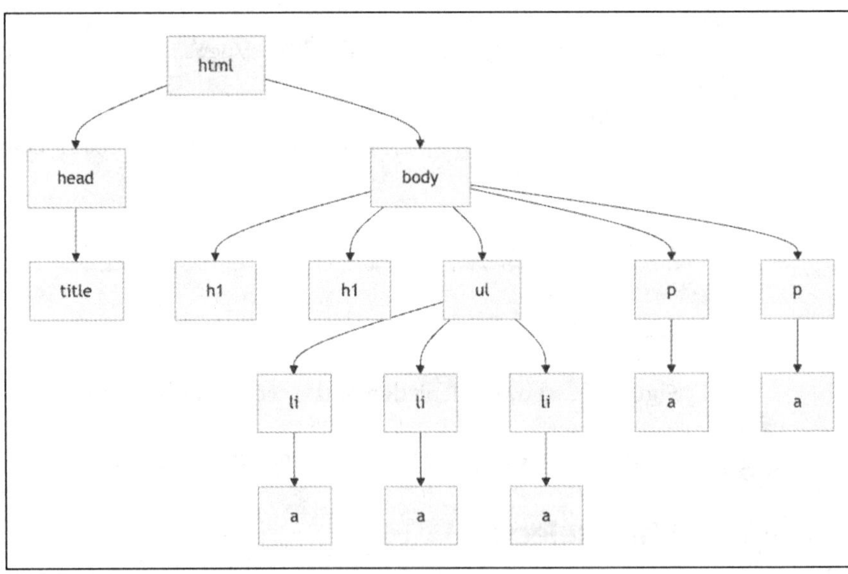

FIGURE 4-4: A family tree of elements.

In the following example, which is shown in Figure 4-5, the anchor tags that are immediate children of the paragraph tags are selected, and those hyperlinks are styled with a red font color and without an underline. The links in the unordered list are not styled because they are children of the list item tag:

```
p > a {
    color: red;
    text-decoration: none;
}
```

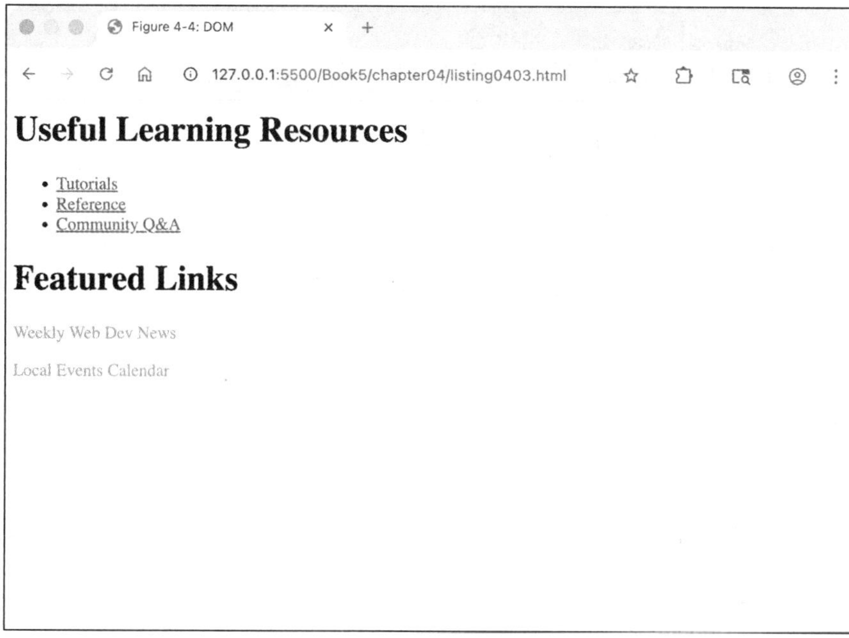

FIGURE 4-5: Child selector used to style the Featured Links.

REMEMBER

If you used just the a selector here, all the links on the page would be styled instead of just a selection.

Descendant selector

The "Useful Learning Resources" links in the code example are descendants, or located within, the unordered list. If you want to style just those links, you can use the *descendant selector*, which selects not just immediate children of a specified element but all elements nested within the specified element. A descendant selector is created by listing the parent selector, a space, and then the descendant selector you want to target.

In the following example, which is shown in Figure 4-6, the anchor tags that are descendants of the unordered list are selected, and those hyperlinks are styled with a blue font color and are crossed out. The "Featured Links" section isn't styled because those links aren't descendants of an unordered list:

```
ul a {
    color: blue;
    text-decoration: line-through;
}
```

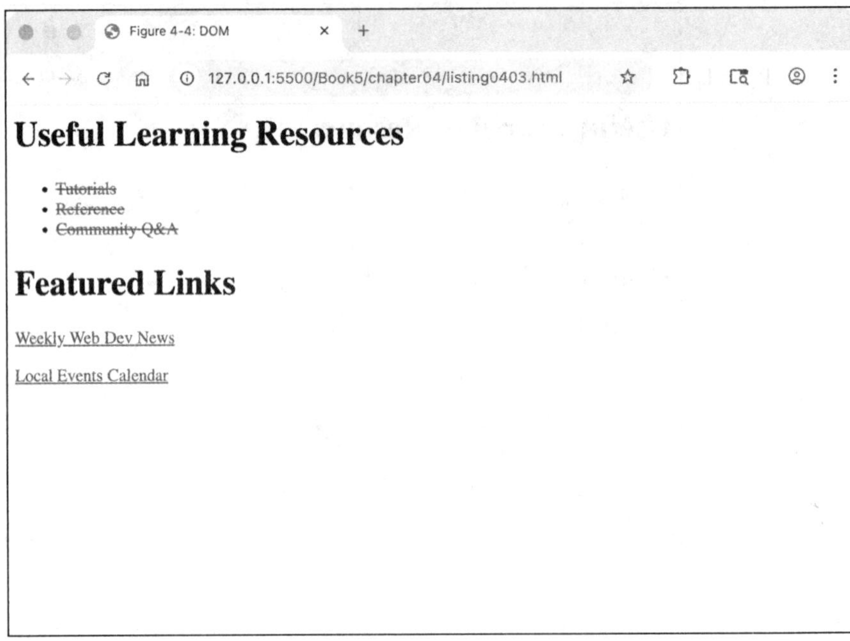

FIGURE 4-6: Child selector used to style the Useful Learning Resources.

Naming HTML elements

Another way of styling specific elements in CSS is to name your HTML elements. You name your code by using either the `id` or `class` attribute, and then style your code by referring to the `id` or `class` selector.

Naming your code using the id attribute

Use the `id` attribute to style one specific element on your web page. The `id` attribute can name any HTML element, and it is always placed in the opening HTML tag. Additionally, each element can have only one `id` attribute value, and the attribute value must appear only once in the HTML file. After you define the attribute in the HTML file, you refer to the HTML element in your CSS by writing a hashtag (`#`) followed by the attribute value.

Using the `id` attribute, the following code styles the "Weekly Web Dev News" link the color red with a yellow background:

HTML:

```
<p> <a href="https://example.com/news" id="featured">Weekly Web Dev News</a>
  </p>
```

CSS:

```
#featured {
    color: red;
    background-color: yellow;
}
```

Naming your code using the class attribute

Use the `class` attribute to style multiple elements on your web page. The `class` attribute can name any HTML element and is always placed in the opening HTML tag. The attribute value need not be unique in the HTML file. After you define the attribute in the HTML file, you refer to the HTML element by writing a period (`.`) followed by the attribute value.

With the `class` attribute, the following code styles all "Useful Learning Resources" links as red with no underline:

HTML:

```
<ul>
  <li>
    <a href="https://example.com/tutorials" class="tech">Tutorials</a>
  </li>
  <li>
    <a href="https://example.com/reference" class="tech">Reference</a>
  </li>
  <li>
    <a href="https://example.com/community" class="tech">Community Q&A</a>
  </li>
</ul>
```

CSS:

```
.tech {
    color: red;
    text-decoration: none;
}
```

TIP

Use a search engine, such as Google, to search for additional CSS effects. For example, if you want to increase the spacing between each list item, open your browser and search for *list item line spacing css.* Links appearing in the top ten results should include the following:

- `www.w3schools.com`: A beginner tutorial site
- `www.stackoverflow.com`: A discussion board for experienced developers
- `https://developer.mozilla.org`: A reference guide that was created by the Mozilla Foundation and is now maintained by a community of developers

Each of these sites is a good place to start; be sure to look for answers that include example code.

Aligning and Laying Out Your Elements

CSS allows you to control not only the formatting of HTML elements but also the placement of these elements on the page, known as the *page layout.* In the past, developers used HTML tables to create page layouts, but the process was tedious, and the developers had to write a great deal of code to ensure consistency across browsers. CSS eliminated the need to use tables to create layouts, helped reduce code bloat, and increased the control of page layouts.

Organizing data on the page

Before diving into code, look at Figure 4-7 and review some of the basic ways we can structure the page and the content on it. Layouts have evolved over time, with some layouts working well on desktop computers but not displaying optimally on tablets or mobile devices.

TIP

Always ask yourself how your intended layout will appear on desktop, tablet, and mobile devices. Left and right navigation toolbars aren't usually seen on mobile devices. Top navigation toolbars are used on both desktop and mobile devices, and bottom navigation toolbars are most common on mobile devices.

Hundreds of different layouts exist, and a few selected page layouts appear here along with example websites. The following examples show real websites with these layouts:

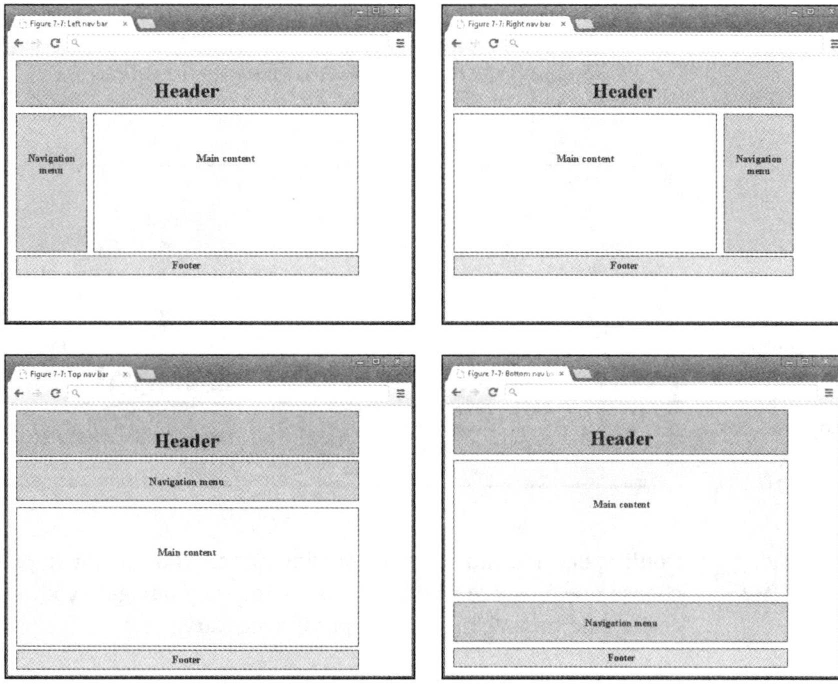

FIGURE 4-7: Vertical and horizontal navigation layouts.

» **Vertical navigation,** which is shown in Figure 4-8, aids reader understanding when a hierarchy or relationship exists between navigational topics.

In the `w3schools.com` example, HTML, JavaScript, Server Side, and XML relate to one another, and related subtopics are below each topic heading.

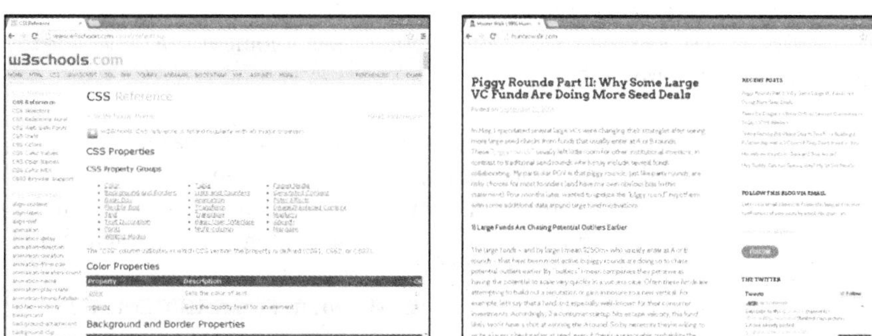

FIGURE 4-8: Use of left and right navigation toolbar on `w3schools.com` (left) and `hunterwalk.com` (right).

» **Horizontal, or menu navigation,** which is shown in Figure 4-9, helps reader navigation when navigational topics have a weak or disparate relationship.

In the eBay example, the Motors, Fashion, and Electronics menu items have different products and appeal to different audiences.

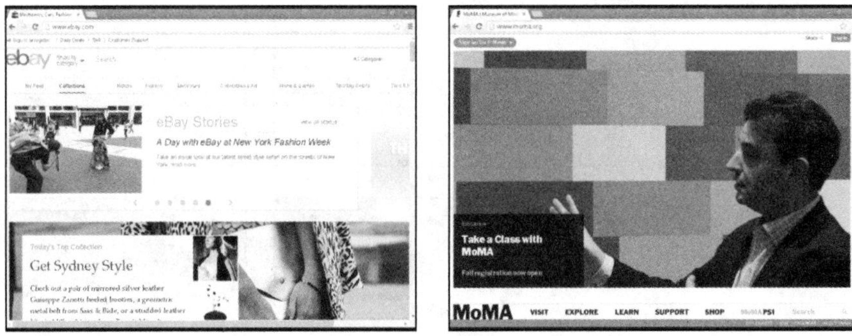

FIGURE 4-9: Use of top and bottom navigation toolbar on `ebay.com` (left) and `moma.org` (right).

TIP

Don't spend too much time worrying about what layout to pick. You can always choose one, observe whether your visitors can navigate your website quickly and easily, and then change the layout if necessary.

Shaping the div

The previous page layouts are collections of elements grouped together. These elements are grouped using rectangular containers created with an opening and closing `<div>` tag, and all of the layouts can be created with these `<div>` tags. By itself, the `<div>` tag doesn't render anything on the screen, but instead serves as a container for content of any type, such as HTML headings, lists, tables, or images.

To see the `<div>` tag in action, take a look at the `Codecademy.com` home page in Figure 4-10.

Note how the page can be divided into three parts — the navigation header, the middle video testimonial, and then additional text user testimonials. `<div>` tags are used to outline these major content areas, and additional nested `<div>` tags within each part are used to group content such as images and text.

In the following example, as shown in Figure 4-11, the HTML `div` elements create two containers, the `id` attribute names each `div`, and CSS sizes and colors the `div` elements.

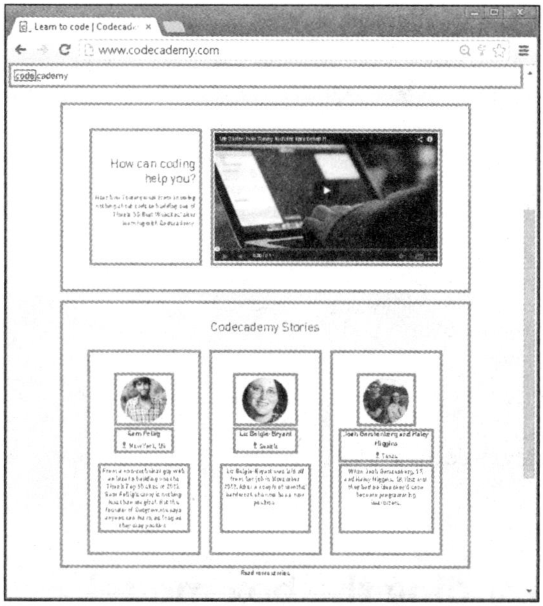

FIGURE 4-10: Codecademy.com home page with visible borders for the <div> tags.

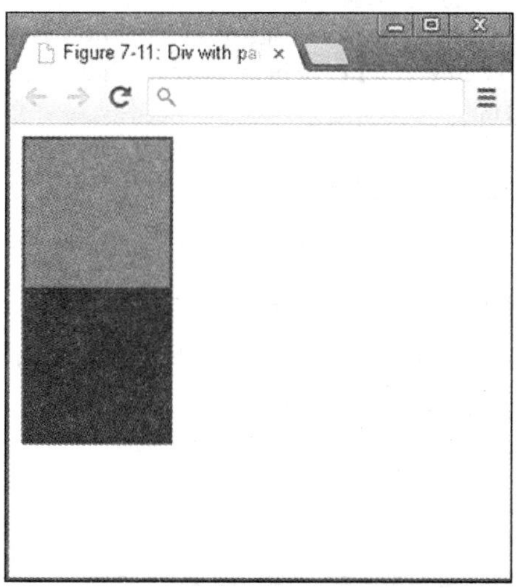

FIGURE 4-11: Two boxes created with HTML <div> tag and styled using CSS.

HTML:

```
<div id="first"></div>
<div id="second"></div>
```

CSS:

```
div {
    height: 100px;
    width: 100px;
    border: 2px solid purple;
}

#first {
    background-color: red;
}

#second {
    background-color: blue;
}
```

Understanding the box model

Just as we created boxes with the preceding tags, CSS creates a box around every single element on the page, even text. Figure 4-12 shows the box model for an image that says, "This is an element." These boxes, which are not always visible, are made up of four parts:

- **`content`:** An HTML tag rendered in the browser
- **`padding`:** Optional spacing between the content and the border
- **`border`:** The edge of the padding; varies in width and visibility
- **`margin`:** Transparent optional spacing surrounding the border

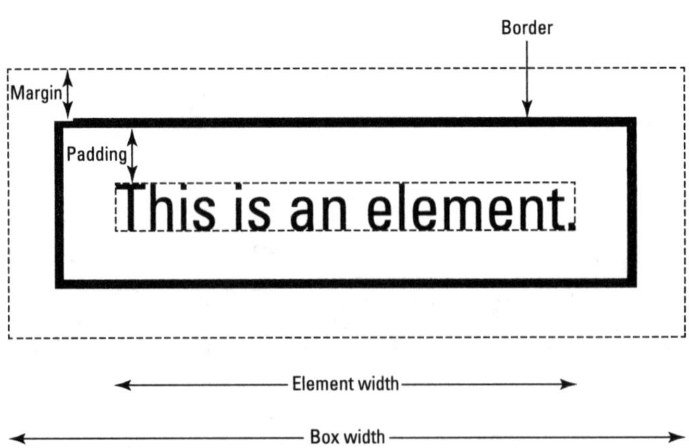

FIGURE 4-12: Box model for the `img` element.

TIP

Using the Chrome browser, navigate to your favorite news website, and then right-click an image and choose Inspect from the context menu. On the right side of the screen, you see three tabs; click the Computed tab. The box model is displayed for the image you right-clicked, showing the content dimensions and dimensions for the padding, border, and margin.

The padding, border, and margin are CSS properties, with a value usually expressed in pixels. In the following code, shown in Figure 4-13, padding and margins are added to separate each `div`.

```
div {
    height: 100px;
    width: 100px;
    border: 1px solid black;
    padding: 10px;
    margin: 10px;
}
```

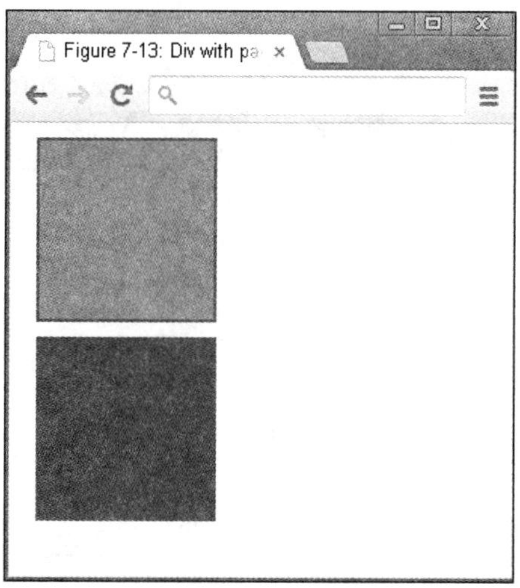

FIGURE 4-13: Padding and margin added to separate each `div`.

Positioning the boxes

Now that you understand how to group elements using HTML and how CSS views elements, the final piece is to position these elements on the page. Various techniques can be used for page layouts. One technique to create the layouts shown in Figure 4-14 is to use the `float` and `clear` properties (as described in Table 4-3).

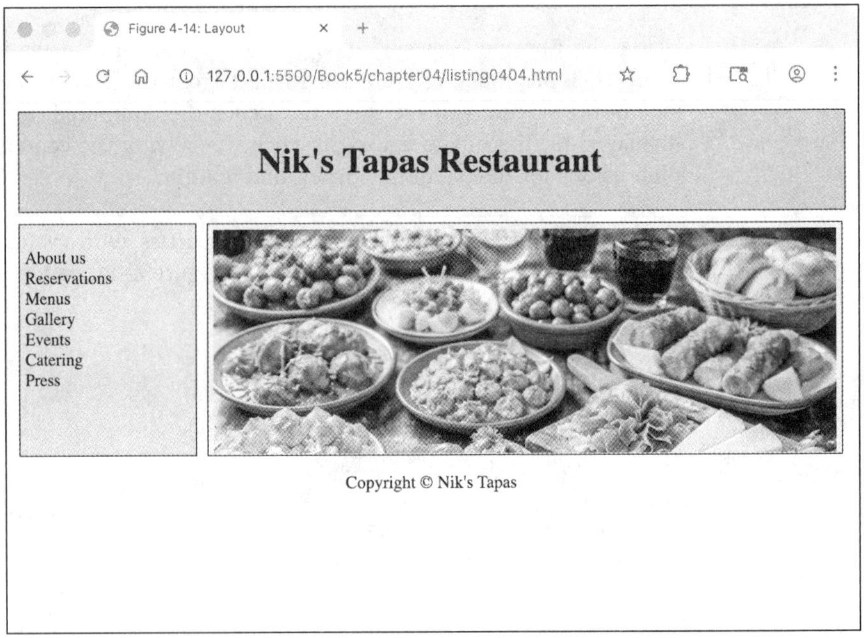

FIGURE 4-14: Left navigation web page layout created using `<div>` tags.

TABLE 4-3 Select CSS Properties and Values for Page Layouts

Property Name	Possible Values	Description

`float`	`left`
	`right`
	none
		Sends an element to the `left` or `right` of the container it is in. The none value specifies that the element should not float.

`clear`	`left`
	`right`
	both
	none
		Specifies on which side of an element not to have other floating elements.

TIP

I include the `float` and `clear` properties here mostly because you'll likely run into them in the wild. At the time of this writing, however, these properties are far less popular choices for creating page layouts than the properties used to create Flexbox layouts and Grid layouts, which you learn about in Chapter 5 of this minibook.

If the width of an element is specified, the `float` property allows elements that would normally appear on separate lines to appear next to each other, such as navigation toolbars and a main content window. The `clear` property prevents any other element from floating on one or both sides of current element; the property is commonly set to both to place web page footers below other elements.

Listing 4-4 uses <div> tags, float, and clear to create a simple left navigation layout, as shown in Figure 4-14:

LISTING 4-4: **Creating a Simple Left Navigation Layout**

```
<!DOCTYPE html>
<html>
  <head>
    <title>Figure 4-14: Layout</title>
    <style>
      #header {
        background-color: #ff8c8c;
        border: 1px solid black;
        padding: 5px;
        margin: 5px;
        text-align: center;
      }

      #navbar {
        background-color: #00e0ff;
        height: 200px;
        width: 20%;
        float: left;
        border: 1px solid black;
        padding: 5px;
        margin: 5px;
        text-align: left;
      }

      div#navbar ul {
        list-style-type: none;
        padding-left: 0;
      }

      #content {
        background-color: #eeeeee;
        height: 200px;
        width: 74%;
        float: left;
        border: 1px solid black;
```

(continued)

LISTING 4-4: *(continued)*

```
        padding: 5px;
        margin: 5px;
        text-align: center;
      }

      #footer {
        clear: both;
        text-align: center;
        padding: 10px;
        margin: 5px;
      }
    </style>
  </head>
  <body>
    <div id="header"><h1>Nik's Tapas Restaurant</h1></div>

    <div id="navbar">
      <ul>
        <li>About us</li>
        <li>Reservations</li>
        <li>Menus</li>
        <li>Gallery</li>
        <li>Events</li>
        <li>Catering</li>
        <li>Press</li>
      </ul>
    </div>

    <div id="content">
      <img src="images/tapas.png" width="100%" alt="Nik's Tapas"/>
    </div>

    <div id="footer">Copyright &copy; Nik's Tapas</div>
  </body>
</html>
```

Typically, after grouping your content using <div> tags, you name each <div> tag using class or id attributes, and then style the div in CSS:

- The CSS is embedded between the opening and closing `<style>` tags, and the HTML is between the opening and closing <body> tags.

» Between the opening and closing <body> tags, I use <div> tags to divide the page into four parts: header, navigation bar, content, and footer.

» The navigation menu is created with an unordered list, which is left-aligned with no marker.

» CSS styles size and color and align each <div> tag.

» The `float` and `clear` CSS properties place the left navigation layout to the left and the footer below the other elements.

Practicing with CSS Selectors

You learned about several different types of selectors in this chapter and the preceding one. CSS provides even more ways to select elements for styling than I can cover in this book. One of the best (and most fun) ways to practice using CSS selectors is by visiting CSS Diner at `https://flukeout.github.io`.

CSS Diner, shown in Figure 4-15, is a free game where your job is to use CSS selectors to select different combinations of things you might find in a restaurant, such as plates, pickles, apples, and bento boxes.

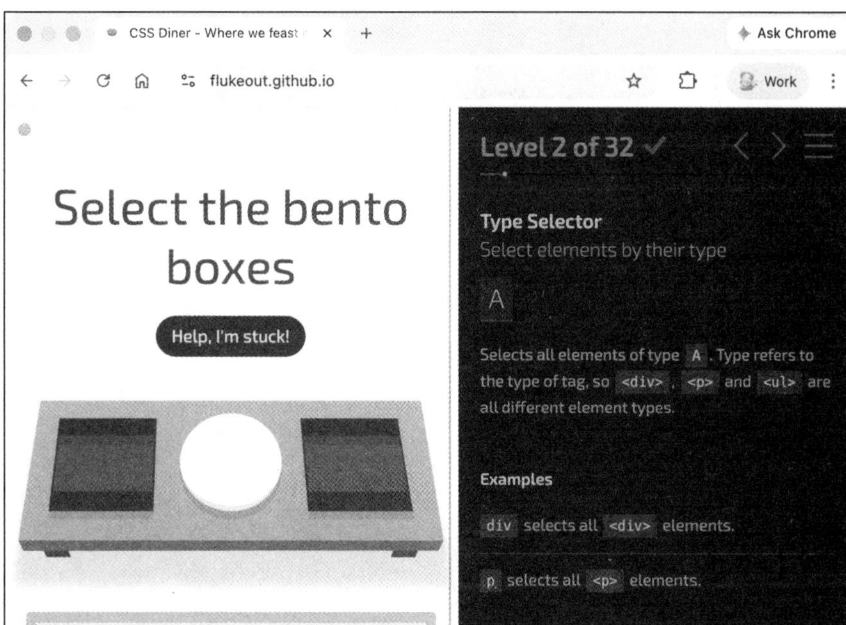

FIGURE 4-15: Practice using CSS selectors at CSS Diner.

IN THIS CHAPTER

» Understanding responsive design and modern layout tools

» Using Flexbox for one-dimensional layouts

» Using CSS Grid for two-dimensional layouts

» Choosing between Flexbox and Grid (and combining them)

Chapter 5
Responsive Layouts with Flexbox and Grid

"The measure of intelligence is the ability to change."

—ALBERT EINSTEIN

In this chapter, you continue building on the knowledge of CSS you gained in Book 2, Chapters 3 and 4. You previously learned how to apply styles to elements and how to do basic web page layout by using CSS. Now it's time to learn two of the newest and most useful features of the latest version of CSS to easily make web pages that look good in any browser on desktop, tablet, or mobile devices.

Introducing Responsive Design

Responsive design is the practice of making web pages and web apps that adjust to fit the width of the browser window in which they appear. In this section, you learn the terminology behind responsive design as well as the reasons for designing responsive web pages.

The web is mobile

In the years since the first edition of this book came out, the web has passed a major milestone. In 2016, the number of web pages viewed on mobile devices surpassed the number of web pages viewed on desktop (including laptop) devices globally. Since then, this trend has continued. Today, mobile devices typically account for a clear majority of global web traffic (often around 60 percent or more, depending on the source, region, and how tablets are counted). This fact is significant because many web pages still don't work well on mobile devices.

Why are so many sites mobile-unfriendly?

Since most web development is done using desktop computers (it's so much easier to code with a large monitor, or even better, with multiple monitors!), an inherent bias in web development exists toward desktop browsers. Many web developers still treat testing their websites on mobile devices as an afterthought.

WARNING

A website built without taking mobile browsers into consideration from the beginning is likely to not work as well on mobile devices as it does on the desktop, or to not be usable at all on mobile. When so many more web pages are being browsed on mobile devices, leaving them behind can result in significantly less traffic to your website and in unhappy customers.

Introducing mobile-first design

In recent years, the trend in web development has begun to reflect reality, and we've entered the age of mobile-first design. In *mobile-first design*, instead of making a web page that's optimized for desktop devices and then scaling it down for mobile devices, we design web pages first for mobile and then scale them up for desktop devices.

Making responsive web pages with the viewport meta tag

The simplest way to design a responsive web page is to write a simple web page that uses the browser's default styling, with no additional positioning CSS or element widths specified, and then add a `viewport` meta tag to the head element. A `viewport` meta tag is an instruction for the web browser that tells it how to scale the virtual window in which web pages display, which is called the *viewport*.

TECHNICAL STUFF

Meta tags are instructions that web developers put in the `<head>` element of HTML pages; they aren't visible to viewers of the web page. Their job is to specify information about the HTML page (also known as *metadata*) or to modify some property of the web page as a whole. In addition to the `viewport` meta tag, other meta tags include the `description` meta tag, which is where you can specify a brief description of your website for search engines, and the `charset` meta tag, which allows you to specify the character encoding for the document.

For example, the HTML document in Listing 5-1 will look just fine (if a bit boring) on desktop devices.

LISTING 5-1: A Non-Responsive Web Page

```
<!DOCTYPE html>
<html>
  <head>
    <title>What's the cat up to?</title>
  </head>
  <body>
    <h1>Here are some of the things my cat is doing this morning:</h1>
    <ul>
      <li>Playing with catnip mouse</li>
      <li>Hiding from the dog</li>
      <li>Jumping on the table</li>
      <li>Getting into the salad</li>
      <li>Rolling on the floor</li>
      <li>Sleeping on the dresser</li>
    </ul>
  </body>
</html>
```

Figure 5-1 shows how this web page looks in Chrome on a desktop computer.

When you open the same web page on a mobile device, however, it appears very small, as shown in Figure 5-2. The reason the web page looks so small on a mobile device is that mobile browsers assume the page is designed for a wide desktop viewport and then zoom out to fit the narrower screen.

The following `viewport` meta tag makes a simple web page display correctly on mobile devices by adjusting the size of the content to fit the size of the viewport:

```
<meta name="viewport" content="width=device-width, initial-scale=1.0">
```

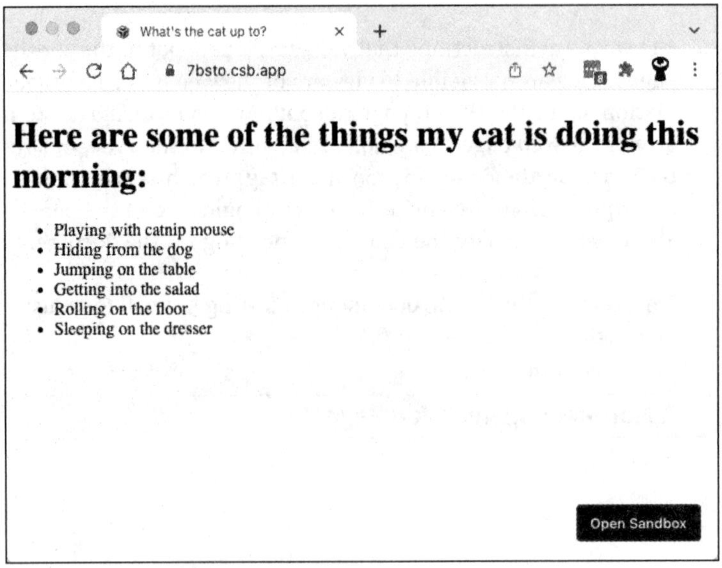

FIGURE 5-1: A simple web page on a desktop browser.

FIGURE 5-2: A nonoptimized web page in a mobile browser.

TIP

The `viewport` meta tag is almost always the same. It's so useful that you should add it to every web page you make.

WARNING

Avoid disabling zoom by adding values such as `user-scalable=no` or `maximum-scale=1` to the `viewport` tag. Users who need magnification (including many low-vision users) rely on pinch-to-zoom.

TECHNICAL STUFF

A full explanation of how the `viewport` tag works is much easier to understand from a video. Check out the excellent video about browser viewports at `www.youtube.com/watch?v=XrMTuTzX4co` to learn more.

With the `viewport` meta tag added, Listing 5-2 shows how the preceding simple web page's code now looks:

LISTING 5-2: Adding the viewport Meta Tag

```
<!DOCTYPE html>
<html>
  <head>
    <title>What's the cat up to?</title>
    <meta name="viewport" content="width=device-width, initial-scale=1.0">
  </head>
  <body>
    <h1>Here are some of the things my cat is doing this morning:</h1>
    <ul>
      <li>Playing with catnip mouse</li>
      <li>Hiding from the dog</li>
      <li>Jumping on the table</li>
      <li>Getting into the salad</li>
      <li>Rolling on the floor</li>
      <li>Sleeping on the dresser</li>
    </ul>
  </body>
</html>
```

This page will look the same in a desktop browser as it did in Figure 5-1. Figure 5-3 shows how it looks in a mobile browser now.

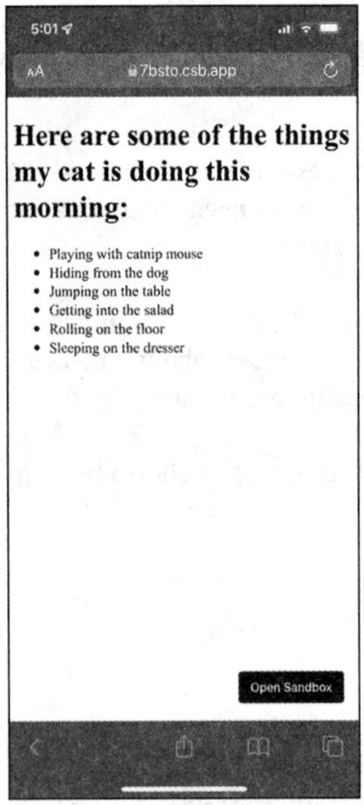

FIGURE 5-3: A simple mobile web page.

Using Flexbox

By default, web browsers display the elements in an HTML document in what is called a *normal flow*, which is from left to right and from top to bottom. By using the CSS `float` and `position` properties, you can modify this normal flow of HTML or even remove elements from the normal flow of a document and position them wherever you want in the viewport. However, these positioning tools can be complex, and achieving the results you want and getting them to work correctly on different devices can be tricky — especially when you're trying to align elements or create responsive layouts.

Another problem with normal flow is that not all languages are written from left to right. So-called normal flow is backward to the Arabic-speaking world, for example.

Flexbox was created to fix the many issues with web page layout using older CSS properties like `float` and `position`. The first things you need to know about Flexbox are

- All Flexbox layout happens in Flexbox containers (also known as *boxes*).
- Flexbox is one-dimensional. When you work with Flexbox, you deal with only the x-axis (rows) or the y-axis (columns) at any one time.
- Flexbox doesn't assume that the text direction (also known as the *writing mode*) is left to right.
- Flexbox containers and the items inside them are flexible. (It's right there in the name!)

In the following sections, you learn more about each of these points and see plenty of example code that you can try out to get comfortable with using Flexbox.

Creating boxes

To get started with Flexbox, you first need to define what part or parts of your web page will use it. The way to do this is to set the `display` property of an element to `flex`. By default, a container will flow elements inside it horizontally (in a row). For example, in the following code, the `div` element with the `id` of gallery is a Flexbox that will flow horizontally:

```
<!DOCTYPE html>
<html>
  <head>
    <title>Creating a container</title>
    <style>
      #gallery {
        display: flex;
      }
    </style>
  </head>
  <body>
    <div id="gallery"> </div>
  </body>
</html>
```

The preceding code won't display anything in the browser just yet, because there's no content in the Flexbox container. To see what Flexbox can do, you can put something in the Flexbox. An element inside a Flexbox container is called an *item.*

Just as a cardboard box doesn't make a lot of sense for holding just one thing (unless you're a certain online retailer, in which case the bigger the box and the smaller the item inside, the better!), a Flexbox with only one item isn't impressive.

To see what simply creating a container and putting things in it can do, we need several items in the box. The code in Listing 5-3 creates three `div` elements in the Flexbox container and styles them with a solid black border and margins of 10 pixels:

LISTING 5-3: Creating a Row of Boxes

```
<!DOCTYPE html>
<html>
  <head>
    <title>A flexible row of boxes</title>
    <style>
      #gallery {
        display: flex;
      }
      .box {
        border: 4px solid black;
        margin: 10px;
        width: 100px;
        height: 100px;
        font-size: 36px;
      }
    </style>
  </head>
  <body>
    <div id="gallery">
      <div class="box">1</div>
      <div class="box">2</div>
      <div class="box">3</div>
    </div>
  </body>
</html>
```

When displayed in a web browser, the preceding code will present three boxes arranged in a neat row, as shown in Figure 5-4.

Thinking in one dimension

When we say that Flexbox layout is one-dimensional, what we mean is that Flexbox deals with only layout in rows or layout in columns. This is different from a grid layout, in which you can position objects in rows or columns at the same time.

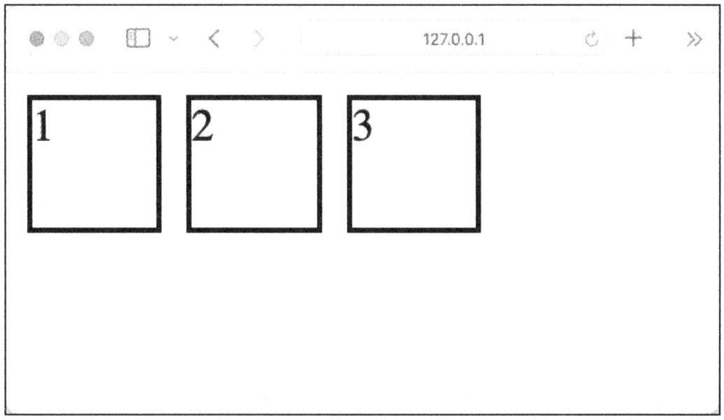

FIGURE 5-4: Little boxes all the same.

To change the dimension that a container flows its items in, we use the `flex-direction` property. This property has four possible values: `row` (the default), `row-reverse`, `column`, and `column-reverse`.

In Listing 5-4, the layout direction of the items has been changed to `column`, which displays them as vertically stacked boxes:

LISTING 5-4: Displaying Boxes in a Column

```
<!DOCTYPE html>
<html>
  <head>
    <title>Demonstrating flex-direction</title>
    <style>
      #gallery {
        display: flex;
        flex-direction: column;
      }
      .box {
        border: 4px solid black;
        margin: 10px;
        width: 100px;
        height: 100px;
        font-size: 36px;
      }
    </style>
  </head>
  <body>
    <div id="gallery">
```

(continued)

LISTING 5-4: *(continued)*

```
      <div class="box">1</div>
      <div class="box">2</div>
      <div class="box">3</div>
    </div>
  </body>
</html>
```

To reverse the order of the items in the box, use one of the `-reverse` values, as shown in Listing 5-5 and in Figure 5-5:

LISTING 5-5: **Reversing the Order of Items**

```
<!DOCTYPE html>
<html>
  <head>
    <title>Demonstrating flex-direction</title>
    <style>
      #gallery {
        display: flex;
        flex-direction: row-reverse;
      }
      .box {
        border: 4px solid black;
        margin: 10px;
        width: 100px;
        height: 100px;
        font-size: 36px;
      }
    </style>
  </head>
  <body>
    <div id="gallery">
      <div class="box">1</div>
      <div class="box">2</div>
      <div class="box">3</div>
    </div>
  </body>
</html>
```

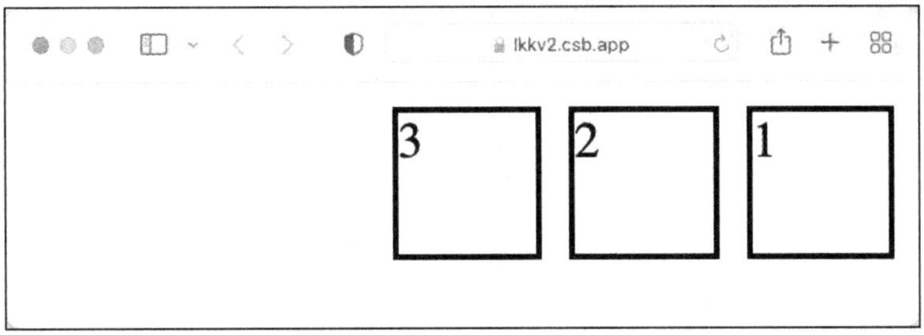

FIGURE 5-5: Reversing a Flexbox container.

Using multiline containers

By default, the items in a Flexbox container will all be on one line. If you want to create a multiline container in which items will wrap to new lines in the container when a line of items in a container fills up, you can use the `flex-wrap` property.

In Listing 5-6, the `flex-wrap` property is set to `wrap`, which creates an additional line when the previous line fills up with items:

LISTING 5-6: Wrapping Items in a Flexbox

```
<!DOCTYPE html>
<html>
   <head>
     <title>Demonstrating flex-wrap</title>
     <style>
       #gallery {
         display: flex;
         flex-wrap: wrap;
       }
       .box {
         border: 4px solid black;
         margin: 10px;
         font-size: 36px;
         width: 100px;
         height: 100px;
         font-size: 36px;
       }
     </style>
   </head>
   <body>
     <div id="gallery">
       <div class="box">1</div>
```

(continued)

LISTING 5-6: ***(continued)***

```
        <div class="box">2</div>
        <div class="box">3</div>
        <div class="box">4</div>
        <div class="box">5</div>
        <div class="box">6</div>
      </div>
    </body>
</html>
```

Figure 5-6 shows what the preceding code looks like rendered in a browser whose viewport is less than the total width of the six items in the container.

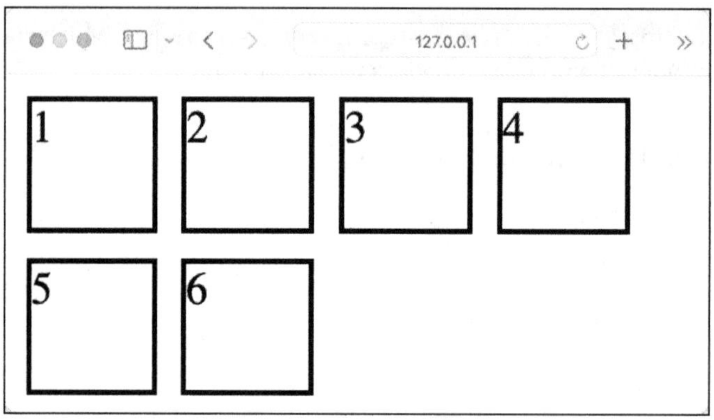

FIGURE 5-6: Wrapping items.

TIP

Wrapping items in a container is one of the best ways to create a responsive layout with Flexbox. With wrapping, when a multiple-column layout doesn't fit the width of the viewport, the items that don't fit will just drop down to a new line, rather than going off the page or shrinking down to fit.

Make no assumptions

If you're working in a language with a left-to-right writing mode, your Flexbox containers will flow their items from left to right by default. If you're working in a language with a right-to-left writing mode, your Flexbox containers will flow their items from right to left by default.

The terminology used by Flexbox is careful not to play favorites. When we talk about the position where a row or column of items begins, we use the term *start.*

Likewise, when we talk about the position where a row or column of items stops, we use the term *end.* The start and end positions could be at the top, bottom, left, or right of the screen. All that's important is that the items in a Flexbox container flow from the start to the end by default. If you use a `-reverse` value for the `flex-direction` property, the items will flow from the end to the start.

By default, items are aligned to the start position on their axis. You can see that in Figure 5-4, where the row of boxes starts at the left and moves to the right.

Aligning on the cross-axis

One of the greatest features of Flexbox is that you can modify the alignment of items on their axis or on their cross-axis. The cross-axis refers to the other axis. To set the cross-axis alignment of items, use the `align-items` property. The `align-items` property can have one of four possible values:

- **`stretch`:** The items are the same size (along the cross-axis) as the largest one. This is the default value. For example, Figure 5-7 shows three boxes of different sizes. Using the `stretch` value of `align-items`, all the boxes will be the same height as the tallest one.
- **`flex-start`:** The items are different heights, and their start points are aligned.
- **`flex-end`:** The end points of the items are aligned.
- **`center`:** The items are centered vertically if the `flex-direction` is set to `row` or `row-reverse`, as shown in Figure 5-8.

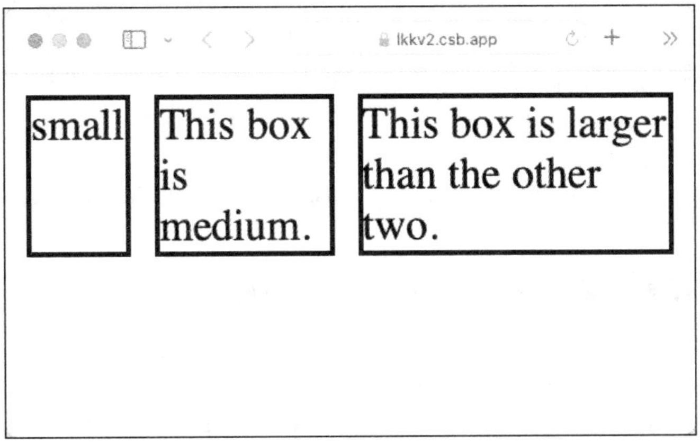

FIGURE 5-7: Stretching items.

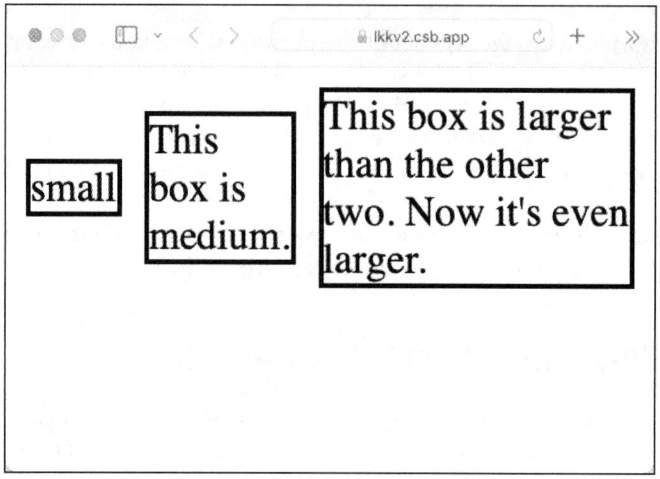

FIGURE 5-8: Centering on the cross-axis.

Aligning on the main axis

To align items on their main axis, use the `justify-content` property. The possible values of `justify-content` are

- **`flex-start`:** Items will be justified with the start of the container.
- **`flex-end`:** Items will be justified with the end of the container.
- **`center`:** Items will be centered in the container.
- **`space-around`:** Items are evenly distributed on the line with equal space around each item.
- **`space-between`:** Items are distributed so that the space between them is equal.
- **`space-evenly`:** Items are distributed so that the space between the items and the space to the edges are even.

Figure 5-9 illustrates each of the possible values of the `justify-content` property.

Modifying flexible boxes

All the Flexbox properties you've seen so far are applied to the container. Each item in the container can also have Flexbox properties applied to it. For example, you may want to modify the sizes or the relative sizes of items in a Flexbox. The three properties that can be applied Flexbox items to affect their size are:

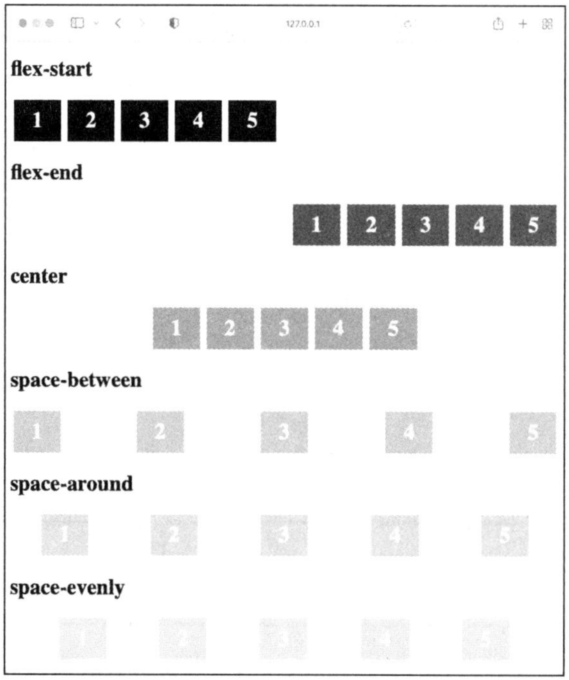

FIGURE 5-9: The different ways to justify content in a container.

» **`flex-basis`:** Defines the initial size of a flex item.

» **`flex-grow`:** Specifies how much a flex item should grow relative to the other flex items in the container when there is more space than the combined initial sizes (as defined by `flex-basis`) of the items.

» **`flex-shrink`:** Specifies how much a flex item will shrink relative to other flex items in the container when there isn't enough space in the container for the flex items to be the `flex-basis` size.

flex-basis

The `flex-basis` property specifies the initial size of an item before the available space in the container is taken into consideration. By default, `flex-basis` is set to `auto`, which tells the item to look at its `width` or `height` property. You can also set the `flex-basis` property to any other size by specifying a `length` (for example, 100px or 80%).

flex-grow

The `flex-grow` property is a number that indicates what share of the available space an item will get when it's distributed. For example, if each item in the container has flex-grow set to 1, the available space will be distributed evenly between them. But if there are three items and two have flex-grow set to 1 and the other has flex-grow set to 2, the one with flex-grow set to 2 will get twice as much of the available space as the others, as shown in the following code and in Figure 5-10:

```
<div style="display: flex;">
  <div class="box" style="flex-grow: 1;"> </div>
  <div class="box" style="flex-grow: 2;"> </div>
  <div class="box" style="flex-grow: 1;"> </div>
</div>
```

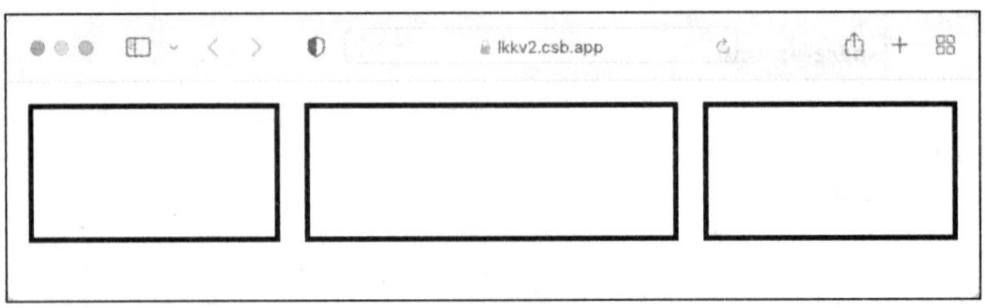

FIGURE 5-10: Distributing available space with flex-grow.

flex-shrink

The flex-shrink property behaves the same way as flex-grow, but it determines how much an item will shrink if there isn't enough space available for the items. In the following code and the example in Figure 5-11, the middle item will shrink twice as much as the other two:

```
<div style="display: flex;">
   <div class="box" style="flex-shrink: 1;"> </div>
   <div class="box" style="flex-shrink: 2;"> </div>
   <div class="box" style="flex-shrink: 1;"> </div>
</div>
```

The flex property

Although you can specify the flex-basis, flex-grow, and flex-shrink properties individually for each item, it's more common for developers to use a shorthand property that sets all three at the same time. The shorthand property for setting these three is the flex property.

FIGURE 5-11: Using `flex-shrink`.

The `flex` property takes up to three values. The first one, which is the only value required, is the number for the `flex-grow` property. The second one is the number for the `flex-shrink` property. The third value is the value for `flex-basis`. There's no difference between using the shorthand property and using the individual properties, except in the amount of typing you need to do.

Here's how you can set `flex-grow` to `2`, `flex-shrink` to `1`, and `flex-basis` to `100px`, all in one line of CSS:

```
flex: 2 1 100px;
```

If you want to set only the `flex-grow` property, you can just use one number:

```
flex: 1;
```

If you only want to set `flex-grow` and `flex-basis`, you can use two values:

```
flex: 1 100px;
```

TECHNICAL STUFF

Note that there's no way to use two values to set only `flex-shrink` and `flex-basis`. If that's what you want to do, you need to use three values and set `flex-grow` as well.

Changing the order of items

By default, items appear in a container in the same order in which they appear in the code. If you want to modify the order of the items, you can do so using the `order` property.

The `order` property takes a number value, which is the order in which the item should appear. Items that have the same number for the `order` property will be laid out in the order in which they appear in the source code. By default, all items have an `order` value of `0`.

WARNING

Be cautious when using `order`. Changing the visual order can create a mismatch between what sighted users see and what keyboard and screen-reader users experience because the tab order and reading order usually follow the source HTML. If you need a different order at different window widths, it's often better to change the HTML structure (or use Grid placement) than to rely heavily on `order`.

Listing 5-7 and Figure 5-12 demonstrate the use of `order` to make an element that comes last in the source code appear first in the browser window:

LISTING 5-7: Changing the Order of Items

```
<!DOCTYPE html>
<html>
  <head>
    <title>The order property</title>
    <style>
      #gallery {
        display: flex;
      }
      .box {
        border: 4px solid black;
        margin: 10px;
        font-size: 36px;
        width: 100px;
        height: 100px;
      }
    </style>
  </head>
  <body>
    <div id="gallery">
      <div class="box" style="order: 2;">
        1
      </div>
      <div class="box" style="order: 3;">
        2
      </div>
      <div class="box" style="order: 1;">
```

```
        3
      </div>
    </div>
  </body>
</html>
```

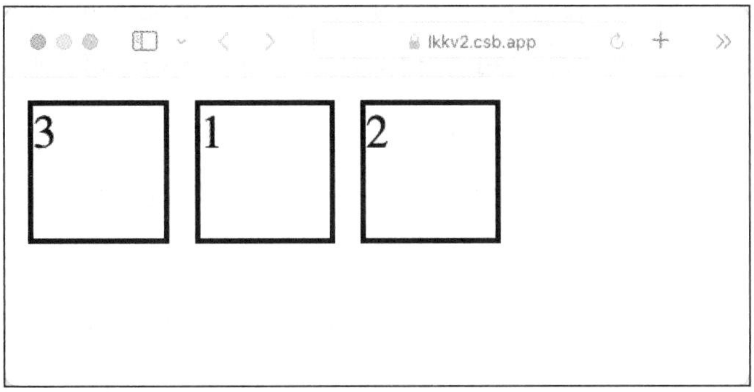

FIGURE 5-12: Changing the order of items in a container.

Using CSS Grid

CSS Grid is the modern layout system for *two-dimensional design:* It lets you control rows and columns at the same time. Flexbox is still ideal for *one-dimensional design* (a row *or* a column), such as navigation bars, button rows, and aligning items within a component.

In many real-world sites, you'll combine them: Grid for the overall page layout and Flexbox inside individual sections or cards. As a general rule:

- Use Flexbox when you're laying items out in a single row or column and want them to flex (grow, shrink, wrap) based on available space.
- Use Grid when you need consistent alignment in both directions, for example, a grid of *cards* — small, self-contained content blocks such as product tiles — with aligned rows, full-page layouts, dashboards, and forms with aligned labels or fields.
- Combine Flexbox and Grid when the page is a grid of regions, but each region needs internal alignment, for example, a grid of product cards where each card uses Flexbox for its header or footer alignment.

Key Grid properties for building a layout

To create a CSS Grid layout, you turn an element into a *grid container* and then define the grid's columns and rows (which are called *tracks*). Once the tracks exist, the browser can automatically place items into the grid, or you can place items explicitly. Following are the CSS properties used in creating grid layouts:

- **`display: grid`:** Creates a grid formatting context on the container.
- **`grid-template-columns` (and `grid-template-rows`):** Defines the grid tracks. For example, `grid-template-columns: 200px 1fr;` creates a fixed sidebar plus a flexible content column.
- **`gap` (or `row-gap` and `column-gap`):** Sets spacing between grid cells without needing margins on items.
- **`repeat()`:** A helper function you can use inside `grid-template-columns/grid-template-rows` to avoid repetition. For example, `repeat(3, 1fr)` creates three equal columns.
- **`minmax()`:** Gives tracks a minimum and maximum size. You'll often see this written as something like `minmax(220px, 1fr)`: The track won't get narrower than 220px, but it can grow. The `fr` unit means *fraction of the available (free) space* in the grid container after fixed-size tracks and gaps are accounted for. So `1fr` means to take one share of the remaining space; multiple `fr`-sized tracks split that remaining space proportionally (for example, `1fr 2fr` gives the second track twice as much).
- **`auto-fit` and `auto-fill`:** Used with `repeat()` to create as many columns as will fit. You see auto-fit in the next example.

Two more concepts are useful as soon as you move beyond the basics:

- **Implicit tracks:** If you place more items than you have defined rows for, Grid will create new rows automatically. Use `grid-auto-rows` to control the size of those implicit rows.
- **Auto-placement and alignment:** Grid will place items for you in row-major order by default. Row-major order is what you typically expect when placing items in a grid. Unpositioned items are placed in the first available empty cell starting from the top left, moving horizontally across columns in the current row, and then wrapping to the next row when the current row is full. You can influence that behavior with `grid-auto-flow`. For alignment, the container-level properties `justify-items` and `align-items` control how items sit inside their cells (similar to Flexbox, but applied to grid cells).

Here's the basic pattern you'll use again and again for responsive grids:

```
.grid {
  display: grid;
  gap: 16px;
  grid-template-columns: repeat(auto-fit, minmax(220px, 1fr));
}
```

That `grid-template-columns` line tells the browser: Make as many columns as will fit, but don't let a column get narrower than 220px; if there's extra space, distribute it evenly. The next section applies this pattern to a grid of content blocks.

A CSS Grid example

One of the most useful Grid patterns is a layout that automatically chooses how many columns will fit. The example in Listing 5-1 creates a set of cards that are displayed in multiple columns on wide screens and collapse to fewer columns (and eventually one column) on narrow screens.

LISTING 5-8: **A CSS Grid Example**

```
<!DOCTYPE html>
<html lang="en">
  <head>
    <meta charset="UTF-8"/>
    <meta name="viewport" content="width=device-width,
  initial-scale=1.0"/>
    <title>CSS Grid Example</title>
    <style>
      .card-grid {
        display: grid;
        gap: 16px;
        grid-template-columns: repeat(auto-fit,
  minmax(220px, 1fr));
      }
      .card {
        border: 2px solid black;
        padding: 12px;
      }
    </style>
  </head>
```

(continued)

LISTING 5-8: *(continued)*

```
  <body>
    <div class="card-grid">
      <div class="card">Card 1</div>
      <div class="card">Card 2</div>
      <div class="card">Card 3</div>
      <div class="card">Card 4</div>
      <div class="card">Card 5</div>
      <div class="card">Card 6</div>
    </div>
  </body>
</html>
```

Figure 5-13 shows the grid created by the preceding code when displayed in a web browser.

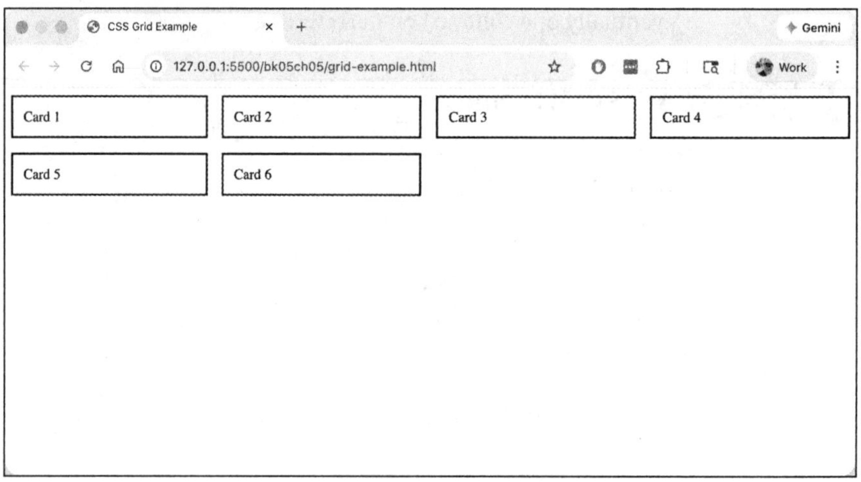

FIGURE 5-13: A simple responsive grid layout.

Practicing with CSS Grids

In the preceding chapter, you visited CSS Diner to practice using selectors. A similar game for practicing with CSS Grid is Grid Garden (`www.cssgridgarden.com`), shown in Figure 5-14.

At Grid Garden, you use CSS Grid properties to tend to a virtual carrot garden. In the process, you learn all about how to place items on a grid in CSS.

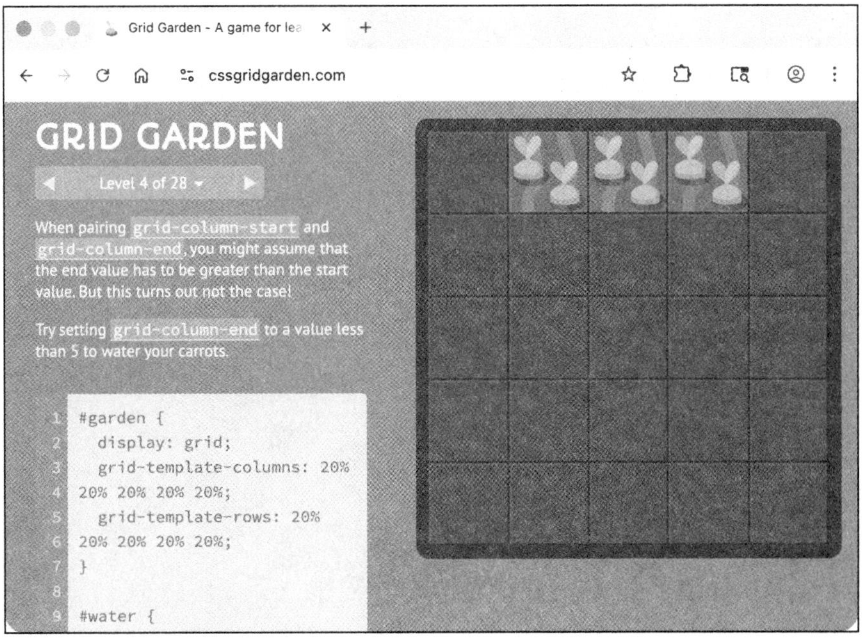

FIGURE 5-14: Grow your CSS skills in Grid Garden.

6

JavaScript Fundamentals

Contents at a Glance

IN THIS CHAPTER

- » Learning the basics of JavaScript syntax
- » Setting up your development environment
- » Writing and running your first program
- » Using JavaScript in a browser

Chapter 1
Jumping into JavaScript

"Trust thyself: every heart vibrates to that iron string."

—RALPH WALDO EMERSON

Because it's built into every web browser, JavaScript is the most widely used programming language today. In this chapter, you learn how JavaScript completes the web language trilogy, learn the fundamentals of its syntax, and set up the tools you'll use throughout this book. Then you write and run your first few lines of JavaScript and learn to use the browser console as a fast and easy place to experiment and debug.

JavaScript, the Basics

Like Python, which you can learn about in Book 2, JavaScript is executed from source code rather than distributed as a compiled executable file. When it runs in a web browser, the code that the browser downloads when you visit a web page is source code. What this means is that it's possible for anyone who accesses any website to read and download the code (including HTML, CSS, and JavaScript) that makes the website's user interface work.

This isn't a flaw; it's by design. The creators of the early web and web browsers built on a philosophy of openness and ease of development and debugging that we still benefit from today. However, to write secure JavaScript code, you do need to understand how the web works and the difference between frontend code and backend code.

How the web works

The internet is a network made up of millions of computers that can all talk to each other using a set of protocols called TCP/IP (Transmission Control Protocol/ Internet Protocol). *TCP/IP* specifies how data is routed around the internet and how any computer can locate any other computer connected to the network.

Each computer connected to the internet may have applications running on it that send data over the internet. One such application is called an HTTP server, which uses HTTP (Hypertext Transfer Protocol) (or more commonly today, its encrypted version, HTTPS) to respond to requests for web pages and other files required by web pages.

TECHNICAL STUFF

Other applications running on web servers include email, streaming media services, file-sharing services, and the domain name service, which translates internet protocol addresses (the *IP* in TCP/IP) like 93.184.216.34 to domain names like `www.example.com` and back.

Requests to web servers are often (but not exclusively) made by programs called *web browsers*. Figure 1-1 illustrates the process of a web browser making a request for a web page and a web server responding.

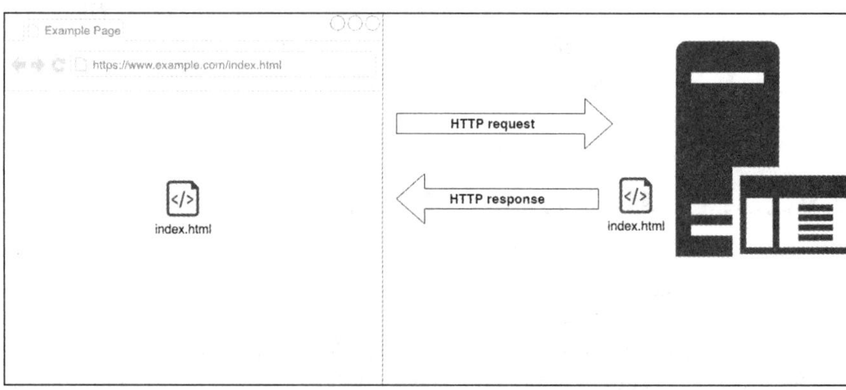

FIGURE 1-1: HTTP request and response.

Describing the technical details of how this request and response are made is beyond the scope of this chapter, but fear not — I cover it in more detail in Chapter 1 of Book 7.

Frontend and backend

A computer (such as your laptop, desktop, or mobile phone) that uses a program like a web browser to make HTTP requests is called a *client.* Code that runs on the client is called *frontend code.* A computer that responds to requests from clients is called a *server.* Code that runs on a server is called *backend code.*

Before JavaScript came along, web clients were what are known as *thin clients* (or sometimes *dumb clients,* which was the punchline for a lot of jokes between those of us working on the web back then). A thin client's job is to receive data from a server and display it in some form. When you click a link or type an address in your browser's address bar, you're telling your client application (your web browser) to make a request from a server.

For example, if you request a web page at `http://www.example.com/about.html`, you're telling the browser to request the document named `about.html` from the IP address that matches up with the `www.example.com` domain name. The HTTP request looks like this:

```
GET /about.html HTTP/1.1
User-Agent: Mozilla/5.0 (Macintosh; Intel Mac OS X 10_15_7)
  AppleWebKit/537.36 (KHTML, like Gecko) Chrome/102.0.0.0
  Safari/537.36
Host: www.example.com
Accept-Language: en-us
Accept-Encoding: gzip, deflate
Connection: Keep-Alive
```

This request says to use the HTTP `GET` method to access the file named `about.html` from the domain name `www.example.com`. The request also contains information about your browser, its language, and what kinds of encoding your browser accepts. The `Keep-Alive` instruction allows the connection between your browser and the server to stay active for multiple requests.

If the file your browser requested exists, the server's response includes the contents of `about.html`. It's up to your web browser to determine how to display that content and to make additional HTTP requests to download any images or other resources (such as CSS files) specified in the HTML page.

When JavaScript came onto the scene, browsers gained more capabilities to manipulate the data received from the server. Now, rather than simply displaying the HTML file delivered by the server, browsers can download scripts and data from the server that allow you to process the data, reorganize it, and much more. Think about web-based applications such as Gmail, for example. If you leave a browser window open with Gmail in it, new messages are automatically downloaded. You can sort and filter your messages, compose new messages, and much more. This is JavaScript at work. Because of the capability to run JavaScript code, web browsers changed from being merely thin clients to being thick clients.

The frontend is open and the backend is closed

Today, word processors, spreadsheets, sophisticated social media apps, image-editing programs, and more run inside web browsers. And, to return to my original point, the code that runs in the browser for each of these applications is available for anyone to read if they want to — no one at Facebook or Google cares if you view the code or even if you copy it.

The reason for this seeming lack of concern for the secrecy of frontend code is that it's not the browser-based code that makes a web application valuable. Without its backend data and algorithms that index and search the data, `Google.com` would be just a simple web-based form that anyone who has watched a video about HTML could do a decent job of writing.

The same goes for Amazon, ChatGPT, and every other website you can think of. These companies vigorously protect their proprietary data, AI models, and customer lists as well as the secret sauce that makes people use them. This code lives on web servers, where you absolutely can't access it except through the HTTPS protocol.

Follow these steps to view the source code that runs in your web browser when you go to `Google.com`:

1. **Open your Chrome web browser and go to `www.google.com`.**
2. **Press Ctrl+Shift+I (Windows) or ⌘+Option+I (macOS) to open the Chrome developer tools.**

   You can open the developer tools also by clicking the Chrome menu (the three stacked dots in the upper-right corner of the browser) and then choosing More Tools ⇨ Developer Tools.

   When you open the developer tools, a pane opens in your browser, as shown in Figure 1-2.
3. **Examine the code on the Elements tab.**

   This tab shows the HTML and CSS that make up the current page in the browser. If you scroll through this source code, you see script elements, which contain either a link to JavaScript code or the JavaScript itself, as shown in Figure 1-3.

FIGURE 1-2: The Chrome developer tools.

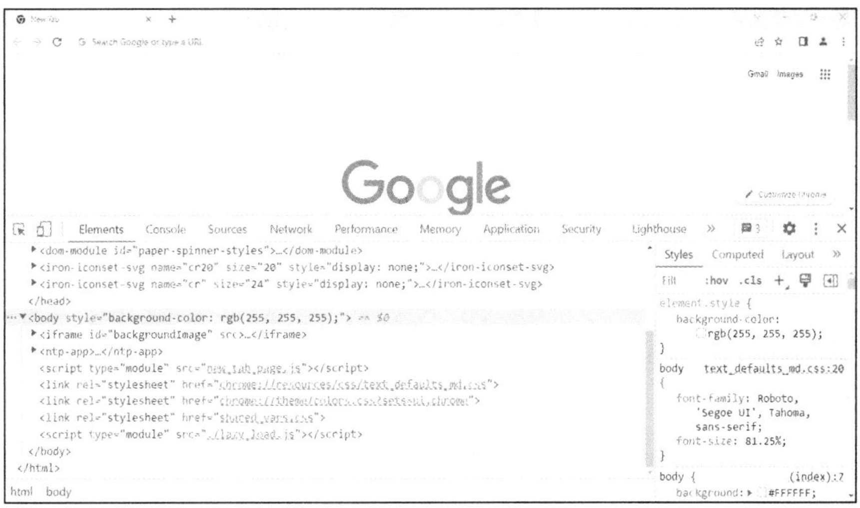

FIGURE 1-3: Viewing the code at `Google.com`.

The Elements tab shows you the HTML and CSS behind a web page. The Sources tab is where you can view the JavaScript code. Click the Sources tab, and you see a list of files on the left, some additional sections at the bottom, and a large main window to the right, as shown in Figure 1-4.

When you start expanding directories on the left, you see a number of files with strange names. When you click some of the JavaScript files, you see a lot of code that all runs together without formatting, as shown in Figure 1-5.

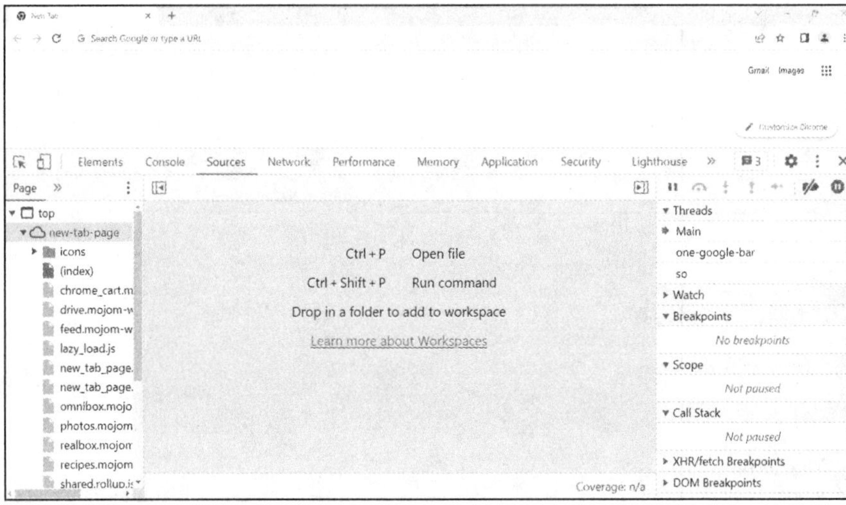

FIGURE 1-4: The Sources tab in the developer tools.

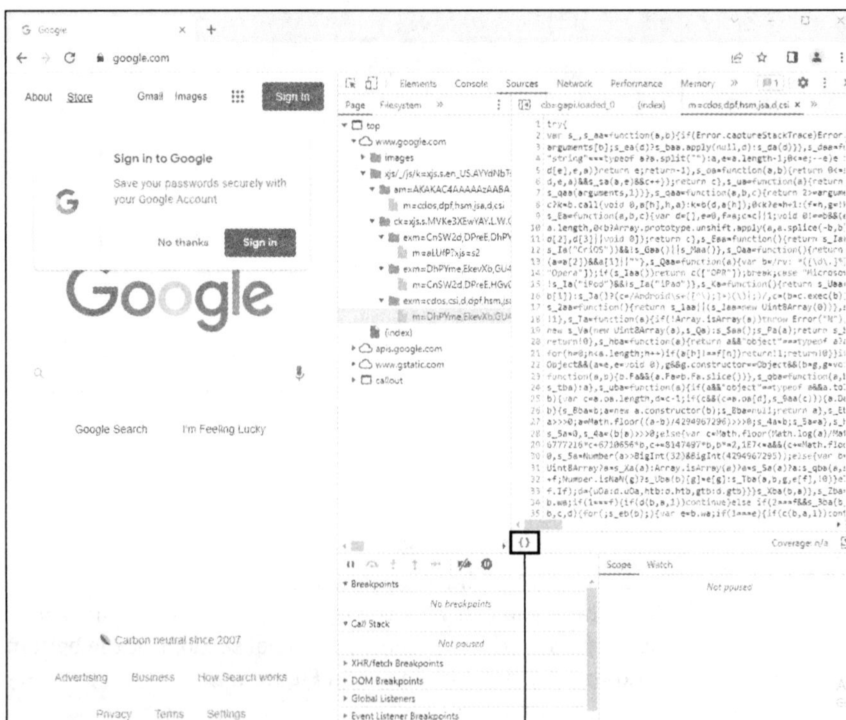

FIGURE 1-5: Viewing JavaScript code on the Sources tab.

The code in Figure 1-5 is optimized to download and run faster in the browser through a process called minifying. *Minified code* has all its unnecessary spaces, line breaks, and comments removed, and variable names replaced with shorter names. The process is like compressing a file on your computer.

To reformat the minified code, click the {} icon in the lower-left corner of the main window on the Sources tab shown in Figure 1-5. Now the code is much easier to understand, as shown in Figure 1-6.

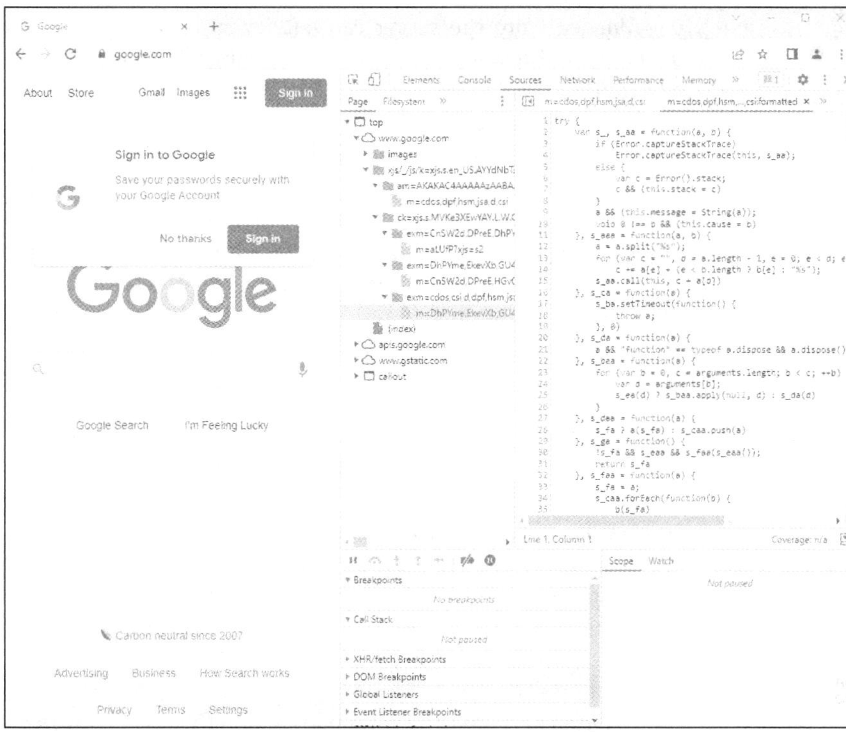

FIGURE 1-6: Google.com's JavaScript, prettified.

The code is still optimized for the browser, and it doesn't contain the useful variable names and comments that the original source code contained. If you study it hard enough, though, even a nonprogrammer can pick out parts that make sense.

The value of a service

If all the client-side code of a web application is visible to anyone who cares to look, doesn't that create a security problem? Could someone with bad intentions view the source code and figure out how to use the app for a purpose for which it wasn't intended?

Yes, in theory. But web browsers have built-in limitations and security precautions to prevent this. For example, a web page downloaded from a server can't access data from just any web server — it must be from the same domain as the original HTTP request or be specifically permitted by the server to access data. Also, web browsers operate in what's called a *sandbox:* The code running in a web browser can't access anything outside the browser (such as files, other programs on your computer, or your operating system) unless you allow it (as you might do when a web page asks to use your location).

The fact that every web application developer knows that their code and the data downloaded from the server can be viewed also helps to increase security. One of the jobs of a web application programmer is to ensure that no personal data or data that would allow someone to possibly access someone else's data is ever stored in the web browser and that all sensitive data is encrypted as it's transferred from the server to the client.

Banks and other businesses that regularly handle personal data always store and process that data on the server, where the code isn't visible to anyone except authorized people and where firewalls and other security precautions can be implemented. Programs that handle logins, credit card processing, data retrieval, and much more on web servers are called *server-side services.*

JavaScript on the server

The capability to run client-side JavaScript is built into every web browser. But JavaScript programs can also run on the server. Node.js is a runtime environment that runs JavaScript outside a web browser. It makes it possible to use the same JavaScript language you use to write frontend user interfaces to write services on the backend.

Like frontend JavaScript running in a browser, backend JavaScript running in Node.js uses just-in-time compilation, and the JavaScript files are stored as plain text. The difference between frontend JavaScript and backend JavaScript running in Node.js is that web browsers never see the JavaScript that runs on the server — they only receive the results of those programs running.

As a result, backend JavaScript doesn't have to operate in a sandbox. It can access the server's operating system, other programs running on the server, and databases to do what it needs to do to process data and return results to web browsers.

Starting Your Development Environment

A *development environment* is the combination of tools used by a programmer to write programs. The most essential tool for any programmer is a code editor. This is where you write the source code that makes up your programs.

Visual Studio Code, or VS Code, is an all-purpose open-source code editor. VS Code can be used with many different programming languages, and you learn how to use it to write Python code in Book 2 and to create web pages in Book 5. See Chapter 1 of Book 2 for instructions on downloading and installing VS Code.

TIP

If you want to try out other code editors, I encourage you to do that. Search the web for *best JavaScript code editors* to find a current list.

You spend a lot of time working in your code editor, so it's a good idea to get to know it. Even if you've used Visual Studio Code before, I encourage you to read this section, because chances are good that you'll learn something new.

Creating a project

On the Get Started page, when you start VS Code, you see a section in the upper left called Start. Generally, when you start a new project, you choose the Open Folder option. This action opens a file browser, as shown in Figure 1-7, and you can select or create a folder for your new project.

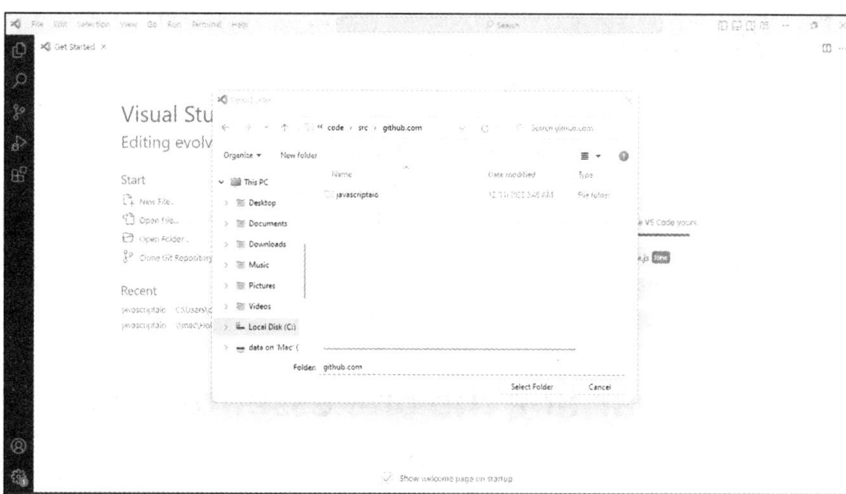

FIGURE 1-7: Choosing the Open Folder option.

WARNING

When you're working on multiple projects, not being able to easily find the project you want to open is frustrating. So I recommend having a system for organizing your code and keeping it separate from everything else on your computer.

My system for organizing my code (which I borrowed from someone else a long time ago and which you're welcome to borrow, too) is to create a folder called `code` in my user home folder (which is called `chrisminnick`).

Inside this folder, I have a folder called `src` (short for source code). Inside the `src` folder, I have a folder for `github.com` (where most of my projects are stored) as well as for other hosted code repositories (such as `gitlab.com` and `bitbucket.com`). I talk about version control and the importance of using it in Chapter 2 of this minibook.

This may seem like a lot of layers of nested directories, but when I'm working on a lot of different projects, I appreciate the fact that I know exactly where to look for anything I need.

For now, I recommend that you create a folder in your `code/src` folder called `codingaio` and create a new folder inside that folder named `javascript`. I show you how to set up Git in Chapter 2 of this minibook, and at that point you'll want to create a `github.com` folder.

TECHNICAL STUFF

You can use the terms *folder* and *directory* interchangeably. (Windows and macOS use the term *folders,* and Linux uses *directories.*) I'll typically use the term *folder* when I'm talking about something on your computer and *directory* when I'm talking about something that is on a server or will be deployed to a server.

TECHNICAL STUFF

Make your life slightly easier by ensuring that the path to your `code` folder, and all the folders inside it, do not have spaces.

The first time you open a folder in VS Code, you may see a message, as shown in Figure 1-8, asking whether you trust the authors of the files in the folder. Select the checkbox to indicate that you do, and then click the Yes button.

When you open an empty folder, the File Explorer pane is displayed with the name of your folder at the top.

Learning the one essential command

If you could save hundreds of hours by just remembering a single keyboard combination, would you do it? VS Code has a command that will save you countless hours of work over your life as a JavaScript developer. Are you ready?

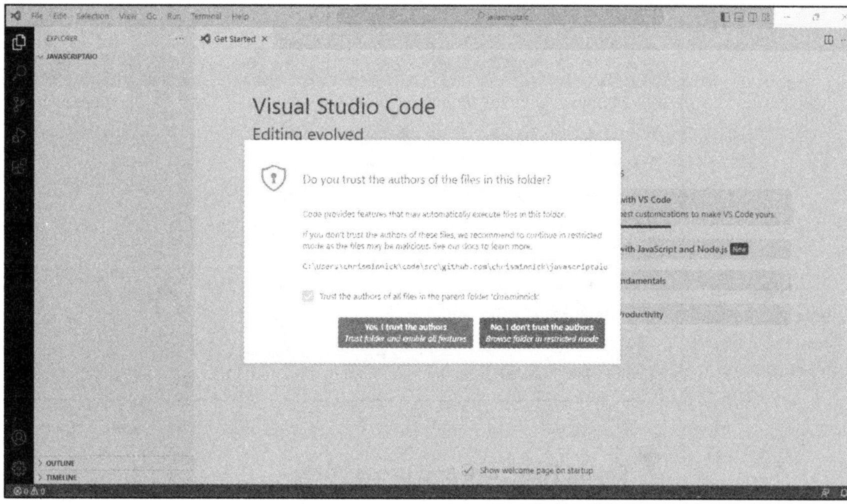

FIGURE 1-8: You can trust me.

The command is Ctrl+Shift+P on Windows and Linux and ⌘+Shift+P on macOS.

When you press this magic key combination, a search box opens at the top of the VS Code interface, along with a list below it of the most recent commands you've run. The search box and list that opens when you press Ctrl+Shift+P (or ⌘+Shift+P) is called the *command palette.* You can scroll through this list or start typing to find or do just about anything in VS Code. Follow these steps to see what I mean:

1. **Press Ctrl+Shift+P (Windows) or ⌘+Shift+P (macOS) to open the command palette.**
2. **Start typing** new file.

   As you type, the options below the search box change, and after a few characters, the top option is Create: New File, as shown in Figure 1-9.
3. **Select Create New File and then press the Enter key.**

   A new set of options appears. These options depend on the extensions you've installed.
4. **Select Text File to create a new text file.**

   A new untitled text file appears.
5. **Press Ctrl+Shift+P (Windows) or ⌘+Shift+P (macOS) to open the command palette again.**
6. **Start typing File: Save.**

   As before, the options under the search box change as you type.

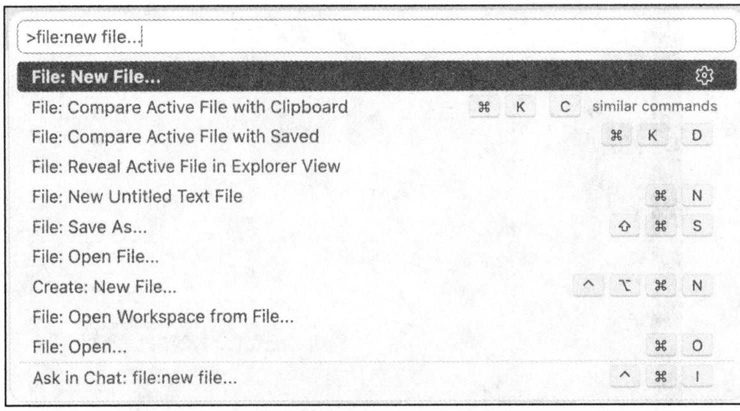

FIGURE 1-9: Selecting Create New File from the command palette.

7. **Select File: Save and press Enter.**

   The Save As dialog opens.

8. **Type** index.html **to name the file and specify that it's an HTML file, and then press Enter or click Save to save it.**

   You have your first saved file in the File Explorer pane.

9. **In your file, type an exclamation point (!) and press Tab.**

   This is another shortcut that creates a blank HTML template, as shown in Figure 1-10.

   TIP

   If the !-followed-by-tab combination doesn't work, type ! and press Ctrl+space. A menu opens, and the first option should be the ! Emmet abbreviation. Select it and press Enter. *Emmet abbreviations* are a set of shortcuts for writing HTML and CSS that are built into VS Code. Once you learn a few of them, you can use them to dramatically reduce the amount of typing you need to do.

10. **Save your `index.html` file.**

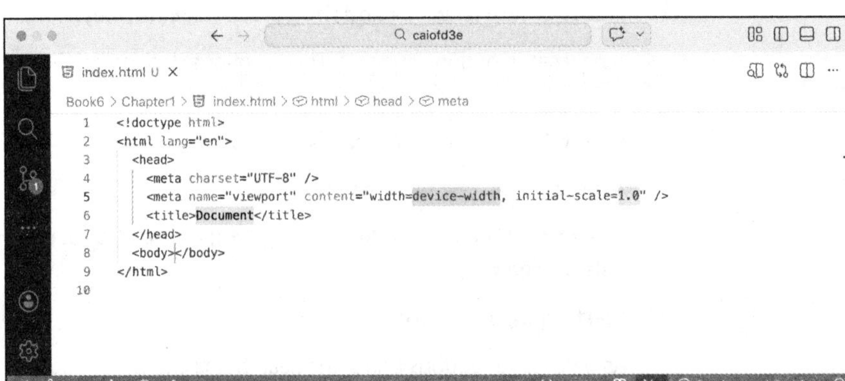

FIGURE 1-10: A new HTML file, created using the command palette.

Keyboard shortcuts are a helpful time-saver, and they also help developers keep their focus by not having to poke around in the menus, looking for what they want to do. Most actions in VS Code have their own keyboard shortcuts, and you'll learn the important ones the more you use VS Code.

Now that you've memorized the command for opening the command palette, you can skip over looking through any of the menus. When you want to do something, just press Ctrl+Shift+P (⌘+Shift+P on macOS) and start typing whatever it is that you want to do.

TIP

The command palette is helpful for finding settings and preferences as well.

Writing Your First JavaScript Program

Now that you have some background and a code editor, it's time to start learning to write JavaScript code. In this section, I start out by explaining the basics of JavaScript syntax. You can then learn a couple different ways to run JavaScript code in a web browser.

Don't worry if you don't understand everything (or anything) at this point about how the code works. After you run the code, I explain what's happening, and then the rest of this minibook explains each facet of JavaScript in detail. The idea right now is to get used to seeing JavaScript code in various environments.

If you've gone through any of the previous minibooks, JavaScript code may look familiar. Most programming languages share common traits, and looking for those commonalities can be a helpful way to start getting a grasp on a language.

Listing 1-1 shows a simple JavaScript program that takes any name (whether it's your name, your dog's name, or your parakeet's name) and turns it into the name of a new programming language by adding *Script* to the end of it.

LISTING 1-1: The Useful JavaScript Name Creator Program

```
let normalName = 'Chris';
let javaScriptName = normalName + 'Script';
console.log('Your JavaScript Name is ' + javaScriptName);
```

Although this first program is simple, it demonstrates a lot of fundamental JavaScript principles.

JavaScript is made of statements

Just as a sentence in a human language is a fundamental building block of any piece of writing, JavaScript has a similar fundamental building block, which is called a *statement*. Listing 1-1 has three separate statements. Each statement ends with a semicolon, and running a statement causes JavaScript to do something. Technically, JavaScript can add missing semicolons automatically in many situations, a feature called *automatic semicolon insertion*. However, many JavaScript programmers use semicolons consistently because they make statement endings clear.

Most people would understand where the preceding paragraph ended, even if I didn't add the period. But my editors probably wouldn't let me do that because it could cause confusion and would look like a typo.

The first two statements, which begin with *let*, tell JavaScript to store a value. The third statement, which begins with *console.log*, tells JavaScript to log (or write) some text to the console in your browser.

Just as English is made up of parts of speech — such as nouns, verbs, and adverbs — JavaScript statements are made up of several parts, as follows:

- **Values:** In Listing 1-1, `'Chris'` is a value.
- **Expressions:** Expressions are units of code that are evaluated and become values. For example, in Listing 1-1, the following is an expression:

  ```
  normalName + 'Script'
  ```

  When `normalName` has a value of `'Chris'`, this expression evaluates to `'ChrisScript'`.
- **Operators:** Operators do something with values. In Listing 1-1, the + operator (known as the *concatenation* operator) joins the value of `normalName` and the literal value `'Script'`.
- **Keywords:** Keywords are parts of JavaScript that have special meaning and cause JavaScript to do something. In Listing 1-1, the word `let` is a keyword that tells JavaScript to store the value on the right side of the = (assignment) operator using the name on the left side of the =.

TECHNICAL STUFF

The process of assigning a value to a name is called *initializing a variable* in programming. You learn much more about initializing variables in Chapter 2 of this minibook.

JavaScript is case-sensitive

Unlike HTML, where browsers consider the tags `<HEAD>` and `<head>` to be identical, JavaScript code is case-sensitive. If you change the capitalization of one character in a JavaScript keyword or a variable name, JavaScript doesn't understand what you're saying. For example, if you type `pizza` in one place and `Pizza` in another, JavaScript thinks these are different values.

WARNING

Incorrect or inconsistent capitalization is by far the biggest source of errors (also known as *bugs*) for beginning coders. These kinds of bugs are often difficult to find. Take your time as you're coding and make it a habit to be precise. It will save you a lot of time later.

JavaScript ignores white space

White space refers to characters such as a tab, a space, and a line break, which produce no visible output when you type them. When you write JavaScript, you often separate statements and the different parts of statements using white space. However, it doesn't matter whether you indent lines with spaces or tabs, include multiple line breaks between statements, or include extra spaces between the parts of a JavaScript statement. For example, it's perfectly fine to write the first statement in Listing 1-1 like this:

```
let normalName =
"Chris";
```

Even though most other JavaScript programmers would look at you funny if they saw this line in your code — and your code formatter will likely fix it for you — JavaScript runs this code the same as if you formatted it in a more traditional way.

Where white space does make a difference is inside quotes. For example, consider the following statement:

```
let normalName = "           Chris ";
```

If you run the program with this statement, the result includes all those spaces.

It's important to use enough space in your code so that it's readable and to be consistent with how you use spaces and tabs. Some people prefer tabs for indenting code, and other people prefer spaces. A code formatter, such as Prettier, which you can learn about shortly, ensures that you're using white space in a consistent and standard way.

Naming practices of JavaScript programmers

Names that you give to variables, files, modules, and functions in JavaScript often consist of more than one word. However, because JavaScript uses spaces to distinguish between the parts of a statement (the same way you use spaces to know when one word ends and another starts), you need another way to make multiple-word names readable.

As long as you don't use spaces or other special characters (see the complete list I give you in Chapter 3 of this minibook), you can name things in JavaScript any way you see fit. However, I suggest that you use the common strategies I describe next.

Camel case

The JavaScript language itself, as well as in JavaScript programs, uses *camel case* extensively. You can use two types of camel case. The first one is *upper camel case,* in which the first word starts with a capital letter and every word after that is capitalized, such as `MyComponent`.

TECHNICAL STUFF

Upper camel case is used in JavaScript for naming classes and components (such as ReactJS components).

The second type of camel case is *lower camel case,* in which the first word is lowercase and every word after that is capitalized, such as `customerFirstName`. Lower camel case is the most common way to name variables you create in your programs.

Underscore

In Book 2, you learn that the preferred way to separate multiple words in Python variable names is with an underscore (_), such as `postal_code`. Many people also use the underscore character between words in JavaScript for some types of variables. For example, if you're getting data from an external source, that data may contain underscore names already, and it makes sense to continue using the same naming scheme in your program. However, in most cases, you should stick with lower camel case.

Hyphens

CSS and HTML frequently use hyphens between words in multiword names. For example, CSS has a property called `border-radius`, and an HTML attribute used with the form element is called `accept-charset`.

WARNING

Naming things with hyphens in JavaScript is problematic and should be avoided because JavaScript interprets the hyphen character as a subtraction operator and your program won't run correctly or at all.

Running Code in the Console

The Chrome browser contains a JavaScript console. The console is the best friend of any JavaScript programmer. (Seriously, we're not known for being the most social bunch!) The console has many uses — and one of those uses is a handy place to test out JavaScript code.

Follow these steps to run the JavaScript Name Creator in your browser console:

1. **Open a new tab in your Chrome browser.**
2. **Press Ctrl+Shift+J (Windows) or ⌘+Option+J (macOS) to open the JavaScript console.**

   The Chrome developer tools window opens, and you see the JavaScript console, as shown in Figure 1-11.

   Every desktop web browser has a JavaScript console. So, even if you're not using Google Chrome, you can still follow along with these instructions by opening your browser's console.

   TIP

   As with everything in programming and the web, the location and steps for opening the developer tools and the console in different web browsers is subject to change. If you want to try out another browser's JavaScript console, a quick web search can tell you how to open it.

3. **Type the code from Listing 1-1 into the JavaScript console.**

   Press Enter after each of the three lines of code and see what happens! If you type everything correctly, your screen should look like Figure 1-12.

WARNING

If you try to paste code into the JavaScript console, you'll get a warning message in Chrome telling you not to paste code that you haven't reviewed into the console. This message protects you from being tricked into pasting code into the console that might compromise your browser. If you see this message, you can manually type the code or type **allow pasting** in the console to disable the warning message.

TIP

If the font size in your console is too small, you can increase it by pressing Ctrl+= (Windows) or ⌘+= (macOS). If you want to make the font size smaller again, press Ctrl+– (Windows) or ⌘+– (macOS).

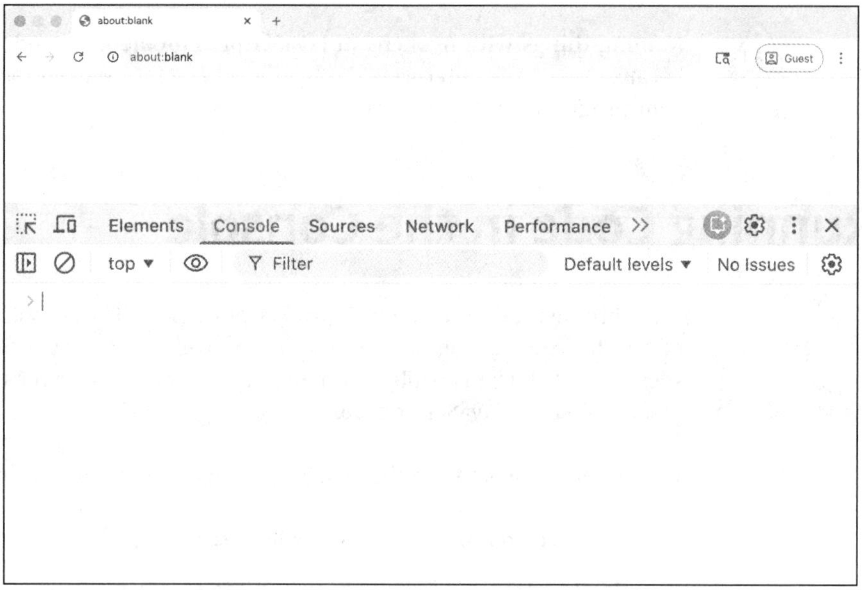

FIGURE 1-11: The JavaScript console.

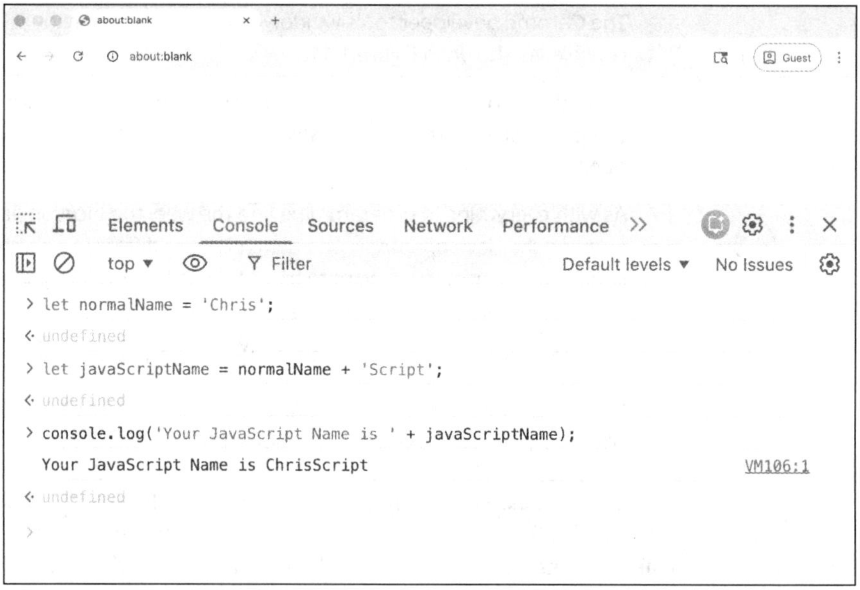

FIGURE 1-12: Running the JavaScript Name Creator code.

The JavaScript console is a direct text-based link to your web browser's JavaScript engine. When you type code into the console and press Enter, the browser runs that code and displays the result. If the line of code doesn't produce a value to display, the console prints `undefined`. In this context, `undefined` means "this code ran, but it didn't return a value."

TIP

If you make a mistake while typing the JavaScript code, you can start over by refreshing the browser window. Reloading clears JavaScript's memory and anything in the console window.

You can enter a single line of code in the console and immediately get a result. However, if you want to change or rerun commands, you need to reenter them.

TIP

If you haven't reloaded the browser window, you can easily return to previous lines of code you entered by pressing the up- and down-arrow keys in the console.

If you want to clear out everything from the console, press the icon above the input/output area that looks like a circle with a line through it. Note that this action doesn't clear out the browser window's memory. If you press the Clear button and then the up- and down-arrows, you'll still see your previously entered code.

To clear out the browser's memory, click the browser's Refresh button or press Ctrl+R (Windows) or ⌘+R (macOS).

Running Code in a Browser Window

Although the JavaScript console is fully capable of running client-side JavaScript, it's limited to running what you type or copy-and-paste into it. To run the hundreds or thousands of lines of code that make up a modern JavaScript program, and to transmit that JavaScript across the internet, JavaScript needs to be connected to an HTML page.

You have three options for including JavaScript in a web page. You can put it

- In an HTML event attribute
- Between the start and end tags of a `script` element
- In a separate file that you import into your HTML document

It's not uncommon to see all three techniques used together in a single web page, or to see multiple instances of each technique in a single file. Let's take a closer look at each of them, along with their pros and cons.

Running JavaScript from HTML event attributes

HTML's *event attributes* were introduced into the language early in JavaScript's life. Their purpose is to detect events happening to HTML elements and to run JavaScript code when those events happen.

Here's what JavaScript attached to an HTML event attribute looks like:

```
<button onclick="alert('Welcome to Coding All-In-One')">
  Click here for an important message
</button>
```

When this button is clicked, the browser pops up a message in an alert. If you want to try it out, go to VS Code and enter the preceding snippet between the <body> and </body> tags in an HTML document. Then save the HTML page and open it in your browser by double-clicking it, dragging it to your browser, or using your browser's Open File menu item.

WARNING

Aside from the first chapters of JavaScript books, alert messages are rarely used in JavaScript. The window alert blocks the execution of JavaScript, is limited in what it can do, and is not attractive. You learn much better ways to display messages to the user in this book.

Avoid using HTML event attributes. That's the old way of responding to events in HTML, and the attributes are kept in HTML mostly for backward-compatibility reasons.

TECHNICAL STUFF

The modern way of responding to events in the browser is by using the addEventListener method, which you learn about in Chapter 10 of this minibook.

Running JavaScript inside script elements

The second method of including JavaScript in HTML is called *inline JavaScript.* To use inline JavaScript, put your JavaScript between an opening <script> tag and a closing </script> tag in your HTML document, as shown in Listing 1-2.

LISTING 1-2: Using Inline JavaScript

```
<!DOCTYPE html>
<html lang="en">
<head>
  <meta charset="UTF-8"/>
```

```
  <meta http-equiv="X-UA-Compatible" content="IE=edge"/>
  <meta name="viewport" content="width=device-width,
   initial-scale=1.0"/>
  <title>Inline JavaScript</title>
</head>
<body>
  <script>
    let personName = prompt('What is your name?');
    alert('Hello, ' + personName);
  </script>
</body>
</html>
```


You can put inline JavaScript in either the head or the body of an HTML document, and you can use as many inline scripts as you need. Inline JavaScript is useful for small bits of JavaScript that need to be run in a single HTML page. The benefit of using inline JavaScript is that it saves a trip to the web server and back, which reduces the load time of your HTML page.

The downside to using inline JavaScript is that, like JavaScript in event attributes, it mixes your HTML and your JavaScript and makes maintaining your application more difficult.

TECHNICAL STUFF

Separation of concerns, which is an important principle in software development, states that your programs should be separated into sections. For example, you shouldn't mix your presentation code (HTML) with your logic (JavaScript). By abiding by the rules of separation of concerns, you make your programs easier to maintain and more modular. I revisit this idea of separation of concerns throughout this book, especially in Book 7 when I tell you about various frontend JavaScript libraries that seem, at first glance, to violate this principle.

WARNING

Listing 1-2 uses a prompt to receive input from a user. Like an alert, a prompt should never be used in a real-life program. It has the same flaws as `alert()`, which is that it is ugly, limited, and blocks the running of your JavaScript.

Including JavaScript files in your HTML

The third method of running JavaScript in a web page is to import a file containing JavaScript code into your HTML document. This is done using the `src` attribute of the `script` element.

This is by far the most common way that JavaScript is used in web pages. To use this method, create a file containing your JavaScript and save it with the `.js` extension, as shown in Listing 1-3.

LISTING 1-3: A JavaScript File

```
const ball = document.getElementById('ball');
document.addEventListener('keydown', handleKeyPress);
let position = 0;
function handleKeyPress(e) {
if (e.code === 'ArrowLeft') {
position = position - 10;
}
if (e.code === 'ArrowRight') {
position = position + 10;
}
if (position < 0) {
position = 0;
}
if (position > 800) {
position = 800;
}
refresh();
}
function refresh() {
ball.style.left = position + 'px';
}
```

The program in Listing 1-3 is the beginning of a simple game, which listens for `keydown` events (it waits for you to press keys on your keyboard, in other words). When you press a key, it checks to see whether that key was the left-arrow key or the right-arrow key. If it was the left arrow, it would subtract 10 from a variable called `position`. If it was the right arrow, it adds 10. This `position` variable is then used to reposition an element called `ball` in the browser window.

Follow these steps to build your own version of this game and try it out:

1. **Make a new file containing the code in Listing 1-3 and save it as `gamelet.js`.**

   TIP

   Although I encourage you to get as much practice as you can with typing code, rather than copying it, you can download all the code listings in this book from the book's website at `www.dummies.com/go/codingaiofd3e`.

2. **Make a new file containing the HTML in Listing 1-4 and save it as `gamelet.html`.**

3. **Right-click the `gamelet.html` file in the Explorer pane of VS Code and choose Reveal in Finder (on macOS) or Reveal in File Explorer (on Windows).**

4. **Double-click the file, drag it to your browser window, or use your browser's Open File command to open it in a browser window.**

   The browser window displays a red ball in the upper-left corner.

5. **Press the right-arrow key on your keyboard several times, and then press the left-arrow key to make the ball move forward and backward.**

LISTING 1-4: The HTML Document for the Game

```
<!DOCTYPE html>
<html lang="en">
<head>
<meta charset="UTF-8"/>
<meta http-equiv="X-UA-Compatible" content="IE=edge"/>
<meta name="viewport" content="width=device-width,
  initial-scale=1.0"/>
<title>Move the ball!</title>
<style>
#ball {
background-color: red;
border-radius: 50%;
width: 20px;
height: 20px;
position: absolute;
}
</style>
</head>
<body>
<div id="ball"></div>
<script src="gamelet.js"></script>
</body>
</html>
```

TIP

You might need to click the mouse inside the browser window to give the window focus before pressing the arrow keys.

Figure 1-13 shows this game running in my browser.

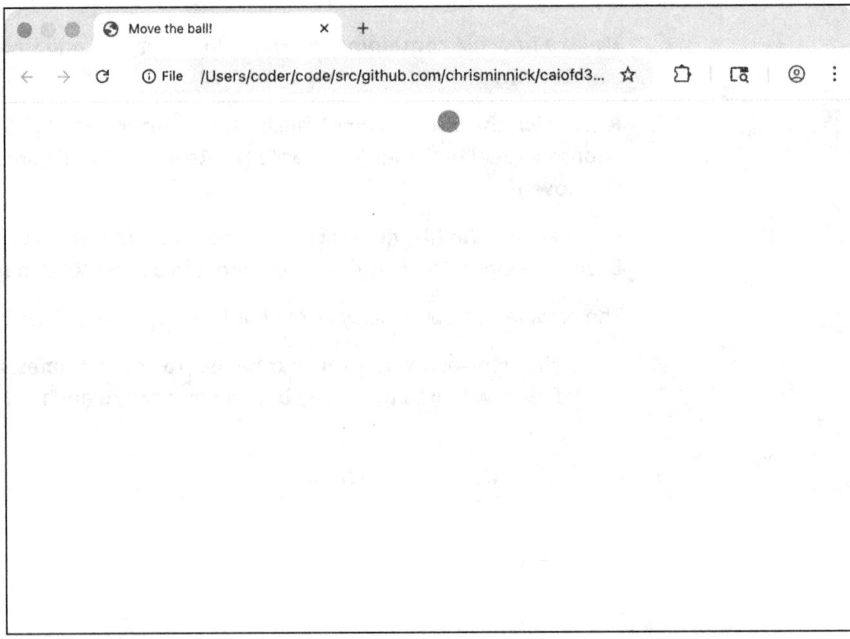

FIGURE 1-13: Running the ball-moving game.

Although this game is far from being functional or fun, it's a good start. See if you can play around with the code and make changes to it. For example:

- Make the ball move a longer distance with each keypress.
- Change the keys that make the ball move.

  TIP

  You can find a complete reference for key codes at `https://developer.mozilla.org/en-US/docs/Web/API/KeyboardEvent/code`.
- Make pressing the up- and down-arrows move the ball up and down. ***Hint:*** You need to change the value of `style.top` to adjust the vertical position.

IN THIS CHAPTER

» Installing and configuring Node.js

» Setting up Visual Studio Code

» Documenting your code

» Writing a README with Markdown

» Practicing responsible coding with Git

Chapter 2 Filling Your JavaScript Toolbox

"As a cook, your station, and its condition, its state of readiness, is an extension of your nervous system."

—ANTHONY BOURDAIN

Though it's technically possible to write JavaScript programs using nothing but an ordinary text editor, I don't recommend it. Computer programming is complex, and JavaScript programming is no exception. Although it used to be popular for web developers to show how elite (or "1337") they were by writing code using the most basic text editor available, someone who codes without making use of certain tools today is more likely to be seen as an amateur who is doing it wrong.

In this chapter, I show you how to install and configure the core tools you'll use throughout this minibook: Node.js, Visual Studio Code, and a handful of essential extensions. I also share a few strategies for getting unstuck when installations go sideways, plus simple habits — like documenting your code, writing a README in Markdown, and using Git — that will save you time, protect your work, and make you a better developer.

Everything in Its Place

Every cook and auto mechanic knows the importance of having the right tools in the right place when you need them. Some tools are essential (like bowls and wrenches), some are useful time-savers (like a mixer or a pneumatic tool), and others are mostly just a waste of space (like a bread machine or a battery-powered tape measure).

In JavaScript development, the number of tools that are freely available is staggering. Unlike in the kitchen or the shop, cheap doesn't mean poor quality. In fact, most professional JavaScript programmers use free and open-source tools exclusively, and in many cases a commercial product that does all the same things isn't available.

The tool chest of the average professional JavaScript developer should include these items:

- A code editor for writing code
- An AI coding assistant. You can use a code editor with AI capabilities built in, like Cursor (`www.cursor.com`), or you can add AI capabilities to a code editor like VS Code by using GitHub Copilot.
- Node.js for running the tools
- A package manager for installing, upgrading, tracking, and removing Node.js software packages
- A build tool for bundling JavaScript files, compiling template code, and automating the build process
- A code beautifier for making sure the code is properly and consistently formatted
- A static code analyzer for checking the code syntax and style
- A debugger for tracking down and eliminating errors
- A testing framework for automating the testing of programs
- A version control system for keeping track of changes and enabling team development

Other categories of tools beyond the ones in this list are available and widely used. I tell you about them later in this book. However, with the listed tools on your belt (or, more realistically, on your desktop or laptop), you'll be ready to code.

I don't tell you how to install all these tools in this chapter. Instead, I start with the most essential ones now and introduce others as you need them. So let's start installing!

Installing Node.js

Node.js is the one essential JavaScript tool that all the other tools depend on. You may already have Node.js installed on your computer. However, updated versions are released regularly, and you'll want to make sure you have a recent version so that everything you learn in this book will work correctly.

To install Node.js or to upgrade the version of Node.js that you may already have installed, go to `https://nodejs.org` and click the link to download the latest version. Once Node.js is downloaded, run the installer to install and configure it. Selecting the default options will work fine in most cases.

REMEMBER

You can learn more about Node.js in Book 8.

Configuring Visual Studio Code

Visual Studio Code (or VS Code, for short) is a flexible and powerful editor. You learn about installing VS Code in Book 2. In Chapter 1 of this minibook, I describe the basic steps of using it for JavaScript coding. You've been using VS Code throughout this book, but to get the most out of it in this minibook, you'll want to install certain extensions and know how to change settings.

Before you start installing extensions, make sure you have a web page you can use to test the extensions. For example, Listing 2-1 shows a simple one you can copy. Save this new page and name it `index.html`. Or, if you have access to an AI chatbot or a coding assistant, you might use that to help you make a more elaborate page.

LISTING 2-1: A Simple HTML Page

```
<!DOCTYPE html>
<html lang="en">
<head>
<meta charset="UTF-8"/>
<meta http-equiv="X-UA-Compatible" content="IE=edge"/>
<meta name="viewport" content="width=device-width,
  initial-scale=1.0"/>
<title>Hello, World!</title>
</head>
<body>
<h1>Hello, World!</h1>
</body>
</html>
```

To get started installing extensions, click the Extensions icon on the left toolbar (which is called the activity bar). The Extensions icon looks like four boxes, with one of them slightly separated from the others. This action brings up the Extensions panel, as shown in Figure 2-1.

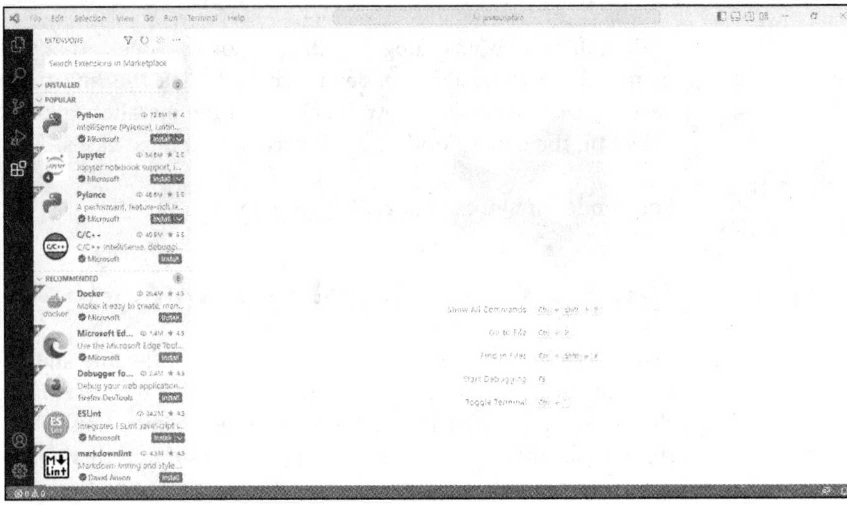

FIGURE 2-1: The VS Code Extensions panel.

Getting prettier

Correctly formatting your code is important for readability and debugging. You can spend a lot of time manually typing spaces or tabs and making everything consistent, or you can let your code editor do it for you. Once you start using a code formatter, you'll never go back, so you might as well start using one today.

Prettier is an *opinionated* code formatter — it doesn't even let you format your code the way you might prefer because it has its own ideas that it thinks are better than yours. And it's probably right, as you'll soon see.

Follow these steps to install and configure Prettier:

1. **In the Extensions panel, type** Prettier **in the search box.**

   A long list of extensions from the Extensions Marketplace appears.

2. **Look for the Prettier extension with the highest number of downloads.**

   At the time I wrote this chapter, for example, the top result, shown in Figure 2-2, had 62 million more downloads than the next most popular.

3. **Click the Install button in the search results or on the Details page for the Prettier extension.**

   After a moment, the Install button changes to the Uninstall button to indicate that the extension has been installed. You also see a new button, named Disable. If you click this button, the extension will be disabled but will still be installed.

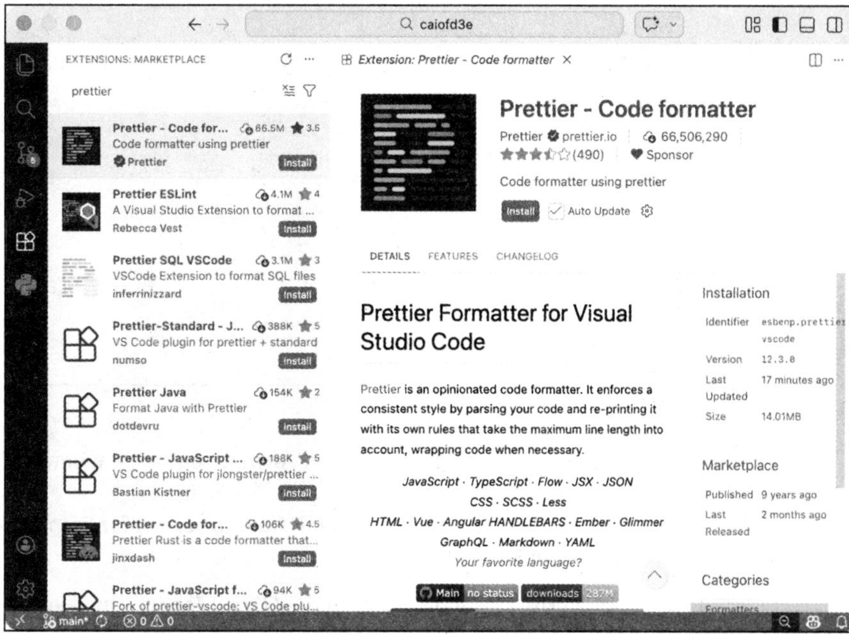

FIGURE 2-2: The Prettier extension.

Now you have Prettier installed, but you have a few things left to configure. To open the settings for an extension, click the gear icon next to the Uninstall button and select Extensions Settings. The settings for Prettier will appear, as shown in Figure 2-3.

The default values on this screen are correct for most people, in my opinion. But it's good to know that you can adjust settings here if you need to. You can even specify your own configuration file for Prettier to use, to make sure that it always formats things just how you want them.

TIP

Note the User and Workspace tabs at the top of the Settings window. If you want to adjust a setting only for a particular project (also called a *workspace*), you can switch to the Workspace tab. Otherwise, I recommend adjusting settings using the User tab so that you don't have to change settings each time you make a new project.

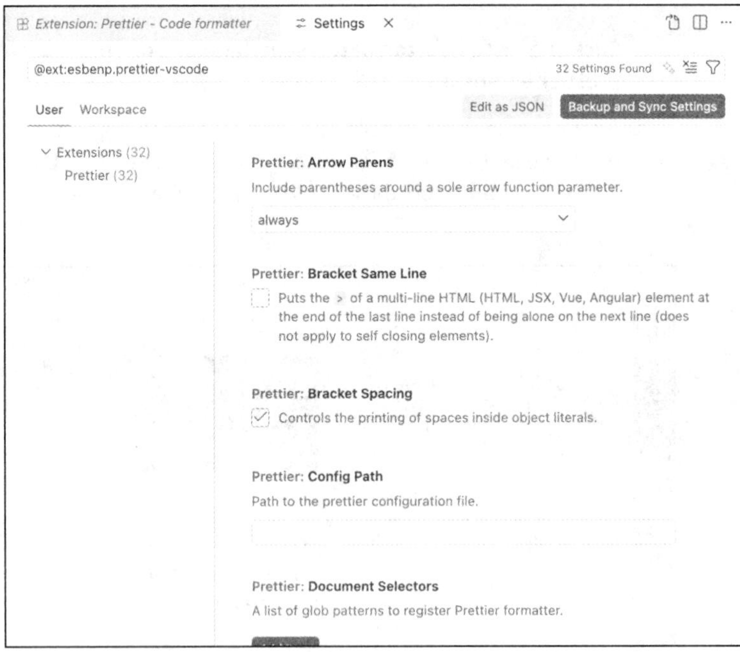

FIGURE 2-3: The Prettier extension settings.

Follow these steps to make Prettier format your code whenever you save:

1. **On the User tab, use the search field to search for** Format on Save**, as shown in Figure 2-4.**
2. **Select the check box next to the Editor: Format on Save setting.**
3. **Search for** default formatter**, and then select Prettier — Code Formatter from the drop-down menu, as shown in Figure 2-5.**
4. **Search for** auto save**. When you find it, choose onFocusChange.**

   TIP

   Your files will be automatically saved when you switch windows. I guarantee that this setting will save you from headaches.
5. **Close the User Settings window (and any other windows you have open in VS Code) by clicking X on the tab.**

After Prettier is installed and you've set it as the default formatter, you'll always have perfectly formatted code that will dazzle everyone who views it. Test it out by following these steps:

1. **Click the File Explorer icon at the top of the activity pane (refer to Figure 2-5) to switch back to viewing your workspace files.**
2. **Open the HTML file you created earlier by double-clicking it.**

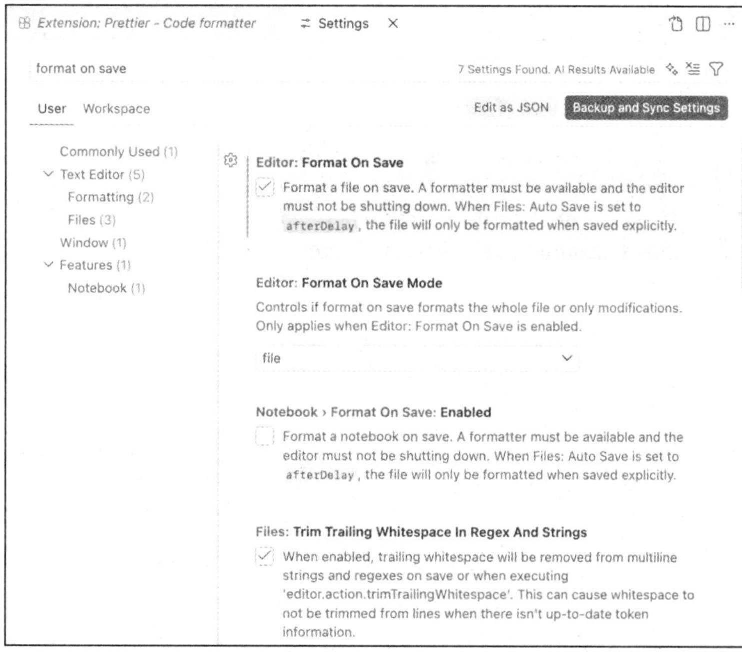

FIGURE 2-4: The Format on Save setting.

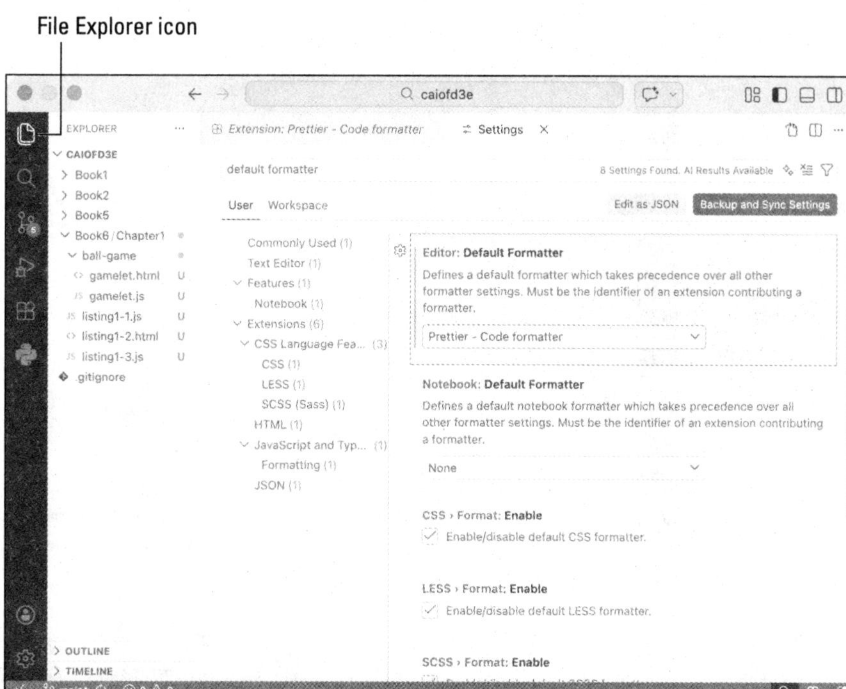

FIGURE 2-5: Setting the default code formatter.

3. **Insert some extra line breaks in the file, change the indentation of some of the lines, and maybe even insert some new HTML markup into the document. Then save the file.**

   As soon as you save, your code is reformatted before your very eyes!

TIP

If your code isn't formatted when you save, close VS Code and restart it, and then ensure that you've adjusted all the right settings in the steps in this section.

Installing Live Server

The next extension you should install is the Live Server extension. Live Server lets you easily preview web applications in a browser.

Follow these steps to install Live Server:

1. **Open the Extensions panel by clicking the Extensions icon.**

   You can instead press Ctrl+Shift+X (Windows) or ⌘+Shift+X (macOS).

2. **Type** Live Server **in the search box to find the extension by Ritwick Dey, as shown in Figure 2-6.**

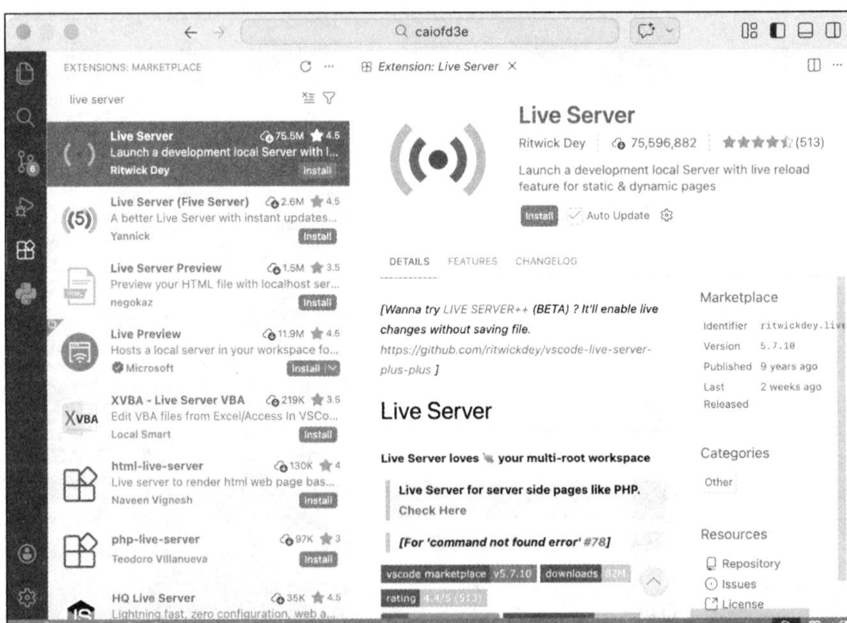

FIGURE 2-6: The Live Server extension.

3. **Click the Install button to install the Live Server extension.**

   Live Server has no configuration options, so there's no need to do anything else!

4. **Return to File Explorer and open any HTML file you've created, or create a new one.**

5. **Right-click the name of the file in the File Explorer pane and choose the Open with Live Server option from the menu that appears.**

6. **Do the following, as needed:**

   - The first time you choose Open with Live Server, you may see a security warning. Approve the extension's access to bypass the security warning. On Windows, approve access for Visual Studio Code to both private and public networks.
   - If you are asked which program you want to use to open the file, choose Google Chrome (or another browser, if you prefer). Select the box that asks whether you want to always use this choice, so that you don't have to choose every time you use Live Server.

   Your web browser opens and connects to Live Server to display your web page. Figure 2-7 shows an over-the-top "Hello, World!" webpage I created with the help of my AI assistant.

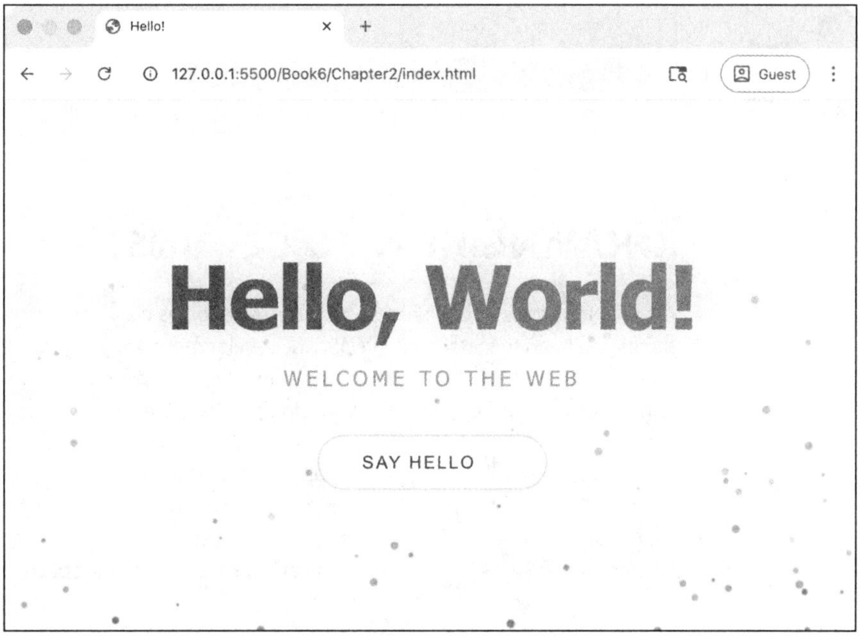

FIGURE 2-7: A web page, served on Live Server.

7. **Return to VS Code, make some changes to your web page, and then save those changes.**

8. **Return to your Chrome browser and note that the page has automatically been updated, as shown in Figure 2-8.**

   The capability for a server to automatically update the content shown in a browser is known as *hot reloading*. Awesome.

FIGURE 2-8: Hot reloading updates the browser for you.

KNOWING HOW TO GET UNSTUCK

A lot of effort goes into making software installation as easy as possible, and most of the things you need to install to do JavaScript development should go smoothly. However, it's inevitable that you'll run into some issues. Here are some of the more common issues that can happen and what you can do to fix them:

- **Not enough disk space:** If you don't have a lot of extra storage, everything you need to install in this chapter won't fit. Delete some extra files, use an online storage service like Dropbox to free up space, or invest in a larger (internal or external) hard drive. Software development can use a lot of storage space, and it's always better to have too much.

* **Network issues:** If you're connected to the internet but still get network errors when installing software, the problem is likely a firewall or another security tool or setting on your computer or network. If you're working on a computer connected to a work network or a public Wi-Fi hotspot, the problem is likely to be a firewall outside your computer. Try connecting to a different network. If you own the computer and control the router, temporarily disable any firewall or security software you've installed or that's part of the operating system.
* **Permissions issues:** By default, operating systems are configured to not allow user changes to certain files or directories. If you're trying to download or install software inside a system directory or one that's restricted, you'll get a permissions error. Try installing the software in your own user directory (`Users/`*`yourname`* on macOS or Windows or `usr/`*`yourname`* on Linux). As a last resort, you can right-click any folder to change its permissions, but you should do this only if you know what you're doing.
* **Software incompatibility:** Each tool you need to install for this book has versions that run on Windows, macOS, and Linux. However, a future version of an operating system or a new processor could change this at any time (at least until the software is updated). If you run into an incompatibility problem, first make sure that you downloaded the right version for your computer's processor and operating system. If that doesn't solve the problem, check with the software's creator to see whether a compatible version is available. (This may be an older version.) If all else fails, consider using a virtualization product like VirtualBox (`virtualbox.org`), VMWare (`vmware.com`), or Parallels (`parallels.com`) to run Linux (I recommend Ubuntu Linux if you're new to Linux) in a virtual computer on your computer.
* **Other errors:** If you encounter other errors, copy the error message you get and paste it into Google or an AI chatbot. Chances are good that someone else has received the same error and that the solution is a quick search away.

Documenting Your Code

Documenting your code is the process of recording what the code does. It's an essential part of any programming task that will save you time and frustration when your program becomes complex and you're trying to remember what each part does. Documentation is also helpful for other programmers who work on your program.

Programmers who get into the habit of documenting their code early on usually gain a deeper understanding of what the code does and are better able to solve problems that occur.

Line comments

The most basic way to add a note to yourself or other programmers is to add a line comment. You create a line comment by placing two (//) slashes together anywhere on a line of code — for example:

```
refresh(); // update the ball's position
```

The line comment tells JavaScript to ignore everything that comes after the two slashes until the end of the line. Use the line comment to include short notes to yourself about what the program does or why a statement is important.

Block comments

When a single-line comment won't do, you can use a block comment, which starts with `/*` and ends with `*/`. JavaScript ignores everything in a block comment.

Block comments are helpful for providing detailed documentation at the beginning of a JavaScript file or for documenting individual functions. For example, Listing 2-2 shows the `gamelet.js` file from Chapter 1 with block comments included.

LISTING 2-2: Gamelet.js with Comments

```
/*
Gamelet: a starting point for writing games
Author: Chris Minnick
Version: 1.0
Instructions:
Include gamelet.js in an HTML document containing
an element with an id of 'ball'.
The script will detect when the left or right arrow
key is pressed and will move the ball element
accordingly.
*/
const ball = document.getElementById("ball"); // get the ball
document.addEventListener("keydown", handleKeyPress); // listen
  for keys
let position = 0; // set initial position
/*
handleKeyPress
responds to certain key presses by updating position.
*/
function handleKeyPress(e) {
```

```
  if (e.code === "ArrowLeft") {
    position = position - 10;
  }
  if (e.code === "ArrowRight") {
    position = position + 10;
  }
  if (position < 0) {
    position = 0;
  }
  refresh(); // reposition the ball
}
/*
refresh
changes the position of the ball
*/
function refresh() {
  ball.style.left = position + "px";
}
```

The README file

Some types of documentation, such as the instructions at the beginning of Listing 2-2, may apply to your entire JavaScript program rather than to a particular file or function. For this kind of documentation, it's helpful to create a `README` file. A `README` file can be written in a simple text file, in an HTML file, or, most commonly, in a markup language called Markdown (I know — it seems like a funny name for a markup language).

The basics of Markdown

To get started with writing your `README` file, make a new file in VS Code and save it with the extension `.md`.

Markdown files generally start with a Level 1 header. To mark text as a level 1 header, preface it with a single # character. Lower-level headers (up to Level 6) are prefaced with additional # symbols.

Let's start the `README` for `gamelet.js` with the following header:

```
# Gamelet
```

After the Level 1 header, you should include a sentence about your project, written as a normal paragraph. To write a paragraph of text in markdown, just separate the paragraph from other text with a blank line. With a description paragraph added, the README file now looks like this:

```
# Gamelet
A starter program for writing JavaScript games.
```

After the description, it's common to add a Level 2 header called `Installation` and one called `Usage`. Because there's no good way to install `Gamelet` yet, just add a `Usage` header. The `Usage` header typically includes a numbered list and code.

To create a numbered list, type a number with a period before the list item. To write code, place three backtick characters (```) followed by the language the code is in (JavaScript or HTML, for example) in front of the code and then place three backticks at the end of the code block.

Just by knowing how to write headers, paragraphs, numbered lists, and code in Markdown, you can create a useful and readable README file. Listing 2-3 shows the finished README for `Gamelet`.

LISTING 2-3: The README file for Gamelet

````
# Gamelet
A starter program for writing JavaScript games.
## Usage
1. Include gamelet.js in an HTML document containing an
element with an id of 'ball'.
```html
<div id="ball">@</div>
<script src="gamelet.js"></script>
```
2. The script will detect when the left or right arrow
keys are pressed and will move the ball element
accordingly.
````

To see what your `README.md` file looks like when it's rendered, click the Open Preview to the Side icon in the upper-right corner of the VS Code editor window, labeled in Figure 2-9.

A rendered preview of the Markdown code appears in a new window to the right of your original `README.md` file, as shown in Figure 2-10.

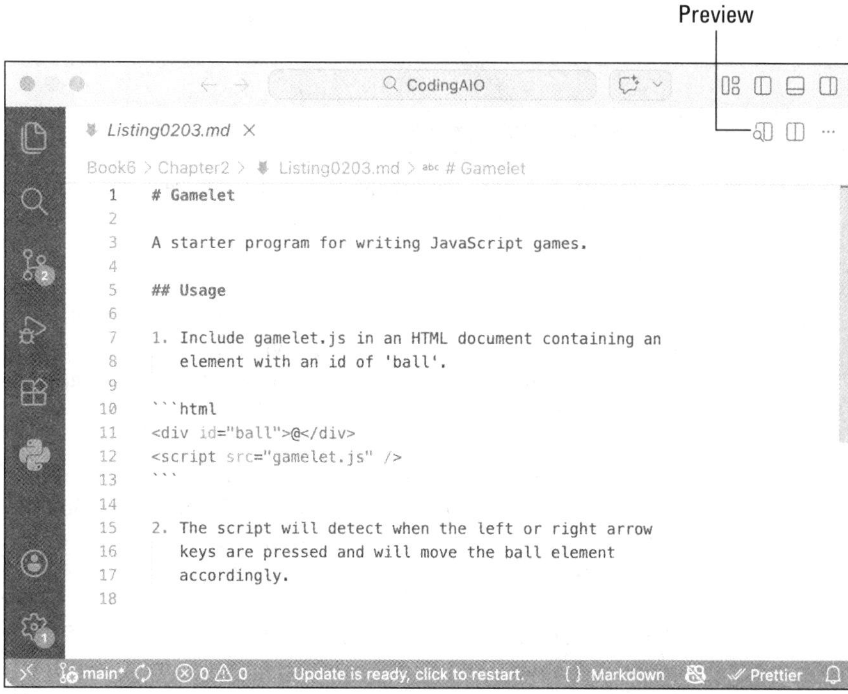

FIGURE 2-9: Click the icon to see your rendered README.md file.

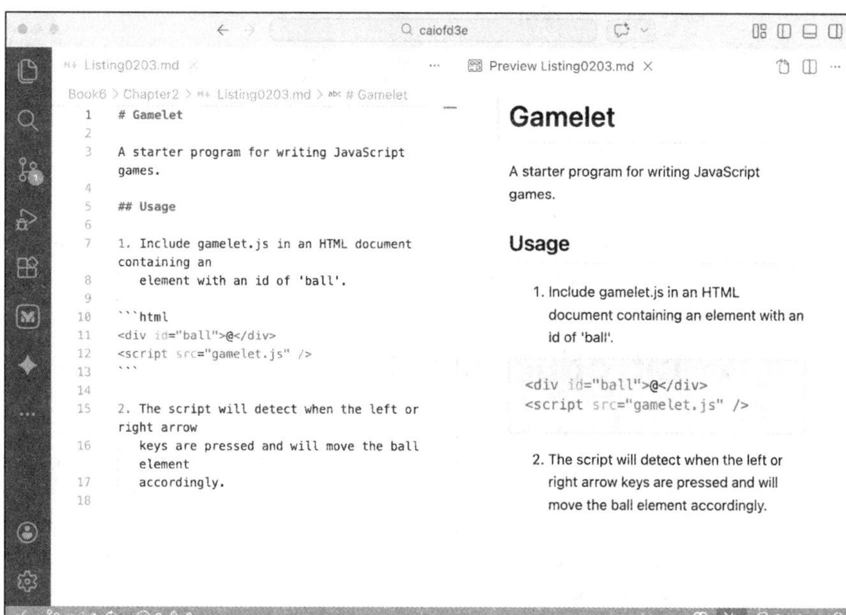

FIGURE 2-10: Previewing README.md in VS Code.

Coding Responsibly with Git

Every programmer has had the experience of creating a document (maybe a paper or a book or an email) and something happens — the power goes out or the coffee spills on your laptop or you simply forgot to save before you turned off your computer. The resulting lost work is a frustrating waste of time, and you may never get that data back or be able to re-create the magic.

For me, it was a computer's power supply that experienced a power surge and exploded in the middle of the night, frying the hard drive and causing me to nearly lose 50 percent of a book I was writing. Fortunately, I had sent most of my work to my editor and was able to recover quickly.

Problems that cause data loss in programming and in writing can also be the result of good intentions. Maybe you spend weeks traveling down a path that you think is right, but it turns out to be wrong, and you wish you could go back to where you were when you first came up with that harebrained idea.

Maybe you work with another programmer or a team of programmers, and you discover that both of you are working on the same file at the same time. How do you figure out how to merge your changes and end up with a single version of the code?

To prevent these situations, programmers (and many writers) use version control systems. *Version control* tracks the changes to a file over time, giving you a record of what each individual file in a project looked like at any point and allowing you to return to any point in the life of your project.

Version control makes team software development possible, but it's also an indispensable tool for individual developers working on their own. The most popular version control system in use today is Git.

Introducing Git

Git is a free and open-source version control system that you can use in every kind of project, from very small to very large. Unlike other version control systems, Git doesn't store complete copies of each file with each version. Instead, it creates snapshots of a project containing only the files that have changed in each version. If a file never changes after it's created, Git needs to store only one copy of that file.

Because of this system of creating snapshots, Git uses much less storage space and is faster than other version control systems.

Installing Git

If you're using macOS or Linux, Git is installed on your computer already. If you're using Windows, you can download Git at `https://git-scm.com/downloads`.

The order of steps you complete to install Git is likely to change, so I don't walk you through each step. As you're installing, make sure to select the options that are selected in Figure 2-11.

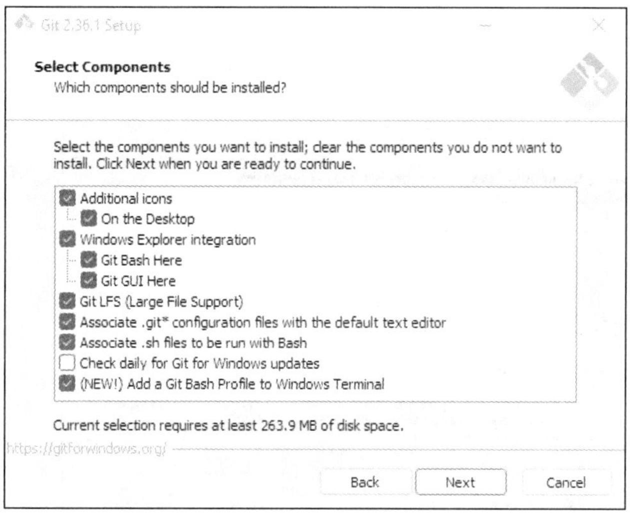

FIGURE 2-11: Select all but one box when installing Git for Windows.

You can select the single unchecked box shown in Figure 2-11 if you like, but I prefer to leave it deselected so I can choose when to update Git myself.

When you reach the step in the process where you choose the default editor used by Git, select Visual Studio Code, as shown in Figure 2-12.

If you're asked whether you want to adjust the name of the initial branch in new repositories, select Override the Default Branch Name for New Repositories and make sure it's set to `main`, as shown in Figure 2-13.

You can safely choose the default settings in the other steps in the installation process.

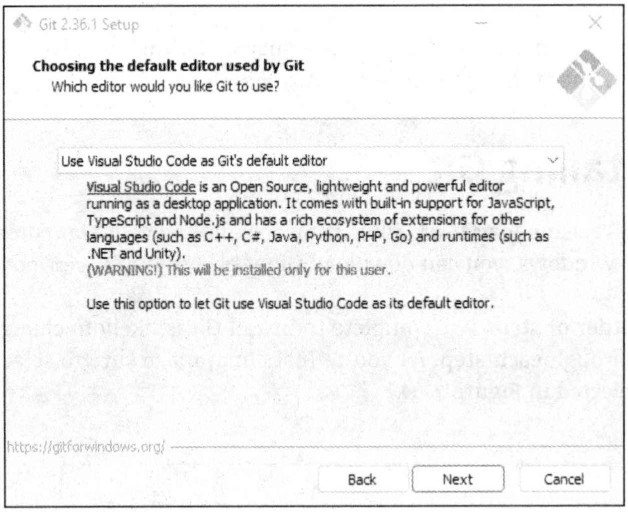

FIGURE 2-12: Select Visual Studio Code as the default editor.

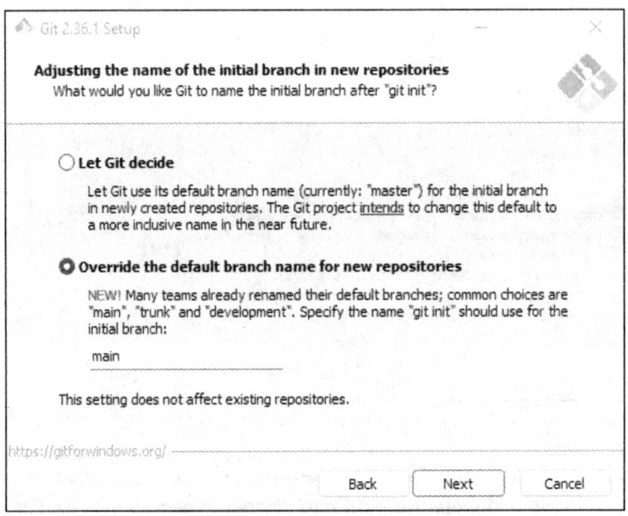

FIGURE 2-13: Setting the default branch name.

Configuring and testing Git

Follow these steps to configure Visual Studio Code to recognize and use Git:

1. **If you have Visual Studio Code open, shut it down and restart it.**

   This step ensures that you're using the latest version. Like Google Chrome, Visual Studio Code checks for updates as you're using it and installs new versions when you restart.

2. **Choose Terminal ➪ New Terminal.**

   A new terminal window opens.

3. **In Terminal, type** git --version **and press Enter.**

   The current version number of Git on your computer is displayed. It should be higher than Version 2. If it's not, or if you don't get a version number, you may need to reinstall Git.

4. **Type the following two commands, replacing the placeholder data in quotes with your own info:**

```
git config --global user.email "you@example.com"
git config --global user.name "Your Name"
```

5. **Click the Source Control icon on the left side of VS Code.**

   The Source Control panel opens, as shown in Figure 2-14.

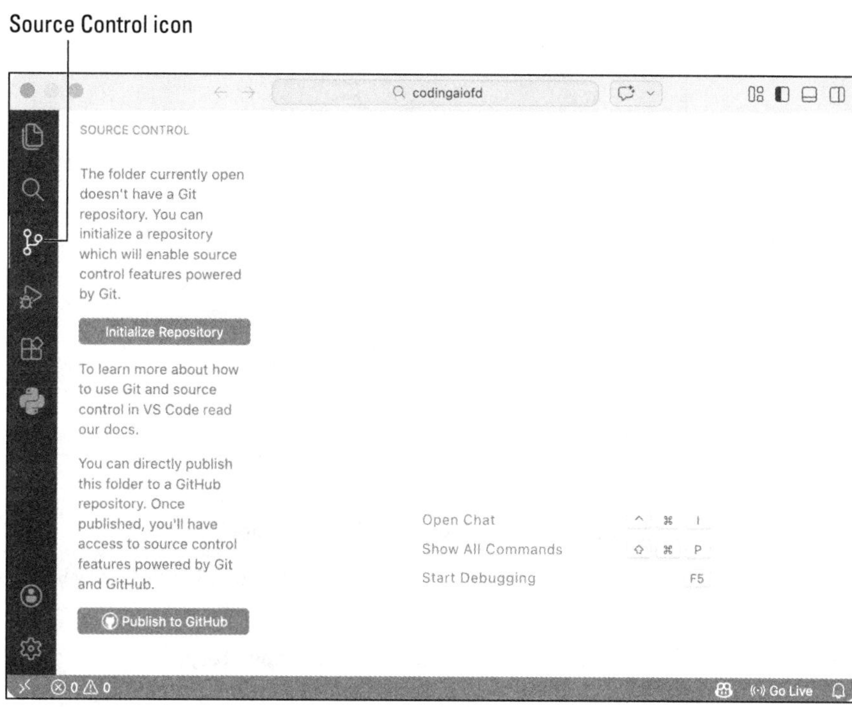

FIGURE 2-14: The Source Control panel in VS Code.

6. **Click the Publish to GitHub button.**

   If you see a pop-up asking for permission for Visual Studio Code to sign in using GitHub, click Allow. Your browser will open and go to the `https://github.com` login page.

7. **If you have a GitHub account already, sign in on this page. If you don't have an account, click the Create an Account link and follow the instructions to create one.**

8. **When the screen shown in Figure 2-15 opens, click the green Authorize button to authorize Visual Studio Code to access your GitHub account.**

   When VS Code has finished authorizing, the screen returns to VS Code.

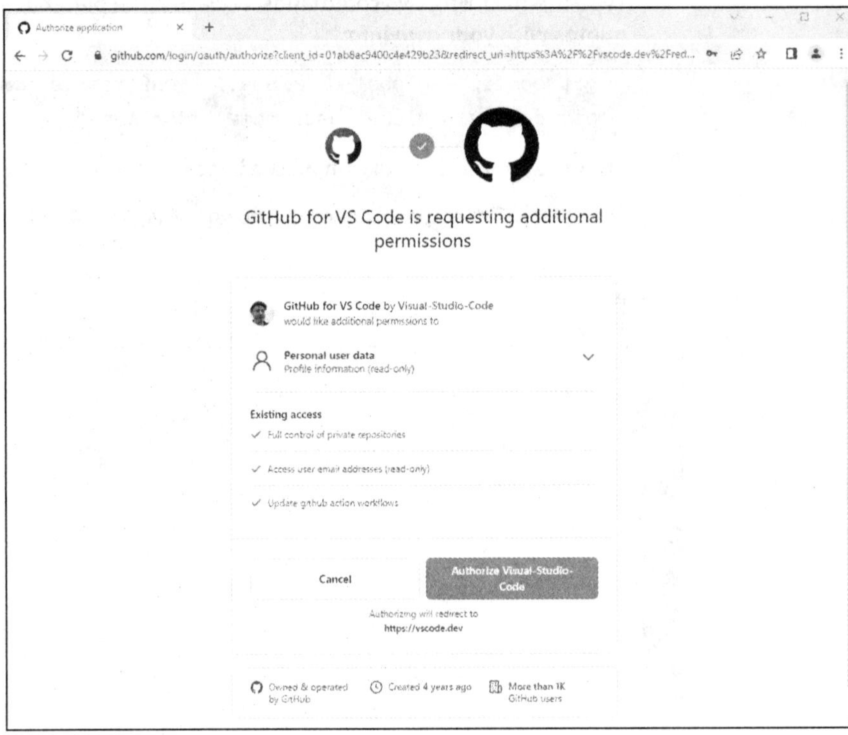

FIGURE 2-15: Authorize Visual Studio Code to access your GitHub account.

9. **Click the Publish to GitHub button again.**

   A drop-down menu appears at the top of VS Code, giving you the option of publishing to a private repository or a public one.

10. **Select Publish to GitHub Public Repository.**

    Public repositories can be viewed by anyone. Private repositories can be viewed only by you and the people you choose to share with.

11. **When asked which files you want to include in the repository, make your selection and then click OK.**

By default, all files in your current workspace are selected. You can change this setting or leave it alone.

The Source Control panel appears, displaying a text area where you can enter a message.

12. **In the text area, type** Initial commit **and then click Commit.**

VS Code displays a notification when it has finished.

After you have a Git repository, it's time to learn the basics of how Git works and how to use it, as I explain next.

Learning the basics of Git

To track your files, Git keeps a database in a folder named `.git` in your project. There's no need to see or change this folder manually, so VS Code hides it from you by default.

In Git, your files can be in three states:

- **Modified** means you've changed a file but haven't yet committed it to the Git database.
- **Staged** means you've marked a modified file to be part of your next commit.
- **Committed** means a file is stored in your local Git database.

Follow these steps to take a file in your repository through all three states:

1. **In the same workspace where you initialized your Git repository, create a new file named `README.md` or open your existing `README.md` file.**

   Make sure the `README.md` file isn't inside a subfolder of your repository. Files and folders that aren't inside any other folders in your project are said to be at the *root* of your project.

2. **Give your `README.md` file a Level 1 header and a description by entering the following:**

```
# Coding All-in-One For Dummies
I'm learning Python, HTML, CSS, JavaScript, React, Vue,
   and Node
from Coding All-in-One For Dummies
```

3. **Save the file.**

   Note that the Source Control icon on the left side of VS Code now has a number (or a larger number).

4. **Click the Source Control icon to open the Source Control panel.**

   You see a list of files. Your new README file is under the Changes heading, as shown in Figure 2-16.

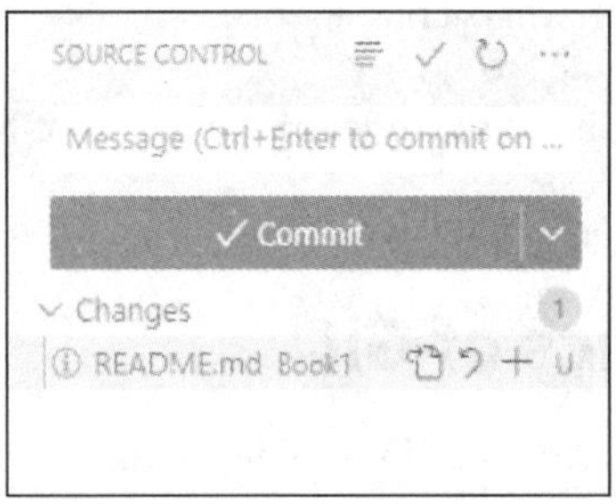

FIGURE 2-16: The Source Control panel, with `README.md` under the Changes heading.

5. **Click the plus sign (+) to the right of your changed (modified) file to stage it.**

   The file moves to the Staged Changes list.

6. **Look for the text box at the top of the Source Control panel. If you don't see it, click the checkmark icon at the top of the Source Control panel.**

7. **Enter a commit message and then press Enter.**

   A commit message should describe what you've changed in your project. But, for your first commit, you can just type **added a README**.

If everything worked correctly, your files are now safely stored in your local Git database. But they're still only on your computer. To publish your files to GitHub, click the Sync Changes button, which appears in the Source Control panel when all your files are checked in. If a confirmation dialog box appears, click OK.

Once your files are published to GitHub, open your web browser and go to your new repository at `https://github.com`. You should see your `README` file rendered below a list of the files in your repository, as shown in Figure 2-17.

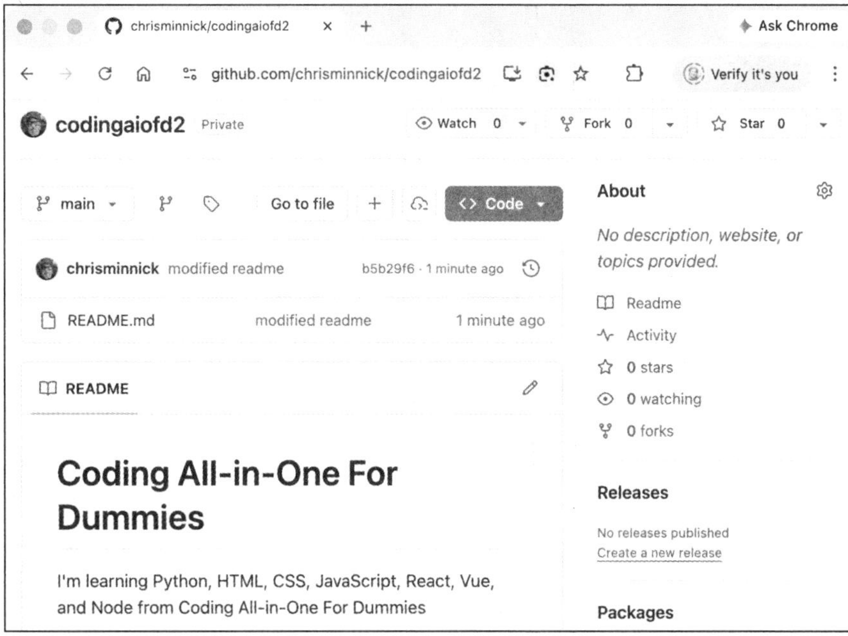

FIGURE 2-17: Viewing your repository's page on GitHub.

Moving forward with Git and GitHub

Now that you know the basics of staging, committing, and publishing your files, it's important to continue doing it regularly — at least once a day, but the more often, the better.

There's a lot more to learn about Git than what you can find in the space available in this book. When you're ready to learn more about the ins and outs of Git, check out the excellent and free book, *Pro Git,* written by Scott Chacon and Ben Straub. It's available at `https://git-scm.com/book/en/v2`.

WARNING

Besides keeping your project's files safe, you have another important reason to check your files regularly, especially if you plan to look for a job: Recruiters and hiring managers will check your GitHub contribution activity (which appears on your GitHub page). Frequent commit activity shows that you're serious about coding.

IN THIS CHAPTER

» Using `let` and `const` to store data

» Introducing JavaScript's data types

» Creating and using objects

» Storing lists with arrays

» Understanding JavaScript scope

Chapter 3
Storing and Wrangling Data

"A foolish consistency is the hobgoblin of little minds."

—RALPH WALDO EMERSON

At its most basic level, programming is the process of changing values. Sometimes, however, you don't want to change certain values. In this chapter, you create variables with `let` and constants with `const`, take a guided tour of JavaScript's core data types, and learn when values are copied versus shared. You also start building complex structures with objects and arrays. I wrap up the chapter with a discussion of scope, so your variables will be where you expect them to be.

Making Variables by Using let

Variables are names that represent values in a program. JavaScript has the `let` keyword for creating a variable.

Declaring variables

Creating a variable is known as *declaring* a variable. To declare a variable by using `let`, simply write the `let` keyword followed by what you want to name the variable, like this:

```
let phoneNumber;
```

This line creates a new empty variable named `phoneNumber`.

TECHNICAL STUFF

Technically, a newly declared variable isn't empty. JavaScript automatically assigns it a value of `undefined`. I talk about this `undefined` value later in the chapter.

Once you've declared a variable, you can assign it a value like this:

```
phoneNumber = '503-555-5555';
```

Initializing variables

Assigning a value to a variable for the first time is called *initializing a variable.* You can combine the declaration and initialization of a variable into one statement, like this:

```
let favoriteColor = 'red';
```

Variables are what make it possible to have computer programs do more than one thing. For example, consider the following tiny JavaScript program:

```
let seven = 7;
let eight = 8;
let sum = seven + eight;
```

This JavaScript program demonstrates how to create a variable and give it a value, though no one would ever write this program (except me, of course). It simply results in the `sum` variable having a value of `15` each time I run the program.

Using variables

You can think of a variable as a box that holds a single item. This box might have a label that describes its contents; the more descriptive the label, the easier it is to know what should be kept in that box. Variables are typically named according to the purpose of the values they store. Constants (I talk about them in the next section) are typically named in a way that identifies the value they store.

To use the value of a variable in a statement, use the variable's name. To see this concept in action (and to try out the following examples), open the JavaScript console in your browser and try declaring and initializing variables. Figure 3-1 shows some things you might want to try.

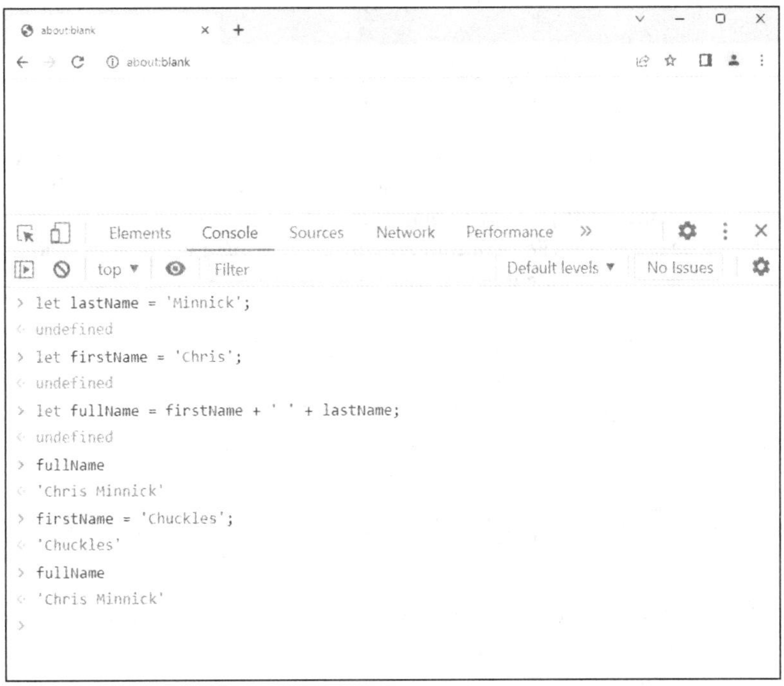

FIGURE 3-1: Using `let` to declare and initialize variables.

TECHNICAL STUFF

Did you expect that the value of `fullName` in Figure 3-1 would change when the value of `firstName` was changed? Can you explain what's happening here? Keep reading, because I explain what's going on in the section about data types!

You can make the preceding program that only added 7 and 8 into a general-purpose program for adding two numbers by setting the values of the numbers using the result of user input, like this:

```
let firstNumber = prompt("Pick a number");
let secondNumber = prompt("Pick another number");
let sum = Number(firstNumber) + Number(secondNumber);
alert(sum);
```

When you run this program, your browser pops up a prompt and waits for your answer. It then pops up a second prompt. When you enter a number into the second prompt, your browser displays an alert with the sum of the numbers.

TECHNICAL STUFF

If you've written or worked with JavaScript previously, you've most likely seen and used the `var` keyword. Creating variables with `var` works the same way as with `let`. However, using `var` is no longer considered to be a good practice by most JavaScript programmers, for reasons I explain later in this chapter, in the "Getting a Handle on Scope" section.

Naming variables

Always make your variable names descriptive and write them in camel case. Two-word variable names are usually more descriptive than single-word names, and using multiple words makes it less likely that you'll have two variables with the same name. For example, if you're creating a variable to hold a street address, it's better to name it `streetAddress` than simply `address`.

If you stick to the rule of naming variables in camel case, you will reduce typos. You won't accidentally type `streetaddress` in one place, `StreetAddress` in another, and `streetAddress` in another, for example.

Making Constants by Using const

Many times, you need easy access to a value in your JavaScript program, but once it's created, you won't need to change it. For this reason, JavaScript has the `const` keyword.

Constants created using `const` work similarly to variables created with `let`, with one important difference: Once declared, a constant can't be reassigned. If you attempt to change a constant, JavaScript gives you an error, as shown in Figure 3-2.

Because a constant can't be assigned a new value after it's created, you must always declare and initialize a constant at the same time:

```
const likesTacos = true;
```

FIGURE 3-2: Attempting to change a constant results in an error.

TECHNICAL STUFF

Technically speaking, `const` doesn't create values that can't be changed (you call these *immutable* values) — it creates a read-only reference to a value. What this means in practice is that if you assign a value to a `const` that includes other values (as happens with arrays and objects, which you start learning about later in the chapter), you can still change the inner values of the `const` — just not the value the `const` refers to.

Knowing when to use constants

Anytime you have a value that you know won't change during the life of a program, and that you need to use more than once, you should make it a constant. It's common, for example, to have configuration variables that are used throughout a program. These may include elements like URL paths, theme colors set by the developer, and error messages. By setting these as constants at the beginning of your program (or in a separate module), you can make sure that they don't get changed and that you have a centralized place for managing them as you code.

Naming constants

Non-changing values should be named using all capital letters and be defined either in a separate module or at the beginning of your JavaScript file or module. If a constant's name is more than one word, it's a well-established practice to name it using *upper snake case*, or `UPPER_SNAKE_CASE`.

TECHNICAL STUFF

As you'll see when you start working with JavaScript objects, arrays, and modules, there are exceptions to every rule.

Taking a Look at Data Types

Variables and constants all have two things in common: a value and a type. You've already seen examples of values. These are the bits of data that you want to store in the variable. In this section, I talk about type.

A variable's *data type* is the kind of data a variable can hold. The data type determines whether 97103-4534 is a postal code or a mathematical operation that results in 92569.

JavaScript is loose and dynamic

JavaScript is a *loosely typed* language, which means you can store any type of data in a variable or constant without having to tell JavaScript in advance the type of data.

JavaScript is also a *dynamically typed* language, which means you can change the type of data stored in a variable. You might initialize a variable using a number but later store text in it. Although changing the type of a variable is unusual and generally should be avoided, JavaScript tries to be friendly and doesn't complain.

To see a value's or variable's data type, use the `typeof` operator. To try it out, open your JavaScript console and enter the following expressions:

```
>> typeof "1"
>> typeof 0
>> typeof true
>> typeof "true"
>> typeof a
>> typeof "a"
```

The result of running these expressions is shown in Figure 3-3.

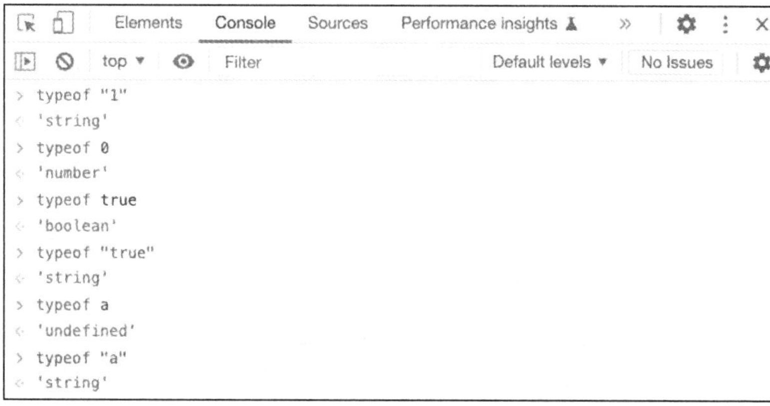

FIGURE 3-3: Using `typeof` to get the data type.

Passing by value

JavaScript has seven basic data types, which are known as the primitive data types. *Primitive data types* are passed by value. When you create a new variable from an existing primitive variable, the value of the existing variable is copied to the new one. Let's look at an example to better understand the implications of this concept.

Start out by creating a variable called `firstName` that will hold a person's first name, and another variable called `lastName` that will hold the person's last name:

```
let firstName = "Andrea";
let lastName = "Wallace";
```

Now you can create a variable called `fullName` that combines the values of `firstName` and `lastName` (and adds a space between them):

```
let fullName = firstName + ' ' + lastName;
```

When you create `fullName`, the values of `firstName` and `lastName` are copied and concatenated. If you change the values of `firstName` and `lastName` after `fullName` is created, `fullName` doesn't know about that, in the same way that a picture you take of someone doesn't change when they get a haircut.

String data type

A *string* is any literal text. It can be made up of any number of characters, including letters, numbers, symbols, and white space. To create a string, enclose a value in matching single or double quotes, like this:

```
let catName = "Mr. Furley";
```

Whether you use single or double quotes doesn't matter, as long as you end your string with the same type of quote you began it with. If you use double quotes to create your string, you can't use double quotes within that string. If you define your string using single quotes, you can't use single quotes inside that string. Consider the following code, which causes an error in JavaScript:

```
let famousQuote = ""Nothing great was ever achieved
  without enthusiasm."";
```

The intention in the preceding example is for the quotation marks to show up around the words. But the result is that JavaScript thinks the string starts with the quotation mark (") and ends with the second quotation mark and therefore contains nothing. The rest of the characters are seen by JavaScript as just a mess of typos.

Escaping characters

When you need to use double quotes in a double-quoted string, you can *escape* them by prefacing the offending symbol with a backslash (\). To correctly store the preceding quote, including the quotation marks, you can write it like this:

```
let famousQuote = "\"Nothing great was ever achieved without
  enthusiasm.\"";
```

Alternatively, you can define your string with single quotes and then use the double quotes inside it as much as you like:

```
let famousQuote = '"Nothing great was ever achieved without
  enthusiasm."';
```

TIP

Once you decide on your own preference (or adopt a standard style of coding) for whether to use single quotes or double quotes for strings, stick with it. Consistency reduces the potential for bugs.

In addition to single quotes and double quotes needing to be escaped, several other special characters can't be used in a string unless you use an escape code. Most of these are things you'll never have a need to use, but others, like backslash and newline, can be useful. These characters are shown in Table 3-1.

Creating strings with template literal notation

Another way to create strings is to use template literal notation. *Template literals* start and end with the backtick (`) character (which is in the upper-left corner of the keyboard).

TABLE 3-1 **JavaScript Special Characters**

Code	Output
\'	Single quote
\"	Double quote
\\	Backslash
\n	New line
\r	Carriage return
\t	Tab
\b	Backspace
\f	Form feed

The useful thing about template literals is that you can include JavaScript expressions inside them by surrounding the expression with curly braces ({}) preceded by a dollar sign ($).

Listing 3-1 shows how to use a template literal string to compile a message to be displayed after someone places an order.

LISTING 3-1: Using a Template Literal String

```
let orderTotal = 39.99;
let itemPurchased = 'JavaScript All-in-One For Dummies';
let customer = 'Joe Q. Developer';
let thankYou = `${customer}, thank you for your order of ${itemPurchased}. Your
  payment of ${orderTotal} was successful.`;
```

Before template literals came along, writing a string that included variable data required the use of the concatenation operator (+), and the resulting statement was confusing and error-prone.

Working with string functions

Once you've created a string, you can use any of JavaScript's built-in string functions with it. Some of the most common string functions are listed in this section.

REMEMBER

You can try out these string functions yourself and see the result. Open your JavaScript console and enter the following statements:

- `charAt` tells you the character at a specified position (starting with position 0):

  ```
  let randomLetters = 'pdfsdj';
  randomLetters.charAt(4);
  ```

- `concat` combines two or more strings and returns the result:

  ```
  let houseNumber = '555';
  let streetName = 'Shady Lane';
  houseNumber.concat(' ', streetName);
  ```

- `indexOf` searches your string and returns the position of the first occurrence of the character or string you specify:

  ```
  let typeOfTree = 'Pine';
  typeOfTree.indexOf('e');
  ```

- `split` splits strings into an array of substrings:

  ```
  let vowelsList = 'a,e,i,o,u';
  vowelsList.split(',');
  ```

- `substring` extracts the characters in a string between two specified positions. If the first number is larger than the second, substring reverses them:

  ```
  let phoneNumber = '313-555-1234';
  phoneNumber.substring(12, 4);
  ```

- `slice` works the same as `substring`, but it returns an empty string (`""`) if the first number is larger than the second:

  ```
  let phoneNumber = '313-555-1234';
  phoneNumber.slice(12, 4);
  ```

- `replace` finds a string and replaces it with another string:

  ```
  let message = 'Learn FORTRAN.';
  message.replace('FORTRAN', 'JavaScript');
  ```

- `toLowerCase` returns a string with all the characters converted to lowercase:

  ```
  let username = 'ChrisMinnick';
  username.toLowerCase();
  ```

- `toUpperCase` returns a string with all the characters converted to uppercase:

  ```
  let stateName = 'texas';
  stateName.toUpperCase();
  ```

Number data type

To make a variable with the `number` data type, assign any number (without quotes) or an expression that evaluates to a number (for example, `1+1`) to a variable or constant.

JavaScript stores numbers as 64-bit floating-point values. This means that, in theory, the `number` data type can store any number between 2^{-1074} and 2^{1024}. In practice, however, you should use the `number` data type to store numbers only between -2^{53-1} and 2^{53-1}.

These numbers are called the maximum and minimum safe integers.

TECHNICAL STUFF

The reason this range is considered safe is that JavaScript numbers are 64-bit doubles, which only have 53 bits of precision for integers, so numbers beyond that range can't always be represented exactly.

For numbers that are larger or smaller than this range, you can use the `BigInt` data type.

Working with number functions

Like the `string` data type, the `number` data type includes several helpful functions (also known as *methods*) for working with numbers:

- `parseInt` converts a number to an integer by discarding everything after the decimal point:

  ```
  parseInt(5.343235);
  ```

- `parseFloat` specifically tells JavaScript to treat a number as a float, meaning that it will include the portion after a decimal point:

  ```
  parseFloat(10.00);
  ```

One of the most common uses for `parseInt` and `parseFloat` is to convert strings to numbers. For example, if the user of your web app enters a number into a text field, that value is received by your program as a string.

Knowing when to convert between strings and numbers

To understand the importance of converting string input into numbers, consider the following example:

```
let orderTotal = tip + tax + total;
```

If the user provides the value for `tip` using an online form, it will be a string containing a number. Let's try this calculation using the following values:

```
let tip = "8.50";
let total = 40;
let tax = 0;
let orderTotal = tip + tax + total;
```

Try out this code in your JavaScript console, and then check the value of `orderTotal`. Can you explain what happened? The tax and total get added normally, but then that result gets concatenated with the string contained in the `tip` variable, and the result is a string with a value of `8.50040`, instead of what you expected to get, which is the number `48.50`.

Try changing the order of the variables on the right side of the statement that declares and initializes the `orderTotal` to see what happens if the string `"tip"` isn't first. JavaScript sometimes does strange things, which is why it's best to explicitly convert to the data type you want something to be.

To fix the code in the preceding example, use `parseFloat`, as shown here:

```
let tip = "8.50";
let total = 40;
let tax = 0;
let orderTotal = parseFloat(tip) + tax + total;
```

Now the program returns the expected result.

BigInt data type

If you need to use numbers that are larger or smaller than the maximum and minimum numbers that can be held by the number data type, you can use the `BigInt` data type.

To create a `BigInt`, just add an `n` to the end of a number. For example, here's a number that's larger than the maximum safe number for the `number` data type:

```
let kilometersToAndromedaGalaxy = 23651826000000000000n;
```

Boolean data type

Boolean variables store one of two possible values: either `true` or `false`.

TECHNICAL STUFF

The word *Boolean* comes from George Boole (1815–1864), who created an algebraic system of logic.

When you compare items in JavaScript, the result is a Boolean. To see this concept in action, try typing the following expressions into the JavaScript console:

- `3 < 10`
- `90 < 10`
- `true === false`
- `0! == "0"`
- `"apples" === "oranges"`

Converting to Boolean

Any value in JavaScript can be converted to a Boolean by using the `!!` operator. You can try out this conversion by going back to the JavaScript console and typing some values with `!!` in front of them:

- `!!"JavaScript is awesome"`
- `!!"I am the best JavaScript programmer"`
- `!!0`
- `!!""`
- `!!99`
- `!!null`

Note that some of the values in this list convert to `true` and others convert to `false`. How do you know which is which? The answer lies in the idea of *Truthy* and *Falsy* values.

TECHNICAL STUFF

The ! (usually pronounced "bang") operator is the logical NOT operator. Using one ! to the left of a value returns its Boolean opposite. So, two !s returns the double opposite, which is how !! can be used to convert a value to its associated Boolean value.

Getting Truthy and Falsy

You can know whether a value converted to a Boolean will be `true` or `false` by remembering a short list of items that always convert to `false`. These values are called *falsy* in JavaScript:

- `false`
- `0` (zero)
- `-0`
- `0n` (`bigInt` zero)
- `""` or `''` or ` `` ` (an empty string)
- `null`
- `undefined`
- `null`

Everything else is `true` when converted to Boolean.

Why is this knowledge useful? The idea of truthy and falsy allows you to simplify the code for many operations in JavaScript. For example, it's common to need to determine whether a variable has a value before trying to do something with it. One way to do this is to write something like the following statement:

```
if (city === ''){
alert('City is a required field.');
}
```

This code might be used to determine whether someone forgot to fill out the `city` field on a form. Another way to write this same thing is to just use the `city` variable in the parentheses, which converts `city` to a Boolean. If it has a value, it will be `true`. If it doesn't have a value, it will be `false`. Because you want to know whether city is `false`, you can invert the Boolean to say "If city is not truthy," like this:

```
if (!city) {
alert('City is a required field.');
}
```

NaN

`NaN` stands for Not a Number. `NaN` is (confusingly) a special value of the Number data type. It's what you get when you try to perform impossible mathematical operations or when you try to perform mathematical operations with strings.

Following are examples of operations that return `NaN`:

- Math operations where the result is not a real number, such as trying to calculate the square root of a negative number:

  ```
  Math.sqrt(-1)
  ```

- Attempting any mathematical operation involving a string, other than with the addition operator:

  ```
  "yarn" / "cats"
  ```

- Attempting to convert a string to a number:

  ```
  parseInt("sandwich")
  ```

Undefined data type

Undefined is the default data type and value of a variable that's been declared but not initialized in JavaScript. It's also the value that will be returned by a statement or function that doesn't specifically return a value.

You can see this default return value in action by entering a variable declaration in the JavaScript console in your browser. Whenever you run a JavaScript statement or expression in the console, JavaScript must return a value. If the statement you run doesn't specifically have a return value, the returned value is `undefined`.

Symbol data type

The *symbol* data type is used to create unique identifiers in JavaScript. Unlike the other data types, even if two symbols appear to be identical and have the same name, JavaScript guarantees that they'll be unique.

To see this unique nature of symbol in action, enter the following snippet in your browser's JavaScript console:

```
let symbol1 = Symbol("mysymbol");
let symbol2 = Symbol("mysymbol");
symbol1===symbol2
```

Wrangling the Object: The Complex Data Type

In addition to its seven primitive data types, JavaScript also has a complex data type called object. An *object* is a container for related data and functionality. For example, an object called `customerInfo` might contain a name, an address, and various other values related to a particular customer.

An object is called a complex data type because it's made up of the other data types. You can think of an object as your opportunity to create any data type you need. Although a simple number data type is useful for storing the score in a game or the number of times someone has played the game, many things in life are more complex and need multiple values to fully describe them.

To make an object, place curly braces (`{}`) around a comma-separated list of name:value pairs. The customer object I described might be created and assigned to a constant, like this:

```
const customer = {
name: 'Laura Wigfall',
address: '3427 Crummit Lane',
city: 'Providence',
state: 'RI',
zipcode: '02905',
customerId: 4,
isInLoyaltyClub: true,
};
```

Here are two important aspects you may have noticed about this object:

- » **The values inside an object (*properties*) can be any combination of the other data types.** In fact, these values can be (and often are) objects themselves.
- » **Objects are commonly declared as constants (`const`).** The result is that the object itself is unchangeable, though the values inside it can still be changed. You explore this interesting facet of JavaScript and its implications much more in Chapter 7 of this minibook.

You can access the properties of an object by using what's called *dot notation*. To see dot notation in action, open your JavaScript console and enter the previous object (or any other object). Then enter the name of the object (`customer`), followed by a period (`.`), followed by the name of one of the object's properties. For example, type `customer.city` into the console after creating the `customer` object.

JavaScript returns the value of that property in response. You can use dot notation to create and change properties as well.

Examining the Array — a Special Kind of Object

Arrays aren't primitive data types, but they aren't the same as other objects, either. *Arrays* are used to store lists of items using a single name. The items inside an array are its *elements*, and the number you can use to access or modify elements is the *index*. Arrays are created using square brackets (`[]`) containing comma-separated values.

The following example creates an array called `favoriteCities`:

```
const favoriteCities = [
'Rome',
'Berlin',
'New York',
'Paris',
'Astoria',
];
```

You can access the elements in an array by using the name of the array followed by square brackets containing the index position of the element you want. For example, to get the name of my second-favorite city, you would use the following line:

```
favoriteCities[1];
```

The reason the index of my second favorite city is 1 is that array index numbers in JavaScript, like Python lists, start with index number 0. You can learn much more about arrays in Chapter 6 of this minibook.

Getting a Handle on Scope

The location where you declare a variable determines where your program can make use of that variable. This concept is called *variable scope*. JavaScript has three kinds of variable scope:

- *Global-scoped* variables can be used anywhere inside a program.
- *Function-scoped* variables can be used anywhere in the function where they was declared. You can read about functions in Chapter 8 of this minibook. You create function-scoped variables by using the `var` keyword.
- *Block-scoped* variables are variables created using the `let` or `const` keyword and initialized inside of a block. A *block* in JavaScript is a unit of code that starts with a left curly brace (`{`) and ends with a right curly brace (`}`). Block-scoped variables can be used anywhere in the block where they are declared.

IN THIS CHAPTER

- » Building expressions
- » Setting values with the assignment operator
- » Testing with the comparison operators
- » Working with arithmetic and string operators
- » Thinking through the logical operators

Chapter 4

Working with Operators and Expressions

"But do your work, and I shall know you."

—RALPH WALDO EMERSON

JavaScript operators and expressions are the building blocks of JavaScript programs. With operators and expressions, you can perform math, compare values, set and change variables, and much more.

In this chapter, you learn about JavaScript's operators and use them to build expressions and statements. You also discover how to combine operators and how to choose which operators to use when multiple operators can produce the same results.

Building Expressions

An *expression* is a piece of code that resolves to a value. There are two types of expressions, both of which you may have already seen in this book: those that affect something else (for example, the expression `chapter = 4` assigns the value `4` to the `chapter` variable) and those that simply resolve to a value (for example, the expression `99 - 1`).

In most cases, when you write JavaScript code, you combine these two types of expressions to form statements. For example:

```
x = x + 1;
```

This statement consists of two expressions. The first adds `1` to the value of `x`, and the second assigns that new value to `x`. The result is that the value of `x` is incremented by `1`.

EXPRESS YOURSELF

You often have multiple ways to write expressions that do the same thing by using different operators. For example, you can achieve the same result as saying `x = x + 1` with any of the following statements:

```
x += 1;
++x;
x=(-(~x));
```

If each of these statements will produce the same result, how do you know which one you should use? Your choice might be determined by several factors, including which one is easiest for you to read and understand, which one is easier for others to understand, which one is shortest, or which one will execute the fastest when run by a JavaScript engine. Sometimes even looking cool to your JavaScript friends comes into play, as in the case of that last statement, which no one in their right mind would ever use but that might give someone a chuckle if they saw it. Ask your friendly AI chatbot how it works.

My advice is to use whatever statement is easiest for you to read and understand, without worrying about what might be small differences in performance or conciseness. As you become more experienced with JavaScript, your style will naturally evolve.

Operators: The Lineup

The symbols or keywords that make expressions do their work are called *operators.* They operate on values, also called *operands,* to produce the final value of an expression. Examples of operators include =, +, and +=. This section discusses some of the more common operators.

Operator precedence

Statements often contain multiple operators. For example, look at the following statement:

```
x = 5 - 1 / 2;
```

Depending on the order in which JavaScript performs each of the three operations (assignment, subtraction, and division) in this statement, the final value of x may be 5, 2, or 4.5.

The key to understanding statements with multiple operators is operator precedence. *Operator precedence* assigns a number from 1 to 18 to each operator. In a statement containing multiple operators, the operator with the highest number runs first.

The multiplication (*) and division (/) operators have a precedence value of 12, addition (+) and subtraction (-) have precedence values of 11, and assignment (=) has a precedence of 2. Because all three operators in this statement have different precedence values, it's a simple matter to work out the final value of x, as shown here:

1. 1 will be divided by 2, resulting in .5.
2. .5 will be subtracted from 5, resulting in 4.5.
3. 4.5 will be assigned to x.

If you haven't done so already, you can verify these values by using your browser's JavaScript console.

But what happens when a statement has multiple operators that have the same precedence level, such as this one:

```
x = 4-5-2/2*2
```

To handle this case, JavaScript assigns an associativity to each operator. *Associativity* is the direction in which expressions that use the operator are evaluated. *Left associativity* means that the left side of the operator is evaluated first. *Right associativity* means that the right side of the operator is evaluated first.

Arithmetic operators have left associativity (except for the special case of the exponentiation operator), and assignment operators have right associativity. By using associativity and operator precedence together, you can work out the final value of x in the preceding statement, like this:

1. `2/2 = 1`
2. `1*2 = 2`
3. `4-5 = -1`
4. `-1-2`
5. `x = -3`

TECHNICAL STUFF

You can see all the operators and their operator precedence by visiting `https://developer.mozilla.org/en-US/docs/Web/JavaScript/Reference/Operators/Operator_Precedence#table`.

Using parentheses

Remembering and figuring out operator precedence is a job that's best left to JavaScript. It's helpful to know the associativity and relative precedence for a few operators (such as the arithmetic and assignment operators), but there's only one operator you need to know to make sure your statements always do things in the order you want. This magical operator is the grouping operator, which is made up of opening and closing parentheses.

The *grouping operator* controls the order of evaluation of statements, and it has the highest precedence of all JavaScript operators. By using the grouping operator, you can override the default operator precedence rules and evaluate expressions in any order you want.

For example, in the following statement, the division and multiplication would normally happen first:

```
x = 4-5-2 / 2*2
```

If you wanted the left and right sides of the division operator to run before the division is done, you could use the grouping operator like this:

```
x = (4-5-2) / (2*2);
```

The result of this statement is `-3/4`, or `-.75`.

Assignment operators

The assignment operator assigns a value to the operand on the left based on the operand on the right:

```
x = 10;
```

You can also chain assignment operators. For example:

```
x = y = z = 0;
```

Remember that the associativity of the assignment operator is from right to left. So, the way JavaScript executes this expression is by assigning `0` to `z`, and then the value of `z` to `y`, and then the value of `y` to `x`. In the end, all three variables are `0`.

Comparison operators

The comparison operators compare the left and right operands and return a Boolean (`true` or `false`) value. Table 4-1 shows the complete list of comparison operators.

TABLE 4-1 JavaScript Comparison Operators

Operator	Description	Example
`==`	Equality	`3 == "3" // true`
`!=`	Inequality	`3 != 3 // false`
`===`	Strict equality	`3 === "3" // false`
`!==`	Strict inequality	`3 !== "3" // true`
`>`	Greater than	`7 > 1 // true`
`>=`	Greater than or equal to	`7 >= 7 // true`
`<`	Less than	`7 < 10 // true`
`<=`	Less than or equal to	`2 <= 2 // true`

The equality and inequality operators (== and !=, respectively) compare only the values of the left and right operands. When possible, they change the type of the operand on the right to match the operand on the left. From the standpoint of JavaScript, this behavior is friendly, but it results in some strange behaviors that can cause bugs in a program.

For example, using the equality operator, the following statement evaluates to `true`:

```
0 == "0"
```

In reality, the number `0` is not the same as a string containing a `0`. Relying on JavaScript to automatically convert a string (for example, from a form input) to a number might not break your program, but it's bad coding practice to use a string where you mean to use a number (or vice versa). For this reason, most JavaScript developers never use the == and != operators. Instead, you should explicitly convert strings to numbers (by using `parseInt()` or `parseFloat()`) or convert numbers to strings (using `toString()`) and use the strict equality and strict inequality operators, like this:

```
a = parseInt("3");
b = parseInt("3");
a === b
```

Arithmetic operators

The arithmetic operators perform mathematical operations and return the results. Table 4-2 shows the complete list of arithmetic operators.

TABLE 4-2 **Arithmetic Operators**

Operator	Description	Example
+	Addition	`a = 1 + 1`
-	Subtraction	`a = 10 - 1`
*	Multiplication	`a = 2 * 2`
/	Division	`a = 8 / 2`
%	Remainder	`a = 5 % 2`

Operator	Description	Example
++	Increment	a = ++b a = b++ a++
--	Decrement	a = --b a = b-- a--
**	Exponentiation operator	2 ** 2

Concatenation operator

The concatenation operator uses the same symbol as the addition operator (+). When used with two strings, this operator joins the strings:

```
let yourName = "Marcellus L. Benfield";
let welcomeMessage = "Welcome, " + yourName;
```

Like the equality operator, the concatenation operator attempts to do type coercion whenever possible. For example:

```
let numberOfHats = 10;
console.log('Harriet has ' + numberOfHats + ' hats.');
```

As with the equality operator, however, there is danger in not specifically converting all values in an expression to the correct type. For example, if you try to add two numbers and one of the operators is a string, the results may not be what you want:

```
let sum = 1+"1"; // result: "11"
```

To avoid this common problem, you can explicitly convert operands to the correct type:

```
let sum = 1 + parseInt("1"); // result: 2
```

Logical operators

Logical operators evaluate an expression for truthiness or falsiness. There are three logical operators, as shown in Table 4-3.

TABLE 4-3 **Logical Operators**

Operator	What It Means	What It Does
&&	AND	Returns the first falsy operand. If all values are truthy, it returns the value of the last operand.
||	OR	Returns the value of the first truthy operand. If all the operands evaluate to false, it returns the last operand.
!	NOT	Takes only one operand. Returns `false` if its operand can be converted to `true`. Otherwise, it returns `true`.

The logical AND and OR operators also have clever additional uses. You can use the `||` operator to set a variable to a default value, like this:

```
let language = userPreference.language || 'English';
```

This statement sets the language to the user-specified language if the user has set one; otherwise, it sets language to `'English'`.

The `&&` operator can be used to choose between two paths, like this:

```
let logInScreen = !loggedIn && showLogInScreen();
```

In this example, if the `loggedIn` variable is falsy, the `showLogInScreen()` function will run. This way of using `&&` to switch between two paths is commonly used in JavaScript to do conditional rendering. In *conditional rendering*, some piece of the user interface (such as a login form) should be displayed in the browser only if a certain condition is `true`. In the preceding example, the condition you're testing for is whether the value of `loggedIn` is `false`.

TECHNICAL STUFF

The `||` and `&&` operators are known as *short-circuit* operators because they stop executing and return a value when they find a truthy value (in the case of `||`) or a falsy value (in the case of `&&`).

The logical NOT operator (`!`) is often used to test whether a variable hasn't been initialized or is `false`:

```
if (!isRegistered) { alert ("Register now!"); }
```

You can use two NOT operators to convert any value to its Boolean equivalent:

```
!!"I like cheese" // returns true
```

Combining operators

You can combine the assignment operator with other operators as a shorthand method of assigning the result of an expression to a variable or constant. For example, the following statements are equivalent:

```
score = score + 1;
score += 1;
```

To form the combination operators, the assignment operator is always on the right, and the other operator is on the left.

Other Operators

JavaScript contains many other operators in addition to the ones mentioned here. Many of these operators are used when working with arrays and objects, which are described in Chapters 6 and 7, respectively, of this minibook.

Some operators that are part of JavaScript are rarely used by JavaScript developers. For example, the bitwise operators can be used to work with data at the level of its individual bits. Working with numbers as bits is faster than using JavaScript's built-in number and math functions. However, few JavaScript programmers ever need to use bitwise operators, and using them is likely to confuse other people who read your code. (For example, two bitwise operator symbols are `|` and `&`, which are easily confused with the logical OR and AND operators.)

IN THIS CHAPTER

» Using `if` and `else`

» Considering your options with `switch`

» Creating loops

» Breaking and continuing loops

Chapter 5 Controlling Flow

"When you have to make a choice and don't make it, that is in itself a choice."

—WILLIAM JAMES

In previous chapters, you may have read about JavaScript variables, expressions, and statements. These are the essential building blocks of every JavaScript program. However, without the capability to make decisions between various statements, or to repeat statements, programming would be much less interesting. In this chapter, you learn about looping and branching statements.

Choosing a Path

Conditional statements, also known as *branching statements,* allow you to write code that performs various actions based on various conditions.

if . . . else statements

The `if` and `else` statements evaluate an expression and then run one block of code if the expression is truthy and another block of code if it's falsy. For example, if you want to customize the display of the current temperature, you could write the following statement:

```
if (country === "United States" || country === "Liberia"){
temperature = temperature + "F";
} else {
temperature = (temperature - 32) * 5 / 9 + "C";
}
```

Sometimes, you want to either do something or not do it, rather than make a choice between two options. In that case, you can just use an `if` statement:

```
if (coffeeMakerIsOff) {
turnOnCoffeeMaker();
}
```

Multiple paths with if else

At other times, you may want to choose between several options. For this, you can string together `if` and `else` statements. For example:

```
if (pet === 'cat') {
greeting = 'Good kitty';
} else if (pet === 'dog') {
greeting = 'Who\'s a good boy or girl?';
} else if (pet === 'parrot') {
greeting = 'Wanna cracker?';
} else {
greeting = 'Hi.';
}
```

The ternary operator

Conditional statements can also be written using the conditional (or ternary) operator. The conditional operator shortens `if ... else` statements to a single expression, which is often useful when doing conditional rendering with ReactJS, Vue.js, or Svelte.

To use the conditional operator, write a condition followed by a question mark. After the question mark comes the expression that will run if the condition is `true`. Follow that expression with a colon and then the expression to run if the condition is `false`:

```
const dt = new Date();
const hours = dt.getHours();
let msg;
msg = hours < 12 ? ('Good morning!') : ('Welcome');
console.log(msg);
```

Assuming that the `hours` variable uses the 24-hour clock, the preceding example returns `'Good morning!'` before noon and a generic greeting otherwise.

REMEMBER

You can try out this code by typing or pasting it into your JavaScript console. All the code from this book is also available for download at `www.dummies.com/go/codingaiofd3e`.

Note that the ternary operator can be used only to switch between two choices. If your code needs to decide between more than two outcomes, use the `if ... else` statements or the `switch` statement, which you can read about in the next section.

Switch statements

The `switch` statement decides which statement to run based on the result of a single expression. Each possible outcome of a `switch` statement is called a `case`. Here's the syntax for the `switch` statement:

```
switch(expression){
case x:
// code to run when expression === x
break;
case y:
// code to run when expression === y
break;
default:
// code to run if nothing else matches expression
}
```

In Listing 5-1, I created a program that displays a different holiday based on the current month of the year. In addition to showing how the `switch` statement works, this example demonstrates how to use JavaScript to display text in a web browser. To try it out, use VS Code to save it as an `.html` file and then open it in a web browser. To view the file in a browser, right-click the filename in the VS Code Explorer pane and select Open in Live Server.

LISTING 5-1: **Using the switch Statement**

```
<!DOCTYPE html>
<html lang="en">
  <head>
    <meta charset="UTF-8"/>
    <meta http-equiv="X-UA-Compatible" content="IE=edge"/>
    <meta name="viewport" content="width=device-width,
   initial-scale=1.0"/>
    <title>Holiday Finder</title>
  </head>
  <body>
    <div id="message"></div>
    <script>
      const dt = new Date();
      const month = dt.getMonth();
      let msg;
      switch (month) {
        case 0:
          msg = "January 4 is National Spaghetti Day!";
          break;
        case 1:
          msg = "February 9 is National Pizza Day!";
          break;
        case 2:
          msg = "March 26 is National Spinach Day!";
          break;
        case 3:
          msg = "April 26 is National Pretzel Day!";
          break;
        default:
          msg = "No holidays this month.";
      }
      const el = document.getElementById("message");
      el.innerHTML = msg;
    </script>
  </body>
</html>
```

Let's walk through this code in detail to understand how `switch` works and to start learning how to write front-end web applications. A *front-end web application* is code that runs in the browser and interacts directly with the web page — making the page respond to user actions, display messages, or update content. Unlike running JavaScript commands in the console, writing JavaScript for a front-end web application means your code connects with the website itself, creating an interactive experience for users.

TIP

Read this section carefully — I introduce a lot of new topics that are important to understanding how front-end JavaScript works. I cover all these topics in much more detail throughout this book, but I'm introducing them here so that you can start working with more complex examples in Chapter 6.

Just above the <script> tag, note the `div` element with an `id` of `message`. Inside this element is where you display the program's output.

After the message `div` element is the `script` element that contains the program. The fact that the `script` element comes after the HTML element where its output will be rendered is important. Because the code in an HTML file is interpreted from top (the beginning of the file) to bottom (the end of the file), if you want to output something inside the HTML code, you have to wait until that HTML code has been read and rendered by the browser first.

The first line of the JavaScript program uses the `Date()` function to find out the current date on the user's computer:

```
const dt = new Date();
```

`Date()` is what's known as a *constructor* function in JavaScript: When you use it with the `new` keyword, it returns a new date object. The date object contains the current date as well as properties and functionality having to do with dates.

The `getMonth()` function runs with the returned date:

```
const month = dt.getMonth();
```

The `getMonth()` function is part of every date object. To use it, attach it to any `date` object with a period (`.`), and don't forget to add the parentheses after it. The parentheses tell JavaScript to make a function do its thing.

REMEMBER

JavaScript counts from 0, so the first month of the year is number 0!

Next, a variable named `msg` is declared but not initialized.

TECHNICAL STUFF

Putting the script after the HTML that it affects is one way to cause the browser to wait until the HTML document is rendered before running the JavaScript. It's often the simplest way, however, so it's commonly used.

Next, the switch statement begins, and the month variable's value is passed into it:

```
switch(month){
```

REMEMBER

The curly braces set off a block of JavaScript. In this case, the block contains the switch statement's cases.

The first case says what to do if the value of month is 0:

```
case 0:
```

If the value of month is 0, any statements after the colon at the end of the case are run, until JavaScript encounters either a break statement (which stops execution of the switch statement) or the ending curly brace containing the switch cases.

Next, we set the value of msg:

```
msg = 'January 4 is National Spaghetti Day!';
```

The break statement ends the evaluation of the switch statement and jumps directly to the next statement after the closing curly bracket.

WARNING

One common cause of bugs in JavaScript is forgetting to include a break statement before each case in a switch statement. If you don't include the break statement, the switch statement runs the code after each case after one of them evaluates to true.

If none of the cases match the value of month, the default case runs and sets the value of msg to a default message:

```
default:
msg = 'No holidays this month.';
```

Note that the break statement isn't required after the default case because there are no more cases after it to skip over.

The next statement locates the HTML element where you want to render the message and assigns it to a constant named el.

```
const el = document.getElementById('message');
```

The `innerHTML` property, which contains the HTML between the element's starting and ending tags, is changed to the value of the `msg` variable:

```
el.innerHTML = msg;
```

Because nothing now appears between the `<div id="message">` and `</div>` tags, the message is just inserted between them. What do you think would happen if there was already text between the starting and ending `div` tags, like this:

```
<div id="message">put some message here</div>
```

Once you have a guess, go ahead and try it. Modify your HTML file to put some text between the starting and ending `div` tags. If you have the file open in your browser using Live Server, you should see the result instantly. Or, rather, you should see no difference. By changing the `innerHTML` property of the `div` element, you overwrite what was there with the new value.

REMEMBER

This simple example demonstrates the fundamental technique used by every front-end JavaScript library to modify the content displayed in the browser window.

Making Loops

One thing that makes computers so useful is that they can do the same thing over and over without getting bored. *Looping statements*, also known as *iterative statements*, make telling a computer to do the same thing over and over much easier.

Imagine that you want to write a program to count to 100 and output each number to the browser console. One way (one very tedious and inefficient way, I should say) would be to write 101 statements, like this:

```
let x = 0;
console.log(++x);
console.log(++x);
console.log(++x);
console.log(++x);
// you get the idea
```

Note that the increment (++) operator in the preceding code example appears in front of the variable it's incrementing. This is called *prefix notation*, in which the operation (adding `1` to `x`) is done before logging the value of `x` to the console. If you put the `++` after `x` (`x++`), that's called *postfix notation*. Try changing this example to use postfix notation, and then run it in your browser console to see what happens.

To make repeating statements easier, JavaScript provides several different types of looping statements, including these:

- `for`
- `for...in`
- `for...of`
- `do...while`
- `while`

for loops

The `for` statement uses three expressions in parentheses after the `for` keyword to create a loop:

- **Initialization:** The initial value of a variable. This variable is usually a counter.
- **Condition:** A Boolean expression that determines whether to run the loop's statements.
- **Final expression:** An expression to be evaluated following each iteration of the loop. This expression is typically used to increment a counter.

The `for` loop is usually used to loop over code a predetermined number of times. Here's how you can write a `for` loop to do the counting-to-100 example from the earlier section "Making Loops:"

```
for(let i=1; i <= 100; i++) {
console.log(i);
}
```

Here's how this loop works. First, a new block-scoped variable called `i` is initialized with a value of `1`.

Then the second expression tests the variable to see whether it's less than or equal to 100. If it is, the statements in the block are executed. If it isn't, the loop exits.

Note that because the i variable is block-scoped, it's available only inside the for loop. This is a good thing.

After the code in the for block executes, the final expression runs, incrementing the counter. Then the test is repeated.

TIP

In practice, for loops are unpopular with experienced JavaScript developers. Like using the var keyword, for loops are an old way to do things and shouldn't be used. There's usually a more modern and simpler syntax for doing the same thing that for loops do. You can learn about some of these in this chapter, and learn about other methods that are better for looping through arrays in Chapter 6.

for . . . in loops

The for . . . in loop iterates over the properties of an object and the properties it inherits from its parent object. Because arrays are types of objects, it's possible to use for . . . in loops to loop over the elements in an array as well.

REMEMBER

Objects contain multiple values, called *properties*, which may hold any type of JavaScript data, including strings, numbers, Booleans, arrays, and even other objects.

To see how for . . . in works, start with the following simple object:

```
const house = {sqft:800, bdRooms:2, bthRooms:1}
```

Listing 5-2 shows how you could write a web page that displays all the properties of this object.

LISTING 5-2: Using for . . . in to Display an Object's Properties

```
<!DOCTYPE html>
<html lang="en">
  <head>
    <meta charset="UTF-8"/>
    <meta http-equiv="X-UA-Compatible" content="IE=edge"/>
    <meta name="viewport" content="width=device-width, initial-scale=1.0"/>
    <title>House Details</title>
  </head>
  <body>
    <div id="root"></div>
    <script>
      const house = { sqft: 800, bdRooms: 2, bthRooms: 1 };
```

(continued)

LISTING 5-2: (continued)

```
      let houseDetails = "<h2>Information about this house</h2>";
      for (let prop in house) {
        houseDetails = `${houseDetails}<br>${prop}:${house[prop]}<br>`;
        document.getElementById("root").innerHTML = houseDetails;
      }
    </script>
  </body>
</html>
```

WARNING

Like for loops, for . . . in loops aren't often used in JavaScript, because you can find better and more modern ways to do anything that you might want to use for . . . in to do. Also, for . . . in loops loop over the properties of their parent object, which is usually not what you want to do. In practice, for . . . in loops are mostly useful for debugging your code.

for . . . of loops

The for . . . of loop creates a loop by iterating over any iterable object. What's an iterable object, you ask? An *iterable object* is an object that can be iterated over. Examples of iterable objects include arrays and strings.

Before for . . . of was introduced into JavaScript in 2015, the way to iterate over arrays was by using the for loop, for . . . in, or the forEach method. Here's an example of using a for . . . of loop to loop over the elements of an array:

```
const pets = ['cat', 'dog', 'chicken'];
for (let pet of pets) {
console.log(pet);
}
```

The result of running the preceding code in the JavaScript console is shown in Figure 5-1.

```
> const pets = ['cat','dog','chicken'];
< undefined
> for (let pet of pets) {
      console.log(pet);
  }
  cat                                                    VM215:2
  dog                                                    VM215:2
  chicken                                                VM215:2
< undefined
```

FIGURE 5-1: Looping over an array's elements.

Strings can be treated as arrays of characters, so the same syntax that's used to loop over an array can be also used for strings:

```
let text = "spell me.";
for (let character of text) {
console.log(character);
}
```

Figure 5-2 shows what this snippet does when run in the JavaScript console.

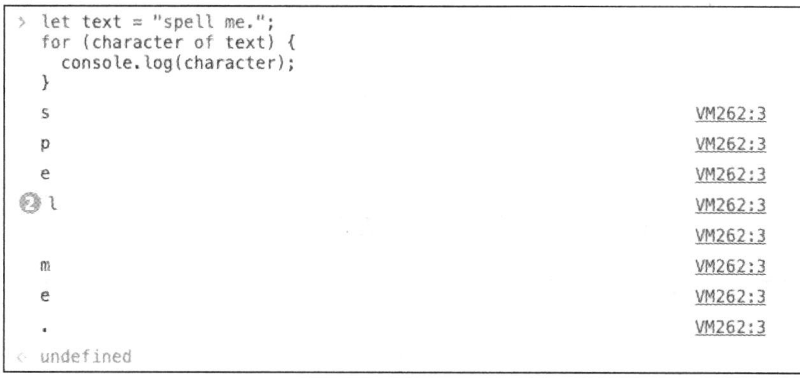

FIGURE 5-2: Iterating over a string.

while loops

The `while` statement creates a loop that repeats a block of code if a specified condition evaluates to `true`. In Listing 5-3, a loop created using `while` generates a random number between 0 and 99 on every pass through the loop. The loop continues until the random number is 71, and then the loop exits and outputs however many loops it needed to make.

LISTING 5-3: A Random-Number Guessing Game

```
<!DOCTYPE html>
<html lang="en">
  <head>
    <meta charset="UTF-8"/>
    <meta http-equiv="X-UA-Compatible" content="IE=edge"/>
    <meta name="viewport" content="width=device-width, initial-scale=1.0"/>
    <title>Random Number with a while Loop</title>
  </head>
  <body>
    <div id="root"></div>
```

(continued)

LISTING 5-3: (continued)

```
    <script>
      let guessNumber = 0;
      let numberToGuess = 71;
      let guess;
      while (guess != numberToGuess) {
        guess = Math.floor(Math.random() * 100);
        guessNumber++;
      }
      document.getElementById("root").innerHTML = `
<h2>I guessed it!</h2>
<p>It only took me ${guessNumber} guesses!</p>`;
    </script>
  </body>
</html>
```

do . . . while loops

A `do . . . while` loop works the same as a `while` loop, except that the condition goes after the code block. As a result, the code between the `do . . . while`'s curly braces is guaranteed to run at least once.

Listing 5-4 shows an improved version of the number guessing game. The difference here is that with the standard `while` loop, the answer is checked before the first random number is created. In a `do . . . while` loop, a random number is first created and then tested.

LISTING 5-4: A Random-Number Guessing Game with do . . . while

```
<!DOCTYPE html>
<html lang="en">
  <head>
    <meta charset="UTF-8"/>
    <meta http-equiv="X-UA-Compatible" content="IE=edge"/>
    <meta name="viewport" content="width=device-width, initial-scale=1.0"/>
    <title>Random Number with a do ... while Loop</title>
  </head>
  <body>
    <div id="root"></div>
    <script>
      let guessNumber = 0;
      let numberToGuess = 71;
      let guess;
```

```
      do {
        guess = Math.floor(Math.random() * 100);
        guessNumber++;
      } while (guess != numberToGuess);
      document.getElementById("root").innerHTML = `
        <h2>I guessed it!</h2>
        <p>It only took me ${guessNumber} guesses!</p>`;
    </script>
  </body>
</html>
```


break and continue statements

The `break` and `continue` statements can be used to interrupt the execution of a loop. The `break` statement causes the current loop or control statement to exit. I described *break* earlier in the chapter, where I tell you about the `switch` statement.

The `continue` statement halts execution of the current iteration of the loop and goes directly to the next one. For example, in the following code, `continue` is used to loop over the digits in a phone number and remove hyphens from it:

```
let phoneNumber = "555-757-1212";
for (let digit of phoneNumber) {
if (digit==='-') continue;
console.log(digit);
}
```

IN THIS CHAPTER

» **Creating, accessing, and modifying arrays**

» **Removing array elements**

» **Programming and looping with array methods**

» **Destructuring and spreading arrays**

Chapter 6
Using Arrays

"I am large. I contain multitudes."

—WALT WHITMAN

Most of the data I describe how to work with earlier in this minibook is in the form of simple variables and constants that store a single value. However, it's common in programming, and in life, to need to store lists of related items under a single name. Think about the following common lists that many people use daily:

- Mailing lists and contacts
- Grocery lists
- To-do lists
- Lists of favorite songs
- The list of items on an invoice or a receipt
- The list of chapters in a book

In each case, without the ability to collect individual pieces of data into a list, you'd just have sticky notes scattered all over the place and in no order (a bit like my desk).

Think for a moment about your favorite apps and websites. Whether it's a blog, a social media site, or your daily run log app, a large part of the app is dedicated to presenting data as lists. The data that powers these apps behind the scenes is stored in databases, which are nothing but sophisticated ways of storing lists. Server-side code retrieves data from these databases and sends it as a list to the front-end JavaScript program, which transforms this raw list data and displays it to you.

To make lists of data in JavaScript, we use a special type of object called an array. In this chapter, you learn how arrays work, and how to create them, add and remove items, and access their elements. You also discover how arrays can help you organize and manipulate lists of data efficiently in your programs.

Introducing Arrays

Arrays are made up of elements. If an array is like a list, an element is like a single item in the list. Arrays keep track of their elements by assigning each element a number, called the *index*.

For example, you can create an array of color names, like this:

```
const colors = ['red','green','blue'];
```

If you enter this statement into your JavaScript console, an array with three elements is created, as you can verify by entering the name of the array into the console, as shown in Figure 6-1.

```
> const colors = ['red','green','blue'];
< undefined
> colors
< ▾(3) ['red', 'green', 'blue']
      0: "red"
      1: "green"
      2: "blue"
      length: 3
    ▸ [[Prototype]]: Array(0)
>
```

FIGURE 6-1: Creating and viewing an array in the console.

In Figure 6-1, you can see a few important aspects of this array and about arrays in general:

- This array has three elements, so it's said to have a *length* of 3.
- The array's elements are numbered starting with 0, which is called *zero-based* numbering.
- Every array shares certain *properties* (or things it has, such as a size or a length) and *methods* (things you can do with it or it can do, such as sort). Arrays have so much in common because they share a common parent, or *prototype*. The prototype for an array is the `Array` object. When you create an array (or any object), JavaScript makes a copy of the `Array` object. You can see these properties and methods that an array inherits from its prototype by clicking the arrow in the console to expand the `Prototype` object, as shown in Figure 6-2.

```
▾ [[Prototype]]: Array(0)
  ▸ at: ƒ at()
  ▸ concat: ƒ concat()
  ▸ constructor: ƒ Array()
  ▸ copyWithin: ƒ copyWithin()
  ▸ entries: ƒ entries()
  ▸ every: ƒ every()
  ▸ fill: ƒ fill()
  ▸ filter: ƒ filter()
  ▸ find: ƒ find()
  ▸ findIndex: ƒ findIndex()
  ▸ findLast: ƒ findLast()
  ▸ findLastIndex: ƒ findLastIndex()
  ▸ flat: ƒ flat()
  ▸ flatMap: ƒ flatMap()
  ▸ forEach: ƒ forEach()
```

FIGURE 6-2: Viewing the properties of the `Array` object.

REMEMBER

The properties and methods of the `Array` object are what make arrays useful. You read later in this chapter about the most important of these properties and how they're used in JavaScript programming.

In the preceding example, the `color` array stores three strings. Arrays aren't limited to storing just one type of data, however. Elements in an array can contain any combination of different data types.

The upper limit of the number of elements an array can hold is over 4 million. So, unless you are extremely popular and have a giant address book or are extremely busy and have the world's longest to-do list, you're unlikely to exceed the maximum.

You'll likely run into performance problems trying to work with a huge array long before you run up against the upper limit of array elements. If you do need to store more than the maximum number of elements a single array can hold, it might be time to look at breaking that list into smaller categories.

Creating Arrays

JavaScript contains three ways to create arrays. You can use:

- The `Array()` constructor
- Array literal notation
- Functions that return arrays, such as `split()`

Using the Array() constructor

A *constructor* function is one that creates and initializes an object. In the case of the `Array()` constructor, it returns a new array object. To use a constructor function, use the `new` operator with the name of the constructor function followed by open and close parentheses:

```
new Array();
```

To make this new array usable, you need to assign it to a variable or constant:

```
const myArray = new Array();
```

You can create elements in the array by passing a list of values to the function, like this:

```
const myArray = new Array('January','February','March');
```

REMEMBER

Programmers commonly use `const` to define array variables. The constant value is the array itself, not the elements inside the array, which you can change.

TECHNICAL STUFF

Programmers say that the array assigned to a constant is *immutable* and that the elements in the array are *mutable*.

The constructor function is a perfectly fine way to make arrays. In fact, the constructor function can be used to make strings, numbers, and Booleans as well. However, most JavaScript programmers don't use constructor functions for these basic data types because they have simpler ways to do the same thing — namely, by assigning the values using literal notation.

Using array literal notation

Array *literal notation* uses a comma-separated list of values inside square brackets to create and initialize an array, like this:

```
const myArray = ["eggs","bacon","toast"];
```

Unlike with the constructor function method, array literal notation doesn't require you to use the `new` operator, so you have one less opportunity to make a typo.

Using the split function

The `split()` function makes an array out of a string. To use `split()`, give it the character (or characters) that you want to use to split the string. For example, if you have a text file containing comma-separated values, you can turn it into an array by splitting it on the comma:

```
let customerData = 'Barb Seibert,3739 Sheila
  Lane,Goldfield,NV,89013';
const customerDataArray = customerData.split(',');
```

Comma-separated value files (also known as CSV files) can be created from spreadsheets or database tables, and knowing how to use `split()` to turn CSV data into arrays that you can work with in JavaScript is important for any programmer.

Be careful when splitting comma-separated data. If any values in the string contain commas and you split it on commas, you'll corrupt the data. For example, try splitting the following string:

```
let customerData = "Barb Seibert, Esq.,3739 Sheila
  Lane,Goldfield,NV,89013";
```

Do you see the problem with this string? A human reading this file will know that `, Esq.` is meant to be part of the name, but the `split()` function doesn't distinguish between commas.

For this reason, comma-separated files should also enclose each value in quotes. You might think you can then split the string based on a comma surrounded by quotes, like this:

```
let customerData = "'Barb Seibert, Esq.','3739 Sheila Lane',
   'Goldfield','NV','89013'";
let customerDataArray = customerData.split("','");
```

However, this method will produce the following array:

```
["'Barb Seibert, Esq.", '3739 Sheila Lane', 'Goldfield', 'NV',
   "89013'"]
```

The quotes at the beginning of the first element and at the end of the last element weren't stripped out by the `slice()` function.

Writing a statement to successfully convert any type of comma-separated data into a string can become complicated. For that reason, you're better off finding a tried-and-true method, such as `convert-csv-to-array`, which is available at `www.npmjs.com/package/convert-csv-to-array`.

Accessing Array Elements

Once you have an array, the next thing to know is how to find out the values of specific elements. To get the value of a single element, use the array name followed by square brackets containing the index number of the element you want to find out.

For example, if you create this array:

```
const myArray = [43,299,34];
```

you can get the second number by using the following expression:

```
myArray[1];
```

It's common to need to know how many elements are in an array before you access its elements. To do this, you can use the `length` property of the array, like this:

```
myArray.length;
```

This statement returns the number of elements in the array. The index number of the array is the length minus 1. So, if you want to use a `for` loop to loop over all elements in an array and add them, you can do it like this:

```
const myArray = [3434,56,2];
let sum = 0;
for (let i = 0; i<myArray.length; i++){
sum += myArray[i];
}
console.log(`The sum is ${sum}`);
```

The best way to loop over an array to calculate a sum, however, is to use the `reduce()` method, which I describe later in the chapter.

Modifying Arrays

To modify the values of array elements or add elements to arrays, you can use the assignment operator. For example, to change the value of the element with an index number of 1 to `'sandwich'`, use the following statement:

```
myArray[1] = 'sandwich';
```

You can use this same technique to add elements to an array:

```
myArray[3] = 'burrito';
```

When adding elements to an array, it's not a requirement to always add it using the next index number. If you have an array with three elements in it, for example, you can use the following statement to add an element with an index number of 1000:

```
myArray[1000] = 'sushi';
```

However, when you do this, JavaScript automatically creates all the elements between the previously highest index number and the new one and gives them values of `undefined`. You can test this statement by checking the `length` property on the array:

```
myArray.length // returns 1001
```

An array with elements inside it that are `undefined` is called a *sparse array.*

Deleting Array Elements

In day-to-day code, you usually remove items from arrays by using array methods that either change the original array on purpose or return a new array.

WARNING

Avoid making "holes" in arrays (sparse arrays) because they can lead to confusing results when you loop over the array.

Following are the two best ways to remove array elements:

- **Remove by index (changes the array).** Use `splice()` to remove one or more elements. For example:

```
myArray.splice(3, 1); // removes one element at index 3
```

- **Remove without changing the original array.** Use `toSpliced()` or `filter()` to produce a new array. For example:

```
const newArray = myArray.toSpliced(3, 1); // returns a new array with
   index 3 removed
```

Avoid `delete myArray[index]` for array elements; it leaves an empty slot and creates a sparse array. Also avoid changing the length to remove items unless you want to truncate an array (for example, clearing a working array or dropping everything after a cutoff). You learn more about the methods mentioned in this section in the next section.

Programming with Array Methods

Arrays include numerous functions that make accomplishing tasks with them easier. Although it's possible to use various loops, operators, and conditional statements to do everything that built-in array functions can do, knowing how to use the most important array functions will make your life easier.

Table 6-1 lists the most-used array functions, along with descriptions of what they do or the values they produce.

TABLE 6-1 JavaScript Array Methods

Method	Return Value
concat()	A new array made up of the current array, joined with other arrays or values or both
every()	true if every element in the given array satisfies the provided testing function
filter()	A new array with all the elements of a current array that test true by the given function
forEach()	Completes the function once for each element in the array
includes()	Determines whether an array includes a specified value and returns true or false
indexOf()	Finds the first occurrence of the specified value within the array; returns -1 if the value is not found
join()	Joins all elements of an array into a string
lastIndexOf()	Finds the last occurrence of the specified value within the array; returns -1 if the value is not found
map()	Creates a new array with the result of a provided function on every element in the array
pop()	Removes the last element in an array
push()	Adds new items to the end of an array
reduce()	Reduces the values in an array to a single value by applying a function to them (from left to right)
reverse()	Reverses the order of elements in an array
shift()	Removes the first element from an array and returns that element, resulting in a change in the length of an array
slice()	Selects a portion of an array and returns it as a new array
some()	Returns true if one or more elements satisfy the provided testing function
sort()	Sorts an array in place and returns a reference to the same sorted array
splice()	Returns a new array composed of elements that were added or removed from a given array
toString()	Converts an array to a string
unshift()	Returns a new array with a new length by the addition of one or more elements

In the following sections, I explain and demonstrate the array methods that you're most likely to encounter or need. If you want to follow along in your JavaScript console, start by creating an array to work with. I'll use the following array, containing the ingredients for a frittata, for all examples in this section:

```
const ingredients = ['eggs','milk','cheese','garlic','onion','kale','salt',
    'pepper'];
```

Pushing and popping

Pushing and popping aren't dance moves; they're what programmers call the processes of, respectively, adding elements to and removing elements from the end of an array. The `push()` function pushes items into the list, and `pop()` pops them out.

The `pop()` method removes the last element and returns the removed element. If all you want to do is remove the last element, you can do that like this:

```
ingredients.pop();
```

After calling `pop()`, the `ingredients` array is one item shorter, as shown in Figure 6-3.

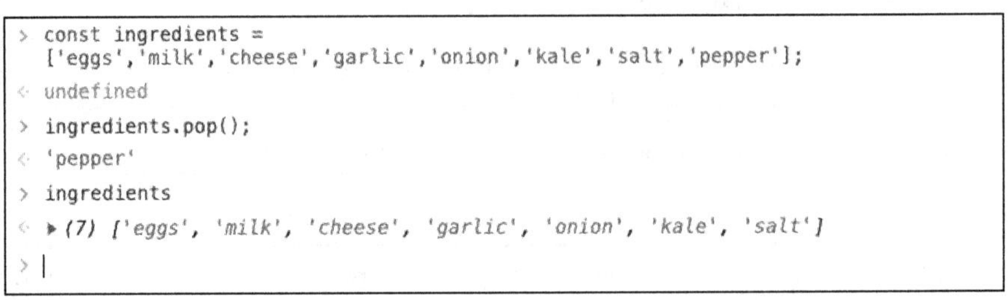

FIGURE 6-3: Popping removes the last element.

If you want to remove the last element and then do something with the removed element, you can assign the result of the pop method to a new variable:

```
let removedElement = ingredients.pop();
```

The `push` method adds a value as a new element and returns the new length of the array:

```
ingredients.push('chili flakes');
```

Figure 6-4 shows the result of pushing chili flakes into the ingredients list.

```
> ingredients.push('chili flakes');
< 8
> ingredients
< ▸(8) ['eggs', 'milk', 'cheese', 'garlic', 'onion', 'kale', 'salt', 'chili fla
  kes']
> |
```

FIGURE 6-4: Pushing adds a new element.

Shifting and unshifting

Shifting works the same as popping and pushing, but it does its work at the beginning of the array. The `shift()` method removes the first element and returns the removed value.

You can use `shift()` the same way you use `pop()`:

```
ingredients.shift();
```

Figure 6-5 shows the result of shifting an array.

WHAT'S THE DEAL WITH THESE METHOD NAMES?

Push, pop, `shift`, and `unshift` are some of the method names that are the hardest to keep straight in JavaScript. It would have been so much easier if `push()` were named `append()` and `unshift()` were named `prepend()`.

These names date to the early days of computing, when the terms referred to operations done to the stack. You can think of an array as a stack of plates; to get to a plate in the middle of the stack, you have to move the ones above it first. If you want the most recently added item, you can just pop it off the top. The same goes for adding plates — when you push a new plate onto the stack, it goes on top.

If you remove a plate from the bottom of the stack, all the plates above it shift downward. Adding a plate to the bottom unshifts the plates above it. I don't know whether anyone has ever come up with a good explanation for that name, except that unshifting is the opposite of shifting.

```
> ingredients.shift();
<· 'eggs'
> ingredients
<· ▸(7) ['milk', 'cheese', 'garlic', 'onion', 'kale', 'salt', 'chili flakes']
> |
```

FIGURE 6-5: Shifting removes an element from the beginning of an array.

Just as push() adds an element to the end of an array and returns the new length, unshift() adds an element to the beginning and returns the new length. Let's say you realize that it was a mistake to remove the eggs from the frittata recipe:

```
ingredients.unshift('eggs');
```

Figure 6-6 shows the result.

```
> ingredients.unshift('eggs');
<· 8
> ingredients
<· ▸(8) ['eggs', 'milk', 'cheese', 'garlic', 'onion', 'kale', 'salt', 'chili fla
   kes']
>
```

FIGURE 6-6: Unshifting adds an element to the beginning of the array.

Slicing an array

The slice() method selects a portion of the array and returns a new array with just that portion. To use slice(), give it the starting element's index number and the ending element's index number. The new array contains everything from the starting element to the element before the ending element.

REMEMBER

Think of the process as asking for three slices of pizza by saying "I'd like from this slice to this slice." The difference, however, is that when using slice(), the original array isn't modified:

```
ingredients.slice(3,6);
```

Figure 6-7 shows how to make a new array from the middle of the ingredients array.

```
> ingredients.slice(3,6);
<· ▸(3) ['garlic', 'onion', 'kale']
> ingredients
<· ▸(8) ['eggs', 'milk', 'cheese', 'garlic', 'onion', 'kale', 'salt', 'chili fla
   kes']
>
```

FIGURE 6-7: Slicing returns a portion of an array as a new array.

Splicing an array

The `splice()` method takes a starting element and a number of elements to remove and removes those elements from an array, returning the removed elements:

```
ingredients.splice(3,3);
```

Figure 6-8 shows how you can use `splice()` to separate an array into two arrays.

```
> const produce = ingredients.splice(3,3);
< undefined
> produce
< ▶ (3) ['garlic', 'onion', 'kale']
> ingredients
< ▶ (5) ['eggs', 'milk', 'cheese', 'salt', 'pepper']
```

FIGURE 6-8: Splicing removes a number of elements from an array.

Looping with Array Methods

Several array methods make looping over the elements in an array easier. In front-end libraries such as ReactJS, Vue.js, and Svelte, you're sure to need a couple of these daily, so it pays to learn them.

Passing callback functions to array methods

Each of the methods in this section loops over an array and uses a callback function to do its work. You can read much more about functions and callback functions in Chapter 8.

A *function* is a program within your program. It receives data and does something with it. As with any program, a function stops running when it's done with its job, and it may return some data to the rest of the program.

So far in this minibook, I've told you how to use functions that are built into JavaScript — such as array functions, string functions, number functions, and Boolean functions.

You can also write custom functions in JavaScript. In fact, writing custom functions is one of the most important and common things you'll do as a JavaScript programmer. Here's an example of a simple function that receives a number as an argument and returns the square of that number:

```
function squareIt(num){
return num*num;
}
```

To use this function, you run it by using its name (squareIt) followed by parentheses. Using a function is also called *invoking* or *calling* the function. You pass data into the function by placing it between the parentheses.

For example, to use the custom squareIt() function to square the number 3, you'd call the function like this:

```
squareIt(3);
```

To get the value returned by the function out of the function, however, you also need to assign it to a variable:

```
let threeSquared = squareIt(3);
```

A *callback function* is a function you pass to another function. Callback functions make functions much more flexible because you can pass not only values but also new functionality into the function.

For example, the following is a function that takes a value and a callback function:

```
function doMath(value,mathToDo){
let result = mathToDo(value);
return result;
}
```

With this function, the doMath() function can have multiple purposes. For example, if you wanted to use it to calculate the circumference of a circle from its radius, you could invoke the function like this:

```
const circumference = doMath(4,function(radius){return 2*Math.PI*radius});
```

The result of running this function is shown in Figure 6-9.

```
> function doMath(value,mathToDo){
    let result = mathToDo(value);
    return result;
  }
<· undefined
> const circumference = doMath(4,function(radius){return 2*Math.PI*radius});
<· undefined
> circumference
<· 25.132741228718345
> |
```

FIGURE 6-9: Using a callback function.

Reducing an array

The `reduce()` function runs a reducer function on each element of an array. A *reducer function* reduces an array from multiple values to a single value. For example, we can use a reducer function to calculate the total from a list of prices in an array:

```
let prices = [4.99,3,98,54.99];
let total = 0;
total = prices.reduce(
function(previousValue,currentValue){
return previousValue + currentValue;
}
);
```


This function creates an array of prices and initializes the total to 0. Then it calls the `reduce()` function on the `prices` array and passes it a function that adds the current value to the previous value.

The `reduce()` function calls the passed-in reducer function once for each element in the array and then passes the result of each run into the next call of the function.

You can simplify the code for the `reduce()` function in a couple of ways. First, you can specify an initial value for `previousValue` by passing it as the second value to the `reduce()` function. This approach eliminates the need to initialize `total` to 0 before running `reduce()`:

```
let total = prices.reduce(
function(previousValue,currentValue){
return previousValue + currentValue;
},0
);
```

The second way to simplify calling `reduce()` (and any function that takes a callback function, in fact) is to use arrow syntax for your callback function. *Arrow syntax* (also sometimes called *fat arrow syntax*) uses a symbol created with = and > that looks like an arrow. Here's what calling `reduce()` and passing it an arrow function looks like:

```
let total = prices.reduce(
(previousValue,currentValue) => previousValue + currentValue,0);
```

Mapping an array

The `map()` array function takes a callback function and returns a new array with the result of applying the callback function to each element in the array.

`Array.map()` is used extensively for generating HTML from JavaScript arrays. For example, using the `ingredients` array from earlier in this chapter, you can use `map()` to generate HTML list item elements from the items, like this:

```
const ingredients = [
'eggs',
'milk',
'cheese',
'garlic',
'onion',
'kale',
'salt',
'pepper',
];
let listItems = ingredients.map(
(singleIngredient) => `<li>${singleIngredient}</li>`
);
```

In this example, the new `listItems` array can be used to populate a template and produce a list in the browser. Listing 6-1 shows one way to do that.

LISTING 6-1: Generating an HTML List from an Array

```
<!doctype html>
<html lang="en">
  <head>
    <meta charset="UTF-8"/>
    <meta http-equiv="X-UA-Compatible" content="IE=edge"/>
    <meta name="viewport" content="width=device-width,
          initial-scale=1.0"/>
```

```
    <title>Ingredients List</title>
  </head>
  <body>
    <ul id="ingredients"></ul>
    <script>
      const ingredients = [
        "eggs",
        "milk",
        "cheese",
        "garlic",
        "onion",
        "kale",
        "salt",
        "pepper",
      ];
      let listItems = ingredients
        .map((singleIngredient) => `<li>${singleIngredient}</li>`)
        .join("");
      document.getElementById("ingredients").innerHTML =
  listItems;
    </script>
  </body>
</html>
```

Listing 6-1 uses the `map()` function to create an array of list item elements, and then it uses the `join()` function to join the elements. The `join()` function takes a character to use to separate the items and returns a string. In this case, I used an empty string to join the elements, which creates a string with all list items joined.

Note that in Listing 6-1, the `join()` function is just tacked to the end of the call to `map()`. This is called *chaining function calls.* The result of the `map()` function, in this case, gets passed to the `join()` function.

Filtering arrays

The `filter()` method applies a test to each element of an array and returns a new array with just the elements that passed the test. In the following example, `filter()`finds only the words that start with the letter *a*:

```
const animalNames = [
  'aardvark',
  'alligator',
  'alpaca',
```

```
  'bear',
  'beaver',
  'cat',
  'dog',
  'elephant',
];
const animalsStartingWithA =
  animalNames.filter((animal) => animal.startsWith('a')
);
```

Destructuring Arrays

Destructuring is the process of unpacking values from an array or an object into separate variables. One way to destructure an array is to just create multiple new variables and assign elements from an array to them, like this:

```
const person = ['Russell C. Guy','3447 Twin House Lane','Neosho','MO'];
let personName = person[0];
let address = person[1];
let city = person[2];
let state = person[3];
```

But there's an easier way to initialize these individual variables, all in one step: use destructuring syntax. To use *array destructuring syntax*, create a list of variable names in square brackets on the left side of the assignment operator and specify an array on the right:

```
let [personName,address,city,state] = person;
```

JavaScript extracts elements from the array and assigns their values to the variables in square brackets, starting with the first element and going until the array runs out of elements or the square brackets run out of variables.

Spreading Arrays

Spread syntax expands (or spreads) an iterable object (such as an array) into its component parts. To use spread syntax, preface the name of an array with three dots (`...`). Spread syntax is often used to pass all values of an array into a function or to copy the values from one array into another:

```
const firstArray = ['a','b','c'];
const secondArray = [...firstArray,'d'];
```

A copy of an array created using spread syntax is called a *shallow copy* because it contains just the values from the original array and has no reference to the original array.

Try the following steps in your JavaScript console to understand the importance of shallow copies:

1. **Create an array:**

   ```
   const fruits = ['apple','orange','banana'];
   ```

2. **Make a copy of the array by using the assignment operator:**

   ```
   const fruitsCopy = fruits;
   ```

3. **Add a new element to the copy:**

   ```
   fruitsCopy.push('watermelon');
   ```

4. **Print the elements of the original array:**

   ```
   fruits
   ```

The result of these steps is shown in Figure 6-10.

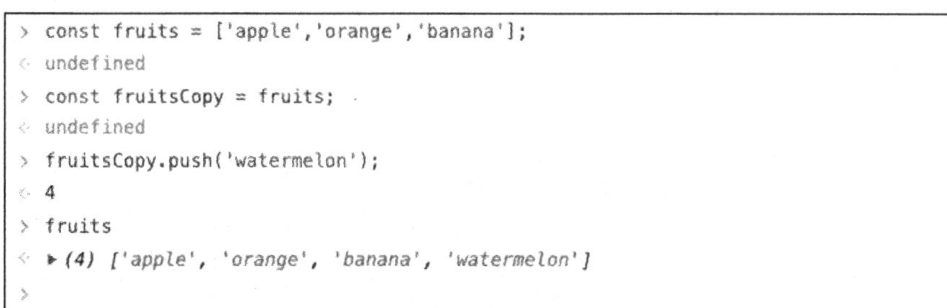

FIGURE 6-10: A copy of an array (or another object) is a reference to the original.

The variable created in the preceding list is a reference to the original array. Frequently, however, you don't want or need a copy of an array to reference the original array. Here's how to make a shallow copy with spread syntax:

```
const fruitsShallowCopy = [...fruits];
```

Now the new array is its own array and the changes you make to it won't affect the original array.

IN THIS CHAPTER

» Understanding objects

» Creating objects in several ways

» Modifying objects using dot or bracket notation

» Comparing and copying objects

Chapter 7

Making and Using Objects

"You can find the entire cosmos lurking in its least remarkable objects."

—WISLAWA SZYMBORSKA

Data is rarely as simple as it seems. To understand any concept or physical object often requires multiple data points. A full description of a toaster, for example, would include its size, color, and power requirements as well as a description of what it does. None of the data types I describe earlier in this minibook can be used to describe a toaster by themselves, but in combination, they can.

In this chapter, you learn how to create, modify, compare, and copy objects in JavaScript. By the end of the chapter, you'll be able to use objects to organize and manage complex data and functionality in your programs.

Objects: The Basics

Objects are reusable components that contain data and functionality. Objects in real life have characteristics that define what they are. For example, a pencil has a length, a diameter, a color, and other characteristics that describe it. A pencil also has things you can do with it, such as write, erase, sharpen, and break.

In JavaScript, both the data and functionality encapsulated by an object are called *properties*. If a property has a function value, it's also known as a *method*. JavaScript objects can be used to describe not only physical objects but also abstract ideas.

A JavaScript object to describe a pencil might look something like this:

```
const pencil = {
length: "7.5 inches",
shape: "hexagonal",
diameter: "1/4 inch",
write: function(){/*do writing*/},
erase: function(){/*do erasing*/},
sharpen: function(){/*do sharpening*/},
}
```

You might create this `pencil` object to describe a pencil in your exciting new simulation game called Pencil Adventure.

Once you create a `pencil` object, you can find out about it and make use of its functions by using dot notation. For example, to sharpen the `pencil`, you can invoke the `sharpen()` method of the `pencil`:

```
pencil.sharpen();
```

Of course, sharpening the `pencil` makes it shorter, so you need to update its length. You can do so by changing the value of the `length` property of the `pencil`:

```
pencil.length = "7 inches";
```

Sharpening `pencil` also gives it another property you should keep track of, which I call `sharpness`. To add this new property, just assign it:

```
pencil.sharpness = "sharp";
```

Another thing you can do with a `pencil` object is to make copies of it. For example, you might have a box of pencils and want to track their properties and be able to use them separately. As with arrays, one way to make a shallow copy of an object is by using the spread syntax:

```
const newPencil = {...pencil};
```

I offer plenty of examples of objects earlier in this book. For example, the `document` object represents an HTML page in a web browser. It contains methods like `getElementById` and properties such as `title`.

TECHNICAL STUFF

One key to gaining a deep understanding of JavaScript is to know that arrays and functions are objects. Also, while numbers, strings, and Booleans are primitive data types (as you learn in Chapter 3 of this minibook), JavaScript lets you access methods on them by temporarily wrapping (or *boxing*) them in object form. In general, avoid creating wrapper objects with `new Number()`, `new String()`, or `new Boolean()` because doing so can lead to confusing behavior.

Creating Objects

JavaScript has four ways to create objects from scratch:

- Use object literal notation.
- Use the `new` keyword.
- Define a class.
- Use `Object.create()`.

Each method produces in the same result. But some methods are more convenient or offer capabilities that others don't, so it's important to be familiar with each of them.

Making objects using literal notation

To make an object using literal notation, use curly braces containing comma-separated *name*:*value* pairs, where *name* is how you access the property, and *value* is any valid JavaScript value, including other objects.

Here's a simple object written using object literal notation:

```
const person = {eyes: 2, feet: 2, eyeColor: 'brown'};
```

You can also initialize an object as an empty object and use dot notation to add properties to it afterward:

```
const person = {};
person.hair = 'black';
person.hands = 2;
person.fullName = {firstName:'Lamont',lastName:'Rudnick'};
```

Making objects using a constructor function

A *constructor* function is one that can be called with the `new` keyword to create (or *construct*) an object. Listing 7-1 shows an example of using a constructor function.

LISTING 7-1: Using a Constructor Function

```
function Cat(name, type){
  this.name = name;
  this.type = type;
}
const ourCat = new Cat('Murray', 'domestic short hair');
```

You can use constructor functions to create multiple objects, and each object created using the `Cat()` constructor function will have the `name` and `type` properties.

The keyword `this` in Listing 7-1 (and elsewhere in this chapter) refers to the context in which a function, such as the constructor function, is running. When you create an object by using the `new` operator and the `Cat()` constructor function in Listing 7-1, `this` refers to the new object.

For example, in the following statement, the `this` keyword refers to the object named `ourCat`:

```
const ourCat = new Cat('Murray','domestic short hair');
```

When the Cat() constructor function runs, it does basically the same thing (with some technical differences) as writing the following:

```
const ourCat = {};
ourCat.name = 'Murray';
ourCat.type = 'domestic short hair';
```

You can read more about the this keyword in Chapter 8 of this minibook.

Making objects with class

A *class* is a template for objects. Many other languages have the idea of classes; but JavaScript didn't have classes when it was designed. Class syntax was introduced into JavaScript in 2015 to provide programmers moving to JavaScript with a more familiar way to create objects.

To write a class, start with the class keyword followed by any name you want. By convention, class names start with an uppercase letter. The name of the class is followed by a left curly brace:

```
class Cat {
```

After the class header, you can (but don't have to) specify a constructor function.

Methods in classes can be written using method notation. In method notation, the colon between the name and the value is removed, and the function name and the body of the function are combined. When you write a constructor function, it's usually written using method notation:

```
constructor(name,type){
  this.name = name;
  this.type = type;
}
```

When a class (or a constructor function outside a class) is called, the values passed to the function are assigned to properties of the object inside the constructor. That's what's going on with the statements that start with this. Inside an object, the this keyword refers to the object in the same way.

REMEMBER

Understanding the this keyword is another one of those difficult but essential keys to understanding JavaScript. You can read much more about this in Chapter 8 of this minibook.

Listing 7-2 shows a simple example of using a class.

LISTING 7-2: Using a Class

```
class Pet {
constructor(name,type){
  this.name = name;
  this.type = type;
}
}
const ourDog = new Pet('Chauncey','AmStaff');
```

At this point, you might wonder why someone would use a class when just using a constructor function appears to require fewer characters to do the same thing. You find out why in Chapter 9 of this minibook, which covers classes in much more detail.

Making objects with Object.create()

The `Object.create()` method makes a new object and uses an existing object as the new object's prototype. Note that the *O* in `Object.create()` is capitalized. That's because `create()` is a method of the `Object` class. To use `Object.create()`, pass an object to it as an argument, as shown in Listing 7-3.

LISTING 7-3: Creating an Object using Object.create()

```
const computer = {memory: "16GB", HD:"8TB"}
const laptop = Object.create(computer);
```

Modifying Objects

Once you've created an object, you can access, modify, and add new properties using one of two methods: dot notation or square brackets notation.

Using dot notation

In *dot notation*, the name of a property is followed by a period, which is followed by the name of a property or method. One useful thing about dot notation is that it makes accessing properties and methods of nested objects simple.

Programmers commonly create objects that contain multiple levels of nested objects. For example, Listing 7-4 shows an object that contains a property that's an object.

LISTING 7-4: An Object with Nested Properties

```
const myLocation = {
  city: {
    id: 2643743,
    name: "London",
    coord: {
      lon: -0.1258,
      lat: 51.5085,
    },
    country: "GB",
    population: 9820000,
    timezone: 3600,
  },
};
```

To get the latitude from the object in Listing 7-4, you can use the following line:

```
myLocation.city.coord.lat;
```

To set the value of a property using dot notation, just assign a value to a property. If the property you assign the value to doesn't exist, it's created in the object.

Using square brackets notation

Square brackets notation uses square brackets after the object name to get and set property values. The name of the property between the brackets is a string, either a literal string or the name of a string variable. Using the object from Listing 7-4, you can get the `city` property using the following:

```
myLocation['city']
```

Square brackets notation is often used with dot notation to access nested properties, like this:

```
myLocation.city['name']
```

You can also put sets of square brackets together to access nested properties:

```
myLocation['city']['name']
```

Square brackets notation is useful when you want to access multiple properties in an object by using the same statement, because it allows you to use a variable for the property name. For example, in Listing 7-5, a loop is used to get the names of the properties of the web browser's `document` object. Using square brackets notation, you can print all the properties without having to know what they are in advance.

LISTING 7-5: Printing the Properties of an Object

```
const pet = { name: "Murray", type: "domestic short hair" };
for (const property in pet) {
  console.log(`${property}: ${pet[property]}`);
}
```

Comparing and Copying Objects

When you make a copy of an object by using the assignment operator or by passing the object into a function, the value that's copied is the object, not the values inside the object. This concept is one of the most useful ones to understand about objects (and arrays). Whereas primitive data types (like strings and numbers) are copied by *value*, objects are copied by *reference*. To understand this difference, let's compare some objects.

Because an object is a value that contains other values, when you compare objects using the triple equals operator (===), what's compared is the object, not its values. For example, create the following two objects in your JavaScript console:

```
const firstObject = {prop1:'test', prop2:'test2'};
const secondObject = {prop1:'test', prop2:'test2'};
```

These two objects appear to be identical, but when you compare them, you see an interesting result:

```
firstObject === secondObject
```

Whereas a comparison of two primitive variables returns `true` if the values of the variables are the same, a comparison of two objects with identical properties returns `false`. This is because the two objects are not the same object, even though they have the same properties and those properties have the same values.

If you compare properties of these two objects, you'll find that they're compared as the primitives they are:

```
firstObject.prop1 === secondObject.prop1
```

Now that you understand how objects are compared, try copying an object. Type the following line into the same JavaScript console window where you created the `firstObject` and `secondObject` objects:

```
const thirdObject = secondObject;
```

As you would expect, this line creates a new constant named `thirdObject`. Next, try changing the value of `thirdObject.prop1`:

```
thirdObject.prop1 = 'orange';
```

With that done, you can now type `thirdObject.prop1` into the console to get back the value you set it to (`'orange'`). If you compare `secondObject.prop1` to `thirdObject.prop1`, you'd expect to get back `false`. But that's not what happens:

```
secondObject.prop1 === thirdObject.prop1;
```

This statement returns `true` because `thirdObject` is a reference to `secondObject`, not to its own object. What do you think happens if you add a new property to `thirdObject`?

```
thirdObject.prop3 = 'claw hammer';
```

If you check the value of `thirdObject.prop3` now, you find that, sure enough, it has been set as you wanted. But what if you check the value of `secondObject.prop3`? You'll find that `secondObject`, as if by magic, now has an identical property named `prop3`.

At this point, you might be suspicious of all objects and decide to check the value of `firstObject.prop3`, like this:

```
firstObject.prop3
```

But you'll find that this line returns `undefined`.

If you compare secondObject and thirdObject, what's happening here becomes obvious:

```
secondObject === thirdObject
```

This expression returns true because thirdObject is secondObject — it's just referencing it using a different name.

The reference nature of objects is extremely useful in JavaScript. It means that you can pass references to objects into a function and the function can modify the values in the object.

However, if you are creating an object from an existing object and don't want the new object to affect the original, you need to do the same thing I show you how to do when making copies of arrays (in the section on spreading arrays in Chapter 6 of this minibook) — make a shallow copy. As with arrays, the easiest way to create a shallow copy of an object is by using the spread operator.

REMEMBER

The spread operator separates, or spreads, an iterable object into its component parts.

Here's how you can make a new object, named fourthObject, that starts its life with the same properties as secondObject:

```
const fourthObject = {...secondObject};
```

Now if you compare fourthObject and secondObject, you get a result of false:

```
fourthObject === secondObject
```

The object named fourthObject is its own object, free to modify its properties and add and delete properties without affecting anything else.

Note that the spread syntax makes only a shallow copy: If the object contains nested objects or arrays, those nested values are still shared by reference. When you need a deep copy, you can use JavaScript's built-in global function, structuredClone(). To use structuredClone(), just pass it the object you want to clone and assign the result to a new variable, like this:

```
const newObject = structuredClone(oldObject);
```

WARNING

While structuredClone() is good for creating clones of objects that have nested values, it's unable to copy functions that are properties of objects.

IN THIS CHAPTER

» Writing and naming functions

» Passing arguments to and returning values from functions

» Understanding `this` and context

» Linking functions in a chain

Chapter 8

Writing and Running Functions

"What I do has to be a function of what I can do, not a function of what people ask me to do."

—TIM BERNERS-LEE

Functions are the objects that make your programs do things. They also serve an important organizational purpose: Just as objects organize data into reusable containers, functions organize statements into reusable functionality.

In this chapter, you learn what a function is in JavaScript, how to use some of the most common JavaScript built-in functions, and the different methods JavaScript provides for writing custom functions. Along the way, you discover some essentials of modern JavaScript, including rest parameters, the spread operator, and arrow functions. I finish the chapter with a discussion of more advanced concepts in JavaScript, such as understanding the `this` keyword and chaining functions.

Functions: An Introduction

A *function* is a group of statements that perform a task. In other words, a function is like a smaller program inside your program.

Functions usually receive data and then return data based on the input. For example, the `String()` function in JavaScript receives a value of any data type and returns a string. To use a function, you specify the name of a function followed by parentheses. Between the parentheses, you can, optionally, supply one or more values. The values you specify between the parentheses are called *arguments*.

For example, in the case of `String()`, if you want to convert the number 10 to a string, you can do so like this:

```
String(10);
```

JavaScript has many built-in functions, but you can also create JavaScript functions. Here's a simple function to add two numbers:

```
function addNumbers(num1, num2){
  return num1 + num2;
}
```

You can use a custom function the same way you use a built-in function. To use `addNumbers()`, just supply it with two numbers, like this:

```
addNumbers(2, 4);
```

Before I delve much deeper into talking about functions, I need to define a few important terms:

- Creating a function is called *defining a function.*
- The code that defines a function is called the *function definition.*
- The names listed between parentheses in a function definition are the function's *parameters.*
- Telling a function to execute its statements is known as *calling the function*.
- Supplying arguments to a function when you call it is called *passing* arguments to the function.
- The values you pass into a function when you call it are called *arguments.*

- When you call a function with arguments (the values you pass to the function), the parameters (the list of names in the function declaration) are initialized as variables inside the function.
- A function inside an object is called a *method.*

You've seen and used many different functions already in this book — both Python functions (in Book 2) and now JavaScript functions. Many of those functions are built into the language. JavaScript contains two types of built-in functions:

- Top-level functions
- Methods of built-in objects

Using top-level functions

Top-level functions are functions that aren't part of an object. You can define your own top-level functions, and JavaScript has a handful of top-level functions already defined for you. You can use these built-in, top-level functions anywhere in your programs.

Table 8-1 describes the built-in top-level functions.

TABLE 8-1 The Built-In Top-Level Functions in JavaScript

Function	What It Does
`Boolean()`	Converts a non-Boolean value to Boolean
`Number()`	Converts a non-number value to a number
`String()`	Converts a non-string value to a string
`eval()`	Runs JavaScript code passed to it as a string (generally discouraged for security and performance reasons)
`isFinite()`	Determines whether the value passed to it is a finite number
`isNaN()`	Determines whether a value passed to it is NaN
`parseFloat()`	Converts a string to a floating-point number
`parseInt()`	Converts a string to an integer
`decodeURI()`	Decodes a string that has been encoded by `encodeURI()`

(continued)

TABLE 8-1 *(continued)*

Function	What It Does
decodeURIComponent()	Decodes a string that has been encoded using encodeURIComponent()
encodeURI()	Replaces certain characters (for example, spaces, quotes, and slashes) in a string with escape sequences to create a valid Uniform Resource Identifier, which are the addresses used to locate web pages and other resources on the web
encodeURIComponent()	Does the same thing as encodeURI() but encodes the entire string, whereas encodeURI() leaves characters that have a special meaning in a URI unescaped.

Using methods of built-in objects

The objects that make JavaScript work all have methods built into them. For example, when you create a string, these methods become available for working with the string. The same goes for the Boolean and number data types, and for arrays and objects.

In Chapter 4 of this minibook, you can read about methods like `split()` and `trim()` for working with strings. The full names of these methods are `String.prototype.split()` and `String.prototype.trim()`. If you've already read the section on prototypes in Chapter 7 of this minibook, you know why: As with objects you create from the base `Object` prototype in JavaScript, strings created from the base `String` prototype have access to properties and methods they inherit.

Methods that your objects inherit from their parents are called *instance methods.* You call them by specifying the object name followed by the name of the method followed by parentheses, which may contain arguments.

Other methods of built-in JavaScript objects can't be called in this way because they don't operate on instances of the base object. Instead, they operate as utilities provided by the base object. These methods are called *static methods.*

An example of a static method is the `Number.parseInt()` method. You can't call `Number.parseInt()` on a variable or value, like this:

```
myString.parseInt() // parseInt() is not a function
```

Instead, you pass the number to the `parseInt()` method, and the return value is an integer, like this:

```
Number.parseInt(myString);
```

TECHNICAL STUFF

Some of the most common static methods of JavaScript built-in objects are duplicates of the global (also known as *top-level*) functions with the same name. For example, `parseInt()` is also a global function that does the same thing as calling `Number.parseInt()`.

Passing by value

When you call a function using arguments that are primitive data types (such as string, number, and Boolean), the values you pass into the function are copied. This is called *passing by value.* Listing 8-1 shows how passing an argument creates a local variable using the name of the parameter.

LISTING 8-1: Passing by Value

```
const favoriteFood = 'tacos';
makeDinner(favoriteFood);
function makeDinner(whatToMake) {
  console.log(`I see you want ${whatToMake}.`);
  whatToMake = 'salad';
  console.log(`I've decided to make ${whatToMake} instead.`);
}
```

In Listing 8-1, the value of `favoriteFood` is copied to a new variable named `whatToMake` when the function is invoked. Because this new variable is scoped to the function, it doesn't exist outside the function. Because the value of `favoriteFood` is passed by value, changing the value of `whatToMake` inside the function doesn't affect `favoriteFood`. In other words, your favorite food remains the same no matter what the `makeDinner()` function decides to do.

Passing by reference

Technically, everything in JavaScript is passed by value. However, when you pass an array or object to a function, the reference to the array or object — not a copy of its contents — is copied into the function.

Just as when you make a copy of an object using the = operator, the copy of an object passed to a function maintains its link to the object outside the function. As a result, if you change the properties of an object passed to a function, those changes are visible outside the function, as shown in Listing 8-2.

LISTING 8-2: Passing an Object to a Function

```
const user = { username: 'funguy37', status: 'active' };
const loginStatus = login(user);
console.log(loginStatus);
console.log(`The status is now ${user.status}`);
function login(userCredentials) {
  if (userCredentials.status === 'active') {
    let randomString = Math.random().toString(36).slice(-16);
    userCredentials.status = randomString;
    return `Status was updated.`;
  }
  return 'Logged In';
}
```

Writing Functions

A *function declaration* is made up of the following parts, written in this order:

- The `function` keyword
- The name of the function
- Parentheses, which may contain a list of parameters
- Curly braces surrounding one or more statements

Functions can be short and simple, or they can be as large and complex as you need them to be. A simple function might simply call another function or write some value to the browser window, such as this one:

```
function updatePageTitle(title){
  document.title = title;
}
```

Try entering this function in your browser console and then call it, passing in a string as the title, like this:

```
updatePageTitle("Welcome to my web page");
```

If you look at the title on your browser tab, note that it has changed to the string you passed to the function. Note also that when you created the function and when you ran the function, `undefined` was written to the console.

Every statement in JavaScript has a return value. If you perform an operation that doesn't return anything, such as declaring a function or running a function, JavaScript returns the default return value, `undefined`.

Naming functions

The rules for function names are the same as the rules for variables: They can contain letters, digits, underscores, and dollar signs. As with variable names, it's common to name functions using lower camel case (where the first word in the variable name is lowercased and subsequent words are uppercased).

Because functions are designed to *do* something, one simple good naming practice is to name them starting with a verb. For example, the following function names make clear what the functions do:

- `convertToMp3()`
- `getCurrentDate()`
- `calculateTotal()`
- `signOut()`
- `getFormData()`

Passing arguments

The name between the parentheses in the function header is called a *parameter*. A function can have as many parameters as it needs to have; each one must be separated by a comma.

TIP

If you find that your function has a large number of parameters, you might think about simplifying the function or breaking it into multiple functions to make your code easier to read.

When you call a function, you substitute values for the names in the parameter list. These values are called *arguments*. Arguments you pass into a function become variables inside the function with the names of the parameters.

A function called `getLocalWeather()` might start like this:

```
function getLocalWeather(city, state){
```

When you call a function with arguments, the arguments must be specified in the same order in which the parameters appear in the function definition. For example:

```
getLocalWeather("Detroit","MI");
```

Using rest parameters

If you don't know how many arguments will be passed to a function when you call it, you can use a special parameter called a *rest parameter*. The syntax for a rest parameter uses the same three-dot operator as when you use spread syntax, which you can read about in Chapter 6 of this minibook. A rest parameter places in an array containing all remaining arguments passed to the function.

For example, you might define a function like the following, which has a normal parameter followed by a rest parameter:

```
function sortList(orderBy, ...items){
  // ...
}
```

To call this function, you specify a value for `orderBy` followed by as many additional arguments as needed:

```
sortList('alphabetical','James','Robert','John','Michael',
   'David','William');
```

Inside the function, an array named `items` with six elements is created.

Using the arguments object

Another way to access any number of arguments passed to a function is to use the `arguments` object. The `arguments` object is automatically created as a variable inside every function created using the `function` keyword. It contains all the arguments passed to a function.

The `arguments` object resembles an array in how you access it; however, it is not an array, in that you can't access any array properties and methods except `length`.

You can get the values in an `arguments` object the same way you can get values from an array. For example, Listing 8-3 creates an HTML numbered list from as many items as you pass into it.

LISTING 8-3: Creating a Numbered List from Any Number of Arguments

```
function makeNumberedList() {
  let numberedList = '<ol>';
  for (let i = 0; i < arguments.length; i++) {
    numberedList += `<li>${arguments[i]}</li>`;
  }
  numberedList += '</ol>';
  return numberedList;
}
```

Passing functions as arguments

Any value can be passed to a function as an argument, including other functions. When a function is passed to another function to be invoked by the function it's passed to, the function that's being passed is known as a *callback function*. The function you pass a callback function to is known as the *outer function*.

Callback functions are used for adding functionality to functions or for telling the outer function what to do when it completes its work, as shown in Listing 8-4.

LISTING 8-4: Using a Callback Function

```
function greetInSpanish(name) {
  return `Hola, ${name}`;
}
function getUserName(callback) {
  let firstName = prompt('Enter your first name');
  return callback(firstName);
}
getUserName(greetInSpanish);
```

Setting default parameters

Functions that specify parameters don't need to be called with those parameters. However, if you don't supply an argument for a parameter, that parameter will have a value of `undefined` inside the function's body unless you specify a default value.

To specify default values for parameters, use the assignment operator inside the parameter list, like this:

```
function greetUser(firstName='Valued', lastName='Customer'){
  alert(`Hello, ${firstName} ${lastName}`);
}
```

With default parameter values set, when this function is called without arguments, it will alert `Hello, Valued Customer` rather than `Hello`.

Default parameters can be also used to eliminate errors that can happen when an argument isn't passed to a function. For example, the function in Listing 8-5 expects an array to be passed to it, which it loops over using the `Array.map()` method:

LISTING 8-5: A Function that Takes an Array

```
function makeUnorderedList(array) {
  let listItems = array.map(function (element) {
    return `<li>${element}</li>`;
  });
  return `<ul>${listItems.join(")}</ul>`;
}
```

If you call the function in Listing 8-5 without specifying an array, the function produces an error, as shown in Figure 8-1.

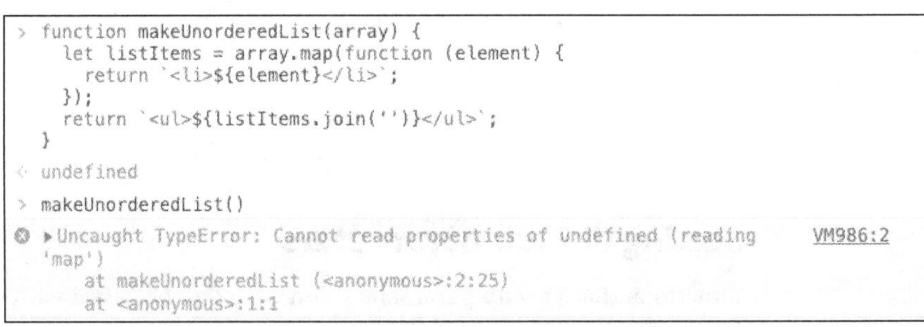

FIGURE 8-1: The result of calling a function that requires an array without passing an array.

TECHNICAL STUFF

When running a function or a program produces an error, programmers say that it *throws* an error.

You can eliminate this potential error by specifying a default value for an empty array:

```
function makeUnorderedList(array=[]){
```

With this change, if you call the function without passing an argument, it just returns an empty (childless) `<ul>` element rather than throwing an error. This isn't a fail-safe method to make the function never throw an error, however. If it's called with a number passed to it, for example, it will still fail. To eliminate this potential error, you can add a check inside the function to verify that the argument is an array before proceeding; if it isn't, you can return an empty string or handle the error gracefully.

Writing a function body

After the first line of the function (sometimes called the *function header*), you can use any combination of other function calls and statements, including additional function definitions. Everything after the function header will be part of the function until you close the function with a closing curly brace.

The part of a function between the curly braces is called the body of the function. The complete `getLocalWeather()` function might look like this:

```
function getLocalWeather(postalCode) {
  const weather = `I don't know what the weather is like in
  ${postalCode}. Maybe try looking out the window.`;
  return weather;
}
```

Returning data

Many functions, such as the `getLocalWeather()` function, have a return value. To return a value from executing a function, use a `return` statement. The `return` statement inside a function halts execution of the function and returns a value.

You can assign the return value to a variable using the assignment operator, or you can pass it into another function. For example, here's how you can get the string returned by `getLocalWeather()`:

```
let weather = getLocalWeather('97103');
```

Using a return value as an argument

If you specify a function call as an argument to another function, the return value of the inner function is passed to the outer function:

```
displayWeatherForecast(getLocalWeather('97103'));
```

Passing function calls as arguments can quickly become confusing, so it's more common to write the preceding statement using two statements:

```
let weather = getLocalWeather('97103');
displayWeatherForecast(weather);
```

The `displayWeatherForecast()` function might look like this:

```
function displayWeatherForecast(forecast){
  const forecastElement = document.getElementById('forecast');
  forecastElement.innerHTML = "Here's the current weather
   forecast: ";
  forecastElement.innerHTML += `${forecast}`;
}
```

Creating conditional code with return

Because `return` halts the execution of a function, it's common to skip writing an `else` clause in an `if/else` statement by simply providing an alternative `return` statement after an `if` statement. For example, if you want to make the `getLocalWeather()` function output something different when an argument isn't provided, you check whether `postalCode` has a value of `undefined` and provide a generic message, like this:

```
function getLocalWeather(postalCode) {
  if (postalCode === undefined) {
    return 'I don't know what the weather is where you are.';
  }
  return `I don't know what the weather is like in
   ${postalCode}. Maybe try looking out the window.`;
}
```

The second `return` statement runs only if `postalCode` is not `undefined`.

Function declaration scope and hoisting

A function declaration can be located anywhere in your program, and it can be run from anywhere in its scope. A *top-level* function is one that's not inside any other block of code. Top-level functions can be called from anywhere in your program. A function that's inside another function or block can be called only from that function or block.

You can call functions that are defined using function declarations before the spot where they're defined in the code. This special power of function declarations is called *hoisting.* Anytime a JavaScript compiler reads your code, it looks for function declarations and then lifts (or hoists) them to the beginning of their scope.

Declaring Anonymous functions

An *anonymous function* is a function declaration that doesn't have a name. Anonymous functions are typically used as callbacks. For example, the following function takes a function as its parameter:

```
function doSomething(callback){
...
}
```

This function can be a named function, but it doesn't need a name, because it is being passed as a parameter and will be assigned a name (`callback`) inside the outer function. Here's how you can pass an anonymous function to the `doSomething()` function:

```
doSomething(function(){console.log('done.');});
```

Defining function expressions

A function *expression* creates a function by assigning an anonymous function to a variable or constant. Listing 8-6 shows an example of using a function expression to define a function.

LISTING 8-6: Defining a Function by Using a Function Expression

```
const convertMilesToKM = function (distanceInMiles) {
  const distanceInKM = distanceInMiles * 1.609;
  return distanceInKM;
};
console.log(convertMilesToKM(5));
```

Unlike function declarations, function expressions are not hoisted. As with any variable declaration, a function created using a function expression can't be used until the expression has been run.

Function expressions are useful for functions that should be created only based on a condition or for functions passed as arguments to other functions. For example, in Listing 8-7, the function that calculates the duration of a trip is declared based on whether the value of a variable named `water` is `true`.

LISTING 8-7: Conditionally Defining a Function by Using an Expression

```
function getThere(distance) {
  let estimatedTripDuration;
  if (water === true) {
    const getSwimTime = function () {
      return distance / 2;
    };
    estimatedTripDuration = getSwimTime();
  } else {
    const getWalkTime = function () {
      return distance / 4;
    };
    estimatedTripDuration = getWalkTime();
  }
  return estimatedTripDuration;
}
let water = true;
let distance = 30;
console.log(`It will take ${getThere(distance)} hours to get there.`);
```

Figure 8-2 shows what the code in Listing 8-7 does when you run it in the JavaScript console.

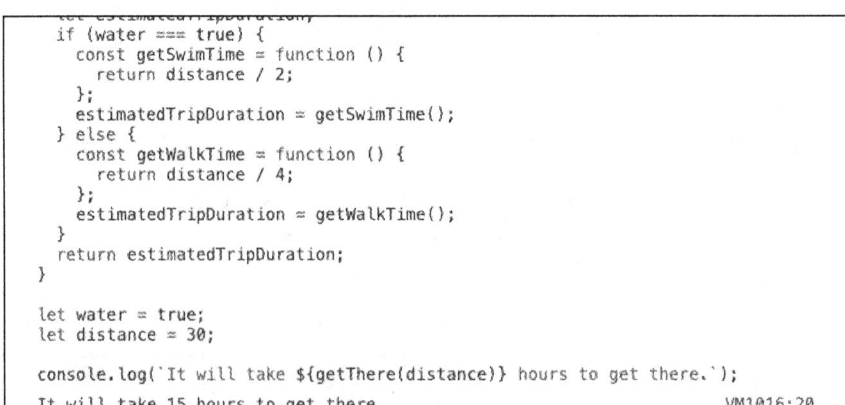

FIGURE 8-2: Creating functions conditionally.

Writing anonymous functions as arrow functions

Anonymous functions can also be written using arrow syntax. *Arrow syntax* doesn't use the `function` keyword. Instead, it uses a combination of symbols that look like an arrow, `=>`, between the parameter list and the body of the function.

To see the difference between using the `function` keyword and using arrow syntax, it's helpful to see the same function written both ways. Here's a function that randomly selects a movie from an array of movie titles, written using the `function` keyword:

```
const pickAMovie = function (choices) {
  let myPick = choices[Math.floor(Math.random() * choices.
   length)];
  return myPick;
};
```

Here's a function that does the same thing as the preceding function but written as an arrow function:

```
const pickAMovie = (choices) => {
  let myPick = choices[Math.floor(Math.random() * choices.
   length)];
  return myPick;
};
```

Simplifying arrow functions

Arrow functions can be simplified even further under certain circumstances:

- If an arrow function takes only one parameter, you don't need to include the parentheses around the parameter list.
- If an arrow function contains only a return statement, you can eliminate the `return` keyword and the curly braces around the function body.

When you apply these two rules, the `pickAMovie()` function can be simplified to the following:

```
const pickAMovie = choices => choices[Math.floor(Math.random() *
   choices.length)];
```

Listing 8-8 shows a simple web application that imports a file containing an array of 100 movies and then randomly chooses one and displays its title.

LISTING 8-8: A Random Movie Picker App

```
<!doctype html>
<html lang="en">
  <head>
    <meta charset="UTF-8"/>
    <meta http-equiv="X-UA-Compatible" content="IE=edge"/>
    <meta name="viewport" content="width=device-width,
  initial-scale=1.0"/>
    <title>Random Movie Picker</title>
    <script type="text/javascript" src="data/movies.js"></script>
  </head>
  <body>
    <button onclick="displayMovieChoice()">Choose a Movie</button>
    <h1>You should watch <span id="movie-choice"></span></h1>
    <script>
      const chooseMovie = (choices) => {
        return choices[Math.floor(Math.random() * choices.
  length)];
      };
      const displayMovieChoice = () => {
        const movieChoice = chooseMovie(movies);
        document.getElementById('movie-choice').innerHTML =
  movieChoice.title;
      };
    </script>
  </body>
</html>
```

Knowing the limits of arrow functions

Arrow functions are a useful shorthand in many cases, such as when writing a callback function. However, they have limitations that make them unsuitable for certain purposes.

Arrow functions don't have the this keyword

Unlike functions created using the `function` keyword, arrow functions don't have their own `this`. Instead, they take on the context of the object in which they're created, and their `this` value doesn't change when they're called in a different context.

Because of this behavior, arrow functions created as methods of an object are said to be lexically bound (sometimes called `autobound`). It's not possible to bind arrow functions to objects using `bind()`, `call()`, or `apply()`.

TIP

See the section "Understanding Context and the this Keyword," later in this chapter, to learn about the `bind()`, `call()`, and `apply()` functions.

Arrow functions don't have the arguments object

Just as with normal functions, you can pass arguments to arrow functions. However, arrow functions don't have their own `arguments` object.

If you need to write an arrow function that can take any number of arguments, however, you can use a rest parameter, like this:

```
const myFunction = (...args) => {
  console.log(`The value of the first argument is ${args[0]}`);
}
```

Writing Methods

A function inside an object is called a *method.* A method can access and modify the other properties of an object by using the `this` keyword.

Methods can be written the same way you write any other property, as in this example:

```
const myCar = {
  speed: 0,
  drive: function (speedLimit) {
    this.speed = speedLimit;
    console.log(`Driving at ${this.speed}mph.`);
  },
};
```

You can also write methods using method notation, which combines the left and right sides of the colon, like this:

```
const myCar = {
  speed: 0,
  drive(speedLimit) {
    this.speed = speedLimit;
```

```
    console.log(`Driving at ${this.speed}mph.`);
  },
};
```

To call the drive() method, append it to the name of its object and pass a value to the speedLimit parameter:

```
myCar.drive(35);
```

The method changes the value of myCar.speed and logs a message to the console. Inside the myCar object, the value of the speed property is now 35, as shown in Figure 8-3.

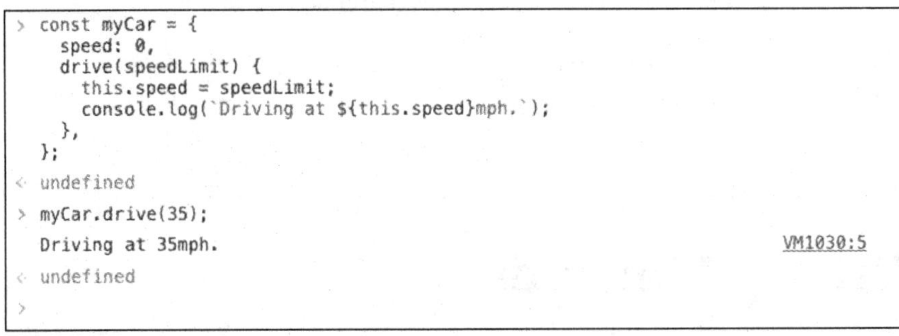

FIGURE 8-3: Methods can change the values of properties.

Understanding Context and the this Keyword

In the preceding section, you can see that the value of this is the object that owns the method. Another name for the object that determines the value of this in a function is *context.*

Functions make it possible to use the same functionality with multiple objects. For example, your program might have numerous objects that can be driven. Rather than define the drive function as a method of each of these objects, you can define a single function outside the objects, as shown in Listing 8-9.

LISTING 8-9: A Function without Context

```
const myTruck = {
  speed: 0,
};
```

```
const myCar = {
  speed: 0,
};
function drive(speedLimit) {
  this.speed = speedLimit;
  console.log(`Driving at ${this.speed}mph.`);
}
```

However, this approach creates a problem, as you'll discover if you try to drive your car now. There's no way to tell `drive()` what to drive. When you call a function that uses the `this` keyword but don't specify an object to call the function on (a *context*, in other words), the `this` keyword will refer to the global object by default, which is the `window` object in a browser.

To solve this problem, you can take one of two approaches:

- Pass the object as a parameter to the function.
- Set the context of the function.

Passing an object to a function

In Chapter 7 of this minibook, you see that passing an object to a function creates a reference to the object (rather than a new object) inside the function. Knowing this, you can add a parameter to the `drive()` function that will be the object that should be driven and then update the statements that use the `this` keyword to use that reference instead, as shown in Listing 8-10.

LISTING 8-10: Passing an Object to a Function

```
const myTruck = {
  speed: 0,
};
const myCar = {
  speed: 0,
};
function drive(vehicle, speedLimit) {
  vehicle.speed = speedLimit;
  console.log(`Driving at ${vehicle.speed}mph.`);
}
```

If you want to drive your truck, you can call `drive()` and pass in `myTruck` as the first argument. If you want to drive your car, you can call the same function but pass `myCar` as the first argument:

```
drive(myCar,55);
drive(myTruck,55);
```

Setting the context of a function

Another way to use the same function with multiple objects is by setting the context of the function (that is, the object it should be called on) using `call()`, `apply()`, or `bind()`.

Using call()

The `call()` method of function objects takes an object as its first parameter. When `call()` is called on a function, that function runs in the context of the object passed to `call()`. After the first parameter, `call()` accepts any number of additional arguments. For example, to call the version of the `drive()` function in Listing 8-10 with the context of the `myCar` object and a `speedLimit` value of 65, you can use the following statement:

```
drive.call(myCar, 65);
```

This statement runs exactly as though you had defined `drive()` inside `myCar` and called it using `myCar.drive(65)`.

Using apply()

The `apply()` method works the same as `call()` but takes an array as its second parameter, which will be passed to the function that `apply()` is applied to.

Using bind()

The `bind()` method works the same as `call()`, with a context object as the first parameter followed by any number of individual arguments. However, rather than return the result of calling the function, `bind()` returns a new function. You can assign this new function to a variable to create a new callable function that includes its context and data. For example, you might want to create a function called `driveMyCarOnTheFreeway()`. To do so, you can use `bind()`, like this:

```
const driveMyCarOnTheFreeway = drive.bind(myCar,65);
```

You can now call the new function and drive on the freeway anytime you like:

```
driveMyCarOnTheFreeway();
```

Passing a function from one object to another

Like any other value in JavaScript, functions can be passed as arguments. This capability makes it easy to share functionality between objects.

Yet another way to use a function with multiple objects is to pass the function as an argument to a method of an object. For example, you might create methods in `myCar` and `myTruck` called `operate()`, which can be used for any sort of operation the vehicle might need to do. Then you can call this function and pass in another function for a specific way to operate the vehicle, like this:

```
const myCar = {
  speed: 0,
  operate(speedLimit, callback) {
    callback(speedLimit);
    console.log(`myCar is driving at ${this.speed}`);
  },
};
function drive(speed) {
  this.speed = speed;
  console.log(`Start driving at ${this.speed}`);
}
myCar.operate(55, drive);
```

However, there's a catch. Figure 8-4 shows what happens when you run this code.

```
> const myCar = {
    speed: 0,
    operate(speedLimit, callback) {
      callback(speedLimit);
      console.log(`myCar is driving at ${this.speed}`);
    },
  };
  function drive(speed) {
    this.speed = speed;
    console.log(`Start driving at ${this.speed}`);
  }
  myCar.operate(55, drive);
  Start driving at 55
  myCar is driving at 0
```

FIGURE 8-4: Attempting to pass a function to a method.

The `this` keyword inside the `drive` function references the global scope (which is the `window` object in a browser) in which it exists.

REMEMBER

Functions are objects, so passing a function into a method and running it isn't the same as creating the function inside the object and running it. You can verify this by typing `window.speed` in the console window.

One way to fix this problem is to bind the callback function that's passed to the `operate()` method to the `this` context of the object, as shown in Listing 8-11.

LISTING 8-11: Using the Same Function in Multiple Objects

```
const myCar = {
  speed: 0,
  operate(speedLimit, callback) {
    const boundCallback = callback.bind(this);
    boundCallback(speedLimit);
    console.log('myCar is driving at ${this.speed}');
  },
};
function drive(speed) {
  this.speed = speed;
  console.log('Driving at ${this.speed}');
}
myCar.operate(55, drive);
```

Passing a function to a child to change the parent

In JavaScript, passing a function as an argument to another function is a powerful technique that allows you to make your code more flexible and reusable. By doing this, you enable one function to control or modify behavior in another context. For example, in Listing 8-12, you might pass a function to handle the removal of a book from the bookstore inventory, allowing the main `bookstore` object to delegate specific actions to other functions as needed. This pattern makes it easier to separate concerns and adapt the behavior of your code without modifying the core logic.

LISTING 8-12: A Bookstore and a Shopping Cart

```
const bookstore = {
  books: ['Ulysses', 'The Great Gatsby'],
  displayBookstore() {
    const renderTarget = document.getElementById('bookstore');
    const bookList = this.books.map((book) => `<p>${book}</p>`);
    renderTarget.innerHTML = bookList.join('');
  },
  removeBook(title) {
    let newList = this.books.filter((book) => book != title);
    this.books = newList;
  },
};
bookstore.removeBook('The Great Gatsby');
```

You can see the `removeBook()` method in action in Figure 8-5.

```
> bookstore.books
<· ▶ (2) ['Ulysses', 'The Great Gatsby']
> bookstore.removeBook('The Great Gatsby');
<· undefined
> bookstore.books
<· ▶ ['Ulysses']
```

FIGURE 8-5: Removing an element from an array.

One reason to remove a book from the bookstore's inventory is that someone purchased it. To give people the ability to buy books, I'll show you how to create a separate object, `shoppingCart`, with a checkout button. When this button is clicked, you need to remove the book from the bookstore's inventory.

The `shoppingCart` object is shown in Listing 8-13.

LISTING 8-13: A Shopping Cart

```
const shoppingCart = {
  itemsInCart: ['The Great Gatsby'],
  displayCart() {
    const renderTarget = document.getElementById('cart');
    const itemsInCart = this.itemsInCart.map((item) =>
                        `<p>${item}</p>`);
```

(continued)

LISTING 8-13: *(continued)*

```
    const checkoutButton = "<button id='checkout'>Check out</
                            button>";
    renderTarget.innerHTML = itemsInCart.join('') +
                              checkoutButton;
  },
};
```

At this point, the shoppingCart's displayCart() method just displays a list of books in the cart and a button that doesn't do anything. To make the button do something, you need to add an event listener to it that will call a function, as shown in Listing 8-14.

LISTING 8-14: **Listening for and Handling a Click Event**

```
const shoppingCart = {
  itemsInCart: ['The Great Gatsby'],
  handleClick() {
    //do something here
  },
  displayCart() {
    const renderTarget = document.getElementById('cart');
    const itemsInCart = this.itemsInCart.map((item) =>
                         `<p>${item}</p>`);
    const checkoutButton = "<button id='checkout'>Check out</
                            button>";
    renderTarget.innerHTML = itemsInCart + checkoutButton;
    document
      .getElementById('checkout')
      .addEventListener('click', () => this.handleClick());
  },
};
```

You can read all about events and event listeners in Chapter 10 in this minibook.

Right now, when you click the button, the shoppingCart.handleClick() function runs, but it doesn't do anything. What you want it to do is remove the book from the bookstore object's books property.

The first thing you need to do is call shoppingCart.displayCart() from the bookstore and pass the removeBook() function as a parameter, as shown in Listing 8-15. Here's the important part, though: Because you want removeBook() to affect data inside the bookstore object, rather than inside the shoppingCart, you need to use `bind()` to bind the context of the function to `bookstore`. You can do that at the same time as you're passing it to `shoppingCart.displayCart()`.

LISTING 8-15: Calling shoppingCart.displayCart() from bookstore

```
const bookstore = {
  books: ['Ulysses', 'The Great Gatsby'],
  removeBook(title) {
    let newList = this.books.filter((book) => book != title);
    this.books = newList;
    this.displayBookstore();
  },
  displayBookstore() {
    const renderTarget = document.getElementById('bookstore');
    const bookList = this.books.map((book) => `<p>${book}</p>`);
    renderTarget.innerHTML = bookList.join('');
    shoppingCart.displayCart(this.removeBook.bind(this));
  },
};
```

Finally, you need to receive the `removeBook()` function inside `shoppingCart.displayCart()` and use it as the event handler, as shown in Listing 8-16.

LISTING 8-16: Using removeBook as the Event Handler

```
const shoppingCart = {
  itemsInCart: ['The Great Gatsby'],
  handleClick(removeBook) {
    removeBook(this.itemsInCart);
  },
  displayCart(clickHandler) {
    const renderTarget = document.getElementById('cart');
    const itemsInCart = this.itemsInCart.map((item) =>
          `<p>${item}</p>`);
    const checkoutButton = "<button id='checkout'>Check out</
          button>";
    renderTarget.innerHTML = itemsInCart.join('') +
          checkoutButton;
    document
      .getElementById('checkout')
      .addEventListener('click', () =>
          this.handleClick(clickHandler));
  },
};
```

To use this bookstore app, you put it in an HTML document and call `bookstore.displayBookstore()`, as shown in Listing 8-17:

LISTING 8-17: Displaying the Bookstore and Cart

```
<!doctype html>
<html lang="en">
  <head>
    <meta charset="UTF-8"/>
    <meta http-equiv="X-UA-Compatible" content="IE=edge"/>
    <meta name="viewport" content="width=device-width,
           initial-scale=1.0"/>
    <title>Amazing JavaScript Bookstore</title>
  </head>
  <body>
    <h1>The Books</h1>
    <div id="bookstore"></div>
    <h1>Your Cart</h1>
    <div id="cart"></div>
    <script>
      const bookstore = {
        books: ['Ulysses', 'The Great Gatsby'],
        removeBook(title) {
          let newList = this.books.filter((book) =>
              book != title);
          this.books = newList;
          this.displayBookstore();
        },
        displayBookstore() {
          const renderTarget = document.getElementById('bookstore');
          const bookList = this.books.map((book) => `<p>${book}</p>`);
          renderTarget.innerHTML = bookList.join('');
          shoppingCart.displayCart(this.removeBook.bind(this));
        },
      };
      const shoppingCart = {
        itemsInCart: ['The Great Gatsby'],
        handleClick(removeBook) {
          removeBook(this.itemsInCart);
        },
        displayCart(clickHandler) {
          const renderTarget = document.getElementById('cart');
```

```
          const itemsInCart = this.itemsInCart.map((item) =>
                `<p>${item}</p>`);
          const checkoutButton = "<button id='checkout'>Check
                Out</button>";
          renderTarget.innerHTML = itemsInCart.join('') +
                checkoutButton;
          document
            .getElementById('checkout')
            .addEventListener('click', () =>
                this.handleClick(clickHandler));
        },
      };
      bookstore.displayBookstore();
    </script>
  </body>
</html>
```

When you run this app in a browser, it displays the bookstore and the cart, as shown in Figure 8-6. When you click the Check Out button, *The Great Gatsby* is removed from `bookstore.books` and then `bookstore.displayBookstore()` is called again to update the browser window with the new list of books, as shown in Figure 8-7.

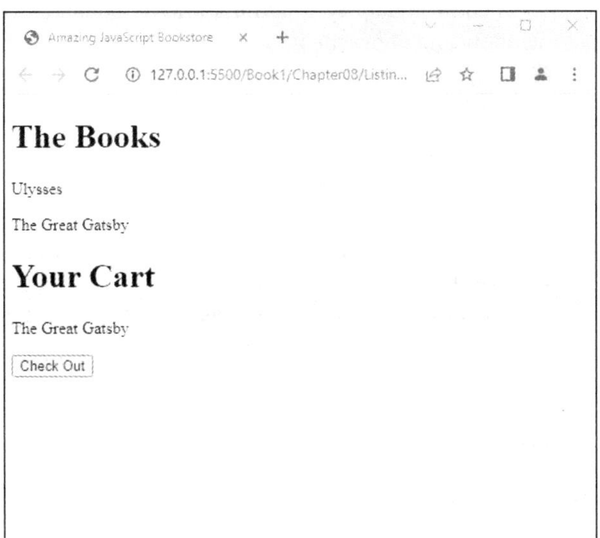

FIGURE 8-6: The finished bookstore app.

FIGURE 8-7: The bookstore, after checkout.

Can you figure out how to also remove the book from the cart when you check out?

To also remove the book from the cart when you check out, you should update the cart object by deleting the selected book from its list. For example, if your cart is an array called `cart.books`, you can use a method such as `cart.removeBook(book)` in your checkout handler. After removing the book from both `bookstore.books` and `cart.books`, call the display functions for the bookstore and cart to refresh the browser window and show the updated lists.

Chaining Functions

Many of JavaScript's built-in functions can be chained so that they run sequentially. For example, to convert a string to uppercase and then trim white space from the beginning and end, you can use the following statement:

```
" my string. ".toUpperCase().trim();
```

The result of running this statement is

```
'MY STRING.'
```

Function chaining works by passing the same object to multiple functions sequentially (in order, from left to right). Function chaining is a design pattern rather than a feature of JavaScript. Using it makes your code more readable and more concise.

To create a chainable function, return `this` from a method. The return value of one method becomes the input for the next method. To understand function chaining, it's helpful to see two ways of doing the same thing. First, here's a series of operations performed using methods of an object named `robot`:

```
let result = robot.walk();
let result2 = robot.talk(result);
let result3 = robot.write(result2);
```

In function chaining, each function returns its `this` value, which becomes the input for the next method in the chain. Here's how you might write the robot object to enable function chaining:

```
const robot = {
  currentActivity: undefined,
  walk() {
    this.currentActivity = 'walking';
    return this;
  },
  talk() {
    this.currentActivity = 'talking';
    return this;
  },
  write() {
    this.currentActivity = 'writing';
    return this;
  },
};
```

To make the robot walk and then talk and then write, you can chain these functions together, like this:

```
robot.walk().talk().write();
```

IN THIS CHAPTER

» Harnessing the power of abstraction and encapsulation

» Getting classy with inheritance and polymorphism

» Deriving classes from base classes

» Constructing constructors

» Understanding properties and methods

Chapter 9
Getting Oriented with Classes

"They can do without architecture who have no olives nor wines in the cellar."

—HENRY DAVID THOREAU

Like constructor functions, classes are templates for objects. At their core, they're built on prototypes (which you can read about in Chapter 6 of this minibook). But their syntax and capabilities go beyond what's available elsewhere in JavaScript. In this chapter, I show you how to harness the power of classes.

Becoming More Classy

The goal with classes is to provide a syntax for working in JavaScript in an object-oriented way. Object-oriented programming is a pattern used in many modern programming languages such as Java and C#. In *object-oriented programming* (also known as OOP), the main focus of a program is its objects and the relationships between them.

The following main concepts in object-oriented programming are described next:

- Encapsulation
- Abstraction
- Inheritance
- Polymorphism

Encapsulation

Encapsulation means that each object in a program has its own private data (called *state*), which only the object can access or modify. An object can also have private functions that only it can invoke.

For example, the private state of a class called `Phone` might include data such as the battery level and whether the display is on. As the user of the phone, you have no direct access to these properties. You can't execute a statement like `myPhone.batteryLevel = 100`.

However, the phone can be plugged in. You can imagine that plugging in a phone is like calling a `myPhone.charge()` method. As the phone charges, the phone updates its private `batteryLevel` property accordingly.

Abstraction

Abstraction means that each object exposes only high-level methods for other objects to be able to work with it. Suppose that you have an object that represents a catalog of products. Other objects don't need to care what happens inside this object — they just need to know that they can call a public method, which might be named `getProducts()`, to get the data from the object.

Abstraction makes complex systems possible. If, to place a phone call, you had to understand how to program your phone and how cellular networks work, you'd have a good excuse for not calling your mom. Fortunately, making a phone call is easy to do because the technical details have been abstracted into a simple user interface.

Inheritance

Inheritance means that new classes can be created that get properties from other classes. For example, a class named `Animal` might have a few properties that describe characteristics of an animal. An object created using the `Animal` class might look like this:

```
{
  domain: 'Eukarya',
  kingdom: 'Animalia',
  structure: 'multicellular'
}
```

If you want to make a new class to describe a fish, you can create a class called `Fish` that has the same properties as the `Animal` class — a better way, however, is to create the `Fish` class by inheriting the properties of the `Animal` class and then adding properties specific to fish.

By using inheritance to create the `Fish` class, it becomes possible for the `Fish` class to access the methods and data common to all animals while also having properties and methods particular to fish (and any classes that inherit from the `Fish` class).

Polymorphism

Polymorphism means that objects of various types can be accessed via the same interface, and that each type of object can provide its own independent implementation of this interface.

For example, suppose that the `Animal` class defines a `move()` method. The `Bird` class could have its own implementation of `move()` that is used when you call `move()` on an object created using the `Bird` class.

Using Base Classes

The most basic syntax for creating a class uses the `class` keyword, followed by a class name, followed by a pair of curly braces, like this:

```
class MyClass {}
```

This class is called a *base* class because objects created by using it don't inherit properties from any other object, other than the base JavaScript object, named `Object`.

Although the basic syntax for creating a class resembles the syntax for creating functions (minus the parameter list, which has been moved to the constructor), an important difference between classes and functions is that classes aren't hoisted. *Hoisting* is the process by which JavaScript moves function and variable declarations to the top of their scope before code execution, allowing you to use them before they are defined in the code. If you try to use a class before it's declared, you get an error. For more on hoisting, see Chapter 6 in this minibook.

Using class expressions

Classes can also be defined by using expressions. To create a class using an expression, assign the class to a variable or constant. When you use an expression to create a class, the name to the right of the `class` keyword is optional. If you do include it, however, it's used as the value for a property of the object called `name`:

```
const MyClass = class MyClass{};
```

Making instances of base classes

To create an object from a class (also known as an *instance* of the class), use the `new` keyword followed by the name of the class:

```
const myObject = new MyClass();
```

As with the constructor function method of creating an object, invoking the name of a class with the `new` keyword causes the class's constructor function to run. If you don't provide your own constructor function inside a base class, JavaScript runs a default constructor, which looks like this:

```
constructor(){}
```

Working with Derived Classes

A *derived* class is one that has a parent class it inherits from. To create a derived class, use the `extends` keyword followed by the name of the class the derived class should be based on, like this:

```
class Coffee extends Beverage {}
```

The derived class is how you implement inheritance (a basic concept of object-oriented programming). A common way to describe a derived class is to say "is a." In this case, `Coffee` is a `Beverage`.

When you invoke a derived class that has no constructor but uses the new keyword, JavaScript supplies the following default constructor:

```
constructor(...args) {
super(...args);
}
```

This constructor accepts any arguments specified when you invoked the class. These arguments are spread into separate parameters (using the spread operator) and passed to the super() function.

The super() function, used inside a constructor, calls the constructor of the parent class.

Understanding Constructors

A *constructor* is a method (always named constructor()) in a class that runs when a class is invoked with new and creates an object instance. It's fully possible, and common, to write classes without explicitly writing a constructor.

If instances of the class need to be initialized with data before other methods can be called, however, you use a constructor.

Constructor functions are written using method notation. The name of the function is followed by a parameter list, followed by curly braces containing statements, like this:

```
class Beverage {
  constructor(){
    // your code here
  }
}
```

If you pass arguments into a class function when you invoke it, those arguments are passed to the constructor function, and you can specify parameters in the constructor's parameter list for expected arguments, like this:

```
class Beverage {
  constructor(size,temperature){
    ...
```

As with a constructor function outside a class, to make the parameters available as properties of the new object, you need to assign them to properties of the new object by using the `this` keyword, as shown in Listing 9-1.

LISTING 9-1: Using the this Keyword in a Class Constructor

```
class Beverage {
  constructor(size, temperature) {
    this.size = size;
    this.temperature = temperature;
  }
}
```

A constructor function in a derived class must have a call to `super()` before any other statements, passing to it the values with which you want to initialize the properties of the parent.

REMEMBER

Calling `super()` is the same as calling the constructor function of the parent class.

For example, Listing 9-2 shows a `Coffee` class derived from the `Beverage` class.

LISTING 9-2: Deriving a Class from a Base Class

```
class Coffee extends Beverage {
  constructor(size, temperature, hasCaffeine, howYouTakeIt) {
    super(size, temperature);
    this.hasCaffeine = hasCaffeine;
    this.howYouTakeIt = howYouTakeIt;
  }
}
```

To create an object from the `Coffee` class, call `Coffee()` with the `new` keyword and pass in arguments for each of the parameters defined by the constructor:

```
const morningCoffee = new Coffee('64oz', 'hot', true, 'black');
```

The new object looks like this:

```
{
  size: '64oz',
  temperature: 'hot',
  hasCaffeine: true,
  howYouTakeIt: 'black'
}
```

Beyond being the place to initialize properties of objects, the class constructor is where you can bind methods to the new object.

Dealing with Properties and Methods

After the constructor, you can define as many properties and methods as you like.

Creating methods in a class

Although the syntax of a class may resemble the syntax of an object literal, they aren't the same. Classes aren't objects; they're functions that you can use to create objects. To create a method inside a class, you can use method notation, the way you would use it inside object literal notation, though the methods have no commas between them.

For example, in the `Beverage` class, you can create a method called `drink()`, as shown in Listing 9-3.

LISTING 9-3: Creating a Method in a Class

```
class Beverage {
  constructor(size, temperature) {
    this.size = size;
    this.temperature = temperature;
  }
  drink() {
    if (this.temperature !== 'scalding') {
      console.log('now drinking');
    }
  }
}
```

Any class derived from `Beverage` will also have access to the `drink()` method.

Overriding methods in a derived class

Because the parent of a derived class is the class's prototype, an object created from a derived class also has access to its parent's methods.

If a derived class has its own version of a method defined in its parent, the derived class's own method is used. For example, the `Coffee` class may have a `drink()` method, as shown in Listing 9-4.

LISTING 9-4: Overriding a Method in a Class

```
class Coffee extends Beverage {
  constructor(size, temperature, hasCaffeine, howYouTakeIt) {
    super(size, temperature);
    this.hasCaffeine = hasCaffeine;
    this.howYouTakeIt = howYouTakeIt;
  }
  drink() {
    if (this.temperature !== 'scalding') {
      console.log('now drinking coffee');
    }
  }
}
```

Defining methods, properties, and fields

Properties created in a class are also known as *fields.* Fields and methods are both called *features,* or *members,* of the class.

The same way that methods in a class are defined without using the `function` keyword, fields in a class are defined without using a `var`, `let`, or `const` keyword, like this:

```
class MyClass {
  publicField = 'this is a public field';
}
```

If you define fields of a class using this syntax (called *class fields syntax*), it's a good practice to first define all class fields in the class, before the constructor. This strategy helps document your class and keep it tidy, as shown here:

```
class Cat {
  paws = 4;
  sound = 'meow';
  constructor(name, favoriteToy) {
```

```
    this.name = name;
    this.favoriteToy = favoriteToy;
  }
}
```

When you define members (methods or fields) outside of the constructor, they're added to the instance before the constructor runs, which means that you can access them from within the constructor.

Public members

By default, members of a class are *public.* Public fields can be accessed by code outside the class. Private fields, on the other hand, can be accessed only from within the class. You don't need to do anything special to declare a public method or field.

Public class members exist on every instance of a class you create. In a derived class, public members that belong to the parent class are added when `super()` is called, which is why `super()` must always be the first statement in a constructor of a derived class.

Private members

To make a member of a class *private,* preface the name of the property or method with the number sign, `#`, as shown in the following snippet:

```
class Cat {
  #isSleeping;
  paws = 4;
  sound = 'meow';
  constructor(name, favoriteToy) {
    this.name = name;
    this.favoriteToy = favoriteToy;
  }
  #takeNap(){
    this.#isSleeping = true;
  }
}
```

Private members of a class can be used by other fields and methods within a class, but are invisible to the world outside the class. As with public members of a class, private members are added whenever a class is constructed or `super()` is called.

Static members

The `static` keyword creates a method or property that can be called only on the class itself — not instances of the class. *Static* methods are commonly used for utilities, and static properties are useful for caches and other class-level data.

In Listing 9-5, `species` is a static property because it needs to be the same for every instance of `Cat`. The static method named `herd()` is static because it's a utility method. I've bolded the `static` members in the following listing to make them easier for you to find.

LISTING 9-5: Creating static Members

```
class Cat {
  static species = 'Felis catus';
  #isSleeping;
  paws = 4;
  sound = 'meow';
  constructor(name, favoriteToy) {
    this.name = name;
    this.favoriteToy = favoriteToy;
  }
  static herd(){
    throw new Error(`You can't do that.`);
  }
  #takeNap(){
    this.#isSleeping = true;
  }
}
```

In the preceding example, both the `species` property and the `herd()` method are public, which means they can be accessed by other JavaScript code by using the name of the class followed by the property or method name.

Private fields can be static as well. Private static fields can be accessed only within the class where they're defined.

REMEMBER

The capability to declare public as well as private fields is part of encapsulation — one of the defining patterns of object-oriented programming, which you can read about at the beginning of this chapter.

Becoming Comfortable with Classes

Fully understanding how to use classes takes some time, and understanding all the ins and outs of various class-related keywords also takes time. Follow these steps to see in action all the various topics you can read about in this chapter:

1. **Open the JavaScript console in your web browser.**
2. **Enter the code in Listing 9-6 to create a class that contains public and private fields as well as static fields.**
3. **Create two instances of the `Cat` class:**

```
const cat1 = new Cat('Mr. Furly', 'tinfoil');
const cat2 = new Cat('Sparky', 'box');
```


LISTING 9-6: Creating a Class with public, private, and static Fields

```
class Cat {
  static species = 'Felis catus';
  #isSleeping;
  paws = 4;
  sound = 'meow';
  constructor(name, favoriteToy) {
    this.name = name;
    this.favoriteToy = favoriteToy;
  }
  static herd() {
    throw new Error(`You can't do that.`);
  }
  play() {
    console.log(`Playing with ${this.favoriteToy}.`);
    this.#takeNap();
  }
  #takeNap() {
    this.#isSleeping = true;
  }
}
```

Once you have the two cats (which are instances of the `Cat` class), you can try running their public methods and see the results. For example, call the `play()` method on one of the cats:

```
cat1.play();
```

4. Type each object name into the console to see the values of its properties and methods:

```
cat1
cat2
```

You can see that the instance of the `Cat` object you called the `play()` method now has its private `isSleeping` property set to `true`. Also note that the `cat1` and `cat2` objects lack the static property `species` and the static method `herd()`, which are defined in the class.

5. Try to access the `isSleeping` property from the console:

```
cat1.#isSleeping
```

You get a syntax error. Now access a public property of one of the `cat` objects:

```
cat1.paws
```

This step works as you'd expect.

6. Call the `herd()` method on the `Cat` class:

```
Cat.herd()
```

The static method called `herd()` runs, and you see an error message (as expected) telling you that you can't herd cats.

7. Make a derived class from `Cat`, named `ShortHair`:

```
class ShortHair extends Cat {
fur = 'short';
constructor(name, favoriteToy){
super(name, favoriteToy);
}
}
```

8. Create an instance of `ShortHair`:

```
const cat3 = new ShortHair('Murray', 'keyboard');
```

9. Check the properties of `cat3`:

```
cat3
```

You see that `cat3` contains all the same properties as `cat1` and `cat2` but also contains a new public property, `fur`, as shown in Figure 9-1.

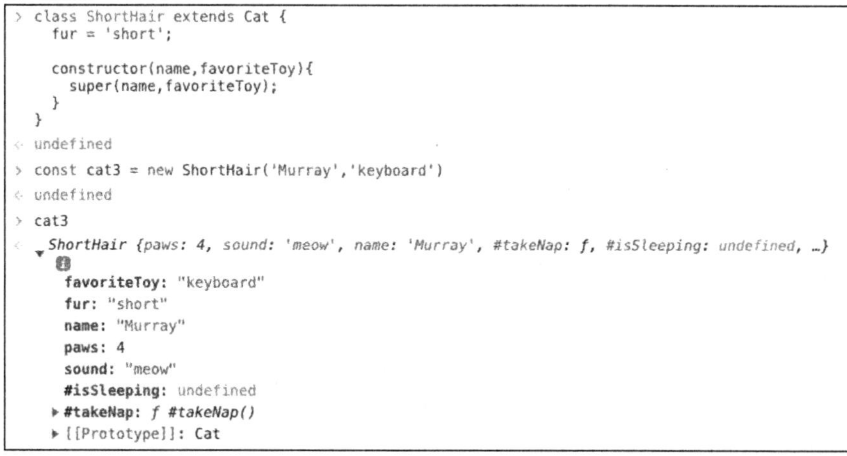

FIGURE 9-1: Making a derived class.

IN THIS CHAPTER

» Stepping through the JavaScript runtime model

» Running through the event loop

» Adding event listeners

Chapter 10

Making Things Happen with Events

"You have power over your mind — not outside events. Realize this, and you will find strength."

—MARCUS AURELIUS

If you've read the earlier chapters in this minibook, you've reached an important milestone in your JavaScript education. Until this point, I've described the JavaScript language itself, largely without considering the environment in which it's running. Now it's time to shift to talking about taking JavaScript to the people.

Events are things that happen outside your program, such as a mouse button click, an HTML element loading, or a timer reaching a certain point. In this chapter, I tell you how events work, how to listen for them from a JavaScript program, and how to run functions in response to events.

Understanding the JavaScript Runtime Model

A programming language's runtime model describes how implementations of the language should run code. In the case of JavaScript, the runtime model is implemented in JavaScript engines, such as Chrome's V8 engine, Mozilla's SpiderMonkey engine, and Apple's JavaScriptCore engine.

At a high level, JavaScript's runtime model is made of these three components: the call stack, the memory heap, and the callback queue. Figure 10-1 shows a visual representation of the JavaScript runtime model.

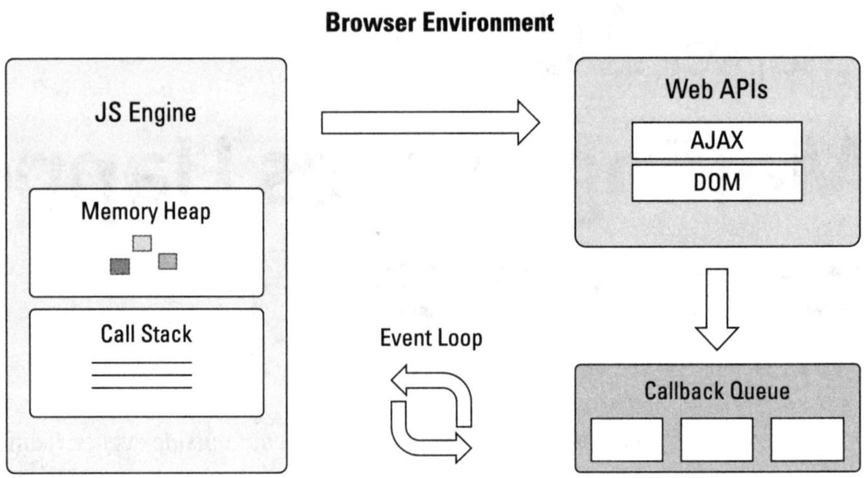

FIGURE 10-1: The JavaScript runtime model.

Stacking function calls

The call stack is made up of *frames*. Each frame is a function call. You can think of them as film frames. JavaScript processes frames one at a time and then moves on to the next one. Along with the heap, the stack is part of the core JavaScript engine (refer to Figure 10-1).

Heaping objects

The *heap* is an area of memory where objects are stored. Unlike the stack, which is ordered based on first-in-first-out (FIFO), the heap is unstructured.

REMEMBER

The names of the heap and the stack are appropriate to how they work. For example, when you remove your clothes from the dryer, they're in an unordered heap. When you stack them, you put them into an order.

Queuing messages

Events, such as the event that happens when you click a button in a web page, create messages. Your browser is generating hundreds of these event messages all the time in response to every mouse movement, page or image load, keystroke, and many other events. These messages all go into the callback queue.

Most of the messages in the queue just exit it without causing anything to happen. But in some cases, the JavaScript engine determines a message to be important and takes some action based on it.

The Event Loop

The *event loop* is a constantly running process in a JavaScript engine that processes messages from the message queue. When JavaScript finds a message it's interested in, it adds function calls to the stack to handle the event. One reason why a message in the queue might be important is that the current program has created an event listener for that event. You can find out how to create event listeners later in this chapter, in the section "Listening for Events."

JavaScript can do only one thing at a time. It might seem to you, however, that it's doing many things simultaneously, because it generally runs very quickly and because it can handle input and output using events and callbacks.

TIP

Events and callbacks are the keys to asynchronous programming, which I tell you about in Chapter 1 of Book 7.

Because JavaScript is single-threaded, it must deal with messages one at a time and process each one until it's done. If a message takes a long time to process, it can hold up everything else. This issue is called *blocking.*

If you've ever visited a web page or run a JavaScript program where you're unable to click anything or even scroll in the web page, and the browser eventually asks you whether you want to continue waiting, JavaScript is trying to handle a message that's blocking execution.

To avoid blocking, most event handler functions are short. Another strategy to avoid blocking is to use asynchronous functions, which hand off execution of code to a process outside the JavaScript engine (such as a networking or data access API) along with a callback function that will be returned to the stack when the outside process finishes its work (such as getting data, waiting for a timer, or making an HTTP request).

Listening for Events

For JavaScript to be able to receive input from users and information about the world outside itself, it needs to run in an environment that can create events. For client-side JavaScript, this environment is most commonly a web browser.

Web browsers contain APIs for interacting with the browser window, web pages, the network, storage, and much more. We use these APIs to write JavaScript programs that do more than just output messages to the console.

To know what's happening in a web browser, the JavaScript program must listen for events produced in the browser. Web developers have three ways to tell a JavaScript program to listen for a specific event:

- HTML event attributes
- Event handler properties
- The `addEventListener()` method

Although all three of these methods are used in JavaScript programming, `addEventListener()` is the recommended and best way.

Listening with HTML event attributes

HTML's *event attributes* are attributes that can be added to HTML elements to run JavaScript in response to events on those elements. For example, the `onclick` attribute can be added to a visible HTML element and will run JavaScript statements or a function when that element is clicked. The following code shows how to use an event attribute:

```
<button onclick="alert('You clicked the button')">Click Here</button>
```

Event attributes were introduced into HTML when JavaScript was created. In addition to `onclick`, there are event attributes for many other browser events, such as `onload`, `onsubmit`, `onkeydown`, and `onmouseover`.

Because they're written in your HTML and apply to only one element, event attributes can quickly become difficult to maintain. They also violate the separation of concerns rule that says JavaScript and HTML should be kept separate.

Because we now have superior ways to handle events in HTML, event attributes are considered obsolete and shouldn't be used.

Listening with event handler properties

Event handler properties are properties available for built-in browser objects that can be used to listen for events. For example, elements have an `onclick` property that you can use like this:

```
const helpButton = document.getElementById('help-button');
function displayHelpWindow(){
  window.open('help.html');
}
helpButton.onclick = displayHelpWindow;
```

Note that, unlike the HTML event attributes, event handler properties properly separate JavaScript code from HTML. Also unlike event attributes, event handler properties take a function, rather than a function call, as their value.

REMEMBER

A function name without parentheses represents the code of the function. A function name with parentheses causes the function to run.

Although using event handler properties is better than using event attributes, they do have their downsides. The biggest problem with event handler properties is that it's impossible to use them to set more than one event of a certain type to an element. In addition, each event handler property can be used for only one type of event, and there aren't built-in event handler attributes for every possible event that can happen.

Using addEventListener()

The `addEventListener()` method is the newest and best way to create event listeners. It can be called on any instance of an object, and it takes two parameters: the event to listen for and a callback function that should run when the event happens on the object.

Here's the basic syntax for `addEventListener()`:

```
EventTarget.addEventListener('event', callback, options);
```

The *event target* is the object the event listener should be attached to. For example, if you want to detect an event that happens in the browser window (such as the `load` event), you can set the event target to `window`. Inside the `window` is the `document` object, which represents the current HTML page. Inside the `document` object are *element nodes,* representing the HTML elements that make up your web page.

An event listener is usually applied to a single element, such as a button or a text input. The most common way to select a single element is by using the `document.getElementById()` method, like this:

```
document.getElementById('submitButton')
```

The value passed to `getElementById()` is a string that should match the value of the `id` attribute for an element in your document.

The first parameter of `addEventListener()`, `'event'`, is the name of the event to listen for. Unlike when you use event attributes or event handler properties, this is just the event name, without the `on` prefix.

The types of events that can be applied to a node depend on the node. Hundreds of different events can be detected by a browser, including mouse events, touch events, keyboard events, speech recognition events, and window scrolling events. Table 10-1 shows some of the more common events that can be applied to HTML element nodes.

TABLE 10-1 **Events Supported by All HTML Elements**

Event	Occurs When This Happens
`abort`	The loading of a file is aborted.
`change`	An element's value has changed since losing and regaining focus.
`click`	A mouse button has been clicked on an element.
`dblclick`	A mouse button has been clicked twice on an element.
`input`	The value of an `<input>` or `<textarea>` element has changed.
`keydown`	A key is pressed.

Event	Occurs When This Happens
keyup	A key is released after being pressed.
mousedown	A mouse button has been pressed.
mouseenter	A mouse pointer is moved onto the element.
mouseleave	A mouse pointer is moved off the element.
mousemove	A mouse pointer has moved.
mouseout	A mouse pointer is moved off the element.
mouseover	A mouse pointer is moved onto the element.
mouseup	A mouse button is released.
reset	A form is reset.
select	Text has been selected.
submit	A form is submitted.

The second parameter of addEventListener() is a callback function. Note that this must be either an anonymous function or the name of a function defined outside the addEventListener() function call. If you add parentheses after the name of the function, the function is invoked, and JavaScript attempts to use the result of invoking the function as the event handler when the event occurs. This is usually a mistake, as shown in the following code example:

```
function handleClick(){
  alert(`I've been clicked!`);
}
document.addEventListener('click', handleClick());
```

If you enter this code into your browser's JavaScript console, you can see that the alert happens right away rather than waiting for a click event.

If you remove the parentheses from after the name of the handleClick() function, the browser waits until it detects a click event anywhere on the current web page before opening the alert window.

The third parameter to addEventListener() is an optional options object. If you include the options object, it can contain any of the following properties:

- **capture:** A Boolean value that, when set to true, causes the event to be dispatched on the element the listener is registered to before being dispatched to elements below it on the DOM tree. By default, capture is set to `false`, and that's almost always what you want to happen.

- **once:** A Boolean value that causes the event listener to be removed from the element automatically after the first time it's invoked. By default, once is set to `false`.
- **`passive`:** A Boolean value indicating that the callback function that handles the event won't call `preventDefault()` to block the default browser event that the event normally triggers. By default, this option is `false`. In some cases, you can set it to `true` to improve the performance of a user interface.
- **`signal`:** Takes an `AbortSignal` as its value. An `AbortSignal` is an object containing an `abort()` method that, when called, removes the event listener.

The `addEventListener()` method has several advantages over the other two methods for handling events:

- You can use it to apply more than one event listener to an element.
- It works with any node in the DOM, not just on elements.
- It gives you more control over when it's activated.

Listing 10-1 shows an example of using `addEventListener()` to detect mouse movements in the browser.

LISTING 10-1: Setting an Event Listener

```
<!doctype html>
<html lang="en">
  <head>
    <meta charset="UTF-8"/>
    <meta http-equiv="X-UA-Compatible" content="IE=edge"/>
    <meta name="viewport" content="width=device-width,
          initial-scale=1.0"/>
    <title>Mouse Tracking</title>
    <script>
      window.addEventListener('load', app);
      function app() {
        const trackingArea = document.getElementById('tracking-area');
        trackingArea.addEventListener('mousemove', onMouseMove);
        function onMouseMove(e) {
```

```
          setPosition({ x: e.offsetX, y: e.offsetY });
        }
      }
      function setPosition(position) {
        const { x, y } = position;
        const positionElement = document.getElementById('current-
            position');
        positionElement.innerHTML = `x: ${x}; y: ${y}`;
      }
    </script>
    <style>
      #tracking-area {
        width: 500px;
        height: 500px;
        border: 1px solid black;
      }
    </style>
  </head>
  <body>
    <h1 id="current-position"></h1>
    <div id="tracking-area">
      Move your mouse in here. If it's not working, click inside
      this box and try again.
    </div>
  </body>
</html>
```

The program in Listing 10-1 uses two calls to `addEventListener()`. The first one waits for the `load` event on the `window` object. The `window` object represents the current browser window. The `load` event is dispatched after an object loads and is displayed in the browser. When this event happens, the `app()` function is called.

Listening for the `load` event is necessary to make sure that the HTML elements that the rest of the program uses are available in the browser window before the `app()` function tries to access them.

TIP

Another way to accomplish the same result is to put your JavaScript block at the bottom of the HTML document.

Inside the `app()` function, the second event listener listens for mouse movements in the `<div>` element with the `ID` of `tracking-area`. When the mouse moves, the onMouseMove() function is called, which gets the current mouse position and updates the value of the <h1> element with an ID of current-position.

The key to how the onMouseMove() function works is the Event object.

The Event object

Note that the onMouseMove() function in Listing 10-1 receives a parameter called e — this is an event object. An *event object* is passed automatically to event handler callback functions. You can give the event object any name you like inside an event handler function, but it's most commonly called e, evt, or event.

The event object contains a wealth of information about the event that happened. To see all the information you can get from the event object, add the following statement inside the onMouseMove() function in Listing 10-1:

```
console.log("event:", e);
```

After you add this line and move your mouse, the generated event objects are logged to the console, as shown in Figure 10-2.

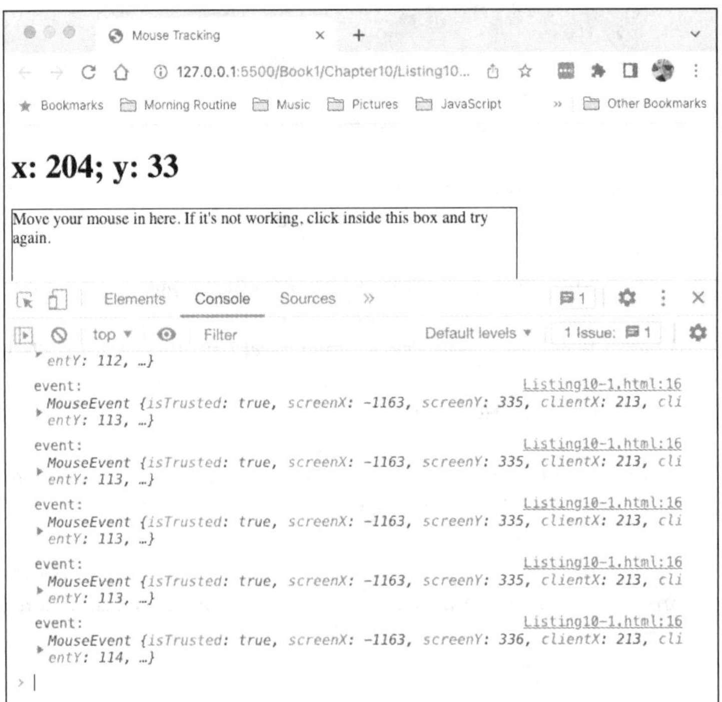

FIGURE 10-2: Viewing the event object.

Listening on multiple targets

Although `addEventListener()` applies an event listener to only a single target, it's possible to use a single `addEventListener()` method call to detect events on multiple events by using event bubbling. *Event bubbling* is the default method that browsers use to detect events on nested elements. Event bubbling refers to the fact that when an event happens on a nested node, such as a button inside a form, the button receives the event first and then bubbles up to the elements that contain the node where the event happened.

To detect events on multiple nodes, you can apply an event listener to an element that contains those nodes. For example, in Listing 10-2, the `<div>` element around the buttons combines them into a group. Because a click on any one of the buttons will bubble up to the `<div>` element, you can detect a click on any one of the buttons by listening for a `click` event on the `<div>` element.

LISTING 10-2: Using Event Bubbling to Detect Events on Multiple Elements

```
<!doctype html>
<html lang="en">
  <head>
    <meta charset="UTF-8"/>
    <meta http-equiv="X-UA-Compatible" content="IE=edge"/>
    <meta name="viewport" content="width=device-width,
         initial-scale=1.0"/>
    <title>Using Bubbling</title>
  </head>
  <body>
    <div id="button-group">
      <button>Click Me</button>
      <button>No, Click Me</button>
    </div>
    <script>
      document
        .getElementById('button-group')
        .addEventListener('click', () => alert('clicked'));
    </script>
  </body>
</html>
```

Dispatching events programmatically

Normally, events happen in response to an action outside your program, such as input from the browser or the user of the web page. Sometimes, however, it's useful to be able to create custom events or dispatch built-in events from your program itself. To accomplish this, you can use the `dispatchEvent()` method.

TECHNICAL STUFF

Unlike events fired by the browser, which invoke event handlers asynchronously by using the event loop, events fired using the `dispatchEvent()` method invoke event handlers synchronously.

To use `dispatchEvent()`, you first have to create an event object to dispatch. To create an event object, use the `new` keyword with the `Event` interface that contains the type of event you want to dispatch. For example, the `MouseEvent` interface can be used to create `click`, `mouseup`, and `mousedown` events, among others. Here's the code to create a simple click event:

```
const clickEvent = new MouseEvent('click');
```

Once you have the `click` event, call `dispatchEvent()` on an event target and pass it the event object you want to dispatch:

```
document.getElementById('my-button').dispatchEvent(clickEvent);
```

If an event listener is registered for that event on the event target, it will be handled.

Listing 10-3 shows how you can use `dispatchEvent()` to fire a `focus` event on an <input> element.

LISTING 10-3: Firing a Built-In Event

```
<!doctype html>
<html lang="en">
  <head>
    <meta charset="UTF-8"/>
    <meta http-equiv="X-UA-Compatible" content="IE=edge"/>
    <meta name="viewport" content="width=device-width,
          initial-scale=1.0"/>
    <title>Document</title>
  </head>
  <body>
    <input id="test-text" type="text" value="this is a test"/>
    <script>
      const focusEvent = new Event('focus');
      const testInput = document.getElementById('test-text');
```

```
    testInput.addEventListener('focus', (e) => {
      console.log(`${e.target.value}`);
    });
    testInput.dispatchEvent(focusEvent);
  </script>
</body>
</html>
```

If you run Listing 10-3 in a browser, you'll see that the event listener runs and logs the value of the input to the console. You might also notice that the `input` element isn't highlighted. If you click your mouse into the `<input>` element, however, the border of the element becomes bold to indicate that the element is active. If you add the following code to the event listener callback, you get a clue about what's going on:

```
console.log(`The active element is: ${document.activeElement.id}`);
```

When you refresh the page with this statement included, you see the following output in the console:

```
this is a test
The active element is:
```

If you click the input element, the event listener fires again, and the following text is added to the console:

```
this is a test
The active element is: test-text
```

Both the programmatically fired event and the event that resulted from clicking the element caused the event listener to run, but only clicking the event changed the state of the input element from unfocused to focused. This is because events are just the messengers. They don't do anything by themselves.

Triggering built-in events

If you want an event fired with `dispatchEvent()` to do something, you have to tell it what to do in the event handler function. Add the following line before the `console.log` statements in the `addEventListener()` callback function in Listing 10-3:

```
testInput.focus();
```

Now, when you look at the console, you see the following output:

```
this is a test
The active element is: test-text
this is a test
The active element is: test-text
```

Can you figure out why the message was printed twice? The `focus()` method of an element gives that element focus and dispatches the focus event. So, by using `dispatchEvent()` and then calling `focus()`, you created two `focus` events.

Creating and triggering custom events

You can use the `dispatchEvent()` method to dispatch custom events containing data as well. To pass data with an event, pass an object to the second parameter of the event interface containing a property called `detail`.

For example, you might want to create an event that passes a date object to the event listener when it's clicked, as in the following example:

```
const event = new CustomEvent('stampedClick', {detail: new Date()});
```

You can then access the `detail` property in the event handler callback:

```
testInput.addEventListener('stampedClick', (e) => {
  console.log(`Clicked at`, e.detail);
});
```

Removing event listeners

To remove an event listener, use the `removeEventListener()` method. To use `removeEventListener()`, pass it the type of event and the listener you want to remove.

If you're going to be using removeEventListener(), you need to create the event handler function outside of the addEventListener() method so that you can pass it to both addEventListener() and removeEventListener():

```
const handleClick = function(e){
console.log('click handled');
}
myButton.addEventListener('click', handleClick);
myButton.removeEventListener('click', handleClick);
```

Preventing default actions

Some elements have default actions that happen when certain events are fired. For example, the <form> element submits a form using HTTP when the submit event fires. If you don't want the default events to happen (as is often the case with the <form> element's default action), you can use the preventDefault() method inside your event handler:

```
e.preventDefault();
```

7 JavaScript Frameworks

Contents at a Glance

IN THIS CHAPTER

» Multitasking with asynchronous JavaScript

» Making promises you can keep

» Putting it all together with AJAX

» Using HTTP to make requests

» Using CORS to make simple and non-simple requests

» Working with JSON

Chapter 1
Writing Asynchronous JavaScript

"Your mind will answer most questions if you learn to relax and wait for the answer."

—WILLIAM S. BURROUGHS

There's no getting around the fact that everything a computer program does takes time. Some actions, like declaring a variable or performing a simple calculation, take such a small amount of time that the action seems instantaneous. But when programs start to involve network requests, database access, and access to resources outside of the web browser, wait times can start to add up.

In this chapter, you learn how asynchronous JavaScript keeps your code responsive, how events and callbacks work (and why nested callbacks become hard to manage), and how promises and async/await help you write clearer asynchronous code. You also use AJAX techniques such as fetch to retrieve data, work with JSON, and understand how CORS affects requests across domains.

Understanding Asynchronous JavaScript

Asynchronous programming is a technique that allows JavaScript to start a process and then continue to run the program while it waits for the result. It might seem confusing that JavaScript is single-threaded but also has a way to do asynchronous programming. To understand, it's helpful to think about asynchronous code in terms of an ordinary human activity such as washing your clothes.

When you wash your clothes by hand, you have to stop everything else you're doing until the clothes are clean. If you use a washing machine, you can turn it on and then go do something else. When the washing cycle is complete, the machine alerts you, and you can move the laundry to the dryer and then get back to work or finish your lunch.

Asynchronous JavaScript works the same way.

Reading synchronous code

All the JavaScript code examples in this book prior to this chapter run synchronously. In synchronous programming, one statement runs, followed by the next statement, and so on until the program is finished running or is stopped.

Listing 1-1 shows an example of a synchronous program.

LISTING 1-1: A Synchronous Program

```
function count(maxNumber) {
  let i = 0;
  while (i < maxNumber) {
    console.log(i);
    i++;
  }
}
count(1000);
```

Note that even though the program in Listing 1-1 contains a loop and a function, you can still follow the execution of the code step-by-step and know the order in which statements will be executed.

Synchronous programming is easy to understand, and there's nothing inherently bad about it. In fact, synchronous code is a necessary part of every JavaScript program.

Problems with synchronous code occur when a process takes a long time to complete. Because JavaScript is single-threaded, statements that take a long time to execute block anything else from happening. The user of such a program perceives that the program is unresponsive.

Events to the rescue

Event handlers provide JavaScript with a way to do asynchronous programming. When you use `addEventListener()`, you tell JavaScript to do something whenever it detects a certain type of event. Without being able to create event listeners, any type of event would have to happen in a particular order, and modern JavaScript user interfaces would be impossible.

Consider, for example, the synchronous user interface in Listing 1-2.

LISTING 1-2: A Synchronous JavaScript User Interface

```
<!doctype html>
<html lang="en">
  <head>
    <meta charset="UTF-8"/>
    <meta http-equiv="X-UA-Compatible" content="IE=edge"/>
    <meta name="viewport" content="width=device-width,
          initial-scale=1.0"/>
    <title>Login Form</title>
    <script>
      alert('Welcome to the login screen');
      const username = prompt('Enter your username:');
      const password = prompt('Enter your password:');
      alert('Click OK to continue logging in');
      doLogin();
      function doLogin() {
        alert(`logging in ${username}...`);
      }
    </script>
  </head>
  <body></body>
</html>
```

In the synchronous login form, the data entry and messages are done using `alert()` and `prompt()`. Both methods are synchronous. Everything in your program stops, and you can't use the browser while they wait for input.

Now consider the asynchronous version of this program, shown in Listing 1-3.

LISTING 1-3: An Asynchronous JavaScript User Interface

```
<!doctype html>
<html lang="en">
  <head>
    <meta charset="UTF-8"/>
    <meta http-equiv="X-UA-Compatible" content="IE=edge"/>
    <meta name="viewport" content="width=device-width,
          initial-scale=1.0"/>
    <title>Login Form</title>
  </head>
  <body>
    <h1 id="status"></h1>
    <label
      >Username
      <input id="username" type="text"/>
    </label>
    <label
      >Password
      <input id="password" type="password"/>
    </label>
    <button id="login">Log In</button>
    <script>
      const username = document.getElementById('username');
      const password = document.getElementById('password');
      const loginBtn = document.getElementById('login');
      const statusMsg = document.getElementById('status');
      loginBtn.addEventListener('click', doLogin);
      function doLogin() {
        statusMsg.innerHTML = `logging in ${username.value}...`;
      }
    </script>
  </body>
</html>
```

On the asynchronous login form, you don't need to enter your username or password in a certain order, and the rest of the program (if there were more JavaScript in this example) can continue to run at the same time.

Calling you back

The `doLogin()` function in Listing 1-3 is passed to `addEventListener()` as a callback function.

REMEMBER

A *callback function* is passed to another function that will be called at a later time. In the case of `addEventListener()`, the callback function is called when the event listener detects an event.

Callback functions are one way to write asynchronous code, but they do present some problems when you need to complete a series of steps instead of just one action.

For example, consider the following series of steps:

1. When the user clicks the button, start the login process.
2. When the login is finished, check to see whether it was successful.
3. If the login wasn't successful, show an error message and exit the steps.
4. If the login was successful, load the members-only screen.
5. When the members screen finishes loading, display it.

Because each of the steps in this process can't be done until some condition is met (such as the button being clicked or the login process finishing), you need to pass the functions that perform each of these steps as callbacks by nesting the callbacks, as shown in Listing 1-4.

LISTING 1-4: Nested Callbacks

```
sendLoginData(
  args,
  function (result) {
    logIn(
      result,
      function (result) {
        loadPage(
          result,
          function () {
            console.log(`result: ${result}`);
          },
          failureCallback,
        );
      },
```

(continued)

LISTING 1-4: (continued)

```
      failureCallback,
    );
  },
  failureCallback,
);
loginBtn.addEventListener('click', sendLoginData);
```

The code in Listing 1-4 is greatly simplified, but you can see that the doLogin() function has multiple levels of nested functions. This type of code is difficult to read and debug. Complex programs written using callbacks can have many more levels of nested functions. Because of the way the nested callbacks form a triangle (if you look at it sideways), nested callbacks have been nicknamed the Pyramid of Doom or the Christmas Tree.

Making Promises

A *promise* is an object (created from JavaScript's built-in Promise interface) that represents the result of an asynchronous operation. A promise lets you work with the result of an asynchronous operation as though it were synchronous and without complex nesting of callbacks.

Promises in JavaScript work like promises in real life — for example, you run a restaurant and a customer promises to pay you Tuesday for a hamburger you give him today.

When the promise is made, the result of the promise is unknown. The only thing you know is that the person will eventually keep the promise or not keep it. In programming, we say that there are three possible *states* for the promise:

- **Pending:** The promise has been made, but the outcome is uncertain.
- **Fulfilled:** The promise was kept, and the customer paid you on Tuesday.
- **Rejected:** The promise wasn't kept.

Promises still use callback functions, but rather than using nesting to pass a value from one finished task to the next, they use a *promise chain.* For example, the nested callbacks from Listing 1-4 can be rewritten with promises, as shown in Listing 1-5.

LISTING 1-5: Creating a Promise Chain

```
doLogin()
  .then((result) => sendLoginData(result))
  .then((result1) => logIn(result1))
  .then((result2) => loadPage(result2))
  .then((result3) => {
    console.log(`final result: ${result3}`);
  })
  .catch(failureCallback);
```

These are the important things to know about using promises:

- Each function in a callback chain must return a promise.
- The `then()` function is actually a type of event handler that executes the function passed to it when the previous function in the chain returns.
- The `catch()` handler runs only when one of the steps in the chain fails.

Writing promises

To create a basic promise, use the `new` keyword with the `Promise` constructor. The `Promise` constructor takes a callback function as its argument. This callback function takes two callback function arguments: `resolve` and `reject`:

```
let myPromise = new Promise((resolve, reject) => {
  someAsynchronousFunction(function () {
    resolve('Success!');
  });
});
```

Once you've created a promise, you can chain it with other promises using `then()`:

```
myPromise.then((result) => {
  // do something with the result
});
```

Listing 1-6 shows a program that uses a promise and the `XMLHttpRequest()` method to load text from a web server and then display it. The `XMLHttpRequest()` method is an older API that's still widely supported. Most modern JavaScript code now uses the `fetch()` method, which you learn about later in this chapter.

LISTING 1-6: Using a Promise to Load Data with XMLHttpRequest()

```
<!doctype html>
<html lang="en">
  <head>
    <meta charset="UTF-8"/>
    <meta http-equiv="X-UA-Compatible" content="IE=edge"/>
    <meta name="viewport" content="width=device-width,
          initial-scale=1.0"/>
    <title>Document</title>
  </head>
  <body>
    <div id="text-display-area"></div>
    <script>
      function bookLoad(url) {
        return new Promise(function (resolve, reject) {
          let request = new XMLHttpRequest();
          request.open('GET', url);
          request.onload = function () {
            if (request.status === 200) {
              resolve(request.response);
            } else {
              reject(
                Error(`The text couldn't be loaded: ${request.
                      statusText}`),
              );
            }
          };
          request.onerror = function () {
            reject(Error('There was a network error.'));
          };
          request.send();
        });
      }
      const displayArea = document.getElementById('text-
           display-area');
      bookLoad('https://www.gutenberg.org/files/2701/2701-0.txt').
        then(
        function (response) {
          displayArea.innerText = response;
        },
        function (err) {
```

```
        console.log(err);
      },
    );
  </script>
</body>
</html>
```

If you try to run the program in Listing 1-6 in your browser, you get an error in the console that looks something like Figure 1-1.

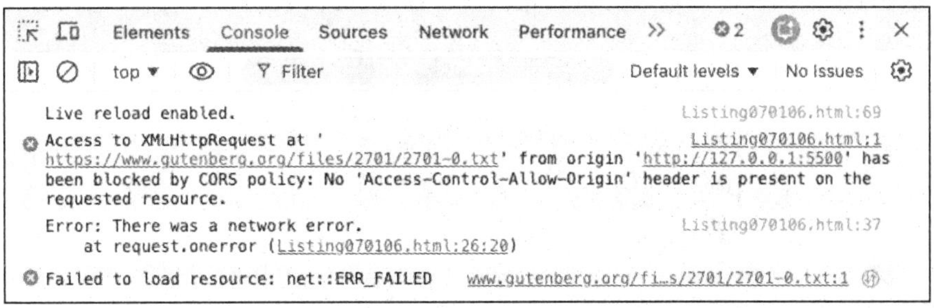

FIGURE 1-1: The error generated when running Listing 1-6.

Your browser is blocking the program from reading the text from the Project Gutenberg server. This happens because web browsers enforce the *same-origin policy:* By default, a page can read data only from the same origin (same protocol, domain, and port) that served the page.

A server can choose to allow cross-origin requests by sending specific HTTP headers. That opt-in mechanism is called *Cross-Origin Resource Sharing* (CORS). Project Gutenberg's text files don't include the CORS headers needed for a browser page to read them directly, so the request fails even though the URL works fine when you visit it in your browser.

Follow these steps to see the same-origin policy in practice and to learn how to make requests succeed by requesting a document from the same location:

1. **Download a local copy of the file you want to load.**

   For example, visit www.gutenberg.org/files/2701/2701-0.txt and save it as `mobydick.txt` in the same folder as your HTML file (the one containing Listing 1-6).

2. **Locate the call to `bookLoad()` near the end of Listing 1-6**

```
bookLoad('https://www.gutenberg.org/files/2701/2701-0.
  txt').then(
```

And change it to this:

```
bookLoad('mobydick.txt').then(
```

This change loads the text from the same origin as your page, which avoids the cross-origin restriction.

3. **Run the page from a local web server.**

   For example, in VS Code, you can right-click the HTML file and choose Open with Live Server. When the page opens in your browser, the script runs. Once `mobydick.txt` is loaded, the promise resolves and the text is displayed, as shown in Figure 1-2.

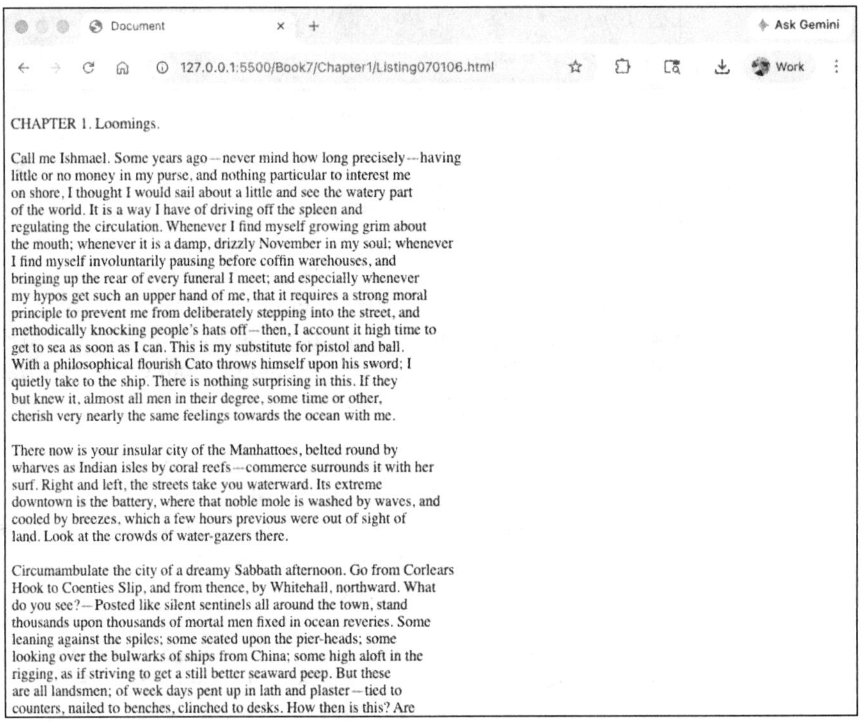

FIGURE 1-2: Loading and displaying a local file.

Introducing async functions

Promises and promise chains are a great improvement over nested callbacks in terms of readability, but there's a better way to write asynchronous code: using async functions.

To write an *async function*, prefix the name of the function with the `async` keyword. Once you do that, you can write expressions using the `await` keyword inside the function:

```
async function getData (){
  const response = await fetch('http://www.example.com/data');
  return response;
}
```

If you want to run asynchronous operations in a sequence, the way you would with nested callbacks or a promise chain, you just write additional `await` expressions. Each `await` expression waits for the asynchronous operation to resolve before allowing the next expression to proceed, as in this example:

```
async function getData (){
  const response = await fetch('http://www.example.com/data');
  const response2 = await processData(response);
  return response2;
}
```

Behind the scenes, async functions use promises. The `await` keyword is essentially a `.then` callback, and the `return` statement in an async function is the final link in a promise chain. Async functions always return a promise.

Async functions make writing asynchronous code as easy and straightforward as writing synchronous code. Once you become comfortable with async functions, you'll want to start rewriting anything that uses nested callbacks or promises. The next two sections show you how to do that.

Converting nested callbacks to async functions

Although newer APIs generally return promises, many common APIs still use callbacks. For example, the `setTimeout()` function causes a browser to wait for a certain number of milliseconds before it invokes a callback. Here's an example of using `setTimeout()`:

```
setTimeout(() => console.log('done!'), 1000);
```

This statement waits 1 second (1000 milliseconds) before invoking an arrow function that will log the word *done* to the console. Granted, it's not an exciting program, but because `setTimeout()` runs asynchronously, if you want to do something else after the message is logged to the console, you need to nest callbacks inside the callback, as shown in Listing 1-7.

LISTING 1-7: Nested setTimeout Calls

```
function doProcessing() {
  var timeout;
  timeout = setTimeout(function () {
    console.log('doing first thing');
    timeout = setTimeout(function () {
      console.log('step 2');
      timeout = setTimeout(function () {
        console.log('step 3');
        setTimeout(function () {
          console.log('last thing!');
        }, 300);
      }, 1000);
    }, 2500);
  }, 3000);
}
doProcessing();
```

Functions that were written to accept callbacks present a problem when you're trying to use them with async/await: They don't return promises. Because async/await is an abstraction of promises, it seems that libraries built using callbacks would necessarily crush your dreams of switching entirely to using async functions.

However, all hope is not lost, because you can "promisify" callback functions! To convert the `doProcessing()` function from Listing 1-7 to promises, you can create a promisified version of `setTimeout()`. To do this, wrap the `Promise` constructor in a function. The `Promise` constructor gets the arguments and passes them to the callback, as shown here:

```
const promisifiedSetTimeout = function (ms) {
  return new Promise(function (res) {
    return setTimeout(res, ms);
  });
};
```

With this new `promisifiedSetTimeout()` function, you can rewrite the `doProcessing()` function using async/await, as shown in Listing 1-8.

LISTING 1-8: Rewriting doProcessing() Using async/await

```
async function doProcessingAsync() {
  await promisifiedSetTimeout(3000);
  console.log('doing first thing');
  await promisifiedSetTimeout(2500);
  console.log('step 2');
  await promisifiedSetTimeout(1000);
  console.log('step 3');
  await promisifiedSetTimeout(300);
  console.log('last thing');
}
doProcessingAsync();
```

REMEMBER

Listing 1-7 and Listing 1-8 produce the same result. Which one do you prefer, in terms of readability and ease of use?

Converting promise chains to async functions

Converting a promise chain to an async function is simply a matter of converting the `.then` functions to `await` expressions and using conditional statements to handle any errors that occur. Listing 1-9 shows the `bookLoad()` function from Listing 1-6 rewritten to use async/await.

LISTING 1-9: Replacing a Promise Chain with an async Function

```
<!doctype html>
<html lang="en">
  <head>
    <meta charset="UTF-8"/>
    <meta http-equiv="X-UA-Compatible" content="IE=edge"/>
    <meta name="viewport" content="width=device-width,
          initial-scale=1.0"/>
    <title>Read a book</title>
  </head>
  <body>
    <div id="text-display-area"></div>
    <script>
      const displayArea = document.getElementById('text-display-
            area');
      async function openBook() {
        const bookText = await bookLoad('mobydick.txt');
```

(continued)

LISTING 1-9: *(continued)*

```
        displayArea.innerText = bookText;
      }
      function bookLoad(url) {
        return new Promise(function (resolve, reject) {
          let request = new XMLHttpRequest();
          request.open('GET', url);
          request.onload = function () {
            if (request.status === 200) {
              resolve(request.response);
            } else {
              reject(
                Error(`The text couldn't be loaded: ${request.
                      statusText}`),
              );
            }
          };
          request.onerror = function () {
            reject(Error('There was a network error.'));
          };
          request.send();
        });
      }
      openBook();
    </script>
  </body>
</html>
```

Handling errors with async/await

Unlike with promise chains, there's no `catch` function for async functions. Instead, you can use a `try/catch` statement — it's made up of a `try` block and either a `catch` block, a `finally` block, or both a `catch` block and a `finally` block. Here's the syntax:

```
try {
  // try to do something
} catch(e) {
  // do something with e, which is an Error object
} finally {
  // something to do whether successful or not
}
```

In an async function, put the `await` expressions in a `try` block, and put error reporting or error-handling code in the `catch` block, as shown here:

```
async function openBook() {
try {
const bookText = await bookLoad('mobydick.txt');
displayArea.innerText = bookText;
} catch(e) {
displayArea.innerText = e;
}
}
```

In this example, when the file is loaded and successfully displayed, the `catch` block is skipped. If the promise returned by `bookLoad()` is rejected, the error is displayed.

Using AJAX

AJAX stands for *a*synchronous *J*avaScript *a*nd *X*ML — the technique that makes dynamic JavaScript user interfaces possible in web browsers. These days (and for most of the time JavaScript programmers have been using this acronym), the primary way it has been used is with JSON data (which I describe shortly) rather than XML. So a more appropriate name for AJAX would be AJAJ.

AJAX uses asynchronous APIs along with the Document Object Model (DOM) to enable the modern web application experience. These are some of the features that AJAX enables:

- Updating only part of a page
- Receiving and sending live data
- Infinitely scrolling user interfaces
- Adding forms with autocomplete capabilities
- Incorporating Like buttons

For the rest of this chapter, I talk about the techniques and APIs that are used for accessing data asynchronously today.

Getting data with the Fetch API

The Fetch API is a way to access files and to make HTTP requests. The most basic form of using the Fetch API is to provide the `fetch()` method with a path to a resource (such as a file or a data stream), like this:

```
fetch('myfile.json');
```

The `fetch()` method returns a promise that resolves to a `Response` object.

A `Response` object represents a response to a request made using the Fetch API. To see an example of a `Response` object, type the following statement into your browser's JavaScript console:

```
const response = await fetch('https://api.github.com/orgs/facebook');
```

This statement fetches information about Facebook's GitHub repositories.

TIP

If for some reason this URL doesn't exist in the future, you can use this same scheme to find information about any public repositories on GitHub.

After you fetch the data from GitHub, you can type the name of the new constant you created (`response`) into the console to see its value. Because you used `await`, the value stored in `response` is a `Response` object (not a promise). The *promise* is returned by `fetch()`; `await` waits for that promise to be fulfilled and gives you the `Response` object, as shown in Figure 1-3.

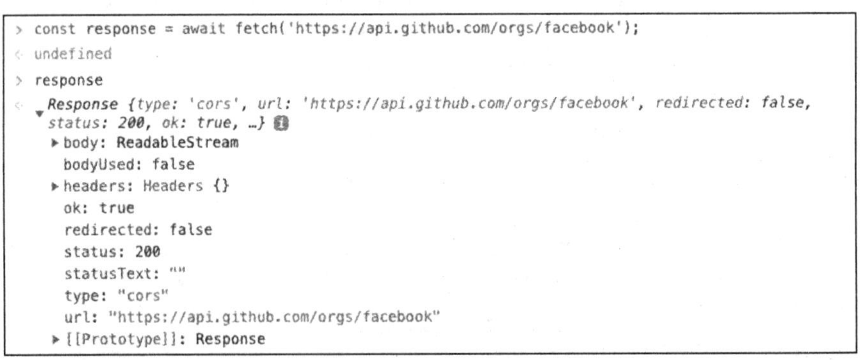

FIGURE 1-3: A fulfilled promise from a `fetch()` call.

If you expand the `Promise` and look at the `Prototype`, you can see that a `Response` has a number of properties and methods. The property of the `Response` object that contains the data returned by the `fetch()` method is the `body` property.

But if you expand the `body` property, you can see that it doesn't seem to contain data you can read. Instead, it tells you that the body is `ReadableStream`. A stream works similarly to how streaming video or audio works. It's not a video file or an audio file itself, but the stream of data can be assembled into video or audio with some parsing. In the same way, you need to do some parsing to convert the response's `body` property to data you can work with in your programs.

Fortunately, the `Response` object provides methods for parsing the response body easily. The method you use to parse this stream retrieved from GitHub is the `json()` method. The `json()` method returns a `Promise` that resolves to the result of parsing the body stream as `json()` data.

I tell you what JSON data is shortly.

In the console window, use the `json()` method on the `Response` object returned by `fetch()`:

```
const data = await response.json();
```

Now, if you type **data** into the console, you see that the response body has been converted into a JavaScript object, as shown in Figure 1-4.

FIGURE 1-4: Converting a response body to an object.

Working with this object is now just like working with any other JavaScript object.

Calling other response methods

The `json()` method of the `Response` object returned by `fetch()` is the most frequently used method. However, the `Response` object provides several other useful methods: `blob()` and `text()`.

If the content returned by the server is file data (such as a video, a PDF file, or an image), use the `blob()` method to convert the ReadableStream returned by the server into a binary file. Like the other response methods that convert the response to a different type of data, `blob()` returns a promise, so it must be called asynchronously, either as part of a promise chain or by using the `await` keyword inside an async function.

TECHNICAL STUFF

Blob is the acronym for *b*inary *l*arge *ob*ject.

The `text()` method returns a promise that resolves to a text representation of the body.

Handling fetch() errors

A `fetch()` promise is rejected only for problems that prevent the request from completing (for example, being offline, a DNS failure, or a connection error). However, many other errors you care about in real applications are still valid HTTP responses. For example, a server can respond with `404` (Not Found) or `500` (Server Error). In that case, `fetch()` still resolves, so your code must check the HTTP status and handle it appropriately.

To detect and handle HTTP-level errors (such as 404 or 500) that happen with a `fetch()` request, check the `Response` object that the promise resolves to. The simplest option is to check the `response.ok` property, which is `true` for successful (2*xx*) responses.

TECHNICAL STUFF

In HTTP, status codes in the `200–299` range indicate success. That's what `response.ok` checks. You'll most commonly see `200` (OK) and `201` (Created), but other 2*xx* codes can appear depending on the request.

Listing 1-10 shows how to capture both network errors and HTTP errors that happen with `fetch()`.

LISTING 1-10: Catching Errors with fetch()

```
async function fetchTheData(url) {
  try {
    const response = await fetch(url);
```

```
    if (response.ok) {
      return response.json();
    } else {
      throw new Error(`HTTP ${response.status}: ${response.
            statusText}`);
    }
  } catch (error) {
    console.log(error);
  }
}
```

To use the function from Listing 1-10, pass it a URL as an argument. There are four possible outcomes from any request that this function will handle:

- The request is successful.
- The request results in a network error.
- The request results in an HTTP error.
- The request isn't made because the browser prevents it due to cross-origin policy restrictions.

Figure 1-5 shows an example of each of these results in the browser console.

FIGURE 1-5: The possible outcomes of an HTTP request.

The fetch init object

The second parameter that the `fetch()` method accepts is an object, called the `init` object, which controls settings for the request. If you're using `fetch()` to do anything more than make a simple `GET` request to a publicly available API (such as GitHub's), you need to set various options for the request to be successful.

These are the most important options you can set with the `init` object:

- **method:** The `method` option is where you specify the HTTP method. See the later section "Introducing HTTP" to find out more about HTTP methods.
- **headers:** The `headers` option takes as its argument an object containing the HTTP headers you want to send with your request.
- **body:** The `body` option is where you can pass data to the server when you're making any type of request other than one done by using the `GET` or `HEAD` method.
- **mode:** The `mode` option is important for being able to make requests to different domains than the web page's origin. The options for `mode` include `cors`, `no-cors`, and `same-origin`.
- **credentials:** The `credentials` option tells the browser whether to send credentials to the server with the request. The possible values for credentials are `omit`, `same-origin`, and `include`.

To know which options you need to use with a `fetch()` request, you need to understand a few more concepts, including how HTTP works and how CORS works.

Introducing HTTP

Hypertext Transfer Protocol (HTTP) is the protocol used to communicate on the web. Every time a web browser fetches a web page, an image, a media file, or any other type of resource from the web, it's using HTTP.

HTTP is a client-server protocol. The client is typically a web browser, and the server is a web server. The client and server communicate with each other using messages.

TECHNICAL STUFF

The client in an HTTP conversation is also known as the *user agent.*

Messages sent by the client are called *requests*, and messages sent by the server are called *responses*.

If you still have your browser window open from doing the `fetch()` in the preceding section, you can see examples of HTTP requests and responses. Chrome Developer Tools has a tab called Network. If you switch to that tab, you see the request you performed, as shown in Figure 1-6.

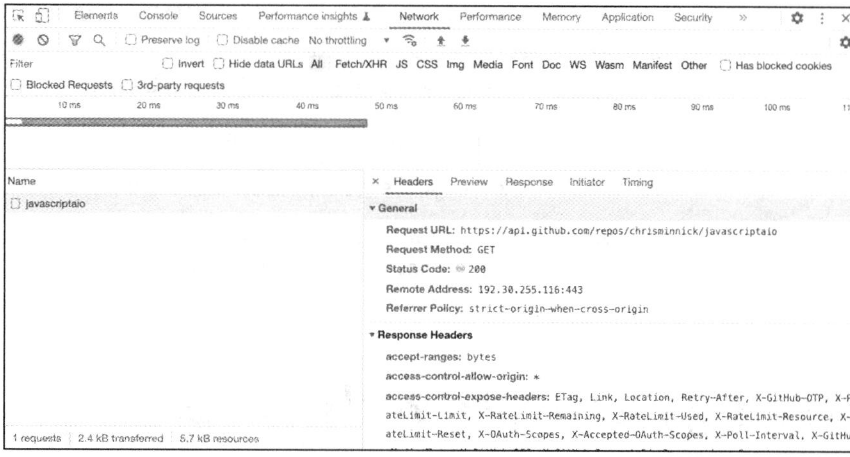

FIGURE 1-6: The Network tab.

If you click the subtabs on the Network tab, you see details about the request and the response. On the Headers tab, you can see the header data, which includes metadata sent by the client and by the server.

The most important pieces of data in the headers are the request method and the status Code.

The request method is usually one of the following:

- **GET:** Gets data from a server. It's the method used by the `fetch()` method when you invoke it with just a single argument.
- **POST:** Submits data to the specified URL. This method is used, for example, when you submit a form on the web.
- **PUT:** Replaces the target resource with the payload of the HTTP request.
- **PATCH:** Makes a partial update to a resource. For example, a request that will result in only some fields of a database record being updated should use PATCH.
- **DELETE:** Deletes the specified resource.

The HTTP status codes indicate whether the HTTP request was successful and tell you what went wrong if it wasn't successful. HTTP status codes range from 100 to

599. In web application development, however, you're likely to see only the following status codes:

- **200:** The request succeeded. This is the status code everyone hopes to see.
- **301:** The requested resource has permanently moved to a new URL, which is given in the response. Think of a 301 redirect as a change-of-address form.
- **400:** A bad request. In web application programming, your request might be missing a piece of data required by the server.
- **401:** Your request isn't authorized. You likely need to provide authentication data.
- **404:** The resource you're looking for can't be found.
- **500:** Internal server error. When you see this error, it often indicates that something went wrong on the server.

Making Requests with CORS

JavaScript's capability to reach out of the browser and fetch data is useful and is an important tool for programming web apps. However, it also has the potential to be misused by malicious scripts. For example, a malicious script embedded in a website might attempt to access sensitive data from another site or API. To reduce this risk, browsers enforce a same-origin policy, which restricts scripts on one origin (such as `www.example.com`) from accessing resources on a different origin (such as `www.evilsite.com`).

However, scripts have legitimate reasons to access resources from other origins. For example, if your web app is located at `www.mywebsite.com` and you have a database server at `database.mywebsite.com`, same-origin policy prevents access to the database server, unless you have some way for the server to tell the browser it's okay. Services such as Google Maps and thousands of publicly available sources of data also rely on the capability to share data across different origins.

The method used by browsers and servers for allowing cross-origin HTTP requests is called the cross-origin resource sharing standard, or *CORS.* CORS uses HTTP headers that let the server tell browsers what origins and types of requests it allows.

Making a simple request

When a browser makes a cross-origin request using the `GET`, `HEAD`, or `POST` method with certain content types (including form data and plain text), it's known as a *simple request.*

In a simple request, the browser makes the request and the server responds with a status code of 200 if the origin of the script is allowed by the value of the server's `Access-Control-Allow-Origin` header.

To see an example of a simple request, type the following statement into your browser console:

```
await fetch('https://api.github.com/repos/chrisminnick/
   javascriptaio');
```

After a second, the promise resolves and the response appears. You can view the HTTP headers by switching to the Network tab, as shown in Figure 1-7.

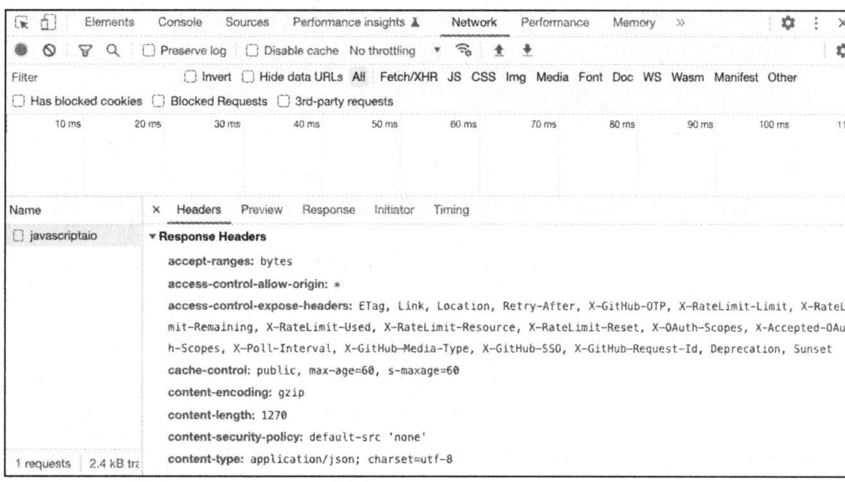

FIGURE 1-7: Viewing the HTTP headers.

If you look at the Response Headers section on the Network tab, you can see the `Access-Control-Allow-Origin` header, with a value of `*`. This indicates that the server allows simple requests from any origin.

Servers may restrict access to just certain domains as well. For example, if this server wanted to allow access only from the `example.com` domain, it could send the following header:

```
Access-Control-Allow-Origin: https://example.com
```

Making a non-simple request

Non-simple requests have the potential to change server data. In these cases, the browser makes a preflight request. The preflight request uses the `OPTIONS` HTTP method. It tells the server the details of the request it wants to make, including the origin of the script, the HTTP method of the request, and the headers it wants to send.

A typical preflight request looks like this:

```
OPTIONS /user HTTP/1.1
Host: example.com
User-Agent: Mozilla/5.0 (Macintosh; Intel Mac OS X 10.15.7)
Accept: application/json
Accept-Language: en-us,en;q=0.9
Accept-Encoding: gzip,deflate
Connection: keep-alive
Origin: https://foo.com
Access-Control-Request-Method: POST
Access-Control-Request-Headers: X-PINGOTHER, Content-Type
```

The server then responds to the request with something like the following:

```
HTTP/1.1 204 No Content
Server: Apache/2
Access-Control-Allow-Origin: https://foo.com
Access-Control-Allow-Methods: POST, GET, OPTIONS
Access-Control-Allow-Headers: X-PINGOTHER, Content-Type
Access-Control-Max-Age: 86400
Vary: Accept-Encoding, Origin
Keep-Alive: timeout=2, max=100
Connection: Keep-Alive
```

If the allowed methods, origin, and headers returned by the server match the requested method, origin, and headers, the browser then proceeds to make the actual request.

If the server is configured correctly, all you need to do to make a request with CORS is to pass the `mode` option with a value of '`cors`':

```
fetch('https://www.example.com/user',{mode:'cors'});
```

Working with JSON Data

The most common format for sending and receiving data to and from JavaScript applications is *JavaScript Object Notation*, or *JSON*. JSON data resembles JavaScript object literal notation, and it's easy to convert between JSON data and JavaScript objects.

Listing 1-11 shows an example of data in JSON format.

LISTING 1-11: JSON Data

```
{
  "coord": {
    "lon": -122.08,
    "lat": 37.39
  },
  "weather": [
    {
      "id": 800,
      "main": "Clear",
      "description": "clear sky",
      "icon": "01d"
    }
  ],
  "base": "stations",
  "main": {
    "temp": 282.55,
    "feels_like": 281.86,
    "temp_min": 280.37,
    "temp_max": 284.26,
    "pressure": 1023,
    "humidity": 100
  },
  "visibility": 10000,
  "wind": {
    "speed": 1.5,
    "deg": 350
  },
  "clouds": {
    "all": 1
  },
  "dt": 1560350645,
```

(continued)

LISTING 1-11: ***(continued)***

```
  "sys": {
    "type": 1,
    "id": 5122,
    "message": 0.0139,
    "country": "US",
    "sunrise": 1560343627,
    "sunset": 1560396563
  },
  "timezone": -25200,
  "id": 420006353,
  "name": "Mountain View",
  "cod": 200
}
```

The code in Listing 1-11 bears a striking resemblance to a JavaScript object. However, if you look closely, you can see that it's not. The first difference is that the left-hand sides of the colons are in quotes. The other difference is that JSON data isn't assigned to a variable or constant. An object isn't any use if it's not assigned a name. JSON data, on the other hand, is extremely useful for sending and receiving data.

TECHNICAL STUFF

JSON can also be used with programming languages besides JavaScript, and most languages include tools for working with JSON data.

Although the data in Listing 1-11 starts and ends with curly braces, it's common to see JSON data that starts and ends with square brackets and therefore turns into an array when it's converted from JSON data.

Getting JSON data

The most common way to get JSON data into your application is by using `fetch()`. Once you have the JSON data, you can use the `Response` object's `json()` method to convert it to data that can be used inside your JavaScript code.

If you don't use `fetch()` to get the JSON data into your program (for example, if you load a JSON file directly into the program), you still need to convert it to

JavaScript before you can use it. You can use JavaScript's built-in `JSON.parse()` method to do this.

To see JSON parse in action, you can create a JSON string like the following:

```
const person = '{"firstName": "Conway","age": 59}';
```

Note that the value of `person` is a string. As such, there's no easy way to extract the individual names or values from it. Here's how to convert a JSON string to an object:

```
const personObject = JSON.parse(person);
```

Sending JSON data

If you have an object in your application that you want to send to a server as JSON data, it needs to be converted to JSON before it can be sent. JavaScript has a built-in method that does this for you, called `JSON.stringify()`.

To use the `stringify()` method, pass an object or value into it. For example, if you followed the steps to create a JSON string and convert it to an object in the preceding section, you can convert it back to a JSON string:

```
const personJSON = JSON.stringify(personObject);
```

IN THIS CHAPTER

» Exporting and importing modules

» Loading modules dynamically

» Using modules with HTML files

Chapter 2

Using JavaScript Modules

"Divide each difficulty into as many parts as is feasible and necessary to resolve it."

—RENE DESCARTES

Until now, every JavaScript program you've written has been in a single file, which is fine for small programs and examples. But, in real-life programming, a program may have thousands of lines of code. Keeping everything in a single file in a large program would make your code impossible to maintain.

To keep your code organized, to enable multiple people to work on a project, and to help you think about your code more easily, JavaScript provides a way to subdivide programs into modules.

In this chapter, you learn how to split your JavaScript programs into modules so you can organize code more effectively and reuse it across files. You learn how to create modules with `export`, how to use them elsewhere with `import` or by importing them into HTML files, and how to work with both named and default exports.

Exporting Modules

A JavaScript *module* is a file whose contents you can import into another file. A module can contain various things, including functions, variables, constants, or classes. In the same way that using functions helps keep your JavaScript files organized, using modules helps keep your JavaScript programs organized.

JavaScript modules are enabled by two keywords: `export` and `import`.

To create a module, you have to export it by using the `export` keyword. For example, one common and simple use for modules is to store constants that are used frequently in your program. To start this file, you might create a file named `constants.js`.

Examples of constants might include the base URL for an API used by your program, color themes, and labels and text used in your application. Listing 2-1 shows what this `constants.js` file might look like.

LISTING 2-1: A File Containing Modules

```
export const API = 'https://api.example.com';
export const colorThemeDark = {
  backgroundColor: '#000',
  textColor: '#EEE',
  headerColor: '#FF0000',
  footerColor: '#FF0000',
};
export const colorThemeLight = {
  backgroundColor: '#fff',
  textColor: '#333',
  headerColor: '#FF0000',
  footerColor: '#FF0000',
};
export const labels = {
  english: {
    supportLink: 'Get Support',
    contactLink: 'Contact Us',
  },
};
```

Modules can be created in one of two ways: as named exports or as default exports, as described next.

Named exports

The export statements in Listing 2-1 are examples of named exports. A *named export* creates a module with the same name as the variable, constant, function, or class that's being exported. One way to create a named export is to preface the declaration of the variable, constant, function, or class with the word *export*. Listing 2-2 shows a named export created from a function.

LISTING 2-2: A Named Function Export

```
export function addOne(input) {
  return input + 1;
}
```

You can also create named exports by using an `export` statement that's separate from the feature you want to export. To create a separate export statement, specify one or more names of variables, constants, functions, or classes surrounded by curly braces and separated by commas. For example, rather than specify an export statement for each of the modules created in Listing 2-1, you can remove the `export` statement that prefaces each constant and just write the following `export` statement:

```
export {API, colorThemeDark, colorThemeLight, labels};
```

REMEMBER

An `export` statement containing all the modules you want to export from a file is typically placed at the end of the file.

Default exports

Default exports specify a single function or class from a file. Unlike named exports, default exports are not associated with a particular name. Instead, a default export is associated with the file it's a part of. (This topic will make more sense if you read the following section, where I show you how to import modules.)

You can create a default export by prefacing the name of a function or class with `export default`. For example, to write the module from Listing 2-2 as a default export, you just need to add `default` after `export`, like this:

```
export default function addOne(input){
return input + 1;
}
```

A file can have only one default export. But a module with a default export can also have multiple named exports. For example, Listing 2-3 shows a file containing several named exports as well as a default export.

LISTING 2-3: A File Containing Named Exports and a Default Export

```
// oregonInfo.js
export const stateName = 'Oregon';
export const capitalCity = 'Salem';
export const stateBird = 'Western meadowlark';
export default function getStateInfo() {
  return { stateName, capitalCity, stateBird };
}
```

Using the `oregonInfo.js` file from Listing 2-3, you can make use of individual constants, or you can import and run the default function to get an object containing data from multiple constants in the file.

The return value of the `getStateInfo()` function in Listing 2-3 demonstrates a shorthand method of using properties of an object where the name and value of the property are the same. In this case, the following `return` statement:

```
return {stateName, capitalCity, stateBird};
```

is equivalent to this one:

```
return {stateName: stateName, capitalCity: capitalCity,
  stateBird: stateBird};
```

For example, when you create named exports, you can also write an export for a default export as a separate statement. A default export just uses the `export` keyword followed by `default`, followed by the name of the variable, constant, function, or class that should be the default export:

```
export default getStateInfo;
```

Importing Modules

After you've created modules by using the `export` statement, you can import them into other JavaScript files by using the `import` keyword. Unlike export statements, which can be placed anywhere at the top level of a file, `import` statements typically appear at the beginning of a file.

Imported modules can be used as though they were created in the same file. However, unlike functions and variables that you create in a JavaScript file, imported modules are read-only.

Importing named exports

Following is the basic syntax for importing named exports:

```
import {moduleName} from 'file path';
```

`moduleName` can be a single exported module or a comma-separated list of module names. `'file path'` is the relative path from the file doing the importing to the file containing the module.

For example, if you keep your modules in a folder called `modules` and the file you want to import them from is outside the `modules` folder, you can import modules from a file inside the `modules` folder by specifying the path as `./modules/filename.js`, where `filename.js` is the name of the file containing the module or modules you want to import. The complete import statement needed to import `stateName` and `capitalCity` from a file named `/modules/oregonInfo.js` would look like this:

```
import {stateName,capitalCity} from './modules/oregonInfo.js';
```

Note that the path to the file you're importing from has the period-slash (`./`) characters before the path. These characters tell the `import` statement to start from the current directory. If the folder you're importing from is at a higher level in the folder structure than the file you're importing to, you use `../` to tell the `import` statement to start one level higher in the folder hierarchy. Likewise, if the folder is two levels higher in the hierarchy, you use `../../`.

Importing default exports

To import a module that was exported as a default export, use the `import` statement without curly braces. Because you're allowed to have only one default export per file, you don't need to specify the same name as the one the function or class has inside the file. For example, you could import the default `getStateInfo()` function from `oregonInfo.js` like this:

```
import oregonStateInfo from './modules/oregonInfo.js';
```

Importing modules dynamically

Normally, modules are imported in the order in which `import` statements appear in the file. Because `import` statements appear at the beginning of a file, all the imported files in a program are loaded before any other code runs, which can lower your program's performance.

By using dynamic module loading, you can tell JavaScript to load modules only when they're needed.

To use dynamic module loading, use the `import` keyword as a function. This function returns a promise object containing a module object. The `import()` function can be called in response to an event.

For example, Listing 2-4 shows how you can import the modules from Listing 2-3 when a button is clicked.

LISTING 2-4: Using Dynamic Loading

```
const stateButton = document.getElementById('oregonButton');
stateButton.addEventListener('click', () =>
  import('./listing2-3.js').then((OregonInfo) => {
    alert(`${OregonInfo.stateName}'s state bird is ${OregonInfo.
        stateBird}.`);
  }),
);
```

Importing modules into HTML

Although modules are most commonly imported into other JavaScript files, you can also import them into HTML files by setting the `type` attribute of a script tag to `module`. Listing 2-5 shows how to import the module from Listing 2-4 into an HTML file.

LISTING 2-5: Importing a Module into an HTML File

```
<!doctype html>
<html lang="en">
  <head>
    <meta charset="UTF-8"/>
    <meta http-equiv="X-UA-Compatible" content="IE=edge"/>
    <meta name="viewport" content="width=device-width,
          initial-scale=1.0"/>
```

```
    <title>Get Oregon Info</title>
  </head>
  <body>
    <button id="oregonButton">Click to find out about Oregon!
          </button>
    <script src="listing2-4.js" type="module"></script>
  </body>
</html>
```

When run in a browser, the preceding HTML file displays a button and loads the event handler code from Listing 2-4. When you click the button, the modules from Listing 2-3 are loaded, and an alert appears, showing information from the modules, as shown in Figure 2-1.

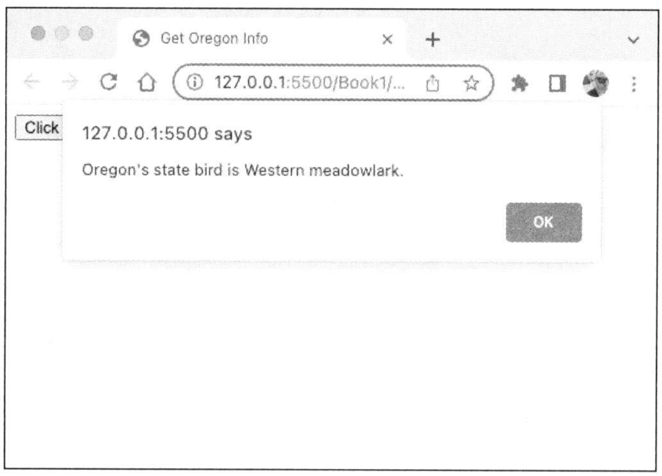

FIGURE 2-1: Loading modules dynamically in response to an event.

IN THIS CHAPTER

» Getting started with React

» Creating your first React project

» Rendering in the browser with ReactDOM

Chapter 3

Getting Started with React

"It's not what happens to you, but how you react to it."

—EPICTETUS

In Chapter 2 of this minibook, you learned how JavaScript modules let you split code into separate files, export what you want to share, and import what you need. React builds on that same idea: instead of organizing your app around a few big scripts, you organize it around small, reusable *components,* and each component is a module that you can import and combine with other components (like building blocks) to build a complete front end.

In this chapter, you get your first hands-on look at React by learning what it is, how it approaches building user interfaces from components, and how to spin up a new React project so you can start rendering components in the browser.

Distilling React

React treats user interfaces as a collection of independent and reusable components, much like how HTML documents are made up of reusable elements. Unlike in HTML, however, you're not limited to using only certain predefined elements. Instead, React allows you to create custom components by combining HTML elements with JavaScript and style rules. These components can be used like custom HTML elements.

You can think of a React user interface as a higher level of abstraction than the user interface created by HTML, as shown in Figure 3-1.

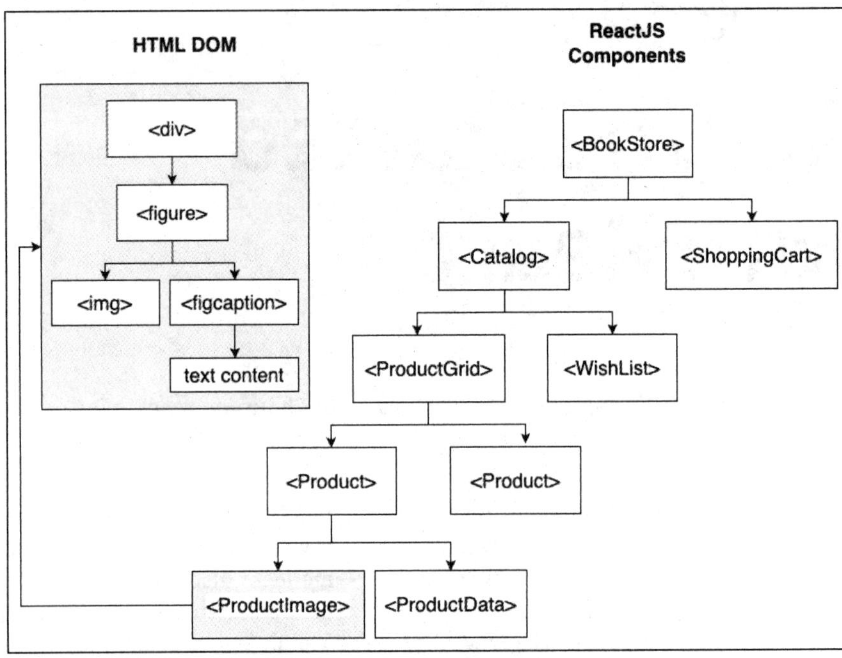

FIGURE 3-1: A React UI is a higher level of abstraction.

Building a React UI

You can understand how React works by learning how to approach building a React app. The process, whether for a small app or a large one, generally follows these five steps:

1. Break up the UI into a component hierarchy.
2. Build a static version in React.
3. Identify the minimal representation of UI state.

4. Identify where the state should live.
5. Add inverse data flow by using events and event handlers.

Step 1: Design the component hierarchy

Figure 3-2 shows a simple and familiar user interface.

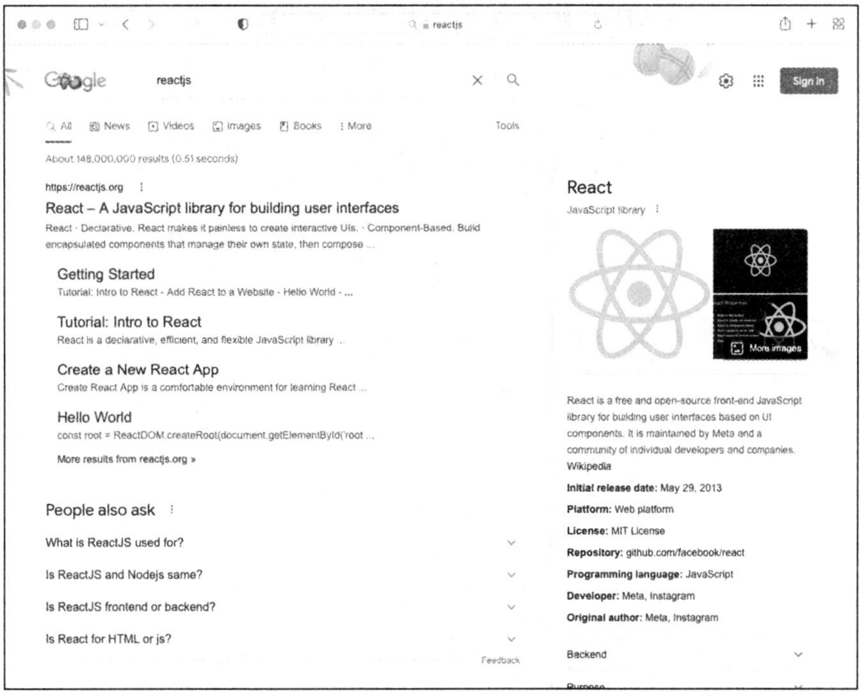

FIGURE 3-2: A user interface mockup.

To translate this user interface into React, your first task is to figure out how to split it up into independent and reusable components. By thinking about independence and reusability, you might decide that the user interface shown in Figure 3-2 should be split into the following components:

- Logo
- Search box
- Sign In button
- Navigation bar
- Search results

- Individual search result
- Sidebar

And just like that, you've finished with the first step in the React development process. Pat yourself on the back and move on!

Step 2: Build a static version in React

Once you've thought about the various components that make up the user interface, your next job is to translate each component into static code. You can think of this step as similar to writing a snippet of HTML for each component, except that you write a JavaScript function that returns parts of a user interface.

For example, Listing 3-1 shows how you might create a simple static version of the navigation bar shown earlier, in Figure 3-2.

LISTING 3-1: A Static Navigation Bar Mockup

```
function TopNavBar() {
  return (
    <nav>
      <ul>
        <li>All</li>
        <li>News</li>
        <li>Videos</li>
        <li>Images</li>
        <li>Books</li>
        <li>More</li>
      </ul>
    </nav>
  );
}
export default TopNavBar;
```

TECHNICAL STUFF

Note that the `return` statement of the preceding component seems to contain just simple HTML code. As you can read about in Chapter 4 of this minibook, this is not HTML. Rather, it's a templating language called JSX that looks like HTML but compiles to JavaScript.

As you make each static component, you can save it in a file with the same name as the function and export the function using a default export. (You can read about creating JavaScript modules in Chapter 2 of this minibook.)

Let's try another static component. Listing 3-2 shows what your completed static mockup for the search box might look like.

LISTING 3-2: A Static Search Box Mockup

```
function SearchBox() {
  return (
    <div>
      <input type="text" placeholder="Search Google or type a URL"/>
    </div>
  );
}
export default SearchBox;
```

Once you've created all the components for your user interface, you need to make a single component that wraps around all of them, in the same way that a `<body>` element wraps around all visible HTML elements in a document. This wrapper component is usually named `App`.

Inside `App` (and the other components as well), you can import components, create instances of them, and put them together (which is called *composition*) to build the structure for your user interface, as shown in Listing 3-3.

LISTING 3-3: Putting Together the Components in App

```
import GoogleLogo from './GoogleLogo';
import SearchBox from './SearchBox';
import SignInButton from './SignInButton';
import TopNavBar from './TopNavBar';
import SearchResults from './SearchResults';
import SideBar from './SideBar';
function App() {
  return (
    <div>
      <div>
        <GoogleLogo/>
        <SearchBox/>
        <SignInButton/>
      </div>
      <TopNavBar/>
      <div>
```

(continued)

LISTING 3-3: *(continued)*

```
        <SearchResults/>
        <SideBar/>
      </div>
    </div>
  );
}
export default App;
```

TIP

If you haven't read Book 6, I highly recommend that you do so before proceeding with learning React. Having a strong understanding of how JavaScript works will make learning React a simple task.

Step 3: Identify the state

The next task in creating a React user interface is to figure out what data should cause the user interface to change. In React, the data that causes the user interface to change is called *state*.

For instance, in the example user interface shown in Figure 3-2, the most basic pieces of data are the search term and the search results. Of these two, the one that causes the user interface to change is the search term entered by the user. The rest of the user interface simply reacts to this key piece of data to generate search results, the sidebar, advertising, and other elements.

A user interface may have just one piece of state, as in this case, or it may have many different stateful values. Once you think you know what values in your UI represent the state, you're done with Step 3.

TIP

It's common for programmers to change their minds about what the state of an application is once they start programming it. The point of Step 3 isn't to set anything in stone but rather to start to get an idea of how your application will change (or react) in response to events.

Step 4: Determine where the state should live

Once you know what the state is, the next step is to figure out which component should hold the state. The state is a private property of an object. Only the component that owns the state property can change it, but the owner of a state property can share it with its children as a read-only value, as shown in Figure 3-3.

The state of an application must be at a higher level in the hierarchy than every component that uses the state. In the search engine example, both the search results and the sidebar make use of the search term. The only component at a higher level in the hierarchy of components is the App component.

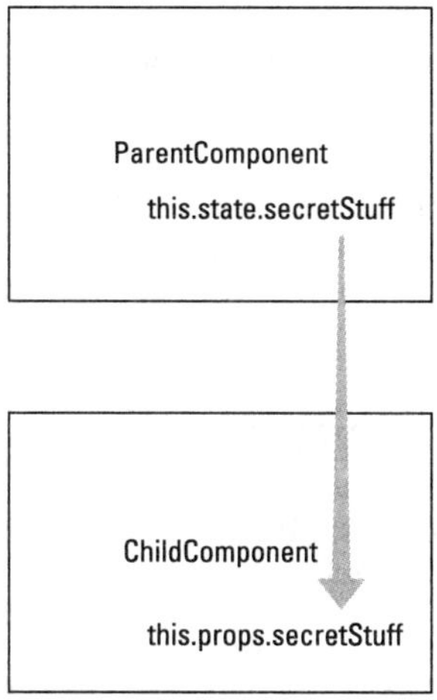

FIGURE 3-3: How state works.

Step 5: Implement inverse data flow

Data in a React application flows from parent components to children. If you need an event in a child component to modify data in its parent component, you have to use a callback function passed to the subcomponent, as shown in Figure 3-4.

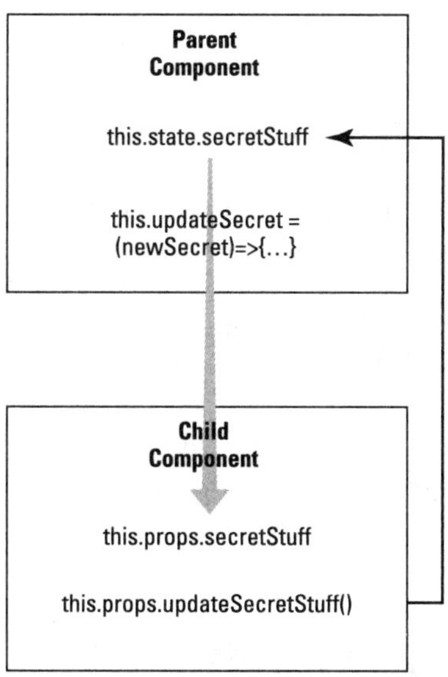

FIGURE 3-4: Pass a function to a child to do inverse data flow.

React calls this a one-way data flow, but it's not any different from how JavaScript normally works. For example, it's not possible to pass data from one module to a module that makes use of it (its parent).

The final step is to listen for events that will cause the state to change and pass callback functions to the children that need to cause the state to be modified. In the search engine example, the event listener can listen for the `submit` event on the `<input>` element in the search component. When this event is detected, the event handler uses a callback function to update the state data in the `App` component with the new value.

React is component-based

When you use React to build a user interface in the browser, you need to use two separate libraries:

- **React:** Renders a tree of components. The React library works similarly to how a browser's rendering engine renders a DOM tree from HTML elements.
- **ReactDOM:** Takes the tree of components from the React library and uses it to update the browser DOM.

As a React programmer, you need to concern yourself only with building components and rendering them using the React library. The work of changing what's shown in the browser window is handled automatically by the ReactDOM library.

React is (mostly) just JavaScript

Until now, you haven't seen any code that's specifically React, but if you've come this far in the book, you already understand most of the code that you'll use to write React applications. This is because React itself is a fairly small library for rendering a tree of components. Unlike some other JavaScript libraries and frameworks, React doesn't have a lot of special functions and tools that you need to learn to be able to use it.

REMEMBER

React developers say that React is *idiomatic JavaScript,* meaning it conforms to the way JavaScript is written rather than creating its own way of working.

Initializing a Project with Vite

You should now have a pretty good understanding of the fundamental ideas behind React programming. In this section, I show you how to build your first React applications in just a few minutes.

Introducing Vite

Using any modern front-end library requires a certain amount of tool setup. The tools and other packages you need to install for React development are the React and ReactDOM libraries, as well as tools for compiling, testing, and running React applications in your development environment.

It's possible to install and configure all these tools individually, but fortunately there are easier ways. Vite is one way to easily start a React project. Using Vite, you can download, install, and run a basic functioning React application in a few minutes (depending on the speed of your internet connection and computer).

Launching the VS Code terminal

Vite is a command-line program, so you must run it using a terminal or command-line interface. For easy access to your terminal, VS Code includes a built-in terminal window.

You can use any code editor to build React applications, but the one I use in this minibook, VS Code, is the same one you've used in the prior minibooks. If you don't have VS Code installed, you can download it from `https://code.visualstudio.com`. See Book 2, Chapter 1 for instructions on installing VS Code.

You can also open a terminal window at any location in your current project by right-clicking a folder name in the VS Code File Explorer pane and choosing Open in Integrated Terminal.

Follow these steps to start a new React project with Vite from the VS Code integrated terminal:

1. **Open an existing VS Code project or create one.**
2. **Open the integrated terminal in VS Code.**

   You can do so by choosing Terminal ➪ New Terminal from the top menu; by pressing Ctrl+` (backtick); or by right-clicking a folder name in the VS Code File Explorer pane and choosing Open in Integrated Terminal.

   A new terminal window opens at the bottom of your VS Code interface, as shown in Figure 3-5.
3. **Type the following command in the integrated terminal:**

   ```
   npm create vite@latest my-react-app -- --template react
   ```

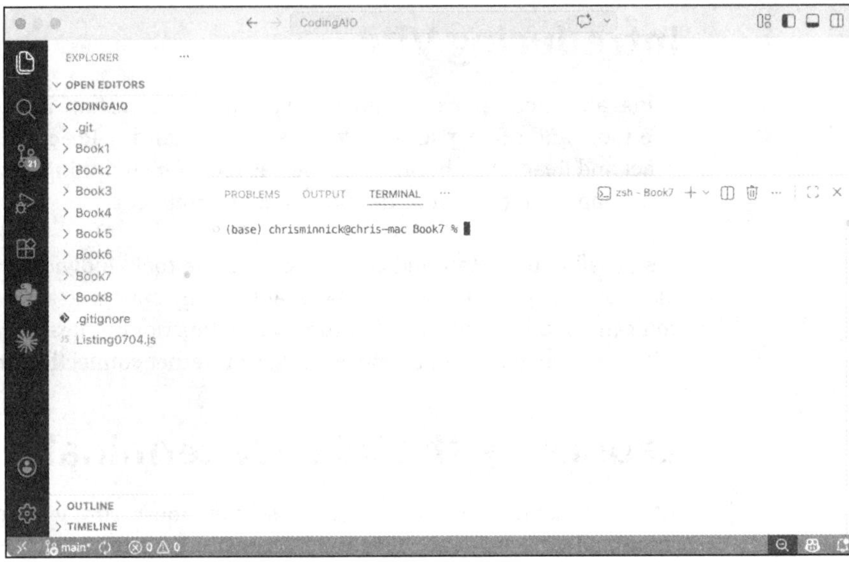

FIGURE 3-5: The VS Code terminal window.

4. **When the installation script asks if you want it to Install with npm and Start Now," answer No.**

   You handle these two steps manually this first time.

5. **If the installation asks you any other questions, just press Enter to choose the default options.**

   Your terminal starts downloading.

6. **When the installation finishes, enter** `cd` **followed by the name of your project to make your new project the current working directory.**

   If you used my instruction from Step 3, you should enter `cd my-react-app`.

7. **Enter** `npm install` **to install the project's dependencies.**

8. **Enter** `npm run` **dev to start the development server.**

   After a moment, you see a message telling you the local development server address. If a browser doesn't automatically start and open that address, you can open your browser and enter the address Vite shows you into the address bar, or you can Ctrl+click (Windows) or ⌘+click (macOS) the link in the VS Code terminal.

Touring the structure of a React app

Figure 3-6 shows the Vite React starter project. You may see something slightly different because this app has changed several times. The look of the starter project isn't important, however, because the idea of a starter project is to give you something to replace with your own app.

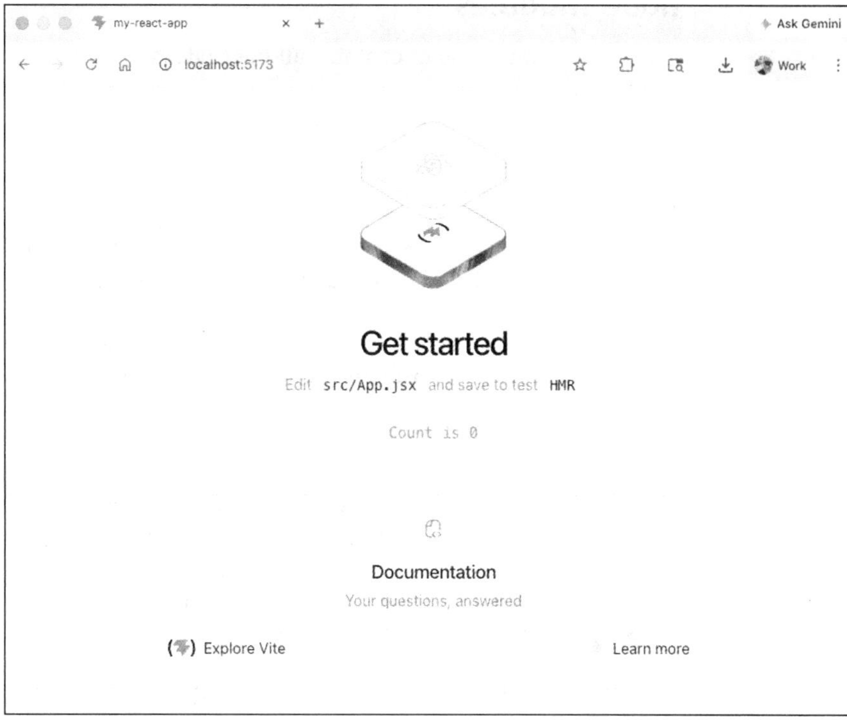

FIGURE 3-6: The default Vite React starter project.

Before you start building an app, let's examine this basic starter app and see what it's made of. If you expand your project in the VS Code File Explorer pane, you can see that the project contains several folders and files at the top level:

- `node_modules`
- `public`
- `src`
- `.gitignore`
- `index.html`
- `package-lock.json`
- `package.json`
- `vite.config.js`

Let's look at each of these folders and files. As you read about them, it may be helpful to open or expand them in VS Code to see their contents.

node_modules

The `node_modules` folder contains all the Node.js modules that were downloaded and installed when you used the `npm install` command. You most likely won't ever need to directly modify anything in this directory.

public

The `public` folder contains *static assets,* which are files that don't need to be compiled to run in the browser, including images and other media files.

Although you may need to occasionally do something with the `public` folder or add files to it, for the most part you won't need to touch the `public` folder.

src

The `src` folder contains your app's source code, including JavaScript modules, CSS, test files, and some configuration files. This is where you will build your app.

If you expand the `src` folder, you'll see that it contains two `.jsx` files, a couple of CSS files, and a subdirectory named `assets`.

REMEMBER

You can name React components using either a `.jsx` file extension or a `.js` extension. Many people prefer to use `.jsx`, and Vite requires it by default.

- The `main.jsx` file is the main JavaScript file for the app. This file is loaded into the browser directly and uses the ReactDOM library to update the browser DOM.
- `App.jsx` contains the module that creates the App component. This component is at the top of the component tree in your React app.
- `App.css` contains CSS code used by the App component.
- Any other files that are in the directory aren't important right now.

.gitignore

The `.gitignore` file is a configuration file that lists file and folder names that shouldn't be tracked in the project's Git repository. If you open `.gitignore`, you can see that it includes the project's `node_modules` folder, some log files, the `dist` directory (generated when you run `npm run build` to create a compiled version of your project for deployment), and some files that are created by your code editor and are important only to your computer.

package-lock.json

The `package-lock.json` file is automatically generated when you install node packages. It describes the tree of dependencies in your `node_modules` folder and is used when you install the project.

package.json

The `package.json` file contains metadata about your project, including general information, such as the name and version, as well as lists of dependencies and scripts (such as `npm run dev` and `npm run build`) you can run. When you install, update, or remove packages, `package.json` is automatically modified. You may need to modify `package.json` yourself sometimes as well.

vite.config.js

The `vite.config.js` file configures the Vite tool. You may need to modify this file at some point, but there's nothing you need to do here now.

Now that you understand what all the different files installed by Vite do, let's make some changes.

Modifying a React Project

Before starting to modify the project, make sure that it's still running in the development server. It isn't necessary for the development server to be running for you to make modifications, but if it is running, you can see the effect that changes to the code have on the browser window as you work. This feature is called *hot reloading.*

You can know whether the development server is running by refreshing the app in the browser or looking at the terminal window in VS Code. If you can't type in the terminal window, your server is likely still running.

REMEMBER

If you want to stop and then restart your development server, click in the terminal window and press Ctrl+C to halt the development server, and then enter `npm run dev` to start it again.

Follow these steps to make some modifications to the default React project:

1. **Open `App.jsx` in VS Code.**

   Note that this component is just a simple JavaScript function. The `return` statement contains something that looks like HTML markup. This is JSX code, which gets compiled to JavaScript. You can learn all about JSX in Chapter 4 of this minibook.

2. **Find the `Get started` text in the `return` statement, and change it to your name.**
3. **Save the file and return to your web browser to see the changes.**
4. **Try making some other changes to `App.jsx`.**

   Here are some suggestions:

   - Remove one of the `img` elements.
   - Open the linked stylesheet, `App.css`, and delete everything inside it, and then note how the view in the browser changes.
   - In `App.jsx`, delete everything between the `<>` and `</>` tags.
   - Insert an `<h1>` element inside the `<>` element and give your page a title — for example, Learning React.

At this point, your React app might look like the one in Figure 3-7.

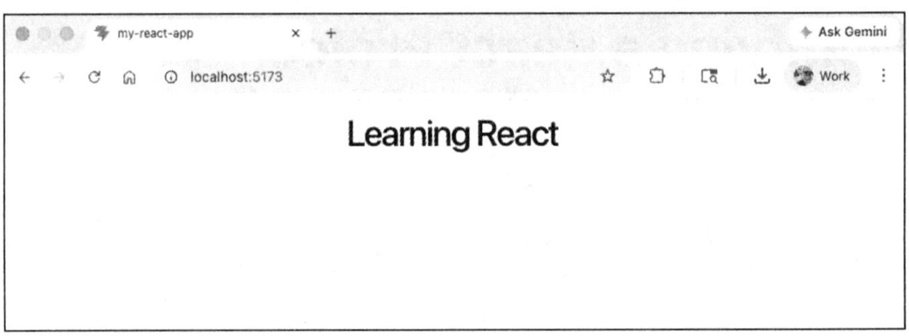

FIGURE 3-7: Your React starter app.

Congratulations on creating your first React App! In the remaining chapters of this minibook, you learn more about React. You can use this starter app as your own playground, where you can try out the tools and techniques that you learn.

IN THIS CHAPTER

» Writing JSX elements

» Using JavaScript in JSX

» Rendering conditionally

» Making lists

» Styling React components

Chapter 4
Writing JSX

"I write to discover what I know."

—FLANNERY O'CONNOR

JSX is a template language for describing user interfaces. In this chapter, I show you how to write JSX to compose views in the browser.

Learning the Fundamentals of JSX

Many people's first reaction to seeing React components is that they seem to violate a fundamental best practice of writing web code: Logic should be separate from presentation. In terms of web pages, there exists a long tradition of placing HTML and JavaScript in different files.

However, React is fundamentally a library for creating user interfaces with reusable components. What's important in a React user interface is the component, not the various languages the component contains.

Rather than enforce a separation of languages, React emphasizes *separation of concerns* by using components that are self-contained and independent parts that can be assembled and used without external dependencies.

JSX is not HTML

Listing 4-1 shows a simple React component.

LISTING 4-1: A Simple React Component

```
function SearchForm() {
  return (
    <form>
      <label htmlFor="searchTerm">
        Search For:
        <input type="text" id="searchTerm"/>
      </label>
      <button>Search</button>
    </form>
  );
}
export default SearchForm;
```

At first glance, it seems that the code in Listing 4-1 combines HTML and JavaScript and that it should generate a syntax error. The key, however, is that the code in the `return` statement isn't HTML — it's JSX.

JSX is XML

JSX is a JavaScript syntax extension that uses XML-like markup to describe UI. When React code is compiled, the JSX code gets transformed into calls to React methods for generating HTML. Listing 4-2 shows what the JSX code in Listing 4-1 compiles to before it runs in the browser.

LISTING 4-2: Compiled JSX

```
React.createElement(
  'form',
  null,
  React.createElement(
    'label',
    { htmlFor: 'searchTerm' },
```

```
    'Search For:',
    React.createElement('input', {
      type: 'text',
      id: 'searchTerm',
    }),
  ),
  React.createElement('button', null, 'Search'),
);
```

You could write your React components by using nested `React.createElement()` methods, but no one does that because it would be much more difficult and there's no benefit to it. Keep in mind that before you test or deploy your React code, it gets translated to pure JavaScript. So, what the browser sees is all JavaScript.

Transpiling with Babel

Babel is a JavaScript package that converts JSX code to JavaScript, though other tools are also widely used today for the same purpose.

Babel is also responsible for making sure your React app will run on every browser someone is likely to use. Because some browsers may not support the latest JavaScript syntax, Babel converts the code you write to the equivalent code in an earlier version of JavaScript that is supported by every browser. This process of converting from one version of JavaScript to another is called *transpilation*. Thanks to transpilation, you usually don't need to worry about browser compatibility when you're writing JavaScript code.

You can see Babel in action and test it out by going to the web-based interface to Babel at `https://babeljs.io/repl`, which is shown in Figure 4-1.

Writing HTML output with JSX

React has a built-in set of components that output HTML elements. To use these elements in the `return` statements of React components, write them using the same element names you use to write the HTML elements they output. For example, to produce an HTML `<div>` element in the browser, use the React `<div>` element, which creates an instance of React's built-in `div` component.

These HTML-equivalent React components have the same attributes as the HTML components they produce, with just a few exceptions, changes, and additions.

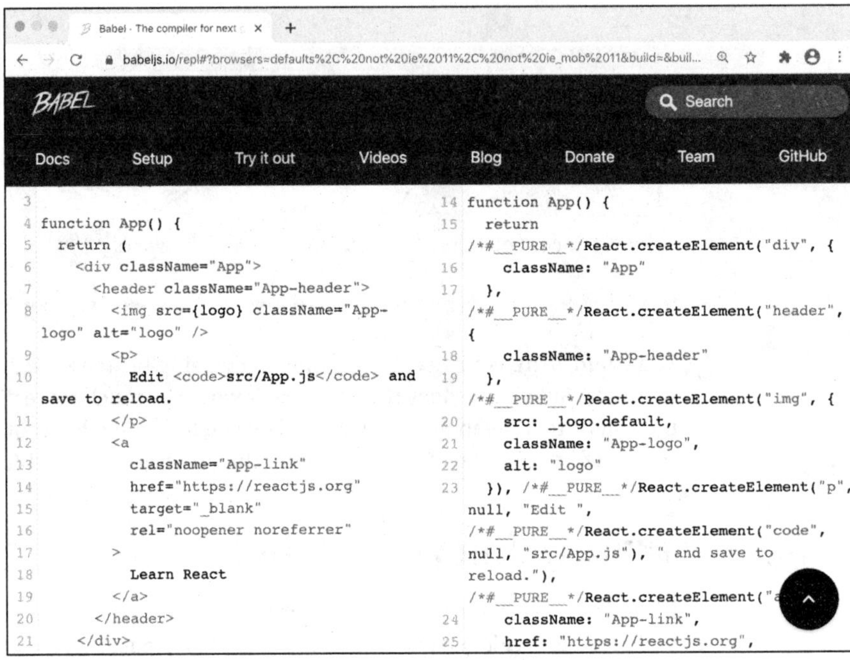

FIGURE 4-1: Using Babel's web-based interface.

Using built-in components

If you look closely at the React components you can see in Chapter 3 of this minibook and in this chapter, several of the differences between using JSX and HTML. These are the most important differences:

- Several attribute names are different in JSX.
- JSX uses camelCase for attribute names.
- JSX elements must be valid XML.

When you write JSX, the `class` attribute in HTML is written as `className`, and the `for` attribute in HTML is written as `htmlFor`. The reason for these two differences is that `class` and `for` are reserved words in JavaScript, and using them in JSX could have unwanted side effects.

JSX attributes are always in camel case, whereas all HTML attributes are in lowercase or use hyphens. For example, the event attributes in HTML are written in JSX as `onClick`, `onSubmit`, or `onChange`.

In JSX, every opening tag must have a closing tag or be self-closing. A self-closing tag has a slash before the closing angle bracket. For example, the `<br>` HTML element is written in JSX as `<br/>`.

HTML doesn't need to conform to the rules of XML. You can write certain HTML elements without a closing tag or a closing slash. These elements are called *empty* elements because they have no content. The HTML `<br>`, `<img>`, and `<input>` elements are examples of empty elements. Here's how you write an `<input>` element in HTML:

```
<input type="text" id="searchTerm">
```

In JSX, this line produces an error because the element isn't closed. To close an element that doesn't require a closing tag in HTML, add a slash at the end of the tag. For instance, to make the preceding HTML `input` element into valid JSX, write it like this:

```
<input type="text" id="searchTerm"/>
```

Using JavaScript Expressions in JSX

To specify that something in JSX should be compiled as JavaScript rather than JSX code, surround it with curly braces. In the following JSX code, the `firstName` variable is inserted into the content of the `<h1>` element:

```
<h1>Welcome, {firstName}</h1>
```

You can use curly braces to insert any JavaScript expression into JSX.

REMEMBER

An *expression* is any unit of code that resolves to a value. JavaScript expressions are covered in Book 6, Chapter 4.

JavaScript expressions can also be passed to elements as values of attributes. For example, in Listing 4-3, the value of the `className` attribute is determined using the result of executing a function.

LISTING 4-3: Specifying an Attribute Value Using an Expression

```
function Message({ messageType, message }) {
  function getMessageClass() {
    if (messageType === 'error') {
      return 'errorStyle';
    } else {
```

(continued)

LISTING 4-3: (continued)

```
      return 'messageStyle';
    }
  }
  return <p className={getMessageClass()}>{message}</p>;
}
export default Message;
```

Although it's possible to use any JavaScript expression inside your JSX code by using curly braces, it's a best practice to limit your use of JavaScript in JSX to *presentational code,* which is code that directly affects what renders in the browser. Code such as event handlers and functions that perform the logic of your app should be outside the `return` statement of your component.

One of the most common things to do with JavaScript in your JSX is conditional rendering, as described next.

Conditionally Rendering JSX

Conditional rendering is the use of a conditional statement to determine whether some piece of JSX should be rendered. You have three main ways to perform conditional rendering in React, by using:

- Element variables
- &&
- The conditional operator

Unlike other libraries, React doesn't provide its own method for doing conditional rendering, so each of these techniques is just plain JavaScript.

Conditional rendering with element variables

JSX tags compile into JavaScript expressions. As with any JavaScript expressions, you can assign JSX code to a variable. Note that because a variable assignment isn't an expression (because it doesn't resolve to a value), creating element variables must be done outside the `return` statement.

In Listing 4-4, a JSX `<h1>` element is assigned to a constant named `header`. The `header` variable can then be used in the `return` statement instead of the `<h1>` element.

LISTING 4-4: Using Element Variables

```
import Message from './Listing0403';
function WelcomeScreen() {
  const header = (
    <h1>
      <Message message="Welcome!" messageType="header"/>
    </h1>
  );
  return header;
}
export default WelcomeScreen;
```

Note the parentheses around the `<h1>` element in Listing 4-4. Although parentheses aren't required when using JSX, it's a good practice to use them anytime you have more than one line of JSX.

To do conditional rendering with element variables, set the value of a variable or constant outside your `return` statement by using a conditional statement, as shown in Listing 4-5.

LISTING 4-5: Conditional Rendering with an Element Variable

```
import Message from './Listing0403';
function WelcomeScreen({ loggedIn }) {
  let header;
  if (loggedIn) {
    header = (
      <h1>
        <Message message="Welcome" messageType="header"/>
      </h1>
    );
  } else {
    header = (
      <header>
        <h1>
          <Message message="Please log in to continue!"
               messageType="header"/>
        </h1>
```

(continued)

LISTING 4-5: (continued)

```
      </header>
    );
  }
  return header;
}
export default WelcomeScreen;
```

Conditional rendering with &&

The && operator evaluates expressions from left to right and returns the value of the first `false` operand, or the last operand if all the values are `true`.

You can use this fact to render JSX conditionally. Because && creates an expression that returns a value, you can use an && expression inside the `return` statement of your component by surrounding the && expression with curly braces, as shown in Listing 4-6.

LISTING 4-6: Conditional Rendering with &&

```
import WelcomeMessage from './WelcomeMessage';
function WelcomeScreen({ loggedIn }) {
  return (
    <div>
      {loggedIn && <WelcomeMessage/>}
      Note: if you don't see the welcome message, you're
            not logged in.
    </div>
  );
}
export default WelcomeScreen;
```

In this example, if the value of `loggedIn` is `false`, that value is returned. A value of `false` doesn't render anything. If the value of `loggedIn` evaluates to `true`, the `<WelcomeMessage/>` element is included in the JSX.

You can string together multiple && expressions to require multiple values to be `true` for some JSX code to be included. For example, Listing 4-7 requires both the `loggedIn` and `isHuman` variables to be `true`.

LISTING 4-7: Using Multiple Conditions with &&

```
import WelcomeMessage from './WelcomeMessage';
function Welcome({ loggedIn, isHuman }) {
  return (
    <div>
      {loggedIn && isHuman && <WelcomeMessage/>}
      Note: If you don't see the welcome message, you're not
             logged in or you're
      a bot.
    </div>
  );
}
export default Welcome;
```

Conditional rendering with the conditional operator

The conditional, or *ternary*, operator can also be used in the `return` statement to choose between different JSX expressions to display. Listing 4-8 shows how to use the conditional operator to choose between two different elements.

LISTING 4-8: Conditional Rendering with the Conditional Operator

```
import WelcomeMessage from './WelcomeMessage';
import Login from './Login';
function Welcome({ loggedIn }) {
  return <div>{loggedIn ? <WelcomeMessage/> : <Login/>}</div>;
}
export default Welcome;
```

Making a List

When you return an array from a React component, it's automatically deconstructed into its individual elements. You can use this fact to easily create lists in the user interface.

For example, it's common for a web API to return JSON data containing an array of objects. Listing 4-9 shows a simple example of this type of JSON string.

LISTING 4-9: A Sample JSON Array of Objects

```
[
  {
    "customerId": "1",
    "address": "234 Pine Street",
    "city": "Pinewood",
    "state": "IL"
  },
  {
    "customerId": "2",
    "address": "456 Elm Street",
    "city": "Elmwood",
    "state": "MI"
  },
  {
    "customerId": "3",
    "address": "678 Maple Street",
    "city": "Maplewood",
    "state": "OH"
  },
  {
    "customerId": "4",
    "address": "901 Chestnut Street",
    "city": "Chestnut",
    "state": "SC"
  }
]
```

The first thing to do to be able to use JSON data is to convert it to JavaScript by using the `JSON.parse()` method, which you can learn about in Chapter 1 of this minibook.

Once you've converted the JSON data to JavaScript, you can convert the resulting array to an HTML list in the browser using JavaScript's `Array.map()` method, as shown in Listing 4-10.

LISTING 4-10: Making a List from an Array

```
function CustomerList({ customers }) {
  return (
    <ul>
```

```
      {customers.map((customer) => (
        <li key={customer.customerId}>
          {customer.address}, {customer.city},{customer.state}
        </li>
      ))}
    </ul>
  );
}
export default CustomerList;
```

In this example, the component receives an array of objects, called `customers`, from its parent component and returns a JSX `<ul>` element containing one `<li>` element for each item in the supplied array.

Note that each `<li>` element generated from the `Array.map()` method has an attribute named `key`. React requires the `key` attribute anytime you create a list, and each `key` must have a unique value. The `key` attribute is used internally in React to make updates to lists more efficient.

Styling React Apps and Components

The first thing to understand about modifying the style of React components is that you can do so globally or locally.

The second thing to know is that, as with nearly everything in React, adding style to components and applications is done using standard JavaScript and CSS techniques.

I tell you first about adding global styles to your React application, and then I discuss how to style individual components.

Adding global styles

You have likely seen examples of using global styles already. In the default `App` component created by Vite, a stylesheet named `App.css` is imported into the `App.jsx` file. The syntax for importing CSS into a React application using this method is straightforward and simple:

```
import './App.css';
```

If you try importing CSS into a JavaScript file, it normally causes an error because CSS isn't valid JavaScript. However, importing CSS into JavaScript is possible because the compilation process that happens when you run a Vite application automatically extracts any imported CSS files and inserts them into the HTML or creates CSS files that are linked to from the `index.html` file.

No matter where in your application you import CSS using this method, it becomes global CSS that affects every component in your application. For your `App.css` file, this behavior is usually desired because the `App` component contains every other component, and its styles should be global.

It's common to include a CSS framework like Bootstrap (`https://getbootstrap.com`) in your `App` component, which makes the styles included in Bootstrap available to every other component.

However, importing global CSS into subcomponents can have unexpected results if you're not aware of the fact that all imported CSS becomes global.

It's generally a good practice to think about global style sheets as being useful for keeping styles that control the layout of components in the application and for styles that manage the overall theme of the application. For anything that's local to a component, such as the layout of elements in a form or the way that headers and figures are styled in a component that displays blog posts, you should use local styles.

Using local styles

React components are meant to be reusable and self-contained parts. Ideally, you should be able to take a React component from one application and use it in another application just by knowing what input it requires. For example, a `DatePicker` component you build for a social media app should be able to be used in an appointment scheduling app.

When components rely on global styles for controlling how they look internally, however, the dependency on some other condition (global styles) breaks this reusability.

To make components more reusable and independent, React encourages the use of JavaScript in a component to style elements that are local to that component. JavaScript styling of components is enabled with the `style` attribute.

Using the style attribute

In HTML, elements that can be styled (which includes any element that produces visible output) have an attribute named `style`, into which you can pass CSS code that is applied only to that element. Passing CSS to a `style` element is known as *inline styling.*

In HTML, the use of inline styles is generally discouraged because it makes maintenance of your web pages more difficult and because inline styles can't be reused.

In React, built-in components that produce visible HTML elements have a `style` attribute. Unlike the HTML `style` attribute, however, the React `style` attribute doesn't take CSS as its value. Instead, it takes a JavaScript object. React converts the properties of this `style` object into JavaScript code that manipulates the CSS Object Model in the browser.

For example, Listing 4-11 shows how to style a paragraph of text in a component by using the `style` attribute.

LISTING 4-11: Using the Style Attribute

```
function BlogPostBody({ blogBodyText }) {
  return (
    <p style={{ fontSize: '100%', marginBottom: '2.2rem', color:
            '#171717' }}>
      {blogBodyText}
    </p>
  );
}
export default BlogPostBody;
```

Although the markup in Listing 4-11 looks similar to inline styling in HTML, it's not the same thing. Keep in mind that when you create a React component that displays a paragraph of text (for example), you're not just styling a single paragraph of text — you're creating a reusable way to style any paragraph of text by simply passing it as an argument to this component.

Using style objects

Note that the value of the `style` attribute in Listing 4-11 is an object literal that's enclosed in curly braces to tell JSX to treat it as literal JavaScript. As a result, double curly braces are around the style properties.

Because the values passed to the style attribute are used to manipulate CSSOM, property names you use must match the names of the CSSOM properties. The biggest difference between CSS properties and CSSOM properties is that multiword CSS properties use hyphens to separate the words (which is sometimes called *kebab case* because it looks sort of like a skewer is going through the words). CSSOM properties, on the other hand, use camel case. For example, in CSS, the roundness of the corners of a border is controlled using the border-radius property, but in JavaScript, you use the borderRadius property.

Two additional differences between CSS rules and style objects are:

- CSS rule sets separate multiple rules using semicolons. In JavaScript, properties are separated using commas.
- In CSS, the values of properties aren't put in quotes. In style objects, the values must be in quotes.

For example, to specify a border radius for an element in CSS, you use the following code line:

```
<div style="border-radius: 8px;">
```

Here's how you can convert the preceding CSS rule to a JavaScript style object and pass it to the style attribute of a React div component:

```
<div style={{borderRadius: "8px"}}>
```

Making style modules

Because style objects are JavaScript objects, you can assign them to variables or constants, and the names of the variables or constants can be passed to the style attribute. Once you've assigned a style object to a constant or variable, you can extract it to a separate file and export it as a module. In this way, you can define styles that have local scope, but that can also be used in multiple components.

One common strategy for using style modules is to make a file containing local styles for each component in a user interface, such as the one shown in Listing 4-12.

LISTING 4-12: Creating Style Modules

```
export const headline = {
  fontSize: '200%',
  color: '#333',
};
```

```
export const authorName = {
  fontWeight: 'bold',
};
export const bodyText = {
  color: '#000',
};
```

You can then import the styles from this module individually or all at once into a React component, as shown in Listing 4-13.

LISTING 4-13: Importing Style Modules

```
import * as styles from './Listing0412.styles.js';
function Article({ headline, authorName, bodyText }) {
  return (
    <div>
      <h2 style={styles.headline}>{headline}</h2>
      <div style={styles.authorName}>by: {authorName}</div>
      <div style={styles.bodyText}>{bodyText}</div>
    </div>
  );
}
export default Article;
```


Other style strategies

Because React doesn't enforce many rules about how components should be assembled, different libraries and techniques have emerged to accomplish similar things. Nowhere is this more obvious, and sometimes confusing, than with styling components.

Every strategy for styling React components is some variation of either using CSS or using style objects. One particularly interesting method that combines the familiarity of writing CSS with the flexibility of using JavaScript is CSS modules.

CSS modules allow you to write ordinary CSS code in a file with the extension `.module.css`. You can then import the styles defined in the `.module.css` file into a React component, where they'll be scoped locally to that component by default.

CSS modules allow you to use not only locally scoped CSS but also a property named `composes`, which gives you the ability to create styles by including properties defined in another style.

Listing 4-14 shows an example of a CSS modules file.

LISTING 4-14: A CSS Modules File

```
.paragraph {
  font-size: 16px;
  font-family: Georgia, serif;
  color: #333;
  text-indent: 25px;
}
.redParagraph {
  composes: paragraph;
  color: red;
}
```

To use the styles from the preceding CSS modules file, import it into a component as an object, as shown in Listing 4-15.

LISTING 4-15: Importing and Using CSS Modules

```
import styles from './Message.module.css';
function Message(props) {
  return <p className={styles.redParagraph}>This text is red.</p>;
}
export default Message;
```

IN THIS CHAPTER

» Writing custom components

» Returning valid data from components

» Passing props and finding the state

» Implementing reactivity with functions and classes

» Hooking into component lifecycle

» Composing with components

Chapter 5

Building React Components

"A good engineer thinks in reverse and asks himself about the stylistic consequences of the components and systems he proposes."

—HELMUT JAHN

React components define React elements. In this chapter, I describe how React components work, how to pass data from parent components to child components, and how to assemble components to build increasingly complex components through a pattern called composition.

Thinking in Components

React components exist to describe an isolated piece of a user interface. So far in this minibook, each component I describe has been a simple JavaScript function that takes an object as an argument and returns a React element. As you will see shortly, components can also be written as JavaScript classes.

Designing your own elements

When you write a React component, you're creating a user-defined element. In a web application, a user-defined element is a way to create a more complex and customized element than those in HTML.

Imagine that you're creating a new search engine, and you want it to have the same functionality as `Bing.com` (shown in Figure 5-1).

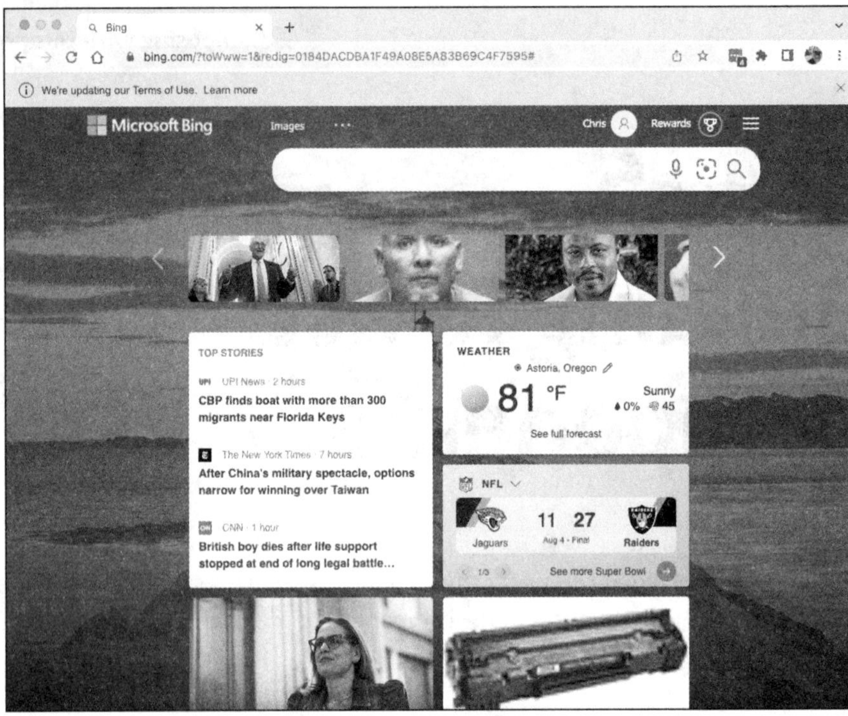

FIGURE 5-1: `Bing.com`.

One important component of `Bing.com` that your new search engine will need is the weather widget. Rather than write all the custom code that powers and styles this widget, wouldn't it be useful if you could include the current local weather on your own search engine home page just by using a `<GetLocalWeather>` HTML element? This is the idea behind React.

Of course, unless you can find a widget that someone else has written (and there's a good chance you can), you still need to write all the logic and presentational code that powers this `<GetLocalWeather>` element. But, by creating a new element, you make it much easier to think about how the application works, and you make the local weather functionality into a reusable part that you could use elsewhere on this website or even on another website.

Thinking about a user interface in terms of high-level components allows you to visualize and work with a user interface as complex as `Bing.com` with just a few elements, as shown in Listing 5-1.

LISTING 5-1: A High-Level View of `Bing.com`

```
export default function Bing() {
  return (
    <Homepage>
      <TopNav/>
      <SearchBox/>
      <NewsImageScroller/>
      <div>
        <div className="leftColumn">
          <TopStories/>
        </div>
        <div className="rightColumn">
          <Weather postalCode="97103"/>
          <Sports/>
        </div>
      </div>
    </Homepage>
  );
}
```

Sure, each of the custom elements shown in Listing 5-1 may consist of hundreds or thousands of lines of code, but when you're putting together the `Bing.com` home page, you don't need to know about how the underlying code works. You just use the elements.

Returning valid values

Following are the valid return values for a component:

» **One JSX element:** Note that the single element returned by a component can be as deeply nested as you need, as long as it has a single element that wraps around all the others.

- **An array:** When a component returns an array (including an array of elements), it's spread into the separate elements.
- **A string:** If the return value is just a string, it must be enclosed in quotes.
- **A number:** If you return a number, don't enclose it in quotes.
- **`undefined`:** If a component doesn't explicitly return a value, it returns `undefined`, which React doesn't render.
- **`null`:** React components can return `null` to intentionally render nothing.

WARNING

Returning an object (including an object that's part of an array) produces an error in React.

Recognizing the Two Types of Data

Two kinds of data make React components work: props and state. Understanding the differences between props and state and when to use each one is the key to making your React components update correctly and quickly.

Passing data with props

Props (short for *properties*) are data that components receive from their parent components. To pass props to a component, specify attributes in React elements. The attribute names become properties of the props object in the component instance the element creates.

For example, Listing 5-2 defines two components: `ParentComponent` and `ChildComponent`. `ParentComponent` creates three instances of `ChildComponent` by using JSX elements. Each `ChildComponent` instance receives a different value for an attribute named `firstName`.

The `firstName` attribute from `ParentComponent` becomes a property of the object passed to `ChildComponent`, and each of the three instances of `ChildComponent` can access and use this property.

LISTING 5-2: Passing Props

```
function ParentComponent() {
  return (
    <div>
      <ChildComponent firstName="Alex"/>
```

```
      <ChildComponent firstName="Mallory"/>
      <ChildComponent firstName="Jennifer"/>
    </div>
  );
}
function ChildComponent(props) {
  return <div>Hi, my name is {props.firstName}.</div>;
}
```

When a parent component passes a value to a child component via an attribute, the resulting property in the child component instance is read-only (or *immutable,* to use a fancier term).

Props are how parent components change the output of child components.

Because props are read-only, a user interface that uses only props never changes. If your goal is to create a static brochure-style web page using React, this approach is fine. But React is called React for a reason — it's designed to react to events (such as user input or data updates) automatically and in real-time. To make React applications reactive, they need data that can change over time or in response to user actions. That type of data is called *state.*

Getting reactive with state

State describes the data in your application that makes things happen. For example, a flashlight typically has two states: on or off. These states are controlled using a switch, and they cause the light to shine or not. If you were programming a React component to operate a flashlight, you'd probably create a variable called `isOn` in your component's state, as shown in Listing 5-3.

LISTING 5-3: A Flashlight Component

```
import { useState } from 'react';
function Flashlight() {
  const [isOn, setIsOn] = useState(false);
  return (
    <div>
      <Lightbulb glowing={isOn}/>
      <button onClick={() => setIsOn(!isOn)}>Change State</button>
      <button onClick={() => setIsOn(false)}>Turn off</button>
    </div>
  );
```

(continued)

LISTING 5-3: (continued)

```
}
export default Flashlight;
function Lightbulb(props) {
  return (
    <div>
      <div
        className="bulb"
        style={{
          width: '100px',
          height: '100px',
          backgroundColor: props.glowing ? 'yellow' : 'black',
        }}
        />
    </div>
  );
}
```

In the preceding example, clicking the button changes the Boolean `isOn` value to its opposite by using the negation operator (`!`). The value of `isOn` is passed to the `Lightbulb` component using an attribute. Inside the `Lightbulb` component, `glowing` is available as a prop.

Just as a real-life light bulb doesn't determine whether it's glowing and can't turn itself on, the `Lightbulb` component has no control over what the value of `glowing` will be.

State isn't always as simple as a Boolean value. Some React user interfaces contain many changing parts and must use a great deal of state data. For example, consider a weather-tracking user interface. To display a live weather-radar map, a user interface must know about temperature, precipitation, wind speed, time, and other factors. All these factors change regularly, and all of them can cause changes to the user interface.

Figure 5-2 shows a weather map widget.

FIGURE 5-2: A weather map widget (source: `www.weatherwidget.io`).

To determine what should be state in this widget, you first must make a list of the various data points needed to generate the user interface. Here's what I came up with:

- Location
- Local date and time
- Sky conditions
- Temperature
- Precipitation type
- Precipitation amount
- Daily forecasted high and low temperatures
- Weather icon
- Unit preference (F or C)

More pieces of data are surely involved, but you get the idea.

Next, ask yourself a few questions about each piece of data:

- Does it change over time?
- Can it be determined or calculated based on another piece of data?
- Is it passed to the component in the props object?

If you answer the first question with "Yes" and the other two questions with "No," that piece of data is likely state.

In my expert opinion (as someone who has experienced all kinds of weather), many of the data points required by this widget should be stored as state. A few of them, however, are likely props. For example, the icon showing the type of weather can be calculated based on a combination of the precipitation data, the time of day, and the temperature. Other data, such as the highs and lows displayed on each day, can be stored in a single state array that might be called `weeklyHighsAndLows`.

How state enables reactivity

Once an instance of a component has been created and is active in the browser, it can be modified only by using a special setter function. In a class component, the function is `setState()`. In a function component, it's a function returned by the `useState()` hook.

When you call one of these setter functions, React makes the change to the state that you request and then re-renders the component using the new state data. The changed state may cause different props to be passed to a component's children, and those components will re-render with different data as well.

The process of re-rendering a component and its children in response to updated state is called *updating.*

Function Components

Function components are JavaScript functions that return a piece of the user interface. In previous versions of React (before React 17), function components were also known as *presentational,* or *dumb,* components because they (like all JavaScript functions) lacked the capability to have data that could persist between invocations.

Listing 5-4 shows a function component that receives data and uses that data to output a list.

LISTING 5-4: A Function Component Example

```
function ToDoList(props) {
  return props.todos.map((todo, index) => <li key={index}>
        {todo}</li>);
}
export default ToDoList;
```

If you call the function from Listing 5-4 and pass in different data, it renders a different list. However, each time you call a function, it's like the function has never been called before. You can't keep track of anything or maintain internal data (what React calls *state*) in a function.

Although nothing has changed about the nature of functions, React has special functions, called *hooks,* that allow function components to store and retrieve data stored outside the function. By using hooks, instances of React function components can keep track of their state from one rendering to the next.

The useState() hook is a method of the React object that can be called from a function component. When you invoke useState(), it returns an array containing two elements: the value of a stateful variable (which lives outside the function) and a function for updating the value of that stateful variable.

By enabling function components to use data that sticks around between invocations, useState() gives function components many of the benefits of classes but without the complexity of classes.

Listing 5-5 shows the simplest possible demonstration of using state in a function component.

TIP

Take your time with this example. When you understand how it works, you'll understand function components.

LISTING 5-5: Using State in a Function Component

```
import { useState } from 'react';
function Counter() {
  const [currentCount, setCurrentCount] = useState(0);
  function incrementCount() {
    const newCount = currentCount + 1; setCurrentCount(newCount);
  }
  return <button onClick={incrementCount}>{currentCount}</button>;
}
export default Counter;
```

As you ponder the simplicity and beauty of Listing 5-5, let me point out a few things:

- **The return value of useState() is deconstructed (using square brackets).** By deconstructing the array, you gain access to two separate values: a stateful variable and a function that updates that variable.
- **The stateful variable and its related function are defined as constants.** This statement is counterintuitive because the point of a stateful variable is to be mutable. However, keep in mind that this constant inside the Counter function must be re-created each time the function runs. When you use the setCurrentCount() function, you're not changing the value of the currentCount constant — you're changing the value of the property stored outside the function that useState() uses to get the value of currentCount.

You can learn about React state and how to manage state in Chapter 6 of this minibook.

Now that function components are no longer second-class citizens (and certainly no one calls them dumb anymore!), most React developers use function components almost exclusively. However, if you studied classes in Book 6, Chapter 9, you are not most React developers! By understanding how class components work, you gain a deeper knowledge of how React works, and then you can decide whether to continue using function components everywhere it's possible or whether you want to use class components.

Class Components

Class components are created by extending the `React.Component` base class. Listing 5-6 shows an example of a simple class component that receives props and renders a to-do list.

LISTING 5-6: A Class Component

```
import React from 'react';
class ToDoList extends React.Component {
  render() {
    return this.props.todos.map((todo, index) => <li key={index}>
           {todo}</li>);
  }
}
export default ToDoList;
```

Compare the class component in Listing 5-6 with the function component in Listing 5-4, and note that the function component is nearly identical to the `render()` method of the class component. The only difference is that when a class component receives the props object, it becomes a property of the class and therefore must be referenced using the `this` keyword.

Also note that the class in Listing 5-6 has no constructor. As you can see in Book 6, Chapter 8, if you don't provide a constructor for a JavaScript class, the constructor is implied. If you don't provide a constructor for a class that extends another class, the constructor and the call to the parent component's constructor (which is done using `super()`) are also implied.

Unlike functions, classes can have their own persistent data. In a React class component, `state` is an object defined in the constructor. Each element created from a class can maintain its own independent `state` property.

Listing 5-7 shows how the `Counter` component from Listing 5-5 can be rewritten as a class component.

LISTING 5-7: Using State in a Class Component

```
import { Component } from 'react';
class Counter extends Component {
  constructor(props) {
    super(props);
    this.state = {
      currentCount: 0,
    };
    this.incrementCount = this.incrementCount.bind(this);
  }
  incrementCount() {
    const newCount = this.state.currentCount + 1;
    this.setState({ currentCount: newCount });
  }
  render() {
    return (
      <button onClick={this.incrementCount}>{this.state.
            currentCount}</button>
    );
  }
}
export default Counter;
```

Here are the important things to note about Listing 5-7:

- The constructor is necessary because we're using it to define the `state` property and to bind the `incrementCount()` method. As you can see in Book 6, Chapter 8, the `bind()` method returns a new function bound to the object you pass to it. In this case, you're binding `incrementCount()` to the current object. The effect is that no matter where you call `incrementCount()`, it affects the properties of the App component.
- In the `incrementCount()` method, you call `setState()`. The `setState()` method is inherited from the base class (Component). The `setState()` method takes an object as its value and merges that object into the `state` object.

See if you can follow the logic of what happens from the construction of an object using the class in Listing 5-7 to when the user clicks the button.

The Component Lifecycle

The life of a component starts when an instance of the component is created, using a JSX element or the `React.createElement()` method. Between creation of the component instance and when it's removed from the DOM, every React component completes a series of phases during its lifetime. These phases are called the *component lifecycle*. The milestones of a component's life are marked by events called *lifecycle events.*

These are the most important events for a component:

- **Mount:** When an instance of a component is created, rendered, and inserted into the browser window
- **Update:** When the component receives new data (as either state or props) that requires it to be re-rendered
- **Unmount:** When a component is removed, or unmounted, from the browser because the component is no longer needed

At each phase (and several subphases) of a component's lifecycle, the component invokes methods, called *lifecycle methods,* in response to the lifecycle events.

In a class component, the default behavior of lifecycle methods can be overridden to perform useful tasks.

Mounting methods

These lifecycle methods run while a component is mounting and afterward:

- `constructor()`
- `getDerivedStateFromProps()`
- `render()`
- `componentDidMount()`

Kicking it off with the constructor

The constructor() method is run whenever an instance of a JavaScript class is created. The constructor is where you can set initial values for an object's properties and bind event handlers. In a React class component, the constructor is where you initialize the state object, as shown in Listing 5-8.

LISTING 5-8: Setting State in the Constructor

```
import React from 'react';
class App extends React.Component {
  constructor(props) {
    super(props);
    this.state = {
      location: {
        coords: { lat: 0, long: 0 },
      },
      temperature: 0,
      windSpeed: 0,
      precipitation: 0,
    };
  }
  render() {
    return <div>Widget Goes Here</div>;
  }
}
export default App;
```

The constructor is the only place in a React class component where you can modify the state object directly, for a very good reason: The constructor() method runs before the render() method. As a result, changes you make to this.state in the constructor() are reflected in the output of the component.

Getting the derived state

The getDerivedStateFromProps() method is a *static* method: It belongs to the class rather than to instances of the class. This method receives the component's props and state and returns an object that will be merged with the state object.

Although it's rarely used, this method exists (as its name implies) for situations where the state depends on changes to props.

WARNING

The official React documentation advises against using this method, so I wouldn't be surprised if it eventually disappears from the library.

Rendering the output

The `render()` method is the only method that's required in every component. In a class component, the `render()` method runs when a component mounts and then again after every update to the `state` object.

TECHNICAL STUFF

A function component is basically just the `render()` method of a class component.

The return value of every component's `render()` method is the piece of the user interface created by the component. The return value is usually described using JSX, although it may also be a string, a number, an array, null, or undefined.

Listing 5-9 shows an example of rendering output that makes use of the state set in the constructor.

LISTING 5-9: Rendering with State Data

```
import React from 'react';
class App extends React.Component {
  constructor(props) {
    super(props);
    this.state = {
      location: 'Chicago',
      current_condition: {
        temp_C: 0,
        windspeedKmph: 0,
        precipMM: 0,
      },
    };
  }
  render() {
    return (
      <div>
        <h1>Today's weather for {this.state.location}</h1>
        <ul>
          <li>temperature: {this.state.current_condition.temp_C} C</li>
          <li>wind speed: {this.state.current_condition.
               windspeedKmph} km/h</li>
          <li>
```

```
            precipitation amount: {this.state.current_condition.
               precipMM} mm
          </li>
        </ul>
      </div>
    );
  }
}
export default App;
```

Finishing the mount

Only after a component has been rendered is it safe to do operations that modify the rendered component. The `componentDidMount` event fires when the component has been rendered and inserted into the browser, and it causes the `componentDidMount()` method to run.

The most common use for this lifecycle method is for kicking off network requests to fetch data. For example, Listing 5-10 shows an example of using the `fetch()` method in `componentDidMount()` to get data from a remote server and using that data to update the state.

LISTING 5-10: Fetching Data Inside componentDidMount()

```
import React from 'react';
class App extends React.Component {
  constructor(props) {
    super(props);
    this.state = {
      location: 'Chicago',
      current_condition: {
        temp_C: 0,
        windspeedKmph: 0,
        precipMM: 0,
      },
    };
  }
  componentDidMount() {
    const getWeatherData = async (city) => {
      const response = await fetch('https://wttr.in/
            ${city}?format=j1');
      const weatherData = await response.json();
```

(continued)

LISTING 5-10: (continued)

```
      this.setState({ current_condition: weatherData.current_
           condition[0] });
    };
    getWeatherData(this.state.location);
  }
  render() {
    return (
      <div>
        <h1>Today's weather for {this.state.location}</h1>
        <ul>
          <li>temp: {this.state.current_condition.temp_C} C</li>
          <li>wind: {this.state.current_condition.windspeedKmph}
                 km/h</li>
          <li>precip amt: {this.state.current_condition.precipMM}
                 mm</li>
        </ul>
      </div>
    );
  }
}
export default App;
```

Updating methods

The updating cycle starts after a component has been mounted.

REMEMBER

Updating happens in response to changes to a component's state.

These are the updating lifecycle methods:

- `getDerivedStateFromProps()`
- `shouldComponentUpdate()`
- `render()`
- `getSnapshotBeforeUpdate()`
- `componentDidUpdate()`

You already know about two of these lifecycle methods: `getDerivedStateFromProps()` and `render()`. They work the same way during updating as they do during mounting. Take a look at the other ones now.

Optimizing with shouldComponentUpdate()

The `shouldComponentUpdate()` method, which is rarely needed nowadays, returns a Boolean value that determines whether the `render()` method is called.

By returning `false` from `shouldComponentUpdate()`, you prevent the re-rendering of a component. This can be useful in cases where you have a component in a tree of components that always renders the same thing when it's passed the same props. Programmers call this type of component a *pure function*. If a component is a pure function, you can compare the previous props to the new props passed to it. If the previous and new props are the same, you can know for certain that re-rendering the component produces the same output, and you can tell the component to skip re-rendering.

The reason `shouldComponentUpdate()` is rarely used now is that there's a better way to determine whether you can skip re-rendering. If you know that your class component always returns the same output when given the same props, you can create the component by extending the `React.PureComponent` class, as shown in Listing 5-11.

LISTING 5-11: Extending React.PureComponent

```
class Message extends React.PureComponent {
  render() {
    return <h1>Hi, {this.props.firstName}</h1>;
  }
}
```

In function components, you can accomplish the same thing as `React.PureComponent` by using `React.memo()`, which caches the return value of a function component and returns the cached value if the inputs to the component are the same as the last time it was rendered. Listing 5-12 shows a function component that does the same thing as the class component in Listing 5-11.

LISTING 5-12: Using React.memo() to Optimize the Rendering of Function Components

```
const Message = React.memo(function Message(props) {
  return <h1>Hi, {props.firstName}</h1>;
});
```

Getting a snapshot

The `getSnapshotBeforeUpdate()` lifecycle method is called right before the DOM is updated during a re-render. This method can be used to capture data about the current state of the browser before things change. For example, if a component is rendering live data inside an element (for example, in a chat application), updating the component resets the scroll position of the chat window. Users find this behavior truly frustrating.

If you capture the scroll position of the chat window before it's updated and return it from `getSnapshotBeforeUpdate()`, the return value is passed to the `componentDidUpdate()` method, where you can return the scroll position to what it was before the update.

Finishing the update

The `componentDidUpdate()` method is the updating phase's equivalent of the `componentDidMount()` method. If you need to update data using a network request or make changes to the DOM directly after a component updates, this is the place to do it.

WARNING

The `componentDidUpdate()` method has the potential to create infinite loops if you're not careful. For example, if you make an HTTP request in `componentDidUpdate()` and update the state using the data from the request, the component re-renders, which causes `componentDidUpdate()` to run, which updates the state, and so on until your component crashes.

To prevent infinite loops, you must wrap any calls to `setState()` inside `componentDidUpdate()` in a conditional statement that checks whether updating the state will result in the same state.

Unmounting a component

The `componentWillUnmount()` lifecycle method is called whenever a component is about to be removed from the browser DOM. Removing a component may happen when a conditional statement causes the component to no longer be rendered, or when you specifically unmount a component by using the `root.unmount()` method.

The purpose of `componentWillUnmount()` is that it gives you a chance to clean up after your component. If your component uses a global method, such as `setInterval()` or `setTimeout()`, you should clear these in `componentWillUnmount()`. If you don't, you could create a memory leak where the `setInterval()` method continues to run even though the component that created it is no longer visible.

Listing 5-13 shows a component that creates a timer to update itself every second and show the current time. Calling `clearInterval()` in the `componentWillUnmount()` method stops the timer from running if the component is unmounted.

LISTING 5-13: Clearing an Interval in componentWillUnmount()

```
import React from 'react';
class ShowClock extends React.Component {
  constructor(props) {
    super(props);
    this.state = { date: new Date() };
  }
  componentDidMount() {
    this.timer = setInterval(() => this.getNewTime(), 1000);
  }
  componentWillUnmount() {
    clearInterval(this.timer);
  }
  getNewTime() {
    this.setState({
      date: new Date(),
    });
  }
  render() {
    return <h1>The current time is {this.state.date.
         toLocaleTimeString()}</h1>;
  }
}
export default ShowClock;
```

Using the Lifecycle in Function Components

Just as you can use state in function components by using the `useState()` hook, you can simulate certain lifecycle methods in function components by using the `useEffect()` hook.

The `useEffect()` hook takes a function as its first argument. By default, this function runs after the component mounts and then after every update of the component. In this way, it functions like a combination of the `componentDidMount()`

and the componentDidUpdate() lifecycle methods in class components. The useEffect() hook allows function components to access data outside themselves (as in the case of asynchronous network requests) or to perform other actions after rendering.

TECHNICAL STUFF

An operation done by a function that affects something outside the function is called a *side effect*. Unlike everything that happens inside a function, performing a side effect can produce an unpredictable result.

Listing 5-14 shows a function component that stores a value in the browser's local storage every time a button is clicked.

TECHNICAL STUFF

Technically, the component in Listing 5-14 stores the value to local storage when the component mounts and every time it updates. Because the only time this component updates is when the value of count changes, this behavior isn't currently a problem. You learn how to run an effect less often in the next section.

LISTING 5-14: Using useEffect to Perform Side Effects

```
import { useEffect, useState } from 'react';
function RecordClicks(props) {
  const [count, setCount] = useState(0);
  useEffect(() => {
    localStorage.setItem('currentCount', count);
  });
  function incrementCount() {
    const incremented = count + 1;
    setCount(incremented);
  }
  return <button onClick={incrementCount}>Increment and Store:
        {count}</button>;
}
export default RecordClicks;
```

Running effects less often

Most of the time, effects should run less often than on every render of a component. For example, a function to load data using a network request may need to run only the first time the component is rendered. Or, you may have a state variable in your function whose value determines whether an effect should run. For these cases, useEffect() takes a second argument, which is an array of dependencies. Here's the syntax of useEffect() with the optional dependency array:

```
useEffect(function, []);
```

If the dependency array is empty, the effect runs only on the first render of the component. This simulates the `componentDidMount()` lifecycle method.

If the dependency array contains one or more dependencies, the effect runs when the component mounts and then every time the value of one of the dependencies changes. In this way, you can use `useEffect()`like `componentDidUpdate()`.

Listing 5-15 shows an improved version of the component from Listing 5-14. In this version, the component attempts to load the value of `count` from the browser's local storage the first time it renders, and then updates the value when the value of the `count` state variable changes.

LISTING 5-15: Creating a Persistent State

```
import { useEffect, useState } from 'react';
function RecordClicks(props) {
  const [count, setCount] = useState(getSavedState());
  function getSavedState() {
    const savedString = localStorage.getItem('currentCount');
    const initialCount = JSON.parse(savedString);
    console.log('currentCount: ${initialCount}');
    return initialCount || 0;
  }
  useEffect(() => {
    localStorage.setItem('currentCount', JSON.stringify(count));
  }, [count]);
  function incrementCount() {
    const incremented = count + 1;
    setCount(incremented);
  }
  return <button onClick={incrementCount}>Increment and Store:
         {count}</button>;
}
export default RecordClicks;
```

By setting a value to local storage and using its value to set the initial value of a stateful variable, you can maintain the state of the application from one browser session to another.

Performing an effect on unmounting

If the function passed to `useEffect()` returns a function, that function runs when the component is no longer rendered (that is, before it unmounts). As with the componentWillUnmount() lifecycle method in class components, this is where you can clean up any timers that the effect has set or unregister event listeners.

Listing 5-16 shows the clock component from Listing 5-13 written as a function component. I've also added a container around the clock component that displays and hides the clock.

LISTING 5-16: A Function Component with a Timer

```
import { useState, useEffect } from 'react';
function ClockContainer(props) {
  const [visible, setVisible] = useState(true);
  return (
    <div>
      <button onClick={() => setVisible(!visible)}>
        Toggle Clock Visibility
      </button>
      {visible && <Clock/>}
    </div>
  );
}
function Clock(props) {
  const [date, setDate] = useState(new Date());
  useEffect(() => {
    const timer = setInterval(() => getNewTime(), 1000);
    return () => {
      console.log('stopping the timer...');
      clearInterval(timer);
    };
  }, []);
  function getNewTime() {
    setDate(new Date());
    console.log('tick...');
  }
  return (
    <div>
      <h1>The current date and time are {date.toLocaleString()}</h1>
    </div>
  );
}
export default ClockContainer;
```

If you run this component in a browser and watch the browser console, you'll see that the messages in the console stop running when the clock isn't visible. Figure 5-3 shows the result of rendering the component and clicking the button to hide the clock.

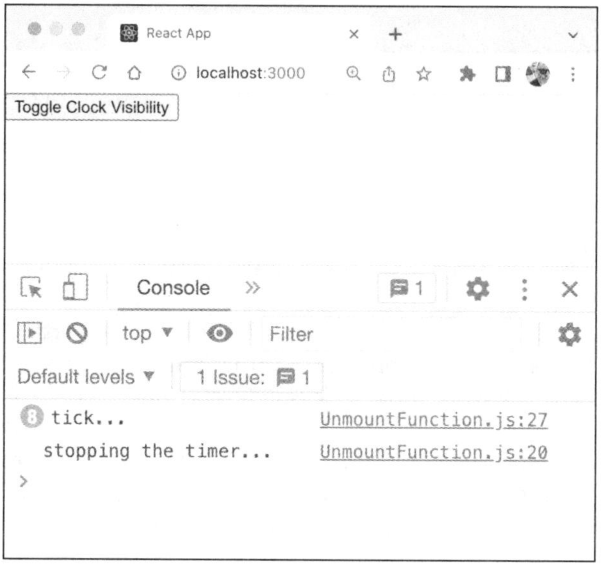

FIGURE 5-3: Returning a function to stop the clock.

Composing Components

Composition is a pattern in React programming where larger components are built by putting together smaller components. The idea behind composition is to reduce duplication of code and increase reusability of components.

How inheritance works in object-oriented programming

When you want to create a class that's a more specific version of an existing class in object-oriented programming, you extend it. For example, if you have a class called `Shape`, you can extend it to create a class called `Circle`, as shown in Listing 5-17.

LISTING 5-17: Extending a Class to Create a More Specific Class

```
class Shape {
  constructor(color) {
    this.color = color;
  }
}
class Circle extends Shape {
  constructor(color, radius) {
    super(color);
    this.radius = radius;
  }
}
const myCircle = new Circle('blue', 3);
```

When you extend a class, the new class inherits the properties and methods of its parent class as well as the properties of that component's parent, and so on to the base class, which is the `Object` class in JavaScript.

When creating user interfaces using React, every component is defined either as a function or as a class that extends `React.Component`. Extending your own classes in React is discouraged. Instead, you use composition.

We use the following three techniques to enable composition:

- Passing props
- Using the `children` prop
- Using custom hooks

Composition using explicit props

Suppose you need to display various types of messages in your application, each with a different style, color, and text. Using inheritance, you might think that the way to do it would be to create a generic `Message` component and then extend it to create `ErrorMessage`, `SuccessMessage`, and `WarningMessage` classes.

However, you can use this approach only with class components, and the resulting components would end up having significant amounts of duplicate code.

Using composition with explicit props, you can create a single `Message` component that takes several props that can be used to configure instances of the `Message` component for the type of message you want to display, as shown in Listing 5-18.

LISTING 5-18: Using Props to Create a More Reusable Component

```
function Message(props) {
  return (
    <div className={props.messageType}>
      <h1>{props.messageText}</h1>
    </div>
  );
}
export default Message;
```

By wrapping this component inside another component, you can create an easily reusable `ErrorMessage` component, as shown in Listing 5-19.

LISTING 5-19: Composing an ErrorMessage Component

```
import Message from './Message';
function ErrorMessage(props) {
  return (
    <Message messageType="error" messageText={props.errorMessage}/>
  );
}
export default ErrorMessage;
```

Composition using the children prop

Another way to compose components is by using the `children` prop. The `children` prop is automatically passed to every instance of a component and contains the children of the React element that creates the component instance.

Using `props.children` allows you to create components that can be wrapped around other components. For example, Listing 5-20 defines two components that use `props.children` to apply their functionality to children.

LISTING 5-20: Creating Components that Use props.children

```
import { useState, useEffect } from 'react';
export function SolidBorderBox(props) {
  return (
    <div style={{ border: '1px solid black', padding: '8px' }}>
      {props.children}
    </div>
  );
}
export function Blink(props) {
  const [visible, setVisible] = useState(true);
  useEffect(() => {
    const blinker = setInterval(() => setVisible(v => !v),
          props.delay);
    return () => clearInterval(blinker);
  });
  return <div>{visible && props.children}</div>;
}
```

The first component defined in Listing 5-20 applies a 1-pixel-wide black border to any component. If you were doing web design in the 1990s, you'll recognize the second component as a replacement for the now out-of-favor HTML `<blink>` element.

To use the components created in Listing 5-20, import them into another component and put their starting and ending tags around any other React elements, as shown in Listing 5-21.

LISTING 5-21: Wrapping Components Around Other Components

```
import { Blink, SolidBorderBox } from './StyleElements';
function App() {
  return (
    <SolidBorderBox>
      <Blink delay={1000}>
        <p>Important Message</p>
      </Blink>
    </SolidBorderBox>
  );
}
export default App;
```

Composition with custom hooks

The third method I talk about for using composition is to extract reusable functionality from components to create custom hooks. Custom hooks aren't technically a feature of React. Instead, they're just JavaScript modules that use React's built-in hooks and can then be imported into function components to easily share functionality.

Listing 5-22 shows a custom hook that returns a list of public GitHub repositories for any GitHub username that's passed to it.

LISTING 5-22: The useGitHubRepos Custom Hook

```
import { useState, useEffect } from 'react';
export default function useGitHubRepos(username) {
  const [repos, setRepos] = useState([]);
  const [isLoading, setIsLoading] = useState(false);
  useEffect(() => {
    const getRepos = async () => {
      try {
        setIsLoading(true);
        let response = await fetch(
          'https://api.github.com/users/${username}/repos',
        );
        let data = await response.json();
        setRepos(data);
        setIsLoading(false);
      } catch (error) {
        console.log(error);
      }
    };
    getRepos();
  }, [username]);
  return [repos, isLoading];
}
```

To use a custom hook in a component, import it and get the return value by invoking the function, as shown in Listing 5-23.

LISTING 5-23: Using a Custom Hook

```
import './App.css';
import useGitHubRepos from './components/Chapter05/
  useGitHubRepos';
function App() {
  const [repos, isLoading] = useGitHubRepos('facebook');
  const reposList = repos.map((repo, index) => (
    <li key={index}>
      <a href={repo.clone_url}>{repo.name}</a>
    </li>
  ));
  return <div>{isLoading ? 'Loading...' : reposList}</div>;
}
export default App;
```

IN THIS CHAPTER

» Handling events

» Setting listeners with event attributes

» Gathering data with forms

» Using controlled and uncontrolled inputs

Chapter 6
Using Data and Events in React

"It is the quality of the moment, not the number of days, or events, or actors, that imports."

—RALPH WALDO EMERSON

In Chapter 3 of this minibook, I cover the React development process, which starts with a static mockup and progresses through building a static version, figuring out what is state, and implementing the state. The last step in the process is to implement the capability for child components to send information to a parent component, and that's what this chapter is about.

Event Handling in React

React's event attributes resemble HTML event attributes. For example, to set an event listener for the click event on a button DOM element, you can pass an `onClick` attribute to a `<button>` element. You can use event attributes on any of React's built-in (HTML equivalent) JSX elements.

Although the JSX event attributes resemble HTML event attributes, HTML event attributes and JSX event attributes have some important differences:

- JSX event attributes are spelled using camel case.
- JSX event attributes take a function as their value, whereas HTML event attributes take a string containing a function invocation.

Although it's tempting to think of JSX event attributes as working the same way as HTML event attributes, they're compiled to calls to `addEventListener()`.

Using event attributes

Using JSX event attributes, you can set event listeners for at least 64 events. These events include mouse events, such as `onClick`, `onDrag`, and `onMouseDown`; the generic `onLoad` and `onError` events; and form events such as `onChange`, `onInput`, and `onSubmit`.

Dispatching synthetic events

React wraps the event object that's always passed to an event handler function with an object it calls the *synthetic event*. The object name of the synthetic event is `SyntheticBaseEvent`. By wrapping native event objects, React can smooth differences in the way browsers handle events as well as make some additional properties available when an event is fired.

Listing 6-1 shows how to capture and view the properties of the `SyntheticBaseEvent` object.

LISTING 6-1: Viewing the Properties of the SyntheticBaseEvent Object

```
function EventProps() {
  const logClick = (e) => {
    console.dir(e);
  };
  return <button onClick={logClick}>Click Me</button>;
}
export default EventProps;
```

Specifying a handler function

The value you pass to an event attribute can be an arrow function, the name of a function declared elsewhere, or a function received by the component via props.

WARNING

A common mistake when setting event handlers is to pass a function call to an event attribute by including parentheses after the function name. Doing so causes the function to be invoked as soon as the component mounts, which can be confusing and hard to debug.

Declaring a function outside the return statement of your component and using its name as the value of the event attribute is the most typical way to set event handlers. Listing 6-2 shows an example of this technique.

LISTING 6-2: Defining a Named Event Handler Function

```
import { useState } from 'react';
function Counter(props) {
  const [counter, setCounter] = useState(0);
  function increment() {
    setCounter(prevCount => prevCount + 1);
  }
  return <button onClick={increment}>{counter}</button>;
}
export default Counter;
```

Passing arguments to an event handler

Because the event attribute takes the value of a function rather than an invocation, you can't simply pass arguments to an event handler function name because that would require you to use parentheses. For example, the following code won't work as intended, because the function is simply invoked when the component mounts:

```
<button onClick={increment(2)}>Add 2</button>
```

To pass arguments (other than the event object) to an event handler, you can define an arrow function that invokes an inner function, as shown in Listing 6-3.

LISTING 6-3: Passing Arguments Using an Inner Function

```
import { useState } from 'react';
function Counter(props) {
  const [counter, setCounter] = useState(0);
  function increment(incrementBy = 1) {
    setCounter(counter + incrementBy);
  }
  return <button onClick={() => increment(2)}>Add 2</button>;
}
export default Counter;
```

Passing functions as props

You don't need to define event handlers in the same component where you use them. As with any value, you can pass event handlers from a parent component to a child component using props.

REMEMBER

Passing functions to subcomponents is how components lower in the component hierarchy can affect state in components higher in the hierarchy.

Defining event handlers in class components

When you define a method in a class component, it can access the component's `this` value. Before you pass a method from a class component to a subcomponent, you have to specify the context in which the function runs.

REMEMBER

When you pass an event handler function to an event attribute of a built-in element, you're passing the function to a subcomponent. For example, in Listing 6-4, the `handleClick` function is defined as a method of the `ToggleVisibility` class component. To set the context in which the function should run, you must bind it to the `ToggleVisibility` class before passing it to the `button` element.

LISTING 6-4: Binding Class Methods before Passing Them as Attributes

```
import React from 'react';
class ToggleVisibility extends React.Component {
  constructor(props) {
    super(props);
    this.state = { visible: true };
  }
```

```
  setVisibility() {
    this.setState({ visible: !this.state.visible });
  }
  render() {
    return (
      <div>
        {this.state.visible ? this.props.children : ''}
        <button onClick={this.setVisibility.bind(this)}>Show/
             Hide</button>
      </div>
    );
  }
}
export default ToggleVisibility;
```

The `ToggleVisibility` class in Listing 6-4 can be wrapped around any component and renders a button that toggles whether the component is rendered or not. Before the function that toggles the `visible` state property can be passed to the `<button>` element, we bind it.

Binding a function can be done directly in the element's event attribute, as shown in Listing 6-4, or it can be done in the constructor.

To bind a function in the constructor, set the value of the function variable to the new function created using the `bind()` method, as shown in Listing 6-5.

LISTING 6-5: Binding a Method in the Constructor

```
import React from 'react';
class ToggleVisibility extends React.Component {
  constructor(props) {
    super(props);
    this.state = { visible: true };
    this.setVisibility = this.setVisibility.bind(this);
  }
  setVisibility() {
    this.setState({ visible: !this.state.visible });
  }
  render() {
    return (
      <div>
        {this.state.visible ? this.props.children : ''}
```

(continued)

LISTING 6-5: (continued)

```
      <button onClick={this.setVisibility}>Show/Hide</button>
    </div>
  );
 }
}
export default ToggleVisibility;
```

Binding event handler methods in the constructor has two benefits:

- If you pass the method to more than one element, it needs to be bound only once.
- Binding the event handler in the event attribute causes the bound function to be re-created with every render. However, the constructor runs only once, and then the function is accessible as long as the class instance exists.

Not binding an event handler in a class component is one of the most common mistakes that React developers make. There are ways to avoid needing to bind methods, however.

Defining methods using arrow syntax

Arrow functions inherit their scope from the scope in which they're defined, which is called *lexical scoping.* Because arrow functions have lexical scope, there's no need to bind them before passing them as arguments.

Functions defined using the `function` keyword, on the other hand, bind their own `this` value, which is why we need to specifically bind them to use them in a different context.

Listing 6-6 shows a class component with its event handler defined as an arrow function and passed to an `<input>` element using an event attribute.

LISTING 6-6: Defining Event Handler Functions By Using Arrow Function Syntax

```
import React from 'react';
class VolumeSlider extends React.Component {
  constructor(props) {
    super(props);
    this.state = { volume: 0 };
  }
```

```
  changeVolume = (e) => {
    this.setState({ volume: e.target.value });
  };
  render() {
    return (
      <>
        <p>Turn the volume up! Current Volume: {this.state.volume}</p>
        <input
          type="range"
          value={this.state.volume}
          min="0"
          max="11"
          onChange={this.changeVolume}
          />
      </>
    );
  }
}
export default VolumeSlider;
```

Passing event handler functions from function components

The other way to avoid having to think about binding event handlers is to use function components. Because function components don't have a `this` value, any function you define inside a function is automatically scoped to that function.

Listing 6-7 shows a function component that does the same thing as the class component in Listing 6-6.

LISTING 6-7: VolumeSlider Written Using a Function Component

```
import { useState } from 'react';
function VolumeSlider(props) {
  const [volume, setVolume] = useState(0);
  function changeVolume(e) {
    setVolume(e.target.value);
  }
  return (
    <>
```

(continued)

LISTING 6-7: *(continued)*

```
      <p>Turn the volume up! Current Volume: {volume}</p>
      <input
        type="range"
        value={volume}
        min="0"
        max="11"
        onChange={changeVolume}
        />
    </>
  );
}
export default VolumeSlider;
```

REMEMBER

Whether you define an event handler function in a function component using the `function` keyword or arrow syntax, you don't need to bind it.

Making Forms with React

HTML form fields, by default, maintain their own internal state. In other words, when you type in an input field, select an option from a drop-down menu, or make a change to any changeable form field, the value of an HTML element changes.

In React applications, however, allowing a form input to maintain its own state makes components less predictable. By default, changing the value of an input doesn't change the underlying data in a component. As a result, it's possible for the content that displays in a form input to be out of sync with the state data of your component.

Other front-end libraries allow your form to automatically update the application's state and allow your application to control the value of the form input. This is what is meant by *two-way data binding.*

React uses *one-way data binding.* What this means is that form inputs can be controlled only by React state. If you want to change the value of an input, you need to do it by updating the state (using an event). The updated state then causes the form input to be updated with the new value. This is called a *controlled input.*

Using controlled inputs

To create a controlled input, specify a `value` attribute for any `<input>`, `<select>`, or `<textarea>` element, like this:

```
<input name="firstName" type="text" value=""/>
```

By itself, this element is useless. It creates an HTML input element that you can't type into. Or, rather, you can type into it, but neither you nor React can see what you're typing.

To make a controlled input useful, first create a stateful variable to hold the value of the input and a function for updating it, like this:

```
const [firstName, setFirstName] = useState('');
```

Next, listen for the `change` event on the input and use it to update the stateful variable, like this:

```
<input name="firstName" type="text" value={firstName}
  onChange={(e)=>setFirstName(e.target.value)}/>
```

Now whenever you type into the input element, it updates the stateful variable, which causes the input element to update its value. Listing 6-8 shows a complete example of using controlled inputs in a function component and demonstrates how to control several different kinds of form elements.

LISTING 6-8: Using Controlled Inputs

```
import { useState } from 'react';
function CustomerServiceSurvey(props) {
  const [yourName, setYourName] = useState('');
  const [yourEmail, setYourEmail] = useState('');
  const [rating, setRating] = useState('Excellent');
  const [comments, setComments] = useState('');
  return (
    <div>
      <div>
        You've entered the following: <br/>
        Rating:{rating}
        <br/>
        Comments:{comments}
```

(continued)

LISTING 6-8: (continued)

```
    <br/>
    Name:{yourName}
    <br/>
    Email:{yourEmail}
    <br/>
  </div>
  <h1>How was your experience with our website today?</h1>
  <select
    name="rating"
    value={rating}
    onChange={(e) => setRating(e.target.value)}
  >
    <option>Excellent</option>
    <option>Pretty Good</option>
    <option>Fair</option>
    <option>Bad</option>
    <option>Horrible</option>
  </select>
  <h1>Would you like to leave any comments?</h1>
  <textarea
    name="comments"
    value={comments}
    onChange={(e) => setComments(e.target.value)}
    />
  <h1>
    Please provide your contact information if you'd like to
        be contacted.
  </h1>
  Your name:
  <input
    type="text"
    name="yourName"
    value={yourName}
    onChange={(e) => setYourName(e.target.value)}
    />
  <br/>
  Your email:
  <input
    type="text"
    name="yourEmail"
    value={yourEmail}
```

```
        onChange={(e) => setYourEmail(e.target.value)}
        />
    </div>
  );
}
export default CustomerServiceSurvey;
```

Note that setting the value of `<select>` inputs and `<textarea>` inputs in React's built-in components is different from how HTML elements work:

- Whereas the value of an HTML `<select>` input is set by setting the `selected` attribute on an `<option>` child, React matches the value of a `value` attribute on the `<select>` input with the value of an `<option>`.
- Whereas the HTML `<textarea>` element uses its content (the content between the beginning and ending tags) as the value, React's built-in `<textarea>` element uses the value of the `value` attribute.

Using uncontrolled forms

Some uses for HTML inputs in a web application don't require user input to be stored in state. In these cases, you can choose to use an *uncontrolled input element*, which is one that maintains, by default, its own internal state in the same way that HTML works.

For example, you might choose to use an uncontrolled input in a long form that simply sends an email rather than anything with the input values inside the user interface. To create an uncontrolled input, omit the `value` attribute.

Listing 6-9 shows an example using a form made with uncontrolled inputs.

LISTING 6-9: Creating Uncontrolled Inputs

```
function CustomerServiceSurvey(props) {
  return (
    <div>
      <h1>How was your experience with our website today?</h1>
      <select name="rating">
        <option>Excellent</option>
        <option>Pretty Good</option>
        <option>Fair</option>
```

(continued)

LISTING 6-9: (continued)

```
        <option>Bad</option>
        <option>Horrible</option>
      </select>
      <h1>Would you like to leave any comments?</h1>
      <textarea name="comments"/>
      <h1>
        Please provide your contact information if you'd like to
              be contacted.
      </h1>
      Your name:
      <input name="yourName"/>
      <br/>
      Your email:
      <input name="yourEmail"/>
    </div>
  );
}
export default CustomerServiceSurvey;
```

In uncontrolled inputs, HTML handles the values of the inputs. One way to get the values of uncontrolled inputs in JavaScript is by using the `id` of the input. The value of the `id` attribute is accessible as a property of the browser's `window` object, as shown in Listing 6-10.

LISTING 6-10: Getting the Values of Uncontrolled Inputs from the Window Object

```
function CustomerServiceSurvey(props) {
  function onSubmit(e) {
    e.preventDefault();
    alert(
      'You rated us ${window.rating.value} and you had the
            following comments: ${window.comments.value}',
    );
  }
  return (
    <div>
      <h1>How was your experience with our website today?</h1>
      <form onSubmit={onSubmit}>
        <select name="rating" id="rating">
          <option>Excellent</option>
          <option>Pretty Good</option>
```

```
          <option>Fair</option>
          <option>Bad</option>
          <option>Horrible</option>
        </select>
        <h1>Would you like to leave any comments?</h1>
        <textarea name="comments" id="comments"/>
        <input type="submit" value="Submit"/>
      </form>
    </div>
  );
}
export default CustomerServiceSurvey;
```

This example uses `alert()` for simplicity so you can quickly see the submitted values without introducing additional UI code. In production applications, you should avoid `alert()` because it blocks the browser and creates a poor user experience. Instead, display results in the page or send them to a server.

WARNING

Although accessing the values of uncontrolled inputs through the DOM can be useful in some circumstances, avoid using the technique shown in Listing 6-10 to change the values of HTML elements in your React components because it bypasses the way React manages updates and produces unexpected results.

Index

Special Characters

A

B

C

D

E

F

G

H

I

J

K

L

M

N

O

P

Q

R

S

T

U

V

W

X

Y

Z

About the Author

Chris Minnick is a prolific author, teacher, and Jack-of-all-trades. He teaches professionals around the world about AI, coding, cybersecurity, agile methodologies, and other related fields. Minnick has authored or co-authored more than 25 technical books for adults and kids, including *A Developer's Guide to Integrating Generative AI into Applications, Microsoft Copilot For Dummies,* and *Coding with AI For Dummies.* When he's not writing or teaching, Chris enjoys doing human things like baking, writing fiction, playing music, and walking the dog in the beautiful Pacific Northwest.

Dedication

To my best canine friend, Chauncey, my best feline friend, Murray, and my best human friend, Jill.

Author's Acknowledgments

Thank you to the authors who contributed chapters to this edition. A giant thank-you to my editor, Susan Pink, who is always a pleasure to work with and without whom this book wouldn't be nearly as good as it is. Thanks to technical editor Guy Hart-Davis, who never fails to catch the code errors I miss and ask the good questions. Thanks to the entire team at Wiley, who work publishing miracles every day. Thank you to associate editor Alicia Sparrow, senior managing editor Kristie Pyles, and production editor Athiyappan Lalith Kumar and everyone at Wiley who had a part in making the third edition of this book possible! Thank you to editorial assistant Shannon Kucaj for your enthusiasm and organizational abilities. Thank you to my agent, Carole Jelen. And, most of all, thank you, the reader, for entrusting me to help guide your learning journey.

Publisher's Acknowledgments

Associate Editor: Alicia Sparrow
Senior Managing Editor: Kristie Pyles
Project and Copy Editor: Susan Pink
Production Editor: Athiyappan Lalith Kumar
Technical Editor: Guy Hart-Davis
Cover Image: Gorodenkoff/stock.adobe.com